P9-CAD-531

Here's

HPE

New Testament

CSB | CHRISTIAN STANDARD BIBLE®   HOLMAN® BIBLES

HOLMAN BIBLE PUBLISHERS
NASHVILLE, TENNESSEE

CSB Here's Hope New Testament
Copyright © 2017 by Holman Bible Publishers
Nashville, Tennessee. All Rights Reserved.

Christian Standard Bible® Copyright © 2017 by Holman Bible Publishers.

Christian Standard Bible® and CSB® are federally registered trademarks
of Holman Bible Publishers.

The text of the Christian Standard Bible may be quoted in any form (written, visual,
electronic, or audio) up to and inclusive of one thousand (1,000) verses without the written
permission of the publisher, provided that the verses quoted do not account for more than
50 percent of the work in which they are quoted, and provided that a complete book of the
Bible is not quoted. Requests for permission are to be directed to and approved in writing by
Holman Bible Publishers, One LifeWay Plaza, Nashville, Tennessee 37234.

When the Christian Standard Bible is quoted, one of the following credit lines must appear
on the copyright page or title page of the work:

Scripture quotations marked CSB have been taken from the Christian Standard Bible®,
Copyright © 2017 by Holman Bible Publishers. Used by permission. Christian Standard
Bible® and CSB® are federally registered trademarks of Holman Bible Publishers.

Unless otherwise noted, all Scripture quotations are taken from the Christian Standard
Bible®, Copyright © 2017 by Holman Bible Publishers. Used by permission. Christian
Standard Bible® and CSB® are federally registered trademarks of Holman Bible Publishers.

The interior of the *CSB Here's Hope New Testament* was designed and typeset using
Bible Serif created by 2K/DENMARK, Højbjerg, Denmark. Proofreading was provided by
Peachtree Editorial Services, Peachtree City, Georgia.

ISBN   978-1-4336-4428-3

Printed in the United States
1 2 3 4 5 — 19 18 17
DP

BOOKS OF THE BIBLE AND CONTENTS

NEW TESTAMENT

Matthew	Mt	1
Mark	Mk	31
Luke	Lk	49
John	Jn	80
Acts	Ac	103
Romans	Rm	132
1 Corinthians	1Co	145
2 Corinthians	2Co	156
Galatians	Gl	163
Ephesians	Eph	167
Philippians	Php	171
Colossians	Col	174
1 Thessalonians	1Th	177
2 Thessalonians	2Th	180
1 Timothy	1Tm	182
2 Timothy	2Tm	185
Titus	Ti	188
Philemon	Phm	190
Hebrews	Heb	191
James	Jms	200
1 Peter	1Pt	203
2 Peter	2Pt	207
1 John	1Jn	209
2 John	2Jn	212
3 John	3Jn	212
Jude	Jd	213
Revelation	Rv	214

FEATURES

Introduction to the CSB	iv
Is There Any Hope?	vii
Where to Find It	viii
Are You Ready to Receive God's Offer of Eternal Life and Hope?	229
What Happens After You Receive Hope From God?	230

INTRODUCTION TO THE CHRISTIAN STANDARD BIBLE®

The Bible is God's revelation to humanity. It is our only source for completely reliable information about God, what happens when we die, and where history is headed. The Bible reveals these things because it is God's inspired Word, inerrant in the original manuscripts. Bible translation brings God's Word from the ancient languages (Hebrew, Greek, and Aramaic) into today's world. In dependence on God's Spirit to accomplish this sacred task, the CSB Translation Oversight Committee and Holman Bible Publishers present the Christian Standard Bible.

TEXTUAL BASE OF THE CSB

The textual base for the New Testament (NT) is the Nestle-Aland *Novum Testamentum Graece*, 28th edition, and the United Bible Societies' *Greek New Testament*, 5th corrected edition. The text for the Old Testament (OT) is the *Biblia Hebraica Stuttgartensia*, 5th edition. Where there are significant differences among Hebrew, Aramaic, or Greek manuscripts, the translators follow what they believe is the original reading and indicate the main alternative(s) in footnotes.

GOALS OF THIS TRANSLATION

- Provide English-speaking people worldwide with an accurate translation in contemporary English.
- Provide an accurate translation for personal study, sermon preparation, private devotions, and memorization.
- Provide a text that is clear and understandable, suitable for public reading, and shareable so that all may access its life-giving message.
- Affirm the authority of Scripture and champion its absolute truth against skeptical viewpoints.

TRANSLATION PHILOSOPHY OF THE CHRISTIAN STANDARD BIBLE

Most discussions of Bible translations speak of two opposite approaches: formal equivalence and dynamic equivalence. However, Bible translations cannot be neatly sorted into these categories. Optimal equivalence capitalizes on the strengths of both approaches.

Optimal equivalence balances contemporary English readability with linguistic precision to the original languages. In the many places throughout the Bible where a word-for-word rendering is understandable, a literal translation is used. When a word-for-word rendering might obscure the meaning for a modern audience, a more dynamic translation is used. This process assures that both the words and the thoughts contained in the original text are conveyed accurately for today's readers. The Christian Standard Bible places equal value on fidelity to the original and readability for a modern audience, resulting in a translation that achieves both goals.

HISTORY OF THE CSB

Holman Bible Publishers assembled an interdenominational team of one hundred scholars, editors, stylists, and proofreaders, all of whom were committed to biblical inerrancy. Working from the original languages, the translation team edited and polished the manuscript, which was first published as the Holman Christian Standard Bible in 2004.

A standing committee maintained the translation, while also seeking ways to improve both readability and accuracy. As with the original translation, the committee that prepared this revision, renamed the Christian Standard Bible, is international and interdenominational, comprising evangelical scholars who honor the inspiration and authority of God's written Word.

FOOTNOTES

Footnotes are used to show readers how the original biblical language has been understood in the CSB.

1. OLD TESTAMENT (OT) TEXTUAL FOOTNOTES

OT textual notes show important differences among Hebrew (Hb) manuscripts and ancient OT versions, such as the Septuagint and the Vulgate. See the list of abbreviations that follows for a list of other ancient versions used.

Some OT textual notes (like NT textual notes) give only an alternate textual reading. However, other OT textual notes also give the support for the reading chosen by the editors as well as for the alternate textual reading. For example, the CSB text of Psalm 12:7 reads,

> You, LORD, will guard us;
> you will protect us[a] from this generation forever.

The textual footnote for this verse reads,

[a]**12:7** Some Hb mss, LXX; other Hb mss read *him*

The textual note in this example means that there are two different readings found in the Hebrew manuscripts: some manuscripts read *us* and others read *him*. The CSB translators chose the reading *us*, which is also found in the Septuagint (LXX), and placed the other Hebrew reading *him* in the footnote.

Two other kinds OT textual notes are:

Alt Hb tradition reads ___   a variation given by scribes in the Hebrew manuscript tradition (known as *Kethiv/Qere* and *Tiqqune Sopherim* readings)

Hb uncertain   when it is unclear what the original Hebrew text was

2. NEW TESTAMENT (NT) TEXTUAL FOOTNOTES

NT textual notes indicate significant differences among Greek manuscripts (mss) and are normally indicated in one of three ways:

> Other mss read _____
> Other mss add _____
> Other mss omit _____

In the NT, some textual footnotes that use the word "add" or "omit" also have square brackets before and after the corresponding verses in the biblical text. Examples of this use of square brackets are Mark 16:9-20 and John 7:53–8:11.

3. OTHER KINDS OF FOOTNOTES

Lit ___ a more literal rendering in English of the Hebrew, Aramaic, or Greek text

Or ___ an alternate or less likely English translation of the same Hebrew, Aramaic, or Greek text

=   an abbreviation for "it means" or "it is equivalent to"

Hb, Aramaic, Gk   the actual Hebrew, Aramaic, or Greek word is given using equivalent English letters

| Hb obscure | the existing Hebrew text is especially difficult to translate |
| emend(ed) to ___ | the original Hebrew text is so difficult to translate that competent scholars have conjectured or inferred a restoration of the original text based on the context, probable root meanings of the words, and uses in comparative languages |

In some editions of the CSB, additional footnotes clarify the meaning of certain biblical texts or explain biblical history, persons, customs, places, activities, and measurements. Cross references are given for parallel passages or passages with similar wording, and in the NT, for passages quoted from the OT.

ABBREVIATIONS IN CSB BIBLES

AD	In the year of our Lord
BC	before Christ
c.	century
ca	circa
chap(s).	chapter(s)
cp.	compare
DSS	Dead Sea Scrolls
e.g.	for example
Eng	English
etc.	et cetera
Gk	Greek
Hb	Hebrew
i.e.	that is
Lat	Latin
lit	literal(ly)
LXX	Septuagint—an ancient translation of the Old Testament into Greek
MT	Masoretic Text
NT	New Testament
ms(s)	manuscript(s)
OT	Old Testament
pl.	plural
Ps(s)	Psalm(s)
Sam	Samaritan Pentateuch
sg.	singular
Sym	Symmachus
Syr	Syriac
Tg	Targum
Theod	Theodotian
v./vv.	verse, verses
Vg	Vulgate—an ancient translation of the Bible into Latin
vol(s).	volume(s)

IS THERE ANY HOPE?

The future is uncertain.
Schools are protected by armed guards.
Many people don't feel safe in their own homes.
Diseases are killing our people.

IS THERE ANY HOPE?

Can we have peace and joy in our heart?
Can we find purpose for our life?
Can we find the strength for tough times?
Does anyone really care?

YES! HERE'S HOPE:
JESUS CARES FOR YOU

The Bible says:

> "*Now may the God of hope fill you with all joy and peace as you believe so that you may overflow with hope by the power of the Holy Spirit*" (Romans 15:13).

In God's Word, the Bible, we find the road to hope. The road is clearly marked in the pages of this New Testament. Read the phrase at the top of each marked page and then the underlined verse. You will find the instructions to the next stop on the road at the bottom of the page. Please read all the verses. The journey begins with Romans 1:16 on page 132.

CAN YOU FIND HOPE IN TODAY'S WORLD?
Turn to Romans 1:16 on page 132.

WHERE TO FIND IT

The Bible is our guide for living   2 Timothy 3:14-17 (Page 186)

Comfort when you are in trouble   John 14:1-18 (Page 95)

Strength for your faith   Hebrews 11:1-40 (Pages 197-198)

Rest when you are weary   Matthew 11:25-30 (Page 10)

How to cope with worry   Matthew 6:25-34 (Page 6)

How to forgive and be forgiven   Matthew 18:21-35 (Page 18)

How to pray   Matthew 6:5-8 (Page 5)

The Beatitudes   Matthew 5:3-12 (Pages 3-4)

The meaning of love   1 Corinthians 13:1-13 (Pages 152-153)

The Christmas story   Luke 2:1-20 (Page 51)

The story of Easter   Luke 24:1-10 (Page 78)

The return of Christ   1 Thessalonians 4:13-18 (Page 178)

The description of heaven   Revelation 21:1-17 (Page 227)

THE NEW TESTAMENT

MATTHEW

THE GENEALOGY OF JESUS CHRIST

1 An account of the genealogy of Jesus Christ, the Son of David, the Son of Abraham:

FROM ABRAHAM TO DAVID

2 Abraham fathered^A Isaac,
Isaac fathered Jacob,
Jacob fathered Judah and his brothers,
3 Judah fathered Perez and Zerah
by Tamar,
Perez fathered Hezron,
Hezron fathered Aram,
4 Aram fathered Amminadab,
Amminadab fathered Nahshon,
Nahshon fathered Salmon,
5 Salmon fathered Boaz by Rahab,
Boaz fathered Obed by Ruth,
Obed fathered Jesse,
6 and Jesse fathered King David.

FROM DAVID TO THE BABYLONIAN EXILE

David fathered Solomon^B
by Uriah's wife,
7 Solomon fathered Rehoboam,
Rehoboam fathered Abijah,
Abijah fathered Asa,^C
8 Asa^C fathered Jehoshaphat,
Jehoshaphat fathered Joram,^D
Joram fathered Uzziah,
9 Uzziah fathered Jotham,
Jotham fathered Ahaz,
Ahaz fathered Hezekiah,
10 Hezekiah fathered Manasseh,
Manasseh fathered Amon,^E
Amon fathered Josiah,
11 and Josiah fathered Jeconiah
and his brothers
at the time of the exile to Babylon.

FROM THE EXILE TO THE CHRIST

12 After the exile to Babylon
Jeconiah fathered Shealtiel,
Shealtiel fathered Zerubbabel,
13 Zerubbabel fathered Abiud,
Abiud fathered Eliakim,
Eliakim fathered Azor,
14 Azor fathered Zadok,
Zadok fathered Achim,
Achim fathered Eliud,
15 Eliud fathered Eleazar,
Eleazar fathered Matthan,
Matthan fathered Jacob,
16 and Jacob fathered Joseph the husband
of Mary,
who gave birth to Jesus who is called
the Christ.

17 So all the generations from Abraham to David were fourteen generations; and from David until the exile to Babylon, fourteen generations; and from the exile to Babylon until the Christ, fourteen generations.

THE NATIVITY OF THE CHRIST

18 The birth of Jesus Christ came about this way: After his mother Mary had been engaged^F to Joseph, it was discovered before they came together that she was pregnant from the Holy Spirit. 19 So her husband Joseph, being a righteous man, and not wanting to disgrace her publicly, decided to divorce her secretly.

20 But after he had considered these things, an angel of the Lord appeared to him in a dream, saying, "Joseph, son of David, don't be afraid to take Mary as your wife, because what has been conceived in her is from the Holy Spirit. 21 She will give birth to a son, and you are to name him Jesus, because he will save his people from their sins."

22 Now all this took place to fulfill what was spoken by the Lord through the prophet:
23 See, the virgin will become pregnant
and give birth to a son,
and they will name him Immanuel,^G
which is translated "God is with us."

24 When Joseph woke up, he did as the Lord's angel had commanded him. He married her 25 but did not have sexual relations with her until she gave birth to a son.^H And he named him Jesus.

WISE MEN VISIT THE KING

2 After Jesus was born in Bethlehem of Judea in the days of King Herod, wise men from the east arrived in Jerusalem, 2 saying, "Where is he who has been born king of the Jews? For we saw his star at its rising and have come to worship him."^I

3 When King Herod heard this, he was deeply disturbed, and all Jerusalem with him. 4 So he assembled all the chief priests and scribes of the people and asked them where the Christ would be born.

5 "In Bethlehem of Judea," they told him, "because this is what was written by the prophet:

---

^A 1:2 In vv. 2-16 either a son, as here, or a later descendant, as in v. 8   ^B 1:6 Other mss add *King*   ^C 1:7,8 Other mss read *Asaph*
^D 1:8 = Jehoram   ^E 1:10 Other mss read *Amos*   ^F 1:18 Or *betrothed*   ^G 1:23 Is 7:14   ^H 1:25 Other mss read *to her firstborn son*
^I 2:2 Or *to pay him homage*

⁶ And you, Bethlehem, in the land
　　of Judah,
are by no means least among the rulers
　　of Judah:
Because out of you will come a ruler
who will shepherd my people Israel."ᴬ

⁷ Then Herod secretly summoned the wise men and asked them the exact time the star appeared. ⁸ He sent them to Bethlehem and said, "Go and search carefully for the child. When you find him, report back to me so that I too can go and worship him."ᴮ

⁹ After hearing the king, they went on their way. And there it was — the star they had seen at its rising. It led them until it came and stopped above the place where the child was. ¹⁰ When they saw the star, they were overwhelmed with joy. ¹¹ Entering the house, they saw the child with Mary his mother, and falling to their knees, they worshiped him.ᶜ Then they opened their treasures and presented him with gifts: gold, frankincense, and myrrh. ¹² And being warned in a dream not to go back to Herod, they returned to their own country by another route.

THE FLIGHT INTO EGYPT

¹³ After they were gone, an angel of the Lord appeared to Joseph in a dream, saying, "Get up! Take the child and his mother, flee to Egypt, and stay there until I tell you. For Herod is about to search for the child to kill him." ¹⁴ So he got up, took the child and his mother during the night, and escaped to Egypt. ¹⁵ He stayed there until Herod's death, so that what was spoken by the Lord through the prophet might be fulfilled: Out of Egypt I called my Son.ᴰ

THE MASSACRE OF THE INNOCENTS

¹⁶ Then Herod, when he realized that he had been outwitted by the wise men, flew into a rage. He gave orders to massacre all the boys in and around Bethlehem who were two years old and under, in keeping with the time he had learned from the wise men. ¹⁷ Then what was spoken through Jeremiah the prophet was fulfilled:
¹⁸ A voice was heard in Ramah,
　　weeping,ᴱ and great mourning,
　　Rachel weeping for her children;
　　and she refused to be consoled,
　　because they are no more.ᶠ

THE RETURN TO NAZARETH

¹⁹ After Herod died, an angel of the Lord appeared in a dream to Joseph in Egypt, ²⁰ saying,

"Get up, take the child and his mother, and go to the land of Israel, because those who intended to kill the child are dead." ²¹ So he got up, took the child and his mother, and entered the land of Israel. ²² But when he heard that Archelaus was ruling over Judea in place of his father Herod, he was afraid to go there. And being warned in a dream, he withdrew to the region of Galilee. ²³ Then he went and settled in a town called Nazareth to fulfill what was spoken through the prophets, that he would be called a Nazarene.

THE HERALD OF THE CHRIST

3 In those days John the Baptist came, preaching in the wilderness of Judea ² and saying, "Repent, because the kingdom of heaven has come near!" ³ For he is the one spoken of through the prophet Isaiah, who said:
A voice of one crying out
　　in the wilderness:
Prepare the way for the Lord;
　　make his paths straight!ᴳ

⁴ Now John had a camel-hair garment with a leather belt around his waist, and his food was locusts and wild honey. ⁵ Then people from Jerusalem, all Judea, and all the vicinity of the Jordan were going out to him, ⁶ and they were baptized by him in the Jordan River, confessing their sins.

⁷ When he saw many of the Pharisees and Sadducees coming to his baptism, he said to them, "Brood of vipers! Who warned you to flee from the coming wrath? ⁸ Therefore produce fruit consistent with" repentance. ⁹ And don't presume to say to yourselves, 'We have Abraham as our father.' For I tell you that God is able to raise up children for Abraham from these stones. ¹⁰ The ax is already at the root of the trees. Therefore, every tree that doesn't produce good fruit will be cut down and thrown into the fire.

¹¹ "I baptize you withⁱ water for repentance, but the one who is coming after me is more powerful than I. I am not worthy to removeʲ his sandals. He himself will baptize you with the Holy Spirit and fire. ¹² His winnowing shovel is in his hand, and he will clear his threshing floor and gather his wheat into the barn. But the chaff he will burn with fire that never goes out."

THE BAPTISM OF JESUS

¹³ Then Jesus came from Galilee to John at the Jordan, to be baptized by him. ¹⁴ But John tried to stop him, saying, "I need to be baptized by you, and yet you come to me?"

ᴬ2:6 Mc 5:2　ᴮ2:8 Or and pay him homage　ᶜ2:11 Or they paid him homage　ᴰ2:15 Hs 11:1　ᴱ2:18 Other mss read Ramah, lamentation, and weeping,　ᶠ2:18 Jr 31:15　ᴳ3:3 Is 40:3　ᴴ3:8 Lit fruit worthy of　ⁱ3:11 Or in　ʲ3:11 Or to carry

[15] Jesus answered him, "Allow it for now, because this is the way for us to fulfill all righteousness." Then John allowed him to be baptized.

[16] When Jesus was baptized, he went up immediately from the water. The heavens suddenly opened for him,[A] and he saw the Spirit of God descending like a dove and coming down on him. [17] And a voice from heaven said: "This is my beloved Son, with whom I am well-pleased."

THE TEMPTATION OF JESUS

4 Then Jesus was led up by the Spirit into the wilderness to be tempted by the devil. [2] After he had fasted forty days and forty nights, he was hungry. [3] Then the tempter approached him and said, "If you are the Son of God, tell these stones to become bread."

[4] He answered, "It is written: **Man must not live on bread alone but on every word that comes from the mouth of God.**"[B]

[5] Then the devil took him to the holy city, had him stand on the pinnacle of the temple, [6] and said to him, "If you are the Son of God, throw yourself down. For it is written:

He will give his angels orders
    concerning you,
and **they will support you**
    with their hands
so that you will not strike
    your foot against a stone."[C]

[7] Jesus told him, "It is also written: **Do not test the Lord your God.**"[D]

[8] Again, the devil took him to a very high mountain and showed him all the kingdoms of the world and their splendor. [9] And he said to him, "I will give you all these things if you will fall down and worship me."[E]

[10] Then Jesus told him, "Go away,[F] Satan! For it is written: **Worship the Lord your God, and serve only him.**"[G]

[11] Then the devil left him, and angels came and began to serve him.

MINISTRY IN GALILEE

[12] When he heard that John had been arrested, he withdrew into Galilee. [13] He left Nazareth and went to live in Capernaum by the sea, in the region of Zebulun and Naphtali. [14] This was to fulfill what was spoken through the prophet Isaiah:

[15] Land of Zebulun and land of Naphtali,
    along the road by the sea,
        beyond the Jordan,
    Galilee of the Gentiles.

[16] The people who live in darkness
    have seen a great light,
and for those living in the land of the
    shadow of death,
a light has dawned.[H,I]

[17] From then on Jesus began to preach, "Repent, because the kingdom of heaven has come near."

THE FIRST DISCIPLES

[18] As he was walking along the Sea of Galilee, he saw two brothers, Simon (who is called Peter), and his brother Andrew. They were casting a net into the sea — for they were fishermen. [19] "Follow me," he told them, "and I will make you fish for[J] people." [20] Immediately they left their nets and followed him.

[21] Going on from there, he saw two other brothers, James the son of Zebedee, and his brother John. They were in a boat with Zebedee their father, preparing their nets, and he called them. [22] Immediately they left the boat and their father and followed him.

TEACHING, PREACHING, AND HEALING

[23] Now Jesus began to go all over Galilee, teaching in their synagogues, preaching the good news of the kingdom, and healing every[K] disease and sickness[L] among the people. [24] Then the news about him spread throughout Syria. So they brought to him all those who were afflicted, those suffering from various diseases and intense pains, the demon-possessed, the epileptics, and the paralytics. And he healed them. [25] Large crowds followed him from Galilee, the Decapolis, Jerusalem, Judea, and beyond the Jordan.

THE SERMON ON THE MOUNT

5 When he saw the crowds, he went up on the mountain, and after he sat down, his disciples came to him. [2] Then[M] he began to teach them, saying:

THE BEATITUDES

[3] "Blessed are the poor in spirit,
    for the kingdom of heaven
        is theirs.
[4] Blessed are those who mourn,
    for they will be comforted.
[5] Blessed are the humble,
    for they will inherit the earth.
[6] Blessed are those who hunger and thirst
    for righteousness,
    for they will be filled.

[A] **3:16** Other mss omit *for him*   [B] **4:4** Dt 8:3   [C] **4:6** Ps 91:11-12   [D] **4:7** Dt 6:16   [E] **4:9** Or *and pay me homage*   [F] **4:10** Other mss read *"Get behind me*   [G] **4:10** Dt 6:13   [H] **4:16** Lit *dawned on them*   [I] **4:15-16** Is 9:1-2   [J] **4:19** Or *you fishers of*   [K] **4:23** Or *every kind of*   [L] **4:23** Or *physical ailment*   [M] **5:2** Lit *Then opening his mouth*

7 Blessed are the merciful,
for they will be shown mercy.
8 Blessed are the pure in heart,
for they will see God.
9 Blessed are the peacemakers,
for they will be called sons of God.
10 Blessed are those who are persecuted
because of righteousness,
for the kingdom of heaven is theirs.

11 "You are blessed when they insult you and persecute you and falsely say every kind of evil against you because of me. 12 Be glad and rejoice, because your reward is great in heaven. For that is how they persecuted the prophets who were before you.

BELIEVERS ARE SALT AND LIGHT

13 "You are the salt of the earth. But if the salt should lose its taste, how can it be made salty?ᴬ It's no longer good for anything but to be thrown out and trampled under people's feet.

14 "You are the light of the world. A city situated on a hill cannot be hidden. 15 No one lights a lamp and puts it under a basket, but rather on a lampstand, and it gives light for all who are in the house. 16 In the same way, let your light shine before others, so that they may see your good works and give glory to your Father in heaven.

CHRIST FULFILLS THE LAW

17 "Don't think that I came to abolish the Law or the Prophets. I did not come to abolish but to fulfill. 18 For truly I tell you, until heaven and earth pass away, not the smallest letterᴮ or one stroke of a letter will pass away from the law until all things are accomplished. 19 Therefore, whoever breaks one of the least of these commands and teaches others to do the same will be called least in the kingdom of heaven. But whoever does and teaches these commands will be called great in the kingdom of heaven. 20 For I tell you, unless your righteousness surpasses that of the scribes and Pharisees, you will never get into the kingdom of heaven.

MURDER BEGINS IN THE HEART

21 "You have heard that it was said to our ancestors, Do not murder,ᶜ and whoever murders will be subject to judgment. 22 But I tell you, everyone who is angry with his brother or sisterᴰ will be subject to judgment. Whoever insultsᴱ his brother or sister, will be subject to the court.ᶠ Whoever says, 'You fool!' will be subject to hellfire.ᴳ 23 So if you are offering your gift on the altar, and there you remember that your brother or sister has something against you, 24 leave your gift there in front of the altar. First go and be reconciled with your brother or sister, and then come and offer your gift. 25 Reach a settlement quickly with your adversary while you're on the way with him to the court, or your adversary will hand you over to the judge, and the judge toᴴ the officer, and you will be thrown into prison. 26 Truly I tell you, you will never get out of there until you have paid the last penny.ᴵ

ADULTERY BEGINS IN THE HEART

27 "You have heard that it was said, Do not commit adultery.ᴶ 28 But I tell you, everyone who looks at a woman lustfully has already committed adultery with her in his heart. 29 If your right eye causes you to sin, gouge it out and throw it away. For it is better that you lose one of the parts of your body than for your whole body to be thrown into hell. 30 And if your right hand causes you to sin, cut it off and throw it away. For it is better that you lose one of the parts of your body than for your whole body to go into hell.

DIVORCE PRACTICES CENSURED

31 "It was also said, Whoever divorces his wife must give her a written notice of divorce.ᴷ 32 But I tell you, everyone who divorces his wife, except in a case of sexual immorality, causes her to commit adultery. And whoever marries a divorced woman commits adultery.

TELL THE TRUTH

33 "Again, you have heard that it was said to our ancestors, You must not break your oath, but you must keep your oaths to the Lord.ᴸ 34 But I tell you, don't take an oath at all: either by heaven, because it is God's throne; 35 or by the earth, because it is his footstool; or by Jerusalem, because it is the city of the great King. 36 Do not swear by your head, because you cannot make a single hair white or black. 37 But let your 'yes' mean 'yes,' and your 'no' mean 'no.' Anything more than this is from the evil one.

ᴬ5:13 Or *how can the earth be salted?*   ᴮ5:18 Or *not one iota; iota* is the smallest letter of the Gk alphabet.   ᶜ5:21 Ex 20:13; Dt 5:17   ᴰ5:22 Other mss add *without a cause*   ᴱ5:22 Lit *Whoever says 'Raca';* an Aramaic term of abuse that puts someone down, insulting one's intelligence   ᶠ5:22 Lit *Sanhedrin*   ᴳ5:22 Lit *the gehenna of fire*   ᴴ5:25 Other mss read *judge will hand you over to*   ᴵ5:26 Lit *quadrans,* the smallest and least valuable Roman coin, worth ⅟₆₄ of a daily wage   ᴶ5:27 Ex 20:14; Dt 5:18   ᴷ5:31 Dt 24:1   ᴸ5:33 Lv 19:12; Nm 30:2; Dt 23:21

GO THE SECOND MILE

38 "You have heard that it was said, **An eye for an eye** and **a tooth for a tooth.**ᴬ **39** But I tell you, don't resistᴮ an evildoer. On the contrary, if anyone slaps you on your right cheek, turn the other to him also. **40** As for the one who wants to sue you and take away your shirt, let him have your coat as well. **41** And if anyone forces you to go one mile, go with him two. **42** Give to the one who asks you, and don't turn away from the one who wants to borrow from you.

LOVE YOUR ENEMIES

43 "You have heard that it was said, **Love your neighbor**ᶜ and hate your enemy. **44** But I tell you, love your enemiesᴰ and pray for those whoᴱ persecute you, **45** so that you may beᶠ children of your Father in heaven. For he causes his sun to rise on the evil and the good, and sends rain on the righteous and the unrighteous. **46** For if you love those who love you, what reward will you have? Don't even the tax collectors do the same? **47** And if you greet only your brothers and sisters, what are you doing out of the ordinary?ᴳ Don't even the Gentilesᴴ do the same? **48** Be perfect, therefore, as your heavenly Father is perfect.

HOW TO GIVE

6 "Be careful not to practice your righteousnessᴵ in front of others to be seen by them. Otherwise, you have no reward with your Father in heaven. **2** So whenever you give to the poor, don't sound a trumpet before you, as the hypocrites do in the synagogues and on the streets, to be applauded by people. Truly I tell you, they have their reward. **3** But when you give to the poor, don't let your left hand know what your right hand is doing, **4** so that your giving may be in secret. And your Father who sees in secret will reward you.ᴶ

HOW TO PRAY

5 "Whenever you pray, you must not be like the hypocrites, because they love to pray standing in the synagogues and on the street corners to be seen by people. Truly I tell you, they have their reward. **6** But when you pray, go into your private room, shut your door, and pray to your Father who is in secret. And your Father who sees in secret will reward you.ᴷ **7** When you pray, don't babble like the Gentiles, since they imagine they'll be heard for their many words. **8** Don't be like them, because your Father knows the things you need before you ask him.

THE MODEL PRAYER

9 "Therefore, you should pray like this:

Our Father in heaven,
your name be honored as holy.
10 Your kingdom come.
Your will be done
11 on earth as it is in heaven.
Give us today our daily bread.ᴸ
12 And forgive us our debts,
as we also have forgiven our debtors.
13 And do not bring us intoᴹ temptation,
but deliver us from the evil one.ᴺ

14 "For if you forgive others their offenses, your heavenly Father will forgive you as well. **15** But if you don't forgive others,ᴼ your Father will not forgive your offenses.

HOW TO FAST

16 "Whenever you fast, don't be gloomy like the hypocrites. For they make their faces unattractiveᴾ so that their fasting is obvious to people. Truly I tell you, they have their reward. **17** But when you fast, put oil on your head and wash your face, **18** so that your fasting isn't obvious to others but to your Father who is in secret. And your Father who sees in secret will reward you.ᴷ

GOD AND POSSESSIONS

19 "Don't store up for yourselves treasuresᵠ on earth, where moth and rust destroy and where thieves break in and steal. **20** But store up for yourselves treasures in heaven, where neither moth nor rust destroys, and where thieves don't break in and steal. **21** For where your treasure is, there your heart will be also.

22 "The eye is the lamp of the body. If your eye is healthy, your whole body will be full of light. **23** But if your eye is bad, your whole body will be full of darkness. So if the light within you is darkness, how deep is that darkness!

24 "No one can serve two masters, since either he will hate one and love the other, or he will be devoted to one and despise the other. You cannot serve both God and money.

ᴬ**5:38** Ex 21:24; Lv 24:20; Dt 19:21   ᴮ**5:39** Or *don't set yourself against,* or *don't retaliate against*   ᶜ**5:43** Lv 19:18   ᴰ**5:44** Other mss add *bless those who curse you, do good to those who hate you,*   ᴱ**5:44** Other mss add *mistreat you and*   ᶠ**5:45** Or *may become,* or *may show yourselves to be*   ᴳ**5:47** Or *doing that is superior;* lit *doing more*   ᴴ**5:47** Other mss read *tax collectors*   ᴵ**6:1** Other mss read *charitable giving*   ᴶ**6:4** Other mss read *will himself reward you openly*   ᴷ**6:6,18** Other mss add *openly*   ᴸ**6:11** Or *our necessary bread,* or *our bread for tomorrow*   ᴹ**6:13** Or *do not cause us to come into*   ᴺ**6:13** Or *from evil;* some later mss add *For yours is the kingdom and the power and the glory forever. Amen.*   ᴼ**6:15** Other mss add *their wrongdoing*   ᴾ**6:16** Or *unrecognizable,* or *disfigured*   ᵠ**6:19** Or *valuables*

THE CURE FOR ANXIETY

25 "Therefore I tell you: Don't worry about your life, what you will eat or what you will drink; or about your body, what you will wear. Isn't life more than food and the body more than clothing? **26** Consider the birds of the sky: They don't sow or reap or gather into barns, yet your heavenly Father feeds them. Aren't you worth more than they? **27** Can any of you add one moment to his life-span[A] by worrying? **28** And why do you worry about clothes? Observe how the wildflowers of the field grow: They don't labor or spin thread. **29** Yet I tell you that not even Solomon in all his splendor was adorned like one of these. **30** If that's how God clothes the grass of the field, which is here today and thrown into the furnace tomorrow, won't he do much more for you — you of little faith? **31** So don't worry, saying, 'What will we eat?' or 'What will we drink?' or 'What will we wear?' **32** For the Gentiles eagerly seek all these things, and your heavenly Father knows that you need them. **33** But seek first the kingdom of God[B] and his righteousness, and all these things will be provided for you. **34** Therefore don't worry about tomorrow, because tomorrow will worry about itself. Each day has enough trouble of its own.

DO NOT JUDGE

7 "Do not judge, so that you won't be judged. **2** For you will be judged by the same standard with which you judge others, and you will be measured by the same measure you use. **3** Why do you look at the splinter in your brother's eye but don't notice the beam of wood in your own eye? **4** Or how can you say to your brother, 'Let me take the splinter out of your eye,' and look, there's a beam of wood in your own eye? **5** Hypocrite! First take the beam of wood out of your eye, and then you will see clearly to take the splinter out of your brother's eye. **6** Don't give what is holy to dogs or toss your pearls before pigs, or they will trample them under their feet, turn, and tear you to pieces.

ASK, SEARCH, KNOCK

7 "Ask, and it will be given to you. Seek, and you will find. Knock, and the door[C] will be opened to you. **8** For everyone who asks receives, and the one who seeks finds, and to the one who knocks, the door will be opened. **9** Who among you, if his son asks him for bread, will give him a stone? **10** Or if he asks for a fish, will give him a snake? **11** If you then, who are evil, know how to give good gifts to your children, how much more will your Father in heaven give good things to those who ask him. **12** Therefore, whatever you want others to do for you, do also the same for them, for this is the Law and the Prophets.

ENTERING THE KINGDOM

13 "Enter through the narrow gate. For the gate is wide and the road broad that leads to destruction, and there are many who go through it. **14** How narrow is the gate and difficult the road that leads to life, and few find it.

15 "Be on your guard against false prophets who come to you in sheep's clothing but inwardly are ravaging wolves. **16** You'll recognize them by their fruit. Are grapes gathered from thornbushes or figs from thistles? **17** In the same way, every good tree produces good fruit, but a bad tree produces bad fruit. **18** A good tree can't produce bad fruit; neither can a bad tree produce good fruit. **19** Every tree that doesn't produce good fruit is cut down and thrown into the fire. **20** So you'll recognize them by their fruit.

21 "Not everyone who says to me, 'Lord, Lord,' will enter the kingdom of heaven, but only the one who does the will of my Father in heaven. **22** On that day many will say to me, 'Lord, Lord, didn't we prophesy in your name, drive out demons in your name, and do many miracles in your name?' **23** Then I will announce to them, 'I never knew you. **Depart from me, you lawbreakers!** '[D,E]

THE TWO FOUNDATIONS

24 "Therefore, everyone who hears these words of mine and acts on them will be like a wise man who built his house on the rock. **25** The rain fell, the rivers rose, and the winds blew and pounded that house. Yet it didn't collapse, because its foundation was on the rock. **26** But everyone who hears these words of mine and doesn't act on them will be like a foolish man who built his house on the sand. **27** The rain fell, the rivers rose, the winds blew and pounded that house, and it collapsed. It collapsed with a great crash."

28 When Jesus had finished saying these things, the crowds were astonished at his teaching, **29** because he was teaching them like one who had authority, and not like their scribes.

A MAN CLEANSED

8 When he came down from the mountain, large crowds followed him. **2** Right away a man with leprosy[F] came up and knelt before him, saying, "Lord, if you are willing, you can make me clean."

[A] **6:27** Or add a single cubit to his height [B] **6:33** Other mss omit of God [C] **7:7** Lit and it [D] **7:23** Lit you who work lawlessness [E] **7:23** Ps 6:8 [F] **8:2** Gk lepros; a term for various skin diseases, also in v. 3; see Lv 13–14

³ Reaching out his hand, Jesus touched him, saying, "I am willing; be made clean." Immediately his leprosy was cleansed. ⁴ Then Jesus told him, "See that you don't tell anyone; but go, show yourself to the priest, and offer the gift that Moses commanded, as a testimony to them."

A CENTURION'S FAITH

⁵ When he entered Capernaum, a centurion came to him, pleading with him, ⁶ "Lord, my servant is lying at home paralyzed, in terrible agony."

⁷ He said to him, "Am I to come and heal him?"ᴬ

⁸ "Lord," the centurion replied, "I am not worthy to have you come under my roof. But just say the word, and my servant will be healed. ⁹ For I too am a man under authority, having soldiers under my command.ᴮ I say to this one, 'Go,' and he goes; and to another, 'Come,' and he comes; and to my servant, 'Do this!' and he does it."

¹⁰ Hearing this, Jesus was amazed and said to those following him, "Truly I tell you, I have not found anyone in Israel with so great a faith. ¹¹ I tell you that many will come from east and west to share the banquetᶜ with Abraham, Isaac, and Jacob in the kingdom of heaven. ¹² But the sons of the kingdom will be thrown into the outer darkness where there will be weeping and gnashing of teeth." ¹³ Then Jesus told the centurion, "Go. As you have believed, let it be done for you." And his servant was healed that very moment.ᴰ

HEALINGS AT CAPERNAUM

¹⁴ Jesus went into Peter's house and saw his mother-in-law lying in bed with a fever. ¹⁵ So he touched her hand, and the fever left her. Then she got up and began to serve him. ¹⁶ When evening came, they brought to him many who were demon-possessed. He drove out the spirits with a word and healed all who were sick, ¹⁷ so that what was spoken through the prophet Isaiah might be fulfilled:

> He himself took our weaknesses
> and carried our diseases.ᴱ

THE COST OF FOLLOWING JESUS

¹⁸ When Jesus saw a large crowdᶠ around him, he gave the order to go to the other side of the sea. ¹⁹ A scribe approached him and said, "Teacher, I will follow you wherever you go."

²⁰ Jesus told him, "Foxes have dens, and birds of the sky have nests, but the Son of Man has no place to lay his head."

²¹ "Lord," another of his disciples said, "first let me go bury my father."

²² But Jesus told him, "Follow me, and let the dead bury their own dead."

WIND AND WAVE OBEY JESUS

²³ As he got into the boat, his disciples followed him. ²⁴ Suddenly, a violent storm arose on the sea, so that the boat was being swamped by the waves — but Jesus kept sleeping. ²⁵ So the disciples came and woke him up, saying, "Lord, save us! We're going to die!"

²⁶ He said to them, "Why are you afraid, you of little faith?" Then he got up and rebuked the winds and the sea, and there was a great calm.

²⁷ The men were amazed and asked, "What kind of man is this? Even the winds and the sea obey him!"

DEMONS DRIVEN OUT BY JESUS

²⁸ When he had come to the other side, to the region of the Gadarenes,ᴳ two demon-possessed men met him as they came out of the tombs. They were so violent that no one could pass that way. ²⁹ Suddenly they shouted, "What do you have to do with us,ᴴ Son of God? Have you come here to torment us before the time?"

³⁰ A long way off from them, a large herd of pigs was feeding. ³¹ "If you drive us out," the demons begged him, "send us into the herd of pigs."

³² "Go!" he told them. So when they had come out, they entered the pigs, and the whole herd rushed down the steep bank into the sea and perished in the water. ³³ Then the men who tended them fled. They went into the city and reported everything, especially what had happened to those who were demon-possessed. ³⁴ At that, the whole town went out to meet Jesus. When they saw him, they begged him to leave their region.

THE SON OF MAN FORGIVES AND HEALS

9 So he got into a boat, crossed over, and came to his own town. ² Just then some men¹ brought to him a paralytic lying on a stretcher. Seeing their faith, Jesus told the paralytic, "Have courage, son, your sins are forgiven."

³ At this, some of the scribes said to themselves, "He's blaspheming!"

⁴ Perceiving their thoughts, Jesus said, "Why are you thinking evil things in your hearts?ᴶ ⁵ For which is easier: to say, 'Your sins are forgiven,' or to say, 'Get up and walk'? ⁶ But so that you may know that the Son of Man has

authority on earth to forgive sins" — then he told the paralytic, "Get up, take your stretcher, and go home." [7] So he got up and went home. [8] When the crowds saw this, they were awestruck[A,B] and gave glory to God, who had given such authority to men.

THE CALL OF MATTHEW

[9] As Jesus went on from there, he saw a man named Matthew sitting at the toll booth, and he said to him, "Follow me," and he got up and followed him.

[10] While he was reclining at the table in the house, many tax collectors and sinners came to eat with Jesus and his disciples. [11] When the Pharisees saw this, they asked his disciples, "Why does your teacher eat with tax collectors and sinners?"

[12] Now when he heard this, he said, "It is not those who are well who need a doctor, but those who are sick. [13] Go and learn what this means: **I desire mercy and not sacrifice.**[C] For I didn't come to call the righteous, but sinners."[D]

A QUESTION ABOUT FASTING

[14] Then John's disciples came to him, saying, "Why do we and the Pharisees fast often, but your disciples do not fast?"

[15] Jesus said to them, "Can the wedding guests[E] be sad while the groom is with them? The time[F] will come when the groom will be taken away from them, and then they will fast. [16] No one patches an old garment with unshrunk cloth, because the patch pulls away from the garment and makes the tear worse. [17] And no one puts[G] new wine into old wineskins. Otherwise, the skins burst, the wine spills out, and the skins are ruined. No, they put new wine into fresh wineskins, and both are preserved."

A GIRL RESTORED AND A WOMAN HEALED

[18] As he was telling them these things, suddenly one of the leaders came and knelt down before him, saying, "My daughter just died,[H] but come and lay your hand on her, and she will live." [19] So Jesus and his disciples got up and followed him.

[20] Just then, a woman who had suffered from bleeding for twelve years approached from behind and touched the end of his robe, [21] for she said to herself, "If I can just touch his robe, I'll be made well."[I]

[22] Jesus turned and saw her. "Have courage, daughter," he said. "Your faith has saved you."[J]

And the woman was made well from that moment.[K]

[23] When Jesus came to the leader's house, he saw the flute players and a crowd lamenting loudly. [24] "Leave," he said, "because the girl is not dead but asleep." And they laughed at him. [25] After the crowd had been put outside, he went in and took her by the hand, and the girl got up. [26] Then news of this spread throughout that whole area.

HEALING THE BLIND

[27] As Jesus went on from there, two blind men followed him, calling out, "Have mercy on us, Son of David!"

[28] When he entered the house, the blind men approached him, and Jesus said to them, "Do you believe that I can do this?"

They said to him, "Yes, Lord."

[29] Then he touched their eyes, saying, "Let it be done for you according to your faith." [30] And their eyes were opened. Then Jesus warned them sternly, "Be sure that no one finds out." [31] But they went out and spread the news about him throughout that whole area.

DRIVING OUT A DEMON

[32] Just as they were going out, a demon-possessed man who was unable to speak was brought to him. [33] When the demon had been driven out, the man who had been mute spoke, and the crowds were amazed, saying, "Nothing like this has ever been seen in Israel!"

[34] But the Pharisees said, "He drives out demons by the ruler of the demons."

THE LORD OF THE HARVEST

[35] Jesus continued going around to all the towns and villages, teaching in their synagogues, preaching the good news of the kingdom, and healing every[L] disease and every sickness.[M,N] [36] When he saw the crowds, he felt compassion for them, because they were distressed and dejected, like sheep without a shepherd. [37] Then he said to his disciples, "The harvest is abundant, but the workers are few. [38] Therefore, pray to the Lord of the harvest to send out workers into his harvest."

COMMISSIONING THE TWELVE

10 Summoning his twelve disciples, he gave them authority over unclean spirits, to drive them out and to heal every[L] disease and sickness.[N] [2] These are the names of the twelve

---

[A] 9:8 Other mss read *amazed*   [B] 9:8 Lit *afraid*   [C] 9:13 Hs 6:6   [D] 9:13 Other mss add *to repentance*   [E] 9:15 Lit *the sons of the bridal chamber*   [F] 9:15 Lit *days*   [G] 9:17 Lit *And they do not put*   [H] 9:18 Lit *daughter has now come to the end*   [I] 9:21 Or *be saved*   [J] 9:22 Or *has made you well*   [K] 9:22 Lit *hour*   [L] 9:35; 10:1 Or *every kind of*   [M] 9:35 Other mss add *among the people*   [N] 9:35; 10:1 Or *physical ailment*

apostles: First, Simon, who is called Peter, and Andrew his brother; James the son of Zebedee, and John his brother; [3] Philip and Bartholomew; Thomas and Matthew the tax collector; James the son of Alphaeus, and Thaddaeus;[A] [4] Simon the Zealot,[B] and Judas Iscariot, who also betrayed him.

[5] Jesus sent out these twelve after giving them instructions: "Don't take the road that leads to the Gentiles, and don't enter any Samaritan town. [6] Instead, go to the lost sheep of the house of Israel. [7] As you go, proclaim: 'The kingdom of heaven has come near.' [8] Heal the sick, raise the dead, cleanse those with leprosy,[C] drive out demons. Freely you received, freely give. [9] Don't acquire gold, silver, or copper for your money-belts. [10] Don't take a traveling bag for the road, or an extra shirt, sandals, or a staff, for the worker is worthy of his food. [11] When you enter any town or village, find out who is worthy, and stay there until you leave. [12] Greet a household when you enter it, [13] and if the household is worthy, let your peace be on it; but if it is unworthy, let your peace return to you. [14] If anyone does not welcome you or listen to your words, shake the dust off your feet when you leave that house or town. [15] Truly I tell you, it will be more tolerable on the day of judgment for the land of Sodom and Gomorrah than for that town.

PERSECUTIONS PREDICTED

[16] "Look, I'm sending you out like sheep among wolves. Therefore be as shrewd as serpents and as innocent as doves. [17] Beware of them, because they will hand you over to local courts[D] and flog you in their synagogues. [18] You will even be brought before governors and kings because of me, to bear witness to them and to the Gentiles. [19] But when they hand you over, don't worry about how or what you are to speak. For you will be given what to say at that hour, [20] because it isn't you speaking, but the Spirit of your Father is speaking through you. [21] "Brother will betray brother to death, and a father his child. Children will rise up against parents and have them put to death. [22] You will be hated by everyone because of my name. But the one who endures to the end will be saved. [23] When they persecute you in one town, flee to another. For truly I tell you, you will not have gone through the towns of Israel before the Son of Man comes. [24] A disciple[E] is not above his teacher, or a slave above his master. [25] It is

enough for a disciple to become like his teacher and a slave like his master. If they called the head of the house 'Beelzebul,' how much more the members of his household!

FEAR GOD

[26] "Therefore, don't be afraid of them, since there is nothing covered that won't be uncovered and nothing hidden that won't be made known. [27] What I tell you in the dark, speak in the light. What you hear in a whisper,[F] proclaim on the housetops. [28] Don't fear those who kill the body but are not able to kill the soul; rather, fear him who is able to destroy both soul and body in hell. [29] Aren't two sparrows sold for a penny?[G] Yet not one of them falls to the ground without your Father's consent.[H] [30] But even the hairs of your head have all been counted. [31] So don't be afraid; you are worth more than many sparrows.

ACKNOWLEDGING CHRIST

[32] "Therefore, everyone who will acknowledge me before others, I will also acknowledge him before my Father in heaven. [33] But whoever denies me before others, I will also deny him before my Father in heaven. [34] Don't assume that I came to bring peace on the earth. I did not come to bring peace, but a sword. [35] For I came to turn

a man against his father,
a daughter against her mother,
a daughter-in-law against her mother-
    in-law;
[36]   and a man's enemies will be
        the members of his household.[I]

[37] The one who loves a father or mother more than me is not worthy of me; the one who loves a son or daughter more than me is not worthy of me. [38] And whoever doesn't take up his cross and follow me is not worthy of me. [39] Anyone who finds his life will lose it, and anyone who loses his life because of me will find it.

A CUP OF COLD WATER

[40] "The one who welcomes you welcomes me, and the one who welcomes me welcomes him who sent me. [41] Anyone who welcomes a prophet because he is a prophet[J] will receive a prophet's reward. And anyone who welcomes a righteous person because he's righteous[K] will receive a righteous person's reward. [42] And whoever gives even a cup of cold water to one of these little ones because he is a disciple,[L] truly I tell you, he will never lose his reward."

[A]**10:3** Other mss read *and Lebbaeus, whose surname was Thaddaeus*   [B]**10:4** Lit *the Cananaean*   [C]**10:8** Gk *lepros* ; a term for various skin diseases; see Lv 13–14   [D]**10:17** Or *sanhedrins*   [E]**10:24** Or *student*   [F]**10:27** Lit *in the ear*   [G]**10:29** Gk *assarion*, a small copper coin   [H]**10:29** Lit *ground apart from your Father*   [I]**10:35-36** Mc 7:6   [J]**10:41** Lit *prophet in the name of a prophet*   [K]**10:41** Lit *person in the name of a righteous person*   [L]**10:42** Lit *little ones in the name of a disciple*

JOHN THE BAPTIST DOUBTS

11 When Jesus had finished giving instructions to his twelve disciples, he moved on from there to teach and preach in their towns. ² Now when John heard in prison what the Christ was doing, he sent a message through his disciples ³ and asked him, "Are you the one who is to come, or should we expect someone else?"

⁴ Jesus replied to them, "Go and report to John what you hear and see: ⁵ The blind receive their sight, the lame walk, those with leprosy^ are cleansed, the deaf hear, the dead are raised, and the poor are told the good news, ⁶ and blessed is the one who isn't offended by me."

⁷ As these men were leaving, Jesus began to speak to the crowds about John: "What did you go out into the wilderness to see? A reed swaying in the wind? ⁸ What then did you go out to see? A man dressed in soft clothes? See, those who wear soft clothes are in royal palaces. ⁹ What then did you go out to see? A prophet? Yes, I tell you, and more than a prophet. ¹⁰ This is the one about whom it is written:

> See, I am sending my messenger
>   ahead of you;
> he will prepare your way before you.^B

¹¹ "Truly I tell you, among those born of women no one greater than John the Baptist has appeared,^C but the least in the kingdom of heaven is greater than he. ¹² From the days of John the Baptist until now, the kingdom of heaven has been suffering violence,^D and the violent have been seizing it by force. ¹³ For all the prophets and the law prophesied until John. ¹⁴ And if you're willing to accept it, he is the Elijah who is to come. ¹⁵ Let anyone who has ears^E listen.

AN UNRESPONSIVE GENERATION

¹⁶ "To what should I compare this generation? It's like children sitting in the marketplaces who call out to other children:

¹⁷ We played the flute for you,
>   but you didn't dance;
>   we sang a lament,
>   but you didn't mourn!^F

¹⁸ For John came neither eating nor drinking, and they say, 'He has a demon!' ¹⁹ The Son of Man came eating and drinking, and they say, 'Look, a glutton and a drunkard, a friend of tax collectors and sinners!' Yet wisdom is vindicated^G by her deeds."^H

²⁰ Then he proceeded to denounce the towns where most of his miracles were done, because they did not repent: ²¹ "Woe to you, Chorazin! Woe to you, Bethsaida! For if the miracles that were done in you had been done in Tyre and Sidon, they would have repented in sackcloth and ashes long ago. ²² But I tell you, it will be more tolerable for Tyre and Sidon on the day of judgment than for you. ²³ And you, Capernaum, will you be exalted to heaven? No, you will go down to Hades. For if the miracles that were done in you had been done in Sodom, it would have remained until today. ²⁴ But I tell you, it will be more tolerable for the land of Sodom on the day of judgment than for you."

THE SON GIVES KNOWLEDGE AND REST

²⁵ At that time Jesus said, "I praise you, Father, Lord of heaven and earth, because you have hidden these things from the wise and intelligent and revealed them to infants. ²⁶ Yes, Father, because this was your good pleasure.^I ²⁷ All things have been entrusted to me by my Father. No one knows the Son except the Father, and no one knows the Father except the Son and anyone to whom the Son desires^J to reveal him.

²⁸ "Come to me, all of you who are weary and burdened, and I will give you rest. ²⁹ Take up my yoke and learn from me, because I am lowly and humble in heart, and you will find rest for your souls. ³⁰ For my yoke is easy and my burden is light."

LORD OF THE SABBATH

12 At that time Jesus passed through the grainfields on the Sabbath. His disciples were hungry and began to pick and eat some heads of grain. ² When the Pharisees saw this, they said to him, "See, your disciples are doing what is not lawful to do on the Sabbath."

³ He said to them, "Haven't you read what David did when he and those who were with him were hungry: ⁴ how he entered the house of God, and they ate^K the bread of the Presence — which is not lawful for him or for those with him to eat, but only for the priests? ⁵ Or haven't you read in the law that on Sabbath days the priests in the temple violate the Sabbath and are innocent? ⁶ I tell you that something greater than the temple is here. ⁷ If you had known what this means, **I desire mercy and not sacrifice,**^L you would not have condemned the innocent. ⁸ For the Son of Man is Lord of the Sabbath."

---

^11:5 Gk *lepros*; a term for various skin diseases; see Lv 13–14   ^11:10 Mal 3:1   ^11:11 Lit *arisen*   ^11:12 Or *has been forcefully advancing*   ^11:15 Other mss add *to hear*   ^11:17 Or *beat your chests in grief*   ^11:19 Or *declared right*   ^11:19 Other mss read *children*   ^11:26 Lit *was well-pleasing in your sight*   ^11:27 Or *wills*, or *chooses*   ^12:4 Other mss read *he ate*   ^12:7 Hs 6:6

THE MAN WITH THE SHRIVELED HAND

[9] Moving on from there, he entered their synagogue. [10] There he saw a man who had a shriveled hand, and in order to accuse him they asked him, "Is it lawful to heal on the Sabbath?"

[11] He replied to them, "Who among you, if he had a sheep that fell into a pit on the Sabbath, wouldn't take hold of it and lift it out? [12] A person is worth far more than a sheep; so it is lawful to do what is good on the Sabbath."

[13] Then he told the man, "Stretch out your hand." So he stretched it out, and it was restored, as good as the other. [14] But the Pharisees went out and plotted against him, how they might kill him.

THE SERVANT OF THE LORD

[15] Jesus was aware of this and withdrew. Large crowds[A] followed him, and he healed them all. [16] He warned them not to make him known, [17] so that what was spoken through the prophet Isaiah might be fulfilled:

[18]   Here is my servant
       whom I have chosen,
    my beloved in whom I delight;
    I will put my Spirit on him,
    and he will proclaim justice
       to the nations.
[19]   He will not argue or shout,
    and no one will hear his voice
       in the streets.
[20]   He will not break a bruised reed,
    and he will not put out
       a smoldering wick,
    until he has led justice to victory.[B]
[21]   The nations will put their hope
       in his name.[C]

A HOUSE DIVIDED

[22] Then a demon-possessed man who was blind and unable to speak was brought to him. He healed him, so that the man[D] could both speak and see. [23] All the crowds were astounded and said, "Could this be the Son of David?"

[24] When the Pharisees heard this, they said, "This man drives out demons only by Beelzebul, the ruler of the demons."

[25] Knowing their thoughts, he told them: "Every kingdom divided against itself is headed for destruction, and no city or house divided against itself will stand. [26] If Satan drives out Satan, he is divided against himself. How then will his kingdom stand? [27] And if I drive out demons by Beelzebul, by whom do your sons drive them out? For this reason they will be your judges. [28] If I drive out demons by the Spirit of God, then the kingdom of God has come upon you. [29] How can someone enter a strong man's house and steal his possessions unless he first ties up the strong man? Then he can plunder his house. [30] Anyone who is not with me is against me, and anyone who does not gather with me scatters. [31] Therefore, I tell you, people will be forgiven every sin and blasphemy, but the blasphemy against[E] the Spirit will not be forgiven.[F] [32] Whoever speaks a word against the Son of Man, it will be forgiven him; but whoever speaks against the Holy Spirit, it will not be forgiven him, either in this age or in the one to come.

A TREE AND ITS FRUIT

[33] "Either make the tree good and its fruit will be good, or make the tree bad[G] and its fruit will be bad; for a tree is known by its fruit. [34] Brood of vipers! How can you speak good things when you are evil? For the mouth speaks from the overflow of the heart. [35] A good person produces good things from his storeroom of good, and an evil person produces evil things from his storeroom of evil. [36] I tell you that on the day of judgment people will have to account for every careless[H] word they speak.[I] [37] For by your words you will be acquitted, and by your words you will be condemned."

THE SIGN OF JONAH

[38] Then some of the scribes and Pharisees said to him, "Teacher, we want to see a sign from you."

[39] He answered them, "An evil and adulterous generation demands a sign, but no sign will be given to it except the sign of the prophet Jonah. [40] For as Jonah was in the belly of the huge fish[J] three days and three nights, so the Son of Man will be in the heart of the earth three days and three nights. [41] The men of Nineveh will stand up at the judgment with this generation and condemn it, because they repented at Jonah's preaching; and look — something greater than Jonah is here. [42] The queen of the south will rise up at the judgment with this generation and condemn it, because she came from the ends of the earth to hear the wisdom of Solomon; and look — something greater than Solomon is here.

AN UNCLEAN SPIRIT'S RETURN

[43] "When an unclean spirit comes out of a person, it roams through waterless places looking for rest but doesn't find any. [44] Then it says,

---

[A]12:15 Other mss read *Many*   [B]12:20 Or *until he has successfully put forth justice*   [C]12:18-21 Is 42:1-4   [D]12:22 Lit *mute*   [E]12:31 Or *of*   [F]12:31 Other mss add *people*   [G]12:33 Or *decayed*; lit *rotten*   [H]12:36 Lit *worthless*   [I]12:36 Lit *will speak*   [J]12:40 Or *sea creature*; Jnh 1:17

'I'll go back to my house that I came from.' Returning, it finds the house vacant, swept, and put in order. [45] Then it goes and brings with it seven other spirits more evil than itself, and they enter and settle down there. As a result, that person's last condition is worse than the first. That's how it will also be with this evil generation."

TRUE RELATIONSHIPS

[46] While he was still speaking with the crowds, his mother and brothers were standing outside wanting to speak to him. [47] Someone told him, "Look, your mother and your brothers are standing outside, wanting to speak to you."[A]

[48] He replied to the one who was speaking to him, "Who is my mother and who are my brothers?" [49] Stretching out his hand toward his disciples, he said, "Here are my mother and my brothers! [50] For whoever does the will of my Father in heaven is my brother and sister and mother."

THE PARABLE OF THE SOWER

13 On that day Jesus went out of the house and was sitting by the sea. [2] Such large crowds gathered around him that he got into a boat and sat down, while the whole crowd stood on the shore.

[3] Then he told them many things in parables, saying: "Consider the sower who went out to sow. [4] As he sowed, some seed fell along the path, and the birds came and devoured them. [5] Other seed fell on rocky ground where it didn't have much soil, and it grew up quickly since the soil wasn't deep. [6] But when the sun came up, it was scorched, and since it had no root, it withered away. [7] Other seed fell among thorns, and the thorns came up and choked it. [8] Still other seed fell on good ground and produced fruit: some a hundred, some sixty, and some thirty times what was sown. [9] Let anyone who has ears[B] listen."

WHY JESUS USED PARABLES

[10] Then the disciples came up and asked him, "Why are you speaking to them in parables?"

[11] He answered, "Because the secrets of the kingdom of heaven have been given for you to know, but it has not been given to them. [12] For whoever has, more will be given to him, and he will have more than enough; but whoever does not have, even what he has will be taken away from him. [13] That is why I speak to them in parables, because looking they do not see, and hearing they do not listen or understand. [14] Isaiah's prophecy is fulfilled in them, which says:

You will listen and listen,
but never understand;
you will look and look,
but never perceive.
[15] For this people's heart
    has grown callous;
their ears are hard of hearing,
and they have shut their eyes;
otherwise they might see
    with their eyes,
and hear with their ears, and
understand with their hearts,
and turn back —
and I would heal them.[C]

[16] "Blessed are your eyes because they do see, and your ears because they do hear. [17] For truly I tell you, many prophets and righteous people longed to see the things you see but didn't see them, to hear the things you hear but didn't hear them.

THE PARABLE OF THE SOWER EXPLAINED

[18] "So listen to the parable of the sower: [19] When anyone hears the word about the kingdom and doesn't understand it, the evil one comes and snatches away what was sown in his heart. This is the one sown along the path. [20] And the one sown on rocky ground — this is one who hears the word and immediately receives it with joy. [21] But he has no root and is short-lived. When distress or persecution comes because of the word, immediately he falls away. [22] Now the one sown among the thorns — this is one who hears the word, but the worries of this age and the deceitfulness[D] of wealth choke the word, and it becomes unfruitful. [23] But the one sown on the good ground — this is one who hears and understands the word, who does produce fruit and yields: some a hundred, some sixty, some thirty times what was sown."

THE PARABLE OF THE WHEAT AND THE WEEDS

[24] He presented another parable to them: "The kingdom of heaven may be compared to a man who sowed good seed in his field. [25] But while people were sleeping, his enemy came, sowed weeds among the wheat, and left. [26] When the plants sprouted and produced grain, then the weeds also appeared. [27] The landowner's servants came to him and said, 'Master, didn't you sow good seed in your field? Then where did the weeds come from?'

[28] " 'An enemy did this,' he told them.

" 'So, do you want us to go and pull them up?' the servants asked him.

[29] " 'No,' he said. 'When you pull up the weeds, you might also uproot the wheat with them.

[A]**12:47** Other mss omit this v.   [B]**13:9** Other mss add *to hear*   [C]**13:14-15** Is 6:9-10   [D]**13:22** Or *pleasure*

[30] Let both grow together until the harvest. At harvest time I'll tell the reapers: Gather the weeds first and tie them in bundles to burn them, but collect the wheat in my barn.'"

THE PARABLES OF THE MUSTARD SEED
AND OF THE LEAVEN

[31] He presented another parable to them: "The kingdom of heaven is like a mustard seed that a man took and sowed in his field. [32] It's the smallest of all the seeds, but when grown, it's taller than the garden plants and becomes a tree, so that the birds of the sky come and nest in its branches."

[33] He told them another parable: "The kingdom of heaven is like leaven[A] that a woman took and mixed into fifty pounds[B] of flour until all of it was leavened."

USING PARABLES FULFILLS PROPHECY

[34] Jesus told the crowds all these things in parables, and he did not tell them anything without a parable, [35] so that what was spoken through the prophet might be fulfilled:

I will open my mouth in parables;
I will declare things kept secret
from the foundation of the world.[C,D]

JESUS INTERPRETS THE PARABLE OF THE WHEAT
AND THE WEEDS

[36] Then he left the crowds and went into the house. His disciples approached him and said, "Explain to us the parable of the weeds in the field."

[37] He replied: "The one who sows the good seed is the Son of Man; [38] the field is the world; and the good seed — these are the children of the kingdom. The weeds are the children of the evil one, [39] and the enemy who sowed them is the devil. The harvest is the end of the age, and the harvesters are angels. [40] Therefore, just as the weeds are gathered and burned in the fire, so it will be at the end of the age. [41] The Son of Man will send out his angels, and they will gather from his kingdom all who cause sin[E] and those guilty of lawlessness.[F] [42] They will throw them into the blazing furnace where there will be weeping and gnashing of teeth. [43] Then the righteous will shine like the sun in their Father's kingdom. Let anyone who has ears[G] listen.

THE PARABLES OF THE HIDDEN TREASURE
AND OF THE PRICELESS PEARL

[44] "The kingdom of heaven is like treasure, buried in a field, that a man found and reburied.

Then in his joy he goes and sells everything he has and buys that field.

[45] "Again, the kingdom of heaven is like a merchant in search of fine pearls. [46] When he found one priceless[H] pearl, he went and sold everything he had and bought it.

THE PARABLE OF THE NET

[47] "Again, the kingdom of heaven is like a large net thrown into the sea. It collected every kind of fish, [48] and when it was full, they dragged it ashore, sat down, and gathered the good fish into containers, but threw out the worthless ones. [49] So it will be at the end of the age. The angels will go out, separate the evil people from the righteous, [50] and throw them into the blazing furnace, where there will be weeping and gnashing of teeth.

THE STOREHOUSE OF TRUTH

[51] "Have you understood all these things?"[I]
They answered him, "Yes."

[52] "Therefore," he said to them, "every teacher of the law[J] who has become a disciple in the kingdom of heaven is like the owner of a house who brings out of his storeroom treasures new and old."

REJECTION AT NAZARETH

[53] When Jesus had finished these parables, he left there. [54] He went to his hometown and began to teach them in their synagogue, so that they were astonished and said, "Where did this man get this wisdom and these miraculous powers? [55] Isn't this the carpenter's son? Isn't his mother called Mary, and his brothers James, Joseph,[K] Simon, and Judas? [56] And his sisters, aren't they all with us? So where does he get all these things?" [57] And they were offended by him.

Jesus said to them, "A prophet is not without honor except in his hometown and in his household." [58] And he did not do many miracles there because of their unbelief.

JOHN THE BAPTIST BEHEADED

14 At that time Herod the tetrarch heard the report about Jesus. [2] "This is John the Baptist," he told his servants. "He has been raised from the dead, and that's why miraculous powers are at work in him."

[3] For Herod had arrested John, chained[L] him, and put him in prison on account of Herodias, his brother Philip's wife, [4] since John had been telling him, "It's not lawful for you to have

---

[A] 13:33 Or yeast   [B] 13:33 Lit three sata; about 40 liters   [C] 13:35 Some mss omit of the world   [D] 13:35 Ps 78:2
[E] 13:41 Or stumbling   [F] 13:41 Or those who do lawlessness   [G] 13:43 Other mss add to hear   [H] 13:46 Or very precious
[I] 13:51 Other mss add Jesus asked them   [J] 13:52 Or every scribe   [K] 13:55 Other mss read Joses; Mk 6:3   [L] 14:3 Or bound

her." [5] Though Herod wanted to kill John, he feared the crowd since they regarded John as a prophet.

[6] When Herod's birthday celebration came, Herodias's daughter danced before them[A] and pleased Herod. [7] So he promised with an oath to give her whatever she asked. [8] Prompted by her mother, she answered, "Give me John the Baptist's head here on a platter." [9] Although the king regretted it, he commanded that it be granted because of his oaths and his guests. [10] So he sent orders and had John beheaded in the prison. [11] His head was brought on a platter and given to the girl, who carried it to her mother. [12] Then his disciples came, removed the corpse,[B] buried it, and went and reported to Jesus.

FEEDING OF THE FIVE THOUSAND

[13] When Jesus heard about it, he withdrew from there by boat to a remote place to be alone. When the crowds heard this, they followed him on foot from the towns. [14] When he went ashore,[C] he saw a large crowd, had compassion on them, and healed their sick.

[15] When evening came, the disciples approached him and said, "This place is deserted, and it is already late.[D] Send the crowds away so that they can go into the villages and buy food for themselves."

[16] "They don't need to go away," Jesus told them. "You give them something to eat."

[17] "But we only have five loaves and two fish here," they said to him.

[18] "Bring them here to me," he said. [19] Then he commanded the crowds to sit down on the grass. He took the five loaves and the two fish, and looking up to heaven, he blessed them. He broke the loaves and gave them to the disciples, and the disciples gave them to the crowds. [20] Everyone ate and was satisfied. They picked up twelve baskets full of leftover pieces. [21] Now those who ate were about five thousand men, besides women and children.

WALKING ON THE WATER

[22] Immediately he[E] made the disciples get into the boat and go ahead of him to the other side, while he dismissed the crowds. [23] After dismissing the crowds, he went up on the mountain by himself to pray. Well into the night, he was there alone. [24] Meanwhile, the boat was already some distance[F] from land,[G] battered

by the waves, because the wind was against them. [25] Jesus came toward them walking on the sea very early in the morning."[26] When the disciples saw him walking on the sea, they were terrified. "It's a ghost!" they said, and they cried out in fear.

[27] Immediately Jesus spoke to them. "Have courage! It is I. Don't be afraid."

[28] "Lord, if it's you," Peter answered him, "command me to come to you on the water."

[29] He said, "Come."

And climbing out of the boat, Peter started walking on the water and came toward Jesus. [30] But when he saw the strength of the wind,[H] he was afraid, and beginning to sink he cried out, "Lord, save me!"

[31] Immediately Jesus reached out his hand, caught hold of him, and said to him, "You of little faith, why did you doubt?"

[32] When they got into the boat, the wind ceased. [33] Then those in the boat worshiped him and said, "Truly you are the Son of God."

MIRACULOUS HEALINGS

[34] When they had crossed over, they came to shore at Gennesaret. [35] When the men of that place recognized him, they alerted the whole vicinity and brought to him all who were sick. [36] They begged him that they might only touch the end of his robe, and as many as touched it were healed.

THE TRADITION OF THE ELDERS

15 Then Jesus was approached by Pharisees and scribes from Jerusalem, who asked, [2] "Why do your disciples break the tradition of the elders? For they don't wash their hands when they eat."[I]

[3] He answered them, "Why do you break God's commandment because of your tradition? [4] For God said:[K] Honor your father and your mother;[L] and, Whoever speaks evil of father or mother must be put to death.[M] [5] But you say, 'Whoever tells his father or mother, "Whatever benefit you might have received from me is a gift committed to the temple," [6] he does not have to honor his father.'[N] In this way, you have nullified the word of God[O] because of your tradition. [7] Hypocrites! Isaiah prophesied correctly about you when he said:

[8]   This people[P] honors me with their lips,
     but their heart is far from me.

---

^ **14:6** Lit *danced in the middle*   ^B **14:12** Other mss read *body*   ^C **14:14** Lit *Coming out* (of the boat)   ^D **14:15** Lit *and the time* (for the evening meal) *has already passed*   ^E **14:22** Other mss read *Jesus*   ^F **14:24** Lit *already many stadia ;* one *stadion* = 600 feet   ^G **14:24** Other mss read *already in the middle of the sea*   ^H **14:25** Lit *fourth watch of the night* = 3 to 6 a.m.   ^I **14:30** Other mss read *saw the wind*   ^J **15:2** Lit *eat bread* = eat a meal   ^K **15:4** Other mss read *commanded, saying*   ^L **15:4** Ex 20:12; Dt 5:16   ^M **15:4** Ex 21:17; Lv 20:9   ^N **15:6** Other mss read *then he does not have to honor his father or mother*   ^O **15:6** Other mss read *commandment*   ^P **15:8** Other mss add *draw near to me with their mouths, and*

⁹ They worship me in vain,
teaching as doctrines
human commands."ᴬ

DEFILEMENT IS FROM WITHIN

¹⁰ Summoning the crowd, he told them, "Listen and understand: ¹¹ It's not what goes into the mouth that defiles a person, but what comes out of the mouth — this defiles a person."

¹² Then the disciples came up and told him, "Do you know that the Pharisees took offense when they heard what you said?"

¹³ He replied, "Every plant that my heavenly Father didn't plant will be uprooted. ¹⁴ Leave them alone! They are blind guides.ᴮ And if the blind guide the blind, both will fall into a pit."

¹⁵ Then Peter said, "Explain this parable to us."

¹⁶ "Do you still lack understanding?" heᶜ asked. ¹⁷ "Don't you realizeᴰ that whatever goes into the mouth passes into the stomach and is eliminated?ᴱ ¹⁸ But what comes out of the mouth comes from the heart, and this defiles a person. ¹⁹ For from the heart come evil thoughts, murders, adulteries, sexual immoralities, thefts, false testimonies, slander. ²⁰ These are the things that defile a person; but eating with unwashed hands does not defile a person."

A GENTILE MOTHER'S FAITH

²¹ When Jesus left there, he withdrew to the area of Tyre and Sidon. ²² Just then a Canaanite woman from that region came and kept crying out,ᶠ "Have mercy on me, Lord, Son of David! My daughter is severely tormented by a demon."

²³ Jesus did not say a word to her. His disciples approached him and urged him, "Send her away because she's crying out after us."

²⁴ He replied, "I was sent only to the lost sheep of the house of Israel."

²⁵ But she came, knelt before him, and said, "Lord, help me!"

²⁶ He answered, "It isn't right to take the children's bread and throw it to the dogs."

²⁷ "Yes, Lord," she said, "yet even the dogs eat the crumbs that fall from their masters' table."

²⁸ Then Jesus replied to her, "Woman, your faith is great. Let it be done for you as you want." And from that momentᴳ her daughter was healed.

HEALING MANY PEOPLE

²⁹ Moving on from there, Jesus passed along the Sea of Galilee. He went up on a mountain and sat there, ³⁰ and large crowds came to him, including the lame, the blind, the crippled, those unable to speak, and many others. They put them at his feet, and he healed them. ³¹ So the crowd was amazed when they saw those unable to speak talking, the crippled restored, the lame walking, and the blind seeing, and they gave glory to the God of Israel.

FEEDING OF THE FOUR THOUSAND

³² Jesus called his disciples and said, "I have compassion on the crowd, because they've already stayed with me three days and have nothing to eat. I don't want to send them away hungry, otherwise they might collapse on the way."

³³ The disciples said to him, "Where could we get enough bread in this desolate place to feed such a crowd?"

³⁴ "How many loaves do you have?" Jesus asked them.

"Seven," they said, "and a few small fish."

³⁵ After commanding the crowd to sit down on the ground, ³⁶ he took the seven loaves and the fish, gave thanks, broke them, and gave them to the disciples, and the disciples gave them to the crowds. ³⁷ They all ate and were satisfied. They collected the leftover pieces — seven large baskets full. ³⁸ Now there were four thousand men who had eaten, besides women and children. ³⁹ After dismissing the crowds, he got into the boat and went to the region of Magadan.ᴴ

THE LEAVEN OF THE PHARISEES AND THE SADDUCEES

16 The Pharisees and Sadducees approached, and tested him, asking him to show them a sign from heaven. ² He replied, "When evening comes you say, 'It will be good weather because the sky is red.' ³ And in the morning, 'Today will be stormy because the sky is red and threatening.' Youᴵ know how to read the appearance of the sky, but you can't read the signs of the times.ᴶ ⁴ An evil and adulterous generation demands a sign, but no sign will be given to it except the sign ofᴷ Jonah." Then he left them and went away.

⁵ The disciples reached the other shore,ᴸ and they had forgotten to take bread. ⁶ Then Jesus told them, "Watch out and beware of the leavenᴹ of the Pharisees and Sadducees."

⁷ They were discussing among themselves, "We didn't bring any bread."

⁸ Aware of this, Jesus said, "You of little faith, why are you discussing among yourselves that

---

ᴬ**15:8-9** Is 29:13 LXX ᴮ**15:14** Other mss add *for the blind* ᶜ**15:16** Other mss read *Jesus* ᴰ**15:17** Other mss add *yet* ᴱ**15:17** Lit *and goes out into the toilet* ᶠ**15:22** Other mss read *and cried out to him* ᴳ**15:28** Lit *hour* ᴴ**15:39** Other mss read *Magdala* ᴵ**16:3** Other mss read *Hypocrites! You* ᴶ**16:2-3** Other mss omit *When* (v. 2) through end of v. 3 ᴷ**16:4** Other mss add *the prophet* ᴸ**16:5** Lit *disciples went to the other side* ᴹ**16:6** Or *yeast*, also in vv. 11,12

you do not have bread? [9] Don't you understand yet? Don't you remember the five loaves for the five thousand and how many baskets you collected? [10] Or the seven loaves for the four thousand and how many large baskets you collected? [11] Why is it you don't understand that when I told you, 'Beware of the leaven of the Pharisees and Sadducees,' it wasn't about bread?" [12] Then they understood that he had not told them to beware of the leaven in bread, but of the teaching of the Pharisees and Sadducees.

PETER'S CONFESSION OF THE MESSIAH

[13] When Jesus came to the region of Caesarea Philippi,[A] he asked his disciples, "Who do people say that the Son of Man is?"[B]

[14] They replied, "Some say John the Baptist; others, Elijah; still others, Jeremiah or one of the prophets."

[15] "But you," he asked them, "who do you say that I am?"

[16] Simon Peter answered, "You are the Messiah, the Son of the living God."

[17] Jesus responded, "Blessed are you, Simon son of Jonah,[C] because flesh and blood did not reveal this to you, but my Father in heaven. [18] And I also say to you that you are Peter, and on this rock I will build my church, and the gates of Hades will not overpower it. [19] I will give you the keys of the kingdom of heaven, and whatever you bind on earth will have been bound[D] in heaven, and whatever you loose on earth will have been loosed[E] in heaven." [20] Then he gave the disciples orders to tell no one that he was[F] the Messiah.

HIS DEATH AND RESURRECTION PREDICTED

[21] From then on Jesus began to point out to his disciples that it was necessary for him to go to Jerusalem and suffer many things from the elders, chief priests, and scribes, be killed, and be raised the third day. [22] Peter took him aside and began to rebuke him, "Oh no,[G] Lord! This will never happen to you!"

[23] Jesus turned and told Peter, "Get behind me, Satan! You are a hindrance to me because you're not thinking about God's concerns[H] but human concerns."

TAKE UP YOUR CROSS

[24] Then Jesus said to his disciples, "If anyone wants to follow after me, let him deny himself, take up his cross, and follow me. [25] For whoever wants to save his life will lose it, but whoever loses his life because of me will find it. [26] For what will it benefit someone if he gains the whole world yet loses his life? Or what will anyone give in exchange for his life? [27] For the Son of Man is going to come with his angels in the glory of his Father, and then he will reward each according to what he has done. [28] Truly I tell you, there are some standing here who will not taste death until they see the Son of Man coming in his kingdom."

THE TRANSFIGURATION

17 After six days Jesus took Peter, James, and his brother John and led them up on a high mountain by themselves. [2] He was transfigured in front of them, and his face shone like the sun; his clothes became as white as the light. [3] Suddenly, Moses and Elijah appeared to them, talking with him. [4] Then Peter said to Jesus, "Lord, it's good for us to be here. I will set up[I] three shelters here: one for you, one for Moses, and one for Elijah."

[5] While he was still speaking, suddenly a bright cloud covered[J] them, and a voice from the cloud said: "This is my beloved Son, with whom I am well-pleased. Listen to him!" [6] When the disciples heard this, they fell facedown and were terrified.

[7] Jesus came up, touched them, and said, "Get up; don't be afraid." [8] When they looked up they saw no one except Jesus alone.

[9] As they were coming down the mountain, Jesus commanded them, "Don't tell anyone about the vision until the Son of Man is raised[K] from the dead."

[10] So the disciples asked him, "Why then do the scribes say that Elijah must come first?"

[11] "Elijah is coming[L] and will restore everything," he replied.[M] [12] "But I tell you: Elijah has already come, and they didn't recognize him. On the contrary, they did whatever they pleased to him. In the same way the Son of Man is going to suffer at their hands." [13] Then the disciples understood that he had spoken to them about John the Baptist.

THE POWER OF JESUS OVER A DEMON

[14] When they reached the crowd, a man approached and knelt down before him. [15] "Lord," he said, "have mercy on my son, because he has seizures[N] and suffers terribly. He often

---

[A]**16:13** A town north of Galilee at the base of Mount Hermon　[B]**16:13** Other mss read *that I, the Son of Man, am*　[C]**16:17** Or *son of John*　[D]**16:19** Or *earth will be bound*　[E]**16:19** Or *earth will be loosed*　[F]**16:20** Other mss add *Jesus*　[G]**16:22** Lit *"Mercy to you = "May God have mercy on you*　[H]**16:23** Lit *about the things of God*　[I]**17:4** Other mss read *Let's make*　[J]**17:5** Or *enveloped*; Ex 40:34-35　[K]**17:9** Other mss read *Man has risen*　[L]**17:11** Other mss add *first*　[M]**17:11** Other mss read *Jesus said to them*　[N]**17:15** Lit *he is moonstruck*; thought to be a form of epilepsy

falls into the fire and often into the water. [16] I brought him to your disciples, but they couldn't heal him."

[17] Jesus replied, "You unbelieving and perverse generation, how long will I be with you? How long must I put up with you? Bring him here to me." [18] Then Jesus rebuked the demon,[A] and it[B] came out of him, and from that moment[C] the boy was healed.

[19] Then the disciples approached Jesus privately and said, "Why couldn't we drive it out?"

[20] "Because of your little faith," he[D] told them. "For truly I tell you, if you have faith the size of[E] a mustard seed, you will tell this mountain, 'Move from here to there,' and it will move. Nothing will be impossible for you."[F]

THE SECOND PREDICTION OF HIS DEATH

[22] As they were gathering together[G] in Galilee, Jesus told them, "The Son of Man is about to be betrayed into the hands of men. [23] They will kill him, and on the third day he will be raised up." And they were deeply distressed.

PAYING THE TEMPLE TAX

[24] When they came to Capernaum, those who collected the temple tax approached Peter and said, "Doesn't your teacher pay the temple tax?"

[25] "Yes," he said.

When he went into the house, Jesus spoke to him first,[H] "What do you think, Simon? From whom do earthly kings collect tariffs or taxes? From their sons or from strangers?"[I]

[26] "From strangers," he said.[J]

"Then the sons are free," Jesus told him. [27] "But, so we won't offend them, go to the sea, cast in a fishhook, and take the first fish that you catch. When you open its mouth you'll find a coin.[K] Take it and give it to them for me and you."

WHO IS THE GREATEST?

18 At that time[C] the disciples came to Jesus and asked, "So who is greatest in the kingdom of heaven?" [2] He called a child and had him stand among them. [3] "Truly I tell you," he said, "unless you turn and become like children, you will never enter the kingdom of heaven. [4] Therefore, whoever humbles himself like this child — this one is the greatest in the kingdom

of heaven. [5] And whoever welcomes[L] one child like this in my name welcomes me.

[6] "But whoever causes one of these little ones who believe in me to fall away — it would be better for him if a heavy millstone were hung around his neck and he were drowned in the depths of the sea. [7] Woe to the world because of offenses. For offenses will inevitably come, but woe to that person by whom the offense comes. [8] If your hand or your foot causes you to fall away, cut it off and throw it away. It is better for you to enter life maimed or lame than to have two hands or two feet and be thrown into the eternal fire. [9] And if your eye causes you to fall away, gouge it out and throw it away. It is better for you to enter life with one eye than to have two eyes and be thrown into hellfire.[M]

THE PARABLE OF THE LOST SHEEP

[10] "See to it that you don't despise one of these little ones, because I tell you that in heaven their angels continually view the face of my Father in heaven."[N] [12] What do you think? If someone has a hundred sheep, and one of them goes astray, won't he leave the ninety-nine on the hillside and go and search for the stray? [13] And if he finds it, truly I tell you, he rejoices over that sheep[O] more than over the ninety-nine that did not go astray. [14] In the same way, it is not the will of your Father in heaven that one of these little ones perish.

RESTORING A BROTHER

[15] "If your brother sins against you,[P] go and rebuke him in private.[Q] If he listens to you, you have won your brother. [16] But if he won't listen, take one or two others with you, so that **by the testimony**[R] **of two or three witnesses every fact may be established.**[S] [17] If he doesn't pay attention to them, tell the church.[T] If he doesn't pay attention even to the church, let him be like a Gentile and a tax collector to you. [18] Truly I tell you, whatever you bind on earth will have been bound[U] in heaven, and whatever you loose on earth will have been loosed[V] in heaven. [19] Again, truly I tell you, if two of you on earth agree about any matter that you[W] pray for, it will be done for you[X] by my Father in heaven. [20] For where two or three are gathered together in my name, I am there among them."

[A]17:18 Lit *rebuked him, or it* [B]17:18 Lit *the demon* [C]17:18; 18:1 Lit *hour* [D]17:20 Other mss read *your unbelief, Jesus*
[E]17:20 Lit *faith like* [F]17:20 Some mss include v. 21: *"However, this kind does not come out except by prayer and fasting."*
[G]17:22 Other mss read *were staying* [H]17:25 Lit *Jesus anticipated him by saying* [I]17:25 Or *foreigners* [J]17:26 Other mss
read *Peter said to him* [K]17:27 Gk *stater*, worth 2 double-drachmas [L]18:5 Or *receives* [M]18:9 Lit *gehenna of fire*
[N]18:10 Some mss include v. 11: *For the Son of Man has come to save the lost.* [O]18:13 Lit *over it* [P]18:15 Other mss omit
against you [Q]18:15 Lit *him between you and him alone* [R]18:16 Lit *mouth* [S]18:16 Dt 19:15 [T]18:17 Or *congregation*
[U]18:18 Or *earth will be bound* [V]18:18 Or *earth will be loosed* [W]18:19 Lit *they* [X]18:19 Lit *for them*

THE PARABLE OF THE UNFORGIVING SERVANT

²¹ Then Peter approached him and asked, "Lord, how many times shall I forgive my brother or sister who sins against me? As many as seven times?"

²² "I tell you, not as many as seven," Jesus replied, "but seventy times seven.ᴬ

²³ "For this reason, the kingdom of heaven can be compared to a king who wanted to settle accounts with his servants. ²⁴ When he began to settle accounts, one who owed ten thousand talentsᴮ was brought before him. ²⁵ Since he did not have the money to pay it back, his master commanded that he, his wife, his children, and everything he had be sold to pay the debt.

²⁶ "At this, the servant fell facedown before him and said, 'Be patient with me, and I will pay you everything.' ²⁷ Then the master of that servant had compassion, released him, and forgave him the loan.

²⁸ "That servant went out and found one of his fellow servants who owed him a hundred denarii.ᶜ He grabbed him, started choking him, and said, 'Pay what you owe!'

²⁹ "At this, his fellow servant fell downᴰ and began begging him, 'Be patient with me, and I will pay you back.' ³⁰ But he wasn't willing. Instead, he went and threw him into prison until he could pay what was owed. ³¹ When the other servants saw what had taken place, they were deeply distressed and went and reported to their master everything that had happened. ³² Then, after he had summoned him, his master said to him, 'You wicked servant! I forgave you all that debt because you begged me. ³³ Shouldn't you also have had mercy on your fellow servant, as I had mercy on you?' ³⁴ And because he was angry, his master handed him over to the jailers to be tortured until he could pay everything that was owed. ³⁵ So also my heavenly Father will do to you unless every one of you forgives his brother or sisterᴱ from yourᶠ heart."

THE QUESTION OF DIVORCE

19 When Jesus had finished saying these things, he departed from Galilee and went to the region of Judea across the Jordan. ² Large crowds followed him, and he healed them there. ³ Some Pharisees approached him to test him. They asked, "Is it lawful for a man to divorce his wife on any grounds?"

⁴ "Haven't you read," he replied, "that he who createdᴳ them in the beginning **made them male and female,**ᴴ ⁵ and he also said, **"For this reason a man will leave his father and mother and be joined to his wife, and the two will become one flesh'?**ᴵ ⁶ So they are no longer two, but one flesh. Therefore, what God has joined together, let no one separate."

⁷ "Why then," they asked him, "did Moses command us to give divorce papers and to send her away?"

⁸ He told them, "Moses permitted you to divorce your wives because of the hardness of your hearts, but it was not like that from the beginning. ⁹ I tell you, whoever divorces his wife, except for sexual immorality, and marries another commits adultery."ᴶ

¹⁰ His disciples said to him, "If the relationship of a man with his wife is like this, it's better not to marry."

¹¹ He responded, "Not everyone can accept this saying, but only those to whom it has been given. ¹² For there are eunuchs who were born that way from their mother's womb, there are eunuchs who were made by men, and there are eunuchs who have made themselves that way because of the kingdom of heaven. The one who is able to accept it should accept it."

BLESSING THE CHILDREN

¹³ Then children were brought to Jesus for him to place his hands on them and pray, but the disciples rebuked them. ¹⁴ Jesus said, "Leave the children alone, and don't try to keep them from coming to me, because the kingdom of heaven belongs to such as these."ᴷ ¹⁵ After placing his hands on them, he went on from there.

THE RICH YOUNG RULER

¹⁶ Just then someone came up and asked him, "Teacher, what good must I do to have eternal life?"

¹⁷ "Why do you ask me about what is good?"ᴸ he said to him. "There is only one who is good.ᴹ If you want to enter into life, keep the commandments."

¹⁸ "Which ones?" he asked him.

Jesus answered: **Do not murder; do not commit adultery; do not steal; do not bear false witness;¹⁹ honor your father and your mother; and love your neighbor as yourself.**ᴺ

ᴬ**18:22** Or *but seventy-seven times* ᴮ**18:24** A talent is worth about 6,000 denarii, or twenty years' wages for a laborer ᶜ**18:28** A denarius = one day's wage ᴰ**18:29** Other mss add *at his feet* ᴱ**18:35** Other mss add *their trespasses* ᶠ**18:35** Lit *his* ᴳ**19:4** Other mss read *made* ᴴ**19:4** Gn 1:27; 5:2 ᴵ**19:5** Gn 2:24 ᴶ**19:9** Other mss add *Also whoever marries a divorced woman commits adultery*; Mt 5:32 ᴷ**19:14** Lit *heaven is of such ones* ᴸ**19:17** Other mss read *"Why do you call me good?"* ᴹ**19:17** Other mss read *"No one is good but one—God* ᴺ**19:18-19** Ex 20:12-16; Lv 19:18; Dt 5:16-20

²⁰ "I have kept all these,"ᴬ the young man told him. "What do I still lack?"

²¹ "If you want to be perfect,"ᴮ Jesus said to him, "go, sell your belongings and give to the poor, and you will have treasure in heaven. Then come, follow me."

²² When the young man heard that, he went away grieving, because he had many possessions.

POSSESSIONS AND THE KINGDOM

²³ Jesus said to his disciples, "Truly I tell you, it will be hard for a rich person to enter the kingdom of heaven. ²⁴ Again I tell you, it is easier for a camel to go through the eye of a needle than for a rich person to enter the kingdom of God."

²⁵ When the disciples heard this, they were utterly astonished and asked, "Then who can be saved?"

²⁶ Jesus looked at them and said, "With man this is impossible, but with God all things are possible."

²⁷ Then Peter responded to him, "See, we have left everything and followed you. So what will there be for us?"

²⁸ Jesus said to them, "Truly I tell you, in the renewal of all things, when the Son of Man sits on his glorious throne, you who have followed me will also sit on twelve thrones, judging the twelve tribes of Israel. ²⁹ And everyone who has left houses or brothers or sisters or father or motherᶜ or children or fields because of my name will receive a hundred times more and will inherit eternal life. ³⁰ But many who are first will be last, and the last first.

THE PARABLE OF THE VINEYARD WORKERS

20 "For the kingdom of heaven is like a landowner who went out early in the morning to hire workers for his vineyard. ² After agreeing with the workers on one denarius,ᴰ he sent them into his vineyard for the day. ³ When he went out about nine in the morning,ᴱ he saw others standing in the marketplace doing nothing. ⁴ He said to them, 'You also go into my vineyard, and I'll give you whatever is right.' So off they went. ⁵ About noon and about three,ᶠ he went out again and did the same thing. ⁶ Then about fiveᴳ he went and found others standing aroundᴴ and said to them, 'Why have you been standing here all day doing nothing?'

⁷ " 'Because no one hired us,' they said to him.
" 'You also go into my vineyard,' he told them.ᴵ

⁸ When evening came, the owner of the vineyard told his foreman, 'Call the workers and give them their pay, starting with the last and ending with the first.'

⁹ "When those who were hired about five came, they each received one denarius. ¹⁰ So when the first ones came, they assumed they would get more, but they also received a denarius each. ¹¹ When they received it, they began to complain to the landowner: ¹² 'These last men put in one hour, and you made them equal to us who bore the burden of the day's work and the burning heat.'

¹³ "He replied to one of them, 'Friend, I'm doing you no wrong. Didn't you agree with me on a denarius? ¹⁴ Take what's yours and go. I want to give this last man the same as I gave you. ¹⁵ Don't I have the right to do what I want with what is mine? Are you jealousᴶ because I'm generous?'ᴷ

¹⁶ "So the last will be first, and the first last."ᴸ

THE THIRD PREDICTION OF HIS DEATH

¹⁷ While going up to Jerusalem, Jesus took the twelve disciples aside privately and said to them on the way, ¹⁸ "See, we are going up to Jerusalem. The Son of Man will be handed over to the chief priests and scribes, and they will condemn him to death. ¹⁹ They will hand him over to the Gentiles to be mocked, flogged,ᴹ and crucified, and on the third day he will be raised."ᴺ

SUFFERING AND SERVICE

²⁰ Then the mother of Zebedee's sons approached him with her sons. She knelt down to ask him for something. ²¹ "What do you want?" he asked her.

"Promise,"ᴼ she said to him, "that these two sons of mine may sit, one on your right and the other on your left, in your kingdom."

²² Jesus answered, "You don't know what you're asking. Are you able to drink the cup that I am about to drink?"ᴾ

"We are able," they said to him.

²³ He told them, "You will indeed drink my cup,ᵠ but to sit at my right and left is not mine to give; instead, it is for those for whom it has been prepared by my Father."

ᴬ**19:20** Other mss add *from my youth*   ᴮ**19:21** Or *complete*   ᶜ**19:29** Other mss add *or wife*   ᴰ**20:2** A denarius = one day's wage, also in vv. 9,10,13   ᴱ**20:3** Lit *about the third hour*   ᶠ**20:5** Lit *about the sixth hour and the ninth hour*   ᴳ**20:6** Lit *about the eleventh hour*, also in v. 9   ᴴ**20:6** Other mss add *doing nothing*   ᴵ**20:7** Other mss add *'and you'll get whatever is right.'*   ᴶ**20:15** Lit *Is your eye evil*; an idiom for jealousy or stinginess   ᴷ**20:15** Lit *good*   ᴸ**20:16** Other mss add *"For many are called, but few are chosen."*   ᴹ**20:19** Or *scourged*   ᴺ**20:19** Other mss read *will rise again*   ᴼ**20:21** Lit *Say*   ᴾ**20:22** Other mss add *and (or) to be baptized with the baptism which I am baptized?"*   ᵠ**20:23** Other mss add *and be baptized with the baptism with which I am baptized.*

²⁴ When the ten disciples heard this, they became indignant with the two brothers. ²⁵ Jesus called them over and said, "You know that the rulers of the Gentiles lord it over them, and those in high positions act as tyrants over them. ²⁶ It must not be like that among you. On the contrary, whoever wants to become great among you must be your servant, ²⁷ and whoever wants to be first among you must be your slave; ²⁸ just as the Son of Man did not come to be served, but to serve, and to give his life as a ransom for many."

TWO BLIND MEN HEALED

²⁹ As they were leaving Jericho, a large crowd followed him. ³⁰ There were two blind men sitting by the road. When they heard that Jesus was passing by, they cried out, "Lord, have mercy on us, Son of David!" ³¹ The crowd demanded that they keep quiet, but they cried out all the more, "Lord, have mercy on us, Son of David!"

³² Jesus stopped, called them, and said, "What do you want me to do for you?"

³³ "Lord," they said to him, "open our eyes."

³⁴ Moved with compassion, Jesus touched their eyes. Immediately they could see, and they followed him.

THE TRIUMPHAL ENTRY

21 When they approached Jerusalem and came to Bethphage at the Mount of Olives, Jesus then sent two disciples, ² telling them, "Go into the village ahead of you. At once you will find a donkey tied there with her foal. Untie them and bring them to me. ³ If anyone says anything to you, say that the Lord needs them, and he will send them at once."

⁴ This took place so that what was spoken through the prophet might be fulfilled:

⁵ **Tell Daughter Zion,**
"See, your King is coming to you,
gentle, and mounted on a donkey,
and on a colt,
the foal of a donkey."ᴬ

⁶ The disciples went and did just as Jesus directed them. ⁷ They brought the donkey and its foal; then they laid their clothes on them, and he sat on them. ⁸ A very large crowd spread their clothes on the road; others were cutting branches from the trees and spreading them on the road. ⁹ Then the crowds who went ahead of him and those who followed shouted:

Hosanna to the Son of David!
Blessed is he who comes in the name
of the Lord!ᴮ
Hosanna in the highest heaven!

¹⁰ When he entered Jerusalem, the whole city was in an uproar, saying, "Who is this?" ¹¹ The crowds were saying, "This is the prophet Jesus from Nazareth in Galilee."

CLEANSING THE TEMPLE

¹² Jesus went into the templeᶜ and threw out all those buying and selling. He overturned the tables of the money changers and the chairs of those selling doves. ¹³ He said to them, "It is written, **my house will be called a house of prayer,**ᴰ but you are making it **a den of thieves!"**ᴱ

CHILDREN PRAISE JESUS

¹⁴ The blind and the lame came to him in the temple, and he healed them. ¹⁵ When the chief priests and the scribes saw the wonders that he did and the children shouting in the temple, "*Hosanna* to the Son of David!" they were indignant ¹⁶ and said to him, "Do you hear what these children are saying?"

Jesus replied, "Yes, have you never read:

You have preparedᶠ **praise**
from the mouths of infants
and nursing babies?"ᴳ

¹⁷ Then he left them, went out of the city to Bethany, and spent the night there.

THE BARREN FIG TREE

¹⁸ Early in the morning, as he was returning to the city, he was hungry. ¹⁹ Seeing a lone fig tree by the road, he went up to it and found nothing on it except leaves. And he said to it, "May no fruit ever come from you again!" At once the fig tree withered.

²⁰ When the disciples saw it, they were amazed and said, "How did the fig tree wither so quickly?"

²¹ Jesus answered them, "Truly I tell you, if you have faith and do not doubt, you will not only do what was done to the fig tree, but even if you tell this mountain, 'Be lifted up and thrown into the sea,' it will be done. ²² And if you believe, you will receive whatever you ask for in prayer."

THE AUTHORITY OF JESUS CHALLENGED

²³ When he entered the temple, the chief priests and the elders of the people came to him as he was teaching and said, "By what authority are you doing these things? Who gave you this authority?"

²⁴ Jesus answered them, "I will also ask you one question, and if you answer it for me, then I will tell you by what authority I do these things.

ᴬ **21:5** Is 62:11; Zch 9:9 ᴮ **21:9** Ps 118:25-26 ᶜ **21:12** Other mss add *of God* ᴰ **21:13** Is 56:7 ᴱ **21:13** Jr 7:11 ᶠ **21:16** Or *restored*
ᴳ **21:16** Ps 8:2

²⁵ Did John's baptism come from heaven, or was it of human origin?"

They discussed it among themselves, "If we say, 'From heaven,' he will say to us, 'Then why didn't you believe him?' ²⁶ But if we say, 'Of human origin,' we're afraid of the crowd, because everyone considers John to be a prophet." ²⁷ So they answered Jesus, "We don't know."

And he said to them, "Neither will I tell you by what authority I do these things.

THE PARABLE OF THE TWO SONS

²⁸ "What do you think? A man had two sons. He went to the first and said, 'My son, go work in the vineyard today.'

²⁹ "He answered, 'I don't want to,' but later he changed his mind and went. ³⁰ Then the man went to the other and said the same thing. 'I will, sir,' he answered, but he didn't go. ³¹ Which of the two did his father's will?"

They said, "The first."

Jesus said to them, "Truly I tell you, tax collectors and prostitutes are entering the kingdom of God before you. ³² For John came to you in the way of righteousness, and you didn't believe him. Tax collectors and prostitutes did believe him; but you, when you saw it, didn't even change your minds then and believe him.

THE PARABLE OF THE VINEYARD OWNER

³³ "Listen to another parable: There was a landowner, who planted a vineyard, put a fence around it, dug a winepress in it, and built a watchtower. He leased it to tenant farmers and went away. ³⁴ When the time came to harvest fruit, he sent his servants to the farmers to collect his fruit. ³⁵ The farmers took his servants, beat one, killed another, and stoned a third. ³⁶ Again, he sent other servants, more than the first group, and they did the same to them. ³⁷ Finally, he sent his son to them. 'They will respect my son,' he said.

³⁸ "But when the tenant farmers saw the son, they said to each other, 'This is the heir. Come, let's kill him and take his inheritance.' ³⁹ So they seized him, threw him out of the vineyard, and killed him. ⁴⁰ Therefore, when the owner of the vineyard comes, what will he do to those farmers?"

⁴¹ "He will completely destroy those terrible men," they told him, "and lease his vineyard to other farmers who will give him his fruit at the harvest."

⁴² Jesus said to them, "Have you never read in the Scriptures:

The stone that the builders rejected
has become the cornerstone.^A
This is what the Lord has done
and it is wonderful in our eyes?^B

⁴³ Therefore I tell you, the kingdom of God will be taken away from you and given to a people producing its fruit. ⁴⁴ Whoever falls on this stone will be broken to pieces; but on whomever it falls, it will shatter him."^C

⁴⁵ When the chief priests and the Pharisees heard his parables, they knew he was speaking about them. ⁴⁶ Although they were looking for a way to arrest him, they feared the crowds, because the people regarded him as a prophet.

THE PARABLE OF THE WEDDING BANQUET

22 Once more Jesus spoke to them in parables: ² "The kingdom of heaven is like a king who gave a wedding banquet for his son. ³ He sent his servants to summon those invited to the banquet, but they didn't want to come. ⁴ Again, he sent out other servants and said, 'Tell those who are invited: See, I've prepared my dinner; my oxen and fattened cattle have been slaughtered, and everything is ready. Come to the wedding banquet.'

⁵ "But they paid no attention and went away, one to his own farm, another to his business, ⁶ while the rest seized his servants, mistreated them, and killed them. ⁷ The king^D was enraged, and he sent out his troops, killed those murderers, and burned down their city.

⁸ "Then he told his servants, 'The banquet is ready, but those who were invited were not worthy. ⁹ Go then to where the roads exit the city and invite everyone you find to the banquet.' ¹⁰ So those servants went out on the roads and gathered everyone they found, both evil and good. The wedding banquet^E was filled with guests.^F ¹¹ When the king came in to see the guests, he saw a man there who was not dressed for a wedding. ¹² So he said to him, 'Friend, how did you get in here without wedding clothes?' The man was speechless.

¹³ "Then the king told the attendants, 'Tie him up hand and foot,^G and throw him into the outer darkness, where there will be weeping and gnashing of teeth.'

¹⁴ "For many are invited, but few are chosen."

GOD AND CAESAR

¹⁵ Then the Pharisees went and plotted how to trap him by what he said."^H ¹⁶ So they sent their disciples to him, along with the Herodians. "Teacher," they said, "we know that you

---

^A **21:42** Lit *the head of the corner* ^B **21:42** Ps 118:22-23 ^C **21:44** Some mss omit this verse ^D **22:7** Other mss read *But when the (that) king heard about it he* ^E **22:10** Other mss read *wedding hall* ^F **22:10** Lit *those reclining* (to eat) ^G **22:13** Other mss add *take him away* ^H **22:15** Lit *trap him in a word*

are truthful and teach truthfully the way of God. You don't care what anyone thinks nor do you show partiality.[A] [17] Tell us, then, what you think. Is it lawful to pay taxes to Caesar or not?"

[18] Perceiving their malicious intent, Jesus said, "Why are you testing me, hypocrites? [19] Show me the coin used for the tax." They brought him a denarius.[B] [20] "Whose image and inscription is this?" he asked them.

[21] "Caesar's," they said to him.

Then he said to them, "Give, then, to Caesar the things that are Caesar's, and to God the things that are God's." [22] When they heard this, they were amazed. So they left him and went away.

THE SADDUCEES AND THE RESURRECTION

[23] That same day some Sadducees, who say there is no resurrection, came up to him and questioned him: [24] "Teacher, Moses said, if a man dies, having no children, his brother is to marry his wife and raise up offspring for his brother.[C] [25] Now there were seven brothers among us. The first got married and died. Having no offspring, he left his wife to his brother. [26] The same thing happened to the second also, and the third, and so on to all seven. [27] Last of all, the woman died. [28] In the resurrection, then, whose wife will she be of the seven? For they all had married her."[D]

[29] Jesus answered them, "You are mistaken, because you don't know the Scriptures or the power of God. [30] For in the resurrection neither marry nor are given in marriage but are like[E] angels in heaven. [31] Now concerning the resurrection of the dead, haven't you read what was spoken to you by God: [32] I am the God of Abraham and the God of Isaac and the God of Jacob?[F] He[G] is not the God of the dead, but of the living."

[33] And when the crowds heard this, they were astonished at his teaching.

THE PRIMARY COMMANDS

[34] When the Pharisees heard that he had silenced the Sadducees, they came together. [35] And one of them, an expert in the law, asked a question to test him: [36] "Teacher, which command in the law is the greatest?"

[37] He said to him, "Love the Lord your God with all your heart, with all your soul, and with all your mind."[38] This is the greatest and most important[H] command. [39] The second is like it: Love your neighbor as yourself.[I] [40] All the Law and the Prophets depend[K] on these two commands."

THE QUESTION ABOUT THE CHRIST

[41] While the Pharisees were together, Jesus questioned them, [42] "What do you think about the Messiah? Whose son is he?"

They replied, "David's."

[43] He asked them, "How is it then that David, inspired by the Spirit,[L] calls him 'Lord':

[44] The Lord declared to my Lord,
   'Sit at my right hand
   until I put your enemies
   under your feet'?[M,N]

[45] "If David calls him 'Lord,' how then can he be his son?" [46] No one was able to answer him at all,[O] and from that day no one dared to question him anymore.

RELIGIOUS HYPOCRITES DENOUNCED

23 Then Jesus spoke to the crowds and to his disciples: [2] "The scribes and the Pharisees are seated in the chair of Moses. [3] Therefore do whatever they tell you, and observe it. But don't do what they do, because they don't practice what they teach. [4] They tie up heavy loads that are hard to carry[P] and put them on people's shoulders, but they themselves aren't willing to lift a finger to move them. [5] They do everything[Q] to be seen by others: They enlarge their phylacteries and lengthen their tassels.[R] [6] They love the place of honor at banquets, the front seats in the synagogues, [7] greetings in the marketplaces, and to be called 'Rabbi' by people.

[8] "But you are not to be called 'Rabbi,' because you have one Teacher,[S] and you are all brothers and sisters. [9] Do not call anyone on earth your father, because you have one Father, who is in heaven. [10] You are not to be called instructors either, because you have one Instructor, the Messiah. [11] The greatest among you will be your servant. [12] Whoever exalts himself will be humbled, and whoever humbles himself will be exalted.

[13] "Woe to you, scribes and Pharisees, hypocrites! You shut the door of the kingdom of heaven in people's faces. For you don't go in, and you don't allow those entering to go in.[T]

[A] 22:16 Lit *don't look on the face of men*   [B] 22:19 A denarius = one day's wage   [C] 22:24 Dt 25:5   [D] 22:28 Lit *all had her*   [E] 22:30 Other mss add *God's*   [F] 22:32 Ex 3:6,15-16   [G] 22:32 Other mss read *God*   [H] 22:37 Dt 6:5   [I] 22:38 Lit *and first*   [J] 22:39 Lv 19:18   [K] 22:40 Or *hang*   [L] 22:43 Lit *David in Spirit*   [M] 22:44 Other mss read *until I make your enemies your footstool*   [N] 22:44 Ps 110:1   [O] 22:46 Lit *answer him a word*   [P] 23:4 Other mss omit *that are hard to carry*   [Q] 23:5 Lit *do all their works*   [R] 23:5 Other mss add *on their robes*   [S] 23:8 Other mss add *the Christ*   [T] 23:13 Some mss include v. 14: *"Woe to you, scribes and Pharisees, hypocrites! You devour widows' houses and make long prayers just for show. This is why you will receive a harsher punishment.*

[15] "Woe to you, scribes and Pharisees, hypocrites! You travel over land and sea to make one convert, and when he becomes one, you make him twice as fit for hell[A] as you are!

[16] "Woe to you, blind guides, who say, 'Whoever takes an oath by the temple, it means nothing. But whoever takes an oath by the gold of the temple is bound by his oath.'[B] [17] Blind fools! For which is greater, the gold or the temple that sanctified the gold? [18] Also, 'Whoever takes an oath by the altar, it means nothing; but whoever takes an oath by the gift that is on it is bound by his oath.' [19] Blind people![C] For which is greater, the gift or the altar that sanctifies the gift? [20] Therefore, the one who takes an oath by the altar takes an oath by it and by everything on it. [21] The one who takes an oath by the temple takes an oath by it and by him who dwells in it. [22] And the one who takes an oath by heaven takes an oath by God's throne and by him who sits on it.

[23] "Woe to you, scribes and Pharisees, hypocrites! You pay a tenth of[D] mint, dill, and cumin, and yet you have neglected the more important matters of the law — justice, mercy, and faithfulness.[E] These things should have been done without neglecting the others. [24] Blind guides! You strain out a gnat, but gulp down a camel!

[25] "Woe to you, scribes and Pharisees, hypocrites! You clean the outside of the cup and dish, but inside they are full of greed[F] and self-indulgence. [26] Blind Pharisee! First clean the inside of the cup,[G] so that the outside of it[H] may also become clean.

[27] "Woe to you, scribes and Pharisees, hypocrites! You are like whitewashed tombs, which appear beautiful on the outside, but inside are full of the bones of the dead and every kind of impurity. [28] In the same way, on the outside you seem righteous to people, but inside you are full of hypocrisy and lawlessness.

[29] "Woe to you, scribes and Pharisees, hypocrites! You build the tombs of the prophets and decorate the graves of the righteous, [30] and you say, 'If we had lived in the days of our ancestors, we wouldn't have taken part with them in shedding the prophets' blood.' [31] So you testify against yourselves that you are descendants of those who murdered the prophets. [32] Fill up, then, the measure of your ancestors' sins!

[33] "Snakes! Brood of vipers! How can you escape being condemned to hell?'[I] [34] This is why I am sending you prophets, sages, and scribes. Some of them you will kill and crucify, and some of them you will flog in your synagogues and pursue from town to town. [35] So all the righteous blood shed on the earth will be charged to you,[J] from the blood of righteous Abel to the blood of Zechariah, son of Berechiah, whom you murdered between the sanctuary and the altar. [36] Truly I tell you, all these things will come on this generation.

JESUS'S LAMENTING OVER JERUSALEM

[37] "Jerusalem, Jerusalem, who kills the prophets and stones those who are sent to her. How often I wanted to gather your children together, as a hen gathers her chicks[K] under her wings, but you were not willing! [38] See, your house is left to you desolate. [39] For I tell you, you will not see me again until you say, 'Blessed is he who comes in the name of the Lord'!"[L]

DESTRUCTION OF THE TEMPLE PREDICTED

24 As Jesus left and was going out of the temple, his disciples came up and called his attention to its buildings. [2] He replied to them, "Do you see all these things? Truly I tell you, not one stone will be left here on another that will not be thrown down."

SIGNS OF THE END OF THE AGE

[3] While he was sitting on the Mount of Olives, the disciples approached him privately and said, "Tell us, when will these things happen? And what is the sign of your coming and of the end of the age?"

[4] Jesus replied to them: "Watch out that no one deceives you. [5] For many will come in my name, saying, 'I am the Messiah,' and they will deceive many. [6] You are going to hear of wars and rumors of wars. See that you are not alarmed, because these things must take place, but the end is not yet. [7] For nation will rise up against nation, and kingdom against kingdom. There will be famines[M] and earthquakes in various places. [8] All these events are the beginning of labor pains.

PERSECUTIONS PREDICTED

[9] "Then they will hand you over to be persecuted, and they will kill you. You will be hated by all nations because of my name. [10] Then many will fall away, betray one another, and hate one another. [11] Many false prophets will rise up and deceive many. [12] Because lawlessness will multiply, the love of many will grow cold. [13] But the one who endures to the end will be saved. [14] This

---

[A] 23:15 Lit *twice the son of gehenna*   [B] 23:16 Lit *is obligated*, also in v. 18   [C] 23:19 Other mss read *Fools and blind*
[D] 23:23 Or *You tithe*   [E] 23:23 Or *faith*   [F] 23:25 Or *full of violence*   [G] 23:26 Other mss add *and dish*   [H] 23:26 Other mss read
of them   [I] 23:33 Lit *escape from the judgment of gehenna*   [J] 23:35 Lit *will come on you*   [K] 23:37 Or *as a mother bird
gathers her young*   [L] 23:39 Ps 118:26   [M] 24:7 Other mss add *epidemics*

good news of the kingdom will be proclaimed in all the world^A as a testimony to all nations, and then the end will come.

THE GREAT TRIBULATION

¹⁵ "So when you see **the abomination of desolation,**^B spoken of by the prophet Daniel, standing in the holy place" (let the reader understand), ¹⁶ "then those in Judea must flee to the mountains. ¹⁷ A man on the housetop^C must not come down to get things out of his house, ¹⁸ and a man in the field must not go back to get his coat. ¹⁹ Woe to pregnant women and nursing mothers in those days! ²⁰ Pray that your escape may not be in winter or on a Sabbath. ²¹ For at that time there will be great distress,^D the kind that hasn't taken place from the beginning of the world until now and never will again. ²² Unless those days were cut short, no one would^E be saved. But those days will be cut short because of the elect.

²³ "If anyone tells you then, 'See, here is the Messiah!' or, 'Over here!' do not believe it. ²⁴ For false messiahs and false prophets will arise and perform great signs and wonders to lead astray, if possible, even the elect. ²⁵ Take note: I have told you in advance. ²⁶ So if they tell you, 'See, he's in the wilderness!' don't go out; or, 'See, he's in the storerooms!' do not believe it. ²⁷ For as the lightning comes from the east and flashes as far as the west, so will be the coming of the Son of Man. ²⁸ Wherever the carcass is, there the vultures^F will gather.

THE COMING OF THE SON OF MAN

²⁹ "Immediately after the distress of those days, the sun will be darkened, and the moon will not shed its light; the stars will fall from the sky, and the powers of the heavens will be shaken. ³⁰ Then the sign of the Son of Man will appear in the sky, and then all the peoples of the earth^G will mourn;^H and they will see the Son of Man coming on the clouds of heaven with power and great glory. ³¹ He will send out his angels with a loud trumpet, and they will gather his elect from the four winds, from one end of the sky to the other.

THE PARABLE OF THE FIG TREE

³² "Learn this lesson from the fig tree: As soon as its branch becomes tender and sprouts leaves, you know that summer is near. ³³ In the same way, when you see all these things, recognize^I that he^J is near — at the door. ³⁴ Truly I tell you, this generation will certainly not pass away until all these things take place. ³⁵ Heaven and earth will pass away, but my words will never pass away.

NO ONE KNOWS THE DAY OR HOUR

³⁶ "Now concerning that day and hour no one knows — neither the angels of heaven nor the Son^K — except the Father alone. ³⁷ As the days of Noah were, so the coming of the Son of Man will be. ³⁸ For in those days before the flood they were eating and drinking, marrying and giving in marriage, until the day Noah boarded the ark. ³⁹ They didn't know until the flood came and swept them all away. This is the way the coming of the Son of Man will be. ⁴⁰ Then two men will be in the field; one will be taken and one left. ⁴¹ Two women will be grinding grain with a hand mill; one will be taken and one left. ⁴² Therefore be alert, since you don't know what day^L your Lord is coming. ⁴³ But know this: If the homeowner had known what time^M the thief was coming, he would have stayed alert and not let his house be broken into. ⁴⁴ This is why you are also to be ready, because the Son of Man is coming at an hour you do not expect.

FAITHFUL SERVICE TO CHRIST

⁴⁵ "Who then is a faithful and wise servant, whom his master has put in charge of his household, to give them food at the proper time? ⁴⁶ Blessed is that servant whom the master finds doing his job when he comes. ⁴⁷ Truly I tell you, he will put him in charge of all his possessions. ⁴⁸ But if that wicked servant says in his heart, 'My master is delayed,' ⁴⁹ and starts to beat his fellow servants, and eats and drinks with drunkards, ⁵⁰ that servant's master will come on a day he does not expect him and at an hour he does not know. ⁵¹ He will cut him to pieces and assign him a place with the hypocrites, where there will be weeping and gnashing of teeth.

THE PARABLE OF THE TEN VIRGINS

25 "At that time the kingdom of heaven will be like ten virgins^N who took their lamps^O and went out to meet the groom. ² Five of them were foolish and five were wise. ³ When the foolish took their lamps, they didn't take oil with them; ⁴ but the wise ones took oil in their flasks with their lamps. ⁵ When the groom was delayed, they all became drowsy and fell asleep.

---

^A24:14 Or *in all the inhabited earth*   ^B24:15 Dn 9:27   ^C24:17 Or *roof*   ^D24:21 Or *tribulation*, also in v. 29   ^E24:22 Lit *short, all flesh would not*   ^F24:28 Or *eagles*   ^G24:30 Or *all the tribes of the land*   ^H24:30 Lit *will beat*; that is, beat their chests   ^I24:33 Or *things, you know*   ^J24:33 Or *it*; that is, summer   ^K24:36 Other mss omit *nor the Son*   ^L24:42 Other mss read *hour*; = time   ^M24:43 Lit *watch*; a division of the night in ancient times   ^N25:1 Or *bridesmaids*   ^O25:1 Or *torches*, also in vv. 3, 4, 7, 8

⁶ "In the middle of the night there was a shout: 'Here's the groom! Come out to meet him.'

⁷ "Then all the virgins got up and trimmed their lamps. ⁸ The foolish ones said to the wise ones, 'Give us some of your oil, because our lamps are going out.'

⁹ "The wise ones answered, 'No, there won't be enough for us and for you. Go instead to those who sell oil, and buy some for yourselves.'

¹⁰ "When they had gone to buy some, the groom arrived, and those who were ready went in with him to the wedding banquet, and the door was shut. ¹¹ Later the rest of the virgins also came and said, 'Master, master, open up for us!'

¹² "He replied, 'Truly I tell you, I don't know you!'

¹³ "Therefore be alert, because you don't know either the day or the hour.^A

THE PARABLE OF THE TALENTS

¹⁴ "For it is just like a man about to go on a journey. He called his own servants and entrusted his possessions to them. ¹⁵ To one he gave five talents,^B to another two talents, and to another one talent, depending on each one's ability. Then he went on a journey. Immediately ¹⁶ the man who had received five talents went, put them to work, and earned five more. ¹⁷ In the same way the man with two earned two more. ¹⁸ But the man who had received one talent went off, dug a hole in the ground, and hid his master's money.

¹⁹ "After a long time the master of those servants came and settled accounts with them. ²⁰ The man who had received five talents approached, presented five more talents, and said, 'Master, you gave me five talents. See, I've earned five more talents.'

²¹ "His master said to him, 'Well done, good and faithful servant! You were faithful over a few things; I will put you in charge of many things. Share your master's joy.'

²² "The man with two talents also approached. He said, 'Master, you gave me two talents. See, I've earned two more talents.'

²³ "His master said to him, 'Well done, good and faithful servant! You were faithful over a few things; I will put you in charge of many things. Share your master's joy.'

²⁴ "The man who had received one talent also approached and said, 'Master, I know you. You're a harsh man, reaping where you haven't sown and gathering where you haven't scattered seed. ²⁵ So I was afraid and went off and hid your talent in the ground. See, you have what is yours.'

²⁶ "His master replied to him, 'You evil, lazy servant! If you knew that I reap where I haven't sown and gather where I haven't scattered, ²⁷ then^C you should have deposited my money with the bankers, and I would have received my money^D back with interest when I returned.

²⁸ "'So take the talent from him and give it to the one who has ten talents. ²⁹ For to everyone who has, more will be given, and he will have more than enough. But from the one who does not have, even what he has will be taken away from him. ³⁰ And throw this good-for-nothing servant into the outer darkness, where there will be weeping and gnashing of teeth.'

THE SHEEP AND THE GOATS

³¹ "When the Son of Man comes in his glory, and all the angels^E with him, then he will sit on his glorious throne. ³² All the nations^F will be gathered before him, and he will separate them one from another, just as a shepherd separates the sheep from the goats. ³³ He will put the sheep on his right and the goats on the left. ³⁴ Then the King will say to those on his right, 'Come, you who are blessed by my Father; inherit the kingdom prepared for you from the foundation of the world.

³⁵ "'For I was hungry and you gave me something to eat; I was thirsty and you gave me something to drink; I was a stranger and you took me in; ³⁶ I was naked and you clothed me; I was sick and you took care of me; I was in prison and you visited me.'

³⁷ "Then the righteous will answer him, 'Lord, when did we see you hungry and feed you, or thirsty and give you something to drink? ³⁸ When did we see you a stranger and take you in, or without clothes and clothe you? ³⁹ When did we see you sick, or in prison, and visit you?'

⁴⁰ "And the King will answer them, 'Truly I tell you, whatever you did for one of the least of these brothers and sisters of mine, you did for me.'

⁴¹ "Then he will also say to those on the left, 'Depart from me, you who are cursed, into the eternal fire prepared for the devil and his angels! ⁴² For I was hungry and you gave me nothing to eat; I was thirsty and you gave me nothing to drink; ⁴³ I was a stranger and you didn't take me in; I was naked and you didn't clothe me, sick and in prison and you didn't take care of me.'

---

^A**25:13** Other mss add *in which the Son of Man is coming.* ^B**25:15** A talent is worth about 6,000 denarii, or twenty years' wages for a laborer ^C**25:26-27** Or *So you knew . . . scattered? Then* (as a question) ^D**25:27** Lit *received what is mine* ^E**25:31** Other mss read *holy angels* ^F**25:32** Or *the Gentiles*

[44] "Then they too will answer, 'Lord, when did we see you hungry, or thirsty, or a stranger, or without clothes, or sick, or in prison, and not help you?'

[45] "Then he will answer them, 'I tell you, whatever you did not do for one of the least of these, you did not do for me.'

[46] "And they will go away into eternal punishment, but the righteous into eternal life."

THE PLOT TO KILL JESUS

26 When Jesus had finished saying all these things, he told his disciples, [2] "You know[A] that the Passover takes place after two days, and the Son of Man will be handed over to be crucified."

[3] Then the chief priests[B] and the elders of the people assembled in the courtyard of the high priest, who was named Caiaphas, [4] and they conspired to arrest Jesus in a treacherous way and kill him. [5] "Not during the festival," they said, "so there won't be rioting among the people."

THE ANOINTING AT BETHANY

[6] While Jesus was in Bethany at the house of Simon the leper,[C] [7] a woman approached him with an alabaster jar of very expensive perfume. She poured it on his head as he was reclining at the table. [8] When the disciples saw it, they were indignant. "Why this waste?" they asked. [9] "This might have been sold for a great deal and given to the poor."

[10] Aware of this, Jesus said to them, "Why are you bothering this woman? She has done a noble thing for me. [11] You always have the poor with you, but you do not always have me. [12] By pouring this perfume on my body, she has prepared me for burial. [13] Truly I tell you, wherever this gospel is proclaimed in the whole world, what she has done will also be told in memory of her."

[14] Then one of the Twelve, the man called Judas Iscariot, went to the chief priests [15] and said, "What are you willing to give me if I hand him over to you?" So they weighed out thirty pieces of silver for him. [16] And from that time he started looking for a good opportunity to betray him.

BETRAYAL AT THE PASSOVER

[17] On the first day of Unleavened Bread the disciples came to Jesus and asked, "Where do you want us to make preparations for you to eat the Passover?"

[18] "Go into the city to a certain man," he said, "and tell him, 'The Teacher says: My time is near; I am celebrating the Passover at your place[D] with my disciples.'" [19] So the disciples did as Jesus had directed them and prepared the Passover. [20] When evening came, he was reclining at the table with the Twelve. [21] While they were eating, he said, "Truly I tell you, one of you will betray me."

[22] Deeply distressed, each one began to say to him, "Surely not I, Lord?"

[23] He replied, "The one who dipped his hand with me in the bowl — he will betray me. [24] The Son of Man will go just as it is written about him, but woe to that man by whom the Son of Man is betrayed! It would have been better for him if he had not been born."

[25] Judas, his betrayer, replied, "Surely not I, Rabbi?"

"You have said it," he told him.

THE FIRST LORD'S SUPPER

[26] As they were eating, Jesus took bread, blessed and broke it, gave it to the disciples, and said, "Take and eat it; this is my body." [27] Then he took a cup, and after giving thanks, he gave it to them and said, "Drink from it, all of you. [28] For this is my blood of the covenant,[E] which is poured out for many for the forgiveness of sins. [29] But I tell you, I will not drink from this fruit of the vine from now on until that day when I drink it new with you in my Father's kingdom." [30] After singing a hymn, they went out to the Mount of Olives.

PETER'S DENIAL PREDICTED

[31] Then Jesus said to them, "Tonight all of you will fall away because of me, for it is written:

> I will strike the shepherd,
> and the sheep of the flock
>   will be scattered.[F]

[32] But after I have risen, I will go ahead of you to Galilee."

[33] Peter told him, "Even if everyone falls away because of you, I will never fall away."

[34] "Truly I tell you," Jesus said to him, "tonight, before the rooster crows, you will deny me three times."

[35] "Even if I have to die with you," Peter told him, "I will never deny you," and all the disciples said the same thing.

THE PRAYER IN THE GARDEN

[36] Then Jesus came with them to a place called Gethsemane, and he told the disciples, "Sit here while I go over there and pray." [37] Taking along Peter and the two sons of Zebedee, he began to be sorrowful and troubled. [38] He said to them,

---

[A] **26:2** Or *Know* (as a command) [B] **26:3** Other mss add *and the scribes* [C] **26:6** Gk *lepros*; a term for various skin diseases; see Lv 13–14 [D] **26:18** Lit *Passover with you* [E] **26:28** Other mss read *new covenant* [F] **26:31** Zch 13:7

"I am deeply grieved[A] to the point of death. Remain here and stay awake with me." [39] Going a little farther, [B] he fell facedown and prayed, "My Father, if it is possible, let this cup pass from me. Yet not as I will, but as you will."

[40] Then he came to the disciples and found them sleeping. He asked Peter, "So, couldn't you stay awake with me one hour? [41] Stay awake and pray, so that you won't enter into temptation. The spirit is willing, but the flesh is weak."

[42] Again, a second time, he went away and prayed, "My Father, if this[C] cannot pass[D] unless I drink it, your will be done." [43] And he came again and found them sleeping, because their eyes could not keep their eyes open.

[44] After leaving them, he went away again and prayed a third time, saying the same thing once more. [45] Then he came to the disciples and said to them, "Are you still sleeping and resting? See, the time is near. The Son of Man is betrayed into the hands of sinners. [46] Get up; let's go. See, my betrayer is near."

JUDAS'S BETRAYAL OF JESUS

[47] While he was still speaking, Judas, one of the Twelve, suddenly arrived. A large mob with swords and clubs was with him from the chief priests and elders of the people. [48] His betrayer had given them a sign: "The one I kiss, he's the one; arrest him." [49] So immediately he went up to Jesus and said, "Greetings, Rabbi!" and kissed him.

[50] "Friend," Jesus asked him, "why have you come?" [E]

Then they came up, took hold of Jesus, and arrested him. [51] At that moment one of those with Jesus reached out his hand and drew his sword. He struck the high priest's servant and cut off his ear.

[52] Then Jesus told him, "Put your sword back in its place because all who take up the sword will perish by the sword. [53] Or do you think that I cannot call on my Father, and he will provide me here and now with more than twelve legions of angels? [54] How, then, would the Scriptures be fulfilled that say it must happen this way?"

[55] At that time Jesus said to the crowds, "Have you come out with swords and clubs, as if I were a criminal,[F] to capture me? Every day I used to sit, teaching in the temple, and you didn't arrest me. [56] But all this has happened so that the writings of the prophets would be fulfilled." Then all the disciples deserted him and ran away.

JESUS FACES THE SANHEDRIN

[57] Those who had arrested Jesus led him away to Caiaphas the high priest, where the scribes and the elders had convened. [58] Peter was following him at a distance right to the high priest's courtyard. He went in and was sitting with the servants to see the outcome.

[59] The chief priests and the whole Sanhedrin were looking for false testimony against Jesus so that they could put him to death, [60] but they could not find any, even though many false witnesses came forward.[G] Finally, two[H] who came forward [61] stated, "This man said, 'I can destroy the temple of God and rebuild it in three days.'"

[62] The high priest stood up and said to him, "Don't you have an answer to what these men are testifying against you?" [63] But Jesus kept silent. The high priest said to him, "I charge you under oath by the living God: Tell us if you are the Messiah, the Son of God."

[64] "You have said it," Jesus told him. "But I tell you, in the future[I] you will see **the Son of Man seated at the right hand** of Power and **coming on the clouds of heaven**."[J]

[65] Then the high priest tore his robes and said, "He has blasphemed! Why do we still need witnesses? See, now you've heard the blasphemy. [66] What is your decision?"

They answered, "He deserves death!" [67] Then they spat in his face and beat him; others slapped him [68] and said, "Prophesy to us, Messiah! Who was it that hit you?"

PETER DENIES HIS LORD

[69] Now Peter was sitting outside in the courtyard. A servant girl approached him and said, "You were with Jesus the Galilean too."

[70] But he denied it in front of everyone: "I don't know what you're talking about."

[71] When he had gone out to the gateway, another woman saw him and told those who were there, "This man was with Jesus the Nazarene!"

[72] And again he denied it with an oath: "I don't know the man!"

[73] After a little while those standing there approached and said to Peter, "You really are one of them, since even your accent[K] gives you away."

[74] Then he started to curse and to swear with an oath, "I don't know the man!" Immediately a rooster crowed, [75] and Peter remembered the words Jesus had spoken, "Before the rooster crows, you will deny me three times." And he went outside and wept bitterly.

[A]**26:38** Lit *"My soul is swallowed up in sorrow*   [B]**26:39** Other mss read *Drawing nearer*   [C]**26:42** Other mss add *cup*
[D]**26:42** Other mss add *from me*   [E]**26:50** Or *Jesus told him, "do what you have come for."*   [F]**26:55** Lit *as against a criminal*
[G]**26:60** Other mss add *they found none*   [H]**26:60** Other mss add *false witnesses*   [I]**26:64** Lit *you, from now*
[J]**26:64** Ps 110:1; Dn 7:13   [K]**26:73** Or *speech*

JESUS HANDED OVER TO PILATE

27 When daybreak came, all the chief priests and the elders of the people plotted against Jesus to put him to death. [2] After tying him up, they led him away and handed him over to Pilate,[A] the governor.

JUDAS HANGS HIMSELF

[3] Then Judas, his betrayer, seeing that Jesus had been condemned, was full of remorse and returned the thirty pieces of silver to the chief priests and elders. [4] "I have sinned by betraying innocent blood," he said.

"What's that to us?" they said. "See to it yourself!" [5] So he threw the silver into the temple and departed. Then he went and hanged himself.

[6] The chief priests took the silver and said, "It's not permitted to put it into the temple treasury, since it is blood money." [7] They conferred together and bought the potter's field with it as a burial place for foreigners. [8] Therefore that field has been called "Blood Field" to this day. [9] Then what was spoken through the prophet Jeremiah was fulfilled: **They took**[B] **the thirty pieces of silver, the price of him whose price was set by the Israelites,** [10] **and they gave**[C] **them for the potter's field, as the Lord directed me.**[D]

JESUS FACES THE GOVERNOR

[11] Now Jesus stood before the governor. "Are you the King of the Jews?" the governor asked him.

Jesus answered, "You say so." [12] While he was being accused by the chief priests and elders, he didn't answer.

[13] Then Pilate said to him, "Don't you hear how much they are testifying against you?" [14] But he didn't answer him on even one charge, so that the governor was quite amazed.

JESUS OR BARABBAS

[15] At the festival the governor's custom was to release to the crowd a prisoner they wanted. [16] At that time they had a notorious prisoner called Barabbas.[E] [17] So when they had gathered together, Pilate said to them, "Who is it you want me to release for you — Barabbas, or Jesus who is called Christ?" [18] For he knew it was because of envy that they had handed him over.

[19] While he was sitting on the judge's bench, his wife sent word to him, "Have nothing to do with that righteous man, for today I've suffered terribly in a dream because of him."

[20] The chief priests and the elders, however, persuaded the crowds to ask for Barabbas and to execute Jesus. [21] The governor asked them, "Which of the two do you want me to release for you?"

"Barabbas!" they answered.

[22] Pilate asked them, "What should I do then with Jesus, who is called Christ?"

They all answered, "Crucify him!"

[23] Then he said, "Why? What has he done wrong?"

But they kept shouting all the more, "Crucify him!"

[24] When Pilate saw that he was getting nowhere, but that a riot was starting instead, he took some water, washed his hands in front of the crowd, and said, "I am innocent of this man's blood.[F] See to it yourselves!"

[25] All the people answered, "His blood be on us and on our children!" [26] Then he released Barabbas to them and, after having Jesus flogged, handed him over to be crucified.

MOCKED BY THE MILITARY

[27] Then the governor's soldiers took Jesus into the governor's residence and gathered the whole company[G] around him. [28] They stripped him and dressed him in a scarlet robe. [29] They twisted together a crown of thorns, put it on his head, and placed a staff in his right hand. And they knelt down before him and mocked him: "Hail, King of the Jews!" [30] Then they spat on him, took the staff, and kept hitting him on the head. [31] After they had mocked him, they stripped him of the robe, put his own clothes on him, and led him away to crucify him.

CRUCIFIED BETWEEN TWO CRIMINALS

[32] As they were going out, they found a Cyrenian man named Simon. They forced him to carry his cross. [33] When they came to a place called *Golgotha* (which means Place of the Skull), [34] they gave him wine[H] mixed with gall to drink. But when he tasted it, he refused to drink it. [35] After crucifying him, they divided his clothes by casting lots.[I] [36] Then they sat down and were guarding him there. [37] Above his head they put up the charge against him in writing: THIS IS JESUS, THE KING OF THE JEWS.

[38] Then two criminals[J] were crucified with him, one on the right and one on the left.

---

^27:2 Other mss read *Pontius Pilate*   [B]27:9 Or *I took*   [C]27:10 Some mss read *I gave*   [D]27:9-10 Jr 32:6-9; Zch 11:12-13
[E]27:16 Other mss read *Jesus Barabbas*, also in v. 17   [F]27:24 Other mss read *this righteous man's blood*   [G]27:27 Lit *cohort*
[H]27:34 Other mss read *sour wine*   [I]27:35 Other mss add *that what was spoken by the prophet might be fulfilled: "They divided my clothes among them, and for my clothing they cast lots."*   [J]27:38 Or *revolutionaries*

39 Those who passed by were yelling insults at[A] him, shaking their heads **40** and saying, "You who would destroy the temple and rebuild it in three days, save yourself! If you are the Son of God, come down from the cross!" **41** In the same way the chief priests, with the scribes and elders,[B] mocked him and said, **42** "He saved others, but he cannot save himself! He is the King of Israel! Let him[C] come down now from the cross, and we will believe in him. **43** He trusts in God; let God rescue him now — if he takes pleasure in him![D] For he said, 'I am the Son of God.'" **44** In the same way even the criminals who were crucified with him taunted him.

THE DEATH OF JESUS

45 From noon until three in the afternoon[E] darkness came over the whole land.[F] **46** About three in the afternoon Jesus cried out with a loud voice, *"Elí, Elí, lemá[G] sabachtháni?"* that is, **"My God, my God, why have you abandoned me?"**[H]

47 When some of those standing there heard this, they said, "He's calling for Elijah." **48** Immediately one of them ran and got a sponge, filled it with sour wine, put it on a stick, and offered him a drink. **49** But the rest said, "Let's see if Elijah comes to save him."

50 But Jesus cried out again with a loud voice and gave up his spirit. **51** Suddenly, the curtain of the sanctuary was torn in two from top to bottom, the earth quaked, and the rocks were split. **52** The tombs were also opened and many bodies of the saints who had fallen asleep were raised. **53** And they came out of the tombs after his resurrection, entered the holy city, and appeared to many.

54 When the centurion and those with him, who were keeping watch over Jesus, saw the earthquake and the things that had happened, they were terrified and said, "Truly this man was the Son of God!"

55 Many women who had followed Jesus from Galilee and looked after him were there, watching from a distance. **56** Among them were Mary Magdalene, Mary the mother of James and Joseph, and the mother of Zebedee's sons.

THE BURIAL OF JESUS

57 When it was evening, a rich man from Arimathea named Joseph came, who himself had also become a disciple of Jesus. **58** He approached Pilate and asked for Jesus's body. Then Pilate ordered that it[I] be released. **59** So Joseph took the body, wrapped it in clean, fine linen, **60** and placed it in his new tomb, which he had cut into the rock. He left after rolling a great stone against the entrance of the tomb. **61** Mary Magdalene and the other Mary were seated there, facing the tomb.

THE CLOSELY GUARDED TOMB

62 The next day, which followed the preparation day, the chief priests and the Pharisees gathered before Pilate **63** and said, "Sir, we remember that while this deceiver was still alive he said, 'After three days I will rise again.' **64** So give orders that the tomb be made secure until the third day. Otherwise, his disciples may come, steal him, and tell the people, 'He has been raised from the dead,' and the last deception will be worse than the first."

65 "You have[J] a guard of soldiers," Pilate told them. "Go and make it as secure as you know how." **66** They went and secured the tomb by setting a seal on the stone and placing the guard.

RESURRECTION MORNING

28 After the Sabbath, as the first day of the week was dawning, Mary Magdalene and the other Mary went to view the tomb. **2** There was a violent earthquake, because an angel of the Lord descended from heaven and approached the tomb. He rolled back the stone and was sitting on it. **3** His appearance was like lightning, and his clothing was as white as snow. **4** The guards were so shaken by fear of him that they became like dead men.

5 The angel told the women, "Don't be afraid, because I know you are looking for Jesus who was crucified. **6** He is not here. For he has risen, just as he said. Come and see the place where he lay. **7** Then go quickly and tell his disciples, 'He has risen from the dead and indeed he is going ahead of you to Galilee; you will see him there.' Listen, I have told you."

8 So, departing quickly from the tomb with fear and great joy, they ran to tell his disciples the news. **9** Just then[K] Jesus met them and said, "Greetings!" They came up, took hold of his feet, and worshiped him. **10** Then Jesus told them, "Do not be afraid. Go and tell my brothers to leave for Galilee, and they will see me there."

[A] **27:39** Lit *passed by blasphemed,* or *were blaspheming*   [B] **27:41** Other mss add *and Pharisees*   [C] **27:42** Other mss read *If he . . . Israel, let him*   [D] **27:43** Or *if he wants him*   [E] **27:45** Lit *From the sixth hour to the ninth hour*   [F] **27:45** Or *whole earth*   [G] **27:46** Some mss read *lama;* other mss read *lima*   [H] **27:46** Ps 22:1   [I] **27:58** Other mss read *that the body*   [J] **27:65** Or *"Take*   [K] **28:9** Other mss add *as they were on their way to tell the news to his disciples*

THE SOLDIERS BRIBED TO LIE

[11] As they were on their way, some of the guards came into the city and reported to the chief priests everything that had happened. [12] After the priests[A] had assembled with the elders and agreed on a plan, they gave the soldiers a large sum of money [13] and told them, "Say this, 'His disciples came during the night and stole him while we were sleeping.' [14] If this reaches the governor's ears, we will deal with[B] him and keep you out of trouble." [15] They took the money and did as they were instructed, and this story has been spread among Jewish people to this day.

THE GREAT COMMISSION

[16] The eleven disciples traveled to Galilee, to the mountain where Jesus had directed them. [17] When they saw him, they worshiped,[C] but some doubted. [18] Jesus came near and said to them, "All authority has been given to me in heaven and on earth. [19] Go, therefore, and make disciples of[D] all nations, baptizing them in the name of the Father and of the Son and of the Holy Spirit, [20] teaching them to observe everything I have commanded you. And remember,[E] I am with you always,[F] to the end of the age."

[A] 28:12 Lit *After they*   [B] 28:14 Lit *will persuade*   [C] 28:17 Other mss add *him*   [D] 28:19 Or *and disciple*   [E] 28:20 Lit *see*
[F] 28:20 Lit *all the days*

MARK

THE MESSIAH'S HERALD

1 The beginning of the gospel of Jesus Christ, the Son of God.^A ² As it is written in Isaiah the prophet:^B

See, I am sending my messenger ahead
    of you;
he will prepare your way.^C,D

³ A voice of one crying out
    in the wilderness:
Prepare the way for the Lord;
    make his paths straight!^E

⁴ John came baptizing^F in the wilderness and proclaiming a baptism of repentance for the forgiveness of sins. ⁵ The whole Judean countryside and all the people of Jerusalem were going out to him, and they were baptized by him in the Jordan River, confessing their sins. ⁶ John wore a camel-hair garment with a leather belt around his waist and ate locusts and wild honey.

⁷ He proclaimed, "One who is more powerful than I am is coming after me. I am not worthy to stoop down and untie the strap of his sandals. ⁸ I baptize you with^G water, but he will baptize you with the Holy Spirit."

THE BAPTISM OF JESUS

⁹ In those days Jesus came from Nazareth in Galilee and was baptized in the Jordan by John. ¹⁰ As soon as he came up out of the water, he saw the heavens being torn open and the Spirit descending on him like a dove. ¹¹ And a voice came from heaven: "You are my beloved Son; with you I am well-pleased."

THE TEMPTATION OF JESUS

¹² Immediately the Spirit drove him into the wilderness. ¹³ He was in the wilderness forty days, being tempted by Satan. He was with the wild animals, and the angels were serving him.

MINISTRY IN GALILEE

¹⁴ After John was arrested, Jesus went to Galilee, proclaiming the good news^H of God: ¹⁵ "The time is fulfilled, and the kingdom of God has come near. Repent and believe the good news!"

THE FIRST DISCIPLES

¹⁶ As he passed alongside the Sea of Galilee, he saw Simon and Andrew, Simon's brother, casting a net into the sea — for they were fishermen. ¹⁷ "Follow me," Jesus told them, "and I will make you fish for^I people." ¹⁸ Immediately they left their nets and followed him. ¹⁹ Going on a little farther, he saw James the son of Zebedee and his brother John in a boat putting their nets in order. ²⁰ Immediately he called them, and they left their father Zebedee in the boat with the hired men and followed him.

DRIVING OUT AN UNCLEAN SPIRIT

²¹ They went into Capernaum, and right away he entered the synagogue on the Sabbath and began to teach. ²² They were astonished at his teaching because he was teaching them as one who had authority, and not like the scribes.

²³ Just then a man with an unclean spirit was in their synagogue. He cried out, ²⁴ "What do you have to do with us, Jesus of Nazareth? Have you come to destroy us? I know who you are — the Holy One of God!"

²⁵ Jesus rebuked him saying, "Be silent, and come out of him!" ²⁶ And the unclean spirit threw him into convulsions, shouted with a loud voice, and came out of him.

²⁷ They were all amazed, and so they began to ask each other: "What is this? A new teaching with authority!^K He commands even the unclean spirits, and they obey him." ²⁸ At once the news about him spread throughout the entire vicinity of Galilee.

HEALINGS AT CAPERNAUM

²⁹ As soon as they left the synagogue, they went into Simon and Andrew's house with James and John. ³⁰ Simon's mother-in-law was lying in bed with a fever, and they told him about her at once. ³¹ So he went to her, took her by the hand, and raised her up. The fever left her,^L and she began to serve them.

³² When evening came, after the sun had set, they brought to him all those who were sick and demon-possessed. ³³ The whole town was assembled at the door, ³⁴ and he healed many who were sick with various diseases and drove out many demons. And he would not permit the demons to speak, because they knew him.

PREACHING IN GALILEE

³⁵ Very early in the morning, while it was still dark, he got up, went out, and made his way to a deserted place; and there he was praying.

---

^A 1:1 Some mss omit *the Son of God* ^B 1:2 Other mss read *in the prophets* ^C 1:2 Other mss add *before you* ^D 1:2 Mal 3:1 ^E 1:3 Is 40:3 ^F 1:4 Or *John the Baptist came* ^G 1:8 Or *in* ^H 1:14 Other mss add *of the kingdom* ^I 1:14 Or *gospel* ^J 1:17 Or *you to become fishers of* ^K 1:27 Other mss read *"What is this? What is this new teaching? For with authority* ^L 1:31 Other mss add *at once*

³⁶ Simon and his companions searched for him, ³⁷ and when they found him they said, "Everyone is looking for you."

³⁸ And he said to them, "Let's go on to the neighboring villages so that I may preach there too. This is why I have come."

A MAN CLEANSED

³⁹ He went into all of Galilee, preaching in their synagogues and driving out demons. ⁴⁰ Then a man with leprosy ᴬ came to him and, on his knees, ᴮ begged him: "If you are willing, you can make me clean." ⁴¹ Moved with compassion, ᶜ Jesus reached out his hand and touched him. "I am willing," he told him. "Be made clean." ⁴² Immediately the leprosy left him, and he was made clean. ⁴³ Then he sternly warned him and sent him away at once, ⁴⁴ telling him, "See that you say nothing to anyone; but go and show yourself to the priest, and offer what Moses commanded for your cleansing, as a testimony to them." ᴰ ⁴⁵ Yet he went out and began to proclaim it widely and to spread the news, with the result that Jesus could no longer enter a town openly. But he was out in deserted places, and they came to him from everywhere.

THE SON OF MAN FORGIVES AND HEALS

2 When he entered Capernaum again after some days, it was reported that he was at home. ² So many people gathered together that there was no more room, not even in the doorway, and he was speaking the word to them. ³ They came to him bringing a paralytic, carried by four of them. ⁴ Since they were not able to bring him to ᴱ Jesus because of the crowd, they removed the roof above him, and after digging through it, they lowered the mat on which the paralytic was lying. ⁵ Seeing their faith, Jesus told the paralytic, "Son, your sins are forgiven."

⁶ But some of the scribes were sitting there, questioning in their hearts: ⁷ "Why does he speak like this? He's blaspheming! Who can forgive sins but God alone?"

⁸ Right away Jesus perceived in his spirit that they were thinking like this within themselves and said to them, "Why are you thinking these things in your hearts? ⁹ Which is easier: to say to the paralytic, 'Your sins are forgiven,' or to say, 'Get up, take your mat, and walk'? ¹⁰ But so that you may know that the Son of Man has authority on earth to forgive sins"— he told the paralytic— ¹¹ "I tell you: get up, take your mat, and go home."

¹² Immediately he got up, took the mat, and went out in front of everyone. As a result, they were all astounded and gave glory to God, saying, "We have never seen anything like this!"

THE CALL OF LEVI

¹³ Jesus went out again beside the sea. The whole crowd was coming to him, and he was teaching them. ¹⁴ Then, passing by, he saw Levi the son of Alphaeus sitting at the toll booth, and he said to him, "Follow me," and he got up and followed him.

¹⁵ While he was reclining at the table in Levi's house, many tax collectors and sinners were eating ᶠ with Jesus and his disciples, for there were many who were following him. ¹⁶ When the scribes who were Pharisees ᴳ saw that he was eating with sinners and tax collectors, they asked his disciples, "Why does he eat" ᴴ with tax collectors and sinners?"

¹⁷ When Jesus heard this, he told them, "It is not those who are well who need a doctor, but those who are sick. I didn't come to call the righteous, but sinners."

A QUESTION ABOUT FASTING

¹⁸ Now John's disciples and the Pharisees ᴵ were fasting. People came and asked him, "Why do John's disciples and the Pharisees' disciples fast, but your disciples do not fast?"

¹⁹ Jesus said to them, "The wedding guests cannot fast while the groom is with them, can they? As long as they have the groom with them, they cannot fast. ²⁰ But the time ᴶ will come when the groom will be taken away from them, and then they will fast on that day. ²¹ No one sews a patch of unshrunk cloth on an old garment. Otherwise, the new patch pulls away from the old cloth, and a worse tear is made. ²² And no one puts new wine into old wineskins. Otherwise, the wine will burst the skins, and the wine is lost as well as the skins. No, new wine is put into fresh wineskins."

LORD OF THE SABBATH

²³ On the Sabbath he was going through the grainfields, and his disciples began to make their way, picking some heads of grain. ²⁴ The Pharisees said to him, "Look, why are they doing what is not lawful on the Sabbath?"

²⁵ He said to them, "Have you never read what David and those who were with him did when he was in need and hungry — ²⁶ how he

---

ᴬ 1:40 Gk *lepros*; a term for various skin diseases, also in v. 42; see Lv 13–14 ᴮ 1:40 Other mss omit *on his knees* ᶜ 1:41 Other mss *Moved with indignation* ᴰ 1:44 Or *against them* ᴱ 2:4 Other mss read *able to get near* ᶠ 2:15 Lit *reclining together* ᴳ 2:16 Other mss read *scribes and Pharisees* ᴴ 2:16 Other mss add *and drink* ᴵ 2:18 Other mss read *The disciples of John and of the Pharisees* ᴶ 2:20 Or *the days*

entered the house of God in the time of Abiathar the high priest and ate the bread of the Presence — which is not lawful for anyone to eat except the priests — and also gave some to his companions?" [27] Then he told them, "The Sabbath was made for[A] man and not man for the Sabbath. [28] So then, the Son of Man is Lord even of the Sabbath."

3 Jesus entered the synagogue again, and a man was there who had a shriveled hand. [2] In order to accuse him, they were watching him closely to see whether he would heal him on the Sabbath. [3] He told the man with the shriveled hand, "Stand before us." [4] Then he said to them, "Is it lawful to do good on the Sabbath or to do evil, to save life or to kill?" But they were silent. [5] After looking around at them with anger, he was grieved at the hardness of their hearts and told the man, "Stretch out your hand." So he stretched it out, and his hand was restored. [6] Immediately the Pharisees went out and started plotting with the Herodians against him, how they might kill him.

MINISTERING TO THE MULTITUDE

[7] Jesus departed with his disciples to the sea, and a large crowd followed from Galilee, and a large crowd followed from Judea, [8] Jerusalem, Idumea, beyond the Jordan, and around Tyre and Sidon. The large crowd came to him because they heard about everything he was doing. [9] Then he told his disciples to have a small boat ready for him, so that the crowd wouldn't crush him. [10] Since he had healed many, all who had diseases were pressing toward him to touch him. [11] Whenever the unclean spirits saw him, they fell down before him and cried out, "You are the Son of God!" [12] And he would strongly warn them not to make him known.

THE TWELVE APOSTLES

[13] Jesus went up the mountain and summoned those he wanted, and they came to him. [14] He appointed twelve, whom he also named apostles,[B] to be with him, to send them out to preach, [15] and to have authority to[C] drive out demons. [16] He appointed the Twelve:[D] To Simon, he gave the name Peter; [17] and to James the son of Zebedee, and to his brother John, he gave the name "Boanerges" (that is, "Sons of Thunder"); [18] Andrew; Philip and Bartholomew; Matthew and Thomas; James the son of Alphaeus, and Thaddaeus; Simon the Zealot, [19] and Judas Iscariot, who also betrayed him.

A HOUSE DIVIDED

[20] Jesus entered a house, and the crowd gathered again so that they were not even able to eat.[E] [21] When his family heard this, they set out to restrain him, because they said, "He's out of his mind."

[22] The scribes who had come down from Jerusalem said, "He is possessed by Beelzebul," and, "He drives out demons by the ruler of the demons."

[23] So he summoned them and spoke to them in parables: "How can Satan drive out Satan? [24] If a kingdom is divided against itself, that kingdom cannot stand. [25] If a house is divided against itself, that house cannot stand. [26] And if Satan opposes himself and is divided, he cannot stand but is finished. [27] But no one can enter a strong man's house and plunder his possessions unless he first ties up the strong man. Then he can plunder his house.

[28] "Truly I tell you, people will be forgiven for all sins and whatever blasphemies they utter. [29] But whoever blasphemes against the Holy Spirit never has forgiveness, but is guilty of an eternal sin"[F] — [30] because they were saying, "He has an unclean spirit."

TRUE RELATIONSHIPS

[31] His mother and his brothers came, and standing outside, they sent word to him and called him. [32] A crowd was sitting around him and told him, "Look, your mother, your brothers, and your sisters[G] are outside asking for you."

[33] He replied to them, "Who are my mother and my brothers?" [34] Looking at those sitting in a circle around him, he said, "Here are my mother and my brothers! [35] Whoever does the will of God is my brother and sister and mother."

THE PARABLE OF THE SOWER

4 Again he began to teach by the sea, and a very large crowd gathered around him. So he got into a boat on the sea and sat down, while the whole crowd was by the sea on the shore. [2] He taught them many things in parables, and in his teaching he said to them: [3] "Listen! Consider the sower who went out to sow. [4] As he sowed, some seed fell along the path, and the birds came and devoured it. [5] Other seed fell on rocky ground where it didn't have much soil, and it grew up quickly, since the soil wasn't deep. [6] When the sun came up, it was scorched, and since it had no root, it withered

---

away. **7** Other seed fell among thorns, and the thorns came up and choked it, and it didn't produce fruit. **8** Still other seed fell on good ground and it grew up, producing fruit that increased thirty, sixty, and a hundred times." **9** Then he said, "Let anyone who has ears to hear listen."

WHY JESUS USED PARABLES

10 When he was alone, those around him with the Twelve, asked him about the parables. **11** He answered them, "The secret of the kingdom of God has been given to you, but to those outside, everything comes in parables **12** so that

they may indeed look,
and yet not perceive;
they may indeed listen,
and yet not understand;
otherwise, they might turn back
and be forgiven."[A,B]

THE PARABLE OF THE SOWER EXPLAINED

13 Then he said to them: "Don't you understand this parable? How then will you understand all of the parables? **14** The sower sows the word. **15** Some are like the word sown on the path. When they hear, immediately Satan comes and takes away the word sown in them.[C] **16** And others are like seed sown on rocky ground. When they hear the word, immediately they receive it with joy. **17** But they have no root; they are short-lived. When distress or persecution comes because of the word, they immediately fall away. **18** Others are like seed sown among thorns; these are the ones who hear the word, **19** but the worries of this age, the deceitfulness[D] of wealth, and the desires for other things enter in and choke the word, and it becomes unfruitful. **20** And those like seed sown on good ground hear the word, welcome it, and produce fruit thirty, sixty, and a hundred times what was sown."

USING YOUR LIGHT

21 He also said to them, "Is a lamp brought in to be put under a basket or under a bed? Isn't it to be put on a lampstand? **22** For there is nothing hidden that will not be revealed, and nothing concealed that will not be brought to light. **23** If anyone has ears to hear, let him listen." **24** And he said to them, "Pay attention to what you hear. By the measure you use, it will be measured to you — and more will be added to you. **25** For whoever has, more will be given to him, and whoever does not have, even what he has will be taken away from him."

THE PARABLE OF THE GROWING SEED

26 "The kingdom of God is like this," he said. "A man scatters seed on the ground. **27** He sleeps and rises night and day; the seed sprouts and grows, although he doesn't know how. **28** The soil produces a crop by itself — first the blade, then the head, and then the full grain on the head. **29** As soon as the crop is ready, he sends for the sickle, because the harvest has come."

THE PARABLE OF THE MUSTARD SEED

30 And he said, "With what can we compare the kingdom of God, or what parable can we use to describe it? **31** It's like a mustard seed that, when sown upon the soil, is the smallest of all the seeds on the ground. **32** And when sown, it comes up and grows taller than all the garden plants, and produces large branches, so that the birds of the sky can nest in its shade."

USING PARABLES

33 He was speaking the word to them with many parables like these, as they were able to understand. **34** He did not speak to them without a parable. Privately, however, he explained everything to his own disciples.

WIND AND WAVE OBEY JESUS

35 On that day, when evening had come, he told them, "Let's cross over to the other side of the sea." **36** So they left the crowd and took him along since he was in the boat. And other boats were with him. **37** A great windstorm arose, and the waves were breaking over the boat, so that the boat was already being swamped. **38** He was in the stern, sleeping on the cushion. So they woke him up and said to him, "Teacher! Don't you care that we're going to die?"

39 He got up, rebuked the wind, and said to the sea, "Silence! Be still!" The wind ceased, and there was a great calm. **40** Then he said to them, "Why are you afraid? Do you still have no faith?"

41 And they were terrified[E] and asked one another, "Who then is this? Even the wind and the sea obey him!"

DEMONS DRIVEN OUT BY JESUS

5 They came to the other side of the sea, to the region of the Gerasenes.[F] **2** As soon as he got out of the boat, a man with an unclean spirit came out of the tombs and met him. **3** He lived in the tombs, and no one was able to restrain him anymore — not even with a chain — **4** because he often had been bound with shackles and chains, but had torn the chains apart

---

[A]**4:12** Other mss read *and their sins be forgiven them*　[B]**4:12** Is 6:9-10　[C]**4:15** Other mss read *in their hearts*
[D]**4:19** Or *seduction*　[E]**4:41** Or *were filled with awe*　[F]**5:1** Some mss read *Gadarenes*; other mss read *Gergesenes*

and smashed the shackles. No one was strong enough to subdue him. [5] Night and day among the tombs and on the mountains, he was always crying out and cutting himself with stones.

[6] When he saw Jesus from a distance, he ran and knelt down before him. [7] And he cried out with a loud voice, "What do you have to do with me, Jesus, Son of the Most High God? I beg you before God, don't torment me!" [8] For he had told him, "Come out of the man, you unclean spirit!"

[9] "What is your name?" he asked him.

"My name is Legion," he answered him, "because we are many." [10] And he begged him earnestly not to send them out of the region.

[11] A large herd of pigs was there, feeding on the hillside. [12] The demons[A] begged him, "Send us to the pigs, so that we may enter them." [13] So he gave them permission, and the unclean spirits came out and entered the pigs. The herd of about two thousand rushed down the steep bank into the sea and drowned there.

[14] The men who tended them[B] ran off and reported it in the town and the countryside, and people went to see what had happened. [15] They came to Jesus and saw the man who had been demon-possessed, sitting there, dressed and in his right mind; and they were afraid. [16] Those who had seen it described to them what had happened to the demon-possessed man and told about the pigs. [17] Then they began to beg him to leave their region.

[18] As he was getting into the boat, the man who had been demon-possessed begged him earnestly that he might remain with him. [19] Jesus did not let him but told him, "Go home to your own people, and report to them how much the Lord has done for you and how he has had mercy on you." [20] So he went out and began to proclaim in the Decapolis how much Jesus had done for him, and they were all amazed.

A GIRL RESTORED AND A WOMAN HEALED

[21] When Jesus had crossed over again by boat[C] to the other side, a large crowd gathered around him while he was by the sea. [22] One of the synagogue leaders, named Jairus, came, and when he saw Jesus, he fell at his feet [23] and begged him earnestly, "My little daughter is dying. Come and lay your hands on her so that she can get well[D] and live." [24] So Jesus went with him, and a large crowd was following and pressing against him.

[25] Now a woman suffering from bleeding for twelve years[26] had endured much under many doctors. She had spent everything she had and was not helped at all. On the contrary, she became worse. [27] Having heard about Jesus, she came up behind him in the crowd and touched his clothing. [28] For she said, "If I just touch his clothes, I'll be made well." [29] Instantly her flow of blood ceased, and she sensed in her body that she was healed of her affliction.

[30] At once Jesus realized in himself that power had gone out from him. He turned around in the crowd and said, "Who touched my clothes?"

[31] His disciples said to him, "You see the crowd pressing against you, and yet you say, 'Who touched me?'"

[32] But he was looking around to see who had done this. [33] The woman, with fear and trembling, knowing what had happened to her, came and fell down before him, and told him the whole truth. [34] "Daughter," he said to her, "your faith has saved you. Go in peace and be healed from your affliction."

[35] While he was still speaking, people came from the synagogue leader's house and said, "Your daughter is dead. Why bother the teacher anymore?"

[36] When Jesus overheard[E] what was said, he told the synagogue leader, "Don't be afraid. Only believe." [37] He did not let anyone accompany him except Peter, James, and John, James's brother. [38] They came to the leader's house, and he saw a commotion — people weeping and wailing loudly. [39] He went in and said to them, "Why are you making a commotion and weeping? The child is not dead but asleep." [40] They laughed at him, but he put them all outside. He took the child's father, mother, and those who were with him, and entered the place where the child was. [41] Then he took the child by the hand and said to her, "*Talitha koum*"[F] (which is translated, "Little girl, I say to you, get up"). [42] Immediately the girl got up and began to walk. (She was twelve years old.) At this they were utterly astounded. [43] Then he gave them strict orders that no one should know about this and told them to give her something to eat.

REJECTION AT NAZARETH

6 He left there and came to his hometown, and his disciples followed him. [2] When the Sabbath came, he began to teach in the synagogue, and many who heard him were astonished. "Where did this man get these things?" they said. "What is this wisdom that has been given to him, and how are these miracles performed by his hands? [3] Isn't this the carpenter, the son of Mary, and the brother of James, Joses, Judas, and Simon? And aren't his sisters here with us?" So they were offended by him.

[A]5:12 Other mss read *All the demons* [B]5:14 Other mss read *tended the pigs* [C]5:21 Other mss omit *by boat* [D]5:23 Or *she might be saved* [E]5:36 Or *ignored* [F]5:41 An Aramaic expression

[4] Jesus said to them, "A prophet is not without honor except in his hometown, among his relatives, and in his household." [5] He was not able to do a miracle there, except that he laid his hands on a few sick people and healed them. [6] And he was amazed at their unbelief. He was going around the villages teaching.

COMMISSIONING THE TWELVE

[7] He summoned the Twelve and began to send them out in pairs and gave them authority over unclean spirits. [8] He instructed them to take nothing for the road except a staff — no bread, no traveling bag, no money in their belts, [9] but to wear sandals and not put on an extra shirt. [10] He said to them, "Whenever you enter a house, stay there until you leave that place. [11] If any place does not welcome you or listen to you, when you leave there, shake the dust off your feet as a testimony against them."[A] [12] So they went out and preached that people should repent. [13] They drove out many demons, anointed many sick people with oil and healed them.

JOHN THE BAPTIST BEHEADED

[14] King Herod heard about it, because Jesus's name had become well known. Some[B] said, "John the Baptist has been raised from the dead, and that's why miraculous powers are at work in him." [15] But others said, "He's Elijah." Still others said, "He's a prophet, like one of the prophets from long ago."

[16] When Herod heard of it, he said, "John, the one I beheaded, has been raised!"

[17] For Herod himself had given orders to arrest John and to chain him in prison on account of Herodias, his brother Philip's wife, because he had married her. [18] John had been telling Herod, "It is not lawful for you to have your brother's wife." [19] So Herodias held a grudge against him and wanted to kill him. But she could not, [20] because Herod feared John and protected him, knowing he was a righteous and holy man. When Herod heard him he would be very perplexed,[C] and yet he liked to listen to him.

[21] An opportune time came on his birthday, when Herod gave a banquet for his nobles, military commanders, and the leading men of Galilee. [22] When Herodias's own daughter[D] came in and danced, she pleased Herod and his guests. The king said to the girl, "Ask me whatever you want, and I'll give it to you." [23] He promised her with an oath: "Whatever you ask me I will give you, up to half my kingdom."

[24] She went out and said to her mother, "What should I ask for?"

"John the Baptist's head," she said.

[25] At once she hurried to the king and said, "I want you to give me John the Baptist's head on a platter immediately." [26] Although the king was deeply distressed, because of his oaths and the guests[E] he did not want to refuse her. [27] The king immediately sent for an executioner and commanded him to bring John's head. So he went and beheaded him in prison, [28] brought his head on a platter, and gave it to the girl. Then the girl gave it to her mother. [29] When John's disciples heard about it, they came and removed his corpse and placed it in a tomb.

FEEDING OF THE FIVE THOUSAND

[30] The apostles gathered around Jesus and reported to him all that they had done and taught. [31] He said to them, "Come away by yourselves to a remote place and rest for a while." For many people were coming and going, and they did not even have time to eat.

[32] So they went away in the boat by themselves to a remote place, [33] but many saw them leaving and recognized them, and they ran on foot from all the towns and arrived ahead of them.[F]

[34] When he went ashore, he saw a large crowd and had compassion on them, because they were like sheep without a shepherd. Then he began to teach them many things.

[35] When it grew late, his disciples approached him and said, "This place is deserted, and it is already late. [36] Send them away so that they can go into the surrounding countryside and villages to buy themselves something to eat."

[37] "You give them something to eat," he responded.

They said to him, "Should we go and buy two hundred denarii[G] worth of bread and give them something to eat?"

[38] He asked them, "How many loaves do you have? Go and see."

When they found out they said, "Five, and two fish." [39] Then he instructed them to have all the people sit down in groups on the green grass. [40] So they sat down in groups of hundreds and fifties. [41] He took the five loaves and the two fish, and looking up to heaven, he blessed and broke the loaves. He kept giving them to his disciples to set before the people. He also divided the two fish among them

---

[A] 6:11 Other mss add *Truly I tell you, it will be more tolerable for Sodom or Gomorrah on judgment day than for that town.*   [B] 6:14 Other mss read *He*   [C] 6:20 Other mss read *When he heard him, he did many things*   [D] 6:22 Other mss read *When his daughter Herodias*   [E] 6:26 Lit *and those reclining at the table*   [F] 6:33 Other mss add *and gathered around him*   [G] 6:37 A denarius = one day's wage

all. [42] Everyone ate and was satisfied. [43] They picked up twelve baskets full of pieces of bread and fish. [44] Now those who had eaten the loaves were five thousand men.

WALKING ON THE WATER

[45] Immediately he made his disciples get into the boat and go ahead of him to the other side, to Bethsaida, while he dismissed the crowd. [46] After he said good-bye to them, he went away to the mountain to pray. [47] Well into the night, the boat was in the middle of the sea, and he was alone on the land. [48] He saw them straining at the oars,[A] because the wind was against them. Very early in the morning[B] he came toward them walking on the sea and wanted to pass by them. [49] When they saw him walking on the sea, they thought it was a ghost and cried out, [50] because they all saw him and were terrified. Immediately he spoke with them and said, "Have courage! It is I. Don't be afraid." [51] Then he got into the boat with them, and the wind ceased. They were completely astounded, [52] because they had not understood about the loaves. Instead, their hearts were hardened.

MIRACULOUS HEALINGS

[53] When they had crossed over, they came to shore at Gennesaret and anchored there. [54] As they got out of the boat, people immediately recognized him. [55] They hurried throughout that region and began to carry the sick on mats to wherever they heard he was. [56] Wherever he went, into villages, towns, or the country, they laid the sick in the marketplaces and begged him that they might touch just the end of his robe. And everyone who touched it was healed.

THE TRADITIONS OF THE ELDERS

7 The Pharisees and some of the scribes who had come from Jerusalem gathered around him. [2] They observed that some of his disciples were eating bread with unclean — that is, unwashed — hands. [3] (For the Pharisees and all the Jews do not eat unless they give their hands a ceremonial washing, keeping the tradition of the elders. [4] When they come from the marketplace, they do not eat unless they have washed. And there are many other customs they have received and keep, like the washing of cups, pitchers, kettles, and dining couches.[C]) [5] So the Pharisees and the scribes asked him,

"Why don't your disciples live according to the tradition of the elders, instead of eating bread with ceremonially unclean[D] hands?"

[6] He answered them, "Isaiah prophesied correctly about you hypocrites, as it is written:

This people honors me with their lips,
    but their heart is far from me.
[7] They worship me in vain,
    teaching as doctrines
        human commands.[E]

[8] Abandoning the command of God, you hold on to human tradition."[F] [9] He also said to them, "You have a fine way of invalidating God's command in order to set up[G] your tradition! [10] For Moses said: Honor your father and your mother;[H] and Whoever speaks evil of father or mother must be put to death.[I] [11] But you say, 'If anyone tells his father or mother: Whatever benefit you might have received from me is corban' " (that is, an offering devoted to God), [12] "you no longer let him do anything for his father or mother. [13] You nullify the word of God by your tradition that you have handed down. And you do many other similar things."

[14] Summoning the crowd again, he told them, "Listen to me, all of you, and understand: [15] Nothing that goes into a person from outside can defile him but the things that come out of a person are what defile him."[J]

[17] When he went into the house away from the crowd, his disciples asked him about the parable. [18] He said to them, "Are you also as lacking in understanding? Don't you realize that nothing going into a person from the outside can defile him? [19] For it doesn't go into his heart but into the stomach and is eliminated" (thus he declared all foods clean[K]). [20] And he said, "What comes out of a person is what defiles him. [21] For from within, out of people's hearts, come evil thoughts, sexual immoralities, thefts, murders, [22] adulteries, greed, evil actions, deceit, self-indulgence, envy,[L] slander, pride, and foolishness. [23] All these evil things come from within and defile a person."

A GENTILE MOTHER'S FAITH

[24] He got up and departed from there to the region of Tyre.[M] He entered a house and did not want anyone to know it, but he could not escape notice. [25] Instead, immediately after hearing about him, a woman whose little daughter had an unclean spirit came and fell at his feet. [26] The woman was a Gentile,[N] a Syrophoenician by birth, and she was asking him to cast the

[A] **6:48** Or *them being battered as they rowed*   [B] **6:48** Lit *Around the fourth watch of the night* = 3 to 6 a.m.   [C] **7:4** Other mss omit *and dining couches*   [D] **7:5** Other mss read *with unwashed*   [E] **7:6-7** Is 29:13   [F] **7:8** Other mss add *The washing of jugs, and cups, and many other similar things you practice.*   [G] **7:9** Or *to maintain*   [H] **7:10** Ex 20:12; Dt 5:16   [I] **7:10** Ex 21:17; Lv 20:9   [J] **7:15** Some mss include v. 16: *"If anyone has ears to hear, let him listen."*   [K] **7:19** Other mss read *is eliminated, making all foods clean"*   [L] **7:22** Or *evil eye*   [M] **7:24** Many early mss add *and Sidon*   [N] **7:26** Or *a Greek (speaker)*

demon out of her daughter. [27] He said to her, "Let the children be fed first, because it isn't right to take the children's bread and throw it to the dogs."

[28] But she replied to him, "Lord, even the dogs under the table eat the children's crumbs."

[29] Then he told her, "Because of this reply, you may go. The demon has left your daughter." [30] When she went back to her home, she found her child lying on the bed, and the demon was gone.

JESUS DOES EVERYTHING WELL

[31] Again, leaving the region of Tyre, he went by way of Sidon to the Sea of Galilee, through[A] the region of the Decapolis. [32] They brought to him a deaf man who had difficulty speaking and begged Jesus to lay his hand on him. [33] So he took him away from the crowd in private. After putting his fingers in the man's ears and spitting, he touched his tongue. [34] Looking up to heaven, he sighed deeply and said to him, *"Ephphatha!"*[B] (that is, "Be opened! "). [35] Immediately his ears were opened, his tongue was loosened, and he began to speak clearly. [36] He ordered them to tell no one, but the more he ordered them, the more they proclaimed it.

[37] They were extremely astonished and said, "He has done everything well. He even makes the deaf hear and the mute speak."

FEEDING FOUR THOUSAND

8 In those days there was again a large crowd, and they had nothing to eat. He called the disciples and said to them, [2] "I have compassion on the crowd, because they've already stayed with me three days and have nothing to eat. [3] If I send them home hungry, they will collapse on the way, and some of them have come a long distance."

[4] His disciples answered him, "Where can anyone get enough bread here in this desolate place to feed these people? "

[5] "How many loaves do you have? " he asked them.

"Seven," they said. [6] He commanded the crowd to sit down on the ground. Taking the seven loaves, he gave thanks, broke them, and gave them to his disciples to set before the people. So they served them to the crowd. [7] They also had a few small fish, and after he had blessed them, he said these were to be served as well. [8] They ate and were satisfied. Then they collected seven large baskets of leftover pieces. [9] About four thousand were there. He dismissed

them. [10] And he immediately got into the boat with his disciples and went to the district of Dalmanutha.

THE LEAVEN OF THE PHARISEES AND HEROD

[11] The Pharisees came and began to argue with him, demanding of him a sign from heaven to test him. [12] Sighing deeply in his spirit, he said, "Why does this generation demand a sign? Truly I tell you, no sign will be given to this generation." [13] Then he left them, got back into the boat, and went to the other side.

[14] The disciples had forgotten to take bread and had only one loaf with them in the boat. [15] Then he gave them strict orders: "Watch out! Beware of the leaven[C] of the Pharisees and the leaven of Herod." [16] They were discussing among themselves that they did not have any bread. [17] Aware of this, he said to them, "Why are you discussing the fact you have no bread? Don't you understand or comprehend? Do you have hardened hearts? [18] **Do you have eyes and not see; do you have ears and not hear?**[D] And do you not remember? [19] When I broke the five loaves for the five thousand, how many baskets full of leftovers did you collect? "

"Twelve," they told him.

[20] "When I broke the seven loaves for the four thousand, how many baskets full of pieces did you collect? "

"Seven," they said.

[21] And he said to them, "Don't you understand yet? "

HEALING A BLIND MAN

[22] They came to Bethsaida. They brought a blind man to him and begged him to touch him. [23] He took the blind man by the hand and brought him out of the village. Spitting on his eyes and laying his hands on him, he asked him, "Do you see anything? "

[24] He looked up and said, "I see people — they look like trees walking."

[25] Again Jesus placed his hands on the man's eyes. The man looked intently and his sight was restored and he saw everything clearly. [26] Then he sent him home, saying, "Don't even go into the village."[E]

PETER'S CONFESSION OF THE MESSIAH

[27] Jesus went out with his disciples to the villages of Caesarea Philippi. And on the road he asked his disciples, "Who do people say that I am? "

[28] They answered him, "John the Baptist; others, Elijah; still others, one of the prophets."

[A] **7:31** Or *into*　[B] **7:34** An Aramaic expression　[C] **8:15** Or *yeast*　[D] **8:18** Jr 5:21; Ezk 12:2　[E] **8:26** Other mss add *or tell anyone in the village*

²⁹ "But you," he asked them, "who do you say that I am?"

Peter answered him, "You are the Messiah." ³⁰ And he strictly warned them to tell no one about him.

HIS DEATH AND RESURRECTION PREDICTED

³¹ Then he began to teach them that it was necessary for the Son of Man to suffer many things and be rejected by the elders, chief priests, and scribes, be killed, and rise after three days. ³² He spoke openly about this. Peter took him aside and began to rebuke him. ³³ But turning around and looking at his disciples, he rebuked Peter and said, "Get behind me, Satan! You are not thinking about God's concerns ᴬ but human concerns."

TAKE UP YOUR CROSS

³⁴ Calling the crowd along with his disciples, he said to them, "If anyone wants to follow after me, let him deny himself, take up his cross, and follow me. ³⁵ For whoever wants to save his life will lose it, but whoever loses his life because of me and the gospel will save it. ³⁶ For what does it benefit someone to gain the whole world and yet lose his life? ³⁷ What can anyone give in exchange for his life? ³⁸ For whoever is ashamed of me and my words in this adulterous and sinful generation, the Son of Man will also be ashamed of him when he comes in the glory of his Father with the holy angels."

9 Then he said to them, "Truly I tell you, there are some standing here who will not taste death until they see the kingdom of God come in power."

THE TRANSFIGURATION

² After six days Jesus took Peter, James, and John and led them up a high mountain by themselves to be alone. He was transfigured in front of them, ³ and his clothes became dazzling — extremely white as no launderer on earth could whiten them. ⁴ Elijah appeared to them with Moses, and they were talking with Jesus. ⁵ Peter said to Jesus, "Rabbi, it's good for us to be here. Let us set up three shelters: one for you, one for Moses, and one for Elijah" — ⁶ because he did not know what to say, since they were terrified. ⁷ A cloud appeared, overshadowing them, and a voice came from the cloud: "This is my beloved Son; listen to him!"

⁸ Suddenly, looking around, they no longer saw anyone with them except Jesus.

⁹ As they were coming down the mountain, he ordered them to tell no one what they had seen until the Son of Man had risen from the dead.

¹⁰ They kept this word to themselves, questioning what "rising from the dead" meant. ¹¹ Then they asked him, "Why do the scribes say that Elijah must come first?"

¹² "Elijah does come first and restores all things," he replied. "Why then is it written that the Son of Man must suffer many things and be treated with contempt? ¹³ But I tell you that Elijah has come, and they did whatever they pleased to him, just as it is written about him."

THE POWER OF FAITH OVER A DEMON

¹⁴ When they came to the disciples, they saw a large crowd around them and scribes disputing with them. ¹⁵ When the whole crowd saw him, they were amazed and ran to greet him. ¹⁶ He asked them, "What are you arguing with them about?"

¹⁷ Someone from the crowd answered him, "Teacher, I brought my son to you. He has a spirit that makes him unable to speak. ¹⁸ Whenever it seizes him, it throws him down, and he foams at the mouth, grinds his teeth, and becomes rigid. I asked your disciples to drive it out, but they couldn't."

¹⁹ He replied to them, "You unbelieving generation, how long will I be with you? How long must I put up with you? Bring him to me." ²⁰ So they brought the boy to him. When the spirit saw him, it immediately threw the boy into convulsions. He fell to the ground and rolled around, foaming at the mouth. ²¹ "How long has this been happening to him?" Jesus asked his father.

"From childhood," he said. ²² "And many times it has thrown him into fire or water to destroy him. But if you can do anything, have compassion on us and help us."

²³ Jesus said to him, " 'If you can'?ᴮ Everything is possible for the one who believes."

²⁴ Immediately the father of the boy cried out, "I do believe; help my unbelief!"

²⁵ When Jesus saw that a crowd was quickly gathering, he rebuked the unclean spirit, saying to it, "You mute and deaf spirit, I command you: Come out of him and never enter him again."

²⁶ Then it came out, shrieking and throwing himᶜ into terrible convulsions. The boy became like a corpse, so that many said, "He's dead." ²⁷ But Jesus, taking him by the hand, raised him, and he stood up.

²⁸ After he had gone into the house, his disciples asked him privately, "Why couldn't we drive it out?"

²⁹ And he told them, "This kind can come out by nothing but prayer."ᴰ

ᴬ**8:33** Or *about the things of God*   ᴮ**9:23** Other mss add *believe*   ᶜ**9:26** Other mss omit *him*   ᴰ**9:29** Other mss add *and fasting*

THE SECOND PREDICTION OF HIS DEATH

[30] Then they left that place and made their way through Galilee, but he did not want anyone to know it. [31] For he was teaching his disciples and telling them, "The Son of Man is going to be betrayed[A] into the hands of men. They will kill him, and after he is killed, he will rise three days later." [32] But they did not understand this statement, and they were afraid to ask him.

WHO IS THE GREATEST?

[33] They came to Capernaum. When he was in the house, he asked them, "What were you arguing about on the way?" [34] But they were silent, because on the way they had been arguing with one another about who was the greatest. [35] Sitting down, he called the Twelve and said to them, "If anyone wants to be first, he must be last and servant of all." [36] He took a child, had him stand among them, and taking him in his arms, he said to them, [37] "Whoever welcomes[B] one little child such as this in my name welcomes me. And whoever welcomes me does not welcome me, but him who sent me."

IN HIS NAME

[38] John said to him, "Teacher, we saw someone[C] driving out demons in your name, and we tried to stop him because he wasn't following us."

[39] "Don't stop him," said Jesus, "because there is no one who will perform a miracle in my name who can soon afterward speak evil of me. [40] For whoever is not against us is for us. [41] And whoever gives you a cup of water to drink in my name, because you belong to Christ — truly I tell you, he will never lose his reward.

WARNINGS FROM JESUS

[42] "But whoever causes one of these little ones who believe in me to fall away — it would be better for him if a heavy millstone were hung around his neck and he were thrown into the sea.

[43] "And if your hand causes you to fall away, cut it off. It is better for you to enter life maimed than to have two hands and go to hell, the unquenchable fire.[D] [45] And if your foot causes you to fall away, cut it off. It is better for you to enter life lame than to have two feet and be thrown into hell.[E] [47] And if your eye causes you to fall away, gouge it out. It is better for you to enter the kingdom of God with one eye than to have two eyes and be thrown into hell, [48] where **their worm does not die, and the fire is not quenched**.[F] [49] For everyone will be salted with fire.[G,H] [50] Salt is good, but if the salt should lose its flavor, how can you season it? Have salt among yourselves, and be at peace with one another."

THE QUESTION OF DIVORCE

10 He set out from there and went to the region of Judea and across the Jordan. Then crowds converged on him again, and as was his custom he taught them again.

[2] Some Pharisees came to test him, asking, "Is it lawful for a man to divorce his wife?"

[3] He replied to them, "What did Moses command you?"

[4] They said, "Moses permitted us to write divorce papers and send her away."

[5] But Jesus told them, "He wrote this command for you because of the hardness of your hearts. [6] But from the beginning of creation God[I] made them male and female.[J] [7] For this reason a man will leave his father and mother[K] [8] and the two will become one flesh.[L] So they are no longer two, but one flesh. [9] Therefore what God has joined together, let no one separate."

[10] When they were in the house again, the disciples questioned him about this matter. [11] He said to them, "Whoever divorces his wife and marries another commits adultery against her. [12] Also, if she divorces her husband and marries another, she commits adultery."

BLESSING THE CHILDREN

[13] People were bringing little children to him in order that he might touch them, but the disciples rebuked them. [14] When Jesus saw it, he was indignant and said to them, "Let the little children come to me. Don't stop them, because the kingdom of God belongs to such as these. [15] Truly I tell you, whoever does not receive[M] the kingdom of God like a little child will never enter it." [16] After taking them in his arms, he laid his hands on them and blessed them.

THE RICH YOUNG RULER

[17] As he was setting out on a journey, a man ran up, knelt down before him, and asked him,

---

[A] 9:31 Or *handed over*   [B] 9:37 Or *"Whoever receives*   [C] 9:38 Other mss add *who didn't go along with us*   [D] 9:43 Some mss include v. 44: *Where their worm does not die, and the fire is not quenched.*   [E] 9:45 Some mss include v. 46: *Where their worm does not die, and the fire is not quenched.*   [F] 9:48 Is 66:24   [G] 9:49 Other mss add *and every sacrifice will be salted with salt*   [H] 9:49 Lv 2:13; Ezk 43:24   [I] 10:6 Other mss omit *God*   [J] 10:6 Gn 1:27; 5:2   [K] 10:7 Some mss add *and be joined to his wife*   [L] 10:7-8 Gn 2:24   [M] 10:15 Or *not welcome*

"Good teacher, what must I do to inherit eternal life?"

[18] "Why do you call me good?" Jesus asked him. "No one is good except God alone. [19] You know the commandments: **Do not murder; do not commit adultery; do not steal; do not bear false witness; do not defraud; honor your father and mother.**"[A]

[20] He said to him, "Teacher, I have kept all these from my youth."

[21] Looking at him, Jesus loved him and said to him, "You lack one thing: Go, sell all you have and give to the poor, and you will have treasure in heaven. Then come,[B] follow me." [22] But he was dismayed by this demand, and he went away grieving, because he had many possessions.

POSSESSIONS AND THE KINGDOM

[23] Jesus looked around and said to his disciples, "How hard it is for those who have wealth to enter the kingdom of God!"

[24] The disciples were astonished at his words. Again Jesus said to them, "Children, how hard it is[C] to enter the kingdom of God! [25] It is easier for a camel to go through the eye of a needle than for a rich person to enter the kingdom of God."

[26] They were even more astonished, saying to one another, "Then who can be saved?"

[27] Looking at them, Jesus said, "With man it is impossible, but not with God, because all things are possible with God."

[28] Peter began to tell him, "Look, we have left everything and followed you."

[29] "Truly I tell you," Jesus said, "there is no one who has left house or brothers or sisters or mother or father[D] or children or fields for my sake and for the sake of the gospel, [30] who will not receive a hundred times more, now at this time — houses, brothers and sisters, mothers and children, and fields, with persecutions — and eternal life in the age to come. [31] But many who are first will be last, and the last first."

THE THIRD PREDICTION OF HIS DEATH

[32] They were on the road, going up to Jerusalem, and Jesus was walking ahead of them. The disciples were astonished, but those who followed him were afraid. Taking the Twelve aside again, he began to tell them the things that would happen to him. [33] "See, we are going up to Jerusalem. The Son of Man will be handed over to the chief priests and the scribes, and they will condemn him to death. Then they will hand him over to the Gentiles, [34] and they will

mock him, spit on him, flog[E] him, and kill him, and he will rise after three days."

SUFFERING AND SERVICE

[35] James and John, the sons of Zebedee, approached him and said, "Teacher, we want you to do whatever we ask you."

[36] "What do you want me to do for you?" he asked them.

[37] They answered him, "Allow us to sit at your right and at your left in your glory."

[38] Jesus said to them, "You don't know what you're asking. Are you able to drink the cup I drink or to be baptized with the baptism I am baptized with?"

[39] "We are able," they told him.

Jesus said to them, "You will drink the cup I drink, and you will be baptized with the baptism I am baptized with. [40] But to sit at my right or left is not mine to give; instead, it is for those for whom it has been prepared."

[41] When the ten disciples heard this, they began to be indignant with James and John. [42] Jesus called them over and said to them, "You know that those who are regarded as rulers of the Gentiles lord it over them, and those in high positions act as tyrants over them. [43] But it is not so among you. On the contrary, whoever wants to become great among you will be your servant, [44] and whoever wants to be first among you will be a slave to all. [45] For even the Son of Man did not come to be served, but to serve, and to give his life as a ransom for many."[F]

A BLIND MAN HEALED

[46] They came to Jericho. And as he was leaving Jericho with his disciples and a large crowd, Bartimaeus (the son of Timaeus), a blind beggar, was sitting by the road. [47] When he heard that it was Jesus of Nazareth, he began to cry out, "Jesus, Son of David, have mercy on me!" [48] Many warned him to keep quiet, but he was crying out all the more, "Have mercy on me, Son of David!"

[49] Jesus stopped and said, "Call him."

So they called the blind man and said to him, "Have courage! Get up; he's calling for you." [50] He threw off his coat, jumped up, and came to Jesus.

[51] Then Jesus answered him, "What do you want me to do for you?"

"*Rabboni*,"[G] the blind man said to him, "I want to see."

[52] Jesus said to him, "Go, your faith has saved you." Immediately he could see and began to follow Jesus on the road.

[A]**10:19** Ex 20:12-16; Dt 5:16-20   [B]**10:21** Other mss add *taking up the cross, and*   [C]**10:24** Other mss add *for those trusting in wealth*   [D]**10:29** Other mss add *or wife*   [E]**10:34** Or *scourge*   [F]**10:45** Or *in the place of many*; Is 53:10-12   [G]**10:51** Hb word for *my lord*

THE TRIUMPHAL ENTRY

11 When they approached Jerusalem, at Bethphage and Bethany near the Mount of Olives, he sent two of his disciples [2] and told them, "Go into the village ahead of you. As soon as you enter it, you will find a colt tied there, on which no one has ever sat. Untie it and bring it. [3] If anyone says to you, 'Why are you doing this?' say, 'The Lord needs it and will send it back here right away.'"

[4] So they went and found a colt outside in the street, tied by a door. They untied it, [5] and some of those standing there said to them, "What are you doing, untying the colt?" [6] They answered them just as Jesus had said; so they let them go.

[7] They brought the donkey to Jesus and threw their clothes on it, and he sat on it. [8] Many people spread their clothes on the road, and others spread leafy branches cut from the fields.[A] [9] Those who went ahead and those who followed shouted:

> *Hosanna!*
> **Blessed is he who comes**
> **in the name of the Lord![B]**
> [10] Blessed is the coming kingdom
> of our father David!
> *Hosanna* in the highest heaven!

[11] He went into Jerusalem and into the temple. After looking around at everything, since it was already late, he went out to Bethany with the Twelve.

THE BARREN FIG TREE IS CURSED

[12] The next day when they went out from Bethany, he was hungry. [13] Seeing in the distance a fig tree with leaves, he went to find out if there was anything on it. When he came to it, he found nothing but leaves; for it was not the season for figs. [14] He said to it, "May no one ever eat fruit from you again!" And his disciples heard it.

CLEANSING THE TEMPLE

[15] They came to Jerusalem, and he went into the temple and began to throw out those buying and selling. He overturned the tables of the money changers and the chairs of those selling doves, [16] and would not permit anyone to carry goods through the temple. [17] He was teaching them: "Is it not written, **My house will be called a house of prayer for all nations?**[C] But you have made it a **den of thieves!**"[D]

[18] The chief priests and the scribes heard it and started looking for a way to kill him. For they were afraid of him, because the whole crowd was astonished by his teaching.

[19] Whenever evening came, they would go out of the city.

THE BARREN FIG TREE IS WITHERED

[20] Early in the morning, as they were passing by, they saw the fig tree withered from the roots up. [21] Then Peter remembered and said to him, "Rabbi, look! The fig tree that you cursed has withered."

[22] Jesus replied to them, "Have faith in God. [23] Truly I tell you, if anyone says to this mountain, 'Be lifted up and thrown into the sea,' and does not doubt in his heart, but believes that what he says will happen, it will be done for him. [24] Therefore I tell you, everything you pray and ask for — believe that you have received[E] it and it will be yours. [25] And whenever you stand praying, if you have anything against anyone, forgive him, so that your Father in heaven will also forgive you your wrongdoing."[F]

THE AUTHORITY OF JESUS CHALLENGED

[27] They came again to Jerusalem. As he was walking in the temple, the chief priests, the scribes, and the elders came [28] and asked him, "By what authority are you doing these things? Who gave you this authority to do these things?"

[29] Jesus said to them, "I will ask you one question; then answer me, and I will tell you by what authority I do these things. [30] Was John's baptism from heaven or of human origin? Answer me."

[31] They discussed it among themselves: "If we say, 'From heaven,' he will say, 'Then why didn't you believe him?' [32] But if we say, 'Of human origin'" — they were afraid of the crowd, because everyone thought that John was truly a prophet. [33] So they answered Jesus, "We don't know."

And Jesus said to them, "Neither will I tell you by what authority I do these things."

THE PARABLE OF THE VINEYARD OWNER

12 He began to speak to them in parables: "A man planted a vineyard, put a fence around it, dug out a pit for a winepress, and built a watchtower. Then he leased it to tenant farmers and went away. [2] At harvest time he sent a servant to the farmers to collect some of the fruit of the vineyard from them. [3] But they took him, beat him, and sent him away empty-handed. [4] Again he sent another servant to them, and they[G] hit him on the head

[A] 11:8 Other mss read *others were cutting leafy branches from the trees and spreading them on the road*   [B] 11:9 Ps 118:26   [C] 11:17 Is 56:7   [D] 11:17 Jr 7:11   [E] 11:24 Some mss read *you receive*; other mss read *you will receive*   [F] 11:25 Some mss include v. 26: *"But if you don't forgive, neither will your Father in heaven forgive your wrongdoing."*   [G] 12:4 Other mss add *threw stones and*

and treated him shamefully.^ [5] Then he sent another, and they killed that one. He also sent many others; some they beat, and others they killed. [6] He still had one to send, a beloved son. Finally he sent him to them, saying, 'They will respect my son.' [7] But those tenant farmers said to one another, 'This is the heir. Come, let's kill him, and the inheritance will be ours.' [8] So they seized him, killed him, and threw him out of the vineyard. [9] What then will the owner[B] of the vineyard do? He will come and kill the farmers and give the vineyard to others. [10] Haven't you read this Scripture:

The stone that the builders rejected
has become the cornerstone.
[11] This came about from the Lord
and is wonderful in our eyes? "[C]

[12] They were looking for a way to arrest him but feared the crowd because they knew he had spoken this parable against them. So they left him and went away.

GOD AND CAESAR

[13] Then they sent some of the Pharisees and the Herodians to Jesus to trap him in his words. [14] When they came, they said to him, "Teacher, we know you are truthful and don't care what anyone thinks, nor do you show partiality but teach the way of God truthfully. Is it lawful to pay taxes to Caesar or not? Should we pay or shouldn't we? "

[15] But knowing their hypocrisy, he said to them, "Why are you testing me? Bring me a denarius[D] to look at." [16] They brought a coin. "Whose image and inscription is this? " he asked them.

"Caesar's," they replied.

[17] Jesus told them, "Give to Caesar the things that are Caesar's, and to God the things that are God's." And they were utterly amazed at him.

THE SADDUCEES AND THE RESURRECTION

[18] Sadducees, who say there is no resurrection, came to him and questioned him: [19] "Teacher, Moses wrote for us that **if a man's brother dies,** leaving a wife behind but **no child, that man should take the wife and raise up offspring for his brother.**[E] [20] There were seven brothers. The first married a woman, and dying, left no offspring. [21] The second also took her, and he died, leaving no offspring. And the third likewise. [22] None of the seven[F] left offspring. Last of all, the woman died too. [23] In

the resurrection, when they rise,[G] whose wife will she be, since the seven had married her? "

[24] Jesus spoke to them, "Isn't this the reason why you're mistaken: you don't know the Scriptures or the power of God? [25] For when they rise from the dead, they neither marry nor are given in marriage but are like angels in heaven. [26] And as for the dead being raised — haven't you read in the book of Moses, in the passage about the burning bush, how God said to him: **I am the God of Abraham and the God of Isaac and the God of Jacob?**[H] [27] He is not the God of the dead but of the living. You are badly mistaken."

THE PRIMARY COMMANDS

[28] One of the scribes approached. When he heard them debating and saw that Jesus answered them well, he asked him, "Which command is the most important of all? "

[29] Jesus answered, "The most important[I] is **Listen, O Israel! The Lord our God, the Lord is one.**[J] [30] **Love the Lord your God with all your heart, with all your soul, with all your mind, and with all your strength.**[K,L] [31] The second is, **Love your neighbor as yourself.**[M] There is no other command greater than these."

[32] Then the scribe said to him, "You are right, teacher. You have correctly said that he is one, and there is no one else except him. [33] And to love him with all your heart, with all your understanding,[N] and with all your strength, and to love your neighbor as yourself, is far more important than all the burnt offerings and sacrifices."

[34] When Jesus saw that he answered wisely, he said to him, "You are not far from the kingdom of God." And no one dared to question him any longer.

THE QUESTION ABOUT THE CHRIST

[35] While Jesus was teaching in the temple, he asked, "How can the scribes say that the Messiah is the son of David? [36] David himself says by the Holy Spirit:

The Lord declared to my Lord,
'Sit at my right hand
until I put your enemies
under your feet.'[O]
[37] David himself calls him 'Lord'; how then can he be his son? " And the large crowd was listening to him with delight.

WARNING AGAINST THE SCRIBES

[38] He also said in his teaching, "Beware of the scribes, who want to go around in long robes

---

^**12:4** Other mss add *and sent him off* [B]**12:9** Or *lord* [C]**12:10-11** Ps 118:22-23 [D]**12:15** A denarius = one day's wage [E]**12:19** Gn 38:8; Dt 25:5 [F]**12:22** Other mss add *had taken her and* [G]**12:23** Other mss omit *when they rise* [H]**12:26** Ex 3:6,15-16 [I]**12:29** Other mss add *of all the commands* [J]**12:29** Or *the Lord our God is Lord alone.* [K]**12:30** Other mss add *This is the first commandment.* [L]**12:30** Dt 6:4-5; Jos 22:5 [M]**12:31** Lv 19:18 [N]**12:33** Other mss add *with all your soul* [O]**12:36** Ps 110:1

and who want greetings in the marketplaces, [39] the best seats in the synagogues, and the places of honor at banquets. [40] They devour widows' houses and say long prayers just for show. These will receive harsher judgment."

THE WIDOW'S GIFT

[41] Sitting across from the temple treasury, he watched how the crowd dropped money into the treasury. Many rich people were putting in large sums. [42] Then a poor widow came and dropped in two tiny coins worth very little. [43] Summoning his disciples, he said to them, "Truly I tell you, this poor widow has put more into the treasury than all the others. [44] For they all gave out of their surplus, but she out of her poverty has put in everything she had — all she had to live on."

DESTRUCTION OF THE TEMPLE PREDICTED

13 As he was going out of the temple, one of his disciples said to him, "Teacher, look! What massive stones! What impressive buildings!"

[2] Jesus said to him, "Do you see these great buildings? Not one stone will be left upon another — all will be thrown down."

SIGNS OF THE END OF THE AGE

[3] While he was sitting on the Mount of Olives across from the temple, Peter, James, John, and Andrew asked him privately, [4] "Tell us, when will these things happen? And what will be the sign when all these things are about to be accomplished?"

[5] Jesus told them, "Watch out that no one deceives you. [6] Many will come in my name, saying, 'I am he,' and they will deceive many. [7] When you hear of wars and rumors of wars, don't be alarmed; these things must take place, but it is not yet the end. [8] For nation will rise up against nation, and kingdom against kingdom. There will be earthquakes in various places, and famines.[A] These are the beginning of birth pains.

PERSECUTIONS PREDICTED

[9] "But you, be on your guard! They will hand you over to local courts,[B] and you will be flogged in the synagogues. You will stand before governors and kings because of me, as a witness to them. [10] And it is necessary that the gospel be preached to all nations. [11] So when they arrest you and hand you over, don't worry beforehand what you will say, but say whatever is given to you at that time, for it isn't you speaking, but the Holy Spirit.

[12] "Brother will betray brother to death, and a father his child. Children will rise up against parents and have them put to death. [13] You will be hated by everyone because of my name, but the one who endures to the end will be saved.

THE GREAT TRIBULATION

[14] "When you see **the abomination of desolation**[C] standing where it should not be" (let the reader understand), "then those in Judea must flee to the mountains. [15] A man on the housetop must not come down or go in to get anything out of his house, [16] and a man in the field must not go back to get his coat. [17] Woe to pregnant women and nursing mothers in those days!

[18] "Pray it[D] won't happen in winter. [19] For those will be days of tribulation, the kind that hasn't been from the beginning of creation until now and never will be again. [20] If the Lord had not cut those days short, no one would be saved. But he cut those days short for the sake of the elect, whom he chose.

[21] "Then if anyone tells you, 'See, here is the Messiah! See, there!' do not believe it. [22] For false messiahs and false prophets will arise and will perform signs and wonders to lead astray, if possible, the elect. [23] And you must watch! I have told you everything in advance.

THE COMING OF THE SON OF MAN

[24] "But in those days, after that tribulation: The sun will be darkened, and the moon will not shed its light; [25] the stars will be falling from the sky, and the powers in the heavens will be shaken. [26] Then they will see the Son of Man coming in clouds with great power and glory. [27] He will send out the angels and gather his elect from the four winds, from the ends of the earth to the ends of heaven.

THE PARABLE OF THE FIG TREE

[28] "Learn this lesson from the fig tree: As soon as its branch becomes tender and sprouts leaves, you know that summer is near. [29] In the same way, when you see these things happening, recognize[E] that he[F] is near — at the door. [30] "Truly I tell you, this generation will certainly not pass away until all these things take place. [31] Heaven and earth will pass away, but my words will never pass away.

NO ONE KNOWS THE DAY OR HOUR

[32] "Now concerning that day or hour no one knows — neither the angels in heaven nor the Son — but only the Father.

[A] 13:8 Other mss add *and disturbances* [B] 13:9 Or *sanhedrins* [C] 13:14 Dn 9:27 [D] 13:18 Other mss read *"Pray that your escape* [E] 13:29 Or *you know* [F] 13:29 Or *it*

[33] "Watch! Be alert! [A] For you don't know when the time is coming.

[34] "It is like a man on a journey, who left his house, gave authority to his servants, gave each one his work, and commanded the doorkeeper to be alert. [35] Therefore be alert, since you don't know when the master of the house is coming — whether in the evening or at midnight or at the crowing of the rooster or early in the morning. [36] Otherwise, when he comes suddenly he might find you sleeping. [37] And what I say to you, I say to everyone: Be alert!"

THE PLOT TO KILL JESUS

14 It was two days before the Passover and the Festival of Unleavened Bread. The chief priests and the scribes were looking for a cunning way to arrest Jesus and kill him. [2] "Not during the festival," they said, "so that there won't be a riot among the people."

THE ANOINTING AT BETHANY

[3] While he was in Bethany at the house of Simon the leper, [B] as he was reclining at the table, a woman came with an alabaster jar of very expensive perfume of pure nard. She broke the jar and poured it on his head. [4] But some were expressing indignation to one another: "Why has this perfume been wasted? [5] For this perfume might have been sold for more than three hundred denarii [C] and given to the poor." And they began to scold her.

[6] Jesus replied, "Leave her alone. Why are you bothering her? She has done a noble thing for me. [7] You always have the poor with you, and you can do what is good for them whenever you want, but you do not always have me. [8] She has done what she could; she has anointed my body in advance for burial. [9] Truly I tell you, wherever the gospel is proclaimed in the whole world, what she has done will also be told in memory of her."

[10] Then Judas Iscariot, one of the Twelve, went to the chief priests to betray Jesus to them. [11] And when they heard this, they were glad and promised to give him money. So he started looking for a good opportunity to betray him.

PREPARATION FOR PASSOVER

[12] On the first day of Unleavened Bread, when they sacrifice the Passover lamb, his disciples asked him, "Where do you want us to go and prepare the Passover so that you may eat it?"

[13] So he sent two of his disciples and told them, "Go into the city, and a man carrying a jar of water will meet you. Follow him. [14] Wherever he enters, tell the owner of the house, 'The Teacher says, "Where is my guest room where I may eat the Passover with my disciples?"' [15] He will show you a large room upstairs, furnished and ready. Make the preparations for us there." [16] So the disciples went out, entered the city, and found it just as he had told them, and they prepared the Passover.

BETRAYAL AT THE PASSOVER

[17] When evening came, he arrived with the Twelve. [18] While they were reclining and eating, Jesus said, "Truly I tell you, one of you will betray me — one who is eating with me."

[19] They began to be distressed and to say to him one by one, "Surely not I?"

[20] He said to them, "It is one of the Twelve — the one who is dipping bread in the bowl with me. [21] For the Son of Man will go just as it is written about him, but woe to that man by whom the Son of Man is betrayed! It would have been better for him if he had not been born."

THE FIRST LORD'S SUPPER

[22] As they were eating, he took bread, blessed and broke it, gave it to them, and said, "Take it; this is my body." [23] Then he took a cup, and after giving thanks, he gave it to them, and they all drank from it. [24] He said to them, "This is my blood of the covenant, [D] which is poured out for many. [25] Truly I tell you, I will no longer drink of the fruit of the vine until that day when I drink it new [E] in the kingdom of God."

[26] After singing a hymn, they went out to the Mount of Olives.

PETER'S DENIAL PREDICTED

[27] Then Jesus said to them, "All of you will fall away, [F] because it is written:

I will strike the shepherd,
and the sheep will be scattered. [G]

[28] But after I have risen, I will go ahead of you to Galilee."

[29] Peter told him, "Even if everyone falls away, I will not."

[30] "Truly I tell you," Jesus said to him, "today, this very night, before the rooster crows twice, you will deny me three times."

[31] But he kept insisting, "If I have to die with you, I will never deny you." And they all said the same thing.

[A] **13:33** Other mss add *and pray*   [B] **14:3** Gk *lepros*; a term for various skin diseases; see Lv 13–14   [C] **14:5** A denarius = one day's wage   [D] **14:24** Other mss read *the new covenant*   [E] **14:25** Or *drink new wine*; lit *drink it new*   [F] **14:27** Other mss add *because of me this night*   [G] **14:27** Zch 13:7

THE PRAYER IN THE GARDEN

³² Then they came to a place named Gethsemane, and he told his disciples, "Sit here while I pray." ³³ He took Peter, James, and John with him, and he began to be deeply distressed and troubled. ³⁴ He said to them, "I am deeply grieved* to the point of death. Remain here and stay awake." ³⁵ He went a little farther, fell to the ground, and prayed that if it were possible, the hour might pass from him. ³⁶ And he said, "*Abba,*" Father! All things are possible for you. Take this cup away from me. Nevertheless, not what I will, but what you will." ³⁷ Then he came and found them sleeping. He said to Peter, "Simon, are you sleeping? Couldn't you stay awake one hour? ³⁸ Stay awake and pray so that you won't enter into temptation.ᶜ The spirit is willing, but the flesh is weak." ³⁹ Once again he went away and prayed, saying the same thing. ⁴⁰ And again he came and found them sleeping, because they could not keep their eyes open. They did not know what to say to him. ⁴¹ Then he came a third time and said to them, "Are you still sleeping and resting? Enough! The time has come. See, the Son of Man is betrayed into the hands of sinners. ⁴² Get up; let's go. See, my betrayer is near."

JUDAS'S BETRAYAL OF JESUS

⁴³ While he was still speaking, Judas, one of the Twelve, suddenly arrived. With him was a mob, with swords and clubs, from the chief priests, the scribes, and the elders. ⁴⁴ His betrayer had given them a signal. "The one I kiss," he said, "he's the one; arrest him and take him away under guard." ⁴⁵ So when he came, immediately he went up to Jesus and said, "Rabbi!" and kissed him. ⁴⁶ They took hold of him and arrested him. ⁴⁷ One of those who stood by drew his sword, struck the high priest's servant, and cut off his ear.

⁴⁸ Jesus said to them, "Have you come out with swords and clubs, as if I were a criminal,ᴰ to capture me? ⁴⁹ Every day I was among you, teaching in the temple, and you didn't arrest me. But the Scriptures must be fulfilled." ⁵⁰ Then they all deserted him and ran away. ⁵¹ Now a certain young man, wearing nothing but a linen cloth, was following him. They caught hold of him, ⁵² but he left the linen cloth behind and ran away naked.

JESUS FACES THE SANHEDRIN

⁵³ They led Jesus away to the high priest, and all the chief priests, the elders, and the scribes assembled. ⁵⁴ Peter followed him at a distance, right into the high priest's courtyard. He was sitting with the servants,ᴱ warming himself by the fire.

⁵⁵ The chief priests and the whole Sanhedrin were looking for testimony against Jesus to put him to death, but they could not find any. ⁵⁶ For many were giving false testimony against him, and the testimonies did not agree. ⁵⁷ Some stood up and gave false testimony against him, stating, ⁵⁸ "We heard him say, 'I will destroy this temple made with human hands, and in three days I will build another not made by hands.'" ⁵⁹ Yet their testimony did not agree even on this.

⁶⁰ Then the high priest stood up before them all and questioned Jesus, "Don't you have an answer to what these men are testifying against you?" ⁶¹ But he kept silent and did not answer. Again the high priest questioned him, "Are you the Messiah, the Son of the Blessed One?"

⁶² "I am," said Jesus, "and you will see the Son of Man seated at the right hand of Power and coming with the clouds of heaven."ᶠ

⁶³ Then the high priest tore his robes and said, "Why do we still need witnesses? ⁶⁴ You have heard the blasphemy. What is your decision?" They all condemned him as deserving death.

⁶⁵ Then some began to spit on him, to blindfold him, and to beat him, saying, "Prophesy!" The temple servants also took him and slapped him.

PETER DENIES HIS LORD

⁶⁶ While Peter was in the courtyard below, one of the high priest's maidservants came. ⁶⁷ When she saw Peter warming himself, she looked at him and said, "You also were with Jesus, the man from Nazareth."

⁶⁸ But he denied it: "I don't know or understand what you're talking about." Then he went out to the entryway,ᴳ and a rooster crowed.ᴴ

⁶⁹ When the maidservant saw him again, she began to tell those standing nearby, "This man is one of them."

⁷⁰ But again he denied it. After a little while those standing there said to Peter again, "You certainly are one of them, since you're also a Galilean."ᴵ

⁷¹ Then he started to curse and swear, "I don't know this man you're talking about!"

⁷² Immediately a rooster crowed a second time, and Peter remembered when Jesus had spoken the word to him, "Before the rooster crows twice, you will deny me three times." And he broke down and wept.

---

*14:34 Or *"My soul is swallowed up in sorrow* *14:36 Aramaic for *father* ᶜ14:38 Or *won't be put to the test*
ᴰ14:48 Or *insurrectionist* ᴱ14:54 Or *temple police,* or *officers,* also in v. 65 ᶠ14:62 Ps 110:1; Dn 7:13 ᴳ14:68 Or *forecourt*
ᴴ14:68 Other mss omit *and a rooster crowed* ᴵ14:70 Other mss add *and your speech shows it*

JESUS FACES PILATE

15 As soon as it was morning, having held a meeting with the elders, scribes, and the whole Sanhedrin, the chief priests tied Jesus up, led him away, and handed him over to Pilate. ² So Pilate asked him, "Are you the King of the Jews?"

He answered him, "You say so."

³ And the chief priests accused him of many things. ⁴ Pilate questioned him again, "Aren't you going to answer? Look how many things they are accusing you of!" ⁵ But Jesus still did not answer, and so Pilate was amazed.

JESUS OR BARABBAS

⁶ At the festival Pilate used to release for the people a prisoner whom they requested. ⁷ There was one named Barabbas, who was in prison with rebels who had committed murder during the rebellion. ⁸ The crowd came up and began to ask Pilate to do for them as was his custom. ⁹ Pilate answered them, "Do you want me to release the King of the Jews for you?" ¹⁰ For he knew it was because of envy that the chief priests had handed him over. ¹¹ But the chief priests stirred up the crowd so that he would release Barabbas to them instead. ¹² Pilate asked them again, "Then what do you want me to do with the one you call the King of the Jews?"

¹³ Again they shouted, "Crucify him!"

¹⁴ Pilate said to them, "Why? What has he done wrong?"

But they shouted all the more, "Crucify him!" ¹⁵ Wanting to satisfy the crowd, Pilate released Barabbas to them; and after having Jesus flogged, he handed him over to be crucified.

MOCKED BY THE MILITARY

¹⁶ The soldiers led him away into the palace (that is, the governor's residence) and called the whole company together. ¹⁷ They dressed him in a purple robe, twisted together a crown of thorns, and put it on him. ¹⁸ And they began to salute him, "Hail, King of the Jews!" ¹⁹ They were hitting him on the head with a stick and spitting on him. Getting down on their knees, they were paying him homage. ²⁰ After they had mocked him, they stripped him of the purple robe and put his clothes on him.

CRUCIFIED BETWEEN TWO CRIMINALS

They led him out to crucify him. ²¹ They forced a man coming in from the country, who was passing by, to carry Jesus's cross. He was Simon of Cyrene, the father of Alexander and Rufus.

²² They brought Jesus to the place called *Golgotha* (which means Place of the Skull). ²³ They tried to give him wine mixed with myrrh, but he did not take it.

²⁴ Then they crucified him and divided his clothes, casting lots for them to decide what each would get. ²⁵ Now it was nine in the morningᴬ when they crucified him. ²⁶ The inscription of the charge written against him was: THE KING OF THE JEWS. ²⁷ They crucified two criminalsᴮ with him, one on his right and one on his left.ᶜ

²⁹ Those who passed by were yelling insults atᴰ him, shaking their heads, and saying, "Ha! The one who would destroy the temple and rebuild it in three days, ³⁰ save yourself by coming down from the cross!" ³¹ In the same way, the chief priests with the scribes were mocking him among themselves and saying, "He saved others, but he cannot save himself! ³² Let the Messiah, the King of Israel, come down now from the cross, so that we may see and believe." Even those who were crucified with him taunted him.

THE DEATH OF JESUS

³³ When it was noon,ᴱ darkness came over the whole land until three in the afternoon.ᶠ ³⁴ And at three Jesus cried out with a loud voice, *"Eloi, Eloi, lemá sabachtháni?"* which is translated, "My God, my God, why have you abandoned me?"ᴳ ³⁵ When some of those standing there heard this, they said, "See, he's calling for Elijah." ³⁶ Someone ran and filled a sponge with sour wine, fixed it on a stick, offered him a drink, and said, "Let's see if Elijah comes to take him down." ³⁷ Jesus let out a loud cry and breathed his last. ³⁸ Then the curtain of the temple was torn in two from top to bottom. ³⁹ When the centurion, who was standing opposite him, saw the way heᴴ breathed his last, he said, "Truly this man was the Son of God!"ᴵ

⁴⁰ There were also women watching from a distance. Among them were Mary Magdalene, Mary the mother of James the younger and of Joses, and Salome. ⁴¹ In Galilee these women followed him and took care of him. Many other women had come up with him to Jerusalem.

THE BURIAL OF JESUS

⁴² When it was already evening, because it was the day of preparation (that is, the day before the Sabbath), ⁴³ Joseph of Arimathea, a prominent member of the Sanhedrin who was himself looking forward to the kingdom of God, came and boldly went to Pilate and asked for Jesus's body. ⁴⁴ Pilate was surprised that he was already

dead. Summoning the centurion, he asked him whether he had already died. [45] When he found out from the centurion, he gave the corpse to Joseph. [46] After he bought some linen cloth, Joseph took him down and wrapped him in the linen. Then he laid him in a tomb cut out of the rock and rolled a stone against the entrance to the tomb. [47] Mary Magdalene and Mary the mother of Joses were watching where he was laid.

RESURRECTION MORNING

16 When the Sabbath was over, Mary Magdalene, Mary the mother of James, and Salome bought spices, so that they could go and anoint him. [2] Very early in the morning, on the first day of the week, they went to the tomb at sunrise. [3] They were saying to one another, "Who will roll away the stone from the entrance to the tomb for us?" [4] Looking up, they noticed that the stone — which was very large — had been rolled away.

[5] When they entered the tomb, they saw a young man dressed in a white robe sitting on the right side; they were alarmed. [6] "Don't be alarmed," he told them. "You are looking for Jesus of Nazareth, who was crucified. He has risen! He is not here. See the place where they put him. [7] But go, tell his disciples and Peter, 'He is going ahead of you to Galilee; you will see him there just as he told you.'"

[8] They went out and ran from the tomb, because trembling and astonishment overwhelmed them. And they said nothing to anyone, since they were afraid.

[Some of the earliest mss conclude with 16:8.][A]

THE LONGER ENDING OF MARK: APPEARANCES OF THE RISEN LORD

[[9] Early on the first day of the week, after he had risen, he appeared first to Mary Magdalene, out of whom he had driven seven demons. [10] She went and reported to those who had been with him, as they were mourning and weeping. [11] Yet, when they heard that he was alive and had been seen by her, they did not believe it.

[12] After this, he appeared in a different form to two of them walking on their way into the country. [13] And they went and reported it to the rest, who did not believe them either.

THE GREAT COMMISSION

[14] Later he appeared to the Eleven themselves as they were reclining at the table. He rebuked their unbelief and hardness of heart, because they did not believe those who saw him after he had risen. [15] Then he said to them, "Go into all the world and preach the gospel to all creation. [16] Whoever believes and is baptized will be saved, but whoever does not believe will be condemned. [17] And these signs will accompany those who believe: In my name they will drive out demons; they will speak in new tongues;[B] [18] they will pick up snakes;[C] if they should drink anything deadly, it will not harm them; they will lay hands on the sick, and they will get well."

THE ASCENSION

[19] So the Lord Jesus, after speaking to them, was taken up into heaven and sat down at the right hand of God. [20] And they went out and preached everywhere, while the Lord worked with them and confirmed the word by the accompanying signs.]

[A]**16:8** Other mss include vv. 9-20 as a longer ending. The following shorter ending is found in some mss between v. 8 and v. 9 and in one ms after v. 8 (each of which omits vv. 9-20): *And all that had been commanded to them they quickly reported to those around Peter. After these things, Jesus himself sent out through them from east to west, the holy and imperishable proclamation of eternal salvation. Amen.*   [B]**16:17** = languages   [C]**16:18** Other mss add *with their hands*

LUKE

1 Many have undertaken to compile a narrative about the events that have been fulfilled^A among us, ² just as the original eyewitnesses and servants of the word handed them down to us. ³ It also seemed good to me, since I have carefully investigated everything from the very first, to write to you in an orderly sequence, most honorable Theophilus, ⁴ so that you may know the certainty of the things about which you have been instructed.^B

GABRIEL PREDICTS JOHN'S BIRTH

⁵ In the days of King Herod of Judea, there was a priest of Abijah's division named Zechariah. His wife was from the daughters of Aaron, and her name was Elizabeth. ⁶ Both were righteous in God's sight, living without blame according to all the commands and requirements of the Lord. ⁷ But they had no children because Elizabeth could not conceive, and both of them were well along in years.

⁸ When his division was on duty and he was serving as priest before God, ⁹ it happened that he was chosen by lot, according to the custom of the priesthood, to enter the sanctuary of the Lord and burn incense. ¹⁰ At the hour of incense the whole assembly of the people was praying outside. ¹¹ An angel of the Lord appeared to him, standing to the right of the altar of incense. ¹² When Zechariah saw him, he was terrified and overcome with fear. ¹³ But the angel said to him: "Do not be afraid, Zechariah, because your prayer has been heard. Your wife Elizabeth will bear you a son, and you will name him John. ¹⁴ There will be joy and delight for you, and many will rejoice at his birth. ¹⁵ For he will be great in the sight of the Lord and will never drink wine or beer. He will be filled with the Holy Spirit while still in his mother's womb. ¹⁶ He will turn many of the children of Israel to the Lord their God. ¹⁷ And he will go before him in the spirit and power of Elijah, to turn the hearts of fathers to their children, and the disobedient to the understanding of the righteous, to make ready for the Lord a prepared people."

¹⁸ "How can I know this?" Zechariah asked the angel. "For I am an old man, and my wife is well along in years."

¹⁹ The angel answered him, "I am Gabriel, who stands in the presence of God, and I was sent to speak to you and tell you this good news. ²⁰ Now listen. You will become silent and unable to speak until the day these things take place, because you did not believe my words, which will be fulfilled in their proper time."

²¹ Meanwhile, the people were waiting for Zechariah, amazed that he stayed so long in the sanctuary. ²² When he did come out, he could not speak to them. Then they realized that he had seen a vision in the sanctuary. He was making signs to them and remained speechless. ²³ When the days of his ministry were completed, he went back home.

²⁴ After these days his wife Elizabeth conceived and kept herself in seclusion for five months. She said, ²⁵ "The Lord has done this for me. He has looked with favor in these days to take away my disgrace among the people."

GABRIEL PREDICTS JESUS'S BIRTH

²⁶ In the sixth month, the angel Gabriel was sent by God to a town in Galilee called Nazareth, ²⁷ to a virgin engaged^C to a man named Joseph, of the house of David. The virgin's name was Mary. ²⁸ And the angel came to her and said, "Greetings, favored woman! The Lord is with you."^D ²⁹ But she was deeply troubled by this statement, wondering what kind of greeting this could be. ³⁰ Then the angel told her: "Do not be afraid, Mary, for you have found favor with God. ³¹ Now listen: You will conceive and give birth to a son, and you will name him Jesus. ³² He will be great and will be called the Son of the Most High, and the Lord God will give him the throne of his father David. ³³ He will reign over the house of Jacob forever, and his kingdom will have no end."

³⁴ Mary asked the angel, "How can this be, since I have not had sexual relations with a man?"^E

³⁵ The angel replied to her: "The Holy Spirit will come upon you, and the power of the Most High will overshadow you. Therefore, the holy one to be born will be called the Son of God. ³⁶ And consider your relative Elizabeth — even she has conceived a son in her old age, and this is the sixth month for her who was called childless. ³⁷ For nothing will be impossible with God."

³⁸ "I am the Lord's servant," said Mary. "May it be done to me according to your word." Then the angel left her.

---

^A **1:1** Or *events that have been accomplished,* or *events most surely believed*   ^B **1:4** Or *informed*   ^C **1:27** Lit *betrothed*
^D **1:28** Other mss add *Blessed are you among women.*   ^E **1:34** Lit *since I do not know a man*

MARY'S VISIT TO ELIZABETH

[39] In those days Mary set out and hurried to a town in the hill country of Judah [40] where she entered Zechariah's house and greeted Elizabeth. [41] When Elizabeth heard Mary's greeting, the baby leaped inside her, and Elizabeth was filled with the Holy Spirit. [42] Then she exclaimed with a loud cry: "Blessed are you among women, and your child be blessed![A] [43] How could this happen to me, that the mother of my Lord should come to me? [44] For you see, when the sound of your greeting reached my ears, the baby leaped for joy inside me. [45] Blessed is she who has believed that the Lord would fulfill what he has spoken to her!"

MARY'S PRAISE

[46] And Mary said:

My soul praises the greatness
    of[B] the Lord,
[47] and my spirit rejoices in God my Savior,
[48] because he has looked with favor
    on the humble condition of his servant.
    Surely, from now on all generations
    will call me blessed,
[49] because the Mighty One
    has done great things for me,
    and his name is holy.
[50] His mercy is from generation
    to generation
    on those who fear him.
[51] He has done a mighty deed with his arm;
    he has scattered the proud
    because of the thoughts of their hearts;
[52] he has toppled the mighty
    from their thrones
    and exalted the lowly.
[53] He has satisfied the hungry
    with good things
    and sent the rich away empty.
[54] He has helped his servant Israel,
    remembering his mercy
[55] to Abraham and his descendants[C] forever,
    just as he spoke to our ancestors.

[56] And Mary stayed with her about three months; then she returned to her home.

THE BIRTH AND NAMING OF JOHN

[57] Now the time had come for Elizabeth to give birth, and she had a son. [58] Then her neighbors and relatives heard that the Lord had shown her his great mercy, and they rejoiced with her.
[59] When they came to circumcise the child on the eighth day, they were going to name him Zechariah, after his father. [60] But his mother responded, "No. He will be called John."

[61] Then they said to her, "None of your relatives has that name." [62] So they motioned to his father to find out what he wanted him to be called. [63] He asked for a writing tablet and wrote: "His name is John." And they were all amazed. [64] Immediately his mouth was opened and his tongue set free, and he began to speak, praising God. [65] Fear came on all those who lived around them, and all these things were being talked about throughout the hill country of Judea. [66] All who heard about him took it to heart, saying, "What then will this child become?" For, indeed, the Lord's hand was with him.

ZECHARIAH'S PROPHECY

[67] Then his father Zechariah was filled with the Holy Spirit and prophesied:
[68] Blessed is the Lord, the God of Israel,
    because he has visited
    and provided redemption
        for his people.
[69] He has raised up a horn of salvation
        for us
    in the house of his servant David,
[70] just as he spoke by the mouth
    of his holy prophets in ancient times;
[71] salvation from our enemies
    and from the hand of those
        who hate us.
[72] He has dealt mercifully with our fathers
    and remembered his holy covenant —
[73] the oath that he swore to our father
    Abraham.
    He has given us the privilege,
[74] since we have been rescued
    from the hand of our enemies,
    to serve him without fear
[75] in holiness and righteousness
    in his presence all our days.
[76] And you, child, will be called
    a prophet of the Most High,
    for you will go before the Lord
    to prepare his ways,
[77] to give his people knowledge
    of salvation
    through the forgiveness of their sins.
[78] Because of our God's merciful
    compassion,
    the dawn from on high will visit us
[79] to shine on those who live in darkness
    and the shadow of death,
    to guide our feet into the way of peace.

[80] The child grew up and became spiritually strong, and he was in the wilderness until the day of his public appearance to Israel.

[A]1:42 Lit *and the fruit of your abdomen* (or *womb*) *is blessed*   [B]1:46 Or *soul magnifies*   [C]1:55 Or *offspring*; lit *seed*

THE BIRTH OF JESUS

2 In those days a decree went out from Caesar Augustus that the whole empire^A should be registered. ² This first registration took place while^B Quirinius was governing Syria. ³ So everyone went to be registered, each to his own town.

⁴ Joseph also went up from the town of Nazareth in Galilee, to Judea, to the city of David, which is called Bethlehem, because he was of the house and family line of David, ⁵ to be registered along with Mary, who was engaged to him^C and was pregnant. ⁶ While they were there, the time came for her to give birth. ⁷ Then she gave birth to her firstborn Son, and she wrapped him tightly in cloth and laid him in a manger,^D because there was no guest room available for them.

THE SHEPHERDS AND THE ANGELS

⁸ In the same region, shepherds were staying out in the fields and keeping watch at night over their flock. ⁹ Then an angel of the Lord stood before them, and the glory of the Lord shone around them, and they were terrified.^E ¹⁰ But the angel said to them, "Don't be afraid, for look, I proclaim to you good news of great joy that will be for all the people:^F ¹¹ Today in the city of David a Savior was born for you, who is the Messiah, the Lord. ¹² This will be the sign for you: You will find a baby wrapped tightly in cloth and lying in a manger."

¹³ Suddenly there was a multitude of the heavenly host^G with the angel, praising God and saying:

¹⁴   Glory to God in the highest heaven,
       and peace on earth to people he favors!^H,I

¹⁵ When the angels had left them and returned to heaven, the shepherds said to one another, "Let's go straight to Bethlehem and see what has happened, which the Lord has made known to us."

¹⁶ They hurried off and found both Mary and Joseph, and the baby who was lying in the manger. ¹⁷ After seeing them, they reported the message they were told about this child, ¹⁸ and all who heard it were amazed at what the shepherds said to them. ¹⁹ But Mary was treasuring up all these things in her heart and meditating on them. ²⁰ The shepherds returned, glorifying and praising God for all the things they had seen and heard, which were just as they had been told.

THE CIRCUMCISION AND PRESENTATION OF JESUS

²¹ When the eight days were completed for his circumcision, he was named Jesus — the name given by the angel before he was conceived. ²² And when the days of their purification according to the law of Moses were finished, they brought him up to Jerusalem to present him to the Lord ²³ (just as it is written in the law of the Lord, **Every firstborn male will be dedicated**^J **to the Lord**^K) ²⁴ and to offer a sacrifice (according to what is stated in the law of the Lord, **a pair of turtledoves or two young pigeons**^L).

SIMEON'S PROPHETIC PRAISE

²⁵ There was a man in Jerusalem whose name was Simeon. This man was righteous and devout, looking forward to Israel's consolation, and the Holy Spirit was on him. ²⁶ It had been revealed to him by the Holy Spirit that he would not see death before he saw the Lord's Messiah. ²⁷ Guided by the Spirit, he entered the temple. When the parents brought in the child Jesus to perform for him what was customary under the law, ²⁸ Simeon took him up in his arms, praised God, and said,

²⁹   Now, Master,
       you can dismiss your servant in peace,
       as you promised.
³⁰   For my eyes have seen your salvation.
³¹   You have prepared it
       in the presence of all peoples —
³²   a light for revelation to the Gentiles^M
       and glory to your people Israel.

³³ His father and mother^N were amazed at what was being said about him. ³⁴ Then Simeon blessed them and told his mother Mary: "Indeed, this child is destined to cause the fall and rise of many in Israel and to be a sign that will be opposed^O — ³⁵ and a sword will pierce your own soul — that the thoughts^P of many hearts may be revealed."

ANNA'S TESTIMONY

³⁶ There was also a prophetess, Anna, a daughter of Phanuel, of the tribe of Asher. She was well along in years, having lived with her husband seven years after her marriage,^Q ³⁷ and was a widow for eighty-four years.^R She did

---

^A 2:1 Or *the whole inhabited world*   ^B 2:2 Or *This registration was the first while*, or *This registration was before*
^C 2:5 Lit *betrothed*   ^D 2:7 Or *feeding trough*, also in vv. 8,16   ^E 2:9 Lit *they feared a great fear*   ^F 2:10 Or *the whole nation*
^G 2:13 Lit *heavenly army*   ^H 2:14 Other mss read *earth good will to people*   ^I 2:14 Or *earth to men of good will*   ^J 2:23 Or *be*
called holy   ^K 2:23 Ex 13:2,12   ^L 2:24 Lv 5:11; 12:8   ^M 2:32 Or *the nations*   ^N 2:33 Other mss read *But Joseph and his mother*
^O 2:34 Or *spoken against*   ^P 2:35 Or *schemes*   ^Q 2:36 Lit *years from her virginity*   ^R 2:37 Or *she was a widow until the age of eighty-four*

not leave the temple, serving God night and day with fasting and prayers. ³⁸ At that very moment,ᴬ she came up and began to thank God and to speak about him to all who were looking forward to the redemption of Jerusalem.ᴮ

THE FAMILY'S RETURN TO NAZARETH

³⁹ When they had completed everything according to the law of the Lord, they returned to Galilee, to their own town of Nazareth. ⁴⁰ The boy grew up and became strong, filled with wisdom, and God's grace was on him.

IN HIS FATHER'S HOUSE

⁴¹ Every year his parents traveled to Jerusalem for the Passover Festival. ⁴² When he was twelve years old, they went up according to the custom of the festival. ⁴³ After those days were over, as they were returning, the boy Jesus stayed behind in Jerusalem, but his parentsᶜ did not know it. ⁴⁴ Assuming he was in the traveling party, they went a day's journey. Then they began looking for him among their relatives and friends. ⁴⁵ When they did not find him, they returned to Jerusalem to search for him. ⁴⁶ After three days, they found him in the temple sitting among the teachers, listening to them and asking them questions. ⁴⁷ And all those who heard him were astounded at his understanding and his answers. ⁴⁸ When his parents saw him, they were astonished, and his mother said to him, "Son, why have you treated us like this? Your father and I have been anxiously searching for you."

⁴⁹ "Why were you searching for me?" he asked them. "Didn't you know that it was necessary for me to be in my Father's house?"ᴰ ⁵⁰ But they did not understand what he said to them.

IN FAVOR WITH GOD AND WITH PEOPLE

⁵¹ Then he went down with them and came to Nazareth and was obedient to them. His mother kept all these things in her heart. ⁵² And Jesus increased in wisdom and stature, and in favor with God and with people.

THE MESSIAH'S HERALD

3 In the fifteenth year of the reign of Tiberius Caesar, while Pontius Pilate was governor of Judea, Herod was tetrarchᴱ of Galilee, his brother Philip tetrarch of the region of Iturea and Trachonitis, and Lysanias tetrarch of Abilene, ² during the high priesthood of Annas and Caiaphas, God's word came to John the son of Zechariah in the wilderness. ³ He went into all the vicinity of the Jordan, proclaiming a baptism of repentance for the forgiveness of sins, ⁴ as it is written in the book of the words of the prophet Isaiah:

A voice of one crying out
   in the wilderness:
Prepare the way for the Lord;
   make his paths straight!
⁵ Every valley will be filled,
   and every mountain and hill will be
      made low;ᶠ
the crooked will become straight,
   and the rough ways smooth,
⁶ and everyone will see the salvation
      of God.ᴳ

⁷ He then said to the crowds who came out to be baptized by him, "Brood of vipers! Who warned you to flee from the coming wrath? ⁸ Therefore produce fruit consistent with repentance. And don't start saying to yourselves, 'We have Abraham as our father,' for I tell you that God is able to raise up children for Abraham from these stones. ⁹ The ax is already at the root of the trees. Therefore, every tree that doesn't produce good fruit will be cut down and thrown into the fire."

¹⁰ "What then should we do?" the crowds were asking him.

¹¹ He replied to them, "The one who has two shirts must share with someone who has none, and the one who has food must do the same."

¹² Tax collectors also came to be baptized, and they asked him, "Teacher, what should we do?"

¹³ He told them, "Don't collect any more than what you have been authorized."

¹⁴ Some soldiers also questioned him, "What should we do?"

He said to them, "Don't take money from anyone by force or false accusation, and be satisfied with your wages."

¹⁵ Now the people were waiting expectantly, and all of them were questioning in their hearts whether John might be the Messiah. ¹⁶ John answered them all, "I baptize you with water, but one who is more powerful than I am is coming. I am not worthy to untie the strap of his sandals. He will baptize you withᴴ the Holy Spirit and fire. ¹⁷ His winnowing shovel is in his hand to clear his threshing floor and gather the wheat into his barn, but the chaff he will burn with fire that never goes out." ¹⁸ Then, along with many other exhortations, he proclaimed good news to the people. ¹⁹ But when John rebuked

ᴬ 2:38 Lit *very hour*   ᴮ 2:38 Other mss read *in Jerusalem*   ᶜ 2:43 Other mss read *but Joseph and his mother*   ᴰ 2:49 Or *be involved in my Father's interests* (or *things*), or *be among my Father's people*   ᴱ 3:1 Or *ruler*   ᶠ 3:5 Lit *be humbled*   ᴳ 3:4-6 Is 40:3-5   ᴴ 3:16 Or *in*

Herod the tetrarch because of Herodias, his brother's wife, and all the evil things he had done, **20** Herod added this to everything else — he locked up John in prison.

THE BAPTISM OF JESUS

21 When all the people were baptized, Jesus also was baptized. As he was praying, heaven opened, **22** and the Holy Spirit descended on him in a physical appearance like a dove. And a voice came from heaven: "You are my beloved Son; with you I am well-pleased."

THE GENEALOGY OF JESUS CHRIST

23 As he began his ministry, Jesus was about thirty years old and was thought to be the
son of Joseph, son of Heli,
24 son of Matthat, son of Levi,
son of Melchi, son of Jannai,
son of Joseph, **25** son of Mattathias,
son of Amos, son of Nahum,
son of Esli, son of Naggai,
26 son of Maath, son of Mattathias,
son of Semein, son of Josech,
son of Joda, **27** son of Joanan,
son of Rhesa, son of Zerubbabel,
son of Shealtiel, son of Neri,
28 son of Melchi, son of Addi,
son of Cosam, son of Elmadam,
son of Er, **29** son of Joshua,
son of Eliezer, son of Jorim,
son of Matthat, son of Levi,
30 son of Simeon, son of Judah,
son of Joseph, son of Jonam,
son of Eliakim, **31** son of Melea,
son of Menna, son of Mattatha,
son of Nathan, son of David,
32 son of Jesse, son of Obed,
son of Boaz, son of Salmon,^A
son of Nahshon, **33** son of Amminadab,
son of Ram,^B son of Hezron,
son of Perez, son of Judah,
34 son of Jacob, son of Isaac,
son of Abraham, son of Terah,
son of Nahor, **35** son of Serug,
son of Reu, son of Peleg,
son of Eber, son of Shelah,
36 son of Cainan, son of Arphaxad,
son of Shem, son of Noah,
son of Lamech, **37** son of Methuselah,
son of Enoch, son of Jared,
son of Mahalalel, son of Cainan,
38 son of Enos, son of Seth,
son of Adam, son of God.

THE TEMPTATION OF JESUS

4 Then Jesus left the Jordan, full of the Holy Spirit, and was led by the Spirit in the wilderness **2** for forty days to be tempted by the devil. He ate nothing during those days, and when they were over, he was hungry. **3** The devil said to him, "If you are the Son of God, tell this stone to become bread."

4 But Jesus answered him, "It is written: **Man must not live on bread alone.**"^C,D

5 So he took him up^E and showed him all the kingdoms of the world in a moment of time. **6** The devil said to him, "I will give you their splendor and all this authority, because it has been given over to me, and I can give it to anyone I want. **7** If you, then, will worship me,^F all will be yours."

8 And Jesus answered him,^G "It is written: **Worship the Lord your God, and serve him only.**"^H

9 So he took him to Jerusalem, had him stand on the pinnacle of the temple, and said to him, "If you are the Son of God, throw yourself down from here. **10** For it is written:

He will give his angels orders
    concerning you,
to protect you,^I **11** and
they will support you
    with their hands,
so that you will not strike
your foot against a stone."^J

12 And Jesus answered him, "It is said: **Do not test the Lord your God.**"^K

13 After the devil had finished every temptation, he departed from him for a time.

MINISTRY IN GALILEE

14 Then Jesus returned to Galilee in the power of the Spirit, and news about him spread throughout the entire vicinity. **15** He was teaching in their synagogues, being praised^L by everyone.

REJECTION AT NAZARETH

16 He came to Nazareth, where he had been brought up. As usual, he entered the synagogue on the Sabbath day and stood up to read. **17** The scroll of the prophet Isaiah was given to him, and unrolling the scroll, he found the place where it was written:
18   The Spirit of the Lord is
            on me,
         because he has anointed me
         to preach good news to the poor.

He has sent me[A]
to proclaim release[B] to the captives
and recovery of sight to the blind,
to set free the oppressed,
¹⁹ to proclaim the year
of the Lord's favor.[C]

²⁰ He then rolled up the scroll, gave it back to the attendant, and sat down. And the eyes of everyone in the synagogue were fixed on him. ²¹ He began by saying to them, "Today as you listen, this Scripture has been fulfilled."

²² They were all speaking well of him[D] and were amazed by the gracious words that came from his mouth; yet they said, "Isn't this Joseph's son?"

²³ Then he said to them, "No doubt you will quote this proverb[E] to me: 'Doctor, heal yourself. What we've heard that took place in Capernaum, do here in your hometown also.'"

²⁴ He also said, "Truly I tell you, no prophet is accepted in his hometown. ²⁵ But I say to you, there were certainly many widows in Israel in Elijah's days, when the sky was shut up for three years and six months while a great famine came over all the land. ²⁶ Yet Elijah was not sent to any of them except a widow at Zarephath in Sidon. ²⁷ And in the prophet Elisha's time, there were many in Israel who had leprosy,[F] and yet not one of them was cleansed except Naaman the Syrian."

²⁸ When they heard this, everyone in the synagogue was enraged. ²⁹ They got up, drove him out of town, and brought him to the edge of the hill that their town was built on, intending to hurl him over the cliff. ³⁰ But he passed right through the crowd and went on his way.

DRIVING OUT AN UNCLEAN SPIRIT

³¹ Then he went down to Capernaum, a town in Galilee, and was teaching them on the Sabbath. ³² They were astonished at his teaching because his message had authority. ³³ In the synagogue there was a man with an unclean demonic spirit who cried out with a loud voice, ³⁴ "Leave us alone! What do you have to do with us, Jesus of Nazareth? Have you come to destroy us? I know who you are — the Holy One of God!"

³⁵ But Jesus rebuked him and said, "Be silent and come out of him!" And throwing him down before them, the demon came out of him without hurting him at all.

³⁶ Amazement came over them all, and they were saying to one another, "What is this message? For he commands the unclean spirits with authority and power, and they come out!" ³⁷ And news about him began to go out to every place in the vicinity.

HEALINGS AT CAPERNAUM

³⁸ After he left the synagogue, he entered Simon's house. Simon's mother-in-law was suffering from a high fever, and they asked him about her. ³⁹ So he stood over her and rebuked the fever, and it left her. She got up immediately and began to serve them.

⁴⁰ When the sun was setting, all those who had anyone sick with various diseases brought them to him. As he laid his hands on each one of them, he healed them. ⁴¹ Also, demons were coming out of many, shouting and saying, "You are the Son of God!" But he rebuked them and would not allow them to speak, because they knew he was the Christ.

⁴² When it was day, he went out and made his way to a deserted place. But the crowds were searching for him. They came to him and tried to keep him from leaving them. ⁴³ But he said to them, "It is necessary for me to proclaim the good news about the kingdom of God to the other towns also, because I was sent for this purpose." ⁴⁴ And he was preaching in the synagogues of Judea.[G]

THE FIRST DISCIPLES

5 As the crowd was pressing in on Jesus to hear God's word, he was standing by Lake Gennesaret. ² He saw two boats at the edge of the lake; the fishermen had left them and were washing their nets. ³ He got into one of the boats, which belonged to Simon, and asked him to put out a little from the land. Then he sat down and was teaching the crowds from the boat.

⁴ When he had finished speaking, he said to Simon, "Put out into deep water and let down your nets for a catch."

⁵ "Master," Simon replied, "we've worked hard all night long and caught nothing. But if you say so, I'll let down the nets."[H]

⁶ When they did this, they caught a great number of fish, and their nets[H] began to tear. ⁷ So they signaled to their partners in the other boat to come and help them; they came and filled both boats so full that they began to sink.

⁸ When Simon Peter saw this, he fell at Jesus's knees and said, "Go away from me, because I'm a sinful man, Lord!" ⁹ For he and all those with him were amazed at the catch of fish they had taken, ¹⁰ and so were James and John, Zebedee's sons, who were Simon's partners.

[A]4:18 Other mss add *to heal the brokenhearted*,   [B]4:18 Or *freedom*, or *forgiveness*   [C]4:18-19 Is 61:1-2   [D]4:22 Or *They were testifying against him*   [E]4:23 Or *parable*   [F]4:27 Gk *lepros*; a term for various skin diseases; see Lv 13–14   [G]4:44 Other mss read *Galilee*   [H]5:5,6 Other mss read *net* (Gk sg)

"Don't be afraid," Jesus told Simon. "From now on you will be catching people." **11** Then they brought the boats to land, left everything, and followed him.

A MAN CLEANSED

12 While he was in one of the towns, a man was there who had leprosy[A] all over him. He saw Jesus, fell facedown, and begged him: "Lord, if you are willing, you can make me clean."

13 Reaching out his hand, Jesus touched him, saying, "I am willing; be made clean," and immediately the leprosy left him. **14** Then he ordered him to tell no one: "But go and show yourself to the priest, and offer what Moses commanded for your cleansing as a testimony to them."

15 But the news[B] about him spread even more, and large crowds would come together to hear him and to be healed of their sicknesses. **16** Yet he often withdrew to deserted places and prayed.

THE SON OF MAN FORGIVES AND HEALS

17 On one of those days while he was teaching, Pharisees and teachers of the law were sitting there who had come from every village of Galilee and Judea, and also from Jerusalem. And the Lord's power to heal was in him. **18** Just then some men came, carrying on a stretcher a man who was paralyzed. They tried to bring him in and set him down before him. **19** Since they could not find a way to bring him in because of the crowd, they went up on the roof and lowered him on the stretcher through the roof tiles into the middle of the crowd before Jesus.

20 Seeing their faith he said, "Friend,[C] your sins are forgiven."

21 Then the scribes and the Pharisees began to think to themselves: "Who is this man who speaks blasphemies? Who can forgive sins but God alone?"

22 But perceiving their thoughts, Jesus replied to them, "Why are you thinking this in your hearts?[D] **23** Which is easier: to say, 'Your sins are forgiven you,' or to say, 'Get up and walk'? **24** But so that you may know that the Son of Man has authority on earth to forgive sins" — he told the paralyzed man, "I tell you: Get up, take your stretcher, and go home."

25 Immediately he got up before them, picked up what he had been lying on, and went home glorifying God. **26** Then everyone was astounded, and they were giving glory to God. And they were filled with awe and said, "We have seen incredible things today."

THE CALL OF LEVI

27 After this, Jesus went out and saw a tax collector named Levi sitting at the tax office, and he said to him, "Follow me." **28** So, leaving everything behind, he got up and began to follow him.

29 Then Levi hosted a grand banquet for him at his house. Now there was a large crowd of tax collectors and others who were guests[E] with them. **30** But the Pharisees and their scribes were complaining to his disciples, "Why do you eat and drink with tax collectors and sinners?"

31 Jesus replied to them, "It is not those who are healthy who need a doctor, but those who are sick. **32** I have not come to call the righteous, but sinners to repentance."

A QUESTION ABOUT FASTING

33 Then they said to him, "John's disciples fast often and say prayers, and those of the Pharisees do the same, but yours eat and drink."[F]

34 Jesus said to them, "You can't make the wedding guests fast while the groom is with them, can you? **35** But the time[G] will come when the groom will be taken away from them — then they will fast in those days."

36 He also told them a parable: "No one tears a patch from a new garment and puts it on an old garment. Otherwise, not only will he tear the new, but also the piece from the new garment will not match the old. **37** And no one puts new wine into old wineskins. Otherwise, the new wine will burst the skins, it will spill, and the skins will be ruined. **38** No, new wine is put into fresh wineskins."[H] **39** And no one, after drinking old wine, wants new, because he says, 'The old is better.'"[I]

LORD OF THE SABBATH

6 On a Sabbath, he passed through the grainfields. His disciples were picking heads of grain, rubbing them in their hands, and eating them. **2** But some of the Pharisees said, "Why are you doing what is not lawful on the Sabbath?"

3 Jesus answered them, "Haven't you read what David and those who were with him did when he was hungry — **4** how he entered the house of God and took and ate the bread of the Presence, which is not lawful for any but the priests to eat? He even gave some to those who were with him." **5** Then he told them, "The Son of Man is Lord of the Sabbath."

6 On another Sabbath he entered the synagogue and was teaching. A man was there whose right hand was shriveled. **7** The scribes

^**5:12** Gk *lepros*; a term for various skin diseases, also in v. 13; see Lv 13–14 ^B**5:15** Lit *the word* ^C**5:20** Lit *"Man* ^D**5:22** Or *minds*
^E**5:29** Lit *were reclining* ^F**5:33** Other mss read *"Why do John's . . . drink?"* (as a question) ^G**5:35** Lit *days* ^H**5:38** Other mss
add *And so both are preserved.* ^I**5:39** Other mss read *is good*

and Pharisees were watching him closely, to see if he would heal on the Sabbath, so that they could find a charge against him. **8** But he knew their thoughts and told the man with the shriveled hand, "Get up and stand here."^A So he got up and stood there. **9** Then Jesus said to them, "I ask you: Is it lawful to do good on the Sabbath or to do evil, to save life or to destroy it?" **10** After looking around at them all, he told him, "Stretch out your hand." He did, and his hand was restored.^B **11** They, however, were filled with rage and started discussing with one another what they might do to Jesus.

THE TWELVE APOSTLES

12 During those days he went out to the mountain to pray and spent all night in prayer to God. **13** When daylight came, he summoned his disciples, and he chose twelve of them, whom he also named apostles: **14** Simon, whom he also named Peter, and Andrew his brother; James and John; Philip and Bartholomew; **15** Matthew and Thomas; James the son of Alphaeus, and Simon called the Zealot; **16** Judas the son of James, and Judas Iscariot, who became a traitor.

TEACHING AND HEALING

17 After coming down with them, he stood on a level place with a large crowd of his disciples and a great number of people from all Judea and Jerusalem and from the seacoast of Tyre and Sidon. **18** They came to hear him and to be healed of their diseases; and those tormented by unclean spirits were made well. **19** The whole crowd was trying to touch him, because power was coming out from him and healing them all.

THE BEATITUDES

20 Then looking up at his disciples, he said:
Blessed are you who are poor,
because the kingdom of God is yours.
21 Blessed are you who are now hungry,
because you will be filled.
Blessed are you who weep now,
because you will laugh.
22 Blessed are you when people hate you,
when they exclude you, insult you,
and slander your name as evil
because of the Son of Man.
23 "Rejoice in that day and leap for joy. Take note — your reward is great in heaven, for this is the way their ancestors used to treat the prophets.

WOE TO THE SELF-SATISFIED

24 But woe to you who are rich,
for you have received your comfort.

25 Woe to you who are now full,
for you will be hungry.
Woe to you^c who are now laughing,
for you will mourn and weep.
26 Woe to you^c
when all people speak well of you,
for this is the way their ancestors
used to treat the false prophets.

LOVE YOUR ENEMIES

27 "But I say to you who listen: Love your enemies, do what is good to those who hate you, **28** bless those who curse you, pray for those who mistreat you. **29** If anyone hits you on the cheek, offer the other also. And if anyone takes away your coat, don't hold back your shirt either. **30** Give to everyone who asks you, and from someone who takes your things, don't ask for them back. **31** Just as you want others to do for you, do the same for them. **32** If you love those who love you, what credit is that to you? Even sinners love those who love them. **33** If you do what is good to those who are good to you, what credit is that to you? Even sinners do that. **34** And if you lend to those from whom you expect to receive, what credit is that to you? Even sinners lend to sinners to be repaid in full. **35** But love your enemies, do what is good, and lend, expecting nothing in return. Then your reward will be great, and you will be children of the Most High. For he is gracious to the ungrateful and evil. **36** Be merciful, just as your Father also is merciful.

DO NOT JUDGE

37 "Do not judge, and you will not be judged. Do not condemn, and you will not be condemned. Forgive, and you will be forgiven. **38** Give, and it will be given to you; a good measure — pressed down, shaken together, and running over — will be poured into your lap. For with the measure you use, it will be measured back to you."

39 He also told them a parable: "Can the blind guide the blind? Won't they both fall into a pit? **40** A disciple is not above his teacher, but everyone who is fully trained will be like his teacher.

41 "Why do you look at the splinter in your brother's eye, but don't notice the beam of wood in your own eye? **42** Or how can you say to your brother, 'Brother, let me take out the splinter that is in your eye,' when you yourself don't see the beam of wood in your own eye? Hypocrite! First take the beam of wood out of your eye, and then you will see clearly to take out the splinter in your brother's eye.

---

^**6:8** Lit *stand in the middle*   ^B **6:10** Other mss add *as sound as the other*   ^c **6:25,26** Other mss omit *to you*

A TREE AND ITS FRUIT

[43] "A good tree doesn't produce bad fruit; on the other hand, a bad tree doesn't produce good fruit.[A] [44] For each tree is known by its own fruit. Figs aren't gathered from thornbushes, or grapes picked from a bramble bush. [45] A good person produces good out of the good stored up in his heart. An evil person produces evil out of the evil stored up in his heart, for his mouth speaks from the overflow of the heart.

THE TWO FOUNDATIONS

[46] "Why do you call me 'Lord, Lord,' and don't do the things I say? [47] I will show you what someone is like who comes to me, hears my words, and acts on them: [48] He is like a man building a house, who dug deep and laid the foundation on the rock. When the flood came, the river crashed against that house and couldn't shake it, because it was well built. [49] But the one who hears and does not act is like a man who built a house on the ground without a foundation. The river crashed against it, and immediately it collapsed. And the destruction of that house was great."

A CENTURION'S FAITH

7 When he had concluded saying all this to the people who were listening, he entered Capernaum. [2] A centurion's servant, who was highly valued by him, was sick and about to die. [3] When the centurion heard about Jesus, he sent some Jewish elders to him, requesting him to come and save the life of his servant. [4] When they reached Jesus, they pleaded with him earnestly, saying, "He is worthy for you to grant this, [5] because he loves our nation and has built us a synagogue."

[6] Jesus went with them, and when he was not far from the house, the centurion sent friends to tell him, "Lord, don't trouble yourself, since I am not worthy to have you come under my roof. [7] That is why I didn't even consider myself worthy to come to you. But say the word, and my servant will be healed.[B] [8] For I too am a man placed under authority, having soldiers under my command. I say to this one, 'Go,' and he goes; and to another, 'Come,' and he comes; and to my servant, 'Do this,' and he does it."

[9] Jesus heard this and was amazed at him, and turning to the crowd following him, he said, "I tell you, I have not found so great a faith even in Israel." [10] When those who had been sent returned to the house, they found the servant in good health.

A WIDOW'S SON RAISED TO LIFE

[11] Afterward he was on his way to a town called Nain. His disciples and a large crowd were traveling with him. [12] Just as he neared the gate of the town, a dead man was being carried out. He was his mother's only son, and she was a widow. A large crowd from the city was also with her. [13] When the Lord saw her, he had compassion on her and said, "Don't weep." [14] Then he came up and touched the open coffin, and the pallbearers stopped. And he said, "Young man, I tell you, get up!"

[15] The dead man sat up and began to speak, and Jesus gave him to his mother. [16] Then fear[C] came over everyone, and they glorified God, saying, "A great prophet has risen among us," and "God has visited[D] his people." [17] This report about him went throughout Judea and all the vicinity.

IN PRAISE OF JOHN THE BAPTIST

[18] Then John's disciples told him about all these things. So John summoned two of his disciples [19] and sent them to the Lord, asking, "Are you the one who is to come, or should we expect someone else?"

[20] When the men reached him, they said, "John the Baptist sent us to ask you, 'Are you the one who is to come, or should we expect someone else?'"

[21] At that time Jesus healed many people of diseases, afflictions, and evil spirits, and he granted sight to many blind people. [22] He replied to them, "Go and report to John what you have seen and heard: The blind receive their sight, the lame walk, those with leprosy[E] are cleansed, the deaf hear, the dead are raised, and the poor are told the good news, [23] and blessed is the one who isn't offended by me."

[24] After John's messengers left, he began to speak to the crowds about John: "What did you go out into the wilderness to see? A reed swaying in the wind? [25] What then did you go out to see? A man dressed in soft clothes? See, those who are splendidly dressed and live in luxury are in royal palaces. [26] What then did you go out to see? A prophet? Yes, I tell you, and more than a prophet. [27] This is the one about whom it is written:

> See, I am sending my messenger
>   ahead of you;
> he will prepare your way before you.[F]

[28] I tell you, among those born of women no one is greater than John,[G] but the least in the kingdom of God is greater than he."

[A] **6:43** Lit *on the other hand, again, a bad tree doesn't produce good fruit*   [B] **7:7** Other mss read *and let my servant be healed*   [C] **7:16** Or *awe*   [D] **7:16** Or *come to help*   [E] **7:22** Gk *lepros* ; a term for various skin diseases; see Lv 13–14   [F] **7:27** Mal 3:1   [G] **7:28** Other mss read *women is not a greater prophet than John the Baptist*

29 (And when all the people, including the tax collectors, heard this, they acknowledged God's way of righteousness, because they had been baptized with John's baptism. 30 But since the Pharisees and experts in the law had not been baptized by him, they rejected the plan of God for themselves.)

AN UNRESPONSIVE GENERATION

31 "To what then should I compare the people of this generation, and what are they like? 32 They are like children sitting in the marketplace and calling to each other:

> We played the flute for you,
> but you didn't dance;
> we sang a lament,
> but you didn't weep!

33 For John the Baptist did not come eating bread or drinking wine, and you say, 'He has a demon!' 34 The Son of Man has come eating and drinking, and you say, 'Look, a glutton and a drunkard, a friend of tax collectors and sinners!' 35 Yet wisdom is vindicated by all her children."

MUCH FORGIVENESS, MUCH LOVE

36 Then one of the Pharisees invited him to eat with him. He entered the Pharisee's house and reclined at the table. 37 And a woman in the town who was a sinner found out that Jesus was reclining at the table in the Pharisee's house. She brought an alabaster jar of perfume 38 and stood behind him at his feet, weeping, and began to wash his feet with her tears. She wiped his feet with her hair, kissing them and anointing them with the perfume.

39 When the Pharisee who had invited him saw this, he said to himself, "This man, if he were a prophet, would know who and what kind of woman this is who is touching him — she's a sinner!"

40 Jesus replied to him, "Simon, I have something to say to you."

He said, "Say it, teacher."

41 "A creditor had two debtors. One owed five hundred denarii,^A and the other fifty. 42 Since they could not pay it back, he graciously forgave them both. So, which of them will love him more?"

43 Simon answered, "I suppose the one he forgave more."

"You have judged correctly," he told him. 44 Turning to the woman, he said to Simon, "Do you see this woman? I entered your house; you gave me no water for my feet, but she, with her tears, has washed my feet and wiped them with her hair. 45 You gave me no kiss, but she hasn't stopped kissing my feet since I came in. 46 You didn't anoint my head with olive oil, but she has anointed my feet with perfume. 47 Therefore I tell you, her many sins have been forgiven; that's why she loved much. But the one who is forgiven little, loves little." 48 Then he said to her, "Your sins are forgiven."

49 Those who were at the table with him began to say among themselves, "Who is this man who even forgives sins?"

50 And he said to the woman, "Your faith has saved you. Go in peace."

MANY WOMEN SUPPORT CHRIST'S WORK

8 Afterward he was traveling from one town and village to another, preaching and telling the good news of the kingdom of God. The Twelve were with him, 2 and also some women who had been healed of evil spirits and sicknesses: Mary, called Magdalene (seven demons had come out of her); 3 Joanna the wife of Chuza, Herod's steward; Susanna; and many others who were supporting them from their possessions.

THE PARABLE OF THE SOWER

4 As a large crowd was gathering, and people were coming to Jesus from every town, he said in a parable: 5 "A sower went out to sow his seed. As he sowed, some seed fell along the path; it was trampled on, and the birds of the sky devoured it. 6 Other seed fell on the rock; when it grew up, it withered away, since it lacked moisture. 7 Other seed fell among thorns; the thorns grew up with it and choked it. 8 Still other seed fell on good ground; when it grew up, it produced fruit: a hundred times what was sown." As he said this, he called out, "Let anyone who has ears to hear listen."

WHY JESUS USED PARABLES

9 Then his disciples asked him, "What does this parable mean?" 10 So he said, "The secrets of the kingdom of God have been given for you to know, but to the rest it is in parables, so that

> **Looking they may not see,**
> **and hearing they may not understand.**^B

THE PARABLE OF THE SOWER EXPLAINED

11 "This is the meaning of the parable: The seed is the word of God. 12 The seed along the path are those who have heard and then the devil comes and takes away the word from their hearts, so that they may not believe and be saved. 13 And the seed on the rock are those who, when they hear, receive the word with joy. Having no root, these believe for a while and

---

^A 7:41 A denarius = one day's wage   ^B 8:10 Is 6:9

fall away in a time of testing. ¹⁴ As for the seed that fell among thorns, these are the ones who, when they have heard, go on their way and are choked with worries, riches, and pleasures of life, and produce no mature fruit. ¹⁵ But the seed in the good ground — these are the ones who, having heard the word with an honest and good heart, hold on to it and by enduring, produce fruit.

USING YOUR LIGHT

¹⁶ "No one, after lighting a lamp, covers it with a basket or puts it under a bed, but puts it on a lampstand so that those who come in may see its light. ¹⁷ For nothing is concealed that won't be revealed, and nothing hidden that won't be made known and brought to light. ¹⁸ Therefore take care how you listen. For whoever has, more will be given to him; and whoever does not have, even what he thinks he has will be taken away from him."

TRUE RELATIONSHIPS

¹⁹ Then his mother and brothers came to him, but they could not meet with him because of the crowd. ²⁰ He was told, "Your mother and your brothers are standing outside, wanting to see you."

²¹ But he replied to them, "My mother and my brothers are those who hear and do the word of God."

WIND AND WAVE OBEY JESUS

²² One day he and his disciples got into a boat, and he told them, "Let's cross over to the other side of the lake." So they set out, ²³ and as they were sailing he fell asleep. Then a fierce windstorm came down on the lake; they were being swamped and were in danger. ²⁴ They came and woke him up, saying, "Master, Master, we're going to die!"

Then he got up and rebuked the wind and the raging waves. So they ceased, and there was a calm. ²⁵ He said to them, "Where is your faith?"

They were fearful and amazed, asking one another, "Who then is this?ᴬ He commands even the winds and the waves, and they obey him!"

DEMONS DRIVEN OUT BY JESUS

²⁶ Then they sailed to the region of the Gerasenes,ᴮ which is opposite Galilee. ²⁷ When he got out on land, a demon-possessed man from the town met him. For a long time he had worn no clothes and did not stay in a house but in the tombs. ²⁸ When he saw Jesus, he cried out,

fell down before him, and said in a loud voice, "What do you have to do with me, Jesus, Son of the Most High God? I beg you, don't torment me!" ²⁹ For he had commanded the unclean spirit to come out of the man. Many times it had seized him, and though he was guarded, bound by chains and shackles, he would snap the restraints and be driven by the demon into deserted places.

³⁰ "What is your name?" Jesus asked him.

"Legion," he said, because many demons had entered him. ³¹ And they begged him not to banish them to the abyss.

³² A large herd of pigs was there, feeding on the hillside. The demons begged him to permit them to enter the pigs, and he gave them permission. ³³ The demons came out of the man and entered the pigs, and the herd rushed down the steep bank into the lake and drowned.

³⁴ When the men who tended them saw what had happened, they ran off and reported it in the town and in the countryside. ³⁵ Then people went out to see what had happened. They came to Jesus and found the man the demons had departed from, sitting at Jesus's feet, dressed and in his right mind. And they were afraid. ³⁶ Meanwhile, the eyewitnesses reported to them how the demon-possessed man was delivered. ³⁷ Then all the people of the Gerasene regionᴮ asked him to leave them, because they were gripped by great fear. So getting into the boat, he returned.

³⁸ The man from whom the demons had departed begged him earnestly to be with him. But he sent him away and said, ³⁹ "Go back to your home, and tell all that God has done for you." And off he went, proclaiming throughout the town how much Jesus had done for him.

A GIRL RESTORED AND A WOMAN HEALED

⁴⁰ When Jesus returned, the crowd welcomed him, for they were all expecting him. ⁴¹ Just then, a man named Jairus came. He was a leader of the synagogue. He fell down at Jesus's feet and pleaded with him to come to his house, ⁴² because he had an only daughter about twelve years old, and she was dying.

While he was going, the crowds were nearly crushing him. ⁴³ A woman suffering from bleeding for twelve years, who had spent all she had on doctorsᶜ and yet could not be healed by any, ⁴⁴ approached from behind and touched the end of his robe. Instantly her bleeding stopped.

⁴⁵ "Who touched me?" Jesus asked.

When they all denied it, Peter^A said, "Master, the crowds are hemming you in and pressing against you."^B

46 "Someone did touch me," said Jesus. "I know that power has gone out from me." **47** When the woman saw that she was discovered, she came trembling and fell down before him. In the presence of all the people, she declared the reason she had touched him and how she was instantly healed. **48** "Daughter," he said to her, "your faith has saved you.^C Go in peace."

49 While he was still speaking, someone came from the synagogue leader's house and said, "Your daughter is dead. Don't bother the teacher anymore."

50 When Jesus heard it, he answered him, "Don't be afraid. Only believe, and she will be saved."^D **51** After he came to the house, he let no one enter with him except Peter, John, James, and the child's father and mother. **52** Everyone was crying and mourning for her. But he said, "Stop crying, because she is not dead but asleep."

53 They laughed at him, because they knew she was dead. **54** So he^E took her by the hand and called out, "Child, get up!" **55** Her spirit returned, and she got up at once. Then he gave orders that she be given something to eat. **56** Her parents were astounded, but he instructed them to tell no one what had happened.

COMMISSIONING THE TWELVE

9 Summoning the Twelve, he gave them power and authority over all the demons and to heal diseases. **2** Then he sent them to proclaim the kingdom of God and to heal the sick.

3 "Take nothing for the road," he told them, "no staff, no traveling bag, no bread, no money; and don't take an extra shirt. **4** Whatever house you enter, stay there and leave from there. **5** If they do not welcome you, when you leave that town, shake off the dust from your feet as a testimony against them." **6** So they went out and traveled from village to village, proclaiming the good news and healing everywhere.

HEROD'S DESIRE TO SEE JESUS

7 Herod the tetrarch heard about everything that was going on. He was perplexed, because some said that John had been raised from the dead, **8** some that Elijah had appeared, and others that one of the ancient prophets had risen. **9** "I beheaded John," Herod said, "but who is this I hear such things about?" And he wanted to see him.

FEEDING OF THE FIVE THOUSAND

10 When the apostles returned, they reported to Jesus all that they had done. He took them along and withdrew privately to a^F town called Bethsaida. **11** When the crowds found out, they followed him. He welcomed them, spoke to them about the kingdom of God, and healed those who needed healing.

12 Late in the day, the Twelve approached and said to him, "Send the crowd away, so that they can go into the surrounding villages and countryside to find food and lodging, because we are in a deserted place here."

13 "You give them something to eat," he told them.

"We have no more than five loaves and two fish," they said, "unless we go and buy food for all these people." **14** (For about five thousand men were there.)

Then he told his disciples, "Have them sit down^G in groups of about fifty each." **15** They did what he said, and had them all sit down. **16** Then he took the five loaves and the two fish, and looking up to heaven, he blessed and broke them. He kept giving them to the disciples to set before the crowd. **17** Everyone ate and was filled. They picked up twelve baskets of leftover pieces.

PETER'S CONFESSION OF THE MESSIAH

18 While he was praying in private and his disciples were with him, he asked them, "Who do the crowds say that I am?"

19 They answered, "John the Baptist; others, Elijah; still others, that one of the ancient prophets has come back."^H

20 "But you," he asked them, "who do you say that I am?"

Peter answered, "God's Messiah."

HIS DEATH AND RESURRECTION PREDICTED

21 But he strictly warned and instructed them to tell this to no one, **22** saying, "It is necessary that the Son of Man suffer many things and be rejected by the elders, chief priests, and scribes, be killed, and be raised the third day."

TAKE UP YOUR CROSS

23 Then he said to them all, "If anyone wants to follow after^I me, let him deny himself, take up his cross daily,^J and follow me. **24** For whoever wants to save his life will lose it, but whoever loses his life because of me will save it. **25** For what does it benefit someone if he gains the whole world, and yet loses or forfeits himself?

---

^A **8:45** Other mss add *and those with him*   ^B **8:45** Other mss add *and you say, 'Who touched me?'*   ^C **8:48** Or *has made you well*   ^D **8:50** Or *she will be made well*   ^E **8:54** Other mss add *having put them all outside*   ^F **9:10** Other mss add *deserted place near a*   ^G **9:14** Lit *them recline*   ^H **9:19** Lit *has risen*   ^I **9:23** Lit *come after*   ^J **9:23** Other mss omit *daily*

26 For whoever is ashamed of me and my words, the Son of Man will be ashamed of him when he comes in his glory and that of the Father and the holy angels. **27** Truly I tell you, there are some standing here who will not taste death until they see the kingdom of God."

THE TRANSFIGURATION

28 About eight days after this conversation, he took along Peter, John, and James and went up on the mountain to pray. **29** As he was praying, the appearance of his face changed, and his clothes became dazzling white. **30** Suddenly, two men were talking with him — Moses and Elijah. **31** They appeared in glory and were speaking of his departure, which he was about to accomplish in Jerusalem.

32 Peter and those with him were in a deep sleep,[A] and when they became fully awake, they saw his glory and the two men who were standing with him. **33** As the two men were departing from him, Peter said to Jesus, "Master, it's good for us to be here. Let us set up three shelters: one for you, one for Moses, and one for Elijah" — not knowing what he was saying.

34 While he was saying this, a cloud appeared and overshadowed them. They became afraid as they entered the cloud. **35** Then a voice came from the cloud, saying: "This is my Son, the Chosen One;[B] listen to him! "

36 After the voice had spoken, Jesus was found alone. They kept silent, and at that time told no one what they had seen.

THE POWER OF JESUS OVER A DEMON

37 The next day, when they came down from the mountain, a large crowd met him. **38** Just then a man from the crowd cried out, "Teacher, I beg you to look at my son, because he's my only child. **39** A spirit seizes him; suddenly he shrieks, and it throws him into convulsions until he foams at the mouth; severely bruising him, it scarcely ever leaves him. **40** I begged your disciples to drive it out, but they couldn't."

41 Jesus replied, "You unbelieving and perverse[C] generation, how long will I be with you and put up with you? Bring your son here."

42 As the boy was still approaching, the demon knocked him down and threw him into severe convulsions. But Jesus rebuked the unclean spirit, healed the boy, and gave him back to his father. **43** And they were all astonished at the greatness of God.

THE SECOND PREDICTION OF HIS DEATH

While everyone was amazed at all the things he was doing, he told his disciples, **44** "Let these words sink in:[D] The Son of Man is about to be betrayed into the hands of men."

45 But they did not understand this statement; it was concealed from them so that they could not grasp it, and they were afraid to ask him about it.

WHO IS THE GREATEST?

46 An argument started among them about who was the greatest of them. **47** But Jesus, knowing their inner thoughts,[E] took a little child and had him stand next to him. **48** He told them, "Whoever welcomes[F] this little child in my name welcomes me. And whoever welcomes me welcomes him who sent me. For whoever is least among you — this one is great."

IN HIS NAME

49 John responded, "Master, we saw someone driving out demons in your name and we tried to stop him because he does not follow us."

50 "Don't stop him," Jesus told him, "because whoever is not against you is for you."[G]

THE JOURNEY TO JERUSALEM

51 When the days were coming to a close for him to be taken up, he determined[H] to journey to Jerusalem. **52** He sent messengers ahead of himself, and on the way they entered a village of the Samaritans to make preparations for him. **53** But they did not welcome him, because he determined to journey to Jerusalem. **54** When the disciples James and John saw this, they said, "Lord, do you want us to call down fire from heaven to consume them?"[I]

55 But he turned and rebuked them,[J] **56** and they went to another village.

FOLLOWING JESUS

57 As they were traveling on the road someone said to him, "I will follow you wherever you go."

58 Jesus told him, "Foxes have dens, and birds of the sky have nests, but the Son of Man has no place to lay his head." **59** Then he said to another, "Follow me."

"Lord," he said, "first let me go bury my father."

60 But he told him, "Let the dead bury their own dead, but you go and spread the news of the kingdom of God."

[A] **9:32** Lit *were weighed down with sleep* [B] **9:35** Other mss read *the Beloved* [C] **9:41** Or *corrupt*, or *perverted*, or *twisted*;
Dt 32:5 [D] **9:44** Lit *"Put these words in your ears* [E] **9:47** Lit *the thoughts of their hearts* [F] **9:48** Or *receives*, throughout
the verse [G] **9:50** Other mss read *against us is for us* [H] **9:51** Lit *he stiffened his face to go*; Is 50:7 [I] **9:54** Other mss add *as
Elijah also did* [J] **9:55-56** Other mss add *and said, "You don't know what kind of spirit you belong to.* [56] *For the Son of Man
did not come to destroy people's lives but to save them,"*

[61] Another said, "I will follow you, Lord, but first let me go and say good-bye to those at my house."

[62] But Jesus said to him, "No one who puts his hand to the plow and looks back is fit for the kingdom of God."

SENDING OUT THE SEVENTY-TWO

10 After this, the Lord appointed seventy-two[A] others, and he sent them ahead of him in pairs to every town and place where he himself was about to go. [2] He told them, "The harvest is abundant, but the workers are few. Therefore, pray to the Lord of the harvest to send out workers into his harvest. [3] Now go; I'm sending you out like lambs among wolves. [4] Don't carry a money-bag, traveling bag, or sandals; don't greet anyone along the road. [5] Whatever house you enter, first say, 'Peace to this household.' [6] If a person of peace is there, your peace will rest on him; but if not, it will return to you. [7] Remain in the same house, eating and drinking what they offer, for the worker is worthy of his wages. Don't move from house to house. [8] When you enter any town, and they welcome you, eat the things set before you. [9] Heal the sick who are there, and tell them, 'The kingdom of God has come near you.' [10] When you enter any town, and they don't welcome you, go out into its streets and say, [11] 'We are wiping off even the dust of your town that clings to our feet as a witness against you. Know this for certain: The kingdom of God has come near.' [12] I tell you, on that day it will be more tolerable for Sodom than for that town.

UNREPENTANT TOWNS

[13] "Woe to you, Chorazin! Woe to you, Bethsaida! For if the miracles that were done in you had been done in Tyre and Sidon, they would have repented long ago, sitting in sackcloth and ashes. [14] But it will be more tolerable for Tyre and Sidon at the judgment than for you. [15] And you, Capernaum, will you be exalted to heaven? No, you will go down to Hades. [16] Whoever listens to you listens to me. Whoever rejects you rejects me. And whoever rejects me rejects the one who sent me."

THE RETURN OF THE SEVENTY-TWO

[17] The seventy-two[B] returned with joy, saying, "Lord, even the demons submit to us in your name."

[18] He said to them, "I watched Satan fall from heaven like lightning. [19] Look, I have given you the authority to trample on snakes and scorpions and over all the power of the enemy; nothing at all will harm you. [20] However, don't rejoice that[C] the spirits submit to you, but rejoice that your names are written in heaven."

THE SON REVEALS THE FATHER

[21] At that time he[D] rejoiced in the Holy[E] Spirit and said, "I praise[F] you, Father, Lord of heaven and earth, because you have hidden these things from the wise and intelligent and revealed them to infants. Yes, Father, because this was your good pleasure.[G] [22] All things have[H] been entrusted to me by my Father. No one knows who the Son is except the Father, and who the Father is except the Son, and anyone to whom the Son desires[I] to reveal him."

[23] Then turning to his disciples he said privately, "Blessed are the eyes that see the things you see! [24] For I tell you that many prophets and kings wanted to see the things you see but didn't see them; to hear the things you hear but didn't hear them."

THE PARABLE OF THE GOOD SAMARITAN

[25] Then an expert in the law stood up to test him, saying, "Teacher, what must I do to inherit eternal life?"

[26] "What is written in the law?" he asked him. "How do you read it?"

[27] He answered, **"Love the Lord your God with all your heart, with all your soul, with all your strength, and with all your mind;"** and **"your neighbor as yourself."**[J]

[28] "You've answered correctly," he told him. "Do this and you will live."

[29] But wanting to justify himself, he asked Jesus, "And who is my neighbor?"

[30] Jesus took up the question and said: "A man was going down from Jerusalem to Jericho and fell into the hands of robbers. They stripped him, beat him up, and fled, leaving him half dead. [31] A priest happened to be going down that road. When he saw him, he passed by on the other side. [32] In the same way, a Levite, when he arrived at the place and saw him, passed by on the other side. [33] But a Samaritan on his journey came up to him, and when he saw the man, he had compassion. [34] He went over to him and bandaged his wounds, pouring on olive oil and wine. Then he put him on his own animal, brought him to an inn, and took care

---

of him. [35] The next day[A] he took out two denarii,[B] gave them to the innkeeper, and said, 'Take care of him. When I come back I'll reimburse you for whatever extra you spend.'

[36] "Which of these three do you think proved to be a neighbor to the man who fell into the hands of the robbers?"

[37] "The one who showed mercy to him," he said.

Then Jesus told him, "Go and do the same."

MARTHA AND MARY

[38] While they were traveling, he entered a village, and a woman named Martha welcomed him into her home.[C] [39] She had a sister named Mary, who also sat at the Lord's[D] feet and was listening to what he said.[E] [40] But Martha was distracted by her many tasks, and she came up and asked, "Lord, don't you care that my sister has left me to serve alone? So tell her to give me a hand."[F]

[41] The Lord[G] answered her, "Martha, Martha, you are worried and upset about many things, [42] but one thing is necessary."[H] Mary has made the right choice,[I] and it will not be taken away from her."

THE MODEL PRAYER

11 He was praying in a certain place, and when he finished, one of his disciples said to him, "Lord, teach us to pray, just as John also taught his disciples."

[2] He said to them, "Whenever you pray, say,
Father,[J]
your name be honored as holy.
Your kingdom come.[K]
[3] Give us each day our daily bread.[L]
[4] And forgive us our sins,
for we ourselves also forgive everyone
in debt to us.[M]
And do not bring us into temptation."[N]

ASK, SEARCH, KNOCK

[5] He also said to them: "Suppose one of you[O] has a friend and goes to him at midnight and says to him, 'Friend, lend me three loaves of bread, [6] because a friend of mine on a journey has come to me, and I don't have anything to offer him.' [7] Then he will answer from inside and say, 'Don't bother me! The door is already locked, and my children and I have gone to bed. I can't get up to give you anything.' [8] I tell you, even though he won't get up and give him anything because he is his friend, yet because of his friend's shameless boldness,[P] he will get up and give him as much as he needs.

[9] "So I say to you, ask, and it will be given to you. Seek, and you will find. Knock, and the door will be opened to you. [10] For everyone who asks receives, and the one who seeks finds, and to the one who knocks, the door will be opened. [11] What father among you, if his son[Q] asks for a fish, will give him a snake instead of a fish? [12] Or if he asks for an egg, will give him a scorpion? [13] If you then, who are evil, know how to give good gifts to your children, how much more will the heavenly Father give the Holy Spirit to those who ask him?"

A HOUSE DIVIDED

[14] Now he was driving out a demon that was mute. When the demon came out, the man who had been mute spoke, and the crowds were amazed. [15] But some of them said, "He drives out demons by Beelzebul, the ruler of the demons." [16] And others, as a test, were demanding of him a sign from heaven.

[17] Knowing their thoughts, he told them, "Every kingdom divided against itself is headed for destruction, and a house divided against itself falls. [18] If Satan also is divided against himself, how will his kingdom stand? For you say I drive out demons by Beelzebul. [19] And if I drive out demons by Beelzebul, by whom do your sons drive them out? For this reason they will be your judges. [20] If I drive out demons by the finger of God, then the kingdom of God has come upon you. [21] When a strong man, fully armed, guards his estate, his possessions are secure. [22] But when one stronger than he attacks and overpowers him, he takes from him all his weapons[R] he trusted in, and divides up his plunder. [23] Anyone who is not with me is against me, and anyone who does not gather with me scatters.

AN UNCLEAN SPIRIT'S RETURN

[24] "When an unclean spirit comes out of a person, it roams through waterless places looking for rest, and not finding rest, it then[S] says, 'I'll go back to my house that I came from.' [25] Returning, it finds the house swept and put in order.

[A]**10:35** Other mss add *as he was leaving*　[B]**10:35** A denarius = one day's wage.　[C]**10:38** Other mss omit *into her home*　[D]**10:39** Other mss read *at Jesus's*　[E]**10:39** Lit *to his word,* or *message*　[F]**10:40** Or *tell her to help me*　[G]**10:41** Other mss read *Jesus*　[H]**10:42** Some mss read *few things are necessary,* or *only one*　[I]**10:42** Lit *has chosen the good part,* or *has chosen the better portion;* = the right meal　[J]**11:2** Other mss read *Our Father in heaven*　[K]**11:2** Other mss add *Your will be done on earth as it is in heaven*　[L]**11:3** Or *our bread for tomorrow*　[M]**11:4** Or *everyone who wrongs us*　[N]**11:4** Other mss add *But deliver us from the evil one*　[O]**11:5** Lit *Who of you*　[P]**11:8** Or *persistence*　[Q]**11:11** Other mss read *son asks for bread, would give him a stone? Or if he*　[R]**11:22** Gk *panoplia,* the armor and weapons of a foot soldier; Eph 6:11,13　[S]**11:24** Other mss omit *then*

26 Then it goes and brings seven other spirits more evil than itself, and they enter and settle down there. As a result, that person's last condition is worse than the first."

TRUE BLESSEDNESS

27 As he was saying these things, a woman from the crowd raised her voice and said to him, "Blessed is the womb that bore you and the one who nursed you! "

28 He said, "Rather, blessed are those who hear the word of God and keep it."

THE SIGN OF JONAH

29 As the crowds were increasing, he began saying: "This generation is an evil generation. It demands a sign, but no sign will be given to it except the sign of Jonah.ᴬ 30 For just as Jonah became a sign to the people of Nineveh, so also the Son of Man will be to this generation. 31 The queen of the south will rise up at the judgment with the men of this generation and condemn them, because she came from the ends of the earth to hear the wisdom of Solomon, and look — something greater than Solomon is here. 32 The men of Nineveh will stand up at the judgment with this generation and condemn it, because they repented at Jonah's preaching, and look — something greater than Jonah is here.

THE LAMP OF THE BODY

33 "No one lights a lamp and puts it in the cellar or under a basket,ᴮ but on a lampstand, so that those who come in may see its light. 34 Your eye is the lamp of the body. When your eye is healthy, your whole body is also full of light. But when it is bad, your body is also full of darkness. 35 Take care, then, that the light in you is not darkness. 36 If, therefore, your whole body is full of light, with no part of it in darkness, it will be entirely illuminated, as when a lamp shines its light on you."

RELIGIOUS HYPOCRISY DENOUNCED

37 As he was speaking, a Pharisee asked him to dine with him. So he went in and reclined at the table. 38 When the Pharisee saw this, he was amazed that he did not first perform the ritual washingᶜ before dinner. 39 But the Lord said to him, "Now you Pharisees clean the outside of the cup and dish, but inside you are full of greed and evil. 40 Fools! Didn't he who made the outside make the inside too? 41 But give from what is within to the poor,ᴰ and then everything is clean for you.

42 "But woe to you Pharisees! You give a tenthᴱ of mint, rue, and every kind of herb, and you bypassᶠ justice and love for God.ᴳ These things you should have done without neglecting the others.

43 "Woe to you Pharisees! You love the front seat in the synagogues and greetings in the marketplaces.

44 "Woe to you!ᴴ You are like unmarked graves; the people who walk over them don't know it."

45 One of the experts in the law answered him, "Teacher, when you say these things you insult us too."

46 Then he said: "Woe also to you experts in the law! You load people with burdens that are hard to carry, and yet you yourselves don't touch these burdens with one of your fingers.

47 "Woe to you! You build tombsᴵ for the prophets, and your fathers killed them. 48 Therefore, you are witnesses that you approveᴶ the deeds of your fathers, for they killed them, and you build their monuments.ᴷ 49 Because of this, the wisdom of God said, 'I will send them prophets and apostles, and some of them they will kill and persecute,' 50 so that this generation may be held responsible for the blood of all the prophets shed since the foundation of the worldᴸ — 51 from the blood of Abel to the blood of Zechariah, who perished between the altar and the sanctuary.

"Yes, I tell you, this generation will be held responsible.ᴹ

52 "Woe to you experts in the law! You have taken away the key to knowledge. You didn't go in yourselves, and you hindered those who were trying to go in."

53 When he left there,ᴺ the scribes and the Pharisees began to oppose him fiercely and to cross-examine him about many things; 54 they were lying in wait for him to trap him in something he said.ᴼ

BEWARE OF RELIGIOUS HYPOCRISY

12 Meanwhile, a crowd of many thousands came together, so that they were trampling on one another. He began to say to his disciples first, "Be on your guard against the leavenᴾ of the Pharisees, which is hypocrisy.

ᴬ**11:29** Other mss add *the prophet*   ᴮ**11:33** Other mss omit *or under a basket*   ᶜ**11:38** Lit *he did not first wash*
ᴰ**11:41** Or *But donate from the heart as charity*   ᴱ**11:42** Or *a tithe*   ᶠ**11:42** Or *neglect*   ᴳ**11:42** Lit *the justice and the love of God*   ᴴ**11:44** Other mss add *scribes and Pharisees, hypocrites!*   ᴵ**11:47** Or *graves*   ᴶ**11:48** Lit *witnesses and approve*
ᴷ**11:48** Other mss omit *their monuments*   ᴸ**11:50** Lit *so that the blood of all . . . world may be required of this generation,*
ᴹ**11:51** Lit *you, it will be required of this generation*   ᴺ**11:53** Other mss read *And as he was saying these things to them*
ᴼ**11:54** Other mss add *so that they might bring charges against him*   ᴾ**12:1** Or *yeast*

2 There is nothing covered that won't be uncovered, nothing hidden that won't be made known. 3 Therefore, whatever you have said in the dark will be heard in the light, and what you have whispered in an ear in private rooms will be proclaimed on the housetops.

FEAR GOD

4 "I say to you, my friends, don't fear those who kill the body, and after that can do nothing more. 5 But I will show you the one to fear: Fear him who has authority to throw people into hell after death. Yes, I say to you, this is the one to fear! 6 Aren't five sparrows sold for two pennies?^ Yet not one of them is forgotten in God's sight. 7 Indeed, the hairs of your head are all counted. Don't be afraid; you are worth more than many sparrows.

ACKNOWLEDGING CHRIST

8 "And I say to you, anyone who acknowledges me before others, the Son of Man will also acknowledge him before the angels of God, 9 but whoever denies me before others will be denied before the angels of God. 10 Anyone who speaks a word against the Son of Man will be forgiven, but the one who blasphemes against the Holy Spirit will not be forgiven. 11 Whenever they bring you before synagogues and rulers and authorities, don't worry about how you should defend yourselves or what you should say. 12 For the Holy Spirit will teach you at that very hour what must be said."

THE PARABLE OF THE RICH FOOL

13 Someone from the crowd said to him, "Teacher, tell my brother to divide the inheritance with me."

14 "Friend,"^B he said to him, "who appointed me a judge or arbitrator over you?" 15 He then told them, "Watch out and be on guard against all greed, because one's life is not in the abundance of his possessions."

16 Then he told them a parable: "A rich man's land was very productive. 17 He thought to himself, 'What should I do, since I don't have anywhere to store my crops? 18 I will do this,' he said. 'I'll tear down my barns and build bigger ones and store all my grain and my goods there. 19 Then I'll say to myself, "You have many goods stored up for many years. Take it easy; eat, drink, and enjoy yourself."'
20 "But God said to him, 'You fool! This very night your life is demanded of you. And the things you have prepared—whose will they be?'

21 "That's how it is with the one who stores up treasure for himself and is not rich toward God."

THE CURE FOR ANXIETY

22 Then he said to his disciples: "Therefore I tell you, don't worry about your life, what you will eat; or about the body, what you will wear. 23 For life is more than food and the body more than clothing. 24 Consider the ravens: They don't sow or reap; they don't have a storeroom or a barn; yet God feeds them. Aren't you worth much more than the birds? 25 Can any of you add one moment to his life-span^C by worrying? 26 If then you're not able to do even a little thing, why worry about the rest?

27 "Consider how the wildflowers grow: They don't labor or spin thread. Yet I tell you, not even Solomon in all his splendor was adorned like one of these. 28 If that's how God clothes the grass, which is in the field today and is thrown into the furnace tomorrow, how much more will he do for you — you of little faith? 29 Don't strive for what you should eat and what you should drink, and don't be anxious. 30 For the Gentile world eagerly seeks all these things, and your Father knows that you need them.

31 "But seek his kingdom, and these things will be provided for you. 32 Don't be afraid, little flock, because your Father delights to give you the kingdom. 33 Sell your possessions and give to the poor. Make money-bags for yourselves that won't grow old, an inexhaustible treasure in heaven, where no thief comes near and no moth destroys. 34 For where your treasure is, there your heart will be also.

READY FOR THE MASTER'S RETURN

35 "Be ready for service^D and have your lamps lit. 36 You are to be like people waiting for their master to return from the wedding banquet so that when he comes and knocks, they can open the door for him at once. 37 Blessed will be those servants the master finds alert when he comes. Truly I tell you, he will get ready,^E have them recline at the table, then come and serve them. 38 If he comes in the middle of the night, or even near dawn,^F and finds them alert, blessed are those servants. 39 But know this: If the homeowner had known at what hour the thief was coming, he would not have let his house be broken into. 40 You also be ready, because the Son of Man is coming at an hour you do not expect."

---

^12:6 Lit two assaria; a small copper coin ^B 12:14 Lit Man ^C 12:25 Or add a cubit to his height ^D 12:35 Lit "Let your loins be girded; an idiom for tying up loose outer clothing in preparation for action; Ex 12:11 ^E 12:37 Lit will gird himself ^F 12:38 Lit even in the second or third watch

REWARDS AND PUNISHMENT

[41] "Lord," Peter asked, "are you telling this parable to us or to everyone?"

[42] The Lord said: "Who then is the faithful and sensible manager his master will put in charge of his household servants to give them their allotted food at the proper time? [43] Blessed is that servant whom the master finds doing his job when he comes. [44] Truly I tell you, he will put him in charge of all his possessions. [45] But if that servant says in his heart, 'My master is delaying his coming,' and starts to beat the male and female servants, and to eat and drink and get drunk, [46] that servant's master will come on a day he does not expect him and at an hour he does not know. He will cut him to pieces[A] and assign him a place with the unfaithful.[B] [47] And that servant who knew his master's will and didn't prepare himself or do it[C] will be severely beaten. [48] But the one who did not know and did what deserved punishment will receive a light beating. From everyone who has been given much, much will be required; and from the one who has been entrusted with much, even more will be expected.[D]

NOT PEACE BUT DIVISION

[49] "I came to bring fire on the earth, and how I wish it were already set ablaze! [50] But I have a baptism to undergo, and how it consumes me until it is finished! [51] Do you think that I came here to bring peace on the earth? No, I tell you, but rather division. [52] From now on, five in one household will be divided: three against two, and two against three.

[53]   They will be divided, father
              against son,
          son against father,
          mother against daughter,
          daughter against mother,
          mother-in-law against her daughter-
              in-law,
          and daughter-in-law against mother-
              in-law."[E]

INTERPRETING THE TIME

[54] He also said to the crowds: "When you see a cloud rising in the west, right away you say, 'A storm is coming,' and so it does. [55] And when the south wind is blowing, you say, 'It's going to be hot,' and it is. [56] Hypocrites! You know how to interpret the appearance of the earth and the sky, but why don't you know how to interpret this present time?

SETTLING ACCOUNTS

[57] "Why don't you judge for yourselves what is right? [58] As you are going with your adversary to the ruler, make an effort to settle with him on the way. Then he won't drag you before the judge, the judge hand you over to the bailiff, and the bailiff throw you into prison. [59] I tell you, you will never get out of there until you have paid the last cent."[F]

REPENT OR PERISH

13 At that time, some people came and reported to him about the Galileans whose blood Pilate had mixed with their sacrifices. [2] And he[G] responded to them, "Do you think that these Galileans were more sinful than all the other Galileans because they suffered these things? [3] No, I tell you; but unless you repent, you will all perish as well. [4] Or those eighteen that the tower in Siloam fell on and killed — do you think they were more sinful than all the other people who live in Jerusalem? [5] No, I tell you; but unless you repent, you will all perish as well."

THE PARABLE OF THE BARREN FIG TREE

[6] And he told this parable: "A man had a fig tree that was planted in his vineyard. He came looking for fruit on it and found none. [7] He told the vineyard worker, 'Listen, for three years I have come looking for fruit on this fig tree and haven't found any. Cut it down! Why should it even waste the soil?'

[8] "But he replied to him, 'Sir,[H] leave it this year also, until I dig around it and fertilize it. [9] Perhaps it will produce fruit next year, but if not, you can cut it down.'"

HEALING A DAUGHTER OF ABRAHAM

[10] As he was teaching in one of the synagogues on the Sabbath, [11] a woman was there who had been disabled by a spirit[I] for over eighteen years. She was bent over and could not straighten up at all.[J] [12] When Jesus saw her, he called out to her,[K] "Woman, you are free of your disability." [13] Then he laid his hands on her, and instantly she was restored and began to glorify God.

[14] But the leader of the synagogue, indignant because Jesus had healed on the Sabbath, responded by telling the crowd, "There are six days when work should be done; therefore come on those days and be healed and not on the Sabbath day."

[15] But the Lord answered him and said, "Hypocrites! Doesn't each one of you untie his ox or donkey from the feeding trough on the Sabbath

---

[A]12:46 Lit *him in two*   [B]12:46 Or *unbelievers*   [C]12:47 Lit *or do toward his will*,   [D]12:48 Or *much*   [E]12:53 Mc 7:6
[F]12:59 Gk *lepton*, the smallest and least valuable copper coin in use   [G]13:2 Other mss read *Jesus*   [H]13:8 Or *Lord*
[I]13:11 Lit *had a spirit of disability*   [J]13:11 Or *straighten up completely*   [K]13:12 Or *he summoned her*

and lead it to water? [16] Satan has bound this woman, a daughter of Abraham, for eighteen years — shouldn't she be untied from this bondage^ on the Sabbath day?"

[17] When he had said these things, all his adversaries were humiliated, but the whole crowd was rejoicing over all the glorious things he was doing.

THE PARABLES OF THE MUSTARD SEED
AND OF THE LEAVEN

[18] He said, therefore, "What is the kingdom of God like, and what can I compare it to? [19] It's like a mustard seed that a man took and sowed in his garden. It grew and became a tree, and the birds of the sky nested in its branches."

[20] Again he said, "What can I compare the kingdom of God to? [21] It's like leaven^B that a woman took and mixed into fifty pounds^C of flour until all of it was leavened."

THE NARROW WAY

[22] He went through one town and village after another, teaching and making his way to Jerusalem. [23] "Lord," someone asked him, "are only a few people going to be saved?"

He said to them, [24] "Make every effort to enter through the narrow door, because I tell you, many will try to enter and won't be able [25] once the homeowner gets up and shuts the door. Then you will stand outside and knock on the door, saying, 'Lord, open up for us!' He will answer you, 'I don't know you or where you're from.' [26] Then you will say, 'We ate and drank in your presence, and you taught in our streets.' [27] But he will say, 'I tell you, I don't know you or where you're from. Get away from me, all you evildoers!' [28] There will be weeping and gnashing of teeth in that place, when you see Abraham, Isaac, Jacob, and all the prophets in the kingdom of God, but yourselves thrown out. [29] They will come from east and west, from north and south, to share the banquet^D in the kingdom of God. [30] Note this: Some who are last will be first, and some who are first will be last."

JESUS AND HEROD ANTIPAS

[31] At that time some Pharisees came and told him, "Go, get out of here. Herod wants to kill you."

[32] He said to them, "Go tell that fox, 'Look, I'm driving out demons and performing healings today and tomorrow, and on the third day I will complete my work.'^E [33] Yet it is necessary that I travel today, tomorrow, and the next day,

because it is not possible for a prophet to perish outside of Jerusalem.

JESUS'S LAMENTATION OVER JERUSALEM

[34] "Jerusalem, Jerusalem, who kills the prophets and stones those who are sent to her. How often I wanted to gather your children together, as a hen gathers her chicks under her wings, but you were not willing! [35] See, your house is abandoned to you. I tell you, you will not see me until the time comes when^F you say, 'Blessed is he who comes in the name of the Lord'! "^G

A SABBATH CONTROVERSY

14 One Sabbath, when he went in to eat^H at the house of one of the leading Pharisees, they were watching him closely. [2] There in front of him was a man whose body was swollen with fluid. [3] In response, Jesus asked the law experts and the Pharisees, "Is it lawful to heal on the Sabbath or not?" [4] But they kept silent. He took the man, healed him, and sent him away. [5] And to them, he said, "Which of you whose son or ox falls into a well, will not immediately pull him out on the Sabbath day?" [6] They could find no answer to these things.

TEACHINGS ON HUMILITY

[7] He told a parable to those who were invited, when he noticed how they would choose the best places for themselves: [8] "When you are invited by someone to a wedding banquet, don't recline at the best place, because a more distinguished person than you may have been invited by your host. [9] The one who invited both of you may come and say to you, 'Give your place to this man,' and then in humiliation, you will proceed to take the lowest place.

[10] "But when you are invited, go and recline in the lowest place, so that when the one who invited you comes, he will say to you, 'Friend, move up higher.' You will then be honored in the presence of all the other guests. [11] For everyone who exalts himself will be humbled, and the one who humbles himself will be exalted."

[12] He also said to the one who had invited him, "When you give a lunch or a dinner, don't invite your friends, your brothers or sisters, your relatives, or your rich neighbors, because they might invite you back, and you would be repaid. [13] On the contrary, when you host a banquet, invite those who are poor, maimed, lame, or blind. [14] And you will be blessed, because they cannot repay you; for you will be repaid at the resurrection of the righteous."

^13:16 Or isn't it necessary that she be untied from this bondage   ^B13:21 Or yeast   ^C13:21 Lit three sata; about forty liters
^D13:29 Lit recline at the table   ^E13:32 Lit I will be finished   ^F13:35 Other mss omit the time comes when
^G13:35 Ps 118:26   ^H14:1 Lit eat bread

THE PARABLE OF THE LARGE BANQUET

¹⁵ When one of those who reclined at the table with him heard these things, he said to him, "Blessed is the one who will eat bread in the kingdom of God!"

¹⁶ Then he told him: "A man was giving a large banquet and invited many. ¹⁷ At the time of the banquet, he sent his servant to tell those who were invited, 'Come, because everything is now ready.'

¹⁸ "But without exception^A they all began to make excuses. The first one said to him, 'I have bought a field, and I must go out and see it. I ask you to excuse me.'

¹⁹ "Another said, 'I have bought five yoke of oxen, and I'm going to try them out. I ask you to excuse me.'

²⁰ "And another said, 'I just got married, and therefore I'm unable to come.'

²¹ "So the servant came back and reported these things to his master. Then in anger, the master of the house told his servant, 'Go out quickly into the streets and alleys of the city, and bring in here the poor, maimed, blind, and lame.'

²² "'Master,' the servant said, 'what you ordered has been done, and there's still room.'

²³ "Then the master told the servant, 'Go out into the highways and hedges and make them come in, so that my house may be filled. ²⁴ For I tell you, not one of those people who were invited will enjoy my banquet.'"

THE COST OF FOLLOWING JESUS

²⁵ Now great crowds were traveling with him. So he turned and said to them: ²⁶ "If anyone comes to me and does not hate his own father and mother, wife and children, brothers and sisters — yes, and even his own life — he cannot be my disciple. ²⁷ Whoever does not bear his own cross and come after me cannot be my disciple.

²⁸ "For which of you, wanting to build a tower, doesn't first sit down and calculate the cost to see if he has enough to complete it? ²⁹ Otherwise, after he has laid the foundation and cannot finish it, all the onlookers will begin to ridicule him, ³⁰ saying, 'This man started to build and wasn't able to finish.'

³¹ "Or what king, going to war against another king, will not first sit down and decide if he is able with ten thousand to oppose the one who comes against him with twenty thousand? ³² If not, while the other is still far off, he sends a delegation and asks for terms of peace. ³³ In the same way, therefore, every one of you who does not renounce^B all his possessions cannot be my disciple.

³⁴ "Now, salt is good, but if salt should lose its taste, how will it be made salty? ³⁵ It isn't fit for the soil or for the manure pile; they throw it out. Let anyone who has ears to hear listen."

THE PARABLE OF THE LOST SHEEP

15 All the tax collectors and sinners were approaching to listen to him. ² And the Pharisees and scribes were complaining, "This man welcomes sinners and eats with them."

³ So he told them this parable: ⁴ "What man among you, who has a hundred sheep and loses one of them, does not leave the ninety-nine in the open field^C and go after the lost one until he finds it? ⁵ When he has found it, he joyfully puts it on his shoulders, ⁶ and coming home, he calls his friends and neighbors together, saying to them, 'Rejoice with me, because I have found my lost sheep!' ⁷ I tell you, in the same way, there will be more joy in heaven over one sinner who repents than over ninety-nine righteous people who don't need repentance.

THE PARABLE OF THE LOST COIN

⁸ "Or what woman who has ten silver coins,^D,E if she loses one coin, does not light a lamp, sweep the house, and search carefully until she finds it? ⁹ When she finds it, she calls her friends and neighbors together, saying, 'Rejoice with me, because I have found the silver coin I lost!' ¹⁰ I tell you, in the same way, there is joy in the presence of God's angels over one sinner who repents."

THE PARABLE OF THE LOST SON

¹¹ He also said: "A man had two sons. ¹² The younger of them said to his father, 'Father, give me the share of the estate I have coming to me.' So he distributed the assets^F to them. ¹³ Not many days later, the younger son gathered together all he had and traveled to a distant country, where he squandered his estate in foolish living. ¹⁴ After he had spent everything, a severe famine struck that country, and he had nothing.^G ¹⁵ Then he went to work for one of the citizens of that country, who sent him into his fields to feed pigs. ¹⁶ He longed to eat his fill from^H the pods that the pigs were eating, but no one would give him anything. ¹⁷ When he came to his senses,^I he said, 'How many of my father's hired workers have more than enough

^A **14:18** Lit *"And from one* (voice)   ^B **14:33** Or *leave*   ^C **15:4** Or *the wilderness*   ^D **15:8** Gk *ten drachmas*   ^E **15:8** A Gk drachma was equivalent to a Roman denarius = one day's wage   ^F **15:12** Or *life,* or *livelihood,* also in v. 30   ^G **15:14** Lit *and he began to be in need*   ^H **15:16** Other mss read *to fill his stomach with*   ^I **15:17** Lit *to himself*

food, and here I am dying of hunger!^A ¹⁸ I'll get up, go to my father, and say to him, "Father, I have sinned against heaven and in your sight. ¹⁹ I'm no longer worthy to be called your son. Make me like one of your hired workers." ' ²⁰ So he got up and went to his father. But while the son was still a long way off, his father saw him and was filled with compassion. He ran, threw his arms around his neck, and kissed him. ²¹ The son said to him, 'Father, I have sinned against heaven and in your sight. I'm no longer worthy to be called your son.'

²² "But the father told his servants, 'Quick! Bring out the best robe and put it on him; put a ring on his finger and sandals on his feet. ²³ Then bring the fattened calf and slaughter it, and let's celebrate with a feast, ²⁴ because this son of mine was dead and is alive again; he was lost and is found!' So they began to celebrate.

²⁵ "Now his older son was in the field; as he came near the house, he heard music and dancing. ²⁶ So he summoned one of the servants, questioning what these things meant. ²⁷ 'Your brother is here,' he told him, 'and your father has slaughtered the fattened calf because he has him back safe and sound.'^B

²⁸ "Then he became angry and didn't want to go in. So his father came out and pleaded with him. ²⁹ But he replied to his father, 'Look, I have been slaving many years for you, and I have never disobeyed your orders, yet you never gave me a goat so that I could celebrate with my friends. ³⁰ But when this son of yours came, who has devoured your assets^c with prostitutes, you slaughtered the fattened calf for him.'

³¹ " 'Son,'^D he said to him, 'you are always with me, and everything I have is yours. ³² But we had to celebrate and rejoice, because this brother of yours was dead and is alive again; he was lost and is found.' "

THE PARABLE OF THE DISHONEST MANAGER

16 Now he said to the disciples: "There was a rich man who received an accusation that his manager was squandering his possessions. ² So he called the manager in and asked, 'What is this I hear about you? Give an account of your management, because you can no longer be my manager.'

³ "Then the manager said to himself, 'What will I do since my master is taking the management away from me? I'm not strong enough to dig; I'm ashamed to beg. ⁴ I know what I'll do so that when I'm removed from management, people will welcome me into their homes.'

⁵ "So he summoned each one of his master's debtors. 'How much do you owe my master?' he asked the first one.

⁶ " 'A hundred measures of olive oil,' he said.

" 'Take your invoice,' he told him, 'sit down quickly, and write fifty.'

⁷ "Next he asked another, 'How much do you owe?'

" 'A hundred measures of wheat,' he said.

" 'Take your invoice,' he told him, 'and write eighty.'

⁸ "The master praised the unrighteous manager because he had acted shrewdly. For the children of this age are more shrewd than the children of light in dealing with their own people.^E ⁹ And I tell you, make friends for yourselves by means of worldly wealth^F so that when it fails,^G they may welcome you into eternal dwellings. ¹⁰ Whoever is faithful in very little is also faithful in much, and whoever is unrighteous in very little is also unrighteous in much. ¹¹ So if you have not been faithful with worldly wealth, who will trust you with what is genuine? ¹² And if you have not been faithful with what belongs to someone else, who will give you what is your own? ¹³ No servant can serve two masters, since either he will hate one and love the other, or he will be devoted to one and despise the other. You cannot serve both God and money."

KINGDOM VALUES

¹⁴ The Pharisees, who were lovers of money, were listening to all these things and scoffing at him. ¹⁵ And he told them, "You are the ones who justify yourselves in the sight of others, but God knows your hearts. For what is highly admired by people is revolting in God's sight.

¹⁶ "The Law and the Prophets were until John; since then, the good news of the kingdom of God has been proclaimed, and everyone is urgently invited to enter it."^H ¹⁷ But it is easier for heaven and earth to pass away than for one stroke of a letter in the law to drop out.

¹⁸ "Everyone who divorces his wife and marries another woman commits adultery, and everyone who marries a woman divorced from her husband commits adultery.

THE RICH MAN AND LAZARUS

¹⁹ "There was a rich man who would dress in purple and fine linen, feasting lavishly every day. ²⁰ But a poor man named Lazarus, covered with sores, was lying at his gate. ²¹ He longed to be filled with what fell from the rich man's

---

^A **15:17** Or *dying in the famine* ; v. 14   ^B **15:27** Lit *him back healthy*   ^c **15:30** Or *life,* or *livelihood*   ^D **15:31** Lit *Child*   ^E **16:8** Lit *own generation*   ^F **16:9** Lit *unrighteous money,* also in v. 11   ^G **16:9** Other mss read *when you fail,* or *pass away*   ^H **16:16** Or *everyone is forcing his way into it*

table, but instead the dogs would come and lick his sores. [22] One day the poor man died and was carried away by the angels to Abraham's side.[A] The rich man also died and was buried. [23] And being in torment in Hades, he looked up and saw Abraham a long way off, with Lazarus at his side. [24] 'Father Abraham!' he called out, 'Have mercy on me and send Lazarus to dip the tip of his finger in water and cool my tongue, because I am in agony in this flame!'

[25] " 'Son,'[B] Abraham said, 'remember that during your life you received your good things, just as Lazarus received bad things, but now he is comforted here, while you are in agony. [26] Besides all this, a great chasm has been fixed between us and you, so that those who want to pass over from here to you cannot; neither can those from there cross over to us.'

[27] " 'Father,' he said, 'then I beg you to send him to my father's house — [28] because I have five brothers — to warn them, so they won't also come to this place of torment.'

[29] "But Abraham said, 'They have Moses and the prophets; they should listen to them.'

[30] " 'No, father Abraham,' he said. 'But if someone from the dead goes to them, they will repent.'

[31] "But he told him, 'If they don't listen to Moses and the prophets, they will not be persuaded if someone rises from the dead.' "

WARNINGS FROM JESUS

17 He said to his disciples, "Offenses will certainly come,[C] but woe to the one through whom they come! [2] It would be better for him if a millstone were hung around his neck and he were thrown into the sea than for him to cause one of these little ones to stumble. [3] Be on your guard. If your brother sins,[D] rebuke him, and if he repents, forgive him. [4] And if he sins against you seven times in a day, and comes back to you seven times, saying, 'I repent,' you must forgive him."

FAITH AND DUTY

[5] The apostles said to the Lord, "Increase our faith."

[6] "If you have faith the size of[E] a mustard seed," the Lord said, "you can say to this mulberry tree, 'Be uprooted and planted in the sea,' and it will obey you.

[7] "Which one of you having a servant tending sheep or plowing will say to him when he comes in from the field, 'Come at once and sit down to eat'? [8] Instead, will he not tell him,

'Prepare something for me to eat, get ready, and serve me while I eat and drink; later you can eat and drink'? [9] Does he thank that servant because he did what was commanded?[F] [10] In the same way, when you have done all that you were commanded, you should say, 'We are worthless servants; we've only done our duty.' "

TEN MEN HEALED

[11] While traveling to Jerusalem, he passed between[G] Samaria and Galilee. [12] As he entered a village, ten men with leprosy[H] met him. They stood at a distance [13] and raised their voices, saying, "Jesus, Master, have mercy on us!"

[14] When he saw them, he told them, "Go and show yourselves to the priests." And while they were going, they were cleansed.

[15] But one of them, seeing that he was healed, returned and, with a loud voice, gave glory to God. [16] He fell facedown at his feet, thanking him. And he was a Samaritan.

[17] Then Jesus said, "Were not ten cleansed? Where are the nine? [18] Didn't any return to give glory to God except this foreigner?" [19] And he told him, "Get up and go on your way. Your faith has saved you."[I]

THE COMING OF THE KINGDOM

[20] Being asked by the Pharisees when the kingdom of God would come, he answered them, "The kingdom of God is not coming with something observable; [21] no one will say,[J] 'See here!' or 'There!' For you see, the kingdom of God is in your midst."[K]

[22] Then he told the disciples: "The days are coming when you will long to see one of the days of the Son of Man, but you won't see it. [23] They will say to you, 'See there!' or 'See here!' Don't follow or run after them. [24] For as the lightning flashes from horizon to horizon and lights up the sky, so the Son of Man will be in his day. [25] But first it is necessary that he suffer many things and be rejected by this generation.

[26] "Just as it was in the days of Noah, so it will be in the days of the Son of Man: [27] People went on eating, drinking, marrying and giving in marriage until the day Noah boarded the ark, and the flood came and destroyed them all. [28] It will be the same as it was in the days of Lot: People went on eating, drinking, buying, selling, planting, building. [29] But on the day Lot left Sodom, fire and sulfur rained from heaven and destroyed them all. [30] It will be like that on the day the Son of Man is revealed. [31] On that day,

a man on the housetop, whose belongings are in the house, must not come down to get them. Likewise the man who is in the field must not turn back. [32] Remember Lot's wife! [33] Whoever tries to make his life secure[A,B] will lose it, and whoever loses his life will preserve it. [34] I tell you, on that night two will be in one bed; one will be taken and the other will be left. [35] Two women will be grinding grain together; one will be taken and the other left."[C]

[37] "Where, Lord?" they asked him.

He said to them, "Where the corpse is, there also the vultures will be gathered."

THE PARABLE OF THE PERSISTENT WIDOW

18 Now he told them a parable on the need for them to pray always and not give up. [2] "There was a judge in a certain town who didn't fear God or respect people. [3] And a widow in that town kept coming to him, saying, 'Give me justice against my adversary.'

[4] "For a while he was unwilling, but later he said to himself, 'Even though I don't fear God or respect people, [5] yet because this widow keeps pestering me,[D] I will give her justice, so that she doesn't wear me out[E] by her persistent coming.'"

[6] Then the Lord said, "Listen to what the unjust judge says. [7] Will not God grant justice to his elect who cry out to him day and night? Will he delay helping them?[F] [8] I tell you that he will swiftly grant them justice. Nevertheless, when the Son of Man comes, will he find faith on earth?"

THE PARABLE OF THE PHARISEE AND THE TAX COLLECTOR

[9] He also told this parable to some who trusted in themselves that they were righteous and looked down on everyone else: [10] "Two men went up to the temple to pray, one a Pharisee and the other a tax collector. [11] The Pharisee was standing and praying like this about himself:[G] 'God, I thank you that I'm not like other people — greedy, unrighteous, adulterers, or even like this tax collector. [12] I fast twice a week; I give a tenth[H] of everything I get.'

[13] "But the tax collector, standing far off, would not even raise his eyes to heaven but kept striking his chest and saying, 'God, have mercy on me,' a sinner!' [14] I tell you, this one went down to his house justified rather than the other; because everyone who exalts himself will be humbled, but the one who humbles himself will be exalted."

BLESSING THE CHILDREN

[15] People were bringing infants to him so he might touch them, but when the disciples saw it, they rebuked them. [16] Jesus, however, invited them: "Let the little children come to me, and don't stop them, because the kingdom of God belongs to such as these. [17] Truly I tell you, whoever does not receive the kingdom of God like a little child will never enter it."

THE RICH YOUNG RULER

[18] A ruler asked him, "Good teacher, what must I do to inherit eternal life?"

[19] "Why do you call me good?" Jesus asked him. "No one is good except God alone. [20] You know the commandments: **Do not commit adultery; do not murder; do not steal; do not bear false witness; honor your father and mother.**"[J]

[21] "I have kept all these from my youth," he said.

[22] When Jesus heard this, he told him, "You still lack one thing: Sell all you have and distribute it to the poor, and you will have treasure in heaven. Then come, follow me."

[23] After he heard this, he became extremely sad, because he was very rich.

POSSESSIONS AND THE KINGDOM

[24] Seeing that he became sad,[K] Jesus said, "How hard it is for those who have wealth to enter the kingdom of God! [25] For it is easier for a camel to go through the eye of a needle than for a rich person to enter the kingdom of God."

[26] Those who heard this asked, "Then who can be saved?"

[27] He replied, "What is impossible with man is possible with God."

[28] Then Peter said, "Look, we have left what we had and followed you."

[29] So he said to them, "Truly I tell you, there is no one who has left a house, wife or brothers or sisters, parents or children because of the kingdom of God, [30] who will not receive many times more at this time, and eternal life in the age to come."

THE THIRD PREDICTION OF HIS DEATH

[31] Then he took the Twelve aside and told them, "See, we are going up to Jerusalem. Everything that is written through the prophets about the Son of Man will be accomplished. [32] For he will be handed over to the Gentiles, and he will be mocked, insulted, spit on; [33] and after they flog him, they will kill him, and he will rise on the third day."

---

^**17:33** Other mss read *to save his life* ^B**17:33** Or *tries to retain his life* ^C**17:35** Some mss include v. 36: *"Two will be in a field: One will be taken, and the other will be left."* ^D**18:5** Lit *widow causes me trouble* ^E**18:5** Or *doesn't ruin my reputation* ^F**18:7** Or *Will he put up with them?* ^G**18:11** Or *by himself* ^H**18:12** Or *give tithes* ^I**18:13** Or *God, turn your wrath from me* ^J**18:20** Ex 20:12-16; Dt 5:16-20 ^K**18:24** Other mss omit *he became sad*

34 They understood none of these things. The meaning of the saying^A was hidden from them, and they did not grasp what was said.

A BLIND MAN RECEIVES HIS SIGHT

35 As he approached Jericho, a blind man was sitting by the road begging. **36** Hearing a crowd passing by, he inquired what was happening. **37** "Jesus of Nazareth is passing by," they told him.

38 So he called out, "Jesus, Son of David, have mercy on me!" **39** Then those in front told him to keep quiet,^B but he kept crying out all the more, "Son of David, have mercy on me!"

40 Jesus stopped and commanded that he be brought to him. When he came closer, he asked him, **41** "What do you want me to do for you?"

"Lord," he said, "I want to see."

42 "Receive your sight." Jesus told him. "Your faith has saved you." **43** Instantly he could see, and he began to follow him, glorifying God. All the people, when they saw it, gave praise to God.

JESUS VISITS ZACCHAEUS

19 He entered Jericho and was passing through. **2** There was a man named Zacchaeus who was a chief tax collector, and he was rich. **3** He was trying to see who Jesus was, but he was not able because of the crowd, since he was a short man. **4** So running ahead, he climbed up a sycamore tree to see Jesus, since he was about to pass that way. **5** When Jesus came to the place, he looked up and said to him, "Zacchaeus, hurry and come down because today it is necessary for me to stay at your house."

6 So he quickly came down and welcomed him joyfully. **7** All who saw it began to complain, "He's gone to stay with a sinful man."

8 But Zacchaeus stood there and said to the Lord, "Look, I'll give half of my possessions to the poor, Lord. And if I have extorted anything from anyone, I'll pay back four times as much."

9 "Today salvation has come to this house," Jesus told him, "because he too is a son of Abraham. **10** For the Son of Man has come to seek and to save the lost."

THE PARABLE OF THE TEN MINAS

11 As they were listening to this, he went on to tell a parable because he was near Jerusalem, and they thought the kingdom of God was going to appear right away.

12 Therefore he said: "A nobleman traveled to a far country to receive for himself authority to be king^C and then to return. **13** He called ten of his servants, gave them ten minas,^D and told them, 'Engage in business until I come back.'

14 "But his subjects hated him and sent a delegation after him, saying, 'We don't want this man to rule over us.'

15 "At his return, having received the authority to be king, he summoned those servants he had given the money to, so that he could find out how much they had made in business. **16** The first came forward and said, 'Master, your mina has earned ten more minas.'

17 "'Well done, good^E servant!' he told him. 'Because you have been faithful in a very small matter, have authority over ten towns.'

18 "The second came and said, 'Master, your mina has made five minas.'

19 "So he said to him, 'You will be over five towns.'

20 "And another came and said, 'Master, here is your mina. I have kept it safe in a cloth **21** because I was afraid of you since you're a harsh man: you collect what you didn't deposit and reap what you didn't sow.'

22 "He told him, 'I will condemn you by what you have said, you evil servant! If you knew I was a harsh man, collecting what I didn't deposit and reaping what I didn't sow, **23** why, then, didn't you put my money in the bank? And when I returned, I would have collected it with interest.' **24** So he said to those standing there, 'Take the mina away from him and give it to the one who has ten minas.'

25 "But they said to him, 'Master, he has ten minas.'

26 "'I tell you, that to everyone who has, more will be given; and from the one who does not have, even what he does have will be taken away. **27** But bring here these enemies of mine, who did not want me to rule over them, and slaughter^F them in my presence.'"

THE TRIUMPHAL ENTRY

28 When he had said these things, he went on ahead, going up to Jerusalem. **29** As he approached Bethphage and Bethany, at the place called the Mount of Olives, he sent two of the disciples **30** and said, "Go into the village ahead of you. As you enter it, you will find a young donkey tied there, on which no one has ever sat. Untie it and bring it. **31** If anyone asks you, 'Why are you untying it?' say this: 'The Lord needs it.'"

32 So those who were sent left and found it just as he had told them. **33** As they were untying the young donkey, its owners said to them, "Why are you untying the donkey?"

---

^**18:34** Lit *This saying*   ^**18:39** Or *those in front rebuked him*   ^**19:12** Lit *to receive for himself a kingdom,* or *sovereignty,* also in v. 15   ^**19:13** = Gk coin worth a hundred drachmas or about a hundred days' wages   ^**19:17** Or *capable*   ^**19:27** Or *execute*

[34] "The Lord needs it," they said. [35] Then they brought it to Jesus, and after throwing their clothes on the donkey, they helped Jesus get on it. [36] As he was going along, they were spreading their clothes on the road. [37] Now he came near the path down the Mount of Olives, and the whole crowd of the disciples began to praise God joyfully with a loud voice for all the miracles they had seen:

[38] **Blessed is the King who comes in the name of the Lord.**[A]
Peace in heaven
and glory in the highest heaven!

[39] Some of the Pharisees from the crowd told him, "Teacher, rebuke your disciples."

[40] He answered, "I tell you, if they were to keep silent, the stones would cry out."

JESUS'S LOVE FOR JERUSALEM

[41] As he approached and saw the city, he wept for it, [42] saying, "If you knew this day what would bring peace — but now it is hidden from your eyes. [43] For the days will come on you when your enemies will build a barricade around you, surround you, and hem you in on every side. [44] They will crush you and your children among you to the ground, and they will not leave one stone on another in your midst, because you did not recognize the time when God visited you."

CLEANSING THE TEMPLE

[45] He went into the temple and began to throw out those who were selling,[B] [46] and he said, "It is written, **my house will be a house of prayer,** but you have made it **a den of thieves!**"[C]

[47] Every day he was teaching in the temple. The chief priests, the scribes, and the leaders of the people were looking for a way to kill him, [48] but they could not find a way to do it, because all the people were captivated by what they heard.

THE AUTHORITY OF JESUS CHALLENGED

20 One day as he was teaching the people in the temple and proclaiming the good news, the chief priests and the scribes, with the elders, came [2] and said to him: "Tell us, by what authority are you doing these things? Who is it who gave you this authority?"

[3] He answered them, "I will also ask you a question. Tell me, [4] was the baptism of John from heaven or of human origin?"

[5] They discussed it among themselves: "If we say, 'From heaven,' he will say, 'Why didn't you believe him?' [6] But if we say, 'Of human origin,' all the people will stone us, because they are convinced that John was a prophet." [7] So they answered that they did not know its origin.

[8] And Jesus said to them, "Neither will I tell you by what authority I do these things."

THE PARABLE OF THE VINEYARD OWNER

[9] Now he began to tell the people this parable: "A man planted a vineyard, leased it to tenant farmers, and went away for a long time. [10] At harvest time he sent a servant to the farmers so that they might give him some fruit from the vineyard. But the farmers beat him and sent him away empty-handed. [11] He sent yet another servant, but they beat that one too, treated him shamefully, and sent him away empty-handed. [12] And he sent yet a third, but they wounded this one too and threw him out.

[13] "Then the owner of the vineyard said, 'What should I do? I will send my beloved son. Perhaps[D] they will respect him.'

[14] "But when the tenant farmers saw him, they discussed it among themselves and said, 'This is the heir. Let's kill him, so that the inheritance will be ours.' [15] So they threw him out of the vineyard and killed him.

"What then will the owner of the vineyard do to them? [16] He will come and kill those farmers and give the vineyard to others."

But when they heard this they said, "That must never happen!"

[17] But he looked at them and said, "Then what is the meaning of this Scripture:[E]

The stone that the builders rejected has become the cornerstone?[F]

[18] Everyone who falls on that stone will be broken to pieces, but on whomever it falls, it will shatter him."

[19] Then the scribes and the chief priests looked for a way to get their hands on him that very hour, because they knew he had told this parable against them, but they feared the people.

GOD AND CAESAR

[20] They watched closely and sent spies who pretended to be righteous,[G] so that they could catch him in what he said, to hand him over to the governor's rule and authority. [21] They questioned him, "Teacher, we know that you speak and teach correctly, and you don't show partiality[H] but teach truthfully the way of God. [22] Is it lawful for us to pay taxes to Caesar or not?"

[A]**19:38** Ps 118:26 [B]**19:45** Other mss add *and buying in it* [C]**19:46** Is 56:7; Jr 7:11 [D]**20:13** Other mss add *when they see him*
[E]**20:17** Lit *"What then is this that is written* [F]**20:17** Ps 118:22 [G]**20:20** Or *upright* [H]**20:21** Lit *you don't receive a face*

²³ But detecting their craftiness, he said to them,ᴬ ²⁴ "Show me a denarius.ᴮ Whose image and inscription does it have?"

"Caesar's," they said.

²⁵ "Well then," he told them, "give to Caesar the things that are Caesar's, and to God the things that are God's."

²⁶ They were not able to catch him in what he said in public, and being amazed at his answer, they became silent.

THE SADDUCEES AND THE RESURRECTION

²⁷ Some of the Sadducees, who say there is no resurrection, came up and questioned him: ²⁸ "Teacher, Moses wrote for us that **if a man's brother** has a wife, and **dies childless, his brother should take the wife and produce offspring for his brother.**ᶜ ²⁹ Now there were seven brothers. The first took a wife and died without children. ³⁰ Also the secondᴰ ³¹ and the third took her. In the same way, all seven died and left no children. ³² Finally, the woman died too. ³³ In the resurrection, therefore, whose wife will the woman be? For all seven had married her."

³⁴ Jesus told them, "The children of this age marry and are given in marriage. ³⁵ But those who are counted worthy to take part in that age and in the resurrection from the dead neither marry nor are given in marriage. ³⁶ For they can no longer die, because they are like angels and are children of God, since they are children of the resurrection. ³⁷ Moses even indicated in the passage about the burning bush that the dead are raised, where he calls the Lord **the God of Abraham and the God of Isaac and the God of Jacob.**ᴱ ³⁸ He is not the God of the dead but of the living, because all are living toᶠ him."

³⁹ Some of the scribes answered, "Teacher, you have spoken well." ⁴⁰ And they no longer dared to ask him anything.

THE QUESTION ABOUT THE CHRIST

⁴¹ Then he said to them, "How can they say that the Christ is the son of David? ⁴² For David himself says in the Book of Psalms:

The Lord declared
    to my Lord,
'Sit at my right hand
⁴³   until I make your enemies
    your footstool.'ᴳ

⁴⁴ David calls him 'Lord'; how then can the Christ be his son?"

WARNING AGAINST THE SCRIBES

⁴⁵ While all the people were listening, he said to his disciples, ⁴⁶ "Beware of the scribes, who want to go around in long robes and who love greetings in the marketplaces, the best seats in the synagogues, and the places of honor at banquets. ⁴⁷ They devour widows' houses and say long prayers just for show. These will receive harsher judgment."ᴴ

THE WIDOW'S GIFT

21 He looked up and saw the rich dropping their offerings into the temple treasury. ² He also saw a poor widow dropping in two tiny coins.ᴵ ³ "Truly I tell you," he said. "This poor widow has put in more than all of them. ⁴ For all these people have put in gifts out of their surplus, but she out of her poverty has put in all she had to live on."

DESTRUCTION OF THE TEMPLE PREDICTED

⁵ As some were talking about the temple, how it was adorned with beautiful stones and gifts dedicated to God, he said, ⁶ "These things that you see — the days will come when not one stone will be left on another that will not be thrown down."

SIGNS OF THE END OF THE AGE

⁷ "Teacher," they asked him, "so when will these things happen? And what will be the sign when these things are about to take place?"

⁸ Then he said, "Watch out that you are not deceived. For many will come in my name, saying, 'I am he,' and, 'The time is near.' Don't follow them. ⁹ When you hear of wars and rebellions,ᴶ don't be alarmed. Indeed, it is necessary that these things take place first, but the end won't come right away."

¹⁰ Then he told them: "Nation will be raised up against nation, and kingdom against kingdom. ¹¹ There will be violent earthquakes, and famines and plagues in various places, and there will be terrifying sights and great signs from heaven. ¹² But before all these things, they will lay their hands on you and persecute you. They will hand you over to the synagogues and prisons, and you will be brought before kings and governors because of my name. ¹³ This will give you an opportunity to bear witness. ¹⁴ Therefore make up your mindsᴷ not to prepare your defense ahead of time, ¹⁵ for I will give you such words and a wisdom that none of your adversaries will be able to resist or contradict. ¹⁶ You

ᴬ**20:23** Other mss add *"Why are you testing me?"*   ᴮ**20:24** A denarius = one day's wage   ᶜ**20:28** Dt 25:5   ᴰ**20:30** Other mss add *took her as wife, and he died without children*   ᴱ**20:37** Ex 3:6,15   ᶠ**20:38** Or *with*   ᴳ**20:42-43** Ps 110:1   ᴴ**20:47** Or *judgment*
ᴵ**21:2** Lit *two lepta*; the *lepton* was the smallest and least valuable Gk coin in use.   ᴶ**21:9** Or *insurrections*, or *revolutions*, or *chaos*
ᴷ**21:14** Lit *Therefore place* (determine) *in your hearts*

will even be betrayed by parents, brothers, relatives, and friends. They will kill some of you. [17] You will be hated by everyone because of my name, [18] but not a hair of your head will be lost. [19] By your endurance, gain[A] your lives.

THE DESTRUCTION OF JERUSALEM

[20] "When you see Jerusalem surrounded by armies, then recognize that its desolation has come near. [21] Then those in Judea must flee to the mountains. Those inside the city must leave it, and those who are in the country must not enter it, [22] because these are days of vengeance to fulfill all the things that are written. [23] Woe to pregnant women and nursing mothers in those days, for there will be great distress in the land[B] and wrath against this people. [24] They will be killed by the sword[C] and be led captive into all the nations, and Jerusalem will be trampled by the Gentiles[D] until the times of the Gentiles are fulfilled.

THE COMING OF THE SON OF MAN

[25] "Then there will be signs in the sun, moon, and stars; and there will be anguish on the earth among nations bewildered by the roaring of the sea and the waves. [26] People will faint from fear and expectation of the things that are coming on the world, because the powers of the heavens will be shaken. [27] Then they will see the Son of Man coming in a cloud with power and great glory. [28] But when these things begin to take place, stand up and lift up your heads, because your redemption is near."

THE PARABLE OF THE FIG TREE

[29] Then he told them a parable: "Look at the fig tree, and all the trees. [30] As soon as they put out leaves you can see for yourselves and recognize that summer is already near. [31] In the same way, when you see these things happening, recognize[E] that the kingdom of God is near. [32] Truly I tell you, this generation will certainly not pass away until all things take place. [33] Heaven and earth will pass away, but my words will never pass away.

THE NEED FOR WATCHFULNESS

[34] "Be on your guard, so that your minds are not dulled[F] from carousing,[G] drunkenness, and worries of life, or that day will come on you unexpectedly [35] like a trap. For it will come on all who live on the face of the whole earth. [36] But be alert at all times, praying that you may have strength[H] to escape all these things that are going to take place and to stand before the Son of Man."

[37] During the day, he was teaching in the temple, but in the evening he would go out and spend the night on what is called the Mount of Olives. [38] Then all the people would come early in the morning to hear him in the temple.

THE PLOT TO KILL JESUS

22 The Festival of Unleavened Bread, which is called Passover, was approaching. [2] The chief priests and the scribes were looking for a way to put him to death, because they were afraid of the people.

[3] Then Satan entered Judas, called Iscariot, who was numbered among the Twelve. [4] He went away and discussed with the chief priests and temple police how he could hand him over to them. [5] They were glad and agreed to give him silver.[I] [6] So he accepted the offer and started looking for a good opportunity to betray him to them when the crowd was not present.

PREPARATION FOR PASSOVER

[7] Then the Day of Unleavened Bread came when the Passover lamb had to be sacrificed. [8] Jesus sent Peter and John, saying, "Go and make preparations for us to eat the Passover."

[9] "Where do you want us to prepare it?" they asked him.

[10] "Listen," he said to them, "when you've entered the city, a man carrying a water jug will meet you. Follow him into the house he enters. [11] Tell the owner of the house, 'The Teacher asks you, "Where is the guest room where I can eat the Passover with my disciples?"' [12] Then he will show you a large, furnished room upstairs. Make the preparations there."

[13] So they went and found it just as he had told them, and they prepared the Passover.

THE FIRST LORD'S SUPPER

[14] When the hour came, he reclined at the table, and the apostles with him. [15] Then he said to them, "I have fervently desired to eat this Passover with you before I suffer. [16] For I tell you, I will not eat it again[J] until it is fulfilled in the kingdom of God." [17] Then he took a cup, and after giving thanks, he said, "Take this and share it among yourselves. [18] For I tell you, from now on I will not drink of the fruit of the vine until the kingdom of God comes."

[19] And he took bread, gave thanks, broke it, gave it to them, and said, "This is my body, which is given for you. Do this in remembrance of me."

[A] 21:19 Other mss read *endurance, you will gain*   [B] 21:23 Or *the earth*   [C] 21:24 Lit *will fall by the edge of the sword*
[D] 21:24 Or *nations*   [E] 21:31 Or *you know*   [F] 21:34 Lit *your hearts are not weighed down*   [G] 21:34 Or *hangovers*
[H] 21:36 Other mss read *you may be counted worthy*   [I] 22:5 Or *money*   [J] 22:16 Other mss omit *again*

²⁰ In the same way he also took the cup after supper and said, "This cup is the new covenant in my blood, which is poured out for you.ᴬ ²¹ But look, the hand of the one betraying me is at the table with me. ²² For the Son of Man will go away as it has been determined, but woe to that man by whom he is betrayed!"

²³ So they began to argue among themselves which of them it could be who was going to do it.

THE DISPUTE OVER GREATNESS

²⁴ Then a dispute also arose among them about who should be considered the greatest. ²⁵ But he said to them, "The kings of the Gentiles lord it over them, and those who have authority over them have themselves calledᴮ 'Benefactors.' ²⁶ It is not to be like that among you. On the contrary, whoever is greatest among you should become like the youngest, and whoever leads, like the one serving. ²⁷ For who is greater, the one at the table or the one serving? Isn't it the one at the table? But I am among you as the one who serves. ²⁸ You are those who stood by me in my trials. ²⁹ I bestow on you a kingdom, just as my Father bestowed one on me, ³⁰ so that you may eat and drink at my table in my kingdom. And you will sit on thrones judging the twelve tribes of Israel.

PETER'S DENIAL PREDICTED

³¹ "Simon, Simon,ᶜ look out. Satan has asked to sift you like wheat. ³² But I have prayed for you that your faith may not fail. And you, when you have turned back, strengthen your brothers."

³³ "Lord," he told him, "I'm ready to go with you both to prison and to death."

³⁴ "I tell you, Peter," he said, "the rooster will not crow today untilᴰ you deny three times that you know me."

BE READY FOR TROUBLE

³⁵ He also said to them, "When I sent you out without money-bag, traveling bag, or sandals, did you lack anything?"

"Not a thing," they said.

³⁶ Then he said to them, "But now, whoever has a money-bag should take it, and also a traveling bag. And whoever doesn't have a sword should sell his robe and buy one. ³⁷ For I tell you, what is written must be fulfilled in me:ᴱ And he was counted among the lawless.ᶠ Yes, what is written about me is coming to its fulfillment."

³⁸ "Lord," they said, "look, here are two swords."

"That is enough!" he told them.

THE PRAYER IN THE GARDEN

³⁹ He went out and made his way as usual to the Mount of Olives, and the disciples followed him. ⁴⁰ When he reached the place, he told them, "Pray that you may not fall into temptation." ⁴¹ Then he withdrew from them about a stone's throw, knelt down, and began to pray, ⁴² "Father, if you are willing, take this cup away from me — nevertheless, not my will, but yours, be done."

⁴³ Then an angel from heaven appeared to him, strengthening him. ⁴⁴ Being in anguish, he prayed more fervently, and his sweat became like drops of blood falling to the ground.ᴳ ⁴⁵ When he got up from prayer and came to the disciples, he found them sleeping, exhausted from their grief. ⁴⁶ "Why are you sleeping?" he asked them. "Get up and pray, so that you won't fall into temptation."

JUDAS'S BETRAYAL OF JESUS

⁴⁷ While he was still speaking, suddenly a mob came, and one of the Twelve named Judas was leading them. He came near Jesus to kiss him, ⁴⁸ but Jesus said to him, "Judas, are you betraying the Son of Man with a kiss?"

⁴⁹ When those around him saw what was going to happen, they asked, "Lord, should we strike with the sword?" ⁵⁰ Then one of them struck the high priest's servant and cut off his right ear.

⁵¹ But Jesus responded, "No more of this!" And touching his ear, he healed him. ⁵² Then Jesus said to the chief priests, temple police, and the elders who had come for him, "Have you come out with swords and clubs as if I were a criminal?"ᴴ ⁵³ Every day while I was with you in the temple, you never laid a hand on me. But this is your hour — and the dominion of darkness."

PETER DENIES HIS LORD

⁵⁴ They seized him, led him away, and brought him into the high priest's house. Meanwhile Peter was following at a distance. ⁵⁵ They lit a fire in the middle of the courtyard and sat down together, and Peter sat among them. ⁵⁶ When a servant saw him sitting in the light, and looked closely at him, she said, "This man was with him too."

⁵⁷ But he denied it: "Woman, I don't know him."

⁵⁸ After a little while, someone else saw him and said, "You're one of them too."

"Man, I am not!" Peter said.

ᴬ22:19-20 Other mss omit *which is given for you* (v. 19) through the end of v. 20 ᴮ22:25 Or *them call themselves* ᶜ22:31 Other mss read *Then the Lord said, "Simon, Simon* ᴰ22:34 Other mss read *before* ᴱ22:37 Or *it is necessary that what is written be fulfilled in me* ᶠ22:37 Is 53:12 ᴳ22:43-44 Other mss omit vv. 43-44 ᴴ22:52 Lit *as against a thief*, or *a bandit*

⁵⁹About an hour later, another kept insisting, "This man was certainly with him, since he's also a Galilean."

⁶⁰But Peter said, "Man, I don't know what you're talking about!" Immediately, while he was still speaking, a rooster crowed. ⁶¹Then the Lord turned and looked at Peter. So Peter remembered the word of the Lord, how he had said to him, "Before the rooster crows today, you will deny me three times." ⁶²And he went outside and wept bitterly.

JESUS MOCKED AND BEATEN

⁶³The men who were holding Jesus started mocking and beating him. ⁶⁴After blindfolding him, they keptᴬasking, "Prophesy! Who was it that hit you?"ᴬ ⁶⁵And they were saying many other blasphemous things to him.

JESUS FACES THE SANHEDRIN

⁶⁶When daylight came, the eldersᴮ of the people, both the chief priests and the scribes, convened and brought him before their Sanhedrin. ⁶⁷They said, "If you are the Messiah, tell us."

But he said to them, "If I do tell you, you will not believe. ⁶⁸And if I ask you, you will not answer. ⁶⁹But from now on, the Son of Man will be seated at the right hand of the power of God."

⁷⁰They all asked, "Are you, then, the Son of God?"

And he said to them, "You say that I am."

⁷¹"Why do we need any more testimony," they said, "since we've heard it ourselves from his mouth?"

JESUS FACES PILATE

23 Then their whole assembly rose up and brought him before Pilate. ²They began to accuse him, saying, "We found this man misleading our nation, opposing payment of taxes to Caesar, and saying that he himself is the Messiah, a king."

³So Pilate asked him, "Are you the king of the Jews?"

He answered him, "You say so."ᶜ

⁴Pilate then told the chief priests and the crowds, "I find no grounds for charging this man."

⁵But they kept insisting, "He stirs up the people, teaching throughout all Judea, from Galilee where he started even to here."

JESUS FACES HEROD ANTIPAS

⁶When Pilate heard this,ᴰ he asked if the man was a Galilean. ⁷Finding that he was under Herod's jurisdiction, he sent him to Herod, who was also in Jerusalem during those days. ⁸Herod was very glad to see Jesus; for a long time he had wanted to see him because he had heard about him and was hoping to see some miracleᴱ performed by him. ⁹So he kept asking him questions, but Jesus did not answer him. ¹⁰The chief priests and the scribes stood by, vehemently accusing him. ¹¹Then Herod, with his soldiers, treated him with contempt, mocked him, dressed him in bright clothing, and sent him back to Pilate. ¹²That very day Herod and Pilate became friends.ᶠ Previously, they had been enemies.

JESUS OR BARABBAS

¹³Pilate called together the chief priests, the leaders, and the people, ¹⁴and said to them, "You have brought me this man as one who misleads the people. But in fact, after examining him in your presence, I have found no grounds to charge this man with those things you accuse him of. ¹⁵Neither has Herod, because he sent him back to us. Clearly, he has done nothing to deserve death. ¹⁶Therefore, I will have him whippedᴳ and then release him."ᴴ

¹⁸Then they all cried out together, "Take this man away! Release Barabbas to us!" ¹⁹(He had been thrown into prison for a rebellion that had taken place in the city, and for murder.)

²⁰Wanting to release Jesus, Pilate addressed them again, ²¹but they kept shouting, "Crucify! Crucify him!"

²²A third time he said to them, "Why? What has this man done wrong? I have found in him no grounds for the death penalty. Therefore, I will have him whipped and then release him."

²³But they kept up the pressure, demanding with loud voices that he be crucified, and their voicesᴵ won out. ²⁴So Pilate decided to grant their demand ²⁵and released the one they were asking for, who had been thrown into prison for rebellion and murder. But he handed Jesus over to their will.

THE WAY TO THE CROSS

²⁶As they led him away, they seized Simon, a Cyrenian, who was coming in from the country, and laid the cross on him to carry behind Jesus. ²⁷A large crowd of people followed him, including women who were mourning and lamenting him. ²⁸But turning to them, Jesus said, "Daughters of Jerusalem, do not weep for me, but weep for yourselves and your children.

ᴬ**22:64** Other mss add *striking him on the face and*   ᴮ**22:66** Or *council of elders*   ᶜ**23:3** Or *"That is true."*   ᴰ**23:6** Other mss read *heard "Galilee"*   ᴱ**23:8** Or *sign*   ᶠ**23:12** Lit *friends with one another*   ᴳ**23:16** Gk *paideuo;* to discipline or "teach a lesson"   ᴴ**23:16** Some mss include v. 17: *For according to the festival he had to release someone to them.*   ᴵ**23:23** Other mss add *and those of the chief priests*

²⁹ Look, the days are coming when they will say, 'Blessed are the women without children, the wombs that never bore, and the breasts that never nursed!' ³⁰ Then they will begin to say to the mountains, 'Fall on us!' and to the hills, 'Cover us!' ^A ³¹ For if they do these things when the wood is green, what will happen when it is dry?"

CRUCIFIED BETWEEN TWO CRIMINALS

³² Two others — criminals — were also led away to be executed with him. ³³ When they arrived at the place called The Skull, they crucified him there, along with the criminals, one on the right and one on the left. ³⁴ Then Jesus said, "Father, forgive them, because they do not know what they are doing." ᴮ And they divided his clothes and cast lots.

³⁵ The people stood watching, and even the leaders were scoffing: "He saved others; let him save himself if this is God's Messiah, the Chosen One!" ³⁶ The soldiers also mocked him. They came offering him sour wine ³⁷ and said, "If you are the King of the Jews, save yourself!"

³⁸ An inscription was above him: ᶜ THIS IS THE KING OF THE JEWS.

³⁹ Then one of the criminals hanging there began to yell insults at ᴰ him: "Aren't you the Messiah? Save yourself and us!"

⁴⁰ But the other answered, rebuking him: "Don't you even fear God, since you are undergoing the same punishment? ⁴¹ We are punished justly, because we're getting back what we deserve for the things we did, but this man has done nothing wrong." ⁴² Then he said, "Jesus, remember me ᴱ when you come into your kingdom."

⁴³ And he said to him, "Truly I tell you, today you will be with me in paradise."

THE DEATH OF JESUS

⁴⁴ It was now about noon, ᶠ and darkness came over the whole land ᴳ until three, ᴴ ⁴⁵ because the sun's light failed. ᴵ The curtain of the sanctuary was split down the middle. ⁴⁶ And Jesus called out with a loud voice, "Father, into your hands I entrust my spirit." ᴶ Saying this, he breathed his last.

⁴⁷ When the centurion saw what happened, he began to glorify God, saying, "This man really was righteous!" ᴷ ⁴⁸ All the crowds that had gathered for this spectacle, when they saw what had taken place, went home, striking their chests. ⁴⁹ But all who knew him, including the women who had followed him from Galilee, stood at a distance, watching these things.

THE BURIAL OF JESUS

⁵⁰ There was a good and righteous man named Joseph, a member of the Sanhedrin, ⁵¹ who had not agreed with their plan and action. He was from Arimathea, a Judean town, and was looking forward to the kingdom of God. ⁵² He approached Pilate and asked for Jesus's body. ⁵³ Taking it down, he wrapped it in fine linen and placed it in a tomb cut into the rock, where no one had ever been placed. ᴸ ⁵⁴ It was the preparation day, and the Sabbath was about to begin. ᴹ ⁵⁵ The women who had come with him from Galilee followed along and observed the tomb and how his body was placed. ⁵⁶ Then they returned and prepared spices and perfumes. And they rested on the Sabbath according to the commandment.

RESURRECTION MORNING

24 On the first day of the week, very early in the morning, they ᴺ came to the tomb, bringing the spices they had prepared. ² They found the stone rolled away from the tomb. ³ They went in but did not find the body of the Lord Jesus. ⁴ While they were perplexed about this, suddenly two men stood by them in dazzling clothes. ⁵ So the women were terrified and bowed down to the ground.

"Why are you looking for the living among the dead?" asked the men. ⁶ "He is not here, but he has risen! Remember how he spoke to you when he was still in Galilee, ⁷ saying, 'It is necessary that the Son of Man be betrayed into the hands of sinful men, be crucified, and rise on the third day'?" ⁸ And they remembered his words.

⁹ Returning from the tomb, they reported all these things to the Eleven and to all the rest. ¹⁰ Mary Magdalene, Joanna, Mary the mother of James, and the other women with them were telling the apostles these things. ¹¹ But these words seemed like nonsense to them, and they did not believe the women. ¹² Peter, however, got up and ran to the tomb. When he stooped to look in, he saw only the linen cloths. ᴼ So he went away, amazed at what had happened.

ᴬ 23:30 Hs 10:8 ᴮ 23:34 Other mss omit Then Jesus said, "Father, forgive them, because they do not know what they are doing." ᶜ 23:38 Other mss add written in Greek, Latin, and Hebrew letters ᴰ 23:39 Or began to blaspheme ᴱ 23:42 Other mss add Lord ᶠ 23:44 Lit about the sixth hour ᴳ 23:44 Or whole earth ᴴ 23:44 Lit the ninth hour ᴵ 23:45 Other mss read three, and the sun was darkened ᴶ 23:46 Ps 31:5 ᴷ 23:47 Or innocent ᴸ 23:53 Or interred, or laid ᴹ 23:54 Lit was dawning ᴺ 24:1 Other mss add and other women with them ᴼ 24:12 Other mss add lying there

THE EMMAUS DISCIPLES

[13] Now that same day two of them were on their way to a village called Emmaus, which was about seven miles^ from Jerusalem. [14] Together they were discussing everything that had taken place. [15] And while they were discussing and arguing, Jesus himself came near and began to walk along with them. [16] But they^ were prevented from recognizing him. [17] Then he asked them, "What is this dispute that you're having^ with each other as you are walking?" And they stopped walking and looked discouraged.

[18] The one named Cleopas answered him, "Are you the only visitor in Jerusalem who doesn't know the things that happened there in these days?"

[19] "What things?" he asked them.

So they said to him, "The things concerning Jesus of Nazareth, who was a prophet powerful in action and speech before God and all the people, [20] and how our chief priests and leaders handed him over to be sentenced to death, and they crucified him. [21] But we were hoping that he was the one who was about to redeem Israel. Besides all this, it's the third day since these things happened. [22] Moreover, some women from our group astounded us. They arrived early at the tomb, [23] and when they didn't find his body, they came and reported that they had seen a vision of angels who said he was alive. [24] Some of those who were with us went to the tomb and found it just as the women had said, but they didn't see him."

[25] He said to them, "How foolish and slow^ you are to believe all that the prophets have spoken! [26] Wasn't it necessary for the Messiah to suffer these things and enter into his glory?" [27] Then beginning with Moses and all the Prophets, he interpreted for them the things concerning himself in all the Scriptures.

[28] They came near the village where they were going, and he gave the impression that he was going farther. [29] But they urged him, "Stay with us, because it's almost evening, and now the day is almost over." So he went in to stay with them.

[30] It was as he reclined at the table with them that he took the bread, blessed and broke it, and gave it to them. [31] Then their eyes were opened, and they recognized him, but he disappeared from their sight. [32] They said to each other,

"Weren't our hearts burning within us while he was talking with us on the road and explaining the Scriptures to us?" [33] That very hour they got up and returned to Jerusalem. They found the Eleven and those with them gathered together, [34] who said, "The Lord has truly been raised and has appeared to Simon!" [35] Then they began to describe what had happened on the road and how he was made known to them in the breaking of the bread.

THE REALITY OF THE RISEN JESUS

[36] As they were saying these things, he himself stood in their midst. He said to them, "Peace to you!" [37] But they were startled and terrified and thought they were seeing a ghost. [38] "Why are you troubled?" he asked them. "And why do doubts arise in your hearts? [39] Look at my hands and my feet, that it is I myself! Touch me and see, because a ghost does not have flesh and bones as you can see I have." [40] Having said this, he showed them his hands and feet. [41] But while they still were amazed and in disbelief because of their joy, he asked them, "Do you have anything here to eat?" [42] So they gave him a piece of a broiled fish,^ [43] and he took it and ate in their presence.

[44] He told them, "These are my words that I spoke to you while I was still with you — that everything written about me in the Law of Moses, the Prophets, and the Psalms must be fulfilled." [45] Then he opened their minds to understand the Scriptures. [46] He also said to them, "This is what is written:^ The Messiah would suffer and rise from the dead the third day, [47] and repentance for^ forgiveness of sins would be proclaimed in his name to all the nations, beginning at Jerusalem. [48] You are witnesses of these things. [49] And look, I am sending you^ what my Father promised. As for you, stay in the city^ until you are empowered^ from on high."

THE ASCENSION OF JESUS

[50] Then he led them out to the vicinity of Bethany, and lifting up his hands he blessed them. [51] And while he was blessing them, he left them and was carried up into heaven. [52] After worshiping him, they returned to Jerusalem with great joy. [53] And they were continually in the temple praising God.^

^**24:13** Lit *about sixty stadia*; one *stadion* = 600 feet   ^**24:16** Lit *their eyes*   ^**24:17** Lit *"What are these words that you are exchanging*   ^**24:25** Lit *slow of heart*   ^**24:42** Other mss add *and some honeycomb*   ^**24:46** Other mss add *and thus it was necessary that*   ^**24:47** Many mss read *repentance and*   ^**24:49** Lit *upon you*   ^**24:49** Other mss add *of Jerusalem*   ^**24:49** Lit *clothed with power*   ^**24:53** Other mss read *praising and blessing God. Amen.*

JOHN

PROLOGUE

1 In the beginning was the Word, and the Word was with God, and the Word was God. ² He was with God in the beginning. ³ All things were created through him, and apart from him not one thing was created that has been created. ⁴ In him was life,ᴬ and that life was the light of men. ⁵ That light shines in the darkness, and yet the darkness did not overcomeᴮ it.

⁶ There was a man sent from God whose name was John.⁷ He came as a witness to testify about the light, so that all might believe through him.ᶜ ⁸ He was not the light, but he came to testify about the light. ⁹ The true light that gives light to everyone, was coming into the world.ᴰ

¹⁰ He was in the world, and the world was created through him, and yet the world did not recognize him. ¹¹ He came to his own, and his own people did not receive him. ¹² But to all who did receive him, he gave them the right to beᴱ children of God, to those who believe in his name, ¹³ who were born, not of natural descent,ᶠ or of the will of the flesh, or of the will of man,ᴳ but of God.

¹⁴ The Word became flesh and dweltᴴ among us. We observed his glory, the glory as the one and only Sonᴵ from the Father, full of grace and truth. ¹⁵ (John testified concerning him and exclaimed, "This was the one of whom I said, 'The one coming after me ranks ahead of me, because he existed before me.' ") ¹⁶ Indeed, we have all received grace uponᴶ grace from his fullness, ¹⁷ for the law was given through Moses; grace and truth came through Jesus Christ. ¹⁸ No one has ever seen God. The one and only Son, who is himself God andᴷ is at the Father's side—he has revealed him.

JOHN THE BAPTIST'S TESTIMONY

¹⁹ This was John's testimony when the Jews from Jerusalem sent priests and Levites to ask him, "Who are you?"

²⁰ He didn't deny it but confessed: "I am not the Messiah."

²¹ "What then?" they asked him. "Are you Elijah?"

"I am not," he said.

"Are you the Prophet?"

"No," he answered.

²² "Who are you, then?" they asked. "We need to give an answer to those who sent us. What can you tell us about yourself?"

²³ He said, "I am a **voice of one crying out in the wilderness: Make straight the way of the Lord**ᴸ—just as Isaiah the prophet said."

²⁴ Now they had been sent from the Pharisees. ²⁵ So they asked him, "Why then do you baptize if you aren't the Messiah, or Elijah, or the Prophet?"

²⁶ "I baptize withᴹ water," John answered them. "Someone stands among you, but you don't know him. ²⁷ He is the one coming after me,ᴺ whose sandal strap I'm not worthy to untie." ²⁸ All this happened in Bethanyᴼ across the Jordan, where John was baptizing.

THE LAMB OF GOD

²⁹ The next day John saw Jesus coming toward him and said, "Here is the Lamb of God, who takes away the sin of the world! ³⁰ This is the one I told you about: 'After me comes a man who ranks ahead of me, because he existed before me.' ³¹ I didn't know him, but I came baptizing with water so he might be revealed to Israel." ³² And John testified, "I saw the Spirit descending from heaven like a dove, and he rested on him. ³³ I didn't know him, but he who sent me to baptize with water told me, 'The one you see the Spirit descending and resting on—he is the one who baptizes with the Holy Spirit.' ³⁴ I have seen and testified that this is the Son of God."ᴾ

³⁵ The next day, John was standing with two of his disciples. ³⁶ When he saw Jesus passing by, he said, "Look, the Lamb of God!"

³⁷ The two disciples heard him say this and followed Jesus. ³⁸ When Jesus turned and noticed them following him, he asked them, "What are you looking for?"

They said to him, "Rabbi" (which means "Teacher"), "where are you staying?"

³⁹ "Come and you'll see," he replied. So they went and saw where he was staying, and they stayed with him that day. It was about four in the afternoon.ᴼ

⁴⁰ Andrew, Simon Peter's brother, was one of the two who heard John and followed him.

ᴬ **1:3-4** Other punctuation is possible: ... *not one thing was created. What was created in him was life* ᴮ **1:5** Or *grasp*, or *comprehend*, or *overtake* ; Jn 12:35 ᶜ **1:7** Or *it (the light)* ᴰ **1:9** Or *The true light who comes into the world gives light to everyone*, or *The true light enlightens everyone coming into the world.* ᴱ **1:12** Or *become* ᶠ **1:13** Lit *blood* ᴳ **1:13** Or *not of human lineage, or of human capacity, or of human volition* ᴴ **1:14** Or *and dwelt in a tent*; lit *and tabernacled* ᴵ **1:14** *Son* is implied from the reference to the Father and from Gk usage. ᴶ **1:16** Or *in place of* ᴷ **1:18** Other mss read *The one and only Son, who* ᴸ **1:23** Is 40:3 ᴹ **1:26** Or *in*, also in vv. 31,33 ᴺ **1:27** Other mss add *who came before me* ᴼ **1:28** Other mss read *in Bethabara* ᴾ **1:34** Other mss read *is the Chosen One of God* ᴼ **1:39** Lit *about the tenth hour*

[41] He first found his own brother Simon and told him, "We have found the Messiah"[A] (which is translated "the Christ"), [42] and he brought Simon to Jesus.

When Jesus saw him, he said, "You are Simon, son of John.[B] You will be called Cephas" (which is translated "Peter"[C]).

PHILIP AND NATHANAEL

[43] The next day Jesus[D] decided to leave for Galilee. He found Philip and told him, "Follow me."

[44] Now Philip was from Bethsaida, the hometown of Andrew and Peter. [45] Philip found Nathanael and told him, "We have found the one Moses wrote about in the law (and so did the prophets): Jesus the son of Joseph, from Nazareth."

[46] "Can anything good come out of Nazareth?" Nathanael asked him.

"Come and see," Philip answered.

[47] Then Jesus saw Nathanael coming toward him and said about him, "Here truly is an Israelite in whom there is no deceit."

[48] "How do you know me?" Nathanael asked.

"Before Philip called you, when you were under the fig tree, I saw you," Jesus answered.

[49] "Rabbi," Nathanael replied, "You are the Son of God; you are the King of Israel!"

[50] Jesus responded to him, "Do you believe because I told you I saw you under the fig tree? You will see greater things than this." [51] Then he said, "Truly I tell you, you will see heaven opened and the angels of God ascending and descending on the Son of Man."

THE FIRST SIGN: TURNING WATER INTO WINE

2 On the third day a wedding took place in Cana of Galilee. Jesus's mother was there, and [2] Jesus and his disciples were invited to the wedding as well. [3] When the wine ran out, Jesus's mother told him, "They don't have any wine."

[4] "What does that have to do with you and me,[E] woman?" Jesus asked. "My hour has not yet come."

[5] "Do whatever he tells you," his mother told the servants.

[6] Now six stone water jars had been set there for Jewish purification. Each contained twenty or thirty gallons.[F]

[7] "Fill the jars with water," Jesus told them. So they filled them to the brim. [8] Then he said to them, "Now draw some out and take it to the headwaiter."[G] And they did.

[9] When the headwaiter tasted the water (after it had become wine), he did not know where it came from — though the servants who had drawn the water knew. He called the groom [10] and told him, "Everyone sets out the fine wine first, then, after people are drunk, the inferior. But you have kept the fine wine until now."

[11] Jesus did this, the first of his signs, in Cana of Galilee. He revealed his glory, and his disciples believed in him.

[12] After this, he went down to Capernaum, together with his mother, his brothers, and his disciples, and they stayed there only a few days.

CLEANSING THE TEMPLE

[13] The Jewish Passover was near, and so Jesus went up to Jerusalem. [14] In the temple he found people selling oxen, sheep, and doves, and he also found the money changers sitting there. [15] After making a whip out of cords, he drove everyone out of the temple with their sheep and oxen. He also poured out the money changers' coins and overturned the tables. [16] He told those who were selling doves, "Get these things out of here! Stop turning my Father's house into a marketplace!"[H]

[17] And his disciples remembered that it is written: Zeal for your house will consume me.[I]

[18] So the Jews replied to him, "What sign will you show us for doing these things?"

[19] Jesus answered, "Destroy this temple,[J] and I will raise it up in three days."

[20] Therefore the Jews said, "This temple took forty-six years to build,[K] and will you raise it up in three days?"

[21] But he was speaking about the temple of his body. [22] So when he was raised from the dead, his disciples remembered that he had said this, and they believed the Scripture and the statement Jesus had made.

[23] While he was in Jerusalem during the Passover Festival, many believed in his name when they saw the signs he was doing. [24] Jesus, however, would not entrust himself to them, since he knew them all [25] and because he did not need anyone to testify about man; for he himself knew what was in man.

JESUS AND NICODEMUS

3 There was a man from the Pharisees named Nicodemus, a ruler of the Jews. [2] This man came to him at night and said, "Rabbi, we know that you are a teacher who has come from God, for no one could perform these signs you do unless God were with him."

[A] **1:41** Both Hb *Messiah* and Gk *Christos* mean "anointed one"   [B] **1:42** Other mss read *"Simon, son of Jonah*   [C] **1:42** Both Aramaic *Cephas* and Gk *Petros* mean "rock"   [D] **1:43** Lit *he*   [E] **2:4** Or *"You and I see things differently*; lit *"What to me and to you*; Mt 8:29; Mk 1:24; 5:7; Lk 8:28   [F] **2:6** Lit *two or three measures*   [G] **2:8** Lit *ruler of the table*   [H] **2:16** Lit *a house of business*   [I] **2:17** Ps 69:9   [J] **2:19** Or *sanctuary*, also in vv. 20,21   [K] **2:20** Or *was built forty-six years ago*

³ Jesus replied, "Truly I tell you, unless someone is born again,ᴬ he cannot see the kingdom of God."

⁴ "How can anyone be born when he is old?" Nicodemus asked him. "Can he enter his mother's womb a second time and be born?"

⁵ Jesus answered, "Truly I tell you, unless someone is born of water and the Spirit, he cannot enter the kingdom of God. ⁶ Whatever is born of the flesh is flesh, and whatever is born of the Spirit is spirit. ⁷ Do not be amazed that I told you that you must be born again. ⁸ The wind blows where it pleases, and you hear its sound, but you don't know where it comes from or where it is going. So it is with everyone born of the Spirit."

⁹ "How can these things be?" asked Nicodemus.

¹⁰ "Are you a teacherᴮ of Israel and don't know these things?" Jesus replied. ¹¹ "Truly I tell you, we speak what we know and we testify to what we have seen, but you do not accept our testimony. ¹² If I have told you about earthly things and you don't believe, how will you believe if I tell you about heavenly things? ¹³ No one has ascended into heaven except the one who descended from heaven — the Son of Man.ᶜ

¹⁴ "Just as Moses lifted up the snake in the wilderness, so the Son of Man must be lifted up, ¹⁵ so that everyone who believes in him mayᴰ have eternal life. ¹⁶ For God loved the world in this way:ᴱ He gaveᶠ his one and only Son, so that everyone who believes in him will not perish but have eternal life. ¹⁷ For God did not send his Son into the world to condemn the world, but to save the world through him. ¹⁸ Anyone who believes in him is not condemned, but anyone who does not believe is already condemned, because he has not believed in the name of the one and only Son of God. ¹⁹ This is the judgment: The light has come into the world, and people loved darkness rather than the light because their deeds were evil. ²⁰ For everyone who does evil hates the light and avoids it,ᴳ so that his deeds may not be exposed. ²¹ But anyone who lives byᴴ the truth comes to the light, so that his works may be shown to be accomplished by God."

JESUS AND JOHN THE BAPTIST

²² After this, Jesus and his disciples went to the Judean countryside, where he spent time with them and baptized.

²³ John also was baptizing in Aenon near Salim, because there was plenty of water there. People were coming and being baptized, ²⁴ since John had not yet been thrown into prison.

²⁵ Then a dispute arose between John's disciples and a Jewⁱ about purification. ²⁶ So they came to John and told him, "Rabbi, the one you testified about, and who was with you across the Jordan, is baptizing — and everyone is going to him."

²⁷ John responded, "No one can receive anything unless it has been given to him from heaven. ²⁸ You yourselves can testify that I said, 'I am not the Messiah, but I've been sent ahead of him.' ²⁹ He who has the bride is the groom. But the groom's friend, who stands by and listens for him, rejoices greatlyⱼ at the groom's voice. So this joy of mine is complete. ³⁰ He must increase, but I must decrease."

THE ONE FROM HEAVEN

³¹ The one who comes from above is above all. The one who is from the earth is earthly and speaks in earthly terms.ᴷ The one who comes from heaven is above all. ³² He testifies to what he has seen and heard, and yet no one accepts his testimony. ³³ The one who has accepted his testimony has affirmed that God is true. ³⁴ For the one whom God sent speaks God's words, since heᴸ gives the Spirit without measure. ³⁵ The Father loves the Son and has given all things into his hands. ³⁶ The one who believes in the Son has eternal life, but the one who rejects the Sonᴹ will not see life; instead, the wrath of God remains on him.

JESUS AND THE SAMARITAN WOMAN

4 When Jesusᴺ learned that the Pharisees had heard he was making and baptizing more disciples than John ² (though Jesus himself was not baptizing, but his disciples were), ³ he left Judea and went again to Galilee. ⁴ He had to travel through Samaria; ⁵ so he came to a town of Samaria called Sychar near the propertyᴼ that Jacob had given his son Joseph. ⁶ Jacob's well was there, and Jesus, worn out from his journey, sat down at the well. It was about noon.ᴾ

⁷ A woman of Samaria came to draw water.

"Give me a drink," Jesus said to her, ⁸ because his disciples had gone into town to buy food.

ᴬ3:3 Or from above, also in v. 7　ᴮ3:10 Or the teacher　ᶜ3:13 Other mss add who is in heaven　ᴰ3:15 Other mss add not perish, but　ᴱ3:16 Or this much　ᶠ3:16 Or For in this way God loved the world, and so he gave, or For God so loved the world that he gave　ᴳ3:20 Lit and does not come to the light　ᴴ3:21 Lit who does　ⁱ3:25 Other mss read and the Jews　ⱼ3:29 Lit with joy rejoices　ᴷ3:31 Or of earthly things　ᴸ3:34 Other mss read since God　ᴹ3:36 Or refuses to believe in the Son, or disobeys the Son　ᴺ4:1 Other mss read the Lord　ᴼ4:5 Lit piece of land　ᴾ4:6 Lit about the sixth hour

⁹ "How is it that you, a Jew, ask for a drink from me, a Samaritan woman?" she asked him. For Jews do not associate withᴬ Samaritans.ᴮ

¹⁰ Jesus answered, "If you knew the gift of God, and who is saying to you, 'Give me a drink,' you would ask him, and he would give you living water."

¹¹ "Sir," said the woman, "you don't even have a bucket, and the well is deep. So where do you get this 'living water'? ¹² You aren't greater than our father Jacob, are you? He gave us the well and drank from it himself, as did his sons and livestock."

¹³ Jesus said, "Everyone who drinks from this water will get thirsty again. ¹⁴ But whoever drinks from the water that I will give him will never get thirsty again. In fact, the water I will give him will become a wellᶜ of water springing up in him for eternal life."

¹⁵ "Sir," the woman said to him, "give me this water so that I won't get thirsty and come here to draw water."

¹⁶ "Go call your husband," he told her, "and come back here."

¹⁷ "I don't have a husband," she answered.

"You have correctly said, 'I don't have a husband,'" Jesus said. ¹⁸ "For you've had five husbands, and the man you now have is not your husband. What you have said is true."

¹⁹ "Sir," the woman replied, "I see that you are a prophet. ²⁰ Our fathers worshiped on this mountain, but you Jews say that the place to worship is in Jerusalem."

²¹ Jesus told her, "Believe me, woman, an hour is coming when you will worship the Father neither on this mountain nor in Jerusalem. ²² You Samaritans worship what you do not know. We worship what we do know, because salvation is from the Jews. ²³ But an hour is coming, and is now here, when the true worshipers will worship the Father in Spirit and in truth.ᴰ Yes, the Father wants such people to worship him. ²⁴ God is spirit, and those who worship him must worship in Spirit and in truth."

²⁵ The woman said to him, "I know that the Messiah is coming" (who is called Christ). "When he comes, he will explain everything to us."

²⁶ Jesus told her, "I, the one speaking to you, am he."

THE RIPENED HARVEST

²⁷ Just then his disciples arrived, and they were amazed that he was talking with a woman. Yet no one said, "What do you want?" or "Why are you talking with her?"

²⁸ Then the woman left her water jar, went into town, and told the people, ²⁹ "Come, see a man who told me everything I ever did. Could this be the Messiah?" ³⁰ They left the town and made their way to him.

³¹ In the meantime the disciples kept urging him, "Rabbi, eat something."

³² But he said, "I have food to eat that you don't know about."

³³ The disciples said to one another, "Could someone have brought him something to eat?"

³⁴ "My food is to do the will of him who sent me and to finish his work," Jesus told them. ³⁵ "Don't you say, 'There are still four more months, and then comes the harvest'? Listen to what I'm telling you: Openᴱ your eyes and look at the fields, because they are readyᶠ for harvest. ³⁶ The reaper is already receiving pay and gathering fruit for eternal life, so that the sower and reaper can rejoice together. ³⁷ For in this case the saying is true: 'One sows and another reaps.' ³⁸ I sent you to reap what you didn't labor for; others have labored, and you have benefited fromᴳ their labor."

THE SAVIOR OF THE WORLD

³⁹ Now many Samaritans from that town believed in him because of what the woman saidᴴ when she testified, "He told me everything I ever did." ⁴⁰ So when the Samaritans came to him, they asked him to stay with them, and he stayed there two days. ⁴¹ Many more believed because of what he said.ᴵ ⁴² And they told the woman, "We no longer believe because of what you said, since we have heard for ourselves and know that this really is the Savior of the world."ᴶ

A GALILEAN WELCOME

⁴³ After two days he left there for Galilee. ⁴⁴ (Jesus himself had testified that a prophet has no honor in his own country.) ⁴⁵ When they entered Galilee, the Galileans welcomed him because they had seen everything he did in Jerusalem during the festival. For they also had gone to the festival.

THE SECOND SIGN: HEALING AN OFFICIAL'S SON

⁴⁶ He went again to Cana of Galilee, where he had turned the water into wine. There was a certain royal official whose son was ill at Capernaum. ⁴⁷ When this man heard that Jesus had come from Judea into Galilee, he went to him and pleaded with him to come down and heal his son, since he was about to die.

ᴬ**4:9** Or *do not share vessels with*   ᴮ**4:9** Other mss omit *For Jews do not associate with Samaritans.*   ᶜ**4:14** Or *spring*
ᴰ**4:23** Or *in spirit and truth,* also in v. 24   ᴱ**4:35** Lit *Raise*   ᶠ**4:35** Lit *white*   ᴳ**4:38** Lit *you have entered into*
ᴴ**4:39** Lit *because of the woman's word*   ᴵ**4:41** Lit *because of his word*   ᴶ**4:42** Other mss add, *the Messiah*

[48] Jesus told him, "Unless you people see signs and wonders, you will not believe."

[49] "Sir," the official said to him, "come down before my boy dies."

[50] "Go," Jesus told him, "your son will live." The man believed what[A] Jesus said to him and departed.

[51] While he was still going down, his servants met him saying that his boy was alive. [52] He asked them at what time he got better. "Yesterday at one in the afternoon[B] the fever left him," they answered. [53] The father realized this was the very hour at which Jesus had told him, "Your son will live." So he himself believed, along with his whole household.

[54] Now this was also the second sign Jesus performed after he came from Judea to Galilee.

THE THIRD SIGN: HEALING THE SICK

5 After this, a Jewish festival took place, and Jesus went up to Jerusalem. [2] By the Sheep Gate in Jerusalem there is a pool, called Bethesda[C] in Aramaic, which has five colonnades. [3] Within these lay a large number of the disabled — blind, lame, and paralyzed.[D]

[5] One man was there who had been disabled for thirty-eight years. [6] When Jesus saw him lying there and realized he had already been there a long time, he said to him, "Do you want to get well?"

[7] "Sir," the disabled man answered, "I have no one to put me into the pool when the water is stirred up, but while I'm coming, someone goes down ahead of me."

[8] "Get up," Jesus told him, "pick up your mat and walk." [9] Instantly the man got well, picked up his mat, and started to walk.

Now that day was the Sabbath, [10] and so the Jews said to the man who had been healed, "This is the Sabbath. The law prohibits you from picking up your mat."

[11] He replied, "The man who made me well told me, 'Pick up your mat and walk.'"

[12] "Who is this man who told you, 'Pick up your mat and walk'?" they asked. [13] But the man who was healed did not know who it was, because Jesus had slipped away into the crowd that was there.[E]

[14] After this, Jesus found him in the temple and said to him, "See, you are well. Do not sin anymore, so that something worse doesn't happen to you." [15] The man went and reported to the Jews that it was Jesus who had made him well. [16] Therefore, the Jews began persecuting Jesus[F] because he was doing these things on the Sabbath.

HONORING THE FATHER AND THE SON

[17] Jesus responded to them, "My Father is still working, and I am working also." [18] This is why the Jews began trying all the more to kill him: Not only was he breaking the Sabbath, but he was even calling God his own Father, making himself equal to God.

[19] Jesus replied, "Truly I tell you, the Son is not able to do anything on his own, but only what he sees the Father doing. For whatever the Father[G] does, the Son likewise does these things. [20] For the Father loves the Son and shows him everything he is doing, and he will show him greater works than these so that you will be amazed. [21] And just as the Father raises the dead and gives them life, so the Son also gives life to whom he wants. [22] The Father, in fact, judges no one but has given all judgment to the Son, [23] so that all people may honor the Son just as they honor the Father. Anyone who does not honor the Son does not honor the Father who sent him.

LIFE AND JUDGMENT

[24] "Truly I tell you, anyone who hears my word and believes him who sent me has eternal life and will not come under judgment but has passed from death to life.

[25] "Truly I tell you, an hour is coming, and is now here, when the dead will hear the voice of the Son of God, and those who hear will live. [26] For just as the Father has life in himself, so also he has granted to the Son to have life in himself. [27] And he has granted him the right to pass judgment, because he is the Son of Man. [28] Do not be amazed at this, because a time is coming when all who are in the graves will hear his voice [29] and come out — those who have done good things, to the resurrection of life, but those who have done wicked things, to the resurrection of condemnation.

[30] "I can do nothing on my own. I judge only as I hear, and my judgment is just, because I do not seek my own will, but the will of him who sent me.

WITNESSES TO JESUS

[31] "If I testify about myself, my testimony is not true. [32] There is another who testifies about me,

---

[A] 4:50 Lit the word   [B] 4:52 Lit at the seventh hour   [C] 5:2 Some mss read Bethzatha; other mss read Bethsaida   [D] 5:3 Some mss include vv. 3b-4: — waiting for the moving of the water, [4]because an angel would go down into the pool from time to time and stir up the water. Then the first one who got in after the water was stirred up recovered from whatever ailment he had.   [E] 5:13 Lit slipped away, there being a crowd in that place   [F] 5:16 Other mss add and trying to kill him   [G] 5:19 Lit whatever that one

and I know that the testimony he gives about me is true. [33] You sent messengers to John, and he testified to the truth. [34] I don't receive human testimony, but I say these things so that you may be saved. [35] John[A] was a burning and shining lamp, and you were willing to rejoice for a while in his light.

[36] "But I have a greater testimony than John's because of the works that the Father has given me to accomplish. These very works I am doing testify about me that the Father has sent me. [37] The Father who sent me has himself testified about me. You have not heard his voice at any time, and you haven't seen his form. [38] You don't have his word residing in you, because you don't believe the one he sent. [39] You pore over the Scriptures because you think you have eternal life in them, and yet they testify about me. [40] But you are not willing to come to me so that you may have life.

[41] "I do not accept glory from people, [42] but I know you — that you have no love for God within you. [43] I have come in my Father's name, and yet you don't accept me. If someone else comes in his own name, you will accept him. [44] How can you believe, since you accept glory from one another but don't seek the glory that comes from the only God? [45] Do not think that I will accuse you to the Father. Your accuser is Moses, on whom you have set your hope. [46] For if you believed Moses, you would believe me, because he wrote about me. [47] But if you don't believe what he wrote, how will you believe my words?"

THE FOURTH SIGN: FEEDING OF THE FIVE THOUSAND

6 After this, Jesus crossed the Sea of Galilee (or Tiberias). [2] A huge crowd was following him because they saw the signs that he was performing by healing the sick. [3] Jesus went up a mountain and sat down there with his disciples.

[4] Now the Passover, a Jewish festival, was near. [5] So when Jesus looked up and noticed a huge crowd coming toward him, he asked Philip, "Where will we buy bread so that these people can eat?" [6] He asked this to test him, for he himself knew what he was going to do.

[7] Philip answered him, "Two hundred denarii[B] worth of bread wouldn't be enough for each of them to have a little."

[8] One of his disciples, Andrew, Simon Peter's brother, said to him, [9] "There's a boy here who has five barley loaves and two fish — but what are they for so many?"

[10] Jesus said, "Have the people sit down."

There was plenty of grass in that place; so they sat down. The men numbered about five thousand. [11] Then Jesus took the loaves, and after giving thanks he distributed them to those who were seated — so also with the fish, as much as they wanted.

[12] When they were full, he told his disciples, "Collect the leftovers so that nothing is wasted." [13] So they collected them and filled twelve baskets with the pieces from the five barley loaves that were left over by those who had eaten.

[14] When the people saw the sign[C] he had done, they said, "This truly is the Prophet who is to come into the world."

[15] Therefore, when Jesus realized that they were about to come and take him by force to make him king, he withdrew again to the mountain by himself.

THE FIFTH SIGN: WALKING ON WATER

[16] When evening came, his disciples went down to the sea, [17] got into a boat, and started across the sea to Capernaum. Darkness had already set in, but Jesus had not yet come to them. [18] A high wind arose, and the sea began to churn. [19] After they had rowed about three or four miles,[D] they saw Jesus walking on the sea. He was coming near the boat, and they were afraid. [20] But he said to them, "It is I.[E] Don't be afraid." [21] Then they were willing to take him on board, and at once the boat was at the shore where they were heading.

THE BREAD OF LIFE

[22] The next day, the crowd that had stayed on the other side of the sea saw there had been only one boat.[F] They also saw that Jesus had not boarded the boat with his disciples, but that his disciples had gone off alone. [23] Some boats from Tiberias came near the place where they had eaten the bread after the Lord had given thanks. [24] When the crowd saw that neither Jesus nor his disciples were there, they got into the boats and went to Capernaum looking for Jesus. [25] When they found him on the other side of the sea, they said to him, "Rabbi, when did you get here?"

[26] Jesus answered, "Truly I tell you, you are looking for me, not because you saw[G] the signs, but because you ate the loaves and were filled. [27] Don't work for the food that perishes but for the food that lasts for eternal life, which the Son of Man will give you, because God the Father has set his seal of approval on him."

[28] "What can we do to perform the works of God?" they asked.

[A] 5:35 Lit *That man*   [B] 6:7 A denarius = one day's wage   [C] 6:14 Other mss read *signs*   [D] 6:19 Lit *twenty-five or thirty stadia*; one *stadion* = 600 feet   [E] 6:20 Lit *"I am*   [F] 6:22 Other mss add *into which his disciples had entered*   [G] 6:26 Or *perceived*

²⁹ Jesus replied, "This is the work of God — that you believe in the one he has sent."

³⁰ "What sign, then, are you going to do so we may see and believe you?" they asked. "What are you going to perform? ³¹ Our ancestors ate the manna in the wilderness, just as it is written: **He gave them bread from heaven to eat.**"ᴬ

³² Jesus said to them, "Truly I tell you, Moses didn't give you the bread from heaven, but my Father gives you the true bread from heaven. ³³ For the bread of God is the one who comes down from heaven and gives life to the world."

³⁴ Then they said, "Sir, give us this bread always."

³⁵ "I am the bread of life," Jesus told them. "No one who comes to me will ever be hungry, and no one who believes in me will ever be thirsty again. ³⁶ But as I told you, you've seen me,ᴮ and yet you do not believe. ³⁷ Everyone the Father gives me will come to me, and the one who comes to me I will never cast out. ³⁸ For I have come down from heaven, not to do my own will, but the will of him who sent me. ³⁹ This is the will of him who sent me: that I should lose none of those he has given me but should raise them up on the last day. ⁴⁰ For this is the will of my Father: that everyone who sees the Son and believes in him will have eternal life, and I will raise him up on the last day."

⁴¹ Therefore the Jews started complaining about him because he said, "I am the bread that came down from heaven." ⁴² They were saying, "Isn't this Jesus the son of Joseph, whose father and mother we know? How can he now say, 'I have come down from heaven'?"

⁴³ Jesus answered them, "Stop complaining among yourselves. ⁴⁴ No one can come to me unless the Father who sent me drawsᶜ him, and I will raise him up on the last day. ⁴⁵ It is written in the Prophets: **And they will all be taught by God.**ᴰ Everyone who has listened to and learned from the Father comes to me — ⁴⁶ not that anyone has seen the Father except the one who is from God. He has seen the Father.

⁴⁷ "Truly I tell you, anyone who believesᴱ has eternal life. ⁴⁸ I am the bread of life. ⁴⁹ Your ancestors ate the manna in the wilderness, and they died. ⁵⁰ This is the bread that comes down from heaven so that anyone may eat of it and not die. ⁵¹ I am the living bread that came down from heaven. If anyone eats of this bread he will live forever. The bread that I will give for the life of the world is my flesh."

⁵² At that, the Jews argued among themselves, "How can this man give us his flesh to eat?"

⁵³ So Jesus said to them, "Truly I tell you, unless you eat the flesh of the Son of Man and drink his blood, you do not have life in yourselves. ⁵⁴ The one who eats my flesh and drinks my blood has eternal life, and I will raise him up on the last day, ⁵⁵ because my flesh is true food and my blood is true drink. ⁵⁶ The one who eats my flesh and drinks my blood remains in me, and I in him. ⁵⁷ Just as the living Father sent me and I live because of the Father, so the one who feeds on me will live because of me. ⁵⁸ This is the bread that came down from heaven; it is not like the mannaᶠ your ancestors ate — and they died. The one who eats this bread will live forever."

⁵⁹ He said these things while teaching in the synagogue in Capernaum.

MANY DISCIPLES DESERT JESUS

⁶⁰ Therefore, when many of his disciples heard this, they said, "This teaching is hard. Who can acceptᴳ it?"

⁶¹ Jesus, knowing in himself that his disciples were complaining about this, asked them, "Does this offend you? ⁶² Then what if you were to observe the Son of Man ascending to where he was before? ⁶³ The Spirit is the one who gives life. The flesh doesn't help at all. The words that I have spoken to you are spirit and are life. ⁶⁴ But there are some among you who don't believe." (For Jesus knew from the beginning those who did not ʰbelieve and the one who would betray him.) ⁶⁵ He said, "This is why I told you that no one can come to me unless it is granted to him by the Father."

⁶⁶ From that momentᴵ many of his disciples turned back and no longer accompanied him. ⁶⁷ So Jesus said to the Twelve, "You don't want to go away too, do you?"

⁶⁸ Simon Peter answered, "Lord, to whom will we go? You have the words of eternal life. ⁶⁹ We have come to believe and know that you are the Holy One of God."ᴶ

⁷⁰ Jesus replied to them, "Didn't I choose you, the Twelve? Yet one of you is a devil." ⁷¹ He was referring to Judas, Simon Iscariot's son,ᴷ one of the Twelve, because he was going to betray him.

THE UNBELIEF OF JESUS'S BROTHERS

7 After this, Jesus traveled in Galilee, since he did not want to travel in Judea because the Jews were trying to kill him. ² The Jewish Festival of Sheltersᴸ was near. ³ So his brothers said to him, "Leave here and go to Judea so your disciples can see your works that you

---

^6:31 Ex 16:4; Ps 78:24 ᴮ6:36 Other mss omit *me* ᶜ6:44 Or *brings*, or *leads* ᴰ6:45 Is 54:13 ᴱ6:47 Other mss add *in me* ᶠ6:58 Other mss omit *the manna* ᴳ6:60 Lit *hear* ʰ6:64 Other mss omit *not* ᴵ6:66 Or *Because of this* ᴶ6:69 Other mss read *you are the Messiah, the Son of the Living God* ᴷ6:71 Or *Judas Iscariot, Simon's son* ᴸ7:2 Or *Tabernacles*, or *Booths*

are doing. **4** For no one does anything in secret while he's seeking public recognition. If you do these things, show yourself to the world." **5** (For not even his brothers believed in him.)

6 Jesus told them, "My time has not yet arrived, but your time is always at hand. **7** The world cannot hate you, but it does hate me because I testify about it — that its works are evil. **8** Go up to the festival yourselves. I'm not going up to this festival,^A because my time has not yet fully come." **9** After he had said these things, he stayed in Galilee.

JESUS AT THE FESTIVAL OF SHELTERS

10 After his brothers had gone up to the festival, then he also went up, not openly but secretly. **11** The Jews were looking for him at the festival and saying, "Where is he?" **12** And there was a lot of murmuring about him among the crowds. Some were saying, "He's a good man." Others were saying, "No, on the contrary, he's deceiving the people." **13** Still, nobody was talking publicly about him for fear of the Jews.

14 When the festival was already half over, Jesus went up into the temple and began to teach. **15** Then the Jews were amazed and said, "How is this man so learned, since he hasn't been trained?"

16 Jesus answered them, "My teaching isn't mine but is from the one who sent me. **17** If anyone wants to do his will, he will know whether the teaching is from God or whether I am speaking on my own. **18** The one who speaks on his own seeks his own glory; but he who seeks the glory of the one who sent him is true, and there is no unrighteousness in him. **19** Didn't Moses give you the law? Yet none of you keeps the law. Why are you trying to kill me?"

20 "You have a demon!" the crowd responded. "Who is trying to kill you?"

21 "I performed one work, and you are all amazed," Jesus answered. **22** "This is why Moses has given you circumcision — not that it comes from Moses but from the fathers — and you circumcise a man on the Sabbath. **23** If a man receives circumcision on the Sabbath so that the law of Moses won't be broken, are you angry at me because I made a man entirely well on the Sabbath? **24** Stop judging according to outward appearances; rather judge according to righteous judgment."

THE IDENTITY OF THE MESSIAH

25 Some of the people of Jerusalem were saying, "Isn't this the man they are trying to kill?

26 Yet, look, he's speaking publicly and they're saying nothing to him. Can it be true that the authorities know he is the Messiah? **27** But we know where this man is from. When the Messiah comes, nobody will know where he is from."

28 As he was teaching in the temple, Jesus cried out, "You know me and you know where I am from. Yet I have not come on my own, but the one who sent me is true. You don't know him; **29** I know him because I am from him, and he sent me."

30 Then they tried to seize him. Yet no one laid a hand on him because his hour had not yet come. **31** However, many from the crowd believed in him and said, "When the Messiah comes, he won't perform more signs than this man has done, will he?" **32** The Pharisees heard the crowd murmuring these things about him, and so the chief priests and the Pharisees sent servants^B to arrest him.

33 Then Jesus said, "I am only with you for a short time. Then I'm going to the one who sent me. **34** You will look for me, but you will not find me; and where I am, you cannot come."

35 Then the Jews said to one another, "Where does he intend to go so we won't find him? He doesn't intend to go to the Jewish people dispersed^C among the Greeks and teach the Greeks, does he? **36** What is this remark he made: 'You will look for me, and you will not find me; and where I am, you cannot come'?"

THE PROMISE OF THE SPIRIT

37 On the last and most important day of the festival, Jesus stood up and cried out, "If anyone is thirsty, let him come to me^D and drink. **38** The one who believes in me, as the Scripture has said, will have streams of living water flow from deep within him." **39** He said this about the Spirit. Those who believed in Jesus were going to receive the Spirit, for the Spirit^E had not yet been given^F because Jesus had not yet been glorified.

THE PEOPLE ARE DIVIDED OVER JESUS

40 When some from the crowd heard these words, they said, "This truly is the Prophet." **41** Others said, "This is the Messiah." But some said, "Surely the Messiah doesn't come from Galilee, does he? **42** Doesn't the Scripture say that the Messiah comes from David's offspring^G and from the town of Bethlehem, where David lived?" **43** So the crowd was divided because of him. **44** Some of them wanted to seize him, but no one laid hands on him.

---

^A**7:8** Other mss add *yet* ^B**7:32** Or *temple police*, or *officers*, also in vv. 45,46 ^C**7:35** Gk *diaspora* ; Jewish people scattered throughout Gentile lands ^D**7:37** Other mss omit *to me* ^E**7:39** Other mss read *Holy Spirit* ^F**7:39** Lit *the Spirit was not yet* ^G**7:42** Lit *seed*

DEBATE OVER JESUS'S CLAIMS

⁴⁵ Then the servants came to the chief priests and Pharisees, who asked them, "Why didn't you bring him?"

⁴⁶ The servants answered, "No man ever spoke like this!"^A

⁴⁷ Then the Pharisees responded to them: "Are you fooled too? ⁴⁸ Have any of the rulers or Pharisees believed in him? ⁴⁹ But this crowd, which doesn't know the law, is accursed."

⁵⁰ Nicodemus — the one who came to him previously and who was one of them — said to them, ⁵¹ "Our law doesn't judge a man before it hears from him and knows what he's doing, does it?"

⁵² "You aren't from Galilee too, are you?" they replied. "Investigate and you will see that no prophet arises from Galilee."

[The earliest mss do not
include 7:53–8:11.]^B

8 [⁵³ Then each one went to his house.
¹ But Jesus went to the Mount of Olives.

AN ADULTERESS FORGIVEN

² At dawn he went to the temple again, and all the people were coming to him. He sat down and began to teach them.

³ Then the scribes and the Pharisees brought a woman caught in adultery, making her stand in the center. ⁴ "Teacher," they said to him, "this woman was caught in the act of committing adultery. ⁵ In the law Moses commanded us to stone such women. So what do you say?" ⁶ They asked this to trap him, in order that they might have evidence to accuse him.

Jesus stooped down and started writing on the ground with his finger. ⁷ When they persisted in questioning him, he stood up and said to them, "The one without sin among you should be the first to throw a stone at her." ⁸ Then he stooped down again and continued writing on the ground. ⁹ When they heard this, they left one by one, starting with the older men. Only he was left, with the woman in the center. ¹⁰ When Jesus stood up, he said to her, "Woman, where are they? Has no one condemned you?"

¹¹ "No one, Lord,"^C she answered.

"Neither do I condemn you," said Jesus. "Go, and from now on do not sin anymore."]

THE LIGHT OF THE WORLD

¹² Jesus spoke to them again: "I am the light of the world. Anyone who follows me will never walk in the darkness but will have the light of life."

¹³ So the Pharisees said to him, "You are testifying about yourself. Your testimony is not valid."

¹⁴ "Even if I testify about myself," Jesus replied, "My testimony is true, because I know where I came from and where I'm going. But you don't know where I come from or where I'm going. ¹⁵ You judge by human standards.^D I judge no one. ¹⁶ And if I do judge, my judgment is true, because it is not I alone who judge, but I and the Father who sent me. ¹⁷ Even in your law it is written that the testimony of two witnesses is true. ¹⁸ I am the one who testifies about myself, and the Father who sent me testifies about me."

¹⁹ Then they asked him, "Where is your Father?"

"You know neither me nor my Father," Jesus answered. "If you knew me, you would also know my Father." ²⁰ He spoke these words by the treasury, while teaching in the temple. But no one seized him, because his hour had not yet come.

JESUS PREDICTS HIS DEPARTURE

²¹ Then he said to them again, "I'm going away; you will look for me, and you will die in your sin. Where I'm going, you cannot come."

²² So the Jews said again, "He won't kill himself, will he, since he says, 'Where I'm going, you cannot come'?"

²³ "You are from below," he told them, "I am from above. You are of this world; I am not of this world. ²⁴ Therefore I told you that you will die in your sins. For if you do not believe that I am he, you will die in your sins."

²⁵ "Who are you?" they questioned.

"Exactly what I've been telling you from the very beginning," Jesus told them. ²⁶ "I have many things to say and to judge about you, but the one who sent me is true, and what I have heard from him — these things I tell the world."

²⁷ They did not know he was speaking to them about the Father. ²⁸ So Jesus said to them, "When you lift up the Son of Man, then you will know that I am he, and that I do nothing on my own. But just as the Father taught me, I say these things. ²⁹ The one who sent me is with me. He has not left me alone, because I always do what pleases him."

---

^A7:46 Other mss read *like this man*   ^B7:53–8:11 Other mss include all or some of the passage after Jn 7:36,44,52; 21:25; or Lk 21:38.   ^C8:11 Or *Sir*; Jn 4:15,49; 5:7; 6:34; 9:36   ^D8:15 Lit *You judge according to the flesh*

TRUTH AND FREEDOM

³⁰ As he was saying these things, many believed in him.

³¹ Then Jesus said to the Jews who had believed him, "If you continue in my word,ᴬ you really are my disciples. ³² You will know the truth, and the truth will set you free."

³³ "We are descendants ᴮ of Abraham," they answered him, "and we have never been enslaved to anyone. How can you say, 'You will become free'?"

³⁴ Jesus responded, "Truly I tell you, everyone who commits sin is a slave of sin. ³⁵ A slave does not remain in the household forever, but a son does remain forever. ³⁶ So if the Son sets you free, you really will be free. ³⁷ I know you are descendants of Abraham, but you are trying to kill me because my word has no place among you. ³⁸ I speak what I have seen in the presence of the Father;ᶜ so then, you do what you have heard from your father."

³⁹ "Our father is Abraham," they replied.

"If you were Abraham's children," Jesus told them, "you would do what Abraham did. ⁴⁰ But now you are trying to kill me, a man who has told you the truth that I heard from God. Abraham did not do this. ⁴¹ You're doing what your father does."

"We weren't born of sexual immorality," they said. "We have one Father — God."

⁴² Jesus said to them, "If God were your Father, you would love me, because I came from God and I am here. For I didn't come on my own, but he sent me. ⁴³ Why don't you understand what I say? Because you cannot listen toᴰ my word. ⁴⁴ You are of your father the devil, and you want to carry out your father's desires. He was a murderer from the beginning and does not stand in the truth, because there is no truth in him. When he tells a lie, he speaks from his own nature,ᴱ because he is a liar and the father of lies. ⁴⁵ Yet because I tell the truth, you do not believe me. ⁴⁶ Who among you can convict me of sin? If I am telling the truth, why don't you believe me? ⁴⁷ The one who is from God listens to God's words. This is why you don't listen, because you are not from God."

JESUS AND ABRAHAM

⁴⁸ The Jews responded to him, "Aren't we right in saying that you're a Samaritan and have a demon?"

⁴⁹ "I do not have a demon," Jesus answered. "On the contrary, I honor my Father and you dishonor me. ⁵⁰ I do not seek my own glory;

there is one who seeks it and judges. ⁵¹ Truly I tell you, if anyone keeps my word, he will never see death."

⁵² Then the Jews said, "Now we know you have a demon. Abraham died and so did the prophets. You say, 'If anyone keeps my word, he will never taste death.' ⁵³ Are you greater than our father Abraham who died? And the prophets died. Who do you claim to be?"

⁵⁴ "If I glorify myself," Jesus answered, "my glory is nothing. My Father — about whom you say, 'He is our God' — he is the one who glorifies me. ⁵⁵ You do not know him, but I know him. If I were to say I don't know him, I would be a liar like you. But I do know him, and I keep his word. ⁵⁶ Your father Abraham rejoiced to see my day; he saw it and was glad."

⁵⁷ The Jews replied, "You aren't fifty years old yet, and you've seen Abraham?"ᶠ

⁵⁸ Jesus said to them, "Truly I tell you, before Abraham was, I am."

⁵⁹ So they picked up stones to throw at him. But Jesus was hiddenᴳ and went out of the temple.ᴴ

THE SIXTH SIGN: HEALING A MAN BORN BLIND

9 As he was passing by, he saw a man blind from birth. ² His disciples asked him: "Rabbi, who sinned, this man or his parents, that he was born blind?"

³ "Neither this man nor his parents sinned," Jesus answered. "This came about so that God's works might be displayed in him. ⁴ Weᴵ must do the works of him who sent meᴶ while it is day. Night is coming when no one can work. ⁵ As long as I am in the world, I am the light of the world."

⁶ After he said these things he spit on the ground, made some mud from the saliva, and spread the mud on his eyes. ⁷ "Go," he told him, "wash in the pool of Siloam" (which means "Sent"). So he left, washed, and came back seeing.

⁸ His neighbors and those who had seen him before as a beggar said, "Isn't this the one who used to sit begging?" ⁹ Some said, "He's the one." Others were saying, "No, but he looks like him."

He kept saying, "I'm the one."

¹⁰ So they asked him, "Then how were your eyes opened?"

¹¹ He answered, "The man called Jesus made mud, spread it on my eyes, and told me, 'Go to Siloam and wash.' So when I went and washed I received my sight."

¹² "Where is he?" they asked.

"I don't know," he said.

ᴬ **8:31** Or *my teaching,* or *my message,* also in v. 37   ᴮ **8:33** Or *offspring ;* lit *seed,* also in v. 37; Jn 7:42   ᶜ **8:38** Other mss read *of my Father*   ᴰ **8:43** Or *cannot hear*   ᴱ **8:44** Lit *from his own things*   ᶠ **8:57** Other mss read *and Abraham has seen you?*   ᴳ **8:59** Or *Jesus hid himself*   ᴴ **8:59** Other mss add *and having gone through their midst, he passed by*   ᴵ **9:4** Other mss read *I*   ᴶ **9:4** Other mss read *us*

THE HEALED MAN'S TESTIMONY

¹³ They brought the man who used to be blind to the Pharisees. ¹⁴ The day that Jesus made the mud and opened his eyes was a Sabbath. ¹⁵ Then the Pharisees asked him again how he received his sight.

"He put mud on my eyes," he told them. "I washed and I can see."

¹⁶ Some of the Pharisees said, "This man is not from God, because he doesn't keep the Sabbath." But others were saying, "How can a sinful man perform such signs?" And there was a division among them.

¹⁷ Again they asked the blind man, "What do you say about him, since he opened your eyes?"

"He's a prophet," he said.

¹⁸ The Jews did not believe this about him — that he was blind and received sight — until they summoned the parents of the one who had received his sight. ¹⁹ They asked them, "Is this your son, the one you say was born blind? How then does he now see?"

²⁰ "We know this is our son and that he was born blind," his parents answered. ²¹ "But we don't know how he now sees, and we don't know who opened his eyes. Ask him; he's of age. He will speak for himself." ²² His parents said these things because they were afraid of the Jews, since the Jews had already agreed that if anyone confessed him as the Messiah, he would be banned from the synagogue. ²³ This is why his parents said, "He's of age; ask him."

²⁴ So a second time they summoned the man who had been blind and told him, "Give glory to God. We know that this man is a sinner."

²⁵ He answered, "Whether or not he's a sinner, I don't know. One thing I do know: I was blind, and now I can see!"

²⁶ Then they asked him, "What did he do to you? How did he open your eyes?"

²⁷ "I already told you," he said, "and you didn't listen. Why do you want to hear it again? You don't want to become his disciples too, do you?"

²⁸ They ridiculed him: "You're that man's disciple, but we're Moses's disciples. ²⁹ We know that God has spoken to Moses. But this man — we don't know where he's from."

³⁰ "This is an amazing thing!" the man told them. "You don't know where he is from, and yet he opened my eyes. ³¹ We know that God doesn't listen to sinners, but if anyone is God-fearing and does his will, he listens to him. ³² Throughout history[A] no one has ever heard of someone opening the eyes of a person born blind. ³³ If this man were not from God, he wouldn't be able to do anything."

³⁴ "You were born entirely in sin," they replied, "and are you trying to teach us?" Then they threw him out.

SPIRITUAL BLINDNESS

³⁵ Jesus heard that they had thrown the man out, and when he found him, he asked, "Do you believe in the Son of Man?"[B]

³⁶ "Who is he, Sir, that I may believe in him?" he asked.

³⁷ Jesus answered, "You have seen him; in fact, he is the one speaking with you."

³⁸ "I believe, Lord!" he said, and he worshiped him.

³⁹ Jesus said, "I came into this world for judgment, in order that those who do not see will see and those who do see will become blind."

⁴⁰ Some of the Pharisees who were with him heard these things and asked him, "We aren't blind too, are we?"

⁴¹ "If you were blind," Jesus told them, "you wouldn't have sin. But now that you say, 'We see,' your sin remains.

THE GOOD SHEPHERD

10 "Truly I tell you, anyone who doesn't enter the sheep pen by the gate but climbs in some other way is a thief and a robber. ² The one who enters by the gate is the shepherd of the sheep. ³ The gatekeeper opens it for him, and the sheep hear his voice. He calls his own sheep by name and leads them out. ⁴ When he has brought all his own outside, he goes ahead of them. The sheep follow him because they know his voice. ⁵ They will never follow a stranger; instead they will run away from him, because they don't know the voice of strangers." ⁶ Jesus gave them this figure of speech, but they did not understand what he was telling them.

⁷ Jesus said again, "Truly I tell you, I am the gate for the sheep. ⁸ All who came before me[C] are thieves and robbers, but the sheep didn't listen to them. ⁹ I am the gate. If anyone enters by me, he will be saved and will come in and go out and find pasture. ¹⁰ A thief comes only to steal and kill and destroy. I have come so that they may have life and have it in abundance.

¹¹ "I am the good shepherd. The good shepherd lays down his life for the sheep. ¹² The hired hand, since he is not the shepherd and doesn't own the sheep, leaves them[D] and runs away when he sees a wolf coming. The wolf then snatches and scatters them. ¹³ This happens because he is a hired hand and doesn't care about the sheep.

¹⁴ "I am the good shepherd. I know my own, and my own know me, ¹⁵ just as the Father

---

[A] 9:32 Lit *From the age*　[B] 9:35 Other mss read *the Son of God*　[C] 10:8 Other mss omit *before me*　[D] 10:12 Lit *leaves the sheep*

knows me, and I know the Father. I lay down my life for the sheep. **16** But I have other sheep that are not from this sheep pen; I must bring them also, and they will listen to my voice. Then there will be one flock, one shepherd. **17** This is why the Father loves me, because I lay down my life so that I may take it up again. **18** No one takes it from me, but I lay it down on my own. I have the right to lay it down, and I have the right to take it up again. I have received this command from my Father."

19 Again the Jews were divided because of these words. **20** Many of them were saying, "He has a demon and he's crazy. Why do you listen to him?" **21** Others were saying, "These aren't the words of someone who is demon-possessed. Can a demon open the eyes of the blind?"

JESUS AT THE FESTIVAL OF DEDICATION

22 Then the Festival of Dedication took place in Jerusalem, and it was winter. **23** Jesus was walking in the temple in Solomon's Colonnade. **24** The Jews surrounded him and asked, "How long are you going to keep us in suspense?^A If you are the Messiah, tell us plainly."^B

25 "I did tell you and you don't believe," Jesus answered them. "The works that I do in my Father's name testify about me. **26** But you don't believe because you are not of my sheep.^C **27** My sheep hear my voice, I know them, and they follow me. **28** I give them eternal life, and they will never perish. No one will snatch them out of my hand. **29** My Father, who has given them to me, is greater than all. No one is able to snatch them out of the Father's hand. **30** I and the Father are one."

RENEWED EFFORTS TO STONE JESUS

31 Again the Jews picked up rocks to stone him. **32** Jesus replied, "I have shown you many good works from the Father. For which of these works are you stoning me?"

33 "We aren't stoning you for a good work," the Jews answered, "but for blasphemy, because you — being a man — make yourself God."

34 Jesus answered them, "Isn't it written in your law,^D I said, you are gods?^E **35** If he called those whom the word of God came to 'gods' — and the Scripture cannot be broken — **36** do you say, 'You are blaspheming' to the one the Father set apart and sent into the world, because I said: I am the Son of God? **37** If I am not doing my Father's works, don't believe me. **38** But if I am doing them and you don't believe me, believe the works. This way

you will know and understand^F that the Father is in me and I in the Father." **39** Then they were trying again to seize him, but he eluded their grasp.

MANY BEYOND THE JORDAN BELIEVE IN JESUS

40 So he departed again across the Jordan to the place where John had been baptizing earlier, and he remained there. **41** Many came to him and said, "John never did a sign, but everything John said about this man was true." **42** And many believed in him there.

LAZARUS DIES AT BETHANY

11 Now a man was sick, Lazarus from Bethany, the village of Mary and her sister Martha. **2** Mary was the one who anointed the Lord with perfume and wiped his feet with her hair, and it was her brother Lazarus who was sick. **3** So the sisters sent a message to him: "Lord, the one you love is sick."

4 When Jesus heard it, he said, "This sickness will not end in death but is for the glory of God, so that the Son of God may be glorified through it." **5** Now Jesus loved Martha, her sister, and Lazarus. **6** So when he heard that he was sick, he stayed two more days in the place where he was. **7** Then after that, he said to the disciples, "Let's go to Judea again."

8 "Rabbi," the disciples told him, "just now the Jews tried to stone you, and you're going there again?"

9 "Aren't there twelve hours in a day?" Jesus answered. "If anyone walks during the day, he doesn't stumble, because he sees the light of this world. **10** But if anyone walks during the night, he does stumble, because the light is not in him."

11 He said this, and then he told them, "Our friend Lazarus has fallen asleep, but I'm on my way to wake him up."

12 Then the disciples said to him, "Lord, if he has fallen asleep, he will get well."

13 Jesus, however, was speaking about his death, but they thought he was speaking about natural sleep. **14** So Jesus then told them plainly, "Lazarus has died. **15** I'm glad for you that I wasn't there so that you may believe. But let's go to him."

16 Then Thomas (called "Twin")^G said to his fellow disciples, "Let's go too so that we may die with him."

THE RESURRECTION AND THE LIFE

17 When Jesus arrived, he found that Lazarus had already been in the tomb four days.

---

^A **10:24** Lit *"How long are you taking away our life?* ^B **10:24** Or *openly*, or *publicly* ^C **10:26** Other mss add *just as I told you* ^D **10:34** Other mss read *in the scripture* ^E **10:34** Ps 82:6 ^F **10:38** Other mss read *know and believe* ^G **11:16** Gk *Didymus*

¹⁸ Bethany was near Jerusalem (less than two miles^ away). ¹⁹ Many of the Jews had come to Martha and Mary to comfort them about their brother.

²⁰ As soon as Martha heard that Jesus was coming, she went to meet him, but Mary remained seated in the house. ²¹ Then Martha said to Jesus, "Lord, if you had been here, my brother wouldn't have died. ²² Yet even now I know that whatever you ask from God, God will give you."

²³ "Your brother will rise again," Jesus told her. ²⁴ Martha said to him, "I know that he will rise again in the resurrection at the last day."

²⁵ Jesus said to her, "I am the resurrection and the life. The one who believes in me, even if he dies, will live. ²⁶ Everyone who lives and believes in me will never die. Do you believe this?"

²⁷ "Yes, Lord," she told him, "I believe you are the Messiah, the Son of God, who comes into the world."

JESUS SHARES THE SORROW OF DEATH

²⁸ Having said this, she went back and called her sister Mary, saying in private, "The Teacher is here and is calling for you."

²⁹ As soon as Mary heard this, she got up quickly and went to him. ³⁰ Jesus had not yet come into the village but was still in the place where Martha had met him. ³¹ The Jews who were with her in the house consoling her saw that Mary got up quickly and went out. They followed her, supposing that she was going to the tomb to cry there.

³² As soon as Mary came to where Jesus was and saw him, she fell at his feet and told him, "Lord, if you had been here, my brother would not have died!"

³³ When Jesus saw her crying, and the Jews who had come with her crying, he was deeply moved^B in his spirit and troubled. ³⁴ "Where have you put him?" he asked.

"Lord," they told him, "come and see."

³⁵ Jesus wept.

³⁶ So the Jews said, "See how he loved him!" ³⁷ But some of them said, "Couldn't he who opened the blind man's eyes also have kept this man from dying?"

THE SEVENTH SIGN: RAISING LAZARUS FROM THE DEAD

³⁸ Then Jesus, deeply moved again, came to the tomb. It was a cave, and a stone was lying against it. ³⁹ "Remove the stone," Jesus said.

Martha, the dead man's sister, told him, "Lord, there is already a stench because he has been dead four days."

⁴⁰ Jesus said to her, "Didn't I tell you that if you believed you would see the glory of God?"

⁴¹ So they removed the stone. Then Jesus raised his eyes and said, "Father, I thank you that you heard me. ⁴² I know that you always hear me, but because of the crowd standing here I said this, so that they may believe you sent me." ⁴³ After he said this, he shouted with a loud voice, "Lazarus, come out!" ⁴⁴ The dead man came out bound hand and foot with linen strips and with his face wrapped in a cloth. Jesus said to them, "Unwrap him and let him go."

THE PLOT TO KILL JESUS

⁴⁵ Therefore, many of the Jews who came to Mary and saw what he did believed in him. ⁴⁶ But some of them went to the Pharisees and told them what Jesus had done.

⁴⁷ So the chief priests and the Pharisees convened the Sanhedrin and were saying, "What are we going to do since this man is doing many signs? ⁴⁸ If we let him go on like this, everyone will believe in him, and the Romans will come and take away both our place and our nation."

⁴⁹ One of them, Caiaphas, who was high priest that year, said to them, "You know nothing at all! ⁵⁰ You're not considering that it is to your^C advantage that one man should die for the people rather than the whole nation perish." ⁵¹ He did not say this on his own, but being high priest that year he prophesied that Jesus was going to die for the nation, ⁵² and not for the nation only, but also to unite the scattered children of God. ⁵³ So from that day on they plotted to kill him.

⁵⁴ Jesus therefore no longer walked openly among the Jews but departed from there to the countryside near the wilderness, to a town called Ephraim, and he stayed there with the disciples.

⁵⁵ Now the Jewish Passover was near, and many went up to Jerusalem from the country to purify themselves before the Passover. ⁵⁶ They were looking for Jesus and asking one another as they stood in the temple: "What do you think? He won't come to the festival, will he?" ⁵⁷ The chief priests and the Pharisees had given orders that if anyone knew where he was, he should report it so that they could arrest him.

THE ANOINTING AT BETHANY

12 Six days before the Passover, Jesus came to Bethany where Lazarus^D was, the one Jesus had raised from the dead. ² So they gave a dinner for him there; Martha was serving

---

^A **11:18** Lit *fifteen stadia* ; one *stadion* = 600 feet   ^B **11:33** Or *angry*, also in v. 38   ^C **11:50** Other mss read *to our*   ^D **12:1** Other mss read *Lazarus who died*

them, and Lazarus was one of those reclining at the table with him. ³ Then Mary took a pound of perfume, pure and expensive nard, anointed Jesus's feet, and wiped his feet with her hair. So the house was filled with the fragrance of the perfume.

⁴ Then one of his disciples, Judas Iscariot (who was about to betray him), said, ⁵ "Why wasn't this perfume sold for three hundred denarii^ and given to the poor?" ⁶ He didn't say this because he cared about the poor but because he was a thief. He was in charge of the money-bag and would steal part of what was put in it.

⁷ Jesus answered, "Leave her alone; she has kept it for the day of my burial. ⁸ For you always have the poor with you, but you do not always have me."

THE DECISION TO KILL LAZARUS

⁹ Then a large crowd of the Jews learned he was there. They came not only because of Jesus but also to see Lazarus, the one he had raised from the dead. ¹⁰ But the chief priests that decided to kill Lazarus also, ¹¹ because he was the reason many of the Jews were deserting them⁸ and believing in Jesus.

THE TRIUMPHAL ENTRY

¹² The next day, when the large crowd that had come to the festival heard that Jesus was coming to Jerusalem, ¹³ they took palm branches and went out to meet him. They kept shouting:

"*Hosanna!*

Blessed is he who comes in the name
of the Lord^c — the King of Israel!"

¹⁴ Jesus found a young donkey and sat on it, just as it is written:

¹⁵ **Do not be afraid,**
Daughter Zion. Look, your King
is coming,
sitting on a donkey's colt.^D

¹⁶ His disciples did not understand these things at first. However, when Jesus was glorified, then they remembered that these things had been written about him and that they had done these things to him.

¹⁷ Meanwhile, the crowd, which had been with him when he called Lazarus out of the tomb and raised him from the dead, continued to testify.^E ¹⁸ This is also why the crowd met him, because they heard he had done this sign. ¹⁹ Then the Pharisees said to one another, "You see? You've accomplished nothing. Look, the world has gone after him!"

JESUS PREDICTS HIS CRUCIFIXION

²⁰ Now some Greeks were among those who went up to worship at the festival. ²¹ So they came to Philip, who was from Bethsaida in Galilee, and requested of him, "Sir, we want to see Jesus." ²² Philip went and told Andrew; then Andrew and Philip went and told Jesus.

²³ Jesus replied to them, "The hour has come for the Son of Man to be glorified. ²⁴ Truly I tell you, unless a grain of wheat falls to the ground and dies, it remains by itself. But if it dies, it produces much fruit. ²⁵ The one who loves his life will lose it, and the one who hates his life in this world will keep it for eternal life. ²⁶ If anyone serves me, he must follow me. Where I am, there my servant also will be. If anyone serves me, the Father will honor him.

²⁷ "Now my soul is troubled. What should I say — Father, save me from this hour? But that is why I came to this hour. ²⁸ Father, glorify your name."^F

Then a voice came from heaven: "I have glorified it, and I will glorify it again."

²⁹ The crowd standing there heard it and said it was thunder. Others said, "An angel has spoken to him."

³⁰ Jesus responded, "This voice came, not for me, but for you. ³¹ Now is the judgment of this world. Now the ruler of this world will be cast out. ³² As for me, if I am lifted up^G from the earth I will draw all people to myself." ³³ He said this to indicate what kind of death he was about to die.

³⁴ Then the crowd replied to him, "We have heard from the law that the Messiah will remain forever. So how can you say, 'The Son of Man must be lifted up'? Who is this Son of Man?"

³⁵ Jesus answered, "The light will be with you only a little longer. Walk while you have the light so that darkness doesn't overtake you. The one who walks in darkness doesn't know where he's going. ³⁶ While you have the light, believe in the light so that you may become children of light." Jesus said this, then went away and hid from them.

ISAIAH'S PROPHECIES FULFILLED

³⁷ Even though he had performed so many signs in their presence, they did not believe in him. ³⁸ This was to fulfill the word of Isaiah the prophet, who said:^H

Lord, who has believed our message?
And to whom has the arm of the Lord
been revealed?^I

---

^**12:5** A denarius = one day's wage   ^**12:11** Lit *going away*   ^**12:13** Ps 118:25-26   ^**12:15** Zch 9:9   ^**12:17** Other mss read *Meanwhile the crowd, which had been with him, continued to testify that he had called Lazarus out of the tomb and raised him from the dead.*   ^**12:28** Other mss read *your Son*   ^**12:32** Or *exalted*, also in v. 34   ^**12:38** Lit *which he said*   ^**12:38** Is 53:1

[39] This is why they were unable to believe, because Isaiah also said:

[40] He has blinded their eyes
and hardened their hearts,
so that they would not see
with their eyes
or understand with their hearts,
and turn,
and I would heal them.[A]

[41] Isaiah said these things because[B] he saw his glory and spoke about him.

[42] Nevertheless, many did believe in him even among the rulers, but because of the Pharisees they did not confess him, so that they would not be banned from the synagogue. [43] For they loved human praise more than praise from God.

A SUMMARY OF JESUS'S MISSION

[44] Jesus cried out, "The one who believes in me believes not in me, but in him who sent me. [45] And the one who sees me sees him who sent me. [46] I have come as light into the world, so that everyone who believes in me would not remain in darkness. [47] If anyone hears my words and doesn't keep them, I do not judge him; for I did not come to judge the world but to save the world. [48] The one who rejects me and doesn't receive my sayings has this as his judge:[C] The word I have spoken will judge him on the last day. [49] For I have not spoken on my own, but the Father himself who sent me has given me a command to say everything I have said. [50] I know that his command is eternal life. So the things that I speak, I speak just as the Father has told me."

JESUS WASHES HIS DISCIPLES' FEET

13 Before the Passover Festival, Jesus knew that his hour had come to depart from this world to the Father. Having loved his own who were in the world, he loved them to the end.

[2] Now when it was time for supper, the devil had already put it into the heart of Judas, Simon Iscariot's son,[D] to betray him. [3] Jesus knew that the Father had given everything into his hands, that he had come from God, and that he was going back to God. [4] So he got up from supper, laid aside his outer clothing, took a towel, and tied it around himself. [5] Next, he poured water into a basin and began to wash his disciples' feet and to dry them with the towel tied around him.

[6] He came to Simon Peter, who asked him, "Lord, are you going to wash my feet?"

[7] Jesus answered him, "What I'm doing you don't realize now, but afterward you will understand."

[8] "You will never wash my feet," Peter said.

Jesus replied, "If I don't wash you, you have no part with me."

[9] Simon Peter said to him, "Lord, not only my feet, but also my hands and my head."

[10] "One who has bathed," Jesus told him, "doesn't need to wash anything except his feet, but he is completely clean. You are clean, but not all of you." [11] For he knew who would betray him. This is why he said, "Not all of you are clean."

THE MEANING OF FOOT WASHING

[12] When Jesus had washed their feet and put on his outer clothing, he reclined again and said to them, "Do you know what I have done for you? [13] You call me Teacher and Lord — and you are speaking rightly, since that is what I am. [14] So if I, your Lord and Teacher, have washed your feet, you also ought to wash one another's feet. [15] For I have given you an example, that you also should do just as I have done for you.

[16] "Truly I tell you, a servant is not greater than his master,[E] and a messenger is not greater than the one who sent him. [17] If you know these things, you are blessed if you do them.

[18] "I'm not speaking about all of you; I know those I have chosen. But the Scripture must be fulfilled: **The one who eats my bread[F] has raised his heel against me.**[G] [19] I am telling you now before it happens, so that when it does happen you will believe that I am he. [20] Truly I tell you, whoever receives anyone I send receives me, and the one who receives me receives him who sent me."

JUDAS'S BETRAYAL PREDICTED

[21] When Jesus had said this, he was troubled in his spirit and testified, "Truly I tell you, one of you will betray me."

[22] The disciples started looking at one another — uncertain which one he was speaking about. [23] One of his disciples, the one Jesus loved, was reclining close beside Jesus.[H] [24] Simon Peter motioned to him to find out who it was he was talking about. [25] So he leaned back against Jesus and asked him, "Lord, who is it?"

[26] Jesus replied, "He's the one I give the piece of bread to after I have dipped it." When he had dipped the bread, he gave it to Judas, Simon Iscariot's son.[D] [27] After Judas ate the piece of bread, Satan entered him. So Jesus told him, "What you're doing, do quickly."

[A] **12:40** Is 6:10　[B] **12:41** Other mss read *when*　[C] **12:48** Lit *has the one judging him*　[D] **13:2,26** Or *Judas Iscariot, Simon's son*　[E] **13:16** Or *lord*　[F] **13:18** Other mss read *eats bread with me*　[G] **13:18** Ps 41:9　[H] **13:23** Lit *reclining at Jesus's breast*; that is, on his right; Jn 1:18

28 None of those reclining at the table knew why he said this to him. 29 Since Judas kept the money-bag, some thought that Jesus was telling him, "Buy what we need for the festival," or that he should give something to the poor. 30 After receiving the piece of bread, he immediately left. And it was night.

THE NEW COMMAND

31 When he had left, Jesus said, "Now the Son of Man is glorified, and God is glorified in him. 32 If God is glorified in him,^A God will also glorify him in himself and will glorify him at once. 33 Children, I am with you a little while longer. You will look for me, and just as I told the Jews, so now I tell you: 'Where I am going, you cannot come.'

34 "I give you a new command: Love one another. Just as I have loved you, you are also to love one another. 35 By this everyone will know that you are my disciples, if you love one another."

PETER'S DENIALS PREDICTED

36 "Lord," Simon Peter said to him, "where are you going?"

Jesus answered, "Where I am going you cannot follow me now, but you will follow later."

37 "Lord," Peter asked, "why can't I follow you now? I will lay down my life for you."

38 Jesus replied, "Will you lay down your life for me? Truly I tell you, a rooster will not crow until you have denied me three times.

THE WAY TO THE FATHER

14 "Don't let your heart be troubled. Believe^B in God; believe also in me. 2 In my Father's house are many rooms; if not, I would have told you. I am going away to prepare a place for you. 3 If I go away and prepare a place for you, I will come again and take you to myself, so that where I am you may be also. 4 You know the way to where I am going."^C

5 "Lord," Thomas said, "we don't know where you're going. How can we know the way?"

6 Jesus told him, "I am the way, the truth, and the life. No one comes to the Father except through me. 7 If you know me, you will also know^D my Father. From now on you do know him and have seen him."

JESUS REVEALS THE FATHER

8 "Lord," said Philip, "show us the Father, and that's enough for us."

9 Jesus said to him, "Have I been among you all this time and you do not know me, Philip? The one who has seen me has seen the Father. How can you say, 'Show us the Father'? 10 Don't you believe that I am in the Father and the Father is in me? The words I speak to you I do not speak on my own. The Father who lives in me does his works. 11 Believe me that I am in the Father and the Father is in me. Otherwise, believe^E because of the works themselves.

PRAYING IN JESUS'S NAME

12 "Truly I tell you, the one who believes in me will also do the works that I do. And he will do even greater works than these, because I am going to the Father. 13 Whatever you ask in my name, I will do it so that the Father may be glorified in the Son. 14 If you ask me^F anything in my name, I will do it.^G

ANOTHER COUNSELOR PROMISED

15 "If you love me, you will keep^H my commands. 16 And I will ask the Father, and he will give you another Counselor^I to be with you forever. 17 He is the Spirit of truth. The world is unable to receive him because it doesn't see him or know him. But you do know him, because he remains with you and will be^J in you.

THE FATHER, THE SON, AND THE HOLY SPIRIT

18 "I will not leave you as orphans; I am coming to you. 19 In a little while the world will no longer see me, but you will see me. Because I live, you will live too. 20 On that day you will know that I am in my Father, you are in me, and I am in you. 21 The one who has my commands and keeps them is the one who loves me. And the one who loves me will be loved by my Father. I also will love him and will reveal myself to him."

22 Judas (not Iscariot) said to him, "Lord, how is it you're going to reveal yourself to us and not to the world?"

23 Jesus answered, "If anyone loves me, he will keep my word. My Father will love him, and we will come to him and make our home with him. 24 The one who doesn't love me will not keep my words. The word that you hear is not mine but is from the Father who sent me.

25 "I have spoken these things to you while I remain with you. 26 But the Counselor, the Holy Spirit, whom the Father will send in my name, will teach you all things and remind you of everything I have told you.

---

^A 13:32 Other mss omit *If God is glorified in him*   ^B 14:1 Or *You believe*   ^C 14:4 Other mss read this verse: *And you know where I am going, and you know the way*   ^D 14:7 Other mss read *If you had known me, you would have known*   ^E 14:11 Other mss read *believe me*   ^F 14:14 Other mss omit *me*   ^G 14:14 Other mss omit all of v. 14   ^H 14:15 Other mss read *"If you love me, keep* (as a command)   ^I 14:16 Or *advocate*, or *comforter*, also in v. 26   ^J 14:17 Other mss read *and is*

JESUS'S GIFT OF PEACE

²⁷ "Peace I leave with you. My peace I give to you. I do not give to you as the world gives. Don't let your heart be troubled or fearful. ²⁸ You have heard me tell you, 'I am going away and I am coming to you.' If you loved me, you would rejoice that I am going to the Father, because the Father is greater than I. ²⁹ I have told you now before it happens so that when it does happen you may believe. ³⁰ I will not talk with you much longer, because the ruler of the world is coming. He has no power over me.^ᴬ ³¹ On the contrary, so that the world may know that I love the Father, I do as the Father commanded me.

"Get up; let's leave this place.

THE VINE AND THE BRANCHES

15 "I am the true vine, and my Father is the gardener. ² Every branch in me that does not produce fruit he removes, and he prunes every branch that produces fruit so that it will produce more fruit. ³ You are already clean because of the word I have spoken to you. ⁴ Remain in me, and I in you. Just as a branch is unable to produce fruit by itself unless it remains on the vine, neither can you unless you remain in me. ⁵ I am the vine; you are the branches. The one who remains in me and I in him produces much fruit, because you can do nothing without me. ⁶ If anyone does not remain in me, he is thrown aside like a branch and he withers. They gather them, throw them into the fire, and they are burned. ⁷ If you remain in me and my words remain in you, ask whatever you want and it will be done for you. ⁸ My Father is glorified by this: that you produce much fruit and prove to be⁸ my disciples.

CHRISTLIKE LOVE

⁹ "As the Father has loved me, I have also loved you. Remain in my love. ¹⁰ If you keep my commands you will remain in my love, just as I have kept my Father's commands and remain in his love.

¹¹ "I have told you these things so that my joy may be in you and your joy may be complete.

¹² "This is my command: Love one another as I have loved you. ¹³ No one has greater love than this: to lay down his life for his friends. ¹⁴ You are my friends if you do what I command you. ¹⁵ I do not call you servants anymore, because a servant doesn't know what his master⁰ is doing. I have called you friends, because I have made known to you everything I have heard from my Father. ¹⁶ You did not choose me, but

I chose you. I appointed you to go and produce fruit and that your fruit should remain, so that whatever you ask the Father in my name, he will give you.

¹⁷ "This is what I command you: Love one another.

PERSECUTIONS PREDICTED

¹⁸ "If the world hates you, understand that it hated me before it hated you. ¹⁹ If you were of the world, the world would love you as its own. However, because you are not of the world, but I have chosen you out of it, the world hates you. ²⁰ Remember the word I spoke to you: 'A servant is not greater than his master.' If they persecuted me, they will also persecute you. If they kept my word, they will also keep yours. ²¹ But they will do all these things to you on account of my name, because they don't know the one who sent me. ²² If I had not come and spoken to them, they would not be guilty of sin. Now they have no excuse for their sin. ²³ The one who hates me also hates my Father. ²⁴ If I had not done the works among them that no one else has done, they would not have sin. Now they have seen and hated both me and my Father. ²⁵ But this happened so that the statement written in their law might be fulfilled: **They hated me for no reason.**ᴰ

THE COUNSELOR'S MINISTRY

²⁶ "When the Counselor comes, the one I will send to you from the Father — the Spirit of truth who proceeds from the Father — he will testify about me. ²⁷ You also will testify, because you have been with me from the beginning.

16 "I have told you these things to keep you from stumbling. ² They will ban you from the synagogues. In fact, a time is coming when anyone who kills you will think he is offering service to God. ³ They will do these things because they haven't known the Father or me. ⁴ But I have told you these things so that when their timeᴱ comes you will remember I told them to you. I didn't tell you these things from the beginning, because I was with you. ⁵ But now I am going away to him who sent me, and not one of you asks me, 'Where are you going?' ⁶ Yet, because I have spoken these things to you, sorrow has filled your heart. ⁷ Nevertheless, I am telling you the truth. It is for your benefit that I go away, because if I don't go away the Counselor will not come to you. If I go, I will send him to you. ⁸ When he comes, he will convict the world about sin, righteousness, and judgment: ⁹ About sin, because they do not believe in me; ¹⁰ about righteousness, because I

---

am going to the Father and you will no longer see me; [11] and about judgment, because the ruler of this world has been judged.

[12] "I still have many things to tell you, but you can't bear them now. [13] When the Spirit of truth comes, he will guide you into all the truth. For he will not speak on his own, but he will speak whatever he hears. He will also declare to you what is to come. [14] He will glorify me, because he will take from what is mine and declare it to you. [15] Everything the Father has is mine. This is why I told you that he takes from what is mine and will declare it to you.

SORROW TURNED TO JOY

[16] "A little while and you will no longer see me; again a little while and you will see me."[A]

[17] Then some of his disciples said to one another, "What is this he's telling us: 'A little while and you will not see me; again a little while and you will see me' and, 'because I am going to the Father'? " [18] They said, "What is this he is saying,[B] 'A little while'? We don't know what he's talking about."

[19] Jesus knew they wanted to ask him, and so he said to them, "Are you asking one another about what I said, 'A little while and you will not see me; again a little while and you will see me'? [20] Truly I tell you, you will weep and mourn, but the world will rejoice. You will become sorrowful, but your sorrow will turn to joy. [21] When a woman is in labor, she has pain because her time has come. But when she has given birth to a child, she no longer remembers the suffering because of the joy that a person has been born into the world. [22] So you also have sorrow[C] now. But I will see you again. Your hearts will rejoice, and no one will take away your joy from you.

[23] "In that day you will not ask me anything. Truly I tell you, anything you ask the Father in my name, he will give you. [24] Until now you have asked for nothing in my name. Ask and you will receive, so that your joy may be complete.

JESUS THE VICTOR

[25] "I have spoken these things to you in figures of speech. A time is coming when I will no longer speak to you in figures, but I will tell you plainly about the Father. [26] On that day you will ask in my name, and I am not telling you that I will ask the Father on your behalf. [27] For the Father himself loves you, because you have loved me and have believed that I came from God.[D] [28] I came from the Father and have come

into the world. Again, I am leaving the world and going to the Father."

[29] His disciples said, "Look, now you're speaking plainly and not using any figurative language. [30] Now we know that you know everything and don't need anyone to question you. By this we believe that you came from God."

[31] Jesus responded to them, "Do you now believe? [32] Indeed, an hour is coming, and has come, when each of you will be scattered to his own home, and you will leave me alone. Yet I am not alone, because the Father is with me. [33] I have told you these things so that in me you may have peace. You will have suffering in this world. Be courageous! I have conquered the world."

JESUS PRAYS FOR HIMSELF

17 Jesus spoke these things, looked up to heaven, and said: "Father, the hour has come. Glorify your Son so that the Son may glorify you, [2] since you gave him authority over all flesh,[E] so that he may give eternal life to everyone you have given him. [3] This is eternal life: that they may know you, the only true God, and the one you have sent — Jesus Christ. [4] I have glorified you on the earth by completing the work you gave me to do. [5] Now, Father, glorify me in your presence with that glory I had with you before the world existed.

JESUS PRAYS FOR HIS DISCIPLES

[6] "I have revealed your name to the people you gave me from the world. They were yours, you gave them to me, and they have kept your word. [7] Now they know that everything you have given is from you, [8] because I have given them the words you gave me. They have received them and have known for certain that I came from you. They have believed that you sent me.

[9] "I pray[F] for them. I am not praying for the world but for those you have given me, because they are yours. [10] Everything I have is yours, and everything you have is mine, and I am glorified in them. [11] I am no longer in the world, but they are in the world, and I am coming to you. Holy Father, protect[G] them by your name that you have given me, so that they may be one as we are one. [12] While I was with them, I was protecting them by your name that you have given me. I guarded them and not one of them is lost, except the son of destruction,[H] so that the Scripture may be fulfilled. [13] Now I am

---

^[16:16] Other mss add *because I am going to the Father*   ^[16:18] Other mss omit *he is saying*   ^[16:22] Other mss read *will have sorrow*   ^[16:27] Other mss read *from the Father*   ^[17:2] Or *people*   ^[17:9] Lit *ask* (throughout this passage)   ^[17:11] Lit *keep* (throughout this passage)   ^[17:12] The one destined for destruction, loss, or perdition

coming to you, and I speak these things in the world so that they may have my joy completed in them. **14** I have given them your word. The world hated them because they are not of the world, just as I am not of the world. **15** I am not praying that you take them out of the world but that you protect them from the evil one. **16** They are not of the world, just as I am not of the world. **17** Sanctify them by the truth; your word is truth. **18** As you sent me into the world, I also have sent them into the world. **19** I sanctify myself for them, so that they also may be sanctified by the truth.

JESUS PRAYS FOR ALL BELIEVERS

20 "I pray not only for these, but also for those who believe in me through their word. **21** May they all be one, as you, Father, are in me and I am in you. May they also be^ in us, so that the world may believe you sent me. **22** I have given them the glory you have given me, so that they may be one as we are one. **23** I am in them and you are in me, so that they may be made completely one, that the world may know you have sent me and have loved them as you have loved me.

24 "Father, I want those you have given me to be with me where I am, so that they will see my glory, which you have given me because you loved me before the world's foundation. **25** Righteous Father, the world has not known you. However, I have known you, and they have known that you sent me. **26** I made your name known to them and will continue to make it known, so that the love you have loved me with may be in them and I may be in them."

JESUS BETRAYED

18 After Jesus had said these things, he went out with his disciples across the Kidron Valley, where there was a garden, and he and his disciples went into it. **2** Judas, who betrayed him, also knew the place, because Jesus often met there with his disciples. **3** So Judas took a company of soldiers and some officials° from the chief priests and the Pharisees and came there with lanterns, torches, and weapons.

4 Then Jesus, knowing everything that was about to happen to him, went out and said to them, "Who is it that you're seeking?"

5 "Jesus of Nazareth," they answered.

"I am he,"ᶜ Jesus told them.

Judas, who betrayed him, was also standing with them. **6** When Jesus told them, "I am he," they stepped back and fell to the ground.

7 Then he asked them again, "Who is it that you're seeking?"

"Jesus of Nazareth," they said.

8 "I told you I am he," Jesus replied. "So if you're looking for me, let these men go." **9** This was to fulfill the words he had said: "I have not lost one of those you have given me."

10 Then Simon Peter, who had a sword, drew it, struck the high priest's servant, and cut off his right ear. (The servant's name was Malchus.) **11** At that, Jesus said to Peter, "Put your sword away! Am I not to drink the cup the Father has given me?"

JESUS ARRESTED AND TAKEN TO ANNAS

12 Then the company of soldiers, the commander, and the Jewish officials arrested Jesus and tied him up. **13** First they led him to Annas, since he was the father-in-law of Caiaphas, who was high priest that year. **14** Caiaphas was the one who had advised the Jews that it would be better for one man to die for the people.

PETER DENIES JESUS

15 Simon Peter was following Jesus, as was another disciple. That disciple was an acquaintance of the high priest; so he went with Jesus into the high priest's courtyard. **16** But Peter remained standing outside by the door. So the other disciple, the one known to the high priest, went out and spoke to the girl who was the doorkeeper and brought Peter in.

17 Then the servant girl who was the doorkeeper said to Peter, "You aren't one of this man's disciples too, are you?"

"I am not." he said. **18** Now the servants and the officials had made a charcoal fire, because it was cold. They were standing there warming themselves, and Peter was standing with them, warming himself.

JESUS BEFORE ANNAS

19 The high priest questioned Jesus about his disciples and about his teaching.

20 "I have spoken openly to the world," Jesus answered him. "I have always taught in the synagogue and in the temple, where all the Jews congregate, and I haven't spoken anything in secret. **21** Why do you question me? Question those who heard what I told them. Look, they know what I said."

22 When he had said these things, one of the officials standing by slapped Jesus, saying, "Is this the way you answer the high priest?"

23 "If I have spoken wrongly," Jesus answered him, "give evidence° about the wrong; but if

---

^**17:21** Other mss add *one*   °**18:3** Or *temple police*, or *officers*, also in vv. 12,18,22   ᶜ**18:5** Lit *I am* ; see note at Jn 8:58.   °**18:23** Or *him, "testify*

rightly, why do you hit me?" **24** Then Annas sent him bound to Caiaphas the high priest.

PETER DENIES JESUS TWICE MORE

25 Now Simon Peter was standing and warming himself. They said to him, "You aren't one of his disciples too, are you?"

He denied it and said, "I am not."

26 One of the high priest's servants, a relative of the man whose ear Peter had cut off, said, "Didn't I see you with him in the garden?" **27** Peter denied it again. Immediately a rooster crowed.

JESUS BEFORE PILATE

28 Then they led Jesus from Caiaphas to the governor's headquarters. It was early morning. They did not enter the headquarters themselves; otherwise they would be defiled and unable to eat the Passover.

29 So Pilate came out to them and said, "What charge do you bring against this man?"

30 They answered him, "If this man weren't a criminal,[A] we wouldn't have handed him over to you."

31 Pilate told them, "You take him and judge him according to your law."

"It's not legal for us to put anyone to death," the Jews declared. **32** They said this so that Jesus's words might be fulfilled indicating what kind of death he was going to die.

33 Then Pilate went back into the headquarters, summoned Jesus, and said to him, "Are you the King of the Jews?"

34 Jesus answered, "Are you asking this on your own, or have others told you about me?"

35 "I'm not a Jew, am I?" Pilate replied. "Your own nation and the chief priests handed you over to me. What have you done?"

36 "My kingdom is not of this world," said Jesus. "If my kingdom were of this world, my servants would fight, so that I wouldn't be handed over to the Jews. But as it is,[B] my kingdom is not from here."

37 "You are a king then?" Pilate asked.

"You say that I'm a king," Jesus replied. "I was born for this, and I have come into the world for this: to testify to the truth. Everyone who is of the truth listens to my voice."

38 "What is truth?" said Pilate.

JESUS OR BARABBAS

After he had said this, he went out to the Jews again and told them, "I find no grounds for charging him. **39** You have a custom that I release one prisoner to you at the Passover. So,

do you want me to release to you the King of the Jews?"

40 They shouted back, "Not this man, but Barabbas!" Now Barabbas was a revolutionary.[C]

JESUS FLOGGED AND MOCKED

19 Then Pilate took Jesus and had him flogged. **2** The soldiers also twisted together a crown of thorns, put it on his head, and clothed him in a purple robe. **3** And they kept coming up to him and saying, "Hail, King of the Jews!" and were slapping his face.

4 Pilate went outside again and said to them, "Look, I'm bringing him out to you to let you know I find no grounds for charging him." **5** Then Jesus came out wearing the crown of thorns and the purple robe. Pilate said to them, "Here is the man!"

PILATE SENTENCES JESUS TO DEATH

6 When the chief priests and the temple servants[D] saw him, they shouted, "Crucify! Crucify!"

Pilate responded, "Take him and crucify him yourselves, since I find no grounds for charging him."

7 "We have a law," the Jews replied to him, "and according to that law he ought to die, because he made himself the Son of God."

8 When Pilate heard this statement, he was more afraid than ever. **9** He went back into the headquarters and asked Jesus, "Where are you from?" But Jesus did not give him an answer. **10** So Pilate said to him, "Do you refuse to speak to me? Don't you know that I have the authority to release you and the authority to crucify you?"

11 "You would have no authority over me at all," Jesus answered him, "if it hadn't been given you from above. This is why the one who handed me over to you has the greater sin."

12 From that moment Pilate kept trying[E] to release him. But the Jews shouted, "If you release this man, you are not Caesar's friend. Anyone who makes himself a king opposes Caesar!"

13 When Pilate heard these words, he brought Jesus outside. He sat down on the judge's seat in a place called the Stone Pavement (but in Aramaic,[F] *Gabbatha*). **14** It was the preparation day for the Passover, and it was about noon.[G] Then he told the Jews, "Here is your king!"

15 They shouted, "Take him away! Take him away! Crucify him!"

Pilate said to them, "Should I crucify your king?"

"We have no king but Caesar!" the chief priests answered.

16 Then he handed him over to be crucified.

[A]**18:30** Lit *an evil doer*   [B]**18:36** Or *But now*   [C]**18:40** Or *robber*; see Jn 10:1,8 for the same Gk word used here   [D]**19:6** Or *temple police*, or *officers*   [E]**19:12** Lit *Pilate was trying*   [F]**19:13** Or *Hebrew*, also in vv. 17,20   [G]**19:14** Lit *about the sixth hour*

THE CRUCIFIXION

Then they took Jesus away.^ ¹⁷Carrying the cross by himself, he went out to what is called Place of the Skull, which in Aramaic is called *Golgotha*. ¹⁸There they crucified him and two others with him, one on either side, with Jesus in the middle. ¹⁹Pilate also had a sign made and put on the cross. It said: JESUS OF NAZARETH, THE KING OF THE JEWS. ²⁰Many of the Jews read this sign, because the place where Jesus was crucified was near the city, and it was written in Aramaic, Latin, and Greek. ²¹So the chief priests of the Jews said to Pilate, "Don't write, 'The King of the Jews,' but that he said, 'I am the King of the Jews.'"

²²Pilate replied, "What I have written, I have written."

²³When the soldiers crucified Jesus, they took his clothes and divided them into four parts, a part for each soldier. They also took the tunic, which was seamless, woven in one piece from the top. ²⁴So they said to one another, "Let's not tear it, but cast lots for it, to see who gets it." This happened that the Scripture might be fulfilled that says: **They divided my clothes among themselves, and they cast lots for my clothing.**⁸ This is what the soldiers did.

JESUS'S PROVISION FOR HIS MOTHER

²⁵Standing by the cross of Jesus were his mother, his mother's sister, Mary the wife of Clopas, and Mary Magdalene. ²⁶When Jesus saw his mother and the disciple he loved standing there, he said to his mother, "Woman, here is your son." ²⁷Then he said to the disciple, "Here is your mother." And from that hour the disciple took her into his home.

THE FINISHED WORK OF JESUS

²⁸After this, when Jesus knew that everything was now finished that the Scripture might be fulfilled, he said, "I'm thirsty." ²⁹A jar full of sour wine was sitting there; so they fixed a sponge full of sour wine on a hyssop branch and held it up to his mouth. ³⁰When Jesus had received the sour wine, he said, "It is finished." Then bowing his head, he gave up his spirit.

JESUS'S SIDE PIERCED

³¹Since it was the preparation day, the Jews did not want the bodies to remain on the cross on the Sabbath (for that Sabbath was a special^ day). They requested that Pilate have the men's legs broken and that their bodies be taken away. ³²So the soldiers came and broke the legs of the first

man and of the other one who had been crucified with him. ³³When they came to Jesus, they did not break his legs since they saw that he was already dead. ³⁴But one of the soldiers pierced his side with a spear, and at once blood and water came out. ³⁵He who saw this has testified so that you also may believe. His testimony is true, and he knows he is telling the truth. ³⁶For these things happened so that the Scripture would be fulfilled: **Not one of his bones will be broken.**^ ³⁷Also, another Scripture says: **They will look at the one they pierced.**^

JESUS'S BURIAL

³⁸After this, Joseph of Arimathea, who was a disciple of Jesus — but secretly because of his fear of the Jews — asked Pilate that he might remove Jesus's body. Pilate gave him permission; so he came and took his body away. ³⁹Nicodemus (who had previously come to him at night) also came, bringing a mixture of about seventy-five pounds^ of myrrh and aloes. ⁴⁰They took Jesus's body and wrapped it in linen cloths with the fragrant spices, according to the burial custom of the Jews. ⁴¹There was a garden in the place where he was crucified. A new tomb was in the garden; no one had yet been placed in it. ⁴²They placed Jesus there because of the Jewish day of preparation and since the tomb was nearby.

THE EMPTY TOMB

20 On the first day of the week Mary Magdalene came to the tomb early, while it was still dark. She saw that the stone had been removed from the tomb. ²So she went running to Simon Peter and to the other disciple, the one Jesus loved, and said to them, "They've taken the Lord out of the tomb, and we don't know where they've put him!"

³At that, Peter and the other disciple went out, heading for the tomb. ⁴The two were running together, but the other disciple outran Peter and got to the tomb first. ⁵Stooping down, he saw the linen cloths lying there, but he did not go in. ⁶Then, following him, Simon Peter also came. He entered the tomb and saw the linen cloths lying there. ⁷The wrapping that had been on his head was not lying with the linen cloths but was folded up in a separate place by itself. ⁸The other disciple, who had reached the tomb first, then also went in, saw, and believed. ⁹For they did not yet understand the Scripture that he must rise from the dead. ¹⁰Then the disciples returned to the place where they were staying.

^19:16 Other mss add *and led him out* ⁸19:24 Ps 22:18 ᶜ19:31 Lit *great* ᴰ19:36 Ex 12:46; Nm 9:12; Ps 34:20 ᴱ19:37 Zch 12:10 ᶠ19:39 Lit *a hundred litrai*; a Roman *litrai* = 12 ounces

MARY MAGDALENE SEES THE RISEN LORD

[11] But Mary stood outside the tomb, crying. As she was crying, she stooped to look into the tomb. [12] She saw two angels in white sitting where Jesus's body had been lying, one at the head and the other at the feet. [13] They said to her, "Woman, why are you crying?"

"Because they've taken away my Lord," she told them, "and I don't know where they've put him."

[14] Having said this, she turned around and saw Jesus standing there, but she did not know it was Jesus. [15] "Woman," Jesus said to her, "why are you crying? Who is it that you're seeking?"

Supposing he was the gardener, she replied, "Sir, if you've carried him away, tell me where you've put him, and I will take him away."

[16] Jesus said to her, "Mary."

Turning around, she said to him in Aramaic,[A] "Rabboni!" — which means "Teacher."

[17] "Don't cling to me," Jesus told her, "since I have not yet ascended to the Father. But go to my brothers and tell them that I am ascending to my Father and your Father, to my God and your God."

[18] Mary Magdalene went and announced to the disciples, "I have seen the Lord!" And she told them what[B] he had said to her.

THE DISCIPLES COMMISSIONED

[19] When it was evening of that first day of the week, the disciples were gathered together with the doors locked because they feared the Jews. Jesus came, stood among them, and said to them, "Peace be with you."

[20] Having said this, he showed them his hands and his side. So the disciples rejoiced when they saw the Lord.

[21] Jesus said to them again, "Peace to you. As the Father has sent me, I also send you." [22] After saying this, he breathed on them and said,[C] "Receive the Holy Spirit. [23] If you forgive the sins of any, they are forgiven them; if you retain the sins of any, they are retained."

THOMAS SEES AND BELIEVES

[24] But Thomas (called "Twin"[D]), one of the Twelve, was not with them when Jesus came. [25] So the other disciples were telling him, "We've seen the Lord!"

But he said to them, "If I don't see the mark of the nails in his hands, put my finger into the mark of the nails, and put my hand into his side, I will never believe."

[26] A week later his disciples were indoors again, and Thomas was with them. Even though the doors were locked, Jesus came and stood among them and said, "Peace be with you."

[27] Then he said to Thomas, "Put your finger here and look at my hands. Reach out your hand and put it into my side. Don't be faithless, but believe."

[28] Thomas responded to him, "My Lord and my God!"

[29] Jesus said, "Because you have seen me, you have believed.[E] Blessed are those who have not seen and yet believe."

THE PURPOSE OF THIS GOSPEL

[30] Jesus performed many other signs in the presence of his disciples that are not written in this book. [31] But these are written so that you may believe that Jesus is the Messiah, the Son of God,[F] and that by believing you may have life in his name.

JESUS'S THIRD APPEARANCE TO THE DISCIPLES

21 After this, Jesus revealed himself again to his disciples by the Sea of Tiberias. He revealed himself in this way: [2] Simon Peter, Thomas (called "Twin"[D]), Nathanael from Cana of Galilee, Zebedee's sons, and two others of his disciples were together. [3] "I'm going fishing," Simon Peter said to them.

"We're coming with you," they told him. They went out and got into the boat, but that night they caught nothing.

[4] When daybreak came, Jesus stood on the shore, but the disciples did not know it was Jesus. [5] "Friends,"[G] Jesus called to them, "you don't have any fish, do you?"

"No," they answered.

[6] "Cast the net on the right side of the boat," he told them, "and you'll find some." So they did,[H] and they were unable to haul it in because of the large number of fish. [7] The disciple, the one Jesus loved, said to Peter, "It is the Lord!"

When Simon Peter heard that it was the Lord, he tied his outer clothing around him (for he had taken it off) and plunged into the sea. [8] Since they were not far from land (about a hundred yards[I] away), the other disciples came in the boat, dragging the net full of fish.

[9] When they got out on land, they saw a charcoal fire there, with fish lying on it, and bread. [10] "Bring some of the fish you've just caught," Jesus told them. [11] So Simon Peter climbed up and hauled the net ashore, full of large fish — 153 of them. Even though there were so many, the net was not torn.

[A] 20:16 Or Hebrew   [B] 20:18 Lit these things   [C] 20:22 Lit he breathed and said to them   [D] 20:24; 21:2 Gk Didymus   [E] 20:29 Or have you believed?   [F] 20:31 Or that the Messiah, the Son of God, is Jesus   [G] 21:5 Lit "Children"   [H] 21:6 Lit they cast   [I] 21:8 Lit about two hundred cubits

¹² "Come and have breakfast," Jesus told them. None of the disciples dared ask him, "Who are you?" because they knew it was the Lord. ¹³ Jesus came, took the bread, and gave it to them. He did the same with the fish. ¹⁴ This was now the third time Jesus appeared[A] to the disciples after he was raised from the dead.

JESUS'S THREEFOLD RESTORATION OF PETER

¹⁵ When they had eaten breakfast, Jesus asked Simon Peter, "Simon, son of John,[B] do you love me more than these?"

"Yes, Lord," he said to him, "you know that I love you."

"Feed my lambs," he told him. ¹⁶ A second time he asked him, "Simon, son of John, do you love me?"

"Yes, Lord," he said to him, "you know that I love you."

"Shepherd my sheep," he told him.

¹⁷ He asked him the third time, "Simon, son of John, do you love me?"

Peter was grieved that he asked him the third time, "Do you love me?" He said, "Lord, you know everything; you know that I love you."

"Feed my sheep," Jesus said. ¹⁸ "Truly I tell you, when you were younger, you would tie your belt and walk wherever you wanted. But when you grow old, you will stretch out your hands and someone else will tie you and carry you where you don't want to go." ¹⁹ He said this to indicate by what kind of death Peter would glorify God. After saying this, he told him, "Follow me."

CORRECTING A FALSE REPORT

²⁰ So Peter turned around and saw the disciple Jesus loved following them, the one who had leaned back against Jesus at the supper and asked, "Lord, who is the one that's going to betray you?" ²¹ When Peter saw him, he said to Jesus, "Lord, what about him?"

²² "If I want him to remain until I come," Jesus answered, "what is that to you? As for you, follow me."

²³ So this rumor[C] spread to the brothers and sisters that this disciple would not die. Yet Jesus did not tell him that he would not die, but, "If I want him to remain until I come, what is that to you?"

EPILOGUE

²⁴ This is the disciple who testifies to these things and who wrote them down. We know that his testimony is true.

²⁵ And there are also many other things that Jesus did, which, if every one of them were written down, I suppose not even the world itself could contain the books[D] that would be written.

[A]21:14 Lit *was revealed* (v. 1) [B]21:15-17 Other mss read *"Simon, son of Jonah*; Mt 16:17; Jn 1:42 [C]21:23 Lit *this word*
[D]21:25 Lit *scroll*

ACTS

PROLOGUE

1 I wrote the first narrative, Theophilus, about all that Jesus began to do and teach ² until the day he was taken up, after he had given instructions through the Holy Spirit to the apostles he had chosen. ³ After he had suffered, he also presented himself alive to them by many convincing proofs, appearing to them over a period of forty days and speaking about the kingdom of God.

THE HOLY SPIRIT PROMISED

⁴ While he was^ with them, he commanded them not to leave Jerusalem, but to wait for the Father's promise. "Which," he said, "you have heard me speak about; ⁵ for John baptized with water, but you will be baptized with the Holy Spirit in a few days."

⁶ So when they had come together, they asked him, "Lord, are you restoring the kingdom to Israel at this time?"

⁷ He said to them, "It is not for you to know times or periods that the Father has set by his own authority. ⁸ But you will receive power when the Holy Spirit has come on you, and you will be my witnesses in Jerusalem, in all Judea and Samaria, and to the end of the earth."

THE ASCENSION

⁹ After he had said this, he was taken up as they were watching, and a cloud took him out of their sight. ¹⁰ While he was going, they were gazing into heaven, and suddenly two men in white clothes stood by them. ¹¹ They said, "Men of Galilee, why do you stand looking up into heaven? This same Jesus, who has been taken from you into heaven, will come in the same way that you have seen him going into heaven."

UNITED IN PRAYER

¹² Then they returned to Jerusalem from the Mount of Olives, which is near Jerusalem — a Sabbath day's journey away. ¹³ When they arrived, they went to the room upstairs where they were staying: Peter, John, James, Andrew, Philip, Thomas, Bartholomew, Matthew, James the son of Alphaeus, Simon the Zealot, and Judas the son of James. ¹⁴ They all were continually united in prayer,^ along with the women, including Mary the mother of Jesus, and his brothers.

MATTHIAS CHOSEN

¹⁵ In those days Peter stood up among the brothers and sisters^ — the number of people who were together was about a hundred and twenty — and said: ¹⁶ "Brothers and sisters, it was necessary that the Scripture be fulfilled that the Holy Spirit through the mouth of David foretold about Judas, who became a guide to those who arrested Jesus. ¹⁷ For he was one of our number and shared in this ministry." ¹⁸ Now this man acquired a field with his unrighteous wages. He fell headfirst, his body burst open and his intestines spilled out. ¹⁹ This became known to all the residents of Jerusalem, so that in their own language that field is called *Hakeldama* (that is, Field of Blood). ²⁰ "For it is written in the Book of Psalms:

Let his dwelling become desolate;
let no one live in it;^ and
Let someone else take his position.^

²¹ "Therefore, from among the men who have accompanied us during the whole time the Lord Jesus went in and out among us — ²² beginning from the baptism of John until the day he was taken up from us — from among these, it is necessary that one become a witness with us of his resurrection."

²³ So they proposed two: Joseph, called Barsabbas, who was also known as Justus, and Matthias. ²⁴ Then they prayed, "You, Lord, know everyone's hearts; show which of these two you have chosen ²⁵ to take the place^ in this apostolic ministry that Judas left to go where he belongs." ²⁶ Then they cast lots for them, and the lot fell to Matthias and he was added to the eleven apostles.

PENTECOST

2 When the day of Pentecost had arrived, they were all together in one place. ² Suddenly a sound like that of a violent rushing wind came from heaven, and it filled the whole house where they were staying. ³ They saw tongues like flames of fire that separated and rested on each one of them. ⁴ Then they were all filled with the Holy Spirit and began to speak in different tongues,^ as the Spirit enabled them.

⁵ Now there were Jews staying in Jerusalem, devout people from every nation under heaven. ⁶ When this sound occurred, a crowd came together and was confused because each one heard them speaking in his own language.

---

^1:4 Or *he was eating*, or *he was lodging*   ^1:14 Other mss add *and petition*   ^1:15 Other mss read *disciples*   ^1:20 Ps 69:25
^1:20 Ps 109:8   ^1:25 Other mss read *to share*   ^2:4 languages, also in v. 11

[7] They were astounded and amazed, saying,[A] "Look, aren't all these who are speaking Galileans? [8] How is it that each of us can hear them in our own native language? [9] Parthians, Medes, Elamites; those who live in Mesopotamia, in Judea and Cappadocia, Pontus and Asia, [10] Phrygia and Pamphylia, Egypt and the parts of Libya near Cyrene; visitors from Rome (both Jews and converts), [11] Cretans and Arabs — we hear them declaring the magnificent acts of God in our own tongues." [12] They were all astounded and perplexed, saying to one another, "What does this mean? " [13] But some sneered and said, "They're drunk on new wine."

PETER'S SERMON

[14] Peter stood up with the Eleven, raised his voice, and proclaimed to them: "Fellow Jews and all you residents of Jerusalem, let me explain this to you and pay attention to my words. [15] For these people are not drunk, as you suppose, since it's only nine in the morning.[B] [16] On the contrary, this is what was spoken through the prophet Joel:

[17] And it will be in the last days, says God,
      that I will pour out my Spirit
        on all people;
      then your sons and your daughters
        will prophesy,
      your young men will see visions,
      and your old men will dream dreams.
[18] I will even pour out my Spirit
      on my servants in those days, both men
        and women
      and they will prophesy.
[19] I will display wonders
        in the heaven above
      and signs on the earth below:
      blood and fire and a cloud of smoke.
[20] The sun will be turned to darkness
      and the moon to blood
      before the great and glorious day of
        the Lord comes.
[21] Then everyone who calls
      on the name of the Lord will be saved.[C]

[22] "Fellow Israelites, listen to these words: This Jesus of Nazareth was a man attested to you by God with miracles, wonders, and signs that God did among you through him, just as you yourselves know. [23] Though he was delivered up according to God's determined plan and foreknowledge, you used[D] lawless people to nail him to a cross and kill him. [24] God raised him up, ending the pains of death, because it

was not possible for him to be held by death. [25] For David says of him:

      I saw the Lord ever before me;
      because he is at my right hand,
      I will not be shaken.
[26] Therefore my heart is glad
      and my tongue rejoices.
      Moreover, my flesh will rest in hope,
[27] because you will not abandon me in
        Hades
      or allow your holy one to see decay.
[28] You have revealed the paths of life to me;
      you will fill me with gladness
      in your presence.[E]

[29] "Brothers and sisters, I can confidently speak to you about the patriarch David: He is both dead and buried, and his tomb is with us to this day. [30] Since he was a prophet, he knew that God had sworn an oath to him to seat one of his descendants[F] on his throne. [31] Seeing what was to come, he spoke concerning the resurrection of the Messiah: He[G] was not abandoned in Hades, and his flesh did not experience decay.[H] [32] "God has raised this Jesus; we are all witnesses of this. [33] Therefore, since he has been exalted to the right hand of God and has received from the Father the promised Holy Spirit, he has poured out what you both see and hear. [34] For it was not David who ascended into the heavens, but he himself says:

      The Lord declared to my Lord,
      'Sit at my right hand
[35] until I make your enemies
        your footstool.'[I]

[36] "Therefore let all the house of Israel know with certainty that God has made this Jesus, whom you crucified, both Lord and Messiah."

CALL TO REPENTANCE

[37] When they heard this, they were pierced to the heart and said to Peter and the rest of the apostles: "Brothers, what should we do? " [38] Peter replied, "Repent and be baptized, each of you, in the name of Jesus Christ for the forgiveness of your sins, and you will receive the gift of the Holy Spirit. [39] For the promise is for you and for your children, and for all who are far off, as many as the Lord our God will call." [40] With many other words he testified and strongly urged them, saying, "Be saved from this corrupt[J] generation!" [41] So those who accepted his message were baptized, and that day about three thousand people were added to them.

[A] 2:7 Other mss add to one another   [B] 2:15 Lit it's the third hour of the day   [C] 2:17-21 Jl 2:28-32   [D] 2:23 Other mss read you have taken   [E] 2:25-28 Ps 16:8-11   [F] 2:30 Other mss add according to the flesh to raise up the Messiah   [G] 2:31 Other mss read His soul   [H] 2:31 Ps 16:10   [I] 2:34-35 Ps 110:1   [J] 2:40 Or crooked, or twisted

A GENEROUS AND GROWING CHURCH

42 They devoted themselves to the apostles' teaching, to the fellowship, to the breaking of bread, and to prayer.

43 Everyone was filled with awe, and many wonders and signs were being performed through the apostles. **44** Now all the believers were together and held all things in common. **45** They sold their possessions and property and distributed the proceeds to all, as any had need. **46** Every day they devoted themselves to meeting together in the temple, and broke bread from house to house. They ate their food with joyful and sincere hearts, **47** praising God and enjoying the favor of all the people. Every day the Lord added to their number[A] those who were being saved.

HEALING OF A LAME MAN

3 Now Peter and John were going up to the temple for the time of prayer at three in the afternoon.[B] **2** A man who was lame from birth was being carried there. He was placed each day at the temple gate called Beautiful, so that he could beg from those entering the temple. **3** When he saw Peter and John about to enter the temple, he asked for money. **4** Peter, along with John, looked straight at him and said, "Look at us." **5** So he turned to them, expecting to get something from them. **6** But Peter said, "I don't have silver or gold, but what I do have, I give you: In the name of Jesus Christ of Nazareth, get up and walk!" **7** Then, taking him by the right hand he raised him up, and at once his feet and ankles became strong. **8** So he jumped up and started to walk, and he entered the temple with them — walking, leaping, and praising God. **9** All the people saw him walking and praising God, **10** and they recognized that he was the one who used to sit and beg at the Beautiful Gate of the temple. So they were filled with awe and astonishment at what had happened to him.

PREACHING IN SOLOMON'S COLONNADE

11 While he[C] was holding on to Peter and John, all the people, utterly astonished, ran toward them in what is called Solomon's Colonnade. **12** When Peter saw this, he addressed the people: "Fellow Israelites, why are you amazed at this? Why do you stare at us, as though we had made him walk by our own power or godliness? **13** The God of Abraham, Isaac, and Jacob, the God of our ancestors, has glorified his servant Jesus, whom you handed over and denied

before Pilate, though he had decided to release him. **14** You denied the Holy and Righteous One and asked to have a murderer released to you. **15** You killed the source[D] of life, whom God raised from the dead; we are witnesses of this. **16** By faith in his name, his name has made this man strong, whom you see and know. So the faith that comes through Jesus has given him this perfect health in front of all of you.

17 "And now, brothers and sisters, I know that you acted in ignorance, just as your leaders also did. **18** In this way God fulfilled what he had predicted through all the prophets — that his Messiah would suffer. **19** Therefore repent and turn back, so that your sins may be wiped out, **20** that seasons of refreshing may come from the presence of the Lord, and that he may send Jesus, who has been appointed for you as the Messiah. **21** Heaven must receive him until the time of the restoration of all things, which God spoke about through his holy prophets from the beginning. **22** Moses said:[E] **The Lord your God will raise up for you a prophet like me from among your brothers and sisters. You must listen to everything he tells you. 23 And everyone who does not listen to that prophet will be completely cut off from the people.[F]**

24 "In addition, all the prophets who have spoken, from Samuel and those after him, have also foretold these days. **25** You are the sons[G] of the prophets and of the covenant that God made with your ancestors, saying to Abraham, **And all the families of the earth will be blessed through your offspring.**[H] **26** God raised up his servant[I] and sent him first to you to bless you by turning each of you from your evil ways."

PETER AND JOHN ARRESTED

4 While they were speaking to the people, the priests, the captain of the temple police, and the Sadducees confronted them, **2** because they were annoyed that they were teaching the people and proclaiming in Jesus the resurrection of the dead. **3** So they seized them and took them into custody until the next day since it was already evening. **4** But many of those who heard the message believed, and the number of the men[J] came to about five thousand.

PETER AND JOHN FACE THE JEWISH LEADERSHIP

5 The next day, their rulers, elders, and scribes assembled in Jerusalem **6** with Annas the high priest, Caiaphas, John, Alexander, and all the members of the high-priestly family. **7** After they had Peter and John stand before them,

---

A **2:47** Other mss read *to the church*   B **3:1** Lit *at the ninth hour*   C **3:11** Other mss read *the lame man who was healed*   D **3:15** Or *the Prince*, or *the Ruler*   E **3:22** Other mss add *to the fathers*   F **3:22-23** Dt 18:15-19   G **3:25** = heirs   H **3:25** Gn 12:3; 18:18; 22:18; 26:4   I **3:26** Other mss add *Jesus*   J **4:4** Or *people*

they began to question them: "By what power or in what name have you done this?"

[8] Then Peter was filled with the Holy Spirit and said to them, "Rulers of the people and elders:[A] [9] If we are being examined today about a good deed done to a disabled man, by what means he was healed, [10] let it be known to all of you and to all the people of Israel, that by the name of Jesus Christ of Nazareth, whom you crucified and whom God raised from the dead — by him this man is standing here before you healthy. [11] This Jesus is

the stone rejected by you builders,
which has become the cornerstone.[B]

[12] There is salvation in no one else, for there is no other name under heaven given to people by which we must be saved."

THE BOLDNESS OF THE DISCIPLES

[13] When they observed the boldness of Peter and John and realized that they were uneducated and untrained men, they were amazed and recognized that they had been with Jesus. [14] And since they saw the man who had been healed standing with them, they had nothing to say in opposition. [15] After they ordered them to leave the Sanhedrin, they conferred among themselves, [16] saying, "What should we do with these men? For an obvious sign has been done through them, clear to everyone living in Jerusalem, and we cannot deny it. [17] But so that this does not spread any further among the people, let's threaten them against speaking to anyone in this name again." [18] So they called for them and ordered them not to speak or teach at all in the name of Jesus.

[19] Peter and John answered them, "Whether it's right in the sight of God for us to listen to you rather than to God, you decide; [20] for we are unable to stop speaking about what we have seen and heard."

[21] After threatening them further, they released them. They found no way to punish them because the people were all giving glory to God over what had been done. [22] For this sign of healing had been performed on a man over forty years old.

PRAYER FOR BOLDNESS

[23] After they were released, they went to their own people and reported everything the chief priests and the elders had said to them. [24] When they heard this, they raised their voices together to God and said, "Master, you are the one who made the heaven, the earth, and the sea, and everything in them. [25] You said through the Holy Spirit, by the mouth of our father David your servant:[C]

Why do the Gentiles rage
and the peoples plot futile things?
[26] The kings of the earth take their stand
and the rulers assemble together
against the Lord and
against his Messiah.[D]

[27] "For, in fact, in this city both Herod and Pontius Pilate, with the Gentiles and the people of Israel, assembled together against your holy servant Jesus, whom you anointed, [28] to do whatever your hand and your will had predestined to take place. [29] And now, Lord, consider their threats, and grant that your servants may speak your word with all boldness, [30] while you stretch out your hand for healing, and signs and wonders are performed through the name of your holy servant Jesus." [31] When they had prayed, the place where they were assembled was shaken, and they were all filled with the Holy Spirit and began to speak the word of God boldly.

ALL THINGS IN COMMON

[32] Now the entire group of those who believed were of one heart and mind, and no one claimed that any of his possessions was his own, but instead they held everything in common. [33] With great power the apostles were giving testimony to the resurrection of the Lord Jesus, and great grace was on all of them. [34] For there was not a needy person among them because all those who owned lands or houses sold them, brought the proceeds of what was sold, [35] and laid them at the apostles' feet. This was then distributed to each person as any had need.

[36] Joseph, a Levite from Cyprus by birth, the one the apostles called Barnabas (which is translated Son of Encouragement), [37] sold a field he owned, brought the money, and laid it at the apostles' feet.

LYING TO THE HOLY SPIRIT

5 But a man named Ananias, with his wife Sapphira, sold a piece of property. [2] However, he kept back part of the proceeds with his wife's knowledge, and brought a portion of it and laid it at the apostles' feet.

[3] "Ananias," Peter asked, "why has Satan filled your heart to lie to the Holy Spirit and keep back part of the proceeds of the land? [4] Wasn't it yours while you possessed it? And after it was sold, wasn't it at your disposal? Why is it that you planned this thing in your heart? You have not lied to people but to God." [5] When he heard these words, Ananias dropped dead, and a great fear came on all who heard. [6] The young

[A] 4:8 Other mss add of Israel   [B] 4:11 Ps 118:22   [C] 4:25 Other mss read through the mouth of David your servant   [D] 4:25-26 Ps 2:1-2

men got up, wrapped his body, carried him out, and buried him.

[7] About three hours later, his wife came in, not knowing what had happened. [8] "Tell me," Peter asked her, "did you sell the land for this price?"

"Yes," she said, "for that price."

[9] Then Peter said to her, "Why did you agree to test the Spirit of the Lord? Look, the feet of those who have buried your husband are at the door, and they will carry you out."

[10] Instantly she dropped dead at his feet. When the young men came in, they found her dead, carried her out, and buried her beside her husband. [11] Then great fear came on the whole church and on all who heard these things.

APOSTOLIC SIGNS AND WONDERS

[12] Many signs and wonders were being done among the people through the hands of the apostles. They were all together in Solomon's Colonnade. [13] No one else dared to join them, but the people spoke well of them. [14] Believers were added to the Lord in increasing numbers — multitudes of both men and women. [15] As a result, they would carry the sick out into the streets and lay them on cots and mats so that when Peter came by, at least his shadow might fall on some of them. [16] In addition, a multitude came together from the towns surrounding Jerusalem, bringing the sick and those who were tormented by unclean spirits, and they were all healed.

IN AND OUT OF PRISON

[17] Then the high priest rose up. He and all who were with him, who belonged to the party of the Sadducees, were filled with jealousy. [18] So they arrested the apostles and put them in the public jail. [19] But an angel of the Lord opened the doors of the jail during the night, brought them out, and said, [20] "Go and stand in the temple, and tell the people all about this life." [21] Hearing this, they entered the temple at daybreak and began to teach.

THE APOSTLES ON TRIAL AGAIN

When the high priest and those who were with him arrived, they convened the Sanhedrin — the full council of the Israelites — and sent orders to the jail to have them brought. [22] But when the servants[A] got there, they did not find them in the jail, so they returned and reported, [23] "We found the jail securely locked, with the guards standing in front of the doors, but when we opened them, we found no one inside." [24] As[B] the captain of the temple police and

the chief priests heard these things, they were baffled about them, wondering what would come of this.

[25] Someone came and reported to them, "Look! The men you put in jail are standing in the temple and teaching the people." [26] Then the commander went with the servants and brought them in without force, because they were afraid the people might stone them. [27] After they brought them in, they had them stand before the Sanhedrin, and the high priest asked, [28] "Didn't we strictly order you not to teach in this name? Look, you have filled Jerusalem with your teaching and are determined to make us guilty of this man's blood."

[29] Peter and the apostles replied, "We must obey God rather than people. [30] The God of our ancestors raised up Jesus, whom you had murdered by hanging him on a tree. [31] God exalted this man to his right hand as ruler and Savior, to give repentance to Israel and forgiveness of sins. [32] We are witnesses of these things, and so is the Holy Spirit whom God has given to those who obey him."

GAMALIEL'S ADVICE

[33] When they heard this, they were enraged and wanted to kill them. [34] But a Pharisee named Gamaliel, a teacher of the law who was respected by all the people, stood up in the Sanhedrin and ordered the men[C] to be taken outside for a little while. [35] He said to them, "Men of Israel, be careful about what you're about to do to these men. [36] Some time ago Theudas rose up, claiming to be somebody, and a group of about four hundred men rallied to him. He was killed, and all his followers were dispersed and came to nothing. [37] After this man, Judas the Galilean rose up in the days of the census and attracted a following. He also perished, and all his followers were scattered. [38] So in the present case, I tell you, stay away from these men and leave them alone. For if this plan or this work is of human origin, it will fail; [39] but if it is of God, you will not be able to overthrow them. You may even be found fighting against God." They were persuaded by him. [40] After they called in the apostles and had them flogged, they ordered them not to speak in the name of Jesus and released them. [41] Then they went out from the presence of the Sanhedrin, rejoicing that they were counted worthy to be treated shamefully on behalf of the Name.[D] [42] Every day in the temple, and in various homes, they continued teaching and proclaiming the good news that Jesus is the Messiah.

SEVEN CHOSEN TO SERVE

6 In those days, as the disciples were increasing in number, there arose a complaint by the Hellenistic Jews against the Hebraic Jews that their widows were being overlooked in the daily distribution. [2] The Twelve summoned the whole company of the disciples and said, "It would not be right for us to give up preaching the word of God to wait on tables. [3] Brothers and sisters, select from among you seven men of good reputation, full of the Spirit and wisdom, whom we can appoint to this duty. [4] But we will devote ourselves to prayer and to the ministry of the word." [5] This proposal pleased the whole company. So they chose Stephen, a man full of faith and the Holy Spirit, and Philip, Prochorus, Nicanor, Timon, Parmenas, and Nicolaus, a convert from Antioch. [6] They had them stand before the apostles, who prayed and laid their hands on them.

[7] So the word of God spread, the disciples in Jerusalem increased greatly in number, and a large group of priests became obedient to the faith.

STEPHEN ACCUSED OF BLASPHEMY

[8] Now Stephen, full of grace and power, was performing great wonders and signs among the people. [9] Opposition arose, however, from some members of the Freedmen's Synagogue, composed of both Cyrenians and Alexandrians, and some from Cilicia and Asia, and they began to argue with Stephen. [10] But they were unable to stand up against his wisdom and the Spirit by whom he was speaking.

[11] Then they secretly persuaded some men to say, "We heard him speaking blasphemous words against Moses and God." [12] They stirred up the people, the elders, and the scribes; so they came, seized him, and took him to the Sanhedrin. [13] They also presented false witnesses who said, "This man never stops speaking against this holy place and the law. [14] For we heard him say that this Jesus of Nazareth will destroy this place and change the customs that Moses handed down to us." [15] And all who were sitting in the Sanhedrin looked intently at him and saw that his face was like the face of an angel.

STEPHEN'S SERMON

7 "Are these things true?" the high priest asked.

[2] "Brothers and fathers," he replied, "listen: The God of glory appeared to our father Abraham when he was in Mesopotamia, before he settled in Haran, [3] and said to him: **Leave your country and relatives, and come to the land that I will show you.**[A]

[4] "Then he left the land of the Chaldeans and settled in Haran. From there, after his father died, God had him move to this land in which you are now living. [5] He didn't give him an inheritance in it — not even a foot of ground — but he promised to give it to him as a possession, and to his descendants after him, even though he was childless. [6] God spoke in this way: **His descendants would be strangers in a foreign country, and they** would **enslave and oppress them for four hundred years.** [7] **I will judge the nation that they will serve as slaves,** God said. **After this, they will come out and worship me in this place.**[B] [8] And so he gave Abraham the covenant of circumcision. After this, he fathered Isaac and circumcised him on the eighth day. Isaac became the father of Jacob, and Jacob became the father of the twelve patriarchs.

THE PATRIARCHS IN EGYPT

[9] "The patriarchs became jealous of Joseph and sold him into Egypt, but God was with him [10] and rescued him out of all his troubles. He gave him favor and wisdom in the sight of Pharaoh, king of Egypt, who appointed him ruler over Egypt and over his whole household. [11] Now a famine and great suffering came over all of Egypt and Canaan, and our ancestors could find no food. [12] When Jacob heard there was grain in Egypt, he sent our ancestors there the first time. [13] The second time, Joseph revealed himself to his brothers, and Joseph's family became known to Pharaoh. [14] Joseph invited his father Jacob and all his relatives, seventy-five people in all, [15] and Jacob went down to Egypt. He and our ancestors died there, [16] were carried back to Shechem, and were placed in the tomb that Abraham had bought for a sum of silver from the sons of Hamor in Shechem.

MOSES, A REJECTED SAVIOR

[17] "As the time was approaching to fulfill the promise that God had made to Abraham, the people flourished and multiplied in Egypt [18] until a different king who did not know Joseph ruled over Egypt.[C] [19] He dealt deceitfully with our race and oppressed our ancestors by making them abandon their infants outside so that they wouldn't survive. [20] At this time Moses was born, and he was beautiful in God's sight. He was cared for in his father's home for three months. [21] When he was put outside, Pharaoh's

---

daughter adopted and raised him as her own son. **22** So Moses was educated in all the wisdom of the Egyptians and was powerful in his speech and actions.

23 "When he was forty years old, he decided to visit his own people, the Israelites. **24** When he saw one of them being mistreated, he came to his rescue and avenged the oppressed man by striking down the Egyptian. **25** He assumed his people would understand that God would give them deliverance through him, but they did not understand. **26** The next day he showed up while they were fighting and tried to reconcile them peacefully, saying, 'Men, you are brothers. Why are you mistreating each other?'

27 "But the one who was mistreating his neighbor pushed Moses aside, saying: **Who appointed you a ruler and a judge over us? 28 Do you want to kill me, the same way you killed the Egyptian yesterday?**^

29 "When he heard this, Moses fled and became an exile in the land of Midian, where he became the father of two sons. **30** After forty years had passed, an angel^ appeared to him in the wilderness of Mount Sinai, in the flame of a burning bush. **31** When Moses saw it, he was amazed at the sight. As he was approaching to look at it, the voice of the Lord came: **32 I am the God of your ancestors — the God of Abraham, of Isaac, and of Jacob.**^ Moses began to tremble and did not dare to look.

33 "The Lord said to him: **Take off the sandals from your feet, because the place where you are standing is holy ground. 34 I have certainly seen the oppression of my people in Egypt; I have heard their groaning and have come down to set them free. And now, come, I will send you to Egypt.**^

35 "This Moses, whom they rejected when they said, **Who appointed you a ruler and a judge?**^ — this one God sent as a ruler and a deliverer through the angel who appeared to him in the bush. **36** This man led them out and performed wonders and signs in the land of Egypt, at the Red Sea, and in the wilderness for forty years.

ISRAEL'S REBELLION AGAINST GOD

37 "This is the Moses who said to the Israelites: **God**^ **will raise up for you a prophet like me from among your brothers and sisters.**^ **38** He is the one who was in the assembly in the wilderness, with the angel who spoke to him on Mount Sinai, and with our ancestors. He received living oracles to give to us.

39 Our ancestors were unwilling to obey him. Instead, they pushed him aside, and in their hearts turned back to Egypt. **40** They told Aaron: **Make us gods who will go before us. As for this Moses who brought us out of the land of Egypt, we don't know what's happened to him.**^ **41** They even made a calf in those days, offered sacrifice to the idol, and were celebrating what their hands had made. **42** God turned away and gave them up to worship the stars of heaven, as it is written in the book of the prophets:

> House of Israel, did you bring me
> offerings and sacrifices
> for forty years in the wilderness?
> **43** You took up the tent of Moloch
> and the star of your god Rephan,
> the images that you made
> to worship.
> So I will send you into exile
> beyond Babylon.^

GOD'S REAL TABERNACLE

44 "Our ancestors had the tabernacle of the testimony in the wilderness, just as he who spoke to Moses commanded him to make it according to the pattern he had seen. **45** Our ancestors in turn received it and with Joshua brought it in when they dispossessed the nations that God drove out before them, until the days of David. **46** He found favor in God's sight and asked that he might provide a dwelling place for the God^ of Jacob. **47** It was Solomon, rather, who built him a house, **48** but the Most High does not dwell in sanctuaries made with hands, as the prophet says:

> **49** Heaven is my throne,
> and the earth my footstool.
> What sort of house will you build
> for me?
> says the Lord,
> or what will be my resting place?
> **50** Did not my hand make all
> these things?^

RESISTING THE HOLY SPIRIT

51 "You stiff-necked people with uncircumcised hearts and ears! You are always resisting the Holy Spirit. As your ancestors did, you do also. **52** Which of the prophets did your ancestors not persecute? They even killed those who foretold the coming of the Righteous One, whose betrayers and murderers you have now become. **53** You received the law under the direction of angels and yet have not kept it."

---

^7:27-28,35 Ex 2:14   ^7:30 Other mss add *of the Lord*   ^7:32 Ex 3:6,15   ^7:33-34 Ex 3:5,7-8,10   ^7:37 Other mss read *The Lord your God*   ^7:37 Dt 18:15   ^7:40 Ex 32:1,23   ^7:42-43 Am 5:25-27   ^7:46 Other mss read *house*   ^7:49-50 Is 66:1-2

THE FIRST CHRISTIAN MARTYR

[54] When they heard these things, they were enraged[A] and gnashed their teeth at him. [55] Stephen, full of the Holy Spirit, gazed into heaven. He saw the glory of God, and Jesus standing at the right hand of God. [56] He said, "Look, I see the heavens opened and the Son of Man standing at the right hand of God!"

[57] They yelled at the top of their voices, covered their ears, and together rushed against him. [58] They dragged him out of the city and began to stone him. And the witnesses laid their garments at the feet of a young man named Saul. [59] While they were stoning Stephen, he called out: "Lord Jesus, receive my spirit!" [60] He knelt down and cried out with a loud voice, "Lord, do not hold this sin against them!" And after saying this, he died.[B]

SAUL THE PERSECUTOR

8 Saul agreed with putting him to death. On that day a severe persecution broke out against the church in Jerusalem, and all except the apostles were scattered throughout the land of Judea and Samaria. [2] Devout men buried Stephen and mourned deeply over him. [3] Saul, however, was ravaging the church. He would enter house after house, drag off men and women, and put them in prison.

PHILIP IN SAMARIA

[4] So those who were scattered went on their way preaching the word. [5] Philip went down to a[C] city in Samaria and proclaimed the Messiah to them. [6] The crowds were all paying attention to what Philip said, as they listened and saw the signs he was performing. [7] For unclean spirits, crying out with a loud voice, came out of many who were possessed, and many who were paralyzed and lame were healed. [8] So there was great joy in that city.

THE RESPONSE OF SIMON

[9] A man named Simon had previously practiced sorcery in that city and amazed the Samaritan people, while claiming to be somebody great. [10] They all paid attention to him, from the least of them to the greatest, and they said, "This man is called the Great Power of God."[D] [11] They were attentive to him because he had amazed them with his sorceries for a long time. [12] But when they believed Philip, as he proclaimed the good news about the kingdom of God and the name of Jesus Christ, both men and women were baptized. [13] Even Simon himself believed.

And after he was baptized, he followed Philip everywhere and was amazed as he observed the signs and great miracles that were being performed.

SIMON'S SIN

[14] When the apostles who were at Jerusalem heard that Samaria had received the word of God, they sent Peter and John to them. [15] After they went down there, they prayed for them so the Samaritans might receive the Holy Spirit because he had not yet come down on any of them. [16] (They had only been baptized in the name of the Lord Jesus.) [17] Then Peter and John laid their hands on them, and they received the Holy Spirit.

[18] When Simon saw that the Spirit[E] was given through the laying on of the apostles' hands, he offered them money, [19] saying, "Give me this power also so that anyone I lay hands on may receive the Holy Spirit."

[20] But Peter told him, "May your silver be destroyed with you, because you thought you could obtain the gift of God with money! [21] You have no part or share in this matter, because your heart is not right before God. [22] Therefore repent of this wickedness of yours, and pray to the Lord that, if possible, your heart's intent may be forgiven. [23] For I see you are poisoned by bitterness and bound by wickedness."

[24] "Pray to the Lord for me," Simon replied, "so that nothing you have said may happen to me."

[25] So, after they had testified and spoken the word of the Lord, they traveled back to Jerusalem, preaching the gospel in many villages of the Samaritans.

THE CONVERSION OF THE ETHIOPIAN OFFICIAL

[26] An angel of the Lord spoke to Philip: "Get up and go south to the road that goes down from Jerusalem to Gaza." (This is the desert road.[F]) [27] So he got up and went. There was an Ethiopian man, a eunuch and high official of Candace, queen of the Ethiopians, who was in charge of her entire treasury. He had come to worship in Jerusalem [28] and was sitting in his chariot on his way home, reading the prophet Isaiah aloud.

[29] The Spirit told Philip, "Go and join that chariot."

[30] When Philip ran up to it, he heard him reading the prophet Isaiah, and said, "Do you understand what you're reading?"

[31] "How can I," he said, "unless someone guides me?" So he invited Philip to come up

---

[A]7:54 Or *were cut to the quick*   [B]7:60 Lit *he fell asleep*   [C]8:5 Other mss read *the*   [D]8:10 Or *"This is the power of God called Great*   [E]8:18 Other mss add *Holy*   [F]8:26 Or *is a desert place*

and sit with him. ³² Now the Scripture passage he was reading was this:

> He was led like a sheep
>   to the slaughter,
> and as a lamb is silent
>   before its shearer,
> so he does not open his mouth.
> ³³ In his humiliation justice
>   was denied him.
> Who will describe
>   his generation?
> For his life is taken
>   from the earth. ^A

³⁴ The eunuch said to Philip, "I ask you, who is the prophet saying this about — himself or someone else?" ³⁵ Philip proceeded to tell him the good news about Jesus, beginning with that Scripture.

³⁶ As they were traveling down the road, they came to some water. The eunuch said, "Look, there's water. What would keep me from being baptized?"^{B 38} So he ordered the chariot to stop, and both Philip and the eunuch went down into the water, and he baptized him. ³⁹ When they came up out of the water, the Spirit of the Lord carried Philip away, and the eunuch did not see him any longer but went on his way rejoicing. ⁴⁰ Philip appeared in^C Azotus,^D and he was traveling and preaching the gospel in all the towns until he came to Caesarea.

THE DAMASCUS ROAD

9 Now Saul was still breathing threats and murder against the disciples of the Lord. He went to the high priest ² and requested letters from him to the synagogues in Damascus, so that if he found any men or women who belonged to the Way, he might bring them as prisoners to Jerusalem. ³ As he traveled and was nearing Damascus, a light from heaven suddenly flashed around him. ⁴ Falling to the ground, he heard a voice saying to him, "Saul, Saul, why are you persecuting me?"

⁵ "Who are you, Lord?" Saul said.

"I am Jesus, the one you are persecuting," he replied. ⁶ "But get up and go into the city, and you will be told what you must do."

⁷ The men who were traveling with him stood speechless, hearing the sound but seeing no one. ⁸ Saul got up from the ground, and though his eyes were open, he could see nothing. So they took him by the hand and led him into Damascus. ⁹ He was unable to see for three days and did not eat or drink.

SAUL'S BAPTISM

¹⁰ There was a disciple in Damascus named Ananias, and the Lord said to him in a vision, "Ananias."

"Here I am, Lord," he replied.

¹¹ "Get up and go to the street called Straight," the Lord said to him, "to the house of Judas, and ask for a man from Tarsus named Saul, since he is praying there. ¹² In a vision^E he has seen a man named Ananias coming in and placing his hands on him so that he may regain his sight."

¹³ "Lord," Ananias answered, "I have heard from many people about this man, how much harm he has done to your saints in Jerusalem. ¹⁴ And he has authority here from the chief priests to arrest all who call on your name."

¹⁵ But the Lord said to him, "Go, for this man is my chosen instrument to take my name to Gentiles, kings, and Israelites. ¹⁶ I will show him how much he must suffer for my name."

¹⁷ Ananias went and entered the house. He placed his hands on him and said, "Brother Saul, the Lord Jesus, who appeared to you on the road you were traveling, has sent me so that you may regain your sight and be filled with the Holy Spirit."

¹⁸ At once something like scales fell from his eyes, and he regained his sight. Then he got up and was baptized. ¹⁹ And after taking some food, he regained his strength.

SAUL PROCLAIMING THE MESSIAH

Saul was with the disciples in Damascus for some time. ²⁰ Immediately he began proclaiming Jesus in the synagogues: "He is the Son of God."

²¹ All who heard him were astounded and said, "Isn't this the man in Jerusalem who was causing havoc for those who called on this name and came here for the purpose of taking them as prisoners to the chief priests?"

²² But Saul grew stronger and kept confounding the Jews who lived in Damascus by proving that Jesus is the Messiah.

²³ After many days had passed, the Jews conspired to kill him, ²⁴ but Saul learned of their plot. So they were watching the gates day and night intending to kill him, ²⁵ but his disciples took him by night and lowered him in a large basket through an opening in the wall.

SAUL IN JERUSALEM

²⁶ When he arrived in Jerusalem, he tried to join the disciples, but they were all afraid of him, since they did not believe he was a disciple.

---

^A**8:32-33** Is 53:7-8   ^B**8:36** Some mss include v. 37: *Philip said, "If you believe with all your heart you may." And he replied, "I believe that Jesus Christ is the Son of God."*   ^C**8:40** Or *Philip was found at,* or *Philip found himself in*   ^D**8:40** Or *Ashdod*
^E**9:12** Other mss omit *In a vision*

²⁷ Barnabas, however, took him and brought him to the apostles and explained to them how Saul had seen the Lord on the road and that the Lord had talked to him, and how in Damascus he had spoken boldly in the name of Jesus. ²⁸ Saul was coming and going with them in Jerusalem, speaking boldly in the name of the Lord. ²⁹ He conversed and debated with the Hellenistic Jews, but they tried to kill him. ³⁰ When the brothers found out, they took him down to Caesarea and sent him off to Tarsus.

THE CHURCH'S GROWTH

³¹ So the church throughout all Judea, Galilee, and Samaria had peace and was strengthened. Living in the fear of the Lord and encouraged by the Holy Spirit, it increased in numbers.

THE HEALING OF AENEAS

³² As Peter was traveling from place to place, he also came down to the saints who lived in Lydda. ³³ There he found a man named Aeneas, who was paralyzed and had been bedridden for eight years. ³⁴ Peter said to him, "Aeneas, Jesus Christ heals you. Get up and make your bed,"^ and immediately he got up. ³⁵ So all who lived in Lydda and Sharon saw him and turned to the Lord.

DORCAS RESTORED TO LIFE

³⁶ In Joppa there was a disciple named Tabitha (which is translated Dorcas). She was always doing good works and acts of charity. ³⁷ About that time she became sick and died. After washing her, they placed her in a room upstairs. ³⁸ Since Lydda was near Joppa, the disciples heard that Peter was there and sent two men to him who urged him, "Don't delay in coming with us." ³⁹ Peter got up and went with them. When he arrived, they led him to the room upstairs. And all the widows approached him, weeping and showing him the robes and clothes that Dorcas had made while she was with them. ⁴⁰ Peter sent them all out of the room. He knelt down, prayed, and turning toward the body said, "Tabitha, get up." She opened her eyes, saw Peter, and sat up. ⁴¹ He gave her his hand and helped her stand up. He called the saints and widows and presented her alive. ⁴² This became known throughout Joppa, and many believed in the Lord. ⁴³ Peter stayed for some time in Joppa with Simon, a leather tanner.

CORNELIUS'S VISION

10 There was a man in Caesarea named Cornelius, a centurion of what was called the Italian Regiment. ² He was a devout man and feared God along with his whole household. He did many charitable deeds for the Jewish people and always prayed to God. ³ About three in the afternoon^B he distinctly saw in a vision an angel of God who came in and said to him, "Cornelius."

⁴ Staring at him in awe, he said, "What is it, Lord?"

The angel told him, "Your prayers and your acts of charity have ascended as a memorial offering before God. ⁵ Now send men to Joppa and call for Simon, who is also named Peter. ⁶ He is lodging with Simon, a tanner, whose house is by the sea."

⁷ When the angel who spoke to him had gone, he called two of his household servants and a devout soldier, who was one of those who attended him. ⁸ After explaining everything to them, he sent them to Joppa.

PETER'S VISION

⁹ The next day, as they were traveling and nearing the city, Peter went up to pray on the roof about noon.^C ¹⁰ He became hungry and wanted to eat, but while they were preparing something, he fell into a trance. ¹¹ He saw heaven opened and an object that resembled a large sheet coming down, being lowered by its four corners to the earth. ¹² In it were all the four-footed animals and reptiles of the earth, and the birds of the sky. ¹³ A voice said to him, "Get up, Peter; kill and eat."

¹⁴ "No, Lord!" Peter said. "For I have never eaten anything impure and ritually unclean."

¹⁵ Again, a second time, the voice said to him, "What God has made clean, do not call impure." ¹⁶ This happened three times, and suddenly the object was taken up into heaven.

PETER VISITS CORNELIUS

¹⁷ While Peter was deeply perplexed about what the vision he had seen might mean, right away the men who had been sent by Cornelius, having asked directions to Simon's house, stood at the gate. ¹⁸ They called out, asking if Simon, who was also named Peter, was lodging there.

¹⁹ While Peter was thinking about the vision, the Spirit told him, "Three men are here looking for you. ²⁰ Get up, go downstairs, and go with them with no doubts at all, because I have sent them."

²¹ Then Peter went down to the men and said, "Here I am, the one you're looking for. What is the reason you're here?"

²² They said, "Cornelius, a centurion, an upright and God-fearing man, who has a good reputation with the whole Jewish nation, was divinely directed by a holy angel to call you to his house and to hear a message from you."

---

^9:34 Or *and get ready to eat*   ^B10:3 Lit *About the ninth hour*   ^C10:9 Lit *about the sixth hour*

23 Peter then invited them in and gave them lodging.

The next day he got up and set out with them, and some of the brothers from Joppa went with him. 24 The following day he entered Caesarea. Now Cornelius was expecting them and had called together his relatives and close friends. 25 When Peter entered, Cornelius met him, fell at his feet, and worshiped him.

26 But Peter lifted him up and said, "Stand up. I myself am also a man." 27 While talking with him, he went in and found a large gathering of people. 28 Peter said to them, "You know it's forbidden for a Jewish man to associate with or visit a foreigner, but God has shown me that I must not call any person impure or unclean. 29 That's why I came without any objection when I was sent for. So may I ask why you sent for me?"

30 Cornelius replied, "Four days ago at this hour, at three in the afternoon,^A I was^B praying in my house. Just then a man in dazzling clothing stood before me 31 and said, 'Cornelius, your prayer has been heard, and your acts of charity have been remembered in God's sight. 32 Therefore send someone to Joppa and invite Simon here, who is also named Peter. He is lodging in Simon the tanner's house by the sea.'^C 33 So I immediately sent for you, and it was good of you to come. So now we are all in the presence of God to hear everything you have been commanded by the Lord."

GOOD NEWS FOR GENTILES

34 Peter began to speak: "Now I truly understand that God doesn't show favoritism, 35 but in every nation the person who fears him and does what is right is acceptable to him. 36 He sent the message to the Israelites, proclaiming the good news of peace through Jesus Christ — he is Lord of all. 37 You know the events that took place throughout all Judea, beginning from Galilee after the baptism that John preached: 38 how God anointed Jesus of Nazareth with the Holy Spirit and with power, and how he went about doing good and healing all who were under the tyranny of the devil, because God was with him. 39 We ourselves are witnesses of everything he did in both the Judean country and in Jerusalem, and yet they killed him by hanging him on a tree. 40 God raised up this man on the third day and caused him to be seen, 41 not by all the people, but by us whom God appointed as witnesses, who ate and drank with him after he rose from the dead. 42 He commanded us to preach to the people and to testify that he is the one appointed by God to be the judge of the living and the dead. 43 All the prophets testify about him that through his name everyone who believes in him receives forgiveness of sins."

GENTILE CONVERSION AND BAPTISM

44 While Peter was still speaking these words, the Holy Spirit came down on all those who heard the message. 45 The circumcised believers who had come with Peter were amazed because the gift of the Holy Spirit had been poured out even on the Gentiles. 46 For they heard them speaking in other tongues^D and declaring the greatness of God.

Then Peter responded, 47 "Can anyone withhold water and prevent these people from being baptized, who have received the Holy Spirit just as we have?" 48 He commanded them to be baptized in the name of Jesus Christ. Then they asked him to stay for a few days.

GENTILE SALVATION DEFENDED

11 The apostles and the brothers and sisters who were throughout Judea heard that the Gentiles had also received the word of God. 2 When Peter went up to Jerusalem, the circumcision party criticized him, 3 saying, "You went to uncircumcised men and ate with them."

4 Peter began to explain to them step by step: 5 "I was in the town of Joppa praying, and I saw, in a trance, an object that resembled a large sheet coming down, being lowered by its four corners from heaven, and it came to me. 6 When I looked closely and considered it, I saw the four-footed animals of the earth, the wild beasts, the reptiles, and the birds of the sky. 7 I also heard a voice telling me, 'Get up, Peter; kill and eat.'

8 " 'No, Lord!' I said. 'For nothing impure or ritually unclean has ever entered my mouth.' 9 But a voice answered from heaven a second time, 'What God has made clean, you must not call impure.'

10 "Now this happened three times, and everything was drawn up again into heaven. 11 At that very moment, three men who had been sent to me from Caesarea arrived at the house where we were. 12 The Spirit told me to accompany them with no doubts at all. These six brothers also accompanied me, and we went into the man's house. 13 He reported to us how he had seen the angel standing in his house and saying, 'Send^E to Joppa, and call for Simon, who is also named Peter. 14 He will speak a message to you by which you and all your household will be saved.'

---

^A **10:30** Lit *at the ninth hour*   ^B **10:30** Other mss add *fasting and*   ^C **10:32** Other mss add *When he arrives, he will speak to you.*
^D **10:46** languages   ^E **11:13** Other mss add *men*

[15] "As I began to speak, the Holy Spirit came down on them, just as on us at the beginning. [16] I remembered the word of the Lord, how he said, 'John baptized with water, but you will be baptized with the Holy Spirit.' [17] If, then, God gave them the same gift that he also gave to us when we believed in the Lord Jesus Christ, how could I possibly hinder God?"

[18] When they heard this they became silent. And they glorified God, saying, "So then, God has given repentance resulting in life even to the Gentiles."

THE CHURCH IN ANTIOCH

[19] Now those who had been scattered as a result of the persecution that started because of Stephen made their way as far as Phoenicia, Cyprus, and Antioch, speaking the word to no one except Jews. [20] But there were some of them, men from Cyprus and Cyrene, who came to Antioch and began speaking to the Greeks^A also, proclaiming the good news about the Lord Jesus. [21] The Lord's hand was with them, and a large number who believed turned to the Lord. [22] News about them reached^B the church in Jerusalem, and they sent out Barnabas to travel^C as far as Antioch. [23] When he arrived and saw the grace of God, he was glad and encouraged all of them to remain true to the Lord with devoted hearts, [24] for he was a good man, full of the Holy Spirit and of faith. And large numbers of people were added to the Lord.

[25] Then he^D went to Tarsus to search for Saul, [26] and when he found him he brought him to Antioch. For a whole year they met with the church and taught large numbers. The disciples were first called Christians at Antioch.

FAMINE RELIEF

[27] In those days some prophets came down from Jerusalem to Antioch. [28] One of them, named Agabus, stood up and predicted by the Spirit that there would be a severe famine throughout the Roman world.^E This took place during the reign of Claudius. [29] Each of the disciples, according to his ability, determined to send relief to the brothers and sisters who lived in Judea. [30] They did this, sending it to the elders by means of Barnabas and Saul.

JAMES MARTYRED AND PETER JAILED

12 About that time King Herod violently attacked some who belonged to the church, [2] and he executed James, John's brother, with the sword. [3] When he saw that it pleased the Jews, he proceeded to arrest Peter too, during the Festival of Unleavened Bread. [4] After the arrest, he put him in prison and assigned four squads of four soldiers each to guard him, intending to bring him out to the people after the Passover. [5] So Peter was kept in prison, but the church was praying fervently to God for him.

PETER RESCUED

[6] When Herod was about to bring him out for trial, that very night Peter, bound with two chains, was sleeping between two soldiers, while the sentries in front of the door guarded the prison. [7] Suddenly an angel of the Lord appeared, and a light shone in the cell. Striking Peter on the side, he woke him up and said, "Quick, get up!" And the chains fell off his wrists. [8] "Get dressed," the angel told him, "and put on your sandals." And he did. "Wrap your cloak around you," he told him, "and follow me." [9] So he went out and followed, and he did not know that what the angel did was really happening, but he thought he was seeing a vision. [10] After they passed the first and second guards, they came to the iron gate that leads into the city, which opened to them by itself. They went outside and passed one street, and suddenly the angel left him.

[11] When Peter came to himself, he said, "Now I know for certain that the Lord has sent his angel and rescued me from Herod's grasp and from all that the Jewish people expected." [12] As soon as he realized this, he went to the house of Mary, the mother of John Mark,^F where many had assembled and were praying. [13] He knocked at the door of the outer gate, and a servant named Rhoda came to answer. [14] She recognized Peter's voice, and because of her joy, she did not open the gate but ran in and announced that Peter was standing at the outer gate.

[15] "You're out of your mind!" they told her. But she kept insisting that it was true, and they said, "It's his angel." [16] Peter, however, kept on knocking, and when they opened the door and saw him, they were amazed.

[17] Motioning to them with his hand to be silent, he described to them how the Lord had brought him out of the prison. "Tell these things to James and the brothers," he said, and he left and went to another place.

[18] At daylight, there was a great commotion among the soldiers as to what had become of Peter. [19] After Herod had searched and did not find him, he interrogated the guards and ordered their execution. Then Herod went down from Judea to Caesarea and stayed there.

---

^A 11:20 Lit *Hellenists*   ^B 11:22 Lit *reached the ears of*   ^C 11:22 Other mss omit *to travel*   ^D 11:25 Other mss read *Barnabas*
^E 11:28 Or *the whole world*   ^F 12:12 Lit *John who was called Mark*

HEROD'S DEATH

[20] Herod had been very angry with the people of Tyre and Sidon. Together they presented themselves before him. After winning over Blastus, who was in charge of the king's bedroom, they asked for peace, because their country was supplied with food from the king's country. [21] On an appointed day, dressed in royal robes and seated on the throne, Herod delivered a speech to them. [22] The assembled people began to shout, "It's the voice of a god and not of a man!" [23] At once an angel of the Lord struck him because he did not give the glory to God, and he was eaten by worms and died.

[24] But the word of God flourished and multiplied. [25] After they had completed their relief mission, Barnabas and Saul returned to^A^ Jerusalem, taking along John who was called Mark.

PREPARING FOR THE MISSION FIELD

13 Now in the church at Antioch there were prophets and teachers: Barnabas, Simeon who was called Niger, Lucius of Cyrene, Manaen, a close friend of Herod the tetrarch, and Saul. [2] As they were worshiping^B^ the Lord and fasting, the Holy Spirit said, "Set apart for me Barnabas and Saul for the work to which I have called them." [3] Then after they had fasted, prayed, and laid hands on them, they sent them off.

THE MISSION TO CYPRUS

[4] So being sent out by the Holy Spirit, they went down to Seleucia, and from there they sailed to Cyprus. [5] Arriving in Salamis, they proclaimed the word of God in the Jewish synagogues. They also had John as their assistant. [6] When they had traveled the whole island as far as Paphos, they came across a sorcerer, a Jewish false prophet named Bar-Jesus. [7] He was with the proconsul, Sergius Paulus, an intelligent man. This man summoned Barnabas and Saul and wanted to hear the word of God. [8] But Elymas the sorcerer (that is the meaning of his name) opposed them and tried to turn the proconsul away from the faith.

[9] But Saul — also called Paul — filled with the Holy Spirit, stared straight at Elymas [10] and said, "You are full of all kinds of deceit and trickery, you son of the devil and enemy of all that is right. Won't you ever stop perverting the straight paths of the Lord? [11] Now, look, the Lord's hand is against you. You are going to be blind, and will not see the sun for a time."

Immediately a mist and darkness fell on him, and he went around seeking someone to lead him by the hand. [12] Then, when he saw what happened, the proconsul believed, because he was astonished at the teaching of the Lord.

PAUL'S SERMON IN ANTIOCH OF PISIDIA

[13] Paul and his companions set sail from Paphos and came to Perga in Pamphylia, but John left them and went back to Jerusalem. [14] They continued their journey from Perga and reached Pisidian Antioch. On the Sabbath day they went into the synagogue and sat down. [15] After the reading of the Law and the Prophets, the leaders of the synagogue sent word to them, saying, "Brothers, if you have any word of encouragement for the people, you can speak."

[16] Paul stood up and motioned with his hand and said: "Fellow Israelites, and you who fear God, listen! [17] The God of this people Israel chose our ancestors, made the people prosper during their stay in the land of Egypt, and led them out of it with a mighty^C^ arm. [18] And for about forty years he put up with them^D^ in the wilderness; [19] and after destroying seven nations in the land of Canaan, he gave them their land as an inheritance. [20] This all took about 450 years. After this, he gave them judges until Samuel the prophet. [21] Then they asked for a king, and God gave them Saul the son of Kish, a man of the tribe of Benjamin, for forty years. [22] After removing him, he raised up David as their king and testified about him: '**I have found David** the son of Jesse to be **a man after my own heart,**^E^ who will carry out all my will.'

[23] "From this man's descendants, as he promised, God brought to Israel the Savior, Jesus.^F^ [24] Before his coming to public attention, John had previously proclaimed a baptism of repentance to all the people of Israel. [25] Now as John was completing his mission, he said, 'Who do you think I am? I am not the one. But one is coming after me, and I am not worthy to untie the sandals on his feet.'

[26] "Brothers and sisters, children of Abraham's race, and those among you who fear God, it is to us that the word of this salvation has been sent. [27] Since the residents of Jerusalem and their rulers did not recognize him or the sayings of the prophets that are read every Sabbath, they have fulfilled their words by condemning him. [28] Though they found no grounds for the death sentence, they asked Pilate to have him killed. [29] When they had carried out all that had been written about him, they

---

^A^12:25 Other mss read *from*   ^B^13:2 Or *were ministering to*   ^C^13:17 Lit *with an uplifted*   ^D^13:18 Other mss read *he cared for them*   ^E^13:22 1Sm 13:14; Ps 89:20   ^F^13:23 Other mss read *brought salvation*

took him down from the tree and put him in a tomb. ³⁰ But God raised him from the dead, ³¹ and he appeared for many days to those who came up with him from Galilee to Jerusalem, who are now his witnesses to the people. ³² And we ourselves proclaim to you the good news of the promise that was made to our ancestors. ³³ God has fulfilled this for us, their children, by raising up Jesus, as it is written in the second Psalm:

You are my Son;
today I have become your Father.ᴬ,ᴮ

³⁴ As to his raising him from the dead, never to return to decay, he has spoken in this way, I will give you the holy and sure promises of David.ᶜ ³⁵ Therefore he also says in another passage, You will not let your Holy One see decay.ᴰ ³⁶ For David, after serving God's purpose in his own generation, fell asleep, was buried with his fathers, and decayed, ³⁷ but the one God raised up did not decay. ³⁸ Therefore, let it be known to you, brothers and sisters, that through this man forgiveness of sins is being proclaimed to you. ³⁹ Everyone who believes is justifiedᴱ through him from everything that you could not be justified from through the law of Moses. ⁴⁰ So beware that what is said in the prophets does not happen to you:

⁴¹ Look, you scoffers,
marvel and vanish away,
because I am doing a work
in your days,
a work that you will never believe,
even if someone were to explain it
to you."ᶠ

PAUL AND BARNABAS IN ANTIOCH

⁴² As they were leaving, the peopleᴳ urged them to speak about these matters the following Sabbath. ⁴³ After the synagogue had been dismissed, many of the Jews and devout converts to Judaism followed Paul and Barnabas, who were speaking with them and urging them to continue in the grace of God.

⁴⁴ The following Sabbath almost the whole town assembled to hear the word of the Lord.ᴴ ⁴⁵ But when the Jews saw the crowds, they were filled with jealousy and began to contradict what Paul was saying, insulting him.

⁴⁶ Paul and Barnabas boldly replied, "It was necessary that the word of God be spoken to you first. Since you reject it and judge yourselves unworthy of eternal life, we are turning to the Gentiles. ⁴⁷ For this is what the Lord has commanded us:

I have made you
a light for the Gentiles
to bring salvation
to the end of the earth."ᴵ

⁴⁸ When the Gentiles heard this, they rejoiced and honored the word of the Lord, and all who had been appointed to eternal life believed. ⁴⁹ The word of the Lord spread through the whole region. ⁵⁰ But the Jews incited the prominent God-fearing women and the leading men of the city. They stirred up persecution against Paul and Barnabas and expelled them from their district. ⁵¹ But Paul and Barnabas shook the dust off their feet against them and went to Iconium. ⁵² And the disciples were filled with joy and the Holy Spirit.

GROWTH AND PERSECUTION IN ICONIUM

14 In Iconium they entered the Jewish synagogue, as usual, and spoke in such a way that a great number of both Jews and Greeks believed. ² But the unbelieving Jews stirred up the Gentiles and poisoned their minds against the brothers. ³ So they stayed there a long time and spoke boldly for the Lord, who testified to the message of his grace by enabling them to do signs and wonders. ⁴ But the people of the city were divided, some siding with the Jews and others with the apostles. ⁵ When an attempt was made by both the Gentiles and Jews, with their rulers, to mistreat and stone them, ⁶ they found out about it and fled to the Lycaonian towns of Lystra and Derbe and to the surrounding countryside. ⁷ There they continued preaching the gospel.

MISTAKEN FOR GODS IN LYSTRA

⁸ In Lystra a man was sitting who was without strength in his feet, had never walked, and had been lame from birth. ⁹ He listened as Paul spoke. After looking directly at him and seeing that he had faith to be healed, ¹⁰ Paul said in a loud voice, "Stand up on your feet!" And he jumped up and began to walk around.

¹¹ When the crowds saw what Paul had done, they shouted, saying in the Lycaonian language, "The gods have come down to us in human form!" ¹² Barnabas they called Zeus, and Paul, Hermes, because he was the chief speaker. ¹³ The priest of Zeus, whose temple was just outside the town, brought bulls and wreaths to the gates because he intended, with the crowds, to offer sacrifice.

¹⁴ The apostles Barnabas and Paul tore their robes when they heard this and rushed into

ᴬ13:33 Or I have begotten you ᴮ13:33 Ps 2:7 ᶜ13:34 Is 55:3 ᴰ13:35 Ps 16:10 ᴱ13:39 Or freed, also later in verse ᶠ13:41 Hab 1:5 ᴳ13:42 Other mss read they were leaving the synagogue of the Jews, the Gentiles ᴴ13:44 Other mss read of God ᴵ13:47 Is 49:6

the crowd, shouting: [15] "People! Why are you doing these things? We are people also, just like you, and we are proclaiming good news to you, that you turn from these worthless things to the living God, **who made the heaven, the earth, the sea, and everything in them.**[A] [16] In past generations he allowed all the nations to go their own way, [17] although he did not leave himself without a witness, since he did what is good by giving you rain from heaven and fruitful seasons and filling you with food and your[B] hearts with joy." [18] Even though they said these things, they barely stopped the crowds from sacrificing to them.

[19] Some Jews came from Antioch and Iconium, and when they won over the crowds, they stoned Paul and dragged him out of the city, thinking he was dead. [20] After the disciples gathered around him, he got up and went into the town. The next day he left with Barnabas for Derbe.

CHURCH PLANTING

[21] After they had preached the gospel in that town and made many disciples, they returned to Lystra, to Iconium, and to Antioch, [22] strengthening the[C] disciples by encouraging them to continue in the faith and by telling them, "It is necessary to go through many hardships to enter the kingdom of God." [23] When they had appointed elders for them in every church and prayed with fasting, they committed them to the Lord in whom they had believed.

[24] They passed through Pisidia and came to Pamphylia. [25] After they had spoken the word in Perga, they went down to Attalia. [26] From there they sailed back to Antioch where they had been commended to the grace of God for the work they had now completed. [27] After they arrived and gathered the church together, they reported everything God had done with them and that he had opened the door of faith to the Gentiles. [28] And they spent a considerable time with the disciples.

DISPUTE IN ANTIOCH

15 Some men came down from Judea and began to teach the brothers: "Unless you are circumcised according to the custom prescribed by Moses, you cannot be saved." [2] After Paul and Barnabas had engaged them in serious argument and debate, Paul and Barnabas and some others were appointed to go up to the apostles and elders in Jerusalem about this issue. [3] When they had been sent on their way by the church, they passed through both Phoenicia and Samaria, describing in detail the conversion of the Gentiles, and they brought great joy to all the brothers and sisters.

[4] When they arrived at Jerusalem, they were welcomed by the church, the apostles, and the elders, and they reported all that God had done with them. [5] But some of the believers who belonged to the party of the Pharisees stood up and said, "It is necessary to circumcise them and to command them to keep the law of Moses."

THE JERUSALEM COUNCIL

[6] The apostles and the elders gathered to consider this matter. [7] After there had been much debate, Peter stood up and said to them: "Brothers and sisters, you are aware that in the early days God made a choice among you,[D] that by my mouth the Gentiles would hear the gospel message and believe. [8] And God, who knows the heart, bore witness to them by giving them the Holy Spirit, just as he also did to us. [9] He made no distinction between us and them, cleansing their hearts by faith. [10] Now then, why are you testing God by putting a yoke on the disciples' necks that neither our ancestors nor we have been able to bear? [11] On the contrary, we believe that we are saved through the grace of the Lord Jesus in the same way they are."

[12] The whole assembly became silent and listened to Barnabas and Paul describe all the signs and wonders God had done through them among the Gentiles. [13] After they stopped speaking, James responded: "Brothers and sisters, listen to me. [14] Simeon[E] has reported how God first intervened to take from the Gentiles a people for his name. [15] And the words of the prophets agree with this, as it is written:

[16]   After these things I will return
       and rebuild David's fallen tent.
       I will rebuild its ruins
       and set it up again,
[17]   so the rest of humanity
       may seek the Lord —
       even all the Gentiles
       who are called by my name —
       declares the Lord
       who makes these things [18] known
       from long ago.[F,G]

[19] Therefore, in my judgment, we should not cause difficulties for those among the Gentiles who turn to God, [20] but instead we should write to them to abstain from things polluted by idols, from sexual immorality, from eating anything that has been strangled, and from blood. [21] For

A**14:15** Ex 20:11; Ps 146:6   B**14:17** Other mss read *our*   C**14:22** Lit *the souls of the*   D**15:7** Other mss read *us*   E**15:14** Simon (Peter)   F**15:17-18** Other mss read *says the Lord who does all these things. Known to God from long ago are all his works.* G**15:16-18** Am 9:11-12; Is 45:21

since ancient times, Moses has had those who proclaim him in every city, and every Sabbath day he is read aloud in the synagogues."

THE LETTER TO THE GENTILE BELIEVERS

²² Then the apostles and the elders, with the whole church, decided to select men who were among them and to send them to Antioch with Paul and Barnabas: Judas, called Barsabbas, and Silas, both leading men among the brothers. ²³ They wrote:

"From the apostles and the elders, your brothers,

To the brothers and sisters among the Gentiles in Antioch, Syria, and Cilicia: Greetings.

²⁴ Since we have heard that some without our authorization went out from us and troubled you with their words and unsettled your hearts,^A ²⁵ we have unanimously decided to select men and send them to you along with our dearly loved Barnabas and Paul, ²⁶ who have risked their lives for the name of our Lord Jesus Christ. ²⁷ Therefore we have sent Judas and Silas, who will personally report the same things by word of mouth. ²⁸ For it was the Holy Spirit's decision — and ours — not to place further burdens on you beyond these requirements: ²⁹ that you abstain from food offered to idols, from blood, from eating anything that has been strangled, and from sexual immorality. You will do well if you keep yourselves from these things. Farewell."

THE OUTCOME OF THE JERUSALEM LETTER

³⁰ So they were sent off and went down to Antioch, and after gathering the assembly, they delivered the letter. ³¹ When they read it, they rejoiced because of its encouragement. ³² Both Judas and Silas, who were also prophets themselves, encouraged the brothers and sisters and strengthened them with a long message. ³³ After spending some time there, they were sent back in peace by the brothers and sisters to those who had sent them.^B,C ³⁵ But Paul and Barnabas, along with many others, remained in Antioch, teaching and proclaiming the word of the Lord.

PAUL AND BARNABAS PART COMPANY

³⁶ After some time had passed, Paul said to Barnabas, "Let's go back and visit the brothers and sisters in every town where we have preached the word of the Lord and see how they're doing." ³⁷ Barnabas wanted to take along John Mark.^D ³⁸ But Paul insisted that they should not take along this man who had deserted them in Pamphylia and had not gone on with them to the work. ³⁹ They had such a sharp disagreement that they parted company, and Barnabas took Mark with him and sailed off to Cyprus. ⁴⁰ But Paul chose Silas and departed, after being commended by the brothers and sisters to the grace of the Lord. ⁴¹ He traveled through Syria and Cilicia, strengthening the churches.

PAUL SELECTS TIMOTHY

16 Paul went on to Derbe and Lystra, where there was a disciple named Timothy, the son of a believing Jewish woman, but his father was a Greek. ² The brothers and sisters at Lystra and Iconium spoke highly of him. ³ Paul wanted Timothy to go with him; so he took him and circumcised him because of the Jews who were in those places, since they all knew that his father was a Greek. ⁴ As they traveled through the towns, they delivered the decisions reached by the apostles and elders at Jerusalem for the people to observe. ⁵ So the churches were strengthened in the faith and grew daily in numbers.

EVANGELIZATION OF EUROPE

⁶ They went through the region of Phrygia and Galatia; they had been forbidden by the Holy Spirit to speak the word in Asia. ⁷ When they came to Mysia, they tried to go into Bithynia, but the Spirit of Jesus did not allow them. ⁸ Passing by Mysia they went down to Troas. ⁹ During the night Paul had a vision in which a Macedonian man was standing and pleading with him, "Cross over to Macedonia and help us!" ¹⁰ After he had seen the vision, we immediately made efforts to set out for Macedonia, concluding that God had called us to preach the gospel to them.

LYDIA'S CONVERSION

¹¹ From Troas we put out to sea and sailed straight for Samothrace, the next day to Neapolis, ¹² and from there to Philippi, a Roman colony and a leading city of the district of Macedonia. We stayed in that city for several days. ¹³ On the Sabbath day we went outside the city gate by the river, where we expected to find a place of prayer. We sat down and spoke to the women gathered there. ¹⁴ A God-fearing woman named Lydia, a dealer in purple cloth from the city of Thyatira, was listening. The Lord opened her heart to respond to what Paul was

---

^A **15:24** Other mss add *by saying, 'Be circumcised and keep the law,'*   ^B **15:33** Other mss read *the brothers to the apostles*   ^C **15:33** Other mss add v. 34: *But Silas decided to stay there.*   ^D **15:37** Lit *John who was called Mark*

saying. [15] After she and her household were baptized, she urged us, "If you consider me a believer in the Lord, come and stay at my house." And she persuaded us.

PAUL AND SILAS IN PRISON

[16] Once, as we were on our way to prayer, a slave girl met us who had a spirit by which she predicted the future. She made a large profit for her owners by fortune-telling. [17] As she followed Paul and us she cried out, "These men, who are proclaiming to you[A] the way of salvation, are the servants of the Most High God." [18] She did this for many days.

Paul was greatly annoyed. Turning to the spirit, he said, "I command you in the name of Jesus Christ to come out of her!" And it came out right away.

[19] When her owners realized that their hope of profit was gone, they seized Paul and Silas and dragged them into the marketplace to the authorities. [20] Bringing them before the chief magistrates, they said, "These men are seriously disturbing our city. They are Jews [21] and are promoting customs that are not legal for us as Romans to adopt or practice." [22] The crowd joined in the attack against them, and the chief magistrates stripped off their clothes and ordered them to be beaten with rods. [23] After they had severely flogged them, they threw them in jail, ordering the jailer to guard them carefully. [24] Receiving such an order, he put them into the inner prison and secured their feet in the stocks.

A MIDNIGHT DELIVERANCE

[25] About midnight Paul and Silas were praying and singing hymns to God, and the prisoners were listening to them. [26] Suddenly there was such a violent earthquake that the foundations of the jail were shaken, and immediately all the doors were opened, and everyone's chains came loose. [27] When the jailer woke up and saw the doors of the prison standing open, he drew his sword and was going to kill himself, since he thought the prisoners had escaped. [28] But Paul called out in a loud voice, "Don't harm yourself, because we're all here!"

[29] The jailer called for lights, rushed in, and fell down trembling before Paul and Silas. [30] He escorted them out and said, "Sirs, what must I do to be saved?"

[31] They said, "Believe in the Lord Jesus, and you will be saved — you and your household." [32] And they spoke the word of the Lord to him along with everyone in his house. [33] He took them the same hour of the night and washed their wounds. Right away he and all his family were baptized. [34] He brought them into his house, set a meal before them, and rejoiced because he had come to believe in God with his entire household.

AN OFFICIAL APOLOGY

[35] When daylight came, the chief magistrates sent the police to say, "Release those men."

[36] The jailer reported these words to Paul: "The magistrates have sent orders for you to be released. So come out now and go in peace."

[37] But Paul said to them, "They beat us in public without a trial, although we are Roman citizens, and threw us in jail. And now are they going to send us away secretly? Certainly not! On the contrary, let them come themselves and escort us out."

[38] The police reported these words to the magistrates. They were afraid when they heard that Paul and Silas were Roman citizens. [39] So they came to appease them, and escorting them from prison, they urged them to leave town. [40] After leaving the jail, they came to Lydia's house, where they saw and encouraged the brothers and sisters, and departed.

A SHORT MINISTRY IN THESSALONICA

17 After they passed through Amphipolis and Apollonia, they came to Thessalonica, where there was a Jewish synagogue. [2] As usual, Paul went into the synagogue, and on three Sabbath days reasoned with them from the Scriptures, [3] explaining and proving that it was necessary for the Messiah to suffer and rise from the dead: "This Jesus I am proclaiming to you is the Messiah." [4] Some of them were persuaded and joined Paul and Silas, including a large number of God-fearing Greeks, as well as a number of the leading women.

RIOT IN THE CITY

[5] But the Jews became jealous, and they brought together some wicked men from the marketplace, formed a mob, and started a riot in the city. Attacking Jason's house, they searched for them to bring them out to the public assembly. [6] When they did not find them, they dragged Jason and some of the brothers before the city officials, shouting, "These men who have turned the world upside down have come here too, [7] and Jason has welcomed them. They are all acting contrary to Caesar's decrees, saying that there is another king — Jesus." [8] The crowd and city officials who heard these things were upset. [9] After taking a security bond from Jason and the others, they released them.

THE BEREANS SEARCH THE SCRIPTURES

[10] As soon as it was night, the brothers and sisters sent Paul and Silas away to Berea. Upon arrival, they went into the synagogue of the Jews. [11] The people here were of more noble character than those in Thessalonica, since they received the word with eagerness and examined the Scriptures daily to see if these things were so. [12] Consequently, many of them believed, including a number of the prominent Greek women as well as men. [13] But when the Jews from Thessalonica found out that the word of God had been proclaimed by Paul at Berea, they came there too, agitating and upsetting[A] the crowds. [14] Then the brothers and sisters immediately sent Paul away to go to the coast, but Silas and Timothy stayed on there. [15] Those who escorted Paul brought him as far as Athens, and after receiving instructions for Silas and Timothy to come to him as quickly as possible, they departed.

PAUL IN ATHENS

[16] While Paul was waiting for them in Athens, he was deeply distressed when he saw that the city was full of idols. [17] So he reasoned in the synagogue with the Jews and with those who worshiped God, as well as in the marketplace every day with those who happened to be there. [18] Some of the Epicurean and Stoic philosophers also debated with him. Some said, "What is this ignorant show-off[B] trying to say?"

Others replied, "He seems to be a preacher of foreign deities" — because he was telling the good news about Jesus and the resurrection. [19] They took him and brought him to the Areopagus,[C] and said, "May we learn about this new teaching you are presenting? [20] Because what you say sounds strange to us, and we want to know what these things mean." [21] Now all the Athenians and the foreigners residing there spent their time on nothing else but telling or hearing something new.

THE AREOPAGUS ADDRESS

[22] Paul stood in the middle of the Areopagus and said: "People of Athens! I see that you are extremely religious in every respect. [23] For as I was passing through and observing the objects of your worship, I even found an altar on which was inscribed: 'To an Unknown God.' Therefore, what you worship in ignorance, this I proclaim to you. [24] The God who made the world and everything in it — he is Lord of heaven and earth — does not live in shrines made by hands. [25] Neither is he served by human hands, as though he needed anything, since he himself gives everyone life and breath and all things. [26] From one man[D] he has made every nationality to live over the whole earth and has determined their appointed times and the boundaries of where they live. [27] He did this so that they might seek God, and perhaps they might reach out and find him, though he is not far from each one of us. [28] For in him we live and move and have our being, as even some of your own poets have said, 'For we are also his offspring.' [29] Since we are God's offspring then, we shouldn't think that the divine nature is like gold or silver or stone, an image fashioned by human art and imagination.

[30] "Therefore, having overlooked the times of ignorance, God now commands all people everywhere to repent, [31] because he has set a day when he is going to judge the world in righteousness by the man he has appointed. He has provided proof of this to everyone by raising him from the dead."

[32] When they heard about the resurrection of the dead, some began to ridicule him, but others said, "We'd like to hear from you again about this." [33] So Paul left their presence. [34] However, some people joined him and believed, including Dionysius the Areopagite, a woman named Damaris, and others with them.

FOUNDING THE CORINTHIAN CHURCH

18 After this, he[E] left Athens and went to Corinth, [2] where he found a Jew named Aquila, a native of Pontus, who had recently come from Italy with his wife Priscilla because Claudius had ordered all the Jews to leave Rome. Paul came to them, [3] and since they were of the same occupation, tentmakers by trade, he stayed with them and worked. [4] He reasoned in the synagogue every Sabbath and tried to persuade both Jews and Greeks.

[5] When Silas and Timothy arrived from Macedonia, Paul devoted himself to preaching the word[F] and testified to the Jews that Jesus is the Messiah. [6] When they resisted and blasphemed, he shook out his clothes and told them, "Your blood is on your own heads! I am innocent.[G] From now on I will go to the Gentiles." [7] So he left there and went to the house of a man named Titius Justus, a worshiper of God, whose house was next door to the synagogue. [8] Crispus, the leader of the synagogue, believed in the Lord, along with his whole household. Many of the Corinthians, when they heard, believed and were baptized.

[A] 17:13 Other mss omit *and upsetting*   [B] 17:18 Lit *this seed picker*   [C] 17:19 Or *Mars Hill*   [D] 17:26 Other mss read *blood*
[E] 18:1 Other mss read *Paul*   [F] 18:5 Other mss read *was urged by the Spirit*   [G] 18:6 Lit *clean*

[9] The Lord said to Paul in a night vision, "Don't be afraid, but keep on speaking and don't be silent. [10] For I am with you, and no one will lay a hand on you to hurt you, because I have many people in this city." [11] He stayed there a year and a half, teaching the word of God among them.

[12] While Gallio was proconsul of Achaia, the Jews made a united attack against Paul and brought him to the tribunal. [13] "This man," they said, " is persuading people to worship God in ways contrary to the law."

[14] As Paul was about to open his mouth, Gallio said to the Jews, "If it were a matter of wrongdoing or of a serious crime, it would be reasonable for me to put up with you Jews. [15] But if these are questions about words, names, and your own law, see to it yourselves. I refuse to be a judge of such things." [16] So he drove them from the tribunal. [17] And they all[A] seized Sosthenes, the leader of the synagogue, and beat him in front of the tribunal, but none of these things mattered to Gallio.

THE RETURN TRIP TO ANTIOCH

[18] After staying for some time, Paul said farewell to the brothers and sisters and sailed away to Syria, accompanied by Priscilla and Aquila. He shaved his head at Cenchreae because of a vow he had taken. [19] When they reached Ephesus he left them there, but he himself entered the synagogue and debated with the Jews. [20] When they asked him to stay for a longer time, he declined, [21] but he said farewell and added,[B] "I'll come back to you again, if God wills." Then he set sail from Ephesus.

[22] On landing at Caesarea, he went up to Jerusalem and greeted the church, then went down to Antioch.

[23] After spending some time there, he set out, traveling through one place after another in the region of Galatia and Phrygia, strengthening all the disciples.

THE ELOQUENT APOLLOS

[24] Now a Jew named Apollos, a native Alexandrian, an eloquent man who was competent in the use of the Scriptures, arrived in Ephesus. [25] He had been instructed in the way of the Lord; and being fervent in spirit,[C] he was speaking and teaching accurately about Jesus, although he knew only John's baptism. [26] He began to speak boldly in the synagogue. After Priscilla and Aquila heard him, they took him aside[D] and explained the way of God to him more accurately. [27] When he wanted to cross over to Achaia, the brothers and sisters wrote to the disciples to welcome him. After he arrived, he was a great help to those who by grace had believed. [28] For he vigorously refuted the Jews in public, demonstrating through the Scriptures that Jesus is the Messiah.

TWELVE DISCIPLES OF JOHN THE BAPTIST

19 While Apollos was in Corinth, Paul traveled through the interior regions and came to Ephesus. He found some disciples [2] and asked them, "Did you receive the Holy Spirit when you believed?"

"No," they told him, "we haven't even heard that there is a Holy Spirit."

[3] "Into what then were you baptized?" he asked them.

"Into John's baptism," they replied.

[4] Paul said, "John baptized with a baptism of repentance, telling the people that they should believe in the one who would come after him, that is, in Jesus."

[5] When they heard this, they were baptized into the name of the Lord Jesus. [6] And when Paul laid his hands on them, the Holy Spirit came on them, and they began to speak in other tongues[E] and to prophesy. [7] Now there were about twelve men in all.

IN THE LECTURE HALL OF TYRANNUS

[8] Paul entered the synagogue and spoke boldly over a period of three months, arguing and persuading them about the kingdom of God. [9] But when some became hardened and would not believe, slandering the Way in front of the crowd, he withdrew from them, taking the disciples, and conducted discussions every day in the lecture hall of Tyrannus. [10] This went on for two years, so that all the residents of Asia, both Jews and Greeks, heard the word of the Lord.

DEMONISM DEFEATED AT EPHESUS

[11] God was performing extraordinary miracles by Paul's hands, [12] so that even facecloths or aprons[F] that had touched his skin were brought to the sick, and the diseases left them, and the evil spirits came out of them.

[13] Now some of the itinerant Jewish exorcists also attempted to pronounce the name of the Lord Jesus over those who had evil spirits, saying, "I command you by the Jesus that Paul preaches!" [14] Seven sons of Sceva, a Jewish high priest, were doing this. [15] The evil spirit answered them, "I know Jesus, and I recognize Paul — but who are you?" [16] Then the man who had the evil spirit jumped on them, overpowered them all, and prevailed against them,

---

[A]18:17 Other mss read *Then all the Greeks* [B]18:21 Other mss add *"By all means it is necessary to keep the coming festival in Jerusalem. But* [C]18:25 Or *in the Spirit* [D]18:26 Lit *they received him* [E]19:6 languages [F]19:12 Or *sweat cloths*

so that they ran out of that house naked and wounded. [17] When this became known to everyone who lived in Ephesus, both Jews and Greeks, they became afraid, and the name of the Lord Jesus was held in high esteem.

[18] And many who had become believers came confessing and disclosing their practices, [19] while many of those who had practiced magic collected their books and burned them in front of everyone. So they calculated their value and found it to be fifty thousand pieces of silver. [20] In this way the word of the Lord flourished and prevailed.

THE RIOT IN EPHESUS

[21] After these events, Paul resolved by the Spirit[A] to pass through Macedonia and Achaia and go to Jerusalem. "After I've been there," he said, "It is necessary for me to see Rome as well." [22] After sending to Macedonia two of those who assisted him, Timothy and Erastus, he himself stayed in Asia for a while.

[23] About that time there was a major disturbance about the Way. [24] For a person named Demetrius, a silversmith who made silver shrines of Artemis, provided a great deal of business for the craftsmen. [25] When he had assembled them, as well as the workers engaged in this type of business, he said: "Men, you know that our prosperity is derived from this business. [26] You see and hear that not only in Ephesus, but in almost all of Asia, this man Paul has persuaded and misled a considerable number of people by saying that gods made by hand are not gods. [27] Not only do we run a risk that our business may be discredited, but also that the temple of the great goddess Artemis may be despised and her magnificence come to the verge of ruin — the very one all of Asia and the world worship."

[28] When they had heard this, they were filled with rage and began to cry out, "Great is Artemis of the Ephesians!" [29] So the city was filled with confusion, and they rushed all together into the amphitheater, dragging along Gaius and Aristarchus, Macedonians who were Paul's traveling companions. [30] Although Paul wanted to go in before the people, the disciples did not let him. [31] Even some of the provincial officials of Asia, who were his friends, sent word to him, pleading with him not to venture[B] into the amphitheater. [32] Some were shouting one thing and some another, because the assembly was in confusion, and most of them did not know why they had come together. [33] Some Jews in the crowd gave instructions to Alexander[C] after they pushed him to the front. Motioning with his hand, Alexander wanted to make his defense to the people. [34] But when they recognized that he was a Jew, they all shouted in unison for about two hours: "Great is Artemis of the Ephesians!"

[35] When the city clerk had calmed the crowd down, he said, "People of Ephesus! What person is there who doesn't know that the city of the Ephesians is the temple guardian of the great[D] Artemis, and of the image that fell from heaven? [36] Therefore, since these things are undeniable, you must keep calm and not do anything rash. [37] For you have brought these men here who are not temple robbers or blasphemers of our[E] goddess. [38] So if Demetrius and the craftsmen who are with him have a case against anyone, the courts are in session, and there are proconsuls. Let them bring charges against one another. [39] But if you seek anything further, it must be decided in a legal assembly. [40] In fact, we run a risk of being charged with rioting for what happened today, since there is no justification that we can give as a reason for this disturbance." [41] After saying this, he dismissed the assembly.

PAUL IN MACEDONIA

20 After the uproar was over, Paul sent for the disciples, encouraged them, and after saying farewell, departed to go to Macedonia. [2] And when he had passed through those areas and offered them many words of encouragement, he came to Greece [3] and stayed three months. The Jews plotted against him when he was about to set sail for Syria, and so he decided to go back through Macedonia. [4] He was accompanied[F] by Sopater son of Pyrrhus[G] from Berea, Aristarchus and Secundus from Thessalonica, Gaius from Derbe, Timothy, and Tychicus and Trophimus from the province of Asia. [5] These men went on ahead and waited for us in Troas, [6] but we sailed away from Philippi after the Festival of Unleavened Bread. In five days we reached them at Troas, where we spent seven days.

EUTYCHUS REVIVED AT TROAS

[7] On the first day of the week, we[H] assembled to break bread. Paul spoke to them, and since he was about to depart the next day, he kept on talking until midnight. [8] There were many lamps in the room upstairs where we were assembled, [9] and a young man named Eutychus

---

[A]**19:21** Or *in his spirit*   [B]**19:31** Lit *not to give himself*   [C]**19:33** Or *thought it was about Alexander*   [D]**19:35** Other mss add *goddess*   [E]**19:37** Other mss read *your*   [F]**20:4** Other mss add *to Asia*   [G]**20:4** Other mss omit *son of Pyrrhus*   [H]**20:7** Other mss read *the disciples*

was sitting on a window sill and sank into a deep sleep as Paul kept on talking. When he was overcome by sleep, he fell down from the third story and was picked up dead. [10] But Paul went down, bent over him, embraced him, and said, "Don't be alarmed, because he's alive." [11] After going upstairs, breaking the bread, and eating, Paul talked a long time until dawn. Then he left. [12] They brought the boy home alive and were greatly comforted.

FROM TROAS TO MILETUS

[13] We went on ahead to the ship and sailed for Assos, where we were going to take Paul on board, because these were his instructions, since he himself was going by land. [14] When he met us at Assos, we took him on board and went on to Mitylene. [15] Sailing from there, the next day we arrived off Chios. The following day we crossed over to Samos, and[A] the day after, we came to Miletus. [16] For Paul had decided to sail past Ephesus to avoid spending time in the province of Asia, because he was hurrying to be in Jerusalem, if possible, for the day of Pentecost.

FAREWELL ADDRESS TO THE EPHESIAN ELDERS

[17] Now from Miletus, he sent to Ephesus and summoned the elders of the church. [18] When they came to him, he said to them: "You know, from the first day I set foot in Asia, how I was with you the whole time, [19] serving the Lord with all humility, with tears, and during the trials that came to me through the plots of the Jews. [20] You know that I did not avoid proclaiming to you anything that was profitable or from teaching you publicly and from house to house. [21] I testified to both Jews and Greeks about repentance toward God and faith in our Lord Jesus.

[22] "And now I am on my way to Jerusalem, compelled by the Spirit,[B] not knowing what I will encounter there, [23] except that in every town the Holy Spirit warns me that chains and afflictions are waiting for me. [24] But I consider my life of no value to myself; my purpose is to finish my course[C] and the ministry I received from the Lord Jesus, to testify to the gospel of God's grace.

[25] "And now I know that none of you, among whom I went about preaching the kingdom, will ever see me again. [26] Therefore I declare to you this day that I am innocent[D] of the blood of all of you, [27] because I did not avoid declaring to you the whole plan of God. [28] Be on guard

for yourselves and for all the flock of which the Holy Spirit has appointed you as overseers, to shepherd the church of God,[E] which he purchased with his own blood. [29] I know that after my departure savage wolves will come in among you, not sparing the flock. [30] Men will rise up even from your own number and distort the truth to lure the disciples into following them. [31] Therefore be on the alert, remembering that night and day for three years I never stopped warning each one of you with tears.

[32] "And now[F] I commit you to God and to the word of his grace, which is able to build you up and to give you an inheritance among all who are sanctified. [33] I have not coveted anyone's silver or gold or clothing. [34] You yourselves know that I worked with my own hands to support myself and those who are with me. [35] In every way I've shown you that it is necessary to help the weak by laboring like this and to remember the words of the Lord Jesus, because he said, 'It is more blessed to give than to receive.'"

[36] After he said this, he knelt down and prayed with all of them. [37] There were many tears shed by everyone. They embraced Paul and kissed him, [38] grieving most of all over his statement that they would never see his face again. And they accompanied him to the ship.

WARNINGS ON THE JOURNEY TO JERUSALEM

21 After we tore ourselves away from them, we set sail straight for Cos, the next day to Rhodes, and from there to Patara. [2] Finding a ship crossing over to Phoenicia, we boarded and set sail. [3] After we sighted Cyprus, passing to the south of it,[G] we sailed on to Syria and arrived at Tyre, since the ship was to unload its cargo there. [4] We sought out the disciples and stayed there seven days. Through the Spirit they told Paul not to go to Jerusalem. [5] When our time had come to an end, we left to continue our journey, while all of them, with their wives and children, accompanied us out of the city. After kneeling down on the beach to pray, [6] we said farewell to one another and boarded the ship, and they returned home.

[7] When we completed our voyage[H] from Tyre, we reached Ptolemais, where we greeted the brothers and sisters and stayed with them for a day. [8] The next day we left and came to Caesarea, where we entered the house of Philip the evangelist, who was one of the Seven, and stayed with him. [9] This man had four virgin daughters who prophesied.

---

^20:15 Other mss add *after staying at Trogyllium*   ^B 20:22 Or *in my spirit*   ^C 20:24 Other mss add *with joy*   ^D 20:26 Lit *clean*
^E 20:28 Some mss read *church of the Lord*; other mss read *church of the Lord and God*   ^F 20:32 Other mss add *brothers and sisters*   ^G 21:3 Lit *leaving it on the left*   ^H 21:7 Or *As we continued our voyage*

[10] After we had been there for several days, a prophet named Agabus came down from Judea. [11] He came to us, took Paul's belt, tied his own feet and hands, and said, "This is what the Holy Spirit says: 'In this way the Jews in Jerusalem will bind the man who owns this belt and deliver him over to the Gentiles.'" [12] When we heard this, both we and the local people pleaded with him not to go up to Jerusalem.

[13] Then Paul replied, "What are you doing, weeping and breaking my heart? For I am ready not only to be bound but also to die in Jerusalem for the name of the Lord Jesus."

[14] Since he would not be persuaded, we said no more except, "The Lord's will be done."

CONFLICT OVER THE GENTILE MISSION

[15] After this we got ready and went up to Jerusalem. [16] Some of the disciples from Caesarea also went with us and brought us to Mnason of Cyprus, an early disciple, with whom we were to stay.

[17] When we reached Jerusalem, the brothers and sisters welcomed us warmly. [18] The following day Paul went in with us to James, and all the elders were present. [19] After greeting them, he reported in detail what God had done among the Gentiles through his ministry.

[20] When they heard it, they glorified God and said, "You see, brother, how many thousands of Jews there are who have believed, and they are all zealous for the law. [21] But they have been informed about you — that you are teaching all the Jews who are among the Gentiles to abandon Moses, telling them not to circumcise their children or to live according to our customs. [22] So what is to be done?[A] They will certainly hear that you've come. [23] Therefore do what we tell you: We have four men who have made a vow. [24] Take these men, purify yourself along with them, and pay for them to get their heads shaved. Then everyone will know that what they were told about you amounts to nothing, but that you yourself are also careful about observing the law. [25] With regard to the Gentiles who have believed, we have written a letter containing our decision that[B] they should keep themselves from food sacrificed to idols, from blood, from what is strangled, and from sexual immorality."

THE RIOT IN THE TEMPLE

[26] So the next day, Paul took the men, having purified himself along with them, and entered the temple, announcing the completion of the purification days when the offering would be made for each of them. [27] When the seven days were nearly over, some Jews from the province of Asia saw him in the temple, stirred up the whole crowd, and seized him, [28] shouting, "Fellow Israelites, help! This is the man who teaches everyone everywhere against our people, our law, and this place. What's more, he also brought Greeks into the temple and has defiled this holy place." [29] For they had previously seen Trophimus the Ephesian in the city with him, and they supposed that Paul had brought him into the temple.

[30] The whole city was stirred up, and the people rushed together. They seized Paul, dragged him out of the temple, and at once the gates were shut. [31] As they were trying to kill him, word went up to the commander of the regiment that all Jerusalem was in chaos. [32] Taking along soldiers and centurions, he immediately ran down to them. Seeing the commander and the soldiers, they stopped beating Paul. [33] Then the commander approached, took him into custody, and ordered him to be bound with two chains. He asked who he was and what he had done. [34] Some in the crowd were shouting one thing and some another. Since he was not able to get reliable information because of the uproar, he ordered him to be taken into the barracks. [35] When Paul got to the steps, he had to be carried by the soldiers because of the violence of the crowd, [36] for the mass of people followed, yelling, "Get rid of him!"

PAUL'S DEFENSE BEFORE THE JERUSALEM MOB

[37] As he was about to be brought into the barracks, Paul said to the commander, "Am I allowed to say something to you?"

He replied, "You know how to speak Greek? [38] Aren't you the Egyptian who started a revolt some time ago and led four thousand men of the Assassins into the wilderness?"

[39] Paul said, "I am a Jewish man from Tarsus of Cilicia, a citizen of an important city. Now I ask you, let me speak to the people."

[40] After he had given permission, Paul stood on the steps and motioned with his hand to the people. When there was a great hush, he **22** addressed them in Aramaic:[C] [1] "Brothers and fathers, listen now to my defense before you." [2] When they heard that he was addressing them in Aramaic,[C] they became even quieter. [3] He continued, "I am a Jew, born in Tarsus of Cilicia but brought up in this city, educated at the feet of Gamaliel according to the law of our ancestors. I was zealous for God, just as all of you are today. [4] I persecuted this Way to the death, arresting and putting both men and women in jail, [5] as both the high priest and

---

[A]21:22 Other mss add *A multitude has to come together, since except that*   [B]21:25 Other mss add *they should observe no such thing,*   [C]21:40; 22:2 Or *Hebrew*

the whole council of elders can testify about me. After I received letters from them to the brothers, I traveled to Damascus to arrest those who were there and bring them to Jerusalem to be punished.

PAUL'S TESTIMONY

[6] "As I was traveling and approaching Damascus, about noon an intense light from heaven suddenly flashed around me. [7] I fell to the ground and heard a voice saying to me, 'Saul, Saul, why are you persecuting me?'

[8] "I answered, 'Who are you, Lord?'

"He said to me, 'I am Jesus of Nazareth, the one you are persecuting.' [9] Now those who were with me saw the light,[A] but they did not hear the voice of the one who was speaking to me.

[10] "I said, 'What should I do, Lord?'

"The Lord told me, 'Get up and go into Damascus, and there you will be told everything that you have been assigned to do.'

[11] "Since I couldn't see because of the brightness of the light,[B] I was led by the hand by those who were with me, and went into Damascus. [12] Someone named Ananias, a devout man according to the law, who had a good reputation with all the Jews living there, [13] came and stood by me and said, 'Brother Saul, regain your sight.' And in that very hour I looked up and saw him. [14] And he said, 'The God of our ancestors has appointed you to know his will, to see the Righteous One, and to hear the words from his mouth, [15] since you will be a witness for him to all people of what you have seen and heard. [16] And now, why are you delaying? Get up and be baptized, and wash away your sins, calling on his name.'

[17] "After I returned to Jerusalem and was praying in the temple, I fell into a trance [18] and saw him telling me, 'Hurry and get out of Jerusalem quickly, because they will not accept your testimony about me.'

[19] "But I said, 'Lord, they know that in synagogue after synagogue I had those who believed in you imprisoned and beaten. [20] And when the blood of your witness Stephen was being shed, I stood there giving approval[C] and guarding the clothes of those who killed him.'

[21] "He said to me, 'Go, because I will send you far away to the Gentiles.'"

PAUL'S ROMAN PROTECTION

[22] They listened to him up to this point. Then they raised their voices, shouting, "Wipe this man off the face of the earth! He should not be allowed to live!"

[23] As they were yelling and flinging aside their garments and throwing dust into the air, [24] the commander ordered him to be brought into the barracks, directing that he be interrogated with the scourge to discover the reason they were shouting against him like this. [25] As they stretched him out for the lash, Paul said to the centurion standing by, "Is it legal for you to scourge a man who is a Roman citizen and is uncondemned?"

[26] When the centurion heard this, he went and reported to the commander, saying, "What are you going to do? For this man is a Roman citizen."

[27] The commander came and said to him, "Tell me, are you a Roman citizen?"

"Yes," he said.

[28] The commander replied, "I bought this citizenship for a large amount of money."

"But I was born a citizen," Paul said.

[29] So those who were about to examine him withdrew from him immediately. The commander too was alarmed when he realized Paul was a Roman citizen and he had bound him.

PAUL BEFORE THE SANHEDRIN

[30] The next day, since he wanted to find out exactly why Paul was being accused by the Jews, he released him[D] and instructed the chief priests and all the Sanhedrin to convene. He brought Paul down and placed him before them. [1] Paul looked straight at the Sanhedrin and said, "Brothers, I have lived my life before God in all good conscience to this day." [2] The high priest Ananias ordered those who were standing next to him to strike him on the mouth. [3] Then Paul said to him, "God is going to strike you, you whitewashed wall! You are sitting there judging me according to the law, and yet in violation of the law are you ordering me to be struck?"

[4] Those standing nearby said, "Do you dare revile God's high priest?"

[5] "I did not know, brothers, that he was the high priest," replied Paul. "For it is written, **You must not speak evil of a ruler of your people.**"[E] [6] When Paul realized that one part of them were Sadducees and the other part were Pharisees, he cried out in the Sanhedrin, "Brothers, I am a Pharisee, a son of Pharisees. I am being judged because of the hope of the resurrection of the dead!" [7] When he said this, a dispute broke out between the Pharisees and the Sadducees, and the assembly was divided. [8] For the Sadducees say there is no resurrection, and neither angel nor spirit, but the Pharisees affirm them all.

[A] 22:9 Other mss add *and were afraid*   [B] 22:11 Lit *the glory of that light*   [C] 22:20 Other mss add *of his murder*   [D] 22:30 Other mss add *from his chains*   [E] 23:5 Ex 22:28

⁹ The shouting grew loud, and some of the scribes of the Pharisees' party got up and argued vehemently: "We find nothing evil in this man. What if a spirit or an angel has spoken to him?"ᴬ

¹⁰ When the dispute became violent, the commander feared that Paul might be torn apart by them and ordered the troops to go down, take him away from them, and bring him into the barracks. ¹¹ The following night, the Lord stood by him and said, "Have courage! For as you have testified about me in Jerusalem, so it is necessary for you to testify in Rome."

THE PLOT AGAINST PAUL

¹² When it was morning, the Jews formed a conspiracy and bound themselves under a curse not to eat or drink until they had killed Paul. ¹³ There were more than forty who had formed this plot. ¹⁴ These men went to the chief priests and elders and said, "We have bound ourselves under a solemn curse that we won't eat anything until we have killed Paul. ¹⁵ So now you, along with the Sanhedrin, make a request to the commander that he bring him down to youᴮ as if you were going to investigate his case more thoroughly. But, before he gets near, we are ready to kill him."

¹⁶ But the son of Paul's sister, hearing about their ambush, came and entered the barracks and reported it to Paul. ¹⁷ Paul called one of the centurions and said, "Take this young man to the commander, because he has something to report to him."

¹⁸ So he took him, brought him to the commander, and said, "The prisoner Paul called me and asked me to bring this young man to you, because he has something to tell you."

¹⁹ The commander took him by the hand, led him aside, and inquired privately, "What is it you have to report to me?"

²⁰ "The Jews," he said, "have agreed to ask you to bring Paul down to the Sanhedrin tomorrow, as though they are going to hold a somewhat more careful inquiry about him. ²¹ Don't let them persuade you, because there are more than forty of them lying in ambush — men who have bound themselves under a curse not to eat or drink until they have killed him. Now they are ready, waiting for your consent."

²² So the commander dismissed the young man and instructed him, "Don't tell anyone that you have informed me about this."

TO CAESAREA BY NIGHT

²³ He summoned two of his centurions and said, "Get two hundred soldiers ready with seventy cavalry and two hundred spearmen to go to Caesarea at nine tonight.ᶜ ²⁴ Also provide mounts for Paul to ride and bring him safely to Felix the governor."

²⁵ He wrote the following letter:ᴰ
²⁶ Claudius Lysias,
To the most excellent governor Felix:
Greetings.
²⁷ When this man had been seized by the Jews and was about to be killed by them, I arrived with my troops and rescued him because I learned that he is a Roman citizen. ²⁸ Wanting to know the charge they were accusing him of, I brought him down before their Sanhedrin. ²⁹ I found out that the accusations were concerning questions of their law, and that there was no charge that merited death or imprisonment. ³⁰ When I was informed that there was a plot against the man,ᴱ I sent him to you right away. I also ordered his accusers to state their case against him in your presence.ᶠ

³¹ So the soldiers took Paul during the night and brought him to Antipatris as they were ordered. ³² The next day, they returned to the barracks, allowing the cavalry to go on with him. ³³ When these men entered Caesarea and delivered the letter to the governor, they also presented Paul to him. ³⁴ After heᶢ read it, he asked what province he was from. When he learned he was from Cilicia, ³⁵ he said, "I will give you a hearing whenever your accusers also get here." He ordered that he be kept under guard in Herod's palace.ᴴ

THE ACCUSATION AGAINST PAUL

24 Five days later Ananias the high priest came down with some elders and a lawyer named Tertullus. These men presented their case against Paul to the governor. ² When Paul was called in, Tertullus began to accuse him and said: "We enjoy great peace because of you, and reforms are taking place for the benefit of this nation because of your foresight. ³ We acknowledge this in every way and everywhere, most excellent Felix, with utmost gratitude. ⁴ But, so that I will not burden you any further, I request that you would be kind enough to give us a brief hearing. ⁵ For we have found this man to be a plague, an agitator among all the Jews

---

ᴬ23:9 Other mss add *Let us not fight God.*   ᴮ23:15 Other mss add *tomorrow*   ᶜ23:23 Lit *at the third hour tonight*
ᴰ23:25 Or *He wrote a letter to this effect:*   ᴱ23:30 Other mss add *by the Jews*   ᶠ23:30 Other mss add *Farewell*
ᴳ23:34 Other mss read *the governor*   ᴴ23:35 Or *headquarters*

throughout the Roman world, and a ringleader of the sect of the Nazarenes. [6] He even tried to desecrate the temple, and so we apprehended him.^ By examining him yourself you will be able to discern the truth about these charges we are bringing against him." [9] The Jews also joined in the attack, alleging that these things were true.

PAUL'S DEFENSE BEFORE FELIX

[10] When the governor motioned for him to speak, Paul replied: "Because I know you have been a judge of this nation for many years, I am glad to offer my defense in what concerns me. [11] You can verify for yourself that it is no more than twelve days since I went up to worship in Jerusalem. [12] They didn't find me arguing with anyone or causing a disturbance among the crowd, either in the temple or in the synagogues or anywhere in the city. [13] Neither can they prove the charges they are now making against me. [14] But I admit this to you: I worship the God of my ancestors according to the Way, which they call a sect, believing everything that is in accordance with the law and written in the prophets. [15] I have a hope in God, which these men themselves also accept, that there will be a resurrection,^ both of the righteous and the unrighteous. [16] I always strive to have a clear conscience toward God and men. [17] After many years, I came to bring charitable gifts and offerings to my people. [18] While I was doing this, some Jews from Asia found me ritually purified in the temple, without a crowd and without any uproar. [19] It is they who ought to be here before you to bring charges, if they have anything against me. [20] Or let these men here state what wrongdoing they found in me when I stood before the Sanhedrin, [21] other than this one statement I shouted while standing among them, 'Today I am on trial before you concerning the resurrection of the dead.'"

THE VERDICT POSTPONED

[22] Since Felix was well informed about the Way, he adjourned the hearing, saying, "When Lysias the commander comes down, I will decide your case." [23] He ordered that the centurion keep Paul under guard, though he could have some freedom, and that he should not prevent any of his friends from meeting^ his needs.

[24] Several days later, when Felix came with his wife Drusilla, who was Jewish, he sent for Paul and listened to him on the subject of faith in Christ Jesus. [25] Now as he spoke about righteousness, self-control, and the judgment to come, Felix became afraid and replied, "Leave for now, but when I have an opportunity I'll call for you." [26] At the same time he was also hoping that Paul would offer him money.^ So he sent for him quite often and conversed with him.

[27] After two years had passed, Porcius Festus succeeded Felix, and because Felix wanted to do the Jews a favor, he left Paul in prison.

APPEAL TO CAESAR

25 Three days after Festus arrived in the province, he went up to Jerusalem from Caesarea. [2] The chief priests and the leaders of the Jews presented their case against Paul to him; and they appealed, [3] asking for a favor against Paul, that Festus summon him to Jerusalem. They were, in fact, preparing an ambush along the road to kill him. [4] Festus, however, answered that Paul should be kept at Caesarea, and that he himself was about to go there shortly. [5] "Therefore," he said, "let those of you who have authority go down with me and accuse him, if he has done anything wrong."

[6] When he had spent not more than eight or ten days among them, he went down to Caesarea. The next day, seated at the tribunal, he commanded Paul to be brought in. [7] When he arrived, the Jews who had come down from Jerusalem stood around him and brought many serious charges that they were not able to prove. [8] Then Paul made his defense: "Neither against the Jewish law, nor against the temple, nor against Caesar have I sinned in any way."

[9] But Festus, wanting to do the Jews a favor, replied to Paul, "Are you willing to go up to Jerusalem to be tried before me there on these charges?"

[10] Paul replied: "I am standing at Caesar's tribunal, where I ought to be tried. I have done no wrong to the Jews, as even you yourself know very well. [11] If then I did anything wrong and am deserving of death, I am not trying to escape death; but if there is nothing to what these men accuse me of, no one can give me up to them. I appeal to Caesar!"

[12] Then after Festus conferred with his council, he replied, "You have appealed to Caesar; to Caesar you will go."

KING AGRIPPA AND BERNICE VISIT FESTUS

[13] Several days later, King Agrippa and Bernice arrived in Caesarea and paid a courtesy call on Festus. [14] Since they were staying there

---

^24:6 Some mss include vv. 6b-8a: *and wanted to judge him according to our law.* [7]*But Lysias the commander came and took him from our hands with great force,* [8]*commanding his accusers to come to you.*　　^24:15 Other mss add *of the dead*　^24:23 Other mss add *or visiting*　^24:26 Other mss add *so that he might release him*

several days, Festus presented Paul's case to the king, saying, "There's a man who was left as a prisoner by Felix. ¹⁵ When I was in Jerusalem, the chief priests and the elders of the Jews presented their case and asked that he be condemned. ¹⁶ I answered them that it is not the Roman custom to give someone up^ before the accused faces the accusers and has an opportunity for a defense against the charges. ¹⁷ So when they had assembled here, I did not delay. The next day I took my seat at the tribunal and ordered the man to be brought in. ¹⁸ The accusers stood up but brought no charge against him of the evils I was expecting. ¹⁹ Instead they had some disagreements with him about their own religion and about a certain Jesus, a dead man Paul claimed to be alive. ²⁰ Since I was at a loss in a dispute over such things, I asked him if he wanted to go to Jerusalem and be tried there regarding these matters. ²¹ But when Paul appealed to be held for trial by the Emperor,ᴮ I ordered him to be kept in custody until I could send him to Caesar."

²² Agrippa said to Festus, "I would like to hear the man myself."

"Tomorrow you will hear him," he replied.

PAUL BEFORE AGRIPPA

²³ So the next day, Agrippa and Bernice came with great pomp and entered the auditorium with the military commanders and prominent men of the city. When Festus gave the command, Paul was brought in. ²⁴ Then Festus said: "King Agrippa and all men present with us, you see this man. The whole Jewish community has appealed to me concerning him, both in Jerusalem and here, shouting that he should not live any longer. ²⁵ I found that he had not done anything deserving of death, but when he himself appealed to the Emperor, I decided to send him. ²⁶ I have nothing definite to write to my lord about him. Therefore, I have brought him before all of you, and especially before you, King Agrippa, so that after this examination is over, I may have something to write. ²⁷ For it seems unreasonable to me to send a prisoner without indicating the charges against him."

PAUL'S DEFENSE BEFORE AGRIPPA

26 Agrippa said to Paul, "You have permission to speak for yourself."

Then Paul stretched out his hand and began his defense: ² "I consider myself fortunate, that it is before you, King Agrippa, I am to make my defense today against all the accusations of the Jews, ³ especially since you are very

knowledgeable about all the Jewish customs and controversies. Therefore I beg you to listen to me patiently.

⁴ "All the Jews know my way of life from my youth, which was spent from the beginning among my own people and in Jerusalem. ⁵ They have known me for a long time, if they are willing to testify, that according to the strictest sect of our religion I lived as a Pharisee. ⁶ And now I stand on trial because of the hope in what God promised to our ancestors, ⁷ the promise our twelve tribes hope to reach as they earnestly serve him night and day. King Agrippa, I am being accused by the Jews because of this hope. ⁸ Why do any of you consider it incredible that God raises the dead? ⁹ In fact, I myself was convinced that it was necessary to do many things in opposition to the name of Jesus of Nazareth. ¹⁰ I actually did this in Jerusalem, and I locked up many of the saints in prison, since I had received authority for that from the chief priests. When they were put to death, I was in agreement against them. ¹¹ In all the synagogues I often punished them and tried to make them blaspheme. Since I was terribly enraged at them, I pursued them even to foreign cities.

PAUL'S ACCOUNT OF HIS CONVERSION AND COMMISSION

¹² "I was traveling to Damascus under these circumstances with authority and a commission from the chief priests. ¹³ King Agrippa, while on the road at midday, I saw a light from heaven brighter than the sun, shining around me and those traveling with me. ¹⁴ We all fell to the ground, and I heard a voice speaking to me in Aramaic,ᶜ 'Saul, Saul, why are you persecuting me? It is hard for you to kick against the goads.'

¹⁵ "I asked, 'Who are you, Lord?'

"And the Lord replied: 'I am Jesus, the one you are persecuting. ¹⁶ But get up and stand on your feet. For I have appeared to you for this purpose, to appoint you as a servant and a witness of what you have seen and will see of me. ¹⁷ I will rescue you from your people and from the Gentiles. I am sending you to themᴰ to open their eyes so that they may turnᴰ from darkness to light and from the power of Satan to God, that they may receive forgiveness of sins and a share among those who are sanctified by faith in me.'

¹⁹ "So then, King Agrippa, I was not disobedient to the heavenly vision. ²⁰ Instead, I preached to those in Damascus first, and to those in Jerusalem and in all the region of Judea, and to the Gentiles, that they should repent and turn

^25:16 Other mss add *to destruction*   ᴮ25:21 Lit *his majesty*, also in v. 25   ᶜ26:14 Or *Hebrew*   ᴰ26:18 Or *to turn them*

to God, and do works worthy of repentance. [21] For this reason the Jews seized me in the temple and were trying to kill me. [22] To this very day, I have had help from God, and I stand and testify to both small and great, saying nothing other than what the prophets and Moses said would take place — [23] that the Messiah must suffer, and that, as the first to rise from the dead, he would proclaim light to our people and to the Gentiles."

AGRIPPA NOT QUITE PERSUADED

[24] As he was saying these things in his defense, Festus exclaimed in a loud voice, "You're out of your mind, Paul! Too much study is driving you mad."

[25] But Paul replied, "I'm not out of my mind, most excellent Festus. On the contrary, I'm speaking words of truth and good judgment. [26] For the king knows about these matters, and I can speak boldly to him. For I am convinced that none of these things has escaped his notice, since this was not done in a corner. [27] King Agrippa, do you believe the prophets? I know you believe."

[28] Agrippa said to Paul, "Are you going to persuade me to become a Christian so easily?"[A]

[29] "I wish before God," replied Paul, "that whether easily or with difficulty,[B] not only you but all who listen to me today might become as I am — except for these chains."

[30] The king, the governor, Bernice, and those sitting with them got up, [31] and when they had left they talked with each other and said, "This man is not doing anything to deserve death or imprisonment."

[32] Agrippa said to Festus, "This man could have been released if he had not appealed to Caesar."

SAILING FOR ROME

27 When it was decided that we were to sail to Italy, they handed over Paul and some other prisoners to a centurion named Julius, of the Imperial Regiment.[C] [2] When we had boarded a ship of Adramyttium, we put to sea, intending to sail to ports along the coast of Asia. Aristarchus, a Macedonian of Thessalonica, was with us. [3] The next day we put in at Sidon, and Julius treated Paul kindly and allowed him to go to his friends to receive their care. [4] When we had put out to sea from there, we sailed along the northern coast[D] of Cyprus because the winds were against us. [5] After sailing through the open sea off Cilicia and Pamphylia, we reached Myra in Lycia. [6] There the

centurion found an Alexandrian ship sailing for Italy and put us on board. [7] Sailing slowly for many days, with difficulty we arrived off Cnidus. Since the wind did not allow us to approach it, we sailed along the south side of Crete off Salmone. [8] With still more difficulty we sailed along the coast and came to a place called Fair Havens near the city of Lasea.

PAUL'S ADVICE IGNORED

[9] By now much time had passed, and the voyage was already dangerous. Since the Day of Atonement[E] was already over, Paul gave his advice [10] and told them, "Men, I can see that this voyage is headed toward disaster and heavy loss, not only of the cargo and the ship but also of our lives." [11] But the centurion paid attention to the captain and the owner of the ship rather than to what Paul said. [12] Since the harbor was unsuitable to winter in, the majority decided to set sail from there, hoping somehow to reach Phoenix, a harbor on Crete facing the southwest and northwest, and to winter there.

STORM-TOSSED SHIP

[13] When a gentle south wind sprang up, they thought they had achieved their purpose. They weighed anchor and sailed along the shore of Crete. [14] But before long, a fierce wind called the "northeaster" rushed down from the island. [15] Since the ship was caught and unable to head into the wind, we gave way to it and were driven along. [16] After running under the shelter of a little island called Cauda,[F] we were barely able to get control of the skiff. [17] After hoisting it up, they used ropes and tackle and girded the ship. Fearing they would run aground on the Syrtis, they lowered the drift-anchor, and in this way they were driven along. [18] Because we were being severely battered by the storm, they began to jettison the cargo the next day. [19] On the third day, they threw the ship's tackle overboard with their own hands. [20] For many days neither sun nor stars appeared, and the severe storm kept raging. Finally all hope was fading that we would be saved.

[21] Since they had been without food for a long time, Paul then stood up among them and said, "You men should have followed my advice not to sail from Crete and sustain this damage and loss. [22] Now I urge you to take courage, because there will be no loss of any of your lives, but only of the ship. [23] For last night an angel of the God I belong to and serve stood by me [24] and said, 'Don't be afraid, Paul. It is necessary for you to appear before Caesar. And indeed, God

[A]26:28 Or *so quickly*   [B]26:29 Or *whether a short time or long*   [C]27:1 Or *Augustan Cohort*   [D]27:4 Lit *sailed under the lee,* also in v. 7   [E]27:9 Lit *the Fast*   [F]27:16 Or *Clauda*

has graciously given you all those who are sailing with you.' ²⁵ So take courage, men, because I believe God that it will be just the way it was told to me. ²⁶ But we have to run aground on some island."

²⁷ When the fourteenth night came, we were drifting in the Adriatic Sea, and about midnight the sailors thought they were approaching land. ²⁸ They took soundings and found it to be a hundred and twenty feet^A deep; when they had sailed a little farther and sounded again, they found it to be ninety feet^B deep. ²⁹ Then, fearing we might run aground on the rocks, they dropped four anchors from the stern and prayed for daylight to come. ³⁰ Some sailors tried to escape from the ship; they had let down the skiff into the sea, pretending that they were going to put out anchors from the bow. ³¹ Paul said to the centurion and the soldiers, "Unless these men stay in the ship, you cannot be saved." ³² Then the soldiers cut the ropes holding the skiff and let it drop away.

³³ When it was about daylight, Paul urged them all to take food, saying, "Today is the fourteenth day that you have been waiting and going without food, having eaten nothing. ³⁴ So I urge you to take some food. For this is for your survival, since none of you will lose a hair from your head." ³⁵ After he said these things and had taken some bread, he gave thanks to God in the presence of all of them, and after he broke it, he began to eat. ³⁶ They all were encouraged and took food themselves. ³⁷ In all there were 276 of us on the ship. ³⁸ When they had eaten enough, they began to lighten the ship by throwing the grain overboard into the sea.

SHIPWRECK

³⁹ When daylight came, they did not recognize the land but sighted a bay with a beach. They planned to run the ship ashore if they could. ⁴⁰ After cutting loose the anchors, they left them in the sea, at the same time loosening the ropes that held the rudders. Then they hoisted the foresail to the wind and headed for the beach. ⁴¹ But they struck a sandbar and ran the ship aground. The bow jammed fast and remained immovable, while the stern began to break up by the pounding of the waves. ⁴² The soldiers' plan was to kill the prisoners so that no one could swim away and escape. ⁴³ But the centurion kept them from carrying out their plan because he wanted to save Paul, and so he ordered those who could swim to jump overboard first and get to land. ⁴⁴ The rest were to follow, some on planks and some on debris from the ship. In this way, everyone safely reached the shore.

MALTA'S HOSPITALITY

28 Once safely ashore, we then learned that the island was called Malta. ² The local people showed us extraordinary kindness. They lit a fire and took us all in, since it was raining and cold. ³ As Paul gathered a bundle of brushwood and put it on the fire, a viper came out because of the heat and fastened itself on his hand. ⁴ When the local people saw the snake hanging from his hand, they said to one another, "This man, no doubt, is a murderer. Even though he has escaped the sea, Justice has not allowed him to live." ⁵ But he shook the snake off into the fire and suffered no harm. ⁶ They expected that he would begin to swell up or suddenly drop dead. After they waited a long time and saw nothing unusual happen to him, they changed their minds and said he was a god.

MINISTRY IN MALTA

⁷ Now in the area around that place was an estate belonging to the leading man of the island, named Publius, who welcomed us and entertained us hospitably for three days. ⁸ Publius's father was in bed suffering from fever and dysentery. Paul went to him, and praying and laying his hands on him, he healed him. ⁹ After this, the rest of those on the island who had diseases also came and were healed. ¹⁰ So they heaped many honors on us, and when we sailed, they gave us what we needed.

ROME AT LAST

¹¹ After three months we set sail in an Alexandrian ship that had wintered at the island, with the Twin Gods^C as its figurehead. ¹² Putting in at Syracuse, we stayed three days. ¹³ From there, after making a circuit along the coast,^D we reached Rhegium. After one day a south wind sprang up, and the second day we came to Puteoli. ¹⁴ There we found brothers and sisters and were invited to stay a week with them. And so we came to Rome. ¹⁵ Now the brothers and sisters from there had heard the news about us and had come to meet us as far as the Forum of Appius and the Three Taverns. When Paul saw them, he thanked God and took courage. ¹⁶ When we entered Rome,^E Paul was allowed to live by himself with the soldier who guarded him.

---

^A **27:28** Lit *twenty fathoms*   ^B **27:28** Lit *fifteen fathoms*   ^C **28:11** Gk *Dioscuri*, twin sons of Zeus, Castor and Pollux   ^D **28:13** Other mss read *From there, casting off*,   ^E **28:16** Other mss add *the centurion turned the prisoners over to the military commander; but*

PAUL'S FIRST INTERVIEW WITH ROMAN JEWS

17 After three days he called together the leaders of the Jews. When they had gathered he said to them: "Brothers, although I have done nothing against our people or the customs of our ancestors, I was delivered as a prisoner from Jerusalem into the hands of the Romans. **18** After they examined me, they wanted to release me, since there was no reason for the death penalty in my case. **19** Because the Jews objected, I was compelled to appeal to Caesar; even though I had no charge to bring against my people. **20** For this reason I've asked to see you and speak to you. In fact, it is for the hope of Israel that I'm wearing this chain."

21 Then they said to him, "We haven't received any letters about you from Judea. None of the brothers has come and reported or spoken anything evil about you. **22** But we want to hear what your views are, since we know that people everywhere are speaking against this sect."

THE RESPONSE TO PAUL'S MESSAGE

23 After arranging a day with him, many came to him at his lodging. From dawn to dusk he expounded and testified about the kingdom of God. He tried to persuade them about Jesus from both the Law of Moses and the Prophets. **24** Some were persuaded by what he said, but others did not believe.

25 Disagreeing among themselves, they began to leave after Paul made one statement:^A "The Holy Spirit was right in saying to your^B ancestors through the prophet Isaiah **26** when he said,

Go to these people and say:
You will always be listening,
but never understanding;
and you will always be looking,
but never perceiving.
27 For the hearts of these people
have grown callous,
their ears are hard of hearing,
and they have shut their eyes;
otherwise they might see
with their eyes
and hear with their ears,
understand with their heart
and turn,
and I would heal them.^C

28 Therefore, let it be known to you that this salvation of God has been sent to the Gentiles; they will listen." ^D

PAUL'S MINISTRY UNHINDERED

30 Paul stayed two whole years in his own rented house. And he welcomed all who visited him, **31** proclaiming the kingdom of God and teaching about the Lord Jesus Christ with all boldness and without hindrance.

---

^A**28:25** Or *after they began to leave, Paul made one statement*   ^B**28:25** Other mss read *our*   ^C**28:26-27** Is 6:9-10
^D**28:28** Some mss include v. 29: *After he said these things, the Jews departed, while engaging in a vigorous debate among themselves.*

ROMANS

THE GOSPEL OF GOD FOR ROME

1 Paul, a servant of Christ Jesus, called as an apostle^A and set apart for the gospel of God — ² which he promised beforehand through his prophets in the Holy Scriptures — ³ concerning his Son, Jesus Christ our Lord, who was a descendant of David^B according to the flesh ⁴ and was appointed to be the powerful Son of God according to the Spirit of holiness^C by the resurrection of the dead. ⁵ Through him we have received grace and apostleship to bring about^D the obedience of faith for the sake of his name among all the Gentiles,^E ⁶ including you who are also called by Jesus Christ.

⁷ To all who are in Rome, loved by God, called as saints.

Grace to you and peace from God our Father and the Lord Jesus Christ.

PAUL'S DESIRE TO VISIT ROME

⁸ First, I thank my God through Jesus Christ for all of you because the news of your faith^F is being reported in all the world. ⁹ God is my witness, whom I serve with my spirit in telling the good news about his Son — that I constantly mention you, ¹⁰ always asking in my prayers that if it is somehow in God's will, I may now at last succeed in coming to you. ¹¹ For I want very much to see you, so that I may impart to you some spiritual gift to strengthen you, ¹² that is, to be mutually encouraged by each other's faith, both yours and mine.

¹³ Now I don't want you to be unaware, brothers and sisters, that I often planned to come to you (but was prevented until now) in order that I might have a fruitful ministry^G among you, just as I have had among the rest of the Gentiles. ¹⁴ I am obligated both to Greeks and barbarians,^H both to the wise and the foolish. ¹⁵ So I am eager to preach the gospel to you also who are in Rome.

THE RIGHTEOUS WILL LIVE BY FAITH

¹⁶ For I am not ashamed of the gospel,^I because it is the power of God for salvation to everyone who believes, first to the Jew, and also to the Greek. ¹⁷ For in it the righteousness of God is revealed from faith to faith,^J just as it is written: The righteous will live by faith.^K,L

THE GUILT OF THE GENTILE WORLD

¹⁸ For God's wrath is revealed from heaven against all godlessness and unrighteousness of people who by their unrighteousness suppress the truth, ¹⁹ since what can be known^M about God is evident among them, because God has shown it to them. ²⁰ For his invisible attributes, that is, his eternal power and divine nature, have been clearly seen since the creation of the world, being understood through what he has made. As a result, people are without excuse. ²¹ For though they knew God, they did not glorify him as God or show gratitude. Instead, their thinking became worthless, and their senseless hearts were darkened. ²² Claiming to be wise, they became fools ²³ and exchanged the glory of the immortal God for images resembling mortal man, birds, four-footed animals, and reptiles.

²⁴ Therefore God delivered them over in the desires of their hearts to sexual impurity, so that their bodies were degraded among themselves. ²⁵ They exchanged the truth of God for a lie, and worshiped and served what has been created instead of the Creator, who is praised forever. Amen.

FROM IDOLATRY TO DEPRAVITY

²⁶ For this reason God delivered them over to disgraceful passions. Their women^N exchanged natural sexual relations^O for unnatural ones. ²⁷ The men^P in the same way also left natural relations with women and were inflamed in their lust for one another. Men committed shameless acts with men and received in their own persons^Q the appropriate penalty of their error.

²⁸ And because they did not think it worthwhile to acknowledge God, God delivered them over to a corrupt mind so that they do what is not right. ²⁹ They are filled with all unrighteousness,^R evil, greed, and wickedness. They are full of envy, murder, quarrels, deceit, and malice. They are gossips, ³⁰ slanderers, God-haters, arrogant, proud, boastful, inventors of evil, disobedient to parents, ³¹ senseless, untrustworthy, unloving,^S and unmerciful. ³² Although they know God's just sentence — that those who practice such things deserve to die^T — they not only do them, but even applaud^U others who practice them.

---

^A1:1 Or *Jesus, a called apostle*   ^B1:3 Lit *was of the seed of David*   ^C1:4 Or *the spirit of holiness*, or *the Holy Spirit*   ^D1:5 Or *him for; lit him into*   ^E1:5 Or *nations*, also in v. 13   ^F1:8 Or *because your faith*   ^G1:13 Lit *have some fruit*   ^H1:14 Or *non-Greeks*   ^I1:16 Other mss add *of Christ*   ^J1:17 Or *revealed out of faith into faith*   ^K1:17 Or *The one who is righteous by faith will live*   ^L1:17 Hab 2:4   ^M1:19 Or *what is known*   ^N1:26 Lit *females*, also in v. 27   ^O1:26 Lit *natural use*, also in v. 27   ^P1:27 Lit *males*, also later in v.   ^Q1:27 Or *in themselves*   ^R1:29 Other mss add *sexual immorality*   ^S1:31 Other mss add *unforgiving*   ^T1:32 Lit *things are worthy of death*   ^U1:32 Lit *even take pleasure in*

See Romans 2:4, page 133

GOD'S RIGHTEOUS JUDGMENT

2 Therefore, every one of you^ who judges is without excuse. For when you judge another, you condemn yourself, since you, the judge, do the same things. ² We know that God's judgment on those who do such things is based on the truth. ³ Do you really think — anyone of you who judges those who do such things yet do the same — that you will escape God's judgment? ⁴ Or do you despise the riches of his kindness, restraint, and patience, not recognizing⁸ that God's kindness is intended to lead you to repentance? ⁵ Because of your hardened and unrepentant heart you are storing up wrath for yourself in the day of wrath, when God's righteous judgment is revealed. ⁶ He will repay each one according to his works:ᶜ ⁷ eternal life to those who by persistence in doing good seek glory, honor, and immortality; ⁸ but wrath and anger to those who are self-seeking and disobey the truth while obeying unrighteousness. ⁹ There will be affliction and distress for every human being who does evil, first to the Jew, and also to the Greek; ¹⁰ but glory, honor, and peace for everyone who does what is good, first to the Jew, and also to the Greek. ¹¹ For there is no favoritism with God.

¹² All who sin without the law will also perish without the law, and all who sin underᴰ the law will be judged by the law. ¹³ For the hearers of the law are not righteous before God, but the doers of the law will be justified.ᴱ ¹⁴ So, when Gentiles, who do not by nature have the law, doᶠ what the law demands, they are a law to themselves even though they do not have the law. ¹⁵ They show that the work of the lawᴳ is written on their hearts. Their consciences confirm this. Their competing thoughts either accuse or even excuse themᴴ ¹⁶ on the day when God judges what people have kept secret, according to my gospel through Christ Jesus.

JEWISH VIOLATION OF THE LAW

¹⁷ Now ifᴵ you call yourself a Jew, and rely on the law, and boast in God, ¹⁸ and know his will, and approve the things that are superior, being instructed from the law, ¹⁹ and if you are convinced that you are a guide for the blind, a light to those in darkness, ²⁰ an instructor of the ignorant, a teacher of the immature, having the embodiment of knowledge and truth in the law — ²¹ you then, who teach another, don't you teach yourself? You who preach, "You must

not steal" — do you steal? ²² You who say, "You must not commit adultery" — do you commit adultery? You who detest idols, do you rob their temples? ²³ You who boast in the law, do you dishonor God by breaking the law? ²⁴ For, as it is written: **The name of God is blasphemed among the Gentiles because of you.**ᴶ

CIRCUMCISION OF THE HEART

²⁵ Circumcision benefits you if you observe the law, but if you are a lawbreaker, your circumcision has become uncircumcision. ²⁶ So if an uncircumcised man keeps the law's requirements, will not his uncircumcision be counted as circumcision? ²⁷ A man who is physically uncircumcised, but who keeps the law, will judge you who are a lawbreaker in spite of having the letter of the law and circumcision. ²⁸ For a person is not a Jew who is one outwardly, and true circumcision is not something visible in the flesh. ²⁹ On the contrary, a person is a Jew who is one inwardly, and circumcision is of the heart — by the Spirit, not the letter.ᴷ That person's praise is not from people but from God.

PAUL ANSWERS AN OBJECTION

3 So what advantage does the Jew have? Or what is the benefit of circumcision? ² Considerable in every way. First, they were entrusted with the very words of God. ³ What then? If some were unfaithful, will their unfaithfulness nullify God's faithfulness? ⁴ Absolutely not! Let God be true, even though everyone is a liar, as it is written:

> That you may be justified
>   in your words
> and triumph when you judge.ᴸ

⁵ But if our unrighteousness highlightsᴹ God's righteousness, what are we to say? I am using a human argument:ᴺ Is God unrighteous to inflict wrath? ⁶ Absolutely not! Otherwise, how will God judge the world? ⁷ But if by my lie God's truth abounds to his glory, why am I also still being judged as a sinner? ⁸ And why not say, just as some people slanderously claim we say, "Let us do what is evil so that good may come"? Their condemnation is deserved!

THE WHOLE WORLD GUILTY BEFORE GOD

⁹ What then? Are we any better off?ᴼ Not at all! For we have already charged that both Jews and Gentilesᴾ are all under sin,ᑫ ¹⁰ as it is written:

---

^2:1 Lit *Therefore, O man, every one*   ᴮ2:4 Or *patience, because you do not recognize*   ᶜ2:6 Ps 62:12; Pr 24:12   ᴰ2:12 Lit *in*
ᴱ2:13 Or *acquitted*   ᶠ2:14 Or *who do not have the law, instinctively do*   ᴳ2:15 The code of conduct required by the law
ᴴ2:15 Internal debate, either in a person or among the pagan moralists   ᴵ2:17 Other mss read *Look* —   ᴶ2:24 Is 52:5
ᴷ2:29 Or *heart — spiritually, not literally*   ᴸ3:4 Ps 51:4   ᴹ3:5 Or *shows,* or *demonstrates*   ᴺ3:5 Lit *I speak as a man*
ᴼ3:9 Are we Jews any better than the Gentiles?   ᴾ3:9 Lit *Greeks*   ᑫ3:9 Under sin's power or dominion

See Romans 3:23, page 134

There is no one righteous,
    not even one.
[11] There is no one who understands;
    there is no one who seeks God.
[12] All have turned away;
    all alike have become worthless.
    There is no one who does
      what is good,
    not even one.[A]
[13] Their throat is an open grave;
    they deceive with their tongues.[B]
    Vipers' venom is under their lips.[C]
[14] Their mouth is full of cursing
    and bitterness.[D]
[15] Their feet are swift to shed blood;
[16] ruin and wretchedness are
    in their paths,
[17] and the path of peace
    they have not known.[E]
[18] There is no fear of God
    before their eyes.[F]

[19] Now we know that whatever the law says, it speaks to those who are subject to the law,[G] so that every mouth may be shut and the whole world may become subject to God's judgment.[H] [20] For no one will be justified[I] in his sight by the works of the law, because the knowledge of sin comes through the law.

THE RIGHTEOUSNESS OF GOD THROUGH FAITH

[21] But now, apart from the law, the righteousness of God has been revealed, attested by the Law and the Prophets.[J] [22] The righteousness of God is through faith in Jesus Christ[K] to all who believe, since there is no distinction. [23] For all have sinned and fall short of the[L] glory of God. [24] They are justified freely by his grace through the redemption that is in Christ Jesus. [25] God presented him as an atoning sacrifice[M] in his blood, received through faith, to demonstrate his righteousness, because in his restraint God passed over the sins previously committed. [26] God presented him to demonstrate his righteousness at the present time, so that he would be righteous and declare righteous[N] the one who has faith in Jesus.

BOASTING EXCLUDED

[27] Where, then, is boasting? It is excluded. By what kind of law?[O] By one of works? No, on the contrary, by a law[P] of faith. [28] For we conclude that a person is justified by faith apart from the works of the law. [29] Or is God the God of Jews only? Is he not the God of Gentiles too? Yes, of Gentiles too, [30] since there is one God who will justify the circumcised by faith and the uncircumcised through faith. [31] Do we then nullify the law through faith? Absolutely not! On the contrary, we uphold the law.

ABRAHAM JUSTIFIED BY FAITH

4 What then will we say that Abraham, our forefather according to the flesh, has found?[Q] [2] If Abraham was justified[R] by works, he has something to boast about — but not before God. [3] For what does the Scripture say? **Abraham believed God, and it was credited to him for righteousness.**[S] [4] Now to the one who works, pay is not credited as a gift, but as something owed. [5] But to the one who does not work, but believes on him who declares the ungodly to be righteous, his faith is credited for righteousness.

DAVID CELEBRATING THE SAME TRUTH

[6] Just as David also speaks of the blessing of the person to whom God credits righteousness apart from works:
[7]   **Blessed are those whose lawless acts**
      are forgiven
    and whose sins are covered.
[8]   **Blessed is the person**
    the Lord will never charge
      with sin.[T]

ABRAHAM JUSTIFIED BEFORE CIRCUMCISION

[9] Is this blessing only for the circumcised, then? Or is it also for the uncircumcised? For we say, **Faith was credited to Abraham for righteousness.**[S] [10] In what way then was it credited — while he was circumcised, or uncircumcised? It was not while he was circumcised, but uncircumcised. [11] And he received the sign of circumcision as a seal of the righteousness that he had by faith[U] while still uncircumcised. This was to make him the father of all who believe but are not circumcised, so that righteousness may be credited to them also. [12] And he became the father of the circumcised, who are not only circumcised but who also follow in the footsteps of the faith

---

[A]3:10-12 Ps 14:1-3; 53:1-3; Ec 7:20 [B]3:13 Ps 5:9 [C]3:13 Ps 140:3 [D]3:14 Ps 10:7 [E]3:15-17 Is 59:7-8 [F]3:18 Ps 36:1 [G]3:19 Lit *those in the law* [H]3:19 Or *become guilty before God, or may be accountable to God* [I]3:20 Or *will be declared righteous, or will be acquitted* [J]3:21 When capitalized, the *Law and the Prophets* = OT [K]3:22 Or *through the faithfulness of Jesus Christ* [L]3:23 Or *and lack the* [M]3:25 Or *a propitiation, or a place of atonement* [N]3:26 Or *and justify, or and acquit* [O]3:27 Or *what principle?* [P]3:27 Or *a principle* [Q]4:1 Or *What then shall we say? Have we found Abraham to be our forefather according to the flesh? or What, then, shall we say that Abraham our forefather found according to the flesh?* [R]4:2 Or *was declared righteous, or was acquitted* [S]4:3,9 Gn 15:6 [T]4:7-8 Ps 32:1-2 [U]4:11 Lit *righteousness of faith*, also in v. 13

See Romans 5:8, page 135

our father Abraham had while he was still uncircumcised.

THE PROMISE GRANTED THROUGH FAITH

[13] For the promise to Abraham or to his descendants that he would inherit the world was not through the law, but through the righteousness that comes by faith. [14] If those who are of the law are heirs, faith is made empty and the promise nullified, [15] because the law produces wrath. And where there is no law, there is no transgression.

[16] This is why the promise is by faith, so that it may be according to grace, to guarantee it to all the descendants — not only to those who are of the law[A] but also to those who are of Abraham's faith. He is the father of us all. [17] As it is written: **I have made you the father of many nations.**[B] He is our father in God's sight, in whom Abraham believed — the God who gives life to the dead and calls things into existence that do not exist. [18] He believed, hoping against hope, so that he became **the father of many nations**[B] according to what had been spoken: **So will your descendants be.**[C] [19] He did not weaken in faith when he considered[D] his own body to be already dead (since he was about a hundred years old) and also the deadness of Sarah's womb. [20] He did not waver in unbelief at God's promise but was strengthened in his faith and gave glory to God, [21] because he was fully convinced that what God had promised, he was also able to do. [22] Therefore, **it was credited to him for righteousness.**[E] [23] Now **it was credited to him**[E] was not written for Abraham alone, [24] but also for us. It will be credited to us who believe in him who raised Jesus our Lord from the dead. [25] He was delivered up for[F] our trespasses and raised for our justification.

FAITH TRIUMPHS

5 Therefore, since we have been declared righteous by faith, we have peace[G] with God through our Lord Jesus Christ. [2] We have also obtained access through him by faith[H] into this grace in which we stand, and we rejoice[I] in the hope of the glory of God. [3] And not only that, but we also rejoice in our afflictions, because we know that affliction produces endurance, [4] endurance produces proven character, and proven character produces hope. [5] This hope will not disappoint us, because God's love has been poured out in our hearts through the Holy Spirit who was given to us.

THOSE DECLARED RIGHTEOUS ARE RECONCILED

[6] For while we were still helpless, at the right time, Christ died for the ungodly. [7] For rarely will someone die for a just person — though for a good person perhaps someone might even dare to die. [8] But God proves his own love for us in that while we were still sinners, Christ died for us. [9] How much more then, since we have now been declared righteous by his blood, will we be saved through him from wrath. [10] For if, while we were enemies, we were reconciled to God through the death of his Son, then how much more, having been reconciled, will we be saved by his life. [11] And not only that, but we also rejoice in God through our Lord Jesus Christ, through whom we have now received this reconciliation.

DEATH THROUGH ADAM AND LIFE THROUGH CHRIST

[12] Therefore, just as sin entered the world through one man, and death through sin, in this way death spread to all people, because all sinned.[J] [13] In fact, sin was in the world before the law, but sin is not charged to a person's account when there is no law. [14] Nevertheless, death reigned from Adam to Moses, even over those who did not sin in the likeness of Adam's transgression. He is a type of the Coming One.

[15] But the gift is not like the trespass. For if by the one man's trespass the many died, how much more have the grace of God and the gift which comes through the grace of the one man Jesus Christ overflowed to the many. [16] And the gift is not like the one man's sin, because from one sin came the judgment, resulting in condemnation, but from many trespasses came the gift, resulting in justification.[K] [17] Since by the one man's trespass, death reigned through that one man, how much more will those who receive the overflow of grace and the gift of righteousness reign in life through the one man, Jesus Christ.

[18] So then, as through one trespass there is condemnation for everyone, so also through one righteous act there is justification leading to life for everyone. [19] For just as through one man's disobedience the many were made sinners, so also through the one man's obedience the many will be made righteous. [20] The law came along to multiply the trespass. But where sin multiplied, grace multiplied even more [21] so that, just as sin reigned in death, so also grace will reign through righteousness, resulting in eternal life through Jesus Christ our Lord.

[A] **4:16** Or *not to those who are of the law only* [B] **4:17,18** Gn 17:5 [C] **4:18** Gn 15:5 [D] **4:19** Other mss read *He did not consider* [E] **4:22,23** Gn 15:6 [F] **4:25** Or *because of* [G] **5:1** Other mss read *faith, let us have peace*, which can also be translated *faith, let us grasp the fact that we have peace* [H] **5:2** Other mss omit *by faith* [I] **5:2** Lit *boast*, also in vv. 3,11 [J] **5:12** Or *have sinned* [K] **5:16** Or *acquittal*

See Romans 6:23, page 136

THE NEW LIFE IN CHRIST

6 What should we say then? Should we continue in sin so that grace may multiply? [2] Absolutely not! How can we who died to sin still live in it? [3] Or are you unaware that all of us who were baptized into Christ Jesus were baptized into his death? [4] Therefore we were buried with him by baptism into death, in order that, just as Christ was raised from the dead by the glory of the Father, so we too may walk in newness[A] of life. [5] For if we have been united with him in the likeness of his death, we will certainly also be[B] in the likeness of his resurrection. [6] For we know that our old self[C] was crucified with him so that the body ruled by sin[D] might be rendered powerless so that we may no longer be enslaved to sin, [7] since a person who has died is freed[E] from sin. [8] Now if we died with Christ, we believe that we will also live with him, [9] because we know that Christ, having been raised from the dead, will not die again. Death no longer rules over him. [10] For the death he died, he died to sin once for all time; but the life he lives, he lives to God. [11] So, you too consider yourselves dead to sin and alive to God in Christ Jesus.[F]

[12] Therefore do not let sin reign in your mortal body, so that you obey[G] its desires. [13] And do not offer any parts[H] of it to sin as weapons for unrighteousness. But as those who are alive from the dead, offer yourselves to God, and all the parts of yourselves to God as weapons for righteousness. [14] For sin will not rule over you, because you are not under the law but under grace.

FROM SLAVES OF SIN TO SLAVES OF GOD

[15] What then? Should we sin because we are not under the law but under grace? Absolutely not! [16] Don't you know that if you offer yourselves to someone[I] as obedient slaves, you are slaves of that one you obey — either of sin leading to death or of obedience leading to righteousness? [17] But thank God that, although you used to be slaves of sin, you obeyed from the heart that pattern of teaching to which you were handed[J] over, [18] and having been set free from sin, you became enslaved to righteousness. [19] I am using a human analogy because of the weakness of your flesh.[K] For just as you offered the parts of yourselves as slaves to impurity, and to greater and greater lawlessness, so now offer them as slaves to righteousness, which results in sanctification. [20] For when you were

slaves of sin, you were free with regard to righteousness.[L] [21] So what fruit was produced[M] then from the things you are now ashamed of? The outcome of those things is death. [22] But now, since you have been set free from sin and have become enslaved to God, you have your fruit, which results in sanctification — and the outcome is eternal life! [23] For the wages of sin is death, but the gift of God is eternal life in Christ Jesus our Lord.

AN ILLUSTRATION FROM MARRIAGE

7 Since I am speaking to those who know the law, brothers and sisters, don't you know that the law rules over someone as long as he lives? [2] For example, a married woman is legally bound to her husband while he lives. But if her husband dies, she is released from the law regarding the husband. [3] So then, if she is married to another man while her husband is living, she will be called an adulteress. But if her husband dies, she is free from that law. Then, if she is married to another man, she is not an adulteress.

[4] Therefore, my brothers and sisters, you also were put to death in relation to the law through the body of Christ so that you may belong to another. You belong to him who was raised from the dead in order that we may bear fruit for God. [5] For when we were in the flesh, the sinful passions aroused through the law were working in us[N] to bear fruit for death. [6] But now we have been released from the law, since we have died to what held us, so that we may serve in the newness of the Spirit and not in the old letter of the law.

SIN'S USE OF THE LAW

[7] What should we say then? Is the law sin? Absolutely not! On the contrary, I would not have known sin if it were not for the law. For example, I would not have known what it is to covet if the law had not said, **Do not covet.**[O] [8] And sin, seizing an opportunity through the commandment, produced in me coveting of every kind. For apart from the law sin is dead. [9] Once I was alive apart from the law, but when the commandment came, sin sprang to life again [10] and I died. The commandment that was meant for life resulted in death for me. [11] For sin, seizing an opportunity through the commandment, deceived me, and through it killed me. [12] So then, the law is holy, and the commandment is holy and just and good. [13] Therefore, did what is good

---

[A]6:4 Or a new way   [B]6:5 Be joined with him   [C]6:6 Lit man   [D]6:6 Lit that the body of sin   [E]6:7 Or justified; lit acquitted [F]6:11 Other mss add our Lord   [G]6:12 Other mss add sin (lit it) in   [H]6:13 Or members, also in v. 19   [I]6:16 Lit that to whom you offer yourselves   [J]6:17 Or entrusted   [K]6:19 Or your human nature   [L]6:20 Lit free to righteousness   [M]6:21 Lit what fruit do you have   [N]7:5 Lit in our members   [O]7:7 Ex 20:17

See Romans 10:9-10 and Romans 10:13, page 139

become death to me? Absolutely not! On the contrary, sin, in order to be recognized as sin, was producing death in me through what is good, so that through the commandment, sin might become sinful beyond measure.

THE PROBLEM OF SIN IN US

[14] For we know that the law is spiritual, but I am of the flesh,[A] sold as a slave to sin.[B] [15] For I do not understand what I am doing, because I do not practice what I want to do, but I do what I hate. [16] Now if I do what I do not want to do, I agree with the law that it is good. [17] So now I am no longer the one doing it, but it is sin living in me. [18] For I know that nothing good lives in me, that is, in my flesh. For the desire to do what is good is with me, but there is no ability to do it. [19] For I do not do the good that I want to do, but I practice the evil that I do not want to do. [20] Now if I do what I do not want, I am no longer the one that does it, but it is the sin that lives in me. [21] So I discover this law:[C] When I want to do what is good,[D] evil is present with me. [22] For in my inner self[E] I delight in God's law, [23] but I see a different law in the parts of my body,[F] waging war against the law of my mind and taking me prisoner to the law of sin in the parts of my body. [24] What a wretched man I am! Who will rescue me from this body of death? [25] Thanks be to God through Jesus Christ our Lord! So then, with my mind I myself am serving the law of God, but with my flesh, the law of sin.

THE LIFE-GIVING SPIRIT

8 Therefore, there is now no condemnation for those in Christ Jesus,[G] [2] because the law of the Spirit of life in Christ Jesus has set you[H] free from the law of sin and death. [3] What the law could not do since it was weakened by the flesh, God did. He condemned sin in the flesh by sending his own Son in the likeness of sinful flesh as a sin offering,[I] [4] in order that the law's requirement would be fulfilled in us who do not walk according to the flesh but according to the Spirit. [5] For those who live according to the flesh have their minds set on the things of the flesh, but those who live according to the Spirit have their minds set on the things of the Spirit. [6] Now the mind-set of the flesh is death, but the mind-set of the Spirit is life and peace. [7] The mind-set of the flesh is hostile to God because it does not submit to God's law. Indeed, it is unable to do so. [8] Those who are in the flesh

cannot please God. [9] You, however, are not in the flesh, but in the Spirit, if indeed the Spirit of God lives in you. If anyone does not have the Spirit of Christ, he does not belong to him. [10] Now if Christ is in you, the body is dead because of sin, but the Spirit[J] gives life[K] because of righteousness. [11] And if the Spirit of him who raised Jesus from the dead lives in you, then he who raised Christ from the dead will also bring your mortal bodies to life through[L] his Spirit who lives in you.

THE HOLY SPIRIT'S MINISTRIES

[12] So then, brothers and sisters, we are not obligated to the flesh to live according to the flesh, [13] because if you live according to the flesh, you are going to die. But if by the Spirit you put to death the deeds of the body, you will live. [14] For all those led by God's Spirit are God's sons. [15] You did not receive a spirit of slavery to fall back into fear. Instead, you received the Spirit of adoption, by whom we cry out, "Abba,[M] Father!" [16] The Spirit himself testifies together with our spirit that we are God's children, [17] and if children, also heirs — heirs of God and coheirs with Christ — if indeed we suffer with him so that we may also be glorified with him.

FROM GROANS TO GLORY

[18] For I consider that the sufferings of this present time are not worth comparing with the glory that is going to be revealed to us. [19] For the creation eagerly waits with anticipation for God's sons to be revealed. [20] For the creation was subjected to futility — not willingly, but because of him who subjected it — in the hope [21] that the creation itself will also be set free from the bondage to decay into the glorious freedom of God's children. [22] For we know that the whole creation has been groaning together with labor pains until now. [23] Not only that, but we ourselves who have the Spirit as the firstfruits — we also groan within ourselves, eagerly waiting for adoption, the redemption of our bodies. [24] Now in this hope we were saved, but hope that is seen is not hope, because who hopes for what he sees? [25] Now if we hope for what we do not see, we eagerly wait for it with patience.

[26] In the same way the Spirit also helps us in our weakness, because we do not know what to pray for as we should, but the Spirit himself intercedes for us[N] with unspoken groanings. [27] And he who searches our hearts knows the

---

[A] 7:14 Or *unspiritual*   [B] 7:14 Lit *under sin*   [C] 7:21 Or *principle*   [D] 7:21 Or *I find with respect to the law that when I want to do good*   [E] 7:22 Lit *inner man*   [F] 7:23 Lit *my members*   [G] 8:1 Other mss add *who do not walk according to the flesh but according to the Spirit*   [H] 8:2 Other mss read *me*   [I] 8:3 Or *for sin*   [J] 8:10 Or *spirit*   [K] 8:10 Or *your spirit is alive*   [L] 8:11 Other mss read *because of*   [M] 8:15 Aramaic for *father*   [N] 8:26 Some mss omit *for us*

mind of the Spirit, because he intercedes for the saints according to the will of God.

[28] We know that all things work together[A] for the good[B] of those who love God, who are called according to his purpose. [29] For those he foreknew he also predestined to be conformed to the image of his Son, so that he would be the firstborn among many brothers and sisters. [30] And those he predestined, he also called; and those he called, he also justified; and those he justified, he also glorified.

THE BELIEVER'S TRIUMPH

[31] What then are we to say about these things? If God is for us, who is against us? [32] He did not even spare his own Son but offered him up for us all. How will he not also with him grant us everything? [33] Who can bring an accusation against God's elect? God is the one who justifies. [34] Who is the one who condemns? Christ Jesus is the one who died, but even more, has been raised; he also is at the right hand of God and intercedes for us. [35] Who can separate us from the love of Christ? Can affliction or distress or persecution or famine or nakedness or danger or sword? [36] As it is written:

> Because of you
> we are being put to death all day long;
> we are counted as sheep
> to be slaughtered.[C]

[37] No, in all these things we are more than conquerors through him who loved us. [38] For I am persuaded that neither death nor life, nor angels nor rulers, nor things present nor things to come, nor powers, [39] nor height nor depth, nor any other created thing will be able to separate us from the love of God that is in Christ Jesus our Lord.

ISRAEL'S REJECTION OF CHRIST

9 I speak the truth in Christ — I am not lying; my conscience testifies to me through the Holy Spirit[D] — [2] that I have great sorrow and unceasing anguish in my heart. [3] For I could wish that I myself were cursed and cut off[E] from Christ for the benefit of my brothers and sisters, my own flesh and blood. [4] They are Israelites, and to them belong the adoption, the glory, the covenants, the giving of the law, the temple service, and the promises. [5] The ancestors are theirs, and from them, by physical descent,[F] came the Christ, who is God over all, praised forever.[G] Amen.

GOD'S GRACIOUS ELECTION OF ISRAEL

[6] Now it is not as though the word of God has failed, because not all who are descended from Israel are Israel. [7] Neither are all of Abraham's children his descendants. [H] On the contrary, **your offspring will be traced**[I] **through Isaac.** [8] That is, it is not the children by physical descent[K] who are God's children, but the children of the promise are considered to be the offspring. [9] For this is the statement of the promise: **At this time I will come, and Sarah will have a son.**[L] [10] And not only that, but Rebekah conceived children through one man, our father Isaac. [11] For though her sons had not been born yet or done anything good or bad, so that God's purpose according to election might stand — [12] not from works but from the one who calls — she was told, **The older will serve the younger.**[M] [13] As it is written: **I have loved Jacob, but I have hated Esau.**[N]

GOD'S SELECTION IS JUST

[14] What should we say then? Is there injustice with God? Absolutely not! [15] For he tells Moses, **I will show mercy to whom I will show mercy, and I will have compassion on whom I will have compassion.**[O] [16] So then, it does not depend on human will or effort but on God who shows mercy. [17] For the Scripture tells Pharaoh, **I raised you up for this reason so that I may display my power in you and that my name may be proclaimed in the whole earth.**[P] [18] So then, he has mercy on whom he wants to have mercy and he hardens whom he wants to harden.

[19] You will say to me, therefore, "Why then does he still find fault? For who can resist his will?" [20] But who are you, a mere man, to talk back to God? Will what is formed say to the one who formed it, "Why did you make me like this?" [21] Or has the potter no right over the clay, to make from the same lump one piece of pottery for honor and another for dishonor? [22] And what if God, wanting to display his wrath and to make his power known, endured with much patience objects of wrath prepared for destruction? [23] And what if he did this to make known the riches of his glory on objects of mercy that he prepared beforehand for glory — [24] on us, the ones he also called, not only from the Jews but also from the Gentiles? [25] As it[O] also says in Hosea,

---

[A] **8:28** Other mss read *that God works together in all things with me by the Holy Spirit* [B] **8:28** The ultimate good [C] **8:36** Ps 44:22 [D] **9:1** Or *testifying* [E] **9:3** Lit *to be anathema* [F] **9:5** Lit *them, according to the flesh* [G] **9:5** Or *the Messiah, the one who is over all, the God who is blessed forever*, or *Messiah. God, who is over all, be blessed forever* [H] **9:7** Lit *seed* [I] **9:7** Lit *called* [J] **9:7** Gn 21:12 [K] **9:8** Lit *children of the flesh* [L] **9:9** Gn 18:10,14 [M] **9:12** Gn 25:23 [N] **9:13** Mal 1:2-3 [O] **9:15** Ex 33:19 [P] **9:17** Ex 9:16 [Q] **9:25** Or *he*

I will call Not my People,
   my People,
and she who is Unloved, Beloved.^A
²⁶ And it will be in the place where
   they were told,
you are not my people,
there they will be called sons
   of the living God.^B

²⁷ But Isaiah cries out concerning Israel,
   Though the number of Israelites
   is like the sand of the sea,
   only the remnant will be saved;
²⁸ since the Lord will execute
   his sentence
   completely and decisively
   on the earth.^C,D

²⁹ And just as Isaiah predicted:
   If the Lord of Hosts^E had not left
   us offspring,
   we would have become
     like Sodom,
   and we would have been made
     like Gomorrah.^F

ISRAEL'S PRESENT STATE

³⁰ What should we say then? Gentiles, who did not pursue righteousness, have obtained righteousness — namely the righteousness that comes from faith. ³¹ But Israel, pursuing the law of righteousness, has not achieved the righteousness of the law.^G ³² Why is that? Because they did not pursue it by faith, but as if it were by works.^H They stumbled over the stumbling stone. ³³ As it is written,

Look, I am putting a stone in Zion
   to stumble over
and a rock to trip over,
and the one who believes on him
   will not be put to shame.^I

RIGHTEOUSNESS BY FAITH ALONE

10 Brothers and sisters, my heart's desire and prayer to God concerning them^J is for their salvation. ² I can testify about them that they have zeal for God, but not according to knowledge. ³ Since they are ignorant of the righteousness of God and attempted to establish their own righteousness, they have not submitted to God's righteousness. ⁴ For Christ is the end^K of the law for righteousness to everyone who believes, ⁵ since Moses writes about the righteousness that is from the law: The one who does these things will live by

them.^L ⁶ But the righteousness that comes from faith speaks like this: **Do not say in your heart, "Who will go up to heaven?"**^M that is, to bring Christ down ⁷ or, **"Who will go down into the abyss?"**^N that is, to bring Christ up from the dead. ⁸ On the contrary, what does it say? **The message is near you, in your mouth and in your heart.**^O This is the message of faith that we proclaim: ⁹ <u>If you confess with your mouth, "Jesus is Lord," and believe in your heart that God raised him from the dead, you will be saved.</u> ¹⁰ <u>One believes with the heart, resulting in righteousness, and one confesses with the mouth, resulting in salvation.</u> ¹¹ For the Scripture says, **Everyone who believes on him will not be put to shame,**^P ¹² since there is no distinction between Jew and Greek, because the same Lord of all richly blesses all who call on him. ¹³ For <u>**everyone who calls on the name of the Lord will be saved.**</u>^Q

ISRAEL'S REJECTION OF THE MESSAGE

¹⁴ How, then, can they call on him they have not believed in? And how can they believe without hearing about him? And how can they hear without a preacher? ¹⁵ And how can they preach unless they are sent? As it is written: **How beautiful**^R **are the feet of those who bring good news.**^S ¹⁶ But not all obeyed the gospel. For Isaiah says, **Lord, who has believed our message?**^T ¹⁷ So faith comes from what is heard, and what is heard comes through the message about Christ.^U ¹⁸ But I ask, "Did they not hear?" Yes, they did:

Their voice has gone out to
   the whole earth,
and their words to the ends
   of the world.^V

¹⁹ But I ask, "Did Israel not understand?" First, Moses said,

I will make you jealous
   of those who are not a nation;
I will make you angry by a nation
   that lacks understanding.^W
²⁰ And Isaiah says boldly,
I was found
   by those who were not looking
     for me;
I revealed myself
   to those who were not asking for me.^X
²¹ But to Israel he says, **All day long I have held out my hands to a disobedient and defiant people.**^Y

---

^A 9:25 Hs 2:23 ^B 9:26 Hs 1:10 ^C 9:28 Or *land* ^D 9:27-28 Is 10:22-23; 28:22; Hs 1:10 ^E 9:29 Gk *Sabaoth* ; or *the Lord of Armies* ^F 9:29 Is 1:9 ^G 9:31 Other mss read *the law for righteousness* ^H 9:32 Other mss add *of the law* ^I 9:33 Is 8:14; 28:16 ^J 10:1 Other mss read *God for Israel* ^K 10:4 Or *goal* ^L 10:5 Lv 18:5 ^M 10:6 Dt 9:4; 30:12 ^N 10:7 Dt 30:13 ^O 10:8 Dt 30:14 ^P 10:11 Is 28:16 ^Q 10:13 Jl 2:32 ^R 10:15 Or *welcome*, or *timely* ^S 10:15 Is 52:7; Nah 1:15 ^T 10:16 Is 53:1 ^U 10:17 Other mss read *God* ^V 10:18 Ps 19:4 ^W 10:19 Dt 32:21 ^X 10:20 Is 65:1 ^Y 10:21 Is 65:2

Turn to back page

ISRAEL'S REJECTION NOT TOTAL

11 I ask, then, has God rejected his people? Absolutely not! For I too am an Israelite, a descendant of Abraham, from the tribe of Benjamin. [2] God has not rejected his people whom he foreknew. Or don't you know what the Scripture says in the passage about Elijah — how he pleads with God against Israel? [3] **Lord, they have killed your prophets and torn down your altars. I am the only one left, and they are trying to take my life!** [A] [4] But what was God's answer to him? **I have left seven thousand for myself who have not bowed down to Baal.** [B] [5] In the same way, then, there is also at the present time a remnant chosen by grace. [6] Now if by grace, then it is not by works; otherwise grace ceases to be grace. [C]

[7] What then? Israel did not find what it was looking for, but the elect did find it. The rest were hardened, [8] as it is written,

> God gave them a spirit of stupor,
> eyes that cannot see
> and ears that cannot hear,
> to this day. [D]

[9] And David says,

> Let their table become a snare
>   and a trap,
> a pitfall and a retribution to them.
> [10] Let their eyes be darkened
>   so that they cannot see,
> and their backs be bent continually. [E]

ISRAEL'S REJECTION NOT FINAL

[11] I ask, then, have they stumbled so as to fall? Absolutely not! On the contrary, by their transgression, salvation has come to the Gentiles to make Israel jealous. [12] Now if their transgression brings riches for the world, and their failure riches for the Gentiles, how much more will their fullness bring!

[13] Now I am speaking to you Gentiles. Insofar as I am an apostle to the Gentiles, I magnify my ministry, [14] if I might somehow make my own people [F] jealous and save some of them. [15] For if their rejection brings reconciliation to the world, what will their acceptance mean but life from the dead? [16] Now if the firstfruits are holy, so is the whole batch. And if the root is holy, so are the branches.

[17] Now if some of the branches were broken off, and you, though a wild olive branch, were grafted in among them and have come to share in the rich root [G] of the cultivated olive tree, [18] do not boast that you are better than those branches. But if you do boast — you do not sustain the root, but the root sustains you. [19] Then you will say, "Branches were broken off so that I might be grafted in." [20] True enough; they were broken off because of unbelief, but you stand by faith. Do not be arrogant, but beware, [H] [21] because if God did not spare the natural branches, he will not spare you either. [22] Therefore, consider God's kindness and severity: severity toward those who have fallen but God's kindness toward you — if you remain in his kindness. Otherwise you too will be cut off. [23] And even they, if they do not remain in unbelief, will be grafted in, because God has the power to graft them in again. [24] For if you were cut off from your native wild olive tree and against nature were grafted into a cultivated olive tree, how much more will these — the natural branches — be grafted into their own olive tree?

[25] I don't want you to be ignorant of this mystery, brothers and sisters, so that you will not be conceited: A partial hardening has come upon Israel until the fullness of the Gentiles has come in. [26] And in this way all [I] Israel will be saved, as it is written,

> The Deliverer will come from Zion;
> he will turn godlessness away
>   from Jacob.
> [27] And this will be my covenant with them [J]
>   when I take away their sins. [K]

[28] Regarding the gospel, they are enemies for your advantage, but regarding election, they are loved because of the patriarchs, [29] since God's gracious gifts and calling are irrevocable. [L] [30] As you once disobeyed God but now have received mercy through their disobedience, [31] so they too have now disobeyed, resulting in mercy to you, so that they also may now [M] receive mercy. [32] For God has imprisoned all in disobedience so that he may have mercy on all.

A HYMN OF PRAISE

> [33] Oh, the depth of the riches
>   both of the wisdom and of the knowledge
>   of God!
> How unsearchable his judgments
> and untraceable his ways!
> [34] **For who has known the mind
>   of the Lord?
> Or who has been his counselor?**
> [35] **And who has ever given to God,
>   that he should be repaid?"** [N]
> [36] For from him and through him
> and to him are all things.
> To him be the glory forever. Amen.

---

^11:3 1Kg 19:10,14   [B]11:4 1Kg 19:18   [C]11:6 Other mss add *But if of works it is no longer grace; otherwise work is no longer work.*   [D]11:8 Dt 29:4; Is 29:10   [E]11:9-10 Ps 69:22-23   [F]11:14 Lit *flesh*   [G]11:17 Other mss read *the root and the richness*   [H]11:20 Lit *fear*   [I]11:26 Or *And then all*   [J]11:26-27 Is 59:20-21   [K]11:27 Jr 31:31-34   [L]11:29 Or *are not taken back*   [M]11:31 Other mss omit *now*   [N]11:34-35 Jb 41:11; Is 40:13; Jr 23:18

A LIVING SACRIFICE

12 Therefore, brothers and sisters, in view of the mercies of God, I urge you to present your bodies as a living sacrifice, holy and pleasing to God; this is your true worship.[A] [2] Do not be conformed to this age, but be transformed by the renewing of your mind, so that you may discern what is the good, pleasing, and perfect will of God.

MANY GIFTS BUT ONE BODY

[3] For by the grace given to me, I tell everyone among you not to think of himself more highly than he should think. Instead, think sensibly, as God has distributed a measure of faith to each one. [4] Now as we have many parts in one body, and all the parts do not have the same function, [5] in the same way we who are many are one body in Christ and individually members of one another. [6] According to the grace given to us, we have different gifts: If prophecy, use it according to the proportion of one's[B] faith; [7] if service, use it in service; if teaching, in teaching; [8] if exhorting, in exhortation; giving, with generosity; leading, with diligence; showing mercy, with cheerfulness.

CHRISTIAN ETHICS

[9] Let love be without hypocrisy. Detest evil; cling to what is good. [10] Love one another deeply as brothers and sisters. Outdo one another in showing honor. [11] Do not lack diligence in zeal; be fervent in the Spirit;[C] serve the Lord. [12] Rejoice in hope; be patient in affliction; be persistent in prayer. [13] Share with the saints in their needs; pursue hospitality. [14] Bless those who persecute you; bless and do not curse. [15] Rejoice with those who rejoice; weep with those who weep. [16] Live in harmony with one another. Do not be proud; instead, associate with the humble. Do not be wise in your own estimation. [17] Do not repay anyone evil for evil. Give careful thought to do what is honorable in everyone's eyes. [18] If possible, as far as it depends on you, live at peace with everyone. [19] Friends, do not avenge yourselves; instead, leave room for God's wrath, because it is written, **Vengeance belongs to me; I will repay,**[D] says the Lord. [20] But

If your enemy is hungry, feed him.
If he is thirsty, give him something
    to drink.
For in so doing
you will be heaping fiery coals
    on his head.[E]

[21] Do not be conquered by evil, but conquer evil with good.

A CHRISTIAN'S DUTIES TO THE STATE

13 Let everyone submit to the governing authorities, since there is no authority except from God, and the authorities that exist are instituted by God. [2] So then, the one who resists the authority is opposing God's command, and those who oppose it will bring judgment on themselves. [3] For rulers are not a terror to good conduct, but to bad. Do you want to be unafraid of the authority? Do what is good, and you will have its approval. [4] For it is God's servant for your good. But if you do wrong, be afraid, because it does not carry the sword for no reason. For it is God's servant, an avenger that brings wrath on the one who does wrong. [5] Therefore, you must submit, not only because of wrath but also because of your conscience. [6] And for this reason you pay taxes, since the authorities are God's servants, continually attending to these tasks.[F] [7] Pay your obligations to everyone: taxes to those you owe taxes, tolls to those you owe tolls, respect to those you owe respect, and honor to those you owe honor.

LOVE, OUR PRIMARY DUTY

[8] Do not owe anyone anything, except to love one another, for the one who loves another has fulfilled the law. [9] The commandments, **Do not commit adultery; do not murder; do not steal;**[G] **do not covet;**[H] and any other commandment, are summed up by this commandment: **Love your neighbor as yourself.**[I] [10] Love does no wrong to a neighbor. Love, therefore, is the fulfillment of the law.

PUT ON CHRIST

[11] Besides this, since you know the time, it is already the hour for you[J] to wake up from sleep, because now our salvation is nearer than when we first believed. [12] The night is nearly over, and the day is near; so let us discard the deeds of darkness and put on the armor of light. [13] Let us walk with decency, as in the daytime: not in carousing and drunkenness; not in sexual impurity and promiscuity; not in quarreling and jealousy. [14] But put on the Lord Jesus Christ, and don't make plans to gratify the desires of the flesh.

THE LAW OF LIBERTY

14 Accept anyone who is weak in faith, but don't argue about disputed matters. [2] One person believes he may eat anything, while one who is weak eats only vegetables. [3] One who eats must not look down on one who does not

---

[A] **12:1** Or *your reasonable service* [B] **12:6** Or *the*, also in v. 19 [C] **12:11** Or *in spirit* [D] **12:19** Dt 32:35 [E] **12:20** Pr 25:21-22
[F] **13:6** Lit *to this very thing* [G] **13:9** Other mss add *do not bear false witness* [H] **13:9** Ex 20:13-17; Dt 5:17-21 [I] **13:9** Lv 19:18
[J] **13:11** Other mss read *for us*

eat, and one who does not eat must not judge one who does, because God has accepted him. [4] Who are you to judge another's household servant? Before his own Lord he stands or falls. And he will stand, because the Lord is able[A] to make him stand.

[5] One person judges one day to be more important than another day. Someone else judges every day to be the same. Let each one be fully convinced in his own mind. [6] Whoever observes the day, observes it for the honor of the Lord.[B] Whoever eats, eats for the Lord, since he gives thanks to God; and whoever does not eat, it is for the Lord that he does not eat it, and he gives thanks to God. [7] For none of us lives for himself, and no one dies for himself. [8] If we live, we live for the Lord; and if we die, we die for the Lord. Therefore, whether we live or die, we belong to the Lord. [9] Christ died and returned to life for this: that he might be Lord over both the dead and the living. [10] But you, why do you judge your brother or sister? Or you, why do you despise your brother or sister? For we will all stand before the judgment seat of God.[C] [11] For it is written,

As I live, says the Lord,
every knee will bow to me,
and every tongue will give praise
    to God.[D]

[12] So then, each of us will give an account of himself to God.

THE LAW OF LOVE

[13] Therefore, let us no longer judge one another. Instead decide never to put a stumbling block or pitfall in the way of your brother or sister. [14] I know and am persuaded in the Lord Jesus that nothing is unclean in itself. Still, to someone who considers a thing to be unclean, to that one it is unclean. [15] For if your brother or sister is hurt by what you eat, you are no longer walking according to love. Do not destroy, by what you eat, someone for whom Christ died. [16] Therefore, do not let your good be slandered, [17] for the kingdom of God is not eating and drinking, but righteousness, peace, and joy in the Holy Spirit. [18] Whoever serves Christ in this way is acceptable to God and receives human approval.

[19] So then, let us pursue what promotes peace and what builds up one another. [20] Do not tear down God's work because of food. Everything is clean, but it is wrong to make someone fall by what he eats. [21] It is a good thing not to eat meat, or drink wine, or do anything that makes your brother or sister stumble.[E] [22] Whatever you believe about these things, keep between yourself and God. Blessed is the one who does not condemn himself by what he approves. [23] But whoever doubts stands condemned if he eats, because his eating is not from faith,[F] and everything that is not from faith is sin.

PLEASING OTHERS, NOT OURSELVES

15 Now we who are strong have an obligation to bear the weaknesses of those without strength, and not to please ourselves. [2] Each one of us is to please his neighbor for his good, to build him up. [3] For even Christ did not please himself. On the contrary, as it is written, **The insults of those who insult you have fallen on me.**[G] [4] For whatever was written in the past was written for our instruction, so that we may have hope through endurance and through the encouragement from the Scriptures. [5] Now may the God who gives[H] endurance and encouragement grant you to live in harmony with one another, according to Christ Jesus, [6] so that you may glorify the God and Father of our Lord Jesus Christ with one mind and one voice.

GLORIFYING GOD TOGETHER

[7] Therefore accept one another, just as Christ also accepted you, to the glory of God. [8] For I say that Christ became a servant of the circumcised[I] on behalf of God's truth, to confirm the promises to the fathers, [9] and so that Gentiles may glorify God for his mercy. As it is written,

Therefore I will praise you
    among the Gentiles,
and I will sing praise to your name.[J]

[10] Again it says, **Rejoice, you Gentiles, with his people!**[K] [11] And again,

Praise the Lord, all you Gentiles;
let all the peoples praise him![L]

[12] And again, Isaiah says,

The root of Jesse will appear,
the one who rises to rule the Gentiles;
the Gentiles will hope in him.[M]

[13] Now may the God of hope fill you with all joy and peace as you believe so that you may overflow with hope by the power of the Holy Spirit.

FROM JERUSALEM TO ILLYRICUM

[14] My brothers and sisters, I myself am convinced about you that you also are full of goodness, filled with all knowledge, and able to instruct one another. [15] Nevertheless, I have

---

[A]14:4 Other mss read *For God has the power*   [B]14:6 Other mss add *but whoever does not observe the day, it is to the Lord that he does not observe it*   [C]14:10 Other mss read *of Christ*   [D]14:11 Is 45:23; 49:18   [E]14:21 Other mss add *or offended or weakened*   [F]14:23 Or *conviction*   [G]15:3 Ps 69:9   [H]15:5 Lit *God of*   [I]15:8 The Jews   [J]15:9 2Sm 22:50; Ps 18:49   [K]15:10 Dt 32:43   [L]15:11 Ps 117:1   [M]15:12 Is 11:10

written to remind you more boldly on some points[A] because of the grace given me by God [16] to be a minister of Christ Jesus to the Gentiles, serving as a priest of the gospel of God. My purpose is that the Gentiles may be an acceptable offering, sanctified by the Holy Spirit. [17] Therefore I have reason to boast in Christ Jesus regarding what pertains to God. [18] For I would not dare say anything except what Christ has accomplished through me by word and deed for the obedience of the Gentiles, [19] by the power of miraculous signs and wonders, and by the power of God's Spirit. As a result, I have fully proclaimed the gospel of Christ from Jerusalem all the way around to Illyricum.[B] [20] My aim is to preach the gospel where Christ has not been named, so that I will not build on someone else's foundation, [21] but, as it is written,

Those who were not told about him
  will see,
and those who have not heard
  will understand.[C]

PAUL'S TRAVEL PLANS

[22] That is why I have been prevented many times from coming to you. [23] But now I no longer have any work to do in these regions,[D] and I have strongly desired for many years to come to you [24] whenever I travel to Spain.[E] For I hope to see you when I pass through and to be assisted by you for my journey there, once I have first enjoyed your company for a while. [25] Right now I am traveling to Jerusalem to serve the saints, [26] because Macedonia and Achaia were pleased to make a contribution for the poor among the saints in Jerusalem. [27] Yes, they were pleased, and indeed are indebted to them. For if the Gentiles have shared in their spiritual benefits, then they are obligated to minister to them in material needs. [28] So when I have finished this and safely delivered the funds[F] to them,[G] I will visit you on the way to Spain. [29] I know that when I come to you, I will come in the fullness of the blessing[H] of Christ.

[30] Now I appeal to you, brothers and sisters, through our Lord Jesus Christ and through the love of the Spirit, to strive together with me in fervent prayers to God on my behalf. [31] Pray that I may be rescued from the unbelievers in Judea, that my ministry to[I] Jerusalem may be acceptable to the saints, [32] and that, by God's will,

I may come to you with joy and be refreshed together with you. [33] May the God of peace be with all of you. Amen.

PAUL'S COMMENDATION OF PHOEBE

16 I commend to you our sister Phoebe, who is a servant[J] of the church in Cenchreae. [2] So you should welcome her in the Lord in a manner worthy of the saints and assist her in whatever matter she may require your help. For indeed she has been a benefactor of many — and of me also.

GREETING TO ROMAN CHRISTIANS

[3] Give my greetings to Prisca[K] and Aquila, my coworkers in Christ Jesus, [4] who risked their own necks for my life. Not only do I thank them, but so do all the Gentile churches. [5] Greet also the church that meets in their home. Greet my dear friend Epaenetus, who is the first convert[L] to Christ from Asia.[M] [6] Greet Mary,[N] who has worked very hard for you.[O] [7] Greet Andronicus and Junia, my fellow Jews[P] and fellow prisoners. They are noteworthy in the eyes of the apostles,[Q] and they were also in Christ before me. [8] Greet Ampliatus, my dear friend in the Lord. [9] Greet Urbanus, our coworker in Christ, and my dear friend Stachys. [10] Greet Apelles, who is approved in Christ. Greet those who belong to the household of Aristobulus. [11] Greet Herodion, my fellow Jew.[R] Greet those who belong to the household of Narcissus who are in the Lord. [12] Greet Tryphaena and Tryphosa, who have worked hard in the Lord. Greet my dear friend Persis, who has worked very hard in the Lord. [13] Greet Rufus, chosen in the Lord; also his mother — and mine. [14] Greet Asyncritus, Phlegon, Hermes, Patrobas, Hermas, and the brothers and sisters who are with them. [15] Greet Philologus and Julia, Nereus and his sister, and Olympas, and all the saints who are with them. [16] Greet one another with a holy kiss. All the churches of Christ send you greetings.

WARNING AGAINST DIVISIVE PEOPLE

[17] Now I urge you, brothers and sisters, to watch out for those who create divisions and obstacles contrary to the teaching that you learned. Avoid them, [18] because such people do not serve our Lord Christ but their own appetites.[S] They

---

[A]15:15 Other mss add *brothers* [B]15:19 A Roman province northwest of Greece on the eastern shore of the Adriatic Sea [C]15:21 Is 52:15 [D]15:23 Lit *now, having no longer a place in these parts* [E]15:24 Other mss add *I will come to you.* [F]15:28 Lit *delivered this fruit* [G]15:28 Or *and placed my seal of approval on this fruit for them* [H]15:29 Other mss add *of the gospel* [I]15:31 Lit *that my service for* [J]16:1 Others interpret this term in a technical sense: *deacon,* or *deaconess,* or *minister,* or *courier* [K]16:3 Traditionally, *Priscilla,* as in Ac 18:2,18,26 [L]16:5 Lit *the firstfruits* [M]16:5 Other mss read *Achaia* [N]16:6 Or *Maria* [O]16:6 Other mss read *us* [P]16:7 Or *family members* [Q]16:7 Or *They are noteworthy among the apostles* [R]16:11 Or *family member* [S]16:18 Lit *belly*

deceive the hearts of the unsuspecting with smooth talk and flattering words.

PAUL'S GRACIOUS CONCLUSION

[19] The report of your obedience has reached everyone. Therefore I rejoice over you, but I want you to be wise about what is good, and yet innocent about what is evil. [20] The God of peace will soon crush Satan under your feet. The grace of our Lord Jesus be with you.

[21] Timothy, my coworker, and Lucius, Jason, and Sosipater, my fellow countrymen, greet you.

[22] I Tertius, who wrote this letter, greet you in the Lord.[A]

[23] Gaius, who is host to me and to the whole church, greets you. Erastus, the city treasurer, and our brother Quartus greet you.[B]

GLORY TO GOD

[25] Now to him who is able to strengthen you according to my gospel and the proclamation about Jesus Christ, according to the revelation of the mystery kept silent for long ages [26] but now revealed and made known through the prophetic Scriptures, according to the command of the eternal God to advance the obedience of faith among all the Gentiles — [27] to the only wise God, through Jesus Christ — to him be the glory forever![C] Amen.

[A]16:22 Or *letter in the Lord, greet you*   [B]16:23 Some mss include v. 24: *The grace of our Lord Jesus Christ be with you all.*
[C]16:25-27 Other mss have these vv. at the end of chap. 14 or 15.

1 CORINTHIANS

GREETING

1 Paul, called as an apostle of Christ Jesus by God's will, and Sosthenes our brother:

[2] To the church of God at Corinth, to those sanctified in Christ Jesus, called as saints, with all those in every place who call on the name of Jesus Christ our Lord — both their Lord and ours.

[3] Grace to you and peace from God our Father and the Lord Jesus Christ.

THANKSGIVING

[4] I always thank my God for you because of the grace of God given to you in Christ Jesus, [5] that you were enriched in him in every way, in all speech and all knowledge. [6] In this way, the testimony about Christ was confirmed among you, [7] so that you do not lack any spiritual gift as you eagerly wait for the revelation of our Lord Jesus Christ. [8] He will also strengthen you to the end, so that you will be blameless in the day of our Lord Jesus Christ. [9] God is faithful; you were called by him into fellowship with his Son, Jesus Christ our Lord.

DIVISIONS AT CORINTH

[10] Now I urge you, brothers and sisters, in the name of our Lord Jesus Christ, that all of you agree in what you say, that there be no divisions among you, and that you be united with the same understanding and the same conviction. [11] For it has been reported to me about you, my brothers and sisters, by members of Chloe's people, that there is rivalry among you. [12] What I am saying is this: One of you says, "I belong to Paul," or "I belong to Apollos," or "I belong to Cephas," or "I belong to Christ." [13] Is Christ divided? Was Paul crucified for you? Or were you baptized in Paul's name? [14] I thank God[A,B] that I baptized none of you except Crispus and Gaius, [15] so that no one can say you were baptized in my name. [16] I did, in fact, baptize the household of Stephanas; beyond that, I don't recall if I baptized anyone else. [17] For Christ did not send me to baptize, but to preach the gospel — not with eloquent wisdom, so that the cross of Christ will not be emptied of its effect.

CHRIST THE POWER AND WISDOM OF GOD

[18] For the word of the cross is foolishness to those who are perishing, but it is the power of God to us who are being saved. [19] For it is written,

I will destroy the wisdom of the wise,
and I will set aside the intelligence
of the intelligent.[C]

[20] Where is the one who is wise? Where is the teacher of the law?[D] Where is the debater of this age? Hasn't God made the world's wisdom foolish? [21] For since, in God's wisdom, the world did not know God through wisdom, God was pleased to save those who believe through the foolishness of what is preached. [22] For the Jews ask for signs and the Greeks seek wisdom, [23] but we preach Christ crucified, a stumbling block to the Jews and foolishness to the Gentiles.[E] [24] Yet to those who are called, both Jews and Greeks, Christ is the power of God and the wisdom of God, [25] because God's foolishness is wiser than human wisdom, and God's weakness is stronger than human strength.

BOASTING ONLY IN THE LORD

[26] Brothers and sisters, consider your calling: Not many were wise from a human perspective,[F] not many powerful, not many of noble birth. [27] Instead, God has chosen what is foolish in the world to shame the wise, and God has chosen what is weak in the world to shame the strong. [28] God has chosen what is insignificant and despised in the world — what is viewed as nothing — to bring to nothing what is viewed as something, [29] so that no one[G] may boast in his presence. [30] It is from him that you are in Christ Jesus, who became wisdom from God for us — our righteousness, sanctification, and redemption, [31] in order that, as it is written: Let the one who boasts, boast in the Lord.[H]

PAUL'S PROCLAMATION

2 When I came to you, brothers and sisters, announcing the mystery[I] of God to you, I did not come with brilliance of speech or wisdom. [2] I decided to know nothing among you except Jesus Christ and him crucified. [3] I came to you in weakness, in fear, and in much trembling. [4] My speech and my preaching were not with persuasive words of wisdom[J] but with a demonstration of the Spirit's power, [5] so that your faith might not be based on human wisdom but on God's power.

SPIRITUAL WISDOM

[6] We do, however, speak a wisdom among the mature, but not a wisdom of this age, or of the

^1:14 Other mss omit *God*   ^1:14 Or *I am thankful*   ^1:19 Is 29:14   ^1:20 Or *scholar*   ^1:23 Other mss read *Greeks*   ^1:26 Lit *wise according to the flesh*   ^1:29 Lit *that not all flesh*   ^1:31 Jr 9:24   ^2:1 Other mss read *testimony*   ^2:4 Other mss read *human wisdom*

rulers of this age, who are coming to nothing. [7] On the contrary, we speak God's hidden wisdom in a mystery, a wisdom God predestined before the ages for our glory. [8] None of the rulers of this age knew this wisdom, because if they had known it, they would not have crucified the Lord of glory. [9] But as it is written,

> What no eye has seen, no ear
>   has heard,
> and no human heart has conceived —
>   God has prepared these things
>   for those who love him.^A

[10] Now God has revealed these things to us by the Spirit, since the Spirit searches everything, even the depths of God. [11] For who knows a person's thoughts^B except his spirit within him? In the same way, no one knows the thoughts of God except the Spirit of God. [12] Now we have not received the spirit of the world, but the Spirit who comes from God, so that we may understand what has been freely given to us by God. [13] We also speak these things, not in words taught by human wisdom, but in those taught by the Spirit, explaining spiritual things to spiritual people.^C [14] But the person without the Spirit^D does not receive what comes from God's Spirit, because it is foolishness to him; he is not able to understand it since it is evaluated^E spiritually. [15] The spiritual person, however, can evaluate^F everything, and yet he himself cannot be evaluated by anyone. [16] For

> who has known the Lord's mind,
>   that he may instruct him?^G

But we have the mind of Christ.

THE PROBLEM OF IMMATURITY

3 For my part, brothers and sisters, I was not able to speak to you as spiritual people but as people of the flesh, as babies in Christ. [2] I gave you milk to drink, not solid food, since you were not yet ready for it. In fact, you are still not ready, [3] because you are still worldly. For since there is envy and strife^H among you, are you not worldly and behaving like mere humans? [4] For whenever someone says, "I belong to Paul," and another, "I belong to Apollos," are you not acting like mere humans?

THE ROLE OF GOD'S SERVANTS

[5] What then is Apollos? What is Paul? They are servants through whom you believed, and each has the role the Lord has given. [6] I planted, Apollos watered, but God gave the growth. [7] So then neither the one who plants nor the one who waters is anything, but only God who gives the growth. [8] Now he who plants and he who waters are one,^I and each will receive his own reward according to his own labor. [9] For we are God's coworkers.^J You are God's field, God's building.

[10] According to God's grace that was given to me, I have laid a foundation as a skilled master builder,^K and another builds on it. But each one is to be careful how he builds on it. [11] For no one can lay any other foundation than what has been laid down. That foundation is Jesus Christ. [12] If anyone builds on the foundation with gold, silver, costly stones, wood, hay, or straw, [13] each one's work will become obvious. For the day will disclose it, because it will be revealed by fire; the fire will test the quality of each one's work. [14] If anyone's work that he has built survives, he will receive a reward. [15] If anyone's work is burned up, he will experience^L loss, but he himself will be saved — but only as through fire.

[16] Don't you yourselves know that you are God's temple and that the Spirit of God lives in you? [17] If anyone destroys God's temple, God will destroy him; for God's temple is holy, and that is what you are.

THE FOLLY OF HUMAN WISDOM

[18] Let no one deceive himself. If anyone among you thinks he is wise in this age, let him become a fool so that he can become wise. [19] For the wisdom of this world is foolishness with God, since it is written, **He catches the wise in their craftiness;**^M [20] and again, **The Lord knows that the reasonings of the wise are futile.**^N [21] So let no one boast in human leaders, for everything is yours — [22] whether Paul or Apollos or Cephas or the world or life or death or things present or things to come — everything is yours, [23] and you belong to Christ, and Christ belongs to God.

THE FAITHFUL MANAGER

4 A person should think of us in this way: as servants of Christ and managers of the mysteries of God. [2] In this regard, it is required that managers be found faithful. [3] It is of little importance to me that I should be judged by you or by any human court.^O In fact, I don't even judge myself. [4] For I am not conscious of anything against myself, but I am not justified by this. It is the Lord who judges me. [5] So don't judge anything prematurely, before the Lord comes, who will both bring to light what is hidden in darkness and reveal the intentions of the hearts. And then praise will come to each one from God.

---

^A **2:9** Is 52:15; 64:4   ^B **2:11** Or *things*   ^C **2:13** Or *things with spiritual words*   ^D **2:14** Lit *natural person*   ^E **2:14** Or *judged, or discerned,* also in v. 15   ^F **2:15** Or *judge, or discern*   ^G **2:16** Is 40:13   ^H **3:3** Other mss add *and divisions*   ^I **3:8** Or *of equal status,* or *united in purpose*   ^J **3:9** Or *are coworkers belonging to God*   ^K **3:10** Or *wise master builder*   ^L **3:15** Or *suffer*   ^M **3:19** Jb 5:13   ^N **3:20** Ps 94:11   ^O **4:3** Lit *a human day*

THE APOSTLES' EXAMPLE OF HUMILITY

⁶ Now, brothers and sisters, I have applied these things to myself and Apollos for your benefit, so that you may learn from us the meaning of the saying: "Nothing beyond what is written." The purpose is that none of you will be arrogant, favoring one person over another. ⁷ For who makes you so superior? What do you have that you didn't receive? If, in fact, you did receive it, why do you boast as if you hadn't received it? ⁸ You are already full! You are already rich! You have begun to reign as kings without us — and I wish you did reign, so that we could also reign with you! ⁹ For I think God has displayed us, the apostles, in last place, like men condemned to die: We have become a spectacle to the world, both to angels and to people. ¹⁰ We are fools for Christ, but you are wise in Christ! We are weak, but you are strong! You are distinguished, but we are dishonored! ¹¹ Up to the present hour we are both hungry and thirsty; we are poorly clothed, roughly treated, homeless; ¹² we labor, working with our own hands. When we are reviled, we bless; when we are persecuted, we endure it; ¹³ when we are slandered, we respond graciously. Even now, we are like the scum of the earth, like everyone's garbage.

PAUL'S FATHERLY CARE

¹⁴ I'm not writing this to shame you, but to warn you as my dear children. ¹⁵ For you may have countless instructors in Christ, but you don't have many fathers. For I became your father in Christ Jesus through the gospel. ¹⁶ Therefore I urge you to imitate me. ¹⁷ This is why I have sent Timothy to you. He is my dearly loved and faithful child in the Lord. He will remind you about my ways in Christ Jesus, just as I teach everywhere in every church.

¹⁸ Now some are arrogant, as though I were not coming to you. ¹⁹ But I will come to you soon, if the Lord wills, and I will find out not the talk, but the power of those who are arrogant. ²⁰ For the kingdom of God is not a matter of talk but of power. ²¹ What do you want? Should I come to you with a rod, or in love and a spirit of gentleness?

IMMORAL CHURCH MEMBERS

5 It is actually reported that there is sexual immorality among you, and the kind of sexual immorality that is not even tolerated^A among the Gentiles — a man is sleeping with his father's wife. ² And you are arrogant! Shouldn't you be filled with grief and remove from your congregation the one who did this?

³ Even though I am absent in the body, I am present in spirit. As one who is present with you in this way, I have already pronounced judgment on the one who has been doing such a thing. ⁴ When you are assembled in the name of our Lord Jesus, and I am with you in spirit, with the power of our Lord Jesus, ⁵ hand that one over to Satan for the destruction of the flesh, so that his spirit may be saved in the day of the Lord.

⁶ Your boasting is not good. Don't you know that a little leaven^B leavens the whole batch of dough? ⁷ Clean out the old leaven so that you may be a new unleavened batch, as indeed you are. For Christ our Passover lamb has been sacrificed.^C ⁸ Therefore, let us observe the feast, not with old leaven or with the leaven of malice and evil, but with the unleavened bread of sincerity and truth.

CHURCH DISCIPLINE

⁹ I wrote to you in a letter not to associate with sexually immoral people. ¹⁰ I did not mean the immoral people of this world or the greedy and swindlers or idolaters; otherwise you would have to leave the world. ¹¹ But actually, I wrote^D you not to associate with anyone who claims to be a brother or sister and is sexually immoral or greedy, an idolater or verbally abusive, a drunkard or a swindler. Do not even eat with such a person. ¹² For what business is it of mine to judge outsiders? Don't you judge those who are inside? ¹³ God judges outsiders. **Remove the evil person from among you.**^E

LAWSUITS AMONG BELIEVERS

6 If any of you has a dispute against another, how dare you take it to court before the unrighteous,^F and not before the saints? ² Or don't you know that the saints will judge the world? And if the world is judged by you, are you unworthy to judge the trivial cases? ³ Don't you know that we will judge angels — how much more matters of this life? ⁴ So if you have such matters, do you appoint as your judges those who have no standing in the church? ⁵ I say this to your shame! Can it be that there is not one wise person among you who is able to arbitrate between fellow believers? ⁶ Instead, brother goes to court against brother, and that before unbelievers!

⁷ As it is, to have legal disputes against one another is already a defeat for you. Why not rather be wronged? Why not rather be cheated? ⁸ Instead, you yourselves do wrong and cheat — and you do this to brothers and sisters! ⁹ Don't you know that the unrighteous will not inherit God's kingdom? Do not be

deceived: No sexually immoral people, idolaters, adulterers, or males who have sex with males,^10 no thieves, greedy people, drunkards, verbally abusive people, or swindlers will inherit God's kingdom. **11** And some of you used to be like this. But you were washed, you were sanctified, you were justified in the name of the Lord Jesus Christ and by the Spirit of our God.

GLORIFYING GOD IN BODY AND SPIRIT

12 "Everything is permissible for me," but not everything is beneficial. "Everything is permissible for me," but I will not be mastered by anything. **13** "Food is for the stomach and the stomach for food," and God will do away with both of them. However, the body is not for sexual immorality but for the Lord, and the Lord for the body. **14** God raised up the Lord and will also raise us up by his power. **15** Don't you know that your bodies are a part of Christ's body? So should I take a part of Christ's body and make it part of a prostitute? Absolutely not! **16** Don't you know that anyone joined to a prostitute is one body with her? For Scripture says, **The two will become one flesh.**^B **17** But anyone joined to the Lord is one spirit with him.

18 Flee sexual immorality! Every other sin^C a person commits is outside the body, but the person who is sexually immoral sins against his own body. **19** Don't you know that your body is a temple of the Holy Spirit who is in you, whom you have from God? You are not your own, **20** for you were bought at a price. So glorify God with your body.^D

PRINCIPLES OF MARRIAGE

7 Now in response to the matters you wrote^E about: "It is good for a man not to use^F a woman for sex." **2** But because sexual immorality is so common,^G each man should have sexual relations with his own wife, and each woman should have sexual relations with her own husband. **3** A husband should fulfill his marital duty to his wife, and likewise a wife to her husband. **4** A wife does not have the right over her own body, but her husband does. In the same way, a husband does not have the right over his own body, but his wife does. **5** Do not deprive one another — except when you agree for a time, to devote yourselves to^H prayer. Then come together again; otherwise, Satan may tempt you because of your lack of self-control. **6** I say this as a concession,

not as a command. **7** I wish that all people were as I am. But each has his own gift from God, one person has this gift, another has that.

A WORD TO THE UNMARRIED

8 I say to the unmarried^I and to widows: It is good for them if they remain as I am. **9** But if they do not have self-control, they should marry, since it is better to marry than to burn with desire.

ABOUT MARRIED PEOPLE

10 To the married I give this command — not I, but the Lord — a wife is not to leave^J her husband. **11** But if she does leave, she must remain unmarried or be reconciled to her husband — and a husband is not to divorce his wife. **12** But I (not the Lord) say to the rest: If any brother has an unbelieving wife and she is willing to live with him, he must not divorce her. **13** Also, if any woman has an unbelieving husband and he is willing to live with her, she must not divorce her husband. **14** For the unbelieving husband is made holy by the wife, and the unbelieving wife is made holy by the husband.^K Otherwise your children would be unclean, but as it is they are holy. **15** But if the unbeliever leaves, let him leave. A brother or a sister is not bound in such cases. God has called you^L to live in peace. **16** Wife, for all you know, you might save your husband. Husband, for all you know, you might save your wife.^M

VARIOUS SITUATIONS OF LIFE

17 Let each one live his life in the situation the Lord assigned when God called him.^N This is what I command in all the churches. **18** Was anyone already circumcised when he was called? He should not undo his circumcision. Was anyone called while uncircumcised? He should not get circumcised. **19** Circumcision does not matter and uncircumcision does not matter. Keeping God's commands is what matters. **20** Let each of you remain in the situation^O in which he was called. **21** Were you called while a slave? Don't let it concern you. But if you can become free, by all means take the opportunity.^P **22** For he who is called by the Lord as a slave is the Lord's freedman. Likewise he who is called as a free man is Christ's slave. **23** You were bought at a price; do not become slaves of people. **24** Brothers and sisters, each person is to remain with God in the situation in which he was called.

---

^A **6:9** Both passive and active participants in homosexual acts   ^B **6:16** Gn 2:24   ^C **6:18** Lit *Every sin*   ^D **6:20** Other mss add *and in your spirit, which belong to God.*   ^E **7:1** Other mss add *to me*   ^F **7:1** Lit *"It is good for a man not to touch a woman*   ^G **7:2** Lit *because of immoralities*   ^H **7:5** Other mss add *fasting and to*   ^I **7:8** Or *widowers*   ^J **7:10** Or *separate from,* or *divorce*   ^K **7:14** Lit *the brother*   ^L **7:15** Other mss read *us*   ^M **7:16** Or *Wife, how do you know that you will save your husband? Husband, how do you know that you will save your wife?*   ^N **7:17** Lit *called each*   ^O **7:20** Lit *in the calling*   ^P **7:21** Or *But even though you can become free, make the most of your position as a slave*

ABOUT THE UNMARRIED AND WIDOWS

[25] Now about virgins:[A] I have no command from the Lord, but I do give an opinion as one who by the Lord's mercy is faithful. [26] Because of the present distress, I think that it is good for a man to remain as he is. [27] Are you bound to a wife? Do not seek to be released. Are you released from a wife? Do not seek a wife. [28] However, if you do get married, you have not sinned, and if a virgin[B] marries, she has not sinned. But such people will have trouble in this life,[C] and I am trying to spare you.

[29] This is what I mean, brothers and sisters: The time is limited, so from now on those who have wives should be as though they had none, [30] those who weep as though they did not weep, those who rejoice as though they did not rejoice, those who buy as though they didn't own anything, [31] and those who use the world as though they did not make full use of it. For this world in its current form is passing away.

[32] I want you to be without concerns. The unmarried man is concerned about the things of the Lord — how he may please the Lord. [33] But the married man is concerned about the things of the world — how he may please his wife — [34] and his interests are divided. The unmarried woman or virgin is concerned about the things of the Lord, so that she may be holy both in body and in spirit. But the married woman is concerned about the things of the world — how she may please her husband. [35] I am saying this for your own benefit, not to put a restraint on you, but to promote what is proper and so that you may be devoted to the Lord without distraction.

[36] If any man thinks he is acting improperly toward the virgin he is engaged to,[D] if she is getting beyond the usual age for marriage, and he feels he should marry — he can do what he wants. He is not sinning; they can get married. [37] But he who stands firm in his heart (who is under no compulsion, but has control over his own will) and has decided in his heart to keep her as his fiancé, will do well. [38] So then he who marries[E] his fiancé does well, but he who does not marry[F] will do better.

[39] A wife is bound[G] as long as her husband is living. But if her husband dies, she is free to be married to anyone she wants — only in the Lord. [40] But she is happier if she remains as she is, in my opinion. And I think that I also have the Spirit of God.

FOOD OFFERED TO IDOLS

8 Now about food sacrificed to idols: We know that "we all have knowledge." Knowledge puffs up, but love builds up. [2] If anyone thinks he knows anything, he does not yet know it as he ought to know it. [3] But if anyone loves God, he is known by him.

[4] About eating food sacrificed to idols, then, we know that "an idol is nothing in the world,"[H] and that "there is no God but one." [5] For even if there are so-called gods, whether in heaven or on earth — as there are many "gods" and many "lords" — [6] yet for us there is one God, the Father. All things are from him, and we exist for him. And there is one Lord, Jesus Christ. All things are through him, and we exist through him.

[7] However, not everyone has this knowledge. Some have been so used to idolatry up until now that when they eat food sacrificed to an idol, their conscience, being weak, is defiled. [8] Food will not bring us close to God.[I] We are not worse off if we don't eat, and we are not better if we do eat. [9] But be careful that this right of yours in no way becomes a stumbling block to the weak. [10] For if someone sees you, the one who has knowledge, dining in an idol's temple, won't his weak conscience be encouraged[J] to eat food offered to idols? [11] So the weak person, the brother or sister for whom Christ died, is ruined[K] by your knowledge. [12] Now when you sin like this against brothers and sisters and wound their weak conscience, you are sinning against Christ. [13] Therefore, if food causes my brother or sister to fall, I will never again eat meat, so that I won't cause my brother or sister to fall.

PAUL'S EXAMPLE AS AN APOSTLE

9 Am I not free? Am I not an apostle? Have I not seen Jesus our Lord? Are you not my work in the Lord? [2] If I am not an apostle to others, at least I am to you, because you are the seal of my apostleship in the Lord.

[3] My defense to those who examine me is this: [4] Don't we have the right to eat and drink? [5] Don't we have the right to be accompanied by a believing wife[L] like the other apostles, the Lord's brothers, and Cephas? [6] Or do only Barnabas and I have no right to refrain from working? [7] Who serves as a soldier at his own expense? Who plants a vineyard and does not eat its fruit? Or who shepherds a flock and does not drink the milk from the flock?

[A] 7:25 Or *betrothed, or those not yet married* [B] 7:28 Or *betrothed woman* [C] 7:28 Lit *in the flesh* [D] 7:36 Or *toward his virgin daughter* [E] 7:38 Or *marries off* [F] 7:38 Or *marry her off* [G] 7:39 Other mss add *by law* [H] 8:4 Or *an idol has no real existence* [I] 8:8 Or *bring us before* (the judgment seat of) *God* [J] 8:10 Or *built up* [K] 8:11 Or *destroyed* [L] 9:5 Lit *a sister as a wife*

⁸ Am I saying this from a human perspective? Doesn't the law also say the same thing? ⁹ For it is written in the law of Moses, **Do not muzzle an ox while it treads out grain.**ᴬ Is God really concerned about oxen? ¹⁰ Isn't he really saying it for our sake? Yes, this is written for our sake, because he who plows ought to plow in hope, and he who threshes should thresh in hope of sharing the crop. ¹¹ If we have sown spiritual things for you, is it too much if we reap material benefits from you? ¹² If others have this right to receive benefits from you, don't we even more? Nevertheless, we have not made use of this right; instead, we endure everything so that we will not hinder the gospel of Christ.

¹³ Don't you know that those who perform the temple services eat the food from the temple, and those who serve at the altar share in the offerings of the altar? ¹⁴ In the same way, the Lord has commanded that those who preach the gospel should earn their living by the gospel.

¹⁵ For my part I have used none of these rights, nor have I written these things that they may be applied in my case. For it would be better for me to die than for anyone to deprive me of my boast! ¹⁶ For if I preach the gospel, I have no reason to boast, because I am compelled to preach ᴮ — and woe to me if I do not preach the gospel! ¹⁷ For if I do this willingly, I have a reward, but if unwillingly, I am entrusted with a commission. ¹⁸ What then is my reward? To preach the gospel and offer it free of charge and not make full use of my rights in the gospel.

¹⁹ Although I am free from all and not anyone's slave, I have made myself a slave to everyone, in order to win more people. ²⁰ To the Jews I became like a Jew, to win Jews; to those under the law, like one under the law — though I myself am not under the lawᶜ — to win those under the law. ²¹ To those who are without the law, like one without the law — though I am not without God's law but under the law of Christ — to win those without the law. ²² To the weak I became weak, in order to win the weak. I have become all things to all people, so that I may by every possible means save some. ²³ Now I do all this because of the gospel, so that I may share in the blessings.

²⁴ Don't you know that the runners in a stadium all race, but only one receives the prize? Run in such a way to win the prize. ²⁵ Now everyone who competes exercises self-control in everything. They do it to receive a perishable crown, but we an imperishable crown. ²⁶ So I do not run like one who runs aimlessly or box like one beating the air. ²⁷ Instead, I discipline my body and bring it under strict control, so that after preaching to others, I myself will not be disqualified.

WARNINGS FROM ISRAEL'S PAST

10 Now I do not want you to be unaware, brothers and sisters, that our ancestors were all under the cloud, all passed through the sea, ² and all were baptized into Moses in the cloud and in the sea. ³ They all ate the same spiritual food, ⁴ and all drank the same spiritual drink. For they drank from the spiritual rock that followed them, and that rock was Christ. ⁵ Nevertheless God was not pleased with most of them, since they were struck down in the wilderness.

⁶ Now these things took place as examples for us, so that we will not desire evil things as they did.ᴰ ⁷ Don't become idolaters as some of them were; as it is written, **The people sat down to eat and drink, and got up to party.**ᴱ,ᶠ ⁸ Let us not commit sexual immorality as some of them did,ᴳ and in a single day twenty-three thousand people died. ⁹ Let us not test Christ as some of them didᴴ and were destroyed by snakes. ¹⁰ And don't complain as some of them did,ᴵ and were killed by the destroyer.ᴶ ¹¹ These things happened to them as examples, and they were written for our instruction, on whom the ends of the agesᴷ have come. ¹² So, whoever thinks he stands must be careful not to fall. ¹³ No temptation has come upon you except what is common to humanity. But God is faithful; he will not allow you to be tempted beyond what you are able, but with the temptation he will also provide a way out so that you may be able to bear it.

WARNING AGAINST IDOLATRY

¹⁴ So then, my dear friends, flee from idolatry. ¹⁵ I am speaking as to sensible people. Judge for yourselves what I am saying. ¹⁶ The cup of blessing that we bless, is it not a sharing in the blood of Christ? The bread that we break, is it not a sharing in the body of Christ? ¹⁷ Because there is one bread, we who are many are one body, since all of us share the one bread. ¹⁸ Consider the people of Israel.ᴸ Do not those who eat the sacrifices participate in the altar? ¹⁹ What am I saying then? That food sacrificed to idols is anything, or that an idol is anything? ²⁰ No, but I do say that what theyᴹ sacrifice, they sacrifice to demons and not to God. I do not want you to be participants with demons! ²¹ You cannot drink the cup of the Lord and the cup of demons. You cannot share in the Lord's table and the table

---

ᴬ**9:9** Dt 25:4 ᴮ**9:16** Lit *because necessity is laid upon me* ᶜ**9:20** Other mss omit *though I myself am not under the law* ᴰ**10:6** Lit *they desired* ᴱ**10:7** Or *to dance* ᶠ**10:7** Ex 32:6 ᴳ**10:8** Lit *them committed sexual immorality* ᴴ**10:9** Lit *them tested* ᴵ**10:10** Lit *them complained* ᴶ**10:10** Or *the destroying angel* ᴷ**10:11** Or *goals of the ages*, or *culmination of the ages* ᴸ**10:18** Lit *Look at Israel according to the flesh* ᴹ**10:20** Other mss read *Gentiles*

of demons. [22] Or are we provoking the Lord to jealousy? Are we stronger than he?

CHRISTIAN LIBERTY

[23] "Everything is permissible,"[A] but not everything is beneficial. "Everything is permissible,"[A] but not everything builds up. [24] No one is to seek his own good, but the good of the other person.

[25] Eat everything that is sold in the meat market, without raising questions for the sake of conscience, [26] since **the earth is the Lord's, and all that is in it.**[B] [27] If any of the unbelievers invites you over and you want to go, eat everything that is set before you, without raising questions for the sake of conscience. [28] But if someone says to you, "This is food from a sacrifice," do not eat it, out of consideration for the one who told you, and for the sake of conscience.[C] [29] I do not mean your own conscience, but the other person's. For why is my freedom judged by another person's conscience? [30] If I partake with thanksgiving, why am I criticized because of something for which I give thanks?

[31] So, whether you eat or drink, or whatever you do, do everything for the glory of God. [32] Give no offense to Jews or Greeks or the church of God, [33] just as I also try to please everyone in everything, not seeking my own benefit, **11** but the benefit of many, so that they may be saved. [1] Imitate me, as I also imitate Christ.

INSTRUCTIONS ABOUT HEAD COVERINGS

[2] Now I praise you[D] because you remember me in everything and hold fast to the traditions just as I delivered them to you. [3] But I want you to know that Christ is the head of every man, and the man is the head of the woman,[E] and God is the head of Christ. [4] Every man who prays or prophesies with something on his head dishonors his head. [5] Every woman who prays or prophesies with her head uncovered dishonors her head, since that is one and the same as having her head shaved. [6] For if a woman doesn't cover her head, she should have her hair cut off. But if it is disgraceful for a woman to have her hair cut off or her head shaved, let her head be covered.

[7] A man should not cover his head, because he is the image and glory of God. So too, woman is the glory of man. [8] For man did not come from woman, but woman came from man. [9] Neither was man created for the sake of woman, but woman for the sake of man. [10] This is why a woman should have a symbol of authority on her head, because of the angels. [11] In the Lord, however, woman is not independent of man, and man is not independent of woman. [12] For just as woman came from man, so man comes through woman, and all things come from God.

[13] Judge for yourselves: Is it proper for a woman to pray to God with her head uncovered? [14] Does not even nature itself teach you that if a man has long hair it is a disgrace to him, [15] but that if a woman has long hair, it is her glory? For her hair is given to her[F] as a covering. [16] If anyone wants to argue about this, we have no other[G] custom, nor do the churches of God.

THE LORD'S SUPPER

[17] Now in giving this instruction I do not praise you, since you come together not for the better but for the worse. [18] For to begin with, I hear that when you come together as a church there are divisions among you, and in part I believe it. [19] Indeed, it is necessary that there be factions among you, so that those who are approved may be recognized among you. [20] When you come together, then, it is not to eat the Lord's Supper. [21] For at the meal, each one eats his own supper.[H] So one person is hungry while another gets drunk! [22] Don't you have homes in which to eat and drink? Or do you despise the church of God and humiliate those who have nothing? What should I say to you? Should I praise you? I do not praise you in this matter!

[23] For I received from the Lord what I also passed on to you: On the night when he was betrayed, the Lord Jesus took bread, [24] and when he had given thanks, broke it, and said,[I] "This is my body, which is[J] for you. Do this in remembrance of me."

[25] In the same way also he took the cup, after supper, and said, "This cup is the new covenant in my blood. Do this, as often as you drink it, in remembrance of me." [26] For as often as you eat this bread and drink the cup, you proclaim the Lord's death until he comes.

SELF-EXAMINATION

[27] So then, whoever eats the bread or drinks the cup of the Lord in an unworthy manner will be guilty of sin against the body[K] and blood of the Lord. [28] Let a person examine himself; in this way let him eat the bread and drink from the cup. [29] For whoever eats and drinks without recognizing the body,[L] eats and drinks judgment on himself. [30] This is why many are sick and ill among you, and many have fallen asleep.

[A] **10:23** Other mss add *for me*   [B] **10:26** Ps 24:1   [C] **10:28** Other mss add *"For the earth is the Lord's and all that is in it."*
[D] **11:2** Other mss add *brothers,*   [E] **11:3** Or *the husband is the head of the wife*   [F] **11:15** Other mss omit *to her*   [G] **11:16** Or *no such*
[H] **11:21** Or *eats his own supper ahead of others*   [I] **11:24** Other mss add *Take, eat.*   [J] **11:24** Other mss add *broken*   [K] **11:27** Lit *be guilty of the body*   [L] **11:29** Other mss read *drinks unworthily, not discerning the Lord's body*

³¹ If we were properly judging ourselves, we would not be judged, ³² but when we are judged by the Lord, we are disciplined, so that we may not be condemned with the world.

³³ Therefore, my brothers and sisters, when you come together to eat, welcome one another.^ ³⁴ If anyone is hungry, he should eat at home, so that when you gather together you will not come under judgment. I will give instructions about the other matters whenever I come.

DIVERSITY OF SPIRITUAL GIFTS

12 Now concerning spiritual gifts:⁸ brothers and sisters, I do not want you to be unaware. ² You know that when you were pagans, you used to be enticed and led astray by mute idols. ³ Therefore I want you to know that no one speaking by the Spirit of God says, "Jesus is cursed," and no one can say, "Jesus is Lord," except by the Holy Spirit.

⁴ Now there are different gifts, but the same Spirit. ⁵ There are different ministries, but the same Lord. ⁶ And there are different activities, but the same God produces each gift in each person. ⁷ A manifestation of the Spirit is given to each person for the common good: ⁸ to one is given a message of wisdom through the Spirit, to another, a message of knowledge by the same Spirit, ⁹ to another, faith by the same Spirit, to another, gifts of healing by the one Spirit, ¹⁰ to another, the performing of miracles, to another, prophecy, to another, distinguishing between spirits, to another, different kinds of tongues,ᶜ to another, interpretation of tongues. ¹¹ One and the same Spirit is active in all these, distributing to each person as he wills.

UNITY YET DIVERSITY IN THE BODY

¹² For just as the body is one and has many parts, and all the parts of that body, though many, are one body — so also is Christ. ¹³ For we were all baptized byᴰ one Spirit into one body — whether Jews or Greeks, whether slaves or free — and we were all given one Spirit to drink. ¹⁴ Indeed, the body is not one part but many. ¹⁵ If the foot should say, "Because I'm not a hand, I don't belong to the body," it is not for that reason any less a part of the body. ¹⁶ And if the ear should say, "Because I'm not an eye, I don't belong to the body," it is not for that reason any less a part of the body. ¹⁷ If the whole body were an eye, where would the hearing be? If the whole body were an ear, where would the sense of smell be? ¹⁸ But as it is, God has arranged each one of the parts in the body just as he wanted. ¹⁹ And if they were all the same part, where would the body be? ²⁰ As it is, there are many parts, but one body. ²¹ The eye cannot say to the hand, "I don't need you! " Or again, the head can't say to the feet, "I don't need you! " ²² On the contrary, those parts of the body that are weaker are indispensable. ²³ And those parts of the body that we consider less honorable, we clothe these with greater honor, and our unrespectable parts are treated with greater respect, ²⁴ which our respectable parts do not need.

Instead, God has put the body together, giving greater honor to the less honorable, ²⁵ so that there would be no division in the body, but that the members would have the same concern for each other. ²⁶ So if one member suffers, all the members suffer with it; if one member is honored, all the members rejoice with it.

²⁷ Now you are the body of Christ, and individual members of it. ²⁸ And God has appointed these in the church: first apostles, second prophets, third teachers, next miracles, then gifts of healing, helping, administrating, various kinds of tongues.ᴱ ²⁹ Are all apostles? Are all prophets? Are all teachers? Do all do miracles? ³⁰ Do all have gifts of healing? Do all speak in other tongues? Do all interpret? ³¹ But desire the greater gifts. And I will show you an even better way.

LOVE: THE SUPERIOR WAY

13 If I speak human or angelic tonguesᶠ but do not have love, I am a noisy gong or a clanging cymbal. ² If I have the gift of prophecy and understand all mysteries and all knowledge, and if I have all faith so that I can move mountains but do not have love, I am nothing. ³ And if I give away all my possessions, and if I give over my body in order to boastᴳ but do not have love, I gain nothing.

⁴ Love is patient, love is kind. Love does not envy, is not boastful, is not arrogant, ⁵ is not rude, is not self-seeking, is not irritable, and does not keep a record of wrongs. ⁶ Love finds no joy in unrighteousness but rejoices in the truth. ⁷ It bears all things, believes all things, hopes all things, endures all things.

⁸ Love never ends. But as for prophecies, they will come to an end; as for tongues, they will cease; as for knowledge, it will come to an end. ⁹ For we know in part, and we prophesy in part, ¹⁰ but when the perfect comes, the partial will come to an end. ¹¹ When I was a child, I spoke like a child, I thought like a child, I reasoned like a child. When I became a man, I put aside childish

---

things. [12] For now we see only a reflection[A] as in a mirror, but then face to face. Now I know in part, but then I will know fully, as I am fully known. [13] Now these three remain: faith, hope, and love — but the greatest of these is love.

PROPHECY: A SUPERIOR GIFT

14 Pursue love and desire spiritual gifts, and especially that you may prophesy. [2] For the person who speaks in another tongue[B] is not speaking to people but to God, since no one understands him; he speaks mysteries in the Spirit.[C] [3] On the other hand, the person who prophesies speaks to people for their strengthening,[D] encouragement, and consolation. [4] The person who speaks in another tongue builds himself up, but the one who prophesies builds up the church. [5] I wish all of you spoke in other tongues,[E] but even more that you prophesied. The person who prophesies is greater than the person who speaks in tongues, unless he interprets so that the church may be built up.

[6] So now, brothers and sisters, if I come to you speaking in other tongues, how will I benefit you unless I speak to you with a revelation or knowledge or prophecy or teaching? [7] Even lifeless instruments that produce sounds — whether flute or harp — if they don't make a distinction in the notes, how will what is played on the flute or harp be recognized? [8] In fact, if the bugle makes an unclear sound, who will prepare for battle? [9] In the same way, unless you use your tongue for intelligible speech, how will what is spoken be known? For you will be speaking into the air. [10] There are doubtless many different kinds of languages in the world, none is without meaning. [11] Therefore, if I do not know the meaning of the language, I will be a foreigner[F] to the speaker, and the speaker will be a foreigner to me. [12] So also you — since you are zealous for spiritual gifts,[G] seek to excel in building up the church.

[13] Therefore the person who speaks in another tongue should pray that he can interpret. [14] For if I pray in another tongue, my spirit prays, but my understanding is unfruitful. [15] What then? I will pray with the spirit, and I will also pray with my understanding. I will sing praise with the spirit, and I will also sing praise with my understanding. [16] Otherwise, if you praise with the spirit,[H] how will the outsider[I] say "Amen" at your giving of thanks, since he does not know what you are saying? [17] For you may very well be giving thanks, but the other person is not being built up. [18] I thank God

that I speak in other tongues more than all of you; [19] yet in the church I would rather speak five words with my understanding, in order to teach others also, than ten thousand words in another tongue.

[20] Brothers and sisters, don't be childish in your thinking, but be infants in regard to evil and adult in your thinking. [21] It is written in the law,

> I will speak to this people
> by people of other tongues
> and by the lips of foreigners,
> and even then, they will not listen
> to me,[J]

says the Lord. [22] Speaking in other tongues, then, is intended as a sign, not for believers but for unbelievers, while prophecy is not for unbelievers but for believers. [23] If, therefore, the whole church assembles together and all are speaking in other tongues and people who are outsiders or unbelievers come in, will they not say that you are out of your minds? [24] But if all are prophesying and some unbeliever or outsider comes in, he is convicted by all and is called to account by all. [25] The secrets of his heart will be revealed, and as a result he will fall facedown and worship God, proclaiming, "God is really among you."

ORDER IN CHURCH MEETINGS

[26] What then, brothers and sisters? Whenever you come together, each one[K] has a hymn, a teaching, a revelation, another tongue, or an interpretation. Everything is to be done for building up. [27] If anyone speaks in another tongue, there are to be only two, or at the most three, each in turn, and let someone interpret. [28] But if there is no interpreter, that person is to keep silent in the church and speak to himself and God. [29] Two or three prophets should speak, and the others should evaluate. [30] But if something has been revealed to another person sitting there, the first prophet should be silent. [31] For you can all prophesy one by one, so that everyone may learn and everyone may be encouraged. [32] And the prophets' spirits are subject to the prophets, [33] since God is not a God of disorder but of peace.

As in all the churches of the saints, [34] the women[L] should be silent in the churches, for they are not permitted to speak, but are to submit themselves, as the law also says. [35] If they want to learn something, let them ask their own husbands at home, since it is disgraceful

[A] **13:12** Lit *we see indirectly*   [B] **14:2** language, also in vv. 4,13,14,19,26,27   [C] **14:2** Or *in spirit,* or *in his spirit*   [D] **14:3** Lit *building up*   [E] **14:5** languages, also in vv. 6,18,21,22,23,39   [F] **14:11** Gk *barbaros,* or *barbarian*   [G] **14:12** Lit *zealous of spirits*   [H] **14:16** Or *praise by the Spirit*   [I] **14:16** Lit *the one filling the place of the uninformed*   [J] **14:21** Is 28:11-12   [K] **14:26** Other mss add *of you*   [L] **14:34** Other mss read *your women*

for a woman to speak in the church. **36** Or did the word of God originate from you, or did it come to you only?

37 If anyone thinks he is a prophet or spiritual, he should recognize that what I write to you is the Lord's command. **38** If anyone ignores this, he will be ignored.^ **39** So then, my brothers and sisters, be eager to prophesy, and do not forbid speaking in other tongues. **40** But everything is to be done decently and in order.

RESURRECTION ESSENTIAL TO THE GOSPEL

15 Now I want to make clear for you, brothers and sisters, the gospel I preached to you, which you received, on which you have taken your stand **2** and by which you are being saved, if you hold to the message I preached to you — unless you believed in vain.^B **3** For I passed on to you as most important what I also received: that Christ died for our sins according to the Scriptures, **4** that he was buried, that he was raised on the third day according to the Scriptures, **5** and that he appeared to Cephas, then to the Twelve. **6** Then he appeared to over five hundred brothers and sisters at one time; most of them are still alive, but some have fallen asleep. **7** Then he appeared to James, then to all the apostles. **8** Last of all, as to one born at the wrong time,^c he also appeared to me.

9 For I am the least of the apostles, not worthy to be called an apostle, because I persecuted the church of God. **10** But by the grace of God I am what I am, and his grace toward me was not in vain. On the contrary, I worked harder than any of them, yet not I, but the grace of God that was with me. **11** Whether, then, it is I or they, so we proclaim and so you have believed.

RESURRECTION ESSENTIAL TO THE FAITH

12 Now if Christ is proclaimed as raised from the dead, how can some of you say, "There is no resurrection of the dead"? **13** If there is no resurrection of the dead, then not even Christ has been raised; **14** and if Christ has not been raised, then our proclamation is in vain, and so is your faith.^D **15** Moreover, we are found to be false witnesses about God, because we have testified wrongly about God that he raised up Christ — whom he did not raise up, if in fact the dead are not raised. **16** For if the dead are not raised, not even Christ has been raised. **17** And if Christ has not been raised, your faith is worthless; you are still in your sins. **18** Those, then, who have fallen asleep in Christ have also

perished. **19** If we have put our hope in Christ for this life only, we should be pitied more than anyone.

CHRIST'S RESURRECTION GUARANTEES OURS

20 But as it is, Christ has been raised from the dead, the firstfruits of those who have fallen asleep. **21** For since death came through a man, the resurrection of the dead also comes through a man. **22** For just as in Adam all die, so also in Christ all will be made alive.

23 But each in his own order: Christ, the firstfruits; afterward, at his coming, those who belong to Christ. **24** Then comes the end, when he hands over the kingdom to God the Father, when he abolishes all rule and all authority and power. **25** For he must reign until he puts all his enemies under his feet. **26** The last enemy to be abolished is death. **27** For **God has put everything under his feet.**^E Now when it says "everything" is put under him, it is obvious that he who puts everything under him is the exception. **28** When everything is subject to Christ, then the Son himself will also be subject to the one who subjected everything to him, so that God may be all in all.

RESURRECTION SUPPORTED BY CHRISTIAN EXPERIENCE

29 Otherwise what will they do who are being baptized for the dead?^F If the dead are not raised at all, then why are people baptized for them?^G **30** Why are we in danger every hour? **31** I face death every day, as surely as I may boast about you, brothers and sisters, in Christ Jesus our Lord. **32** If I fought wild beasts in Ephesus as a mere man, what good did that do me? If the dead are not raised, **Let us eat and drink, for tomorrow we die.**^H **33** Do not be deceived: "Bad company corrupts good morals." **34** Come to your senses^I and stop sinning; for some people are ignorant about God. I say this to your shame.

THE NATURE OF THE RESURRECTION BODY

35 But someone will ask, "How are the dead raised? What kind of body will they have when they come? " **36** You fool! What you sow does not come to life unless it dies. **37** And as for what you sow — you are not sowing the body that will be, but only a seed, perhaps of wheat or another grain. **38** But God gives it a body as he wants, and to each of the seeds its own body. **39** Not all flesh is the same flesh; there is one flesh for humans, another for animals, another for

^**14:38** Other mss read *he should be ignored*   ^B**15:2** Or *believed without careful thought*, or *believed in vain*   ^c**15:8** Or *one whose birth was unusual*   ^D**15:14** Or *proclamation is useless, and your faith also is useless*, or *proclamation is empty, and your faith also is empty*   ^E**15:27** Ps 8:6   ^F**15:29** Or *baptized on account of the dead*   ^G**15:29** Other mss read *for the dead*   ^H**15:32** Is 22:13   ^I**15:34** Lit *Sober up*

birds, and another for fish. [40] There are heavenly bodies and earthly bodies, but the splendor of the heavenly bodies is different from that of the earthly ones. [41] There is a splendor of the sun, another of the moon, and another of the stars; in fact, one star differs from another star in splendor. [42] So it is with the resurrection of the dead: Sown in corruption, raised in incorruption; [43] sown in dishonor, raised in glory; sown in weakness, raised in power; [44] sown a natural body, raised a spiritual body. If there is a natural body, there is also a spiritual body. [45] So it is written, **The first man Adam became a living being;**[A] the last Adam became a life-giving spirit. [46] However, the spiritual is not first, but the natural, then the spiritual.

[47] The first man was from the earth, a man of dust; the second man is[B] from heaven. [48] Like the man of dust, so are those who are of the dust; like the man of heaven, so are those who are of heaven. [49] And just as we have borne the image of the man of dust, we will also bear the image of the man of heaven.

VICTORIOUS RESURRECTION

[50] What I am saying, brothers and sisters, is this: Flesh and blood cannot inherit the kingdom of God, nor can corruption inherit incorruption. [51] Listen, I am telling you a mystery: We will not all fall asleep, but we will all be changed, [52] in a moment, in the twinkling of an eye, at the last trumpet. For the trumpet will sound, and the dead will be raised incorruptible, and we will be changed. [53] For this corruptible body must be clothed with incorruptibility, and this mortal body must be clothed with immortality. [54] When this corruptible body is clothed with incorruptibility, and this mortal body is clothed with immortality, then the saying that is written will take place:

> **Death has been swallowed up in victory.**[C]

[55] **Where, death, is your victory?**
> **Where, death, is your sting?**[D]

[56] The sting of death is sin, and the power of sin is the law. [57] But thanks be to God, who gives us the victory through our Lord Jesus Christ! [58] Therefore, my dear brothers and sisters, be steadfast, immovable, always excelling in the Lord's work, because you know that your labor in the Lord is not in vain.

COLLECTION FOR THE JERUSALEM CHURCH

16 Now about the collection for the saints: Do the same as I instructed the Galatian churches. [2] On the first day of the week, each of you is to set something aside and save in keeping with how he is prospering, so that no collections will need to be made when I come. [3] When I arrive, I will send with letters those you recommend to carry your gift to Jerusalem. [4] If it is suitable for me to go as well, they will travel with me.

PAUL'S TRAVEL PLANS

[5] I will come to you after I pass through Macedonia — for I will be traveling through Macedonia — [6] and perhaps I will remain with you or even spend the winter, so that you may send me on my way wherever I go. [7] I don't want to see you now just in passing, since I hope to spend some time with you, if the Lord allows. [8] But I will stay in Ephesus until Pentecost, [9] because a wide door for effective ministry has opened for me[E] — yet many oppose me. [10] If Timothy comes, see that he has nothing to fear while with you, because he is doing the Lord's work, just as I am. [11] So let no one look down on him. Send him on his way in peace so that he can come to me, because I am expecting him with the brothers.

[12] Now about our brother Apollos: I strongly urged him to come to you with the brothers, but he was not at all willing to come now. However, he will come when he has an opportunity.

FINAL EXHORTATION

[13] Be alert, stand firm in the faith, be courageous,[F] be strong. [14] Do everything in love.

[15] Brothers and sisters, you know the household of Stephanas: They are the firstfruits of Achaia and have devoted themselves to serving the saints. I urge you [16] also to submit to such people, and to everyone who works and labors with them. [17] I am delighted to have Stephanas, Fortunatus, and Achaicus present, because these men have made up for your absence. [18] For they have refreshed my spirit and yours. Therefore recognize such people.

CONCLUSION

[19] The churches of Asia send you greetings. Aquila and Priscilla send you greetings warmly in the Lord, along with the church that meets in their home. [20] All the brothers and sisters send you greetings. Greet one another with a holy kiss.

[21] This greeting is in my own hand — Paul. [22] If anyone does not love the Lord, a curse be on him. Our Lord, come![G] [23] The grace of the Lord Jesus be with you. [24] My love be with all of you in Christ Jesus.

[A] **15:45** Gn 2:7 [B] **15:47** Other mss add *the Lord* [C] **15:54** Is 25:8 [D] **15:55** Hs 13:14 [E] **16:9** Lit *door has opened to me, great and effective* [F] **16:13** Lit *act like men* [G] **16:22** Aramaic *Marana tha*

2 CORINTHIANS

GREETING

1 Paul, an apostle of Christ Jesus by God's will, and Timothy our^A brother:

To the church of God at Corinth, with all the saints who are throughout Achaia.

² Grace to you and peace from God our Father and the Lord Jesus Christ.

THE GOD OF COMFORT

³ Blessed be the God and Father of our Lord Jesus Christ, the Father of mercies and the God of all comfort. ⁴ He comforts us in all our affliction,^B so that we may be able to comfort those who are in any kind of affliction, through the comfort we ourselves receive from God. ⁵ For just as the sufferings of Christ overflow to us, so also through Christ our comfort overflows. ⁶ If we are afflicted, it is for your comfort and salvation. If we are comforted, it is for your comfort, which produces in you patient endurance of the same sufferings that we suffer. ⁷ And our hope for you is firm, because we know that as you share in the sufferings, so you will also share in the comfort.

⁸ We don't want you to be unaware, brothers and sisters, of our affliction that took place in Asia. We were completely overwhelmed — beyond our strength — so that we even despaired of life itself. ⁹ Indeed, we felt that we had received the sentence of death, so that we would not trust in ourselves but in God who raises the dead. ¹⁰ He has delivered us from such a terrible death, and he will deliver us. We have put our hope in him that he will deliver us again ¹¹ while you join in helping us by your prayers. Then many will give thanks on our^C behalf for the gift that came to us through the prayers of many.

A CLEAR CONSCIENCE

¹² Indeed, this is our boast: The testimony of our conscience is that we have conducted ourselves in the world, and especially toward you, with godly sincerity and purity, not by human wisdom but by God's grace. ¹³ For we are writing nothing to you other than what you can read and also understand. I hope you will understand completely — ¹⁴ just as you have partially understood us — that we are your reason for pride, just as you also are ours in the day of our^D Lord Jesus.

A VISIT POSTPONED

¹⁵ Because of this confidence, I planned to come to you first, so that you could have a second benefit,^E ¹⁶ and to visit you on my way to Macedonia, and then come to you again from Macedonia and be helped by you on my journey to Judea. ¹⁷ Now when I planned this, was I of two minds? Or what I plan, do I plan in a purely human^F way so that I say "Yes, yes" and "No, no" at the same time? ¹⁸ As God is faithful, our message to you is not "Yes and no." ¹⁹ For the Son of God, Jesus Christ, whom we proclaimed among you — Silvanus,^G Timothy, and I — did not become "Yes and no." On the contrary, in him it is always "Yes." ²⁰ For every one of God's promises is "Yes" in him. Therefore, through him we also say "Amen" to the glory of God. ²¹ Now it is God who strengthens us together with you in Christ, and who has anointed us. ²² He has also put his seal on us and given us the Spirit in our hearts as a down payment.

²³ I call on God as a witness, on my life, that it was to spare you that I did not come to Corinth. ²⁴ I do not mean that we lord it over your faith, but we are workers with you for your joy, **2** because you stand firm in your faith. ¹ In fact, I made up my mind about this: I would not come to you on another painful visit."² For if I cause you pain, then who will cheer me other than the one being hurt by me?'³ I wrote this very thing so that when I came I wouldn't have pain from those who ought to give me joy, because I am confident about all of you that my joy will also be yours. ⁴ For I wrote to you with many tears out of an extremely troubled and anguished heart — not to cause you pain, but that you should know the abundant love I have for you.

A SINNER FORGIVEN

⁵ If anyone has caused pain, he has caused pain not so much to me but to some degree — not to exaggerate — to all of you. ⁶ This punishment by the majority is sufficient for that person. ⁷ As a result, you should instead forgive and comfort him. Otherwise, he may be overwhelmed by excessive grief. ⁸ Therefore I urge you to reaffirm your love to him. ⁹ I wrote for this purpose: to test your character to see if you are obedient in everything. ¹⁰ Anyone you forgive, I do too. For what I have forgiven — if I have forgiven anything — it is for your benefit in

^A 1:1 Lit *the* ^B 1:4 Or *trouble,* or *tribulation,* or *trials,* or *oppression* ^C 1:11 Other mss read *your* ^D 1:14 Other mss omit *our*
^E 1:15 Other mss read *a second joy* ^F 1:17 Or *a worldly,* or *a fleshly,* or *a selfish* ^G 1:19 Or *Silas*; Ac 15:22-32; 16:19-40; 17:1-16
^H 2:1 Lit *not again in sorrow to come to you* ^I 2:2 Lit *the one pained*

the presence of Christ, [11] so that we may not be taken advantage of by Satan. For we are not ignorant of his schemes.

A TRIP TO MACEDONIA

[12] When I came to Troas to preach the gospel of Christ, even though the Lord opened a door for me, [13] I had no rest in my spirit because I did not find my brother Titus. Instead, I said good-bye to them and left for Macedonia.

A MINISTRY OF LIFE OR DEATH

[14] But thanks be to God, who always leads us in Christ's triumphal procession and through us spreads the aroma of the knowledge of him in every place. [15] For to God we are the fragrance of Christ among those who are being saved and among those who are perishing. [16] To some we are an aroma of death leading to death, but to others, an aroma of life leading to life. Who is adequate for these things? [17] For we do not market the word of God for profit like so many.[A] On the contrary, we speak with sincerity in Christ, as from God and before God.

LIVING LETTERS

3 Are we beginning to commend ourselves again? Or do we need, like some, letters of recommendation to you or from you? [2] You yourselves are our letter, written on our hearts, known and read by everyone. [3] You show that you are Christ's letter, delivered[B] by us, not written with ink but with the Spirit of the living God — not on tablets of stone but on tablets of human hearts.[C]

PAUL'S COMPETENCE

[4] Such is the confidence we have through Christ before God. [5] It is not that we are competent in[D] ourselves to claim anything as coming from ourselves, but our adequacy is from God. [6] He has made us competent to be ministers of a new covenant, not of the letter, but of the Spirit. For the letter kills, but the Spirit gives life.

NEW COVENANT MINISTRY

[7] Now if the ministry that brought death, chiseled in letters on stones, came with glory, so that the Israelites were not able to gaze steadily at Moses's face because of its glory, which was set aside, [8] how will the ministry of the Spirit not be more glorious? [9] For if the ministry that brought condemnation had glory, the ministry that brings righteousness overflows with even more glory. [10] In fact, what had been glorious is not glorious now by comparison because of the glory that surpasses it. [11] For if what was set aside was glorious, what endures will be even more glorious.

[12] Since, then, we have such a hope, we act with great boldness. [13] We are not like Moses, who used to put a veil over his face to prevent the Israelites from gazing steadily until the end[E] of the glory of what was being set aside, [14] but their minds were hardened. For to this day, at the reading of the old covenant, the same veil remains; it is not lifted, because it is set aside only in Christ. [15] Yet still today, whenever Moses is read, a veil lies over their hearts, [16] but whenever a person turns to the Lord, the veil is removed. [17] Now the Lord is the Spirit, and where the Spirit of the Lord is, there is freedom. [18] We all, with unveiled faces, are looking as in a mirror at[F] the glory of the Lord and are being transformed into the same image from glory to glory; this is from the Lord who is the Spirit.[G]

THE LIGHT OF THE GOSPEL

4 Therefore, since we have this ministry because we were shown mercy, we do not give up. [2] Instead, we have renounced secret and shameful things, not acting deceitfully or distorting the word of God, but commending ourselves before God to everyone's conscience by an open display of the truth. [3] But if our gospel is veiled, it is veiled to those who are perishing. [4] In their case, the god of this age has blinded the minds of the unbelievers to keep them from seeing the light of the gospel of the glory of Christ,[H] who is the image of God. [5] For we are not proclaiming ourselves but Jesus Christ as Lord, and ourselves as your servants for Jesus's sake. [6] For God who said, "Let light shine out of darkness," has shone in our hearts to give the light of the knowledge of God's glory in the face of Jesus Christ.

TREASURE IN CLAY JARS

[7] Now we have this treasure in clay jars, so that this extraordinary power may be from God and not from us. [8] We are afflicted in every way but not crushed; we are perplexed but not in despair; [9] we are persecuted but not abandoned; we are struck down but not destroyed. [10] We always carry the death of Jesus in our body, so that the life of Jesus may also be displayed in our body. [11] For we who live are always being given over to death for Jesus's sake, so that Jesus's life may also be displayed in our mortal flesh. [12] So then, death is at work in us, but life in you. [13] And

---

since we have the same spirit of faith in keeping with what is written, **I believed, therefore I spoke,**[A] we also believe, and therefore speak. [14] For we know that the one who raised the Lord Jesus will also raise us with Jesus and present us with you. [15] Indeed, everything is for your benefit so that, as grace extends through more and more people, it may cause thanksgiving to increase to the glory of God.

[16] Therefore we do not give up. Even though our outer person is being destroyed, our inner person is being renewed day by day. [17] For our momentary light affliction is producing for us an absolutely incomparable eternal weight of glory. [18] So we do not focus on what is seen, but on what is unseen. For what is seen is temporary, but what is unseen is eternal.

OUR FUTURE AFTER DEATH

5 For we know that if our earthly tent we live in is destroyed, we have a building from God, an eternal dwelling in the heavens, not made with hands. [2] Indeed, we groan in this tent, desiring to put on our heavenly dwelling, [3] since, when we have taken it off,[B] we will not be found naked. [4] Indeed, we groan while we are in this tent, burdened as we are, because we do not want to be unclothed but clothed, so that mortality may be swallowed up by life. [5] Now the one who prepared us for this very purpose is God, who gave us the Spirit as a down payment.

[6] So we are always confident and know that while we are at home in the body we are away from the Lord. [7] For we walk by faith, not by sight. [8] In fact, we are confident, and we would prefer to be away from the body and at home with the Lord. [9] Therefore, whether we are at home or away, we make it our aim to be pleasing to him. [10] For we must all appear before the judgment seat of Christ, so that each may be repaid for what he has done in the body, whether good or evil.

[11] Therefore, since we know the fear of the Lord, we try to persuade people. What we are is plain to God, and I hope it is also plain to your consciences. [12] We are not commending ourselves to you again, but giving you an opportunity to be proud of us, so that you may have a reply for those who take pride in outward appearance rather than in the heart. [13] For if we are out of our mind, it is for God; if we are in our right mind, it is for you. [14] For the love of Christ compels us, since we have reached this conclusion: If one died for all, then all died. [15] And he

died for all so that those who live should no longer live for themselves, but for the one who died for them and was raised.

THE MINISTRY OF RECONCILIATION

[16] From now on, then, we do not know anyone from a worldly perspective.[C] Even if we have known Christ from a worldly perspective,[D] yet now we no longer know him in this way. [17] Therefore, if anyone is in Christ, he is a new creation; the old has passed away, and see, the new has[E] come! [18] Everything is from God, who has reconciled us to himself through Christ and has given us the ministry of reconciliation. [19] That is, in Christ, God was reconciling the world to himself, not counting their trespasses against them, and he has committed the message of reconciliation to us.

[20] Therefore, we are ambassadors for Christ, since God is making his appeal through us. We plead on Christ's behalf: "Be reconciled to God." [21] He made the one who did not know sin to be sin[F] for us, so that in him we might become the righteousness of God.

6 Working together with him, we also appeal to you, "Don't receive the grace of God in vain." [2] For he says:

> **At an acceptable time I listened to you, and in the day of salvation I helped you.**[G]

See, now is the acceptable time; now is the day of salvation!

THE CHARACTER OF PAUL'S MINISTRY

[3] We are not giving anyone an occasion for offense, so that the ministry will not be blamed. [4] Instead, as God's ministers, we commend ourselves in everything: by great endurance, by afflictions, by hardships, by difficulties, [5] by beatings, by imprisonments, by riots, by labors, by sleepless nights, by times of hunger, [6] by purity, by knowledge, by patience, by kindness, by the Holy Spirit, by sincere love, [7] by the word of truth,[H] by the power of God; through weapons of righteousness for the right hand and the left, [8] through glory and dishonor, through slander and good report; regarded as deceivers, yet true; [9] as unknown, yet recognized; as dying, yet see — we live; as being disciplined, yet not killed; [10] as grieving, yet always rejoicing; as poor, yet enriching many; as having nothing, yet possessing everything. [11] We have spoken openly to you, Corinthians; our heart has been opened wide. [12] We are not withholding our affection from you, but you are withholding

[A] 4:13 Ps 116:10 LXX   [B] 5:3 Other mss read *when we have put on*   [C] 5:16 Lit *anyone according to the flesh*   [D] 5:16 Lit *Christ according to the flesh*   [E] 5:17 Other mss read *look, all new things have*   [F] 5:21 Or *be a sin offering*   [G] 6:2 Is 49:8   [H] 6:7 Or *by truthful speech*

yours from us. ¹³ I speak as to my children; as a proper response, open your heart to us.

SEPARATION TO GOD

¹⁴ Don't become partners with those who do not believe. For what partnership is there between righteousness and lawlessness? Or what fellowship does light have with darkness? ¹⁵ What agreement does Christ have with Belial?ᴬ Or what does a believer have in common with an unbeliever? ¹⁶ And what agreement does the temple of God have with idols? For weᴮ are the temple of the living God, as God said:

I will dwell
and walk among them,
and I will be their God,
and they will be my people.ᶜ

¹⁷ Therefore, come out from among them
and be separate, says the Lord;
do not touch any unclean thing,
and I will welcome you.ᴰ

¹⁸ And I will be a Father to you,
and you will be sons and daughters to me,
says the Lord Almighty.ᴱ

7 So then, dear friends, since we have these promises, let us cleanse ourselves from every impurity of the flesh and spirit, bringing holiness to completionᶠ in the fear of God.

JOY AND REPENTANCE

² Make room for us in your hearts. We have wronged no one, corrupted no one, taken advantage of no one. ³ I don't say this to condemn you, since I have already said that you are in our hearts, to die together and to live together. ⁴ I am very frank with you; I have great pride in you. I am filled with encouragement; I am overflowing with joy in all our afflictions.

⁵ In fact, when we came into Macedonia, weᴳ had no rest. Instead, we were troubled in every way: conflicts on the outside, fears within. ⁶ But God, who comforts the downcast, comforted us by the arrival of Titus, ⁷ and not only by his arrival but also by the comfort he received from you. He told us about your deep longing, your sorrow, and your zeal for me, so that I rejoiced even more. ⁸ For even if I grieved you with my letter, I don't regret it. And if I regretted it — since I saw that the letter grieved you, yet only for a while — ⁹ I now rejoice, not because you were grieved, but because your grief led to repentance. For you were grieved as God willed, so that you didn't experience any loss from us. ¹⁰ For godly grief produces a repentance that leads to salvation without regret, but worldly grief produces death. ¹¹ For consider how much diligence this very thing — this grieving as God wills — has produced in you: what a desire to clear yourselves, what indignation, what fear, what deep longing, what zeal, what justice! In every way you showed yourselves to be pure in this matter. ¹² So even though I wrote to you, it was not because of the one who did wrong, or because of the one who was wronged, but in order that your devotion to us might be made plain to you in the sight of God. ¹³ For this reason we have been comforted.

In addition to our own comfort, we rejoiced even more over the joy Titus had, because his spirit was refreshed by all of you. ¹⁴ For if I have made any boast to him about you, I have not been disappointed; but as I have spoken everything to you in truth, so our boasting to Titus has also turned out to be the truth. ¹⁵ And his affection toward you is even greater as he remembers the obedience of all of you, and how you received him with fear and trembling. ¹⁶ I rejoice that I have complete confidence in you.

APPEAL TO COMPLETE THE COLLECTION

8 We want you to know, brothers and sisters, about the grace of God that was given to the churches of Macedonia: ² During a severe trial brought about by affliction, their abundant joy and their extreme poverty overflowed in a wealth of generosity on their part. ³ I can testify that, according to their ability and even beyond their ability, of their own accord, ⁴ they begged us earnestly for the privilege of sharing in the ministry to the saints, ⁵ and not just as we had hoped. Instead, they gave themselves first to the Lord and then to us by God's will. ⁶ So we urged Titus that just as he had begun, so he should also complete among you this act of grace.

⁷ Now as you excel in everything — in faith, speech, knowledge, and in all diligence, and in your love for usᴴ — excel also in this act of grace. ⁸ I am not saying this as a command. Rather, by means of the diligence of others, I am testing the genuineness of your love. ⁹ For you know the grace of our Lord Jesus Christ: Though he was rich, for your sake he became poor, so that by his poverty you might become rich. ¹⁰ And in this matter I am giving advice because it is profitable for you, who began last year not only to do something but also to want to do it. ¹¹ Now also finish the task, so that just as there was an eager desire, there may also be a completion, according to what you have. ¹² For if the eagerness is there, the gift is acceptable according to what

ᴬ **6:15** Or *Beliar*   ᴮ **6:16** Other mss read *you*   ᶜ **6:16** Lv 26:12; Jr 31:33; 32:38; Ezk 37:26   ᴰ **6:17** Is 52:11   ᴱ **6:18** 2Sm 7:14; Is 43:6; 49:22; 60:4; Hs 1:10   ᶠ **7:1** Or *spirit, perfecting holiness*   ᴳ **7:5** Lit *our flesh*   ᴴ **8:7** Other mss read *in our love for you*

a person has, not according to what he does not have. [13] It is not that there should be relief for others and hardship for you, but it is a question of equality. [A] [14] At the present time your surplus is available for their need, so that their abundance may in turn meet your need, in order that there may be equality. [15] As it is written: **The person who had much did not have too much, and the person who had little did not have too little.** [B]

ADMINISTRATION OF THE COLLECTION

[16] Thanks be to God, who put the same concern for you into the heart of Titus. [17] For he welcomed our appeal and, being very diligent, went out to you by his own choice. [18] We have sent with him the brother who is praised among all the churches for his gospel ministry. [C] [19] And not only that, but he was also appointed by the churches to accompany us with this gracious gift that we are administering for the glory of the Lord himself and to show our eagerness to help. [20] We are taking this precaution so that no one will criticize us about this large sum that we are administering. [21] Indeed, we are giving careful thought to do what is right, not only before the Lord but also before people. [22] We have also sent with them our brother. We have often tested him in many circumstances and found him to be diligent — and now even more diligent because of his great confidence in you. [23] As for Titus, he is my partner and coworker for you; as for our brothers, they are the messengers of the churches, the glory of Christ. [24] Therefore, show them proof before the churches of your love and of our boasting about you.

MOTIVATIONS FOR GIVING

9 Now concerning the ministry to the saints, it is unnecessary for me to write to you. [2] For I know your eagerness, and I boast about you to the Macedonians: "Achaia has been ready since last year," and your zeal has stirred up most of them. [3] But I am sending the brothers so that our boasting about you in this matter would not prove empty, and so that you would be ready just as I said. [4] Otherwise, if any Macedonians come with me and find you unprepared, we, not to mention you, would be put to shame in that situation. [D] [5] Therefore I considered it necessary to urge the brothers to go on ahead to you and arrange in advance the generous gift you promised, so that it will be ready as a gift and not as an extortion.

[6] The point is this: [E] The person who sows sparingly will also reap sparingly, and the person who sows generously will also reap generously. [7] Each person should do as he has decided in his heart — not reluctantly or out of compulsion, since God loves a cheerful giver. [8] And God is able to make every grace overflow to you, so that in every way, always having everything you need, you may excel in every good work. [9] As it is written:

He distributed freely;
he gave to the poor;
his righteousness endures forever. [F]

[10] Now the one who provides seed for the sower and bread for food will also provide and multiply your seed and increase the harvest of your righteousness. [11] You will be enriched in every way for all generosity, which produces thanksgiving to God through us. [12] For the ministry of this service is not only supplying the needs of the saints but is also overflowing in many expressions of thanks to God. [13] Because of the proof provided by this ministry, they will glorify God for your obedient confession of the gospel of Christ, and for your generosity in sharing with them and with everyone. [14] And as they pray on your behalf, they will have deep affection for you because of the surpassing grace of God in you. [15] Thanks be to God for his indescribable gift!

PAUL'S APOSTOLIC AUTHORITY

10 Now I Paul, myself, appeal to you by the meekness and gentleness of Christ — I who am humble among you in person but bold toward you when absent. [2] I beg you that when I am present I will not need to be bold with the confidence by which I plan to challenge certain people who think we are behaving according to the flesh. [3] For although we live in the flesh, we do not wage war according to the flesh, [4] since the weapons of our warfare are not of the flesh, but are powerful through God for the demolition of strongholds. We demolish arguments [5] and every proud thing that is raised up against the knowledge of God, and we take every thought captive to obey Christ. [6] And we are ready to punish any disobedience, once your obedience is complete.

[7] Look at what is obvious. [G] If anyone is confident that he belongs to Christ, let him remind himself of this: Just as he belongs to Christ, so do we. [8] For if I boast a little too much about our authority, which the Lord gave for building you up and not for tearing you down, I will not be put to shame. [9] I don't want to seem as though I am trying to terrify you with my letters. [10] For it is said, "His letters are weighty and powerful, but his physical presence is weak and his public speaking amounts to nothing." [11] Let such a

^8:13 Lit *but from equality* ^B8:15 Ex 16:18 ^C8:18 Lit *churches, in the gospel* ^D9:4 Or *in this confidence* ^E9:6 Lit *And this* ^F9:9 Ps 112:9 ^G10:7 Or *You are looking at things outwardly*

person consider this: What we are in our letters, when we are absent, we will also be in our actions when we are present.

¹² For we don't dare classify or compare ourselves with some who commend themselves. But in measuring themselves by themselves and comparing themselves to themselves, they lack understanding. ¹³ We, however, will not boast beyond measure but according to the measure of the area of ministry that God has assigned to us, which reaches even to you. ¹⁴ For we are not overextending ourselves, as if we had not reached you, since we have come to you with the gospel of Christ. ¹⁵ We are not boasting beyond measure about other people's labors. On the contrary, we have the hope that as your faith increases, our area of ministry will be greatly enlarged, ¹⁶ so that we may preach the gospel to the regions beyond you without boasting about what has already been done in someone else's area of ministry. ¹⁷ So **let the one who boasts, boast in the Lord.**ᴬ ¹⁸ For it is not the one commending himself who is approved, but the one the Lord commends.

PAUL AND THE FALSE APOSTLES

11 I wish you would put up with a little foolishness from me. Yes, do put up with me!ᴮ ² For I am jealous for you with a godly jealousy, because I have promised you in marriage to one husband — to present a pure virgin to Christ. ³ But I fear that, as the serpent deceived Eve by his cunning, your minds may be seduced from a sincere and pureᶜ devotion to Christ. ⁴ For if a person comes and preaches another Jesus, whom we did not preach, or you receive a different spirit, which you had not received, or a different gospel, which you had not accepted, you put up with it splendidly!

⁵ Now I consider myself in no way inferior to those "super-apostles."ᴰ ⁶ Even if I am untrained in public speaking, I am certainly not untrained in knowledge. Indeed, we have in every way made that clear to you in everything. ⁷ Or did I commit a sin by humbling myself so that you might be exalted, because I preached the gospel of God to you free of charge? ⁸ I robbed other churches by taking pay from them to minister to you. ⁹ When I was present with you and in need, I did not burden anyone, since the brothers who came from Macedonia supplied my needs. I have kept myself, and will keep myself, from burdening you in any way. ¹⁰ As the truth of Christ is in me, this boasting of mine will not be stoppedᴰ in the regions of Achaia. ¹¹ Why? Because I don't love you? God knows I do!

¹² But I will continue to do what I am doing, in order to denyᴱ an opportunity to those who want to be regarded as our equals in what they boast about. ¹³ For such people are false apostles, deceitful workers, disguising themselves as apostles of Christ. ¹⁴ And no wonder! For Satan disguises himself as an angel of light. ¹⁵ So it is no great surprise if his servants also disguise themselves as servants of righteousness. Their end will be according to their works.

PAUL'S SUFFERINGS FOR CHRIST

¹⁶ I repeat: Let no one consider me a fool. But if you do, at least accept me as a fool so that I can also boast a little. ¹⁷ What I am saying in this matterᶠ of boasting, I don't speak as the Lord would, but as it were, foolishly. ¹⁸ Since many boast according to the flesh, I will also boast. ¹⁹ For you, being so wise, gladly put up with fools! ²⁰ In fact, you put up with it if someone enslaves you, if someone exploits you, if someone takes advantage of you, if someone is arrogant toward you, if someone slaps you in the face. ²¹ I say this to our shame: We have been too weak for that!

But in whatever anyone dares to boast — I am talking foolishly — I also dare: ²² Are they Hebrews? So am I. Are they Israelites? So am I. Are they the descendants of Abraham? So am I. ²³ Are they servants of Christ? I'm talking like a madman — I'm a better one: with far more labors, many more imprisonments, far worse beatings, many times near death.

²⁴ Five times I received the forty lashes minus one from the Jews. ²⁵ Three times I was beaten with rods. Once I received a stoning. Three times I was shipwrecked. I have spent a night and a day in the open sea. ²⁶ On frequent journeys, I faced dangers from rivers, dangers from robbers, dangers from my own people, dangers from Gentiles, dangers in the city, dangers in the wilderness, dangers at sea, and dangers among false brothers; ²⁷ toil and hardship, many sleepless nights, hunger and thirst, often without food, cold, and without clothing. ²⁸ Not to mentionᴳ other things, there is the daily pressure on me: my concern for all the churches. ²⁹ Who is weak, and I am not weak? Who is made to stumble, and I do not burn with indignation?

³⁰ If boasting is necessary, I will boast about my weaknesses. ³¹ The God and Father of the Lord Jesus, who is blessed forever, knows I am not lying. ³² In Damascus, a rulerᴴ under King Aretas guarded the city of Damascus in order to arrest me. ³³ So I was let down in a basket through a window in the wall and escaped from his hands.

ᴬ10:17 Jr 9:24   ᴮ11:1 Or *Yes, you are putting up with me*   ᶜ11:3 Other mss omit *and pure*   ᴰ11:10 Or *silenced*   ᴱ11:12 Lit *cut off*   ᶠ11:17 Or *business,* or *confidence*   ᴳ11:28 Lit *Apart from*   ᴴ11:32 Gk *ethnarches* ; a leader of an ethnic community

SUFFICIENT GRACE

12 Boasting is necessary. It is not profitable, but I will move on to visions and revelations of the Lord. [2] I know a man in Christ who was caught up to the third heaven fourteen years ago. Whether he was in the body or out of the body, I don't know; God knows. [3] I know that this man — whether in the body or out of the body I don't know; God knows — [4] was caught up into paradise and heard inexpressible words, which a human being is not allowed to speak. [5] I will boast about this person, but not about myself, except of my weaknesses.

[6] For if I want to boast, I wouldn't be a fool, because I would be telling the truth. But I will spare you, so that no one can credit me with something beyond what he sees in me or hears from me, [7] especially because of the extraordinary revelations. Therefore, so that I would not exalt myself, a thorn in the flesh was given to me, a messenger of Satan to torment me so that I would not exalt myself. [8] Concerning this, I pleaded with the Lord three times that it would leave me. [9] But he said to me, "My grace is sufficient for you, for my power is perfected in weakness."

Therefore, I will most gladly boast all the more about my weaknesses, so that Christ's power may reside in me. [10] So I take pleasure in weaknesses, insults, hardships, persecutions, and in difficulties, for the sake of Christ. For when I am weak, then I am strong.

SIGNS OF AN APOSTLE

[11] I have been a fool; you forced it on me. You ought to have commended me, since I am not in any way inferior to those "super-apostles," even though I am nothing. [12] The signs of an apostle were performed with unfailing endurance among you, including signs and wonders and miracles. [13] So in what way are you worse off than the other churches, except that I personally did not burden you? Forgive me for this wrong!

PAUL'S CONCERN FOR THE CORINTHIANS

[14] Look, I am ready to come to you this third time. I will not burden you, since I am not seeking what is yours, but you. For children ought not save up for their parents, but parents for their children. [15] I will most gladly spend and be spent for you.[A] If I love you more, am I to be loved less? [16] Now granted, I did not burden you; yet sly as I am, I took you in by deceit! [17] Did I take advantage of you by any of those I sent you? [18] I urged Titus to go, and I sent the brother with him. Titus didn't take advantage of you,

did he? Didn't we walk in the same spirit and in the same footsteps?

[19] Have you been thinking all along that we were defending ourselves to you? No, in the sight of God we are speaking in Christ, and everything, dear friends, is for building you up. [20] For I fear that perhaps when I come I will not find you to be what I want, and you may not find me to be what you want. Perhaps there will be quarreling, jealousy, angry outbursts, selfish ambitions, slander, gossip, arrogance, and disorder. [21] I fear that when I come my God will again[B] humiliate me in your presence, and I will grieve for many who sinned before and have not repented of the moral impurity, sexual immorality, and sensuality they practiced.

FINAL WARNINGS AND EXHORTATIONS

13 This is the third time I am coming to you. **Every matter must be established by the testimony of two or three witnesses.**[C] [2] I gave a warning when I was present the second time, and now I give a warning while I am absent to those who sinned before and to all the rest: If I come again, I will not be lenient, [3] since you seek proof of Christ speaking in me. He is not weak in dealing with you, but powerful among you. [4] For he was crucified in weakness, but he lives by the power of God. For we also are weak in him, but in dealing with you we will live with him by God's power.

[5] Test yourselves to see if you are in the faith. Examine yourselves. Or do you yourselves not recognize that Jesus Christ is in you? — unless you fail the test.[D] [6] And I hope you will recognize that we ourselves do not fail the test. [7] But we pray to God that you do nothing wrong — not that we may appear to pass the test, but that you may do what is right, even though we may appear to fail. [8] For we can't do anything against the truth, but only for the truth. [9] We rejoice when we are weak and you are strong. We also pray that you become fully mature.[E] [10] This is why I am writing these things while absent, so that when I am there I may not have to deal harshly with you, in keeping with the authority the Lord gave me for building up and not for tearing down.

[11] Finally, brothers and sisters, rejoice.[F] Become mature, be encouraged,[G] be of the same mind, be at peace, and the God of love and peace will be with you. [12] Greet one another with a holy kiss. All the saints send you greetings.

[13] The grace of the Lord Jesus Christ, and the love of God, and the fellowship of the Holy Spirit be with you all.[H]

---

^12:15 Lit *for your souls*, or *for your lives*   ^12:21 Or *come again my God will*   ^13:1 Dt 17:6; 19:15   ^13:5 Or *you are disqualified*, or *you are counterfeit*   ^13:9 Or *become complete*, or *be restored*   ^13:11 Or *farewell*   ^13:11 Or *listen to my appeal*   ^13:12-13 Some translations divide these two vv. into three vv. so that v. 13 begins with *All the saints . . .* and v. 14 begins with *The grace of . . .*

GALATIANS

1 Paul, an apostle — not from men or by man, but by Jesus Christ and God the Father who raised him from the dead — ² and all the brothers who are with me:

To the churches of Galatia.

³ Grace to you and peace from God the Father and our Lord^A Jesus Christ, ⁴ who gave himself for our sins to rescue us from this present evil age, according to the will of our God and Father. ⁵ To him be the glory forever and ever. Amen.

NO OTHER GOSPEL

⁶ I am amazed that you are so quickly turning away from him who called you by the grace of Christ and are turning to a different gospel — ⁷ not that there is another gospel, but there are some who are troubling you and want to distort the gospel of Christ. ⁸ But even if we or an angel from heaven should preach to you a gospel contrary to what we have preached to you, a curse be on him!^B ⁹ As we have said before, I now say again: If anyone is preaching to you a gospel contrary to what you received, a curse be on him!

¹⁰ For am I now trying to persuade people,^C or God? Or am I striving to please people? If I were still trying to please people, I would not be a servant of Christ.

PAUL DEFENDS HIS APOSTLESHIP

¹¹ For I want you to know, brothers and sisters, that the gospel preached by me is not of human origin. ¹² For I did not receive it from a human source and I was not taught it, but it came by a revelation of Jesus Christ.

¹³ For you have heard about my former way of life in Judaism: I intensely persecuted God's church and tried to destroy it. ¹⁴ I advanced in Judaism beyond many contemporaries among my people, because I was extremely zealous for the traditions of my ancestors. ¹⁵ But when God, who from my mother's womb set me apart and called me by his grace, was pleased ¹⁶ to reveal his Son in me, so that I could preach him among the Gentiles, I did not immediately consult with anyone.^D ¹⁷ I did not go up to Jerusalem to those who had become apostles before me; instead I went to Arabia and came back to Damascus.

¹⁸ Then after three years I did go up to Jerusalem to get to know Cephas,^E and I stayed with him fifteen days. ¹⁹ But I didn't see any of the other apostles except James, the Lord's brother. ²⁰ I declare in the sight of God: I am not lying in what I write to you.

²¹ Afterward, I went to the regions of Syria and Cilicia. ²² I remained personally unknown to the Judean churches that are in Christ. ²³ They simply kept hearing: "He who formerly persecuted us now preaches the faith he once tried to destroy." ²⁴ And they glorified God because of me.^F

PAUL DEFENDS HIS GOSPEL AT JERUSALEM

2 Then after fourteen years I went up again to Jerusalem with Barnabas, taking Titus along also. ² I went up according to a revelation and presented to them the gospel I preach among the Gentiles, but privately to those recognized as leaders. I wanted to be sure I was not running, and had not been running, in vain. ³ But not even Titus, who was with me, was compelled to be circumcised, even though he was a Greek. ⁴ This matter arose because some false brothers had infiltrated our ranks to spy on the freedom we have in Christ Jesus in order to enslave us. ⁵ But we did not give up and submit to these people for even a moment, so that the truth of the gospel would be preserved for you.

⁶ Now from those recognized as important (what they^G once were makes no difference to me; God does not show favoritism^H) — they added nothing to me. ⁷ On the contrary, they saw that I had been entrusted with the gospel for the uncircumcised, just as Peter was for the circumcised, ⁸ since the one at work in Peter for an apostleship to the circumcised was also at work in me for the Gentiles. ⁹ When James, Cephas,^E and John — those recognized as pillars — acknowledged the grace that had been given to me, they gave the right hand of fellowship to me and Barnabas, agreeing that we should go to the Gentiles and they to the circumcised. ¹⁰ They asked only that we would remember the poor, which I had made every effort to do.

FREEDOM FROM THE LAW

¹¹ But when Cephas^E came to Antioch, I opposed him to his face because he stood condemned.^I ¹² For he regularly ate with the Gentiles before certain men came from James. However, when they came, he withdrew and separated himself,

---

^A **1:3** Other mss read *God our Father and the Lord* ^B **1:8** Or *you, let him be condemned*, or *you, let him be condemned to hell*; Gk *anathema* ^C **1:10** Or *win the approval of people* ^D **1:16** Lit *flesh and blood* ^E **1:18; 2:9,11** Other mss read *Peter* ^F **1:24** Or *in me* ^G **2:6** Lit *the recognized ones* ^H **2:6** Or *God is not a respecter of persons*; lit *God does not receive the face of man* ^I **2:11** Or *he was in the wrong*

because he feared those from the circumcision party. [13] Then the rest of the Jews joined his hypocrisy, so that even Barnabas was led astray by their hypocrisy. [14] But when I saw that they were deviating from the truth of the gospel, I told Cephas[A] in front of everyone, "If you, who are a Jew, live like a Gentile and not like a Jew, how can you compel Gentiles to live like Jews?"[B]

[15] We are Jews by birth and not "Gentile sinners," [16] and yet because we know that a person is not justified by the works of the law but by faith in Jesus Christ,[C] even we ourselves have believed in Christ Jesus. This was so that we might be justified by faith in Christ[D] and not by the works of the law, because by the works of the law no human being will[E] be justified. [17] But if we ourselves are also found to be "sinners" while seeking to be justified by Christ, is Christ then a promoter[F] of sin? Absolutely not! [18] If I rebuild those things that I tore down, I show myself to be a lawbreaker. [19] For through the law I died to the law, so that I might live for God. [20] I have been crucified with Christ, and I no longer live, but Christ lives in me. The life I now live in the body,[G] I live by faith in the Son of God, who loved me and gave himself for me. [21] I do not set aside the grace of God, for if righteousness comes through the law, then Christ died for nothing.

JUSTIFICATION THROUGH FAITH

3 You foolish Galatians! Who has cast a spell on you,[H] before whose eyes Jesus Christ was publicly portrayed[I] as crucified? [2] I only want to learn this from you: Did you receive the Spirit by the works of the law or by believing what you heard?[J] [3] Are you so foolish? After beginning by the Spirit, are you now finishing by the flesh? [4] Did you experience[K] so much for nothing — if in fact it was for nothing? [5] So then, does God give you the Spirit and work miracles among you by your doing the works of the law? Or is it by believing what you heard — [6] just like Abraham who **believed God, and it was credited to him for righteousness?**[L]

[7] You know, then, that those who have faith, these are Abraham's sons. [8] Now the Scripture saw in advance that God would justify the Gentiles by faith and proclaimed the gospel ahead of time to Abraham, saying, **All the nations**[M] **will be blessed through you.**[N] [9] Consequently those who have faith are blessed with Abraham, who had faith.[O]

LAW AND PROMISE

[10] For all who rely on the works of the law are under a curse, because it is written, **Everyone who does not do everything written in the book of the law is cursed.**[P] [11] Now it is clear that no one is justified before God by the law, because **the righteous will live by faith.**[Q] [12] But the law is not based on faith; instead, **the one who does these things will live by them.**[R] [13] Christ redeemed us from the curse of the law by becoming a curse for us, because it is written, **Cursed is everyone who is hung on a tree.**[S] [14] The purpose was that the blessing of Abraham would come to the Gentiles by Christ Jesus, so that we could receive the promised Spirit through faith.

[15] Brothers and sisters, I'm using a human illustration. No one sets aside or makes additions to a validated human will.[T] [16] Now the promises were spoken to Abraham and to his seed. He does not say "and to seeds," as though referring to many, but referring to one, **and to your seed,**[U] who is Christ. [17] My point is this: The law, which came 430 years later, does not invalidate a covenant previously established by God[V] and thus cancel the promise. [18] For if the inheritance is based on the law, it is no longer based on the promise; but God has graciously given it to Abraham through the promise.

THE PURPOSE OF THE LAW

[19] Why then was the law given? It was added for the sake of transgressions[W] until the Seed to whom the promise was made would come. The law was put into effect through angels by means of a mediator. [20] Now a mediator is not just for one person alone, but God is one. [21] Is the law therefore contrary to God's promises? Absolutely not! For if the law had been granted with the ability to give life, then righteousness would certainly be on the basis of the law. [22] But the Scripture imprisoned everything under sin's power,[X] so that the promise might be given on the basis of faith in Jesus Christ to those who believe. [23] Before this faith came, we were confined under the law, imprisoned until the coming faith was revealed. [24] The law, then, was our guardian until Christ, so that we could be justified by faith. [25] But since that faith has come, we are no longer under a guardian, [26] for through faith you are all sons of God in Christ Jesus.

[A] **2:14** Other mss read *Peter*   [B] **2:14** Some translations continue the quotation through v. 16 or v. 21.   [C] **2:16** Or *by the faithfulness of Jesus Christ*   [D] **2:16** Or *by the faithfulness of Christ*   [E] **2:16** Lit *law all flesh will not*   [F] **2:17** Or *servant*   [G] **2:20** Lit *flesh*   [H] **3:1** Other mss add *not to obey the truth*   [I] **3:1** Other mss add *among you*   [J] **3:2** Lit *hearing with faith*, also in v. 5   [K] **3:4** Or *suffer*   [L] **3:6** Gn 15:6   [M] **3:8** Or *Gentiles*   [N] **3:8** Gn 12:3; 18:18   [O] **3:9** Or *with believing Abraham*   [P] **3:10** Dt 27:26   [Q] **3:11** Hab 2:4   [R] **3:12** Lv 18:5   [S] **3:13** Dt 21:23   [T] **3:15** Or *a human covenant that has been ratified*   [U] **3:16** Gn 12:7; 13:15; 17:8; 24:7   [V] **3:17** Other mss add *in Christ*   [W] **3:19** Or *because of transgressions*   [X] **3:22** Lit *under sin*

SONS AND HEIRS

²⁷ For those of you who were baptized into Christ have been clothed with Christ. ²⁸ There is no Jew or Greek, slave or free, male and female; since you are all one in Christ Jesus. ²⁹ And if you belong to Christ, then you are Abraham's

4 seed, heirs according to the promise. ¹ Now I say that as long as the heir is a child, he differs in no way from a slave, though he is the owner of everything. ² Instead, he is under guardians and trustees until the time set by his father. ³ In the same way we also, when we were children, were in slavery under the elementsᴬ of the world. ⁴ When the time came to completion, God sent his Son, born of a woman, born under the law, ⁵ to redeem those under the law, so that we might receive adoption as sons. ⁶ And because you are sons, God sent the Spirit of his Son into ourᴮ hearts, crying, "*Abba*,ᶜ Father!" ⁷ So you are no longer a slave but a son, and if a son, then God has made you an heir.

PAUL'S CONCERN FOR THE GALATIANS

⁸ But in the past, since you didn't know God, you were enslaved to thingsᴰ that by nature are not gods. ⁹ But now, since you know God, or rather have become known by God, how can you turn back again to the weak and worthless elements? Do you want to be enslaved to them all over again? ¹⁰ You are observing special days, months, seasons, and years. ¹¹ I am fearful for you, that perhaps my labor for you has been wasted.

¹² I beg you, brothers and sisters: Become like me, for I also became like you. You have not wronged me; ¹³ you knowᴱ that previously I preached the gospel to you because of a weakness of the flesh. ¹⁴ You did not despise or reject me though my physical condition was a trial for you.ᶠ On the contrary, you received me as an angel of God, as Christ Jesus himself. ¹⁵ Where, then, is your blessing? For I testify to you that, if possible, you would have torn out your eyes and given them to me. ¹⁶ So then, have I become your enemy because I told you the truth? ¹⁷ They court you eagerly, but not for good. They want to exclude you from me, so that you would pursue them. ¹⁸ But it is always good to be pursuedᴳ in a good manner — and not just when I am with you. ¹⁹ My children, I am again suffering labor pains for you until Christ is formed in you. ²⁰ I would like to be with you right now and change my tone of voice, because I don't know what to do about you.

SARAH AND HAGAR: TWO COVENANTS

²¹ Tell me, you who want to be under the law, don't you hear the law? ²² For it is written that Abraham had two sons, one by a slave and the other by a free woman. ²³ But the one by the slave was born as a result of the flesh, while the one by the free woman was born through promise. ²⁴ These things are being taken figuratively, for the women represent two covenants. One is from Mount Sinai and bears children into slavery — this is Hagar. ²⁵ Now Hagar represents Mount Sinai in Arabia and corresponds to the present Jerusalem, for she is in slavery with her children. ²⁶ But the Jerusalem above is free, and she is our mother. ²⁷ For it is written,

> Rejoice, childless woman,
> unable to give birth.
> Burst into song and shout,
> you who are not in labor,
> for the children of the desolate woman
>   will be many,
> more numerous than those
>   of the woman who has a husband.ᴴ

²⁸ Now you too, brothers and sisters, like Isaac, are children of promise. ²⁹ But just as then the child born as a result of the flesh persecuted the one born as a result of the Spirit, so also now. ³⁰ But what does the Scripture say? "Drive out the slave and her son, for the son of the slave will never be a coheir with the son of the free woman."ᴵ ³¹ Therefore, brothers and sisters, we are not children of a slave but of the free woman.

FREEDOM OF THE CHRISTIAN

5 For freedom, Christ set us free. Stand firm then and don't submit again to a yoke of slavery. ² Take note! I, Paul, am telling you that if you get yourselves circumcised, Christ will not benefit you at all. ³ Again I testify to every man who gets himself circumcised that he is obligated to do the entire law. ⁴ You who are trying to be justified by the law are alienated from Christ; you have fallen from grace. ⁵ For we eagerly await through the Spirit, by faith, the hope of righteousness. ⁶ For in Christ Jesus neither circumcision nor uncircumcision accomplishes anything; what matters is faith working through love.

⁷ You were running well. Who prevented you from being persuaded regarding the truth?ᴶ ⁸ This persuasion does not come from the one who calls you. ⁹ A little leavenᴷ leavens the whole batch of dough. ¹⁰ I myself am persuaded in the Lord you will not accept any other view. But whoever it is that is confusing you will

---

ᴬ**4:3** Or *spirits*, or *principles*　ᴮ**4:6** Other mss read *your*　ᶜ**4:6** Aramaic for *father*　ᴰ**4:8** Or *beings*　ᴱ**4:12-13** Or ¹² *Become like I am, because I — inasmuch as you are brothers and sisters — am not requesting anything of you. You wronged me.*　¹³ *You know*　ᶠ**4:14** Other mss read *me*　ᴳ**4:18** Lit *zealously courted*　ᴴ**4:27** Is 54:1　ᴵ**4:30** Gn 21:10　ᴶ**5:7** Or *obeying the truth*　ᴷ**5:9** Or *yeast*

pay the penalty. [11] Now brothers and sisters, if I still preach circumcision, why am I still persecuted? In that case the offense of the cross has been abolished. [12] I wish those who are disturbing you might also let themselves be mutilated!

[13] For you were called to be free, brothers and sisters; only don't use this freedom as an opportunity[A] for the flesh, but serve one another through love. [14] For the whole law is fulfilled in one statement: **Love your neighbor as yourself.**[B] [15] But if you bite and devour one another, watch out, or you will be consumed by one another.

THE SPIRIT VERSUS THE FLESH

[16] I say then, walk by the Spirit and you will certainly not carry out the desire of the flesh. [17] For the flesh desires what is against the Spirit, and the Spirit desires what is against the flesh; these are opposed to each other, so that you don't do what you want. [18] But if you are led by the Spirit, you are not under the law.

[19] Now the works of the flesh are obvious:[C] sexual immorality, moral impurity, promiscuity, [20] idolatry, sorcery, hatreds, strife, jealousy, outbursts of anger, selfish ambitions, dissensions, factions, [21] envy,[D] drunkenness, carousing, and anything similar. I am warning you about these things — as I warned you before — that those who practice such things will not inherit the kingdom of God.

[22] But the fruit of the Spirit is love, joy, peace, patience, kindness, goodness, faithfulness, [23] gentleness, and self-control. The law is not against such things.[E] [24] Now those who belong to Christ Jesus have crucified the flesh with its passions and desires. [25] If we live by the Spirit, let us also keep in step with the Spirit. [26] Let us not become conceited, provoking one another, envying one another.

CARRY ONE ANOTHER'S BURDENS

6 Brothers and sisters, if someone is overtaken in any wrongdoing, you who are spiritual, restore such a person with a gentle spirit,[F] watching out for yourselves so that you also won't be tempted. [2] Carry one another's burdens; in this way you will fulfill the law of Christ. [3] For if anyone considers himself to be something when he is nothing, he deceives himself. [4] Let each person examine his own work, and then he can take pride in himself alone, and not compare himself with someone else. [5] For each person will have to carry his own load.

[6] Let the one who is taught the word share all his good things with the teacher. [7] Don't be deceived: God is not mocked. For whatever a person sows he will also reap, [8] because the one who sows to his flesh will reap destruction from the flesh, but the one who sows to the Spirit will reap eternal life from the Spirit. [9] Let us not get tired of doing good, for we will reap at the proper time if we don't give up. [10] Therefore, as we have opportunity, let us work for the good of all, especially for those who belong to the household of faith.

CONCLUDING EXHORTATION

[11] Look at what large letters I use as I write to you in my own handwriting. [12] Those who want to make a good impression in the flesh are the ones who would compel you to be circumcised — but only to avoid being persecuted for the cross of Christ. [13] For even the circumcised don't keep the law themselves, and yet they want you to be circumcised in order to boast about your flesh. [14] But as for me, I will never boast about anything except the cross of our Lord Jesus Christ. The world has been crucified to me through the cross, and I to the world. [15] For[G] both circumcision and uncircumcision mean nothing; what matters instead is a new creation. [16] May peace come to all those who follow this standard, and mercy even to the Israel of God!"

[17] From now on, let no one cause me trouble, because I bear on my body the marks of Jesus. [18] Brothers and sisters, the grace of our Lord Jesus Christ be with your spirit. Amen.

---

^5:13 Lit a *pretext*; a military term for abuse of position   ^5:14 Lv 19:18   ^5:19 Other mss add *adultery*,   ^5:21 Other mss add *murders*,   ^5:23 Or *Against such things there is no law*   ^6:1 Or *with the Spirit of gentleness*   ^6:15 Other mss add *in Christ Jesus*   ^6:16 Or *And for those who follow this standard, may peace and mercy be upon them, even upon the Israel of God,* or *And as many who will follow this standard, peace be upon them and mercy even upon the Israel of God.*

EPHESIANS

1 Paul, an apostle of Christ Jesus by God's will: To the faithful saints in Christ Jesus^A at Ephesus.^B

[2] Grace to you and peace from God our Father and the Lord Jesus Christ.

GOD'S RICH BLESSINGS

[3] Blessed is the God and Father of our Lord Jesus Christ, who has blessed us with every spiritual blessing in the heavens in Christ. [4] For he chose us in him, before the foundation of the world, to be holy and blameless in love before him.^C [5] He predestined us to be adopted as sons through Jesus Christ for himself, according to the good pleasure of his will, [6] to the praise of his glorious grace that he lavished on us in the Beloved One.

[7] In him we have redemption through his blood, the forgiveness of our trespasses, according to the riches of his grace [8] that he richly poured out on us with all wisdom and understanding.^D [9] He made known to us the mystery of his will, according to his good pleasure that he purposed in Christ [10] as a plan for the right time^E — to bring everything together in Christ, both things in heaven and things on earth in him.

[11] In him we have also received an inheritance,^F because we were predestined according to the plan of the one who works out everything in agreement with the purpose of his will, [12] so that we who had already put our hope in Christ might bring praise to his glory.

[13] In him you also were sealed with the promised Holy Spirit when you heard the word of truth, the gospel of your salvation, and when you believed. [14] The Holy Spirit is the down payment of our inheritance, until the redemption of the possession, to the praise of his glory.

PRAYER FOR SPIRITUAL INSIGHT

[15] This is why, since I heard about your faith in the Lord Jesus and your love for all the saints, [16] I never stop giving thanks for you as I remember you in my prayers. [17] I pray that the God of our Lord Jesus Christ, the glorious Father,^G would give you the Spirit^H of wisdom and revelation in the knowledge of him. [18] I pray that the eyes of your heart may be enlightened so that you may know what is the hope of his calling, what is the wealth of his glorious inheritance in the saints, [19] and what is the immeasurable greatness of his power toward us who believe, according to the mighty working of his strength.

GOD'S POWER IN CHRIST

[20] He exercised this power in Christ by raising him from the dead and seating him at his right hand in the heavens — [21] far above every ruler and authority, power and dominion, and every title given,^I not only in this age but also in the one to come. [22] And **he subjected everything under his feet**^J and appointed him^K as head over everything for the church, [23] which is his body, the fullness of the one who fills all things in every way.

FROM DEATH TO LIFE

2 And you were dead in your trespasses and sins [2] in which you previously lived according to the ways of this world, according to the ruler of the power of the air, the spirit now working in the disobedient.^L [3] We too all previously lived among them in our fleshly desires, carrying out the inclinations of our flesh and thoughts, and we were by nature children under wrath as the others were also. [4] But God, who is rich in mercy, because of his great love that he had for us,^M [5] made us alive with Christ even though we were dead in trespasses. You are saved by grace! [6] He also raised us up with him and seated us with him in the heavens in Christ Jesus, [7] so that in the coming ages he might display the immeasurable riches of his grace through his kindness to us in Christ Jesus. [8] For you are saved by grace through faith, and this is not from yourselves; it is God's gift — [9] not from works, so that no one can boast. [10] For we are his workmanship, created in Christ Jesus for good works, which God prepared ahead of time for us to do.

UNITY IN CHRIST

[11] So then, remember that at one time you were Gentiles in the flesh — called "the uncircumcised" by those called "the circumcised," which is done in the flesh by human hands. [12] At that time you were without Christ, excluded from the citizenship of Israel, and foreigners to the covenants of promise, without hope and without God in the world. [13] But now in Christ Jesus,

---

^A **1:1** Or *to the saints, the believers in Christ Jesus*   ^B **1:1** Other mss omit *at Ephesus*   ^C **1:4** Or *in his sight. In love*   ^D **1:8** Or *on us. With all wisdom and understanding*   ^E **1:10** Or *the fulfillment of times*   ^F **1:11** Or *In him we are also an inheritance,*   ^G **1:17** Or *the Father of glory*   ^H **1:17** Or *a spirit*   ^I **1:21** Lit *every name named*   ^J **1:22** Ps 8:6   ^K **1:22** Lit *gave him*   ^L **2:2** Lit *sons of disobedience*   ^M **2:4** Lit *love with which he loved us*

you who were far away have been brought near by the blood of Christ. [14] For he is our peace, who made both groups one and tore down the dividing wall of hostility. In his flesh, [15] he made of no effect the law consisting of commands and expressed in regulations, so that he might create in himself one new man from the two, resulting in peace. [16] He did this so that he might reconcile both to God in one body through the cross by which he put the hostility to death.[A] [17] He came and proclaimed the good news of peace to you who were far away and peace to those who were near. [18] For through him we both have access in one spirit to the Father. [19] So then you are no longer foreigners and strangers, but fellow citizens with the saints, and members of God's household, [20] built on the foundation of the apostles and prophets, with Christ Jesus himself as the cornerstone. [21] In him the whole building, being put together, grows into a holy temple in the Lord. [22] In him you are also being built together for God's dwelling in the Spirit.

PAUL'S MINISTRY TO THE GENTILES

3 For this reason, I, Paul, the prisoner of Christ Jesus on behalf of you Gentiles — [2] you have heard, haven't you, about the administration of God's grace that he gave to me for you? [3] The mystery was made known to me by revelation, as I have briefly written above. [4] By reading this you are able to understand my insight into the mystery of Christ. [5] This was not made known to people[B] in other generations as it is now revealed to his holy apostles and prophets by the Spirit: [6] The Gentiles are coheirs, members of the same body, and partners in the promise in Christ Jesus through the gospel. [7] I was made a servant of this gospel by the gift of God's grace that was given to me by the working of his power.

[8] This grace was given to me — the least of all the saints — to proclaim to the Gentiles the incalculable riches of Christ, [9] and to shed light for all about the administration of the mystery hidden for ages in God who created all things. [10] This is so that God's multi-faceted wisdom may now be made known through the church to the rulers and authorities in the heavens. [11] This is according to his eternal purpose accomplished in Christ Jesus our Lord. [12] In him we have boldness and confident access through faith in him.[C] [13] So then I ask you not to be discouraged over my afflictions on your behalf, for they are your glory.

PRAYER FOR SPIRITUAL POWER

[14] For this reason I kneel before the Father[D] [15] from whom every family in heaven and on earth is named. [16] I pray that he may grant you, according to the riches of his glory, to be strengthened with power in your inner being through his Spirit, [17] and that Christ may dwell in your hearts through faith. I pray that you, being rooted and firmly established in love, [18] may be able to comprehend with all the saints what is the length and width, height and depth of God's love, [19] and to know Christ's love that surpasses knowledge, so that you may be filled with all the fullness of God.

[20] Now to him who is able to do above and beyond all that we ask or think according to the power that works in us — [21] to him be glory in the church and in Christ Jesus to all generations, forever and ever. Amen.

UNITY AND DIVERSITY IN THE BODY OF CHRIST

4 Therefore I, the prisoner in the Lord, urge you to live worthy of the calling you have received, [2] with all humility and gentleness, with patience, bearing with one another in love, [3] making every effort to keep the unity of the Spirit through the bond of peace. [4] There is one body and one Spirit — just as you were called to one hope[E] at your calling — [5] one Lord, one faith, one baptism, [6] one God and Father of all, who is above all and through all and in all.

[7] Now grace was given to each one of us according to the measure of Christ's gift. [8] For it says:

> When he ascended on high,
> he took the captives captive;
> he gave gifts to people.[F]

[9] But what does "he ascended" mean except that he[G] also descended to the lower parts of the earth?[H] [10] The one who descended is also the one who ascended far above all the heavens, to fill all things. [11] And he himself gave some to be apostles, some prophets, some evangelists, some pastors and teachers, [12] equipping the saints for the work of ministry, to build up the body of Christ, [13] until we all reach unity in the faith and in the knowledge of God's Son, growing into maturity with a stature measured by Christ's fullness. [14] Then we will no longer be little children, tossed by the waves and blown around by every wind of teaching, by human cunning with cleverness in the techniques of deceit. [15] But speaking the truth in love, let us grow in every way into him who is the head — Christ. [16] From him the whole body, fitted and

---

[A] 2:16 Or *death in himself*   [B] 3:5 Lit *to the sons of men*   [C] 3:12 Or *through his faithfulness*   [D] 3:14 Other mss add *of our Lord Jesus Christ*   [E] 4:4 Lit *called in one hope*   [F] 4:8 Ps 68:18   [G] 4:9 Other mss add *first*   [H] 4:9 Or *the lower parts, namely, the earth*

knit together by every supporting ligament, promotes the growth of the body for building up itself in love by the proper working of each individual part.

LIVING THE NEW LIFE

[17] Therefore, I say this and testify in the Lord: You should no longer live as the Gentiles live, in the futility of their thoughts. [18] They are darkened in their understanding, excluded from the life of God, because of the ignorance that is in them and because[A] of the hardness of their hearts. [19] They became callous and gave themselves over to promiscuity for the practice of every kind of impurity with a desire for more and more.[B]

[20] But that is not how you came to know Christ, [21] assuming you heard about him and were taught by him, as the truth is in Jesus, [22] to take off[C] your former way of life, the old self that is corrupted by deceitful desires, [23] to be renewed[D] in the spirit of your minds, [24] and to put on[E] the new self, the one created according to God's likeness in righteousness and purity of the truth.

[25] Therefore, putting away lying, **speak the truth, each one to his neighbor,**[F] because we are members of one another. [26] **Be angry and do not sin.**[G] Don't let the sun go down on your anger, [27] and don't give the devil an opportunity. [28] Let the thief no longer steal. Instead, he is to do honest work with his own hands, so that he has something to share with anyone in need. [29] No foul language should come from your mouth, but only what is good for building up someone in need,[H] so that it gives grace to those who hear. [30] And don't grieve God's Holy Spirit. You were sealed by him[I] for the day of redemption. [31] Let all bitterness, anger and wrath, shouting and slander be removed from you, along with all malice. [32] And be kind and compassionate to one another, forgiving one another, just as God also forgave you[J] in Christ.

5 Therefore, be imitators of God, as dearly loved children, [2] and walk in love, as Christ also loved us and gave himself for us, a sacrificial and fragrant offering to God. [3] But sexual immorality and any impurity or greed should not even be heard of[K] among you, as is proper for saints. [4] Obscene and foolish talking or crude joking are not suitable, but rather giving thanks. [5] For know and recognize this: Every sexually immoral or impure or greedy person,

who is an idolater, does not have an inheritance in the kingdom of Christ and of God.

LIGHT VERSUS DARKNESS

[6] Let no one deceive you with empty arguments, for God's wrath is coming on the disobedient[L] because of these things. [7] Therefore, do not become their partners. [8] For you were once darkness, but now you are light in the Lord. Live as children of light — [9] for the fruit of the light[M] consists of all goodness, righteousness, and truth — [10] testing what is pleasing to the Lord. [11] Don't participate in the fruitless works of darkness, but instead expose them. [12] For it is shameful even to mention what is done by them in secret. [13] Everything exposed by the light is made visible, [14] for what makes everything visible is light. Therefore it is said:

Get up, sleeper, and rise up from the dead, and Christ will shine on you.

CONSISTENCY IN THE CHRISTIAN LIFE

[15] Pay careful attention, then, to how you live — not as unwise people but as wise — [16] making the most of the time,[N] because the days are evil. [17] So don't be foolish, but understand what the Lord's will is. [18] And don't get drunk with wine, which leads to reckless living, but be filled by the Spirit: [19] speaking to one another in psalms, hymns, and spiritual songs, singing and making music with your heart to the Lord, [20] giving thanks always for everything to God the Father in the name of our Lord Jesus Christ, [21] submitting to one another in the fear of Christ.

WIVES AND HUSBANDS

[22] Wives, submit[O] to your husbands as to the Lord, [23] because the husband is the head of the wife as Christ is the head of the church. He is the Savior of the body. [24] Now as the church submits to Christ, so also wives are to submit to their husbands in everything. [25] Husbands, love your wives, just as Christ loved the church and gave himself for her [26] to make her holy, cleansing[P] her with the washing of water by the word. [27] He did this to present the church to himself in splendor, without spot or wrinkle or anything like that, but holy and blameless. [28] In the same way, husbands are to love their wives as their own bodies. He who loves his wife loves himself. [29] For no one ever hates his own flesh but provides and cares for it, just as Christ does for the church, [30] since we are members of his

---

[A] **4:18** Or *in them because*   [B] **4:19** Lit *with greediness*   [C] **4:21-22** Or *Jesus. This means: take off* (as a command)   [D] **4:22-23** Or *desires; renew* (as a command)   [E] **4:23-24** Or *minds; and put on* (as a command)   [F] **4:25** Zch 8:16   [G] **4:26** Ps 4:4   [H] **4:29** Lit *for the building up of the need*   [I] **4:30** Or *Spirit, by whom you were sealed*   [J] **4:32** Other mss read *us*   [K] **5:3** Or *be named*   [L] **5:6** Lit *sons of disobedience*   [M] **5:9** Other mss read *fruit of the Spirit*   [N] **5:16** Lit *buying back the time*   [O] **5:22** Other mss omit *submit*   [P] **5:26** Or *having cleansed*

body.^A ^31 For this reason a man will leave his father and mother and be joined to his wife, and the two will become one flesh.^B ^32 This mystery is profound, but I am talking about Christ and the church. ^33 To sum up, each one of you is to love his wife as himself, and the wife is to respect her husband.

CHILDREN AND PARENTS

6 Children, obey your parents in the Lord, because this is right. ^2 Honor your father and mother, which is the first commandment with a promise, ^3 so that it may go well with you and that you may have a long life in the land.^C,D ^4 Fathers, don't stir up anger in your children, but bring them up in the training and instruction of the Lord.

SLAVES AND MASTERS

^5 Slaves, obey your human^E masters with fear and trembling, in the sincerity of your heart, as you would Christ. ^6 Don't work only while being watched, as people-pleasers, but as slaves of Christ, do God's will from your heart. ^7 Serve with a good attitude, as to the Lord and not to people, ^8 knowing that whatever good each one does, slave or free, he will receive this back from the Lord. ^9 And masters, treat your slaves the same way, without threatening them, because you know that both their Master and yours is in heaven, and there is no favoritism with him.

CHRISTIAN WARFARE

^10 Finally, be strengthened by the Lord and by his vast strength. ^11 Put on the full armor of God so that you can stand against the schemes of the devil. ^12 For our struggle is not against flesh and blood, but against the rulers, against the authorities, against the cosmic powers of this darkness, against evil, spiritual forces in the heavens. ^13 For this reason take up the full armor of God, so that you may be able to resist in the evil day, and having prepared everything, to take your stand. ^14 Stand, therefore, with truth like a belt around your waist, righteousness like armor on your chest, ^15 and your feet sandaled with readiness for the gospel of peace. ^16 In every situation take up the shield of faith with which you can extinguish all the flaming arrows of the evil one. ^17 Take the helmet of salvation and the sword of the Spirit — which is the word of God. ^18 Pray at all times in the Spirit with every prayer and request, and stay alert with all perseverance and intercession for all the saints. ^19 Pray also for me, that the message may be given to me when I open my mouth to make known with boldness the mystery of the gospel. ^20 For this I am an ambassador in chains. Pray that I might be bold enough to speak about it as I should.

PAUL'S FAREWELL

^21 Tychicus, our dearly loved brother and faithful servant^F in the Lord, will tell you all the news about me so that you may be informed. ^22 I am sending him to you for this very reason, to let you know how we are and to encourage your hearts.

^23 Peace to the brothers and sisters, and love with faith, from God the Father and the Lord Jesus Christ. ^24 Grace be with all who have undying love for our Lord Jesus Christ.^G,H

---

^A **5:30** Other mss add *and of his flesh and of his bones*   ^B **5:31** Gn 2:24   ^C **6:3** Or *life on the earth*   ^D **6:2-3** Ex 20:12
^E **6:5** Lit *according to the flesh*   ^F **6:21** Or *deacon*   ^G **6:24** Other mss add *Amen.*   ^H **6:24** Lit *all who love our Lord Jesus Christ in incorruption*

PHILIPPIANS

1 Paul and Timothy, servants of Christ Jesus: To all the saints in Christ Jesus who are in Philippi, including the overseers and deacons. ² Grace to you and peace from God our Father and the Lord Jesus Christ.

THANKSGIVING AND PRAYER

³ I give thanks to my God for every remembrance of you,^A ⁴ always praying with joy for all of you in my every prayer, ⁵ because of your partnership in the gospel from the first day until now. ⁶ I am sure of this, that he who started a good work in you^B will carry it on to completion until the day of Christ Jesus. ⁷ Indeed, it is right for me to think this way about all of you, because I have you in my heart,^C and you are all partners with me in grace, both in my imprisonment and in the defense and confirmation of the gospel. ⁸ For God is my witness, how deeply I miss all of you with the affection of Christ Jesus. ⁹ And I pray this: that your love will keep on growing in knowledge and every kind of discernment, ¹⁰ so that you may approve the things that are superior and may be pure and blameless in the day of Christ, ¹¹ filled with the fruit of righteousness that comes through Jesus Christ to the glory and praise of God.

ADVANCE OF THE GOSPEL

¹² Now I want you to know, brothers and sisters, that what has happened to me has actually advanced the gospel, ¹³ so that it has become known throughout the whole imperial guard, and to everyone else, that my imprisonment is because I am in Christ. ¹⁴ Most of the brothers have gained confidence in the Lord from my imprisonment and dare even more to speak the word^D fearlessly. ¹⁵ To be sure, some preach Christ out of envy and rivalry, but others out of good will. ¹⁶ These preach out of love, knowing that I am appointed for the defense of the gospel; ¹⁷ the others proclaim Christ out of selfish ambition, not sincerely, thinking that they will cause me trouble in my imprisonment. ¹⁸ What does it matter? Only that in every way, whether from false motives or true, Christ is proclaimed, and in this I rejoice. Yes, and I will continue to rejoice ¹⁹ because I know this will lead to my salvation^E through your prayers and help from the Spirit of Jesus Christ. ²⁰ My eager expectation and hope is that I will not be ashamed about anything, but that now as always, with all courage, Christ will be highly honored in my body, whether by life or by death.

LIVING IS CHRIST

²¹ For me, to live is Christ and to die is gain. ²² Now if I live on in the flesh, this means fruitful work for me; and I don't know which one I should choose. ²³ I am torn between the two. I long to depart and be with Christ — which is far better — ²⁴ but to remain in the flesh is more necessary for your sake. ²⁵ Since I am persuaded of this, I know that I will remain and continue with all of you for your progress and joy in the faith, ²⁶ so that, because of my coming to you again, your boasting in Christ Jesus may abound.

²⁷ Just one thing: As citizens of heaven, live your life worthy of the gospel of Christ. Then, whether I come and see you or am absent, I will hear about you that you are standing firm in one spirit, in one accord,^F contending together for the faith of the gospel, ²⁸ not being frightened in any way by your opponents. This is a sign of destruction for them, but of your salvation — and this is from God. ²⁹ For it has been granted to you on Christ's behalf not only to believe in him, but also to suffer for him, ³⁰ since you are engaged in the same struggle that you saw I had and now hear that I have.

CHRISTIAN HUMILITY

2 If then there is any encouragement in Christ, if any consolation of love, if any fellowship with the Spirit, if any affection and mercy, ² make my joy complete by thinking the same way, having the same love, united in spirit, intent on one purpose. ³ Do nothing out of selfish ambition or conceit, but in humility consider others as more important than yourselves. ⁴ Everyone should look out not only for his own interests, but also for the interests of others.

CHRIST'S HUMILITY AND EXALTATION

⁵ Adopt the same attitude as that of Christ Jesus,
⁶   who, existing in the form of God,
      did not consider equality with God
      as something to be exploited.^G
⁷   Instead he emptied himself
      by assuming the form of a servant,
      taking on the likeness of humanity.
      And when he had come as a man,

---

^A 1:3 Or for your every remembrance of me   ^B 1:6 Or work among you   ^C 1:7 Or because you have me in your heart
^D 1:14 Other mss add of God   ^E 1:19 Or vindication   ^F 1:27 Lit soul   ^G 2:6 Or to be grasped, or to be held on to

⁸ he humbled himself
    by becoming obedient
  to the point of death —
    even to death on a cross.
⁹ For this reason God highly exalted him
    and gave him the name
    that is above every name,
¹⁰ so that at the name of Jesus
    every knee will bow —
  in heaven and on earth
  and under the earth —
¹¹ and every tongue will confess
    that Jesus Christ is Lord,
  to the glory of God the Father.

LIGHTS IN THE WORLD

¹² Therefore, my dear friends, just as you have always obeyed, so now, not only in my presence but even more in my absence, work out your own salvation with fear and trembling. ¹³ For it is God who is working in you both to will and to work according to his good purpose. ¹⁴ Do everything without grumbling and arguing, ¹⁵ so that you may be blameless and pure, children of God who are faultless in a crooked and perverted generation, among whom you shine like stars in the world, ¹⁶ by holding firm to the word of life. Then I can boast in the day of Christ that I didn't run or labor for nothing. ¹⁷ But even if I am poured out as a drink offering on the sacrificial service of your faith, I am glad and rejoice with all of you. ¹⁸ In the same way you should also be glad and rejoice with me.

TIMOTHY AND EPAPHRODITUS

¹⁹ Now I hope in the Lord Jesus to send Timothy to you soon so that I too may be encouraged by news about you. ²⁰ For I have no one else like-minded who will genuinely care about your interests; ²¹ all seek their own interests, not those of Jesus Christ. ²² But you know his proven character, because he has served with me in the gospel ministry like a son with a father. ²³ Therefore, I hope to send him as soon as I see how things go with me. ²⁴ I am confident in the Lord that I myself will also come soon.

²⁵ But I considered it necessary to send you Epaphroditus — my brother, coworker, and fellow soldier, as well as your messenger and minister to my need — ²⁶ since he has been longing for all of you and was distressed because you heard that he was sick. ²⁷ Indeed, he was so sick that he nearly died. However, God had mercy on him, and not only on him but also on me, so that I would not have sorrow upon sorrow. ²⁸ For this reason, I am very eager to send him so that you may rejoice again when you see him and I may be less anxious. ²⁹ Therefore, welcome him in the Lord with great joy and hold people like him in honor, ³⁰ because he came close to death for the work of Christ, risking his life to make up what was lacking in your ministry to me.

KNOWING CHRIST

3 In addition, my brothers and sisters, rejoice in the Lord. To write to you again about this is no trouble for me and is a safeguard for you.

² Watch out for the dogs, watch out for the evil workers, watch out for those who mutilate the flesh. ³ For we are the circumcision, the ones who worship by the Spirit of God, boast in Christ Jesus, and do not put confidence in the flesh — ⁴ although I have reasons for confidence in the flesh. If anyone else thinks he has grounds for confidence in the flesh, I have more: ⁵ circumcised the eighth day; of the nation of Israel, of the tribe of Benjamin, a Hebrew born of Hebrews; regarding the law, a Pharisee; ⁶ regarding zeal, persecuting the church; regarding the righteousness that is in the law, blameless.

⁷ But everything that was a gain to me, I have considered to be a loss because of Christ. ⁸ More than that, I also consider everything to be a loss in view of the surpassing value of knowing Christ Jesus my Lord. Because of him I have suffered the loss of all things and consider them as dung, so that I may gain Christ ⁹ and be found in him, not having a righteousness of my own from the law, but one that is through faith in Christ^A — the righteousness from God based on faith. ¹⁰ My goal is to know him and the power of his resurrection and the fellowship of his sufferings, being conformed to his death, ¹¹ assuming that I will somehow reach the resurrection from among the dead.

REACHING FORWARD TO GOD'S GOAL

¹² Not that I have already reached the goal or am already perfect, but I make every effort to take hold of it because I also have been taken hold of by Christ Jesus. ¹³ Brothers and sisters, I do not^B consider myself to have taken hold of it. But one thing I do: Forgetting what is behind and reaching forward to what is ahead, ¹⁴ I pursue as my goal the prize promised by God's heavenly^C call in Christ Jesus. ¹⁵ Therefore, let all of us who are mature think this way. And if you think differently about anything, God will reveal this also to you. ¹⁶ In any case, we should live up to whatever truth we have attained. ¹⁷ Join in imitating me, brothers and sisters, and pay careful attention to those who live

---

^A 3:9 Or *through the faithfulness of Christ*   ^B 3:13 Other mss read *not yet*   ^C 3:14 Or *upward*

according to the example you have in us. [18] For I have often told you, and now say again with tears, that many live as enemies of the cross of Christ. [19] Their end is destruction; their god is their stomach; their glory is in their shame. They are focused on earthly things, [20] but our citizenship is in heaven, and we eagerly wait for a Savior from there, the Lord Jesus Christ. [21] He will transform the body of our humble condition into the likeness of his glorious body, by the power that enables him to subject everything to himself.

4 So then, my dearly loved and longed for brothers and sisters, my joy and crown, in this manner stand firm in the Lord, dear friends.

PRACTICAL COUNSEL

[2] I urge Euodia and I urge Syntyche to agree in the Lord. [3] Yes, I also ask you, true partner,[A] to help these women who have contended for the gospel at my side, along with Clement and the rest of my coworkers whose names are in the book of life. [4] Rejoice in the Lord always. I will say it again: Rejoice! [5] Let your graciousness[B] be known to everyone. The Lord is near. [6] Don't worry about anything, but in everything, through prayer and petition with thanksgiving, present your requests to God. [7] And the peace of God, which surpasses all understanding, will guard your hearts and minds in Christ Jesus.

[8] Finally[C] brothers and sisters, whatever is true, whatever is honorable, whatever is just, whatever is pure, whatever is lovely, whatever is commendable — if there is any moral excellence and if there is anything praiseworthy — dwell on these things. [9] Do what you have learned and received and heard from me, and seen in me, and the God of peace will be with you.

APPRECIATION OF SUPPORT

[10] I rejoiced in the Lord greatly because once again you renewed your care for me. You were, in fact, concerned about me but lacked the opportunity to show it. [11] I don't say this out of need, for I have learned to be content in whatever circumstances I find myself. [12] I know both how to make do with little, and I know how to make do with a lot. In any and all circumstances I have learned the secret of being content — whether well fed or hungry, whether in abundance or in need. [13] I am able to do all things through him[D] who strengthens me. [14] Still, you did well by partnering with me in my hardship.

[15] And you Philippians know that in the early days of the gospel, when I left Macedonia, no church shared with me in the matter of giving and receiving except you alone. [16] For even in Thessalonica you sent gifts for my need several times. [17] Not that I seek the gift, but I seek the profit[E] that is increasing to your account. [18] But I have received everything in full, and I have an abundance. I am fully supplied,[F] having received from Epaphroditus what you provided — a fragrant offering, an acceptable sacrifice, pleasing to God. [19] And my God will supply all your needs according to his riches in glory in Christ Jesus. [20] Now to our God and Father be glory forever and ever. Amen.

FINAL GREETINGS

[21] Greet every saint in Christ Jesus. The brothers who are with me send you greetings. [22] All the saints send you greetings, especially those who belong to Caesar's household. [23] The grace of the Lord Jesus Christ be with your spirit.[G]

[A] **4:3** Or *true Syzygus*, possibly a person's name   [B] **4:5** Or *gentleness*   [C] **4:8** Or *In addition*   [D] **4:13** Other mss read *Christ*
[E] **4:17** Lit *fruit*   [F] **4:18** Or *Here, then, is my receipt for everything, I have an abundance, for I am fully supplied*
[G] **4:23** Other mss add *Amen.*

COLOSSIANS

GREETING

1 Paul, an apostle of Christ Jesus by God's will, and Timothy our brother:

² To the saints in Christ at Colossae, who are faithful brothers and sisters.

Grace to you and peace from God our Father.[A]

THANKSGIVING

³ We always thank God, the Father of our Lord Jesus Christ, when we pray for you, ⁴ for we have heard of your faith in Christ Jesus and of the love you have for all the saints ⁵ because of the hope reserved for you in heaven. You have already heard about this hope in the word of truth, the gospel ⁶ that has come to you. It is bearing fruit and growing all over the world, just as it has among you since the day you heard it and came to truly appreciate God's grace.[B] ⁷ You learned this from Epaphras, our dearly loved fellow servant. He is a faithful minister of Christ on your[C] behalf, ⁸ and he has told us about your love in the Spirit.

PRAYER FOR SPIRITUAL GROWTH

⁹ For this reason also, since the day we heard this, we haven't stopped praying for you. We are asking that you may be filled with the knowledge of his will in all wisdom and spiritual understanding,[D] ¹⁰ so that you may walk worthy of the Lord, fully pleasing to him: bearing fruit in every good work and growing in the knowledge of God, ¹¹ being strengthened with all power, according to his glorious might, so that you may have great endurance and patience, joyfully ¹² giving thanks to the Father, who has enabled you[E] to share in the saints' inheritance in the light. ¹³ He has rescued us from the domain of darkness and transferred us into the kingdom of the Son he loves. ¹⁴ In him we have redemption,[F] the forgiveness of sins.

THE CENTRALITY OF CHRIST

¹⁵ He is the image of the invisible God,
the firstborn over all creation.
¹⁶ For everything was created by him,
in heaven and on earth,
the visible and the invisible,
whether thrones or dominions
or rulers or authorities —
all things have been created through him
and for him.
¹⁷ He is before all things,
and by him all things hold together.

¹⁸ He is also the head of the body,
the church;
he is the beginning,
the firstborn from the dead,
so that he might come to have
first place in everything.
¹⁹ For God was pleased to have
all his fullness dwell in him,
²⁰ and through him to reconcile
everything to himself,
whether things on earth or things
in heaven,
by making peace
through his blood, shed
on the cross.[G]

²¹ Once you were alienated and hostile in your minds expressed in your evil actions. ²² But now he has reconciled you by his physical body through his death, to present you holy, faultless, and blameless before him — ²³ if indeed you remain grounded and steadfast in the faith and are not shifted away from the hope of the gospel that you heard. This gospel has been proclaimed in all creation under heaven, and I, Paul, have become a servant of it.

PAUL'S MINISTRY

²⁴ Now I rejoice in my sufferings for you, and I am completing in my flesh what is lacking in Christ's afflictions for his body, that is, the church. ²⁵ I have become its servant, according to God's commission that was given to me for you, to make the word of God fully known, ²⁶ the mystery hidden for ages and generations but now revealed to his saints. ²⁷ God wanted to make known among the Gentiles the glorious wealth of this mystery, which is Christ in you, the hope of glory. ²⁸ We proclaim him, warning and teaching everyone with all wisdom, so that we may present everyone mature in Christ. ²⁹ I labor for this, striving with his strength that works powerfully in me.

2 For I want you to know how greatly I am struggling for you, for those in Laodicea, and for all who have not seen me in person. ² I want their hearts to be encouraged and joined together in love, so that they may have all the riches of complete understanding and have the knowledge of God's mystery — Christ.[H] ³ In him are hidden all the treasures of wisdom and knowledge.

[A] 1:2 Other mss add *and the Lord Jesus Christ* [B] 1:6 Or *and truly recognized God's grace* [C] 1:7 Other mss read *our* [D] 1:9 Or *all spiritual wisdom and understanding* [E] 1:12 Other mss read *us* [F] 1:14 Other mss add *through his blood* [G] 1:20 Other mss add *through him* [H] 2:2 Other mss read *mystery of God, both of the Father and of Christ*; other ms variations exist on this v.

CHRIST VERSUS THE COLOSSIAN HERESY

[4] I am saying this so that no one will deceive you with arguments that sound reasonable. [5] For I may be absent in body, but I am with you in spirit, rejoicing to see how well ordered you are and the strength of your faith in Christ.

[6] So then, just as you have received Christ Jesus as Lord, continue to live in him, [7] being rooted and built up in him and established in the faith, just as you were taught, and overflowing with gratitude.

[8] Be careful that no one takes you captive through philosophy and empty deceit based on human tradition, based on the elements of the world, rather than Christ. [9] For the entire fullness of God's nature dwells bodily[A] in Christ, [10] and you have been filled by him, who is the head over every ruler and authority. [11] You were also circumcised in him with a circumcision not done with hands, by putting off the body of flesh, in the circumcision of Christ, [12] when you were buried with him in baptism, in which you were also raised with him through faith in the working of God, who raised him from the dead. [13] And when you were dead in trespasses and in the uncircumcision of your flesh, he made you alive with him and forgave us all our trespasses. [14] He erased the certificate of debt, with its obligations, that was against us and opposed to us, and has taken it away by nailing it to the cross. [15] He disarmed the rulers and authorities and disgraced them publicly; he triumphed over them in him.[B]

[16] Therefore, don't let anyone judge you in regard to food and drink or in the matter of a festival or a new moon or a Sabbath day.[C] [17] These are a shadow of what was to come; the substance is[D] Christ. [18] Let no one condemn[E] you by delighting in ascetic practices and the worship of angels, claiming access to a visionary realm. Such people are inflated by empty notions of their unspiritual[F] mind. [19] He doesn't hold on to the head, from whom the whole body, nourished and held together by its ligaments and tendons, grows with growth from God.

[20] If you died with Christ to the elements of this world, why do you live as if you still belonged to the world? Why do you submit to regulations: [21] "Don't handle, don't taste, don't touch"? [22] All these regulations refer to what is destined to perish by being used up; they are human commands and doctrines. [23] Although these have a reputation for wisdom by promoting self-made religion, false humility, and

severe treatment of the body, they are not of any value in curbing self-indulgence.[G]

THE LIFE OF THE NEW MAN

3 So if you have been raised with Christ, seek the things above, where Christ is, seated at the right hand of God. [2] Set your minds on things above, not on earthly things. [3] For you died, and your life is hidden with Christ in God. [4] When Christ, who is your[H] life, appears, then you also will appear with him in glory.

[5] Therefore, put to death what belongs to your earthly nature: sexual immorality, impurity, lust, evil desire, and greed, which is idolatry. [6] Because of these, God's wrath is coming upon the disobedient,[I] [7] and you once walked in these things when you were living in them. [8] But now, put away all the following: anger, wrath, malice, slander, and filthy language from your mouth. [9] Do not lie to one another, since you have put off the old self with its practices [10] and have put on the new self. You are being renewed in knowledge according to the image of your[J] Creator. [11] In Christ there is not Greek and Jew, circumcision and uncircumcision, barbarian, Scythian, slave and free; but Christ is all and in all.

THE CHRISTIAN LIFE

[12] Therefore, as God's chosen ones, holy and dearly loved, put on compassion, kindness, humility, gentleness, and patience, [13] bearing with one another and forgiving one another if anyone has a grievance against another. Just as the Lord has forgiven you, so you are also to forgive. [14] Above all, put on love, which is the perfect bond of unity. [15] And let the peace of Christ, to which you were also called in one body, rule your hearts. And be thankful. [16] Let the word of Christ dwell richly among you, in all wisdom teaching and admonishing one another through psalms, hymns, and spiritual songs,[K] singing to God with gratitude in your hearts. [17] And whatever you do, in word or in deed, do everything in the name of the Lord Jesus, giving thanks to God the Father through him.

CHRIST IN YOUR HOME

[18] Wives, submit yourselves to your husbands, as is fitting in the Lord. [19] Husbands, love your wives and don't be bitter toward them. [20] Children, obey your parents in everything, for this pleases the Lord. [21] Fathers, do not exasperate your children, so that they won't become discouraged. [22] Slaves, obey your human masters

---

[A] **2:9** Or *nature lives in a human body*   [B] **2:15** Or *them through it*   [C] **2:16** Or *or sabbaths*   [D] **2:17** Or *substance belongs to*   [E] **2:18** Or *disqualify*   [F] **2:18** Lit *fleshly*   [G] **2:23** Lit *value against indulgence of the flesh*   [H] **3:4** Other mss read *our*   [I] **3:6** Other mss omit *upon the disobedient*   [J] **3:10** Lit *his*   [K] **3:16** Or *and songs prompted by the Spirit*

in everything. Don't work only while being watched, as people-pleasers, but work wholeheartedly, fearing the Lord. ²³ Whatever you do, do it from the heart, as something done for the Lord and not for people, ²⁴ knowing that you will receive the reward of an inheritance from the Lord. You serve the Lord Christ. ²⁵ For the wrongdoer will be paid back for whatever wrong he has done, and there is no favoritism.

4 Masters, deal with your slaves justly and fairly, since you know that you too have a Master in heaven.

SPEAKING TO GOD AND OTHERS

² Devote yourselves to prayer; stay alert in it with thanksgiving. ³ At the same time, pray also for us that God may open a door to us for the word, to speak the mystery of Christ, for which I am in chains, ⁴ so that I may make it known as I should. ⁵ Act wisely toward outsiders, making the most of the time. ⁶ Let your speech always be gracious, seasoned with salt, so that you may know how you should answer each person.

FINAL GREETINGS

⁷ Tychicus, our dearly loved brother, faithful minister, and fellow servant in the Lord, will tell you all the news about me. ⁸ I have sent him to you for this very purpose, so that you may know how we are^ and so that he may encourage your hearts. ⁹ He is coming with Onesimus, a faithful and dearly loved brother, who is one of you. They will tell you about everything here.

¹⁰ Aristarchus, my fellow prisoner, sends you greetings, as does Mark, Barnabas's cousin (concerning whom you have received instructions: if he comes to you, welcome him), ¹¹ and so does Jesus who is called Justus. These alone of the circumcised are my coworkers for the kingdom of God, and they have been a comfort to me. ¹² Epaphras, who is one of you, a servant of Christ Jesus, sends you greetings. He is always wrestling for you in his prayers, so that you can stand mature and fully assured^B in everything God wills. ¹³ For I testify about him that he works hard^c for you, for those in Laodicea, and for those in Hierapolis. ¹⁴ Luke, the dearly loved physician, and Demas send you greetings. ¹⁵ Give my greetings to the brothers and sisters in Laodicea, and to Nympha and the church in her home. ¹⁶ After this letter has been read at your gathering, have it read also in the church of the Laodiceans; and see that you also read the letter from Laodicea. ¹⁷ And tell Archippus, "Pay attention to the ministry you have received in the Lord, so that you can accomplish it."

¹⁸ I, Paul, am writing this greeting with my own hand. Remember my chains. Grace be with you.^D

---

^4:8 Other mss read *that he may know how you are*   ^B 4:12 Other mss read *and complete*   ^c 4:13 Other mss read *he has a great zeal*   ^D 4:18 Other mss add *Amen.*

1 THESSALONIANS

GREETING

1 Paul, Silvanus,^ and Timothy:
To the church of the Thessalonians in God the Father and the Lord Jesus Christ.
Grace to you and peace.^B

THANKSGIVING

2 We always thank God for all of you, making mention of you constantly in our prayers. **3** We recall, in the presence of our God and Father, your work produced by faith, your labor motivated by love, and your endurance inspired by hope in our Lord Jesus Christ. **4** For we know, brothers and sisters loved by God, that he has chosen you, **5** because our gospel did not come to you in word only, but also in power, in the Holy Spirit, and with full assurance. You know how we lived among you for your benefit, **6** and you yourselves became imitators of us and of the Lord when, in spite of severe persecution, you welcomed the message with joy from the Holy Spirit. **7** As a result, you became an example to all the believers in Macedonia and Achaia. **8** For the word of the Lord rang out from you, not only in Macedonia and Achaia, but in every place that your faith^C in God has gone out. Therefore, we don't need to say anything, **9** for they themselves report^D what kind of reception we had from you: how you turned to God from idols to serve the living and true God **10** and to wait for his Son from heaven, whom he raised from the dead — Jesus, who rescues us from the coming wrath.

PAUL'S CONDUCT

2 For you yourselves know, brothers and sisters, that our visit with you was not without result. **2** On the contrary, after we had previously suffered and were treated outrageously in Philippi, as you know, we were emboldened by our God to speak the gospel of God to you in spite of great opposition. **3** For our exhortation didn't come from error or impurity or an intent to deceive. **4** Instead, just as we have been approved by God to be entrusted with the gospel, so we speak, not to please people, but rather God, who examines our hearts. **5** For we never used flattering speech, as you know, or had greedy motives — God is our witness — **6** and we didn't seek glory from people, either from you or from others. **7** Although we could have been a burden as Christ's apostles, instead we were gentle^E among you, as a nurse^F nurtures

her own children. **8** We cared so much for you that we were pleased to share with you not only the gospel of God but also our own lives, because you had become dear to us. **9** For you remember our labor and hardship, brothers and sisters. Working night and day so that we would not burden any of you, we preached God's gospel to you. **10** You are witnesses, and so is God, of how devoutly, righteously, and blamelessly we conducted ourselves with you believers. **11** As you know, like a father with his own children, **12** we encouraged, comforted, and implored each one of you to live worthy of God, who calls you into his own kingdom and glory.

RECEPTION AND OPPOSITION TO THE MESSAGE

13 This is why we constantly thank God, because when you received the word of God that you heard from us, you welcomed it not as a human message, but as it truly is, the word of God, which also works effectively in you who believe. **14** For you, brothers and sisters, became imitators of God's churches in Christ Jesus that are in Judea, since you have also suffered the same things from people of your own country, just as they did from the Jews **15** who killed the Lord Jesus and the prophets and persecuted us. They displease God and are hostile to everyone, **16** by keeping us from speaking to the Gentiles so that they may be saved. As a result, they are constantly filling up their sins to the limit, and wrath has overtaken them at last.^G

PAUL'S DESIRE TO SEE THEM

17 But as for us, brothers and sisters, after we were forced to leave you^H for a short time (in person, not in heart), we greatly desired and made every effort to return and see you face to face. **18** So we wanted to come to you — even I, Paul, time and again — but Satan hindered us. **19** For who is our hope or joy or crown of boasting in the presence of our Lord Jesus at his coming? Is it not you? **20** Indeed you are our glory and joy!

ANXIETY IN ATHENS

3 Therefore, when we could no longer stand it, we thought it was better to be left alone in Athens. **2** And we sent Timothy, our brother and God's coworker^I in the gospel of Christ, to strengthen and encourage you concerning your faith, **3** so that no one will be shaken by

---

^1:1 Or *Silas*; Ac 15:22-32; 16:19-40; 17:1-16   ^B1:1 Other mss add *from God our Father and the Lord Jesus Christ*   ^C1:8 Or *in every place news of your faith*   ^D1:9 Lit *report about us*   ^E2:7 Many mss read *infants*   ^F2:7 Or *nursing mother*   ^G2:16 Or *to the end*   ^H2:17 Lit *orphaned from you*   ^I3:2 Other mss read *servant*

these afflictions. For you yourselves know that we are appointed to this. [4] In fact, when we were with you, we told you in advance that we were going to experience affliction, and as you know, it happened. [5] For this reason, when I could no longer stand it, I also sent him to find out about your faith, fearing that the tempter had tempted you and that our labor might be for nothing.

ENCOURAGED BY TIMOTHY

[6] But now Timothy has come to us from you and brought us good news about your faith and love. He reported that you always have good memories of us and that you long to see us, as we also long to see you. [7] Therefore, brothers and sisters, in all our distress and affliction, we were encouraged about you through your faith. [8] For now we live, if you stand firm in the Lord. [9] How can we thank God for you in return for all the joy we experience before our God because of you, [10] as we pray very earnestly night and day to see you face to face and to complete what is lacking in your faith?

PRAYER FOR THE CHURCH

[11] Now may our God and Father himself, and our Lord Jesus, direct our way to you. [12] And may the Lord cause you to increase and overflow with love for one another and for everyone, just as we do for you. [13] May he make your hearts blameless in holiness before our God and Father at the coming of our Lord Jesus with all his saints. Amen.[A]

THE CALL TO SANCTIFICATION

4 Additionally then, brothers and sisters, we ask and encourage you in the Lord Jesus, that as you have received instruction from us on how you should live and please God — as you are doing[B] — do this even more. [2] For you know what commands we gave you through the Lord Jesus.

[3] For this is God's will, your sanctification: that you keep away from sexual immorality, [4] that each of you knows how to control his own body[C] in holiness and honor, [5] not with lustful passions, like the Gentiles, who don't know God. [6] This means one must not transgress against and take advantage of a brother or sister in this manner, because the Lord is an avenger of all these offenses, as we also previously told and warned you. [7] For God has not called us to impurity but to live in holiness. [8] Consequently, anyone who rejects this does not reject man, but God, who gives you his Holy Spirit.

LOVING AND WORKING

[9] About brotherly love: You don't need me to write you because you yourselves are taught by God to love one another. [10] In fact, you are doing this toward all the brothers and sisters in the entire region of Macedonia. But we encourage you, brothers and sisters, to do this even more, [11] to seek to lead a quiet life, to mind your own business,[D] and to work with your own hands, as we commanded you, [12] so that you may behave properly in the presence of outsiders and not be dependent on anyone.[E]

THE COMFORT OF CHRIST'S COMING

[13] We do not want you to be uninformed, brothers and sisters, concerning those who are asleep, so that you will not grieve like the rest, who have no hope. [14] For if we believe that Jesus died and rose again, in the same way, through Jesus, God will bring with him those who have fallen asleep. [15] For we say this to you by a word from the Lord: We who are still alive at the Lord's coming will certainly not precede those who have fallen asleep. [16] For the Lord himself will descend from heaven with a shout,[F] with the archangel's voice, and with the trumpet of God, and the dead in Christ will rise first. [17] Then we who are still alive, who are left, will be caught up together with them in the clouds to meet the Lord in the air, and so we will always be with the Lord. [18] Therefore encourage[G] one another with these words.

THE DAY OF THE LORD

5 About the times and the seasons: Brothers and sisters, you do not need anything to be written to you. [2] For you yourselves know very well that the day of the Lord will come just like a thief in the night. [3] When they say, "Peace and security," then sudden destruction will come upon them, like labor pains on a pregnant woman, and they will not escape. [4] But you, brothers and sisters, are not in the dark, for this day to surprise you like a thief. [5] For you are all children of light and children of the day. We do not belong to the night or to darkness. [6] So then, let us not sleep, like the rest, but let us stay awake and be self-controlled. [7] For those who sleep, sleep at night, and those who get drunk, get drunk at night. [8] But since we belong to the day, let us be self-controlled and put on the armor of faith and love, and a helmet of the hope of salvation. [9] For God did not appoint us to wrath, but to obtain salvation through our Lord Jesus Christ, [10] who died for us, so that whether we are awake or asleep,

---

[A]3:13 Other mss omit *Amen.*   [B]4:1 Lit *walking*   [C]4:4 Or *to acquire his own wife*; lit *to possess his own vessel*   [D]4:11 Lit *to practice one's own things*   [E]4:12 Or *not need anything*, or *not be in need*   [F]4:16 Or *command*   [G]4:18 Or *comfort*

we may live together with him. [11] Therefore encourage one another and build each other up as you are already doing.

EXHORTATIONS AND BLESSINGS

[12] Now we ask you, brothers and sisters, to give recognition to those who labor among you and lead you[A] in the Lord and admonish you, [13] and to regard them very highly in love because of their work. Be at peace among yourselves. [14] And we exhort you, brothers and sisters: warn those who are idle,[B] comfort the discouraged, help the weak, be patient with everyone. [15] See to it that no one repays evil for evil to anyone, but always pursue what is good for one another and for all. [16] Rejoice always, [17] pray constantly, [18] give thanks in everything; for this is God's will for you in Christ Jesus. [19] Don't stifle the Spirit. [20] Don't despise prophecies, [21] but test all things. Hold on to what is good. [22] Stay away from every kind of evil.

[23] Now may the God of peace himself sanctify you completely. And may your whole spirit, soul, and body be kept sound and blameless at the coming of our Lord Jesus Christ. [24] He who calls you is faithful; he will do it. [25] Brothers and sisters, pray for us also. [26] Greet all the brothers and sisters with a holy kiss. [27] I charge you by the Lord that this letter be read to all the brothers and sisters. [28] The grace of our Lord Jesus Christ be with you.

A[5:12] Or *care for you*   B[5:14] Or *who are disorderly,* or *who are undisciplined*

2 THESSALONIANS

1 Paul, Silvanus,^ and Timothy:
To the church of the Thessalonians in God our Father and the Lord Jesus Christ.

[2] Grace to you and peace from God our Father and the Lord Jesus Christ.

GOD'S JUDGMENT AND GLORY

[3] We ought to thank God always for you, brothers and sisters, and rightly so, since your faith is flourishing and the love each one of you has for one another is increasing. [4] Therefore, we ourselves boast about you among God's churches — about your perseverance and faith in all the persecutions and afflictions that you are enduring. [5] It is clear evidence of God's righteous judgment that you will be counted worthy of God's kingdom, for which you also are suffering, [6] since it is just for God to repay with affliction those who afflict you [7] and to give relief to you who are afflicted, along with us. This will take place at the revelation of the Lord Jesus from heaven with his powerful angels, [8] when he takes vengeance with flaming fire on those who don't know God and on those who don't obey the gospel of our Lord Jesus. [9] They will pay the penalty of eternal destruction from the Lord's presence and from his glorious strength [10] on that day when he comes to be glorified by his saints and to be marveled at by all those who have believed, because our testimony among you was believed. [11] In view of this, we always pray for you that our God will make you worthy of his calling, and by his power fulfill your every desire to do good^B and your work produced by faith, [12] so that the name of our Lord Jesus will be glorified by you, and you by him, according to the grace of our God and the Lord Jesus Christ.

THE MAN OF LAWLESSNESS

2 Now concerning the coming of our Lord Jesus Christ and our being gathered to him: We ask you, brothers and sisters, [2] not to be easily upset or troubled, either by a prophecy^C or by a message or by a letter supposedly from us, alleging that the day of the Lord^D has come. [3] Don't let anyone deceive you in any way. For that day will not come unless the apostasy^E comes first and the man of lawlessness^F is revealed, the man doomed to destruction. [4] He opposes and exalts himself above every so-called

god or object of worship, so that he sits^G in God's temple, proclaiming that he himself is God. [5] Don't you remember that when I was still with you I used to tell you about this? [6] And you know what currently restrains him, so that he will be revealed in his time. [7] For the mystery of lawlessness is already at work, but the one now restraining will do so until he is out of the way, [8] and then the lawless one will be revealed. The Lord Jesus will destroy him with the breath of his mouth and will bring him to nothing at the appearance of his coming. [9] The coming of the lawless one is based on Satan's working, with all kinds of false miracles, signs, and wonders, [10] and with every wicked deception among those who are perishing. They perish because they did not accept the love of the truth and so be saved. [11] For this reason God sends them a strong delusion so that they will believe the lie, [12] so that all will be condemned — those who did not believe the truth but delighted in unrighteousness.

STAND FIRM

[13] But we ought to thank God always for you, brothers and sisters loved by the Lord, because from the beginning^H God has chosen you for salvation through sanctification by the Spirit and through belief in the truth. [14] He called you to this through our gospel, so that you might obtain the glory of our Lord Jesus Christ. [15] So then, brothers and sisters, stand firm and hold to the traditions you were taught, whether by what we said or what we wrote.

[16] May our Lord Jesus Christ himself and God our Father, who has loved us and given us eternal encouragement and good hope by grace, [17] encourage your hearts and strengthen you in every good work and word.

PRAY FOR US

3 In addition, brothers and sisters, pray for us that the word of the Lord may spread rapidly and be honored, just as it was with you, [2] and that we may be delivered from wicked and evil people, for not all have faith.^I [3] But the Lord is faithful; he will strengthen and guard you from the evil one. [4] We have confidence in the Lord about you, that you are doing and will continue to do what we command. [5] May the Lord direct your hearts to God's love and Christ's endurance.

---

^1:1 Or *Silas*; Ac 15:22-32; 16:19-40; 17:1-16   ^1:11 Or *power bring to fruition your desire to do good*   ^2:2 Or *spiritual utterance*   ^2:2 Other mss read *Christ*   ^2:3 Or *rebellion*   ^2:3 Other mss read *man of sin*   ^2:4 Other mss add *as God*   ^2:13 Other mss read *because as a firstfruit*   ^3:2 Or *for the faith is not in everyone*

WARNING AGAINST IRRESPONSIBLE BEHAVIOR

6 Now we command you, brothers and sisters, in the name of our Lord Jesus Christ, to keep away from every brother or sister who is idle and does not live according to the tradition received from us. **7** For you yourselves know how you should imitate us: We were not idle among you; **8** we did not eat anyone's food free of charge; instead, we labored and toiled, working night and day, so that we would not be a burden to any of you. **9** It is not that we don't have the right to support, but we did it to make ourselves an example to you so that you would imitate us. **10** In fact, when we were with you, this is what we commanded you: "If anyone isn't willing to work, he should not eat." **11** For we hear that there are some among you who are idle. They are not busy but busybodies. **12** Now we command and exhort such people by the Lord Jesus Christ to work quietly and provide for themselves.^ **13** But as for you, brothers and sisters, do not grow weary in doing good.

14 If anyone does not obey our instruction in this letter, take note of that person; don't associate with him, so that he may be ashamed. **15** Yet don't consider him as an enemy, but warn him as a brother.

FINAL GREETINGS

16 May the Lord of peace himself give you peace always in every way. The Lord be with all of you. **17** I, Paul, am writing this greeting with my own hand, which is an authenticating mark in every letter; this is how I write. **18** The grace of our Lord Jesus Christ be with you all.

---

^**3:12** Lit *they may eat their own bread*

1 TIMOTHY

GREETING

1 Paul, an apostle of Christ Jesus by the command of God our Savior and of Christ Jesus our hope:

[2] To Timothy, my true son in the faith.

Grace, mercy, and peace from God the[A] Father and Christ Jesus our Lord.

FALSE DOCTRINE AND MISUSE OF THE LAW

[3] As I urged you when I went to Macedonia, remain in Ephesus so that you may instruct certain people not to teach false doctrine [4] or to pay attention to myths and endless genealogies. These promote empty speculations rather than God's plan, which operates by faith. [5] Now the goal of our instruction is love that comes from a pure heart, a good conscience, and a sincere faith. [6] Some have departed from these and turned aside to fruitless discussion. [7] They want to be teachers of the law, although they don't understand what they are saying or what they are insisting on. [8] But we know that the law is good, provided one uses it legitimately. [9] We know that the law is not meant for a righteous person, but for the lawless and rebellious, for the ungodly and sinful, for the unholy and irreverent, for those who kill their fathers and mothers, for murderers, [10] for the sexually immoral and homosexuals, for slave traders,[B] liars, perjurers, and for whatever else is contrary to the sound teaching [11] that conforms to the gospel concerning the glory of the blessed God, which was entrusted to me.

PAUL'S TESTIMONY

[12] I give thanks to Christ Jesus our Lord who has strengthened me, because he considered me faithful, appointing me to the ministry — [13] even though I was formerly a blasphemer, a persecutor, and an arrogant man. But I received mercy because I acted out of ignorance in unbelief, [14] and the grace of our Lord overflowed, along with the faith and love that are in Christ Jesus. [15] This saying is trustworthy and deserving of full acceptance: "Christ Jesus came into the world to save sinners" — and I am the worst of them. [16] But I received mercy for this reason, so that in me, the worst of them, Christ Jesus might demonstrate his extraordinary patience as an example to those who would believe in him for eternal life. [17] Now to the King eternal, immortal, invisible, the only[C] God, be honor and glory forever and ever. Amen.

ENGAGE IN BATTLE

[18] Timothy, my son, I am giving you this instruction in keeping with the prophecies previously made about you, so that by recalling them you may fight the good fight, [19] having faith and a good conscience. Some have rejected these and have shipwrecked their faith. [20] Among them are Hymenaeus and Alexander, whom I have delivered to Satan, so that they may be taught not to blaspheme.

INSTRUCTIONS ON PRAYER

2 First of all, then, I urge that petitions, prayers, intercessions, and thanksgivings be made for everyone, [2] for kings and all those who are in authority, so that we may lead a tranquil and quiet life in all godliness and dignity. [3] This is good, and it pleases God our Savior, [4] who wants everyone to be saved and to come to the knowledge of the truth.

[5] For there is one God and one mediator between God and humanity, the man Christ Jesus, [6] who gave himself as a ransom for all, a testimony at the proper time. [7] For this I was appointed a herald, an apostle (I am telling the truth;[D] I am not lying), and a teacher of the Gentiles in faith and truth.

INSTRUCTIONS TO MEN AND WOMEN

[8] Therefore, I want the men in every place to pray, lifting up holy hands without anger or argument. [9] Also, the women are to dress themselves in modest clothing, with decency and good sense, not with elaborate hairstyles, gold, pearls, or expensive apparel, [10] but with good works, as is proper for women who profess to worship God. [11] A woman is to learn quietly with full submission. [12] I do not allow a woman to teach or to have authority over a man; instead, she is to remain quiet. [13] For Adam was formed first, then Eve. [14] And Adam was not deceived, but the woman was deceived and transgressed. [15] But she will be saved through childbearing, if they continue in faith, love, and holiness, with good sense.

QUALIFICATIONS FOR OVERSEERS AND DEACONS

3 This saying is trustworthy: "If anyone aspires to be an overseer,[E] he desires a noble work." [2] An overseer, therefore, must be above reproach, the husband of one wife, self-controlled, sensible, respectable, hospitable, able to teach, [3] not an excessive drinker, not a bully but gentle, not

---

^1:2 Other mss read *our* ^1:10 Or *slave traders* ^1:17 Other mss add *wise* ^2:7 Other mss add *in Christ* ^3:1 Or *bishop, pastor*

quarrelsome, not greedy. **4** He must manage his own household competently and have his children under control with all dignity. **5** (If anyone does not know how to manage his own household, how will he take care of God's church?) **6** He must not be a new convert, or he might become conceited and incur the same condemnation as the devil. **7** Furthermore, he must have a good reputation among outsiders, so that he does not fall into disgrace and the devil's trap.

8 Deacons, likewise, should be worthy of respect, not hypocritical, not drinking a lot of wine, not greedy for money, **9** holding the mystery of the faith with a clear conscience. **10** They must also be tested first; if they prove blameless, then they can serve as deacons. **11** Wives,[A] too, must be worthy of respect, not slanderers, self-controlled, faithful in everything. **12** Deacons are to be husbands of one wife, managing their children and their own households competently. **13** For those who have served well as deacons acquire a good standing for themselves and great boldness in the faith that is in Christ Jesus.

THE MYSTERY OF GODLINESS

14 I write these things to you, hoping to come to you soon. **15** But if I should be delayed, I have written so that you will know how people ought to conduct themselves in God's household, which is the church of the living God, the pillar and foundation of the truth. **16** And most certainly, the mystery of godliness is great:

He[B] was manifested in the flesh,
vindicated in the Spirit,
seen by angels,
preached among the nations,
believed on in the world,
taken up in glory.

DEMONIC INFLUENCE

4 Now the Spirit explicitly says that in later times some will depart from the faith, paying attention to deceitful spirits and the teachings of demons, **2** through the hypocrisy of liars whose consciences are seared. **3** They forbid marriage and demand abstinence from foods that God created to be received with gratitude by those who believe and know the truth. **4** For everything created by God is good, and nothing is to be rejected if it is received with thanksgiving, **5** since it is sanctified by the word of God and by prayer.

A GOOD SERVANT OF JESUS CHRIST

6 If you point these things out to the brothers and sisters, you will be a good servant of Christ Jesus, nourished by the words of the faith and the good teaching that you have followed. **7** But have nothing to do with pointless and silly myths. Rather, train yourself in godliness. **8** For the training of the body has limited benefit, but godliness is beneficial in every way, since it holds promise for the present life and also for the life to come. **9** This saying is trustworthy and deserves full acceptance. **10** For this reason we labor and strive,[C] because we have put our hope in the living God, who is the Savior of all people, especially of those who believe.

INSTRUCTIONS FOR MINISTRY

11 Command and teach these things. **12** Don't let anyone despise your youth, but set an example for the believers in speech, in conduct, in love,[D] in faith, and in purity. **13** Until I come, give your attention to public reading, exhortation, and teaching. **14** Don't neglect the gift that is in you; it was given to you through prophecy, with the laying on of hands by the council of elders. **15** Practice these things; be committed to them, so that your progress may be evident to all. **16** Pay close attention to your life and your teaching; persevere in these things, for in doing this you will save both yourself and your hearers.

5 Don't rebuke an older man, but exhort him as a father, younger men as brothers, **2** older women as mothers, and the younger women as sisters with all purity.

THE SUPPORT OF WIDOWS

3 Support[E] widows who are genuinely in need. **4** But if any widow has children or grandchildren, let them learn to practice godliness toward their own family first and to repay their parents, for this pleases God. **5** The widow who is truly in need and left all alone has put her hope in God and continues night and day in her petitions and prayers; **6** however, she who is self-indulgent is dead even while she lives. **7** Command this also, so that they will be above reproach. **8** But if anyone does not provide for his own family, especially for his own household, he has denied the faith and is worse than an unbeliever.

9 No widow is to be enrolled on the list for support unless she is at least sixty years old, has been the wife of one husband, **10** and is well known for good works — that is, if she has brought up children, shown hospitality, washed the saints' feet, helped the afflicted, and devoted herself to every good work. **11** But refuse to enroll younger widows, for when they are drawn away from Christ by desire, they want to marry **12** and

^3:11 Or *The women*　^3:16 Other mss read *God*　^4:10 Other mss read *and suffer reproach*　^4:12 Other mss add *in spirit,*　^5:3 Lit *Honor*

will therefore receive condemnation because they have renounced their original pledge. [13] At the same time, they also learn to be idle, going from house to house; they are not only idle, but are also gossips and busybodies, saying things they shouldn't say. [14] Therefore, I want younger women to marry, have children, manage their households, and give the adversary no opportunity to accuse us. [15] For some have already turned away to follow Satan. [16] If any[A] believing woman has widows in her family, let her help them. Let the church not be burdened, so that it can help widows in genuine need.

HONORING THE ELDERS

[17] The elders who are good leaders are to be considered worthy of double honor,[B] especially those who work hard at preaching and teaching. [18] For the Scripture says: **Do not muzzle an ox while it is treading out the grain,**[C] and the worker is worthy of his wages.

[19] Don't accept an accusation against an elder unless it is supported by two or three witnesses. [20] Publicly rebuke those who sin, so that the rest will be afraid. [21] I solemnly charge you before God and Christ Jesus and the elect angels to observe these things without prejudice, doing nothing out of favoritism. [22] Don't be too quick to appoint[D] anyone as an elder, and don't share in the sins of others. Keep yourself pure. [23] Don't continue drinking only water, but use a little wine because of your stomach and your frequent illnesses. [24] Some people's sins are obvious, preceding them to judgment, but the sins of others surface[E] later. [25] Likewise, good works are obvious, and those that are not obvious cannot remain hidden.

HONORING MASTERS

6 All who are under the yoke as slaves should regard their own masters[F] as worthy of all respect, so that God's name and his teaching will not be blasphemed. [2] Let those who have believing masters not be disrespectful to them because they are brothers, but serve them even better, since those who benefit from their service are believers and dearly loved.[G]

FALSE DOCTRINE AND HUMAN GREED

Teach and encourage these things. [3] If anyone teaches false doctrine and does not agree with the sound teaching of our Lord Jesus Christ and with the teaching that promotes godliness, [4] he is conceited and understands nothing, but has an unhealthy interest in disputes and arguments over words. From these come envy, quarreling, slander, evil suspicions, [5] and constant disagreement among people whose minds are depraved and deprived of the truth, who imagine that godliness is a way to material gain."[6] But godliness with contentment is great gain. [7] For we brought nothing into the world, and[i] we can take nothing out. [8] If we have food and clothing,[J] we will be content with these. [9] But those who want to be rich fall into temptation, a trap, and many foolish and harmful desires, which plunge people into ruin and destruction. [10] For the love of money is a root[K] of all kinds of evil, and by craving it, some have wandered away from the faith and pierced themselves with many griefs.

FIGHT THE GOOD FIGHT

[11] But you, man of God, flee from these things, and pursue righteousness, godliness, faith, love, endurance, and gentleness. [12] Fight the good fight of the faith. Take hold of eternal life to which you were called and about which you have made a good confession in the presence of many witnesses. [13] In the presence of God, who gives life to all, and of Christ Jesus, who gave a good confession before Pontius Pilate, I charge you [14] to keep this command without fault or failure until the appearing of our Lord Jesus Christ. [15] God will bring this about in his own time. He is the blessed and only Sovereign, the King of kings, and the Lord of lords, [16] who alone is immortal and who lives in unapproachable light, whom no one has seen or can see, to him be honor and eternal power. Amen.

INSTRUCTIONS TO THE RICH

[17] Instruct those who are rich in the present age not to be arrogant or to set their hope on the uncertainty of wealth, but on God,[L] who richly provides us with all things to enjoy. [18] Instruct them to do what is good, to be rich in good works, to be generous and willing to share, [19] storing up treasure for themselves as a good foundation for the coming age, so that they may take hold of what is truly life.

GUARD THE HERITAGE

[20] Timothy, guard what has been entrusted to you, avoiding irreverent and empty speech and contradictions from what is falsely called knowledge. [21] By professing it, some people have departed from the faith.

Grace be with you all.

A 5:16 Other mss add *believing man or*   B 5:17 Or *of respect and remuneration*   C 5:18 Dt 25:4   D 5:22 Lit *to lay hands on*
E 5:24 Lit *follow*   F 6:1 Or *owners*   G 6:2 Or *because, as believers who are dearly loved, they are devoted to others' welfare*
H 6:5 Other mss add *From such people withdraw yourself.*   I 6:7 Other mss add *it is clear that*   J 6:8 Or *food and shelter*
K 6:10 Or *is the root*   L 6:17 Other mss read *on the living God*

2 TIMOTHY

1 Paul, an apostle of Christ Jesus by God's will, for the sake of the promise of life in Christ Jesus:

² To Timothy, my dearly loved son.

Grace, mercy, and peace from God the Father and Christ Jesus our Lord.

THANKSGIVING

³ I thank God, whom I serve with a clear conscience as my ancestors did, when I constantly remember you in my prayers night and day. ⁴ Remembering your tears, I long to see you so that I may be filled with joy. ⁵ I recall your sincere faith that first lived in your grandmother Lois and in your mother Eunice and now, I am convinced, is in you also.

⁶ Therefore, I remind you to rekindle the gift of God that is in you through the laying on of my hands. ⁷ For God has not given us a spirit of fear, but one of power,^ love, and sound judgment.

NOT ASHAMED OF THE GOSPEL

⁸ So don't be ashamed of the testimony about our Lord, or of me his prisoner. Instead, share in suffering for the gospel, relying on the power of God. ⁹ He has saved us and called us with a holy calling, not according to our works, but according to his own purpose and grace, which was given to us in Christ Jesus before time began. ¹⁰ This has now been made evident through the appearing of our Savior Christ Jesus, who has abolished death and has brought life and immortality to light through the gospel. ¹¹ For this gospel I was appointed a herald, apostle, and teacher,ᵇ ¹² and that is why I suffer these things. But I am not ashamed, because I know whom I have believed and am persuaded that he is able to guard what has been entrusted to meᶜ until that day.

BE LOYAL TO THE FAITH

¹³ Hold on to the pattern of sound teaching that you have heard from me, in the faith and love that are in Christ Jesus. ¹⁴ Guard the good deposit through the Holy Spirit who lives in us. ¹⁵ You know that all those in the province of Asia have deserted me, including Phygelus and Hermogenes. ¹⁶ May the Lord grant mercy to the household of Onesiphorus, because he often refreshed me and was not ashamed of my chains. ¹⁷ On the contrary, when he was in Rome, he diligently searched for me and found me. ¹⁸ May the Lord grant that he obtain mercy from him on that day. You know very well how much he ministered at Ephesus.

BE STRONG IN GRACE

2 You, therefore, my son, be strong in the grace that is in Christ Jesus. ² What you have heard from me in the presence of many witnesses, commit to faithful menᴰ who will be able to teach others also.

³ Share in suffering as a good soldier of Christ Jesus. ⁴ No one serving as a soldier gets entangled in the concerns of civilian life; he seeks to please the commanding officer. ⁵ Also, if anyone competes as an athlete, he is not crowned unless he competes according to the rules. ⁶ The hardworking farmer ought to be the first to get a share of the crops. ⁷ Consider what I say, for the Lord will give you understanding in everything.

⁸ Remember Jesus Christ, risen from the dead and descended from David, according to my gospel, ⁹ for which I suffer to the point of being bound like a criminal. But the word of God is not bound. ¹⁰ This is why I endure all things for the elect: so that they also may obtain salvation, which is in Christ Jesus, with eternal glory. ¹¹ This saying is trustworthy:

For if we died with him,
we will also live with him;
¹² if we endure, we will also reign with him;
if we deny him, he will also deny us;
¹³ if we are faithless, he remains faithful,
for he cannot deny himself.

AN APPROVED WORKER

¹⁴ Remind them of these things, and charge them before Godᴱ not to fight about words. This is useless and leads to the ruin of those who listen. ¹⁵ Be diligent to present yourself to God as one approved, a worker who doesn't need to be ashamed, correctly teaching the word of truth. ¹⁶ Avoid irreverent and empty speech, since those who engage in it will produce even more godlessness, ¹⁷ and their teaching will spread like gangrene. Hymenaeus and Philetus are among them. ¹⁸ They have departed from the truth, saying that the resurrection has already taken place, and are ruining the faith of some. ¹⁹ Nevertheless, God's solid foundation

---

^1:7 Or *For the Spirit God gave us does not make us fearful, but gives us power* ᵇ1:11 Other mss add *of the Gentiles* ᶜ1:12 Or *guard what I have entrusted to him*, or *guard my deposit* ᴰ2:2 Or *faithful people* ᴱ2:14 Other mss read *before the Lord*

stands firm, bearing this inscription: **The Lord knows those who are his,**[A] and let everyone who calls on the name of[B] the Lord turn away from wickedness.

²⁰ Now in a large house there are not only gold and silver vessels, but also those of wood and clay; some for honorable[C] use and some for dishonorable.[D] ²¹ So if anyone purifies himself from anything dishonorable,[E] he will be a special[F] instrument, set apart, useful to the Master, prepared for every good work.

²² Flee from youthful passions, and pursue righteousness, faith, love, and peace, along with those who call on the Lord from a pure heart. ²³ But reject foolish and ignorant disputes, because you know that they breed quarrels. ²⁴ The Lord's servant must not quarrel, but must be gentle to everyone, able to teach,[G] and patient, ²⁵ instructing his opponents with gentleness. Perhaps God will grant them repentance leading them to the knowledge of the truth. ²⁶ Then they may come to their senses and escape the trap of the devil, who has taken them captive to do his will.

DIFFICULT TIMES AHEAD

3 But know this: Hard times will come in the last days. ² For people will be lovers of self, lovers of money, boastful, proud, demeaning, disobedient to parents, ungrateful, unholy, ³ unloving, irreconcilable, slanderers, without self-control, brutal, without love for what is good, ⁴ traitors, reckless, conceited, lovers of pleasure rather than lovers of God, ⁵ holding to the form of godliness but denying its power. Avoid these people.

⁶ For among them are those who worm their way into households and deceive gullible women overwhelmed by sins and led astray by a variety of passions, ⁷ always learning and never able to come to a knowledge of the truth. ⁸ Just as Jannes and Jambres resisted Moses, so these also resist the truth. They are men who are corrupt in mind and worthless in regard to the faith. ⁹ But they will not make further progress, for their foolishness will be clear to all, as was the foolishness of Jannes and Jambres.

STRUGGLES IN THE CHRISTIAN LIFE

¹⁰ But you have followed my teaching, conduct, purpose, faith, patience, love, and endurance, ¹¹ along with the persecutions and sufferings that came to me in Antioch, Iconium, and Lystra. What persecutions I endured — and yet the Lord rescued me from them all. ¹² In fact, all who want to live a godly life in Christ Jesus will be persecuted. ¹³ Evil people and impostors will become worse, deceiving and being deceived. ¹⁴ But as for you, continue in what you have learned and firmly believed. You know those who taught you, ¹⁵ and you know that from infancy you have known the sacred Scriptures, which are able to give you wisdom for salvation through faith in Christ Jesus. ¹⁶ All Scripture is inspired by God[H] and is profitable for teaching, for rebuking, for correcting, for training in righteousness, ¹⁷ so that the man of God may be complete, equipped for every good work.

FULFILL YOUR MINISTRY

4 I solemnly charge you before God and Christ Jesus, who is going to judge the living and the dead, and because of his appearing and his kingdom: ² Preach the word; be ready in season and out of season; rebuke, correct, and encourage with great patience and teaching. ³ For the time will come when people will not tolerate sound doctrine, but according to their own desires, will multiply teachers for themselves because they have an itch to hear what they want to hear. ⁴ They will turn away from hearing the truth and will turn aside to myths. ⁵ But as for you, exercise self-control in everything, endure hardship, do the work of an evangelist, fulfill your ministry.

⁶ For I am already being poured out as a drink offering, and the time for my departure is close. ⁷ I have fought the good fight, I have finished the race, I have kept the faith. ⁸ There is reserved for me the crown of righteousness, which the Lord, the righteous Judge, will give me on that day, and not only to me, but to all those who have loved his appearing.[I]

FINAL INSTRUCTIONS

⁹ Make every effort to come to me soon, ¹⁰ because Demas has deserted me, since he loved this present world, and has gone to Thessalonica. Crescens has gone to Galatia, Titus to Dalmatia. ¹¹ Only Luke is with me. Bring Mark with you, for he is useful to me in the ministry. ¹² I have sent Tychicus to Ephesus. ¹³ When you come, bring the cloak I left in Troas with Carpus, as well as the scrolls, especially the parchments. ¹⁴ Alexander the coppersmith did great harm to me. The Lord will repay him according to his works. ¹⁵ Watch out for him yourself because he strongly opposed our words.

[A] 2:19 Nm 16:5　[B] 2:19 Lit *everyone who names the name of*　[C] 2:20 Or *special*　[D] 2:20 Or *ordinary*　[E] 2:21 Lit *from these*　[F] 2:21 Or *an honorable*　[G] 2:24 Or *everyone, skillful in teaching*　[H] 3:16 Lit *breathed out by God*　[I] 4:8 Or *have longed for his appearing*

[16] At my first defense, no one stood by me, but everyone deserted me. May it not be counted against them. [17] But the Lord stood with me and strengthened me, so that I might fully preach the word and all the Gentiles might hear it. So I was rescued from the lion's mouth. [18] The Lord will rescue me from every evil work and will bring me safely into his heavenly kingdom. To him be the glory forever and ever! Amen.

BENEDICTION

[19] Greet Prisca and Aquila, and the household of Onesiphorus. [20] Erastus has remained at Corinth; I left Trophimus sick at Miletus. [21] Make every effort to come before winter. Eubulus greets you, as do Pudens, Linus, Claudia, and all the brothers and sisters.

[22] The Lord be with your spirit. Grace be with you all.

TITUS

1 Paul, a servant of God and an apostle of Jesus Christ, for^A the faith of God's elect and their knowledge of the truth that leads^B to godliness, ² in the hope of eternal life that God, who cannot lie, promised before time began. ³ In his own time he has revealed his word in the preaching with which I was entrusted by the command of God our Savior:

⁴ To Titus, my true son in our common faith.

Grace and peace from God the Father and Christ Jesus our Savior.

TITUS'S MINISTRY IN CRETE

⁵ The reason I left you in Crete was to set right what was left undone and, as I directed you, to appoint elders in every town. ⁶ An elder must be blameless: the husband of one wife, with faithful^C children who are not accused of wildness or rebellion. ⁷ As an overseer of God's household, he must be blameless: not arrogant, not hot-tempered, not an excessive drinker, not a bully, not greedy for money, ⁸ but hospitable, loving what is good, sensible, righteous, holy, self-controlled, ⁹ holding to the faithful message as taught, so that he will be able both to encourage with sound teaching and to refute those who contradict it.

¹⁰ For there are many rebellious people, full of empty talk and deception, especially those from the circumcision party. ¹¹ It is necessary to silence them; they are ruining entire households by teaching what they shouldn't in order to get money dishonestly. ¹² One of their very own prophets said, "Cretans are always liars, evil beasts, lazy gluttons." ¹³ This testimony is true. For this reason, rebuke them sharply, so that they may be sound in the faith ¹⁴ and may not pay attention to Jewish myths and the commands of people who reject the truth.

¹⁵ To the pure, everything is pure, but to those who are defiled and unbelieving nothing is pure; in fact, both their mind and conscience are defiled. ¹⁶ They claim to know God, but they deny him by their works. They are detestable, disobedient, and unfit for any good work.

SOUND TEACHING AND CHRISTIAN LIVING

2 But you are to proclaim things consistent with sound teaching. ² Older men are to be self-controlled, worthy of respect, sensible, and sound in faith, love, and endurance. ³ In the same way, older women are to be reverent in behavior, not slanderers, not slaves to excessive drinking. They are to teach what is good, ⁴ so that they may encourage the young women to love their husbands and to love their children, ⁵ to be self-controlled, pure, workers at home, kind, and in submission to their husbands, so that God's word will not be slandered.

⁶ In the same way, encourage the young men to be self-controlled⁷ in everything. Make yourself an example of good works with integrity and dignity^D in your teaching. ⁸ Your message is to be sound beyond reproach, so that any opponent will be ashamed, because he doesn't have anything bad to say about us.

⁹ Slaves are to submit to their masters in everything, and to be well-pleasing, not talking back ¹⁰ or stealing, but demonstrating utter faithfulness, so that they may adorn the teaching of God our Savior in everything.

¹¹ For the grace of God has appeared, bringing salvation^E for all people, ¹² instructing us to deny godlessness and worldly lusts and to live in a sensible, righteous, and godly way in the present age, ¹³ while we wait for the blessed hope, the appearing of the glory of our great God and Savior, Jesus Christ. ¹⁴ He gave himself for us to redeem us from all lawlessness and to cleanse for himself a people for his own possession, eager to do good works.

¹⁵ Proclaim these things; encourage and rebuke with all authority. Let no one disregard^F you.

CHRISTIAN LIVING AMONG OUTSIDERS

3 Remind them to submit to rulers and authorities, to obey, to be ready for every good work, ² to slander no one, to avoid fighting, and to be kind, always showing gentleness to all people. ³ For we too were once foolish, disobedient, deceived, enslaved by various passions and pleasures, living in malice and envy, hateful, detesting one another.

⁴ But when the kindness of God our Savior and his love for mankind appeared, ⁵ he saved us — not by works of righteousness that we had done, but according to his mercy — through the washing of regeneration and renewal by the Holy Spirit. ⁶ He poured out his Spirit on us abundantly through Jesus Christ our Savior ⁷ so that, having been justified by his grace, we may become heirs with the hope

---

^A 1:1 Or *according to* ^B 1:1 Or *corresponds* ^C 1:6 Or *believing* ^D 2:7 Other mss add *and incorruptibility* ^E 2:11 Or *appeared with saving power* ^F 2:15 Or *despise*

of eternal life. [8] This saying is trustworthy. I want you to insist on these things, so that those who have believed God might be careful to devote themselves to good works. These are good and profitable for everyone. [9] But avoid foolish debates, genealogies, quarrels, and disputes about the law, because they are unprofitable and worthless. [10] Reject a divisive person after a first and second warning. [11] For you know that such a person has gone astray and is sinning; he is self-condemned.

FINAL INSTRUCTIONS AND CLOSING

[12] When I send Artemas or Tychicus to you, make every effort to come to me in Nicopolis, because I have decided to spend the winter there. [13] Diligently help Zenas the lawyer and Apollos on their journey, so that they will lack nothing.

[14] Let our people learn to devote themselves to good works for pressing needs, so that they will not be unfruitful. [15] All those who are with me send you greetings. Greet those who love us in the faith. Grace be with all of you.

PHILEMON

P aul, a prisoner of Christ Jesus, and Timothy our brother:

To Philemon our dear friend and coworker,
[2] to Apphia our sister,[A] to Archippus our fellow soldier, and to the church that meets in
your home.

[3] Grace to you and peace from God our Father
and the Lord Jesus Christ.

PHILEMON'S LOVE AND FAITH

[4] I always thank my God when I mention you
in my prayers, [5] because I hear of your love for
all the saints and the faith that you have in the
Lord Jesus. [6] I pray that your participation in
the faith may become effective through knowing every good thing that is in us[B] for the glory
of Christ. [7] For I have great joy and encouragement from your love, because the hearts of
the saints have been refreshed through you,
brother.

AN APPEAL FOR ONESIMUS

[8] For this reason, although I have great boldness in Christ to command you to do what is
right, [9] I appeal to you, instead, on the basis of
love. I, Paul, as an elderly man[C] and now also as
a prisoner of Christ Jesus, [10] appeal to you for
my son, Onesimus.[D] I became his father while
I was in chains. [11] Once he was useless to you,
but now he is useful both to you and to me. [12] I
am sending him back to you — I am sending
my very own heart.[E,F] [13] I wanted to keep him
with me, so that in my imprisonment for the
gospel he might serve me in your place. [14] But
I didn't want to do anything without your consent, so that your good deed might not be out
of obligation, but of your own free will. [15] For
perhaps this is why he was separated from you
for a brief time, so that you might get him back
permanently, [16] no longer as a slave, but more
than a slave — as a dearly loved brother. He is
especially so to me, but how much more to you,
both in the flesh and in the Lord.

[17] So if you consider me a partner, welcome
him as you would me. [18] And if he has wronged
you in any way, or owes you anything, charge
that to my account. [19] I, Paul, write this with
my own hand: I will repay it — not to mention to you that you owe me even your very
self. [20] Yes, brother, may I benefit from you in
the Lord; refresh my heart in Christ. [21] Since I
am confident of your obedience, I am writing
to you, knowing that you will do even more
than I say. [22] Meanwhile, also prepare a guest
room for me, since I hope that through your
prayers I will be restored to you.

FINAL GREETINGS

[23] Epaphras, my fellow prisoner in Christ Jesus,
sends you greetings, and so do [24] Mark, Aristarchus, Demas, and Luke, my coworkers.

[25] The grace of the Lord[G] Jesus Christ be with
your spirit.

[A]2 Other mss read *our beloved*   [B]6 Other mss read *in you*   [C]9 Or *an ambassador*   [D]10 In Gk, *Onesimus* means "useful"
[E]12 Other mss read *him back. Receive him, my own heart.*   [F]12 Lit *you — that is, my own heart*   [G]25 Other mss read
our Lord

HEBREWS

THE NATURE OF THE SON

1 Long ago God spoke to the fathers by the prophets at different times and in different ways. [2] In these last days, he has spoken to us by his Son. God has appointed him heir of all things and made the universe[A] through him. [3] The Son is the radiance[B] of God's glory and the exact expression[C] of his nature, sustaining all things by his powerful word. After making purification for sins,[D] he sat down at the right hand of the Majesty on high.[E] [4] So he became superior to the angels, just as the name he inherited is more excellent than theirs.

THE SON SUPERIOR TO ANGELS

[5] For to which of the angels did he ever say,

You are my Son;
today I have become your Father,[F,G]

or again,

I will be his Father,
and he will be my Son?[H]

[6] Again, when he[I] brings his firstborn into the world, he says,

And let all God's angels worship him.[J]

[7] And about the angels he says:

He makes his angels winds,[K]
and his servants[L] a fiery flame,[M]

[8] but to[N] the Son:

Your throne, O God,
is forever and ever,
and the scepter of your kingdom
is a scepter of justice.
[9] You have loved righteousness
and hated lawlessness;
this is why God, your God,
has anointed you
with the oil of joy
beyond your companions.[O,P]

[10] And:

In the beginning, Lord,
you established the earth,
and the heavens are the works
of your hands;
[11] they will perish, but you remain.
They will all wear out like clothing;
[12] you will roll them up like a cloak,[O]
and they will be changed like clothing.
But you are the same,
and your years will never end.[R]

[13] Now to which of the angels has he ever said:

Sit at my right hand
until I make your enemies
your footstool?[S]

[14] Are they not all ministering spirits sent out to serve those who are going to inherit salvation?

WARNING AGAINST NEGLECT

2 For this reason, we must pay attention all the more to what we have heard, so that we will not drift away. [2] For if the message spoken through angels was legally binding[T] and every transgression and disobedience received a just punishment, [3] how will we escape if we neglect such a great salvation? This salvation had its beginning when it was spoken of by the Lord, and it was confirmed to us by those who heard him. [4] At the same time, God also testified by signs and wonders, various miracles, and distributions of gifts from the Holy Spirit according to his will.

JESUS AND HUMANITY

[5] For he has not subjected to angels the world to come that we are talking about. [6] But someone somewhere has testified:

What is man that you remember him,
or the son of man that you care
for him?
[7] You made him lower than the angels
for a short time;
you crowned him with glory
and honor[U]
[8] and subjected everything
under his feet.[V]

For in **subjecting everything** to him, he left nothing that is not subject to him. As it is, we do not yet see **everything subjected** to him. [9] But we do see Jesus — **made lower than the angels for a short time** so that by God's grace he might taste death for everyone — **crowned with glory and honor** because he suffered death.

[10] For in bringing many sons and daughters to glory, it was entirely appropriate that God — for whom and through whom all things exist — should make the source[W] of their salvation perfect through sufferings. [11] For the one who sanctifies and those who are sanctified all have

---

[A] **1:2** Lit *ages* [B] **1:3** Or *reflection* [C] **1:3** Or *representation*, or *copy*, or *reproduction* [D] **1:3** Other mss read *for our sins by himself* [E] **1:3** Or *he sat down on high at the right hand of the Majesty* [F] **1:5** Or *have begotten you* [G] **1:5** Ps 2:7 [H] **1:5** 2Sm 7:14; 1Ch 17:13 [I] **1:6** Or *When he again* [J] **1:6** Dt 32:43 LXX; Ps 97:7 [K] **1:7** Or *spirits* [L] **1:7** Or *ministers* [M] **1:7** Ps 104:4 [N] **1:8** Or *about* [O] **1:9** Or *associates* [P] **1:8-9** Ps 45:6-7 [Q] **1:12** Other mss omit *like a cloak* [R] **1:10-12** Ps 102:25-27 [S] **1:13** Ps 110:1 [T] **2:2** Or *valid*, or *reliable* [U] **2:7** Other mss add *and set him over the works of your hands* [V] **2:6-8** Ps 8:5-7 LXX [W] **2:10** Or *pioneer*, or *leader*

one Father.^A That is why Jesus is not ashamed to call them brothers and sisters, [12] saying:

> I will proclaim your name
> to my brothers and sisters;
> I will sing hymns to you
> in the congregation.^B

[13] Again, I will trust in him.^C And again, Here I am with the children God gave me.^D

[14] Now since the children have flesh and blood in common, Jesus also shared in these, so that through his death he might destroy the one holding the power of death — that is, the devil — [15] and free those who were held in slavery all their lives by the fear of death. [16] For it is clear that he does not reach out to help angels, but to help Abraham's offspring. [17] Therefore, he had to be like his brothers and sisters in every way, so that he could become a merciful and faithful high priest in matters^E pertaining to God, to make atonement^F for the sins of the people. [18] For since he himself has suffered when he was tempted, he is able to help those who are tempted.

OUR APOSTLE AND HIGH PRIEST

3 Therefore, holy brothers and sisters, who share in a heavenly calling, consider Jesus, the apostle and high priest of our confession. [2] He was faithful to the one who appointed him, just as Moses was in all God's household. [3] For Jesus is considered worthy of more glory than Moses, just as the builder has more honor than the house. [4] Now every house is built by someone, but the one who built everything is God. [5] Moses was faithful as a servant in all God's household, as a testimony to what would be said in the future. [6] But Christ was faithful as a Son over his household. And we are that household if we hold on to our confidence and the hope in which we boast.^G

WARNING AGAINST UNBELIEF

[7] Therefore, as the Holy Spirit says:

> Today, if you hear his voice,
> [8] do not harden your hearts
>   as in the rebellion,
> on the day of testing in the wilderness,
> [9] where your fathers tested me, tried me,
>   and saw my works [10] for forty years.
> Therefore I was provoked to anger
>   with that generation
> and said, "They always go astray
>   in their hearts,
> and they have not known my ways."

[11] So I swore in my anger,
> "They will not enter my rest."^H

[12] Watch out, brothers and sisters, so that there won't be in any of you an evil, unbelieving heart that turns away from the living God. [13] But encourage each other daily, while it is still called today, so that none of you is hardened by sin's deception. [14] For we have become participants in Christ if we hold firmly until the end the reality^I that we had at the start. [15] As it is said:

> Today, if you hear his voice,
> do not harden your hearts
>   as in the rebellion.^J

[16] For who heard and rebelled? Wasn't it all who came out of Egypt under Moses? [17] With whom was God angry for forty years? Wasn't it with those who sinned, whose bodies fell in the wilderness? [18] And to whom did he swear that they would not enter his rest, if not to those who disobeyed? [19] So we see that they were unable to enter because of unbelief.

THE PROMISED REST

4 Therefore, since the promise to enter his rest remains, let us beware^K that none of you be found to have fallen short.^L [2] For we also have received the good news just as they did. But the message they heard did not benefit them, since they were not united with those who heard it in faith.^M [3] For we who have believed enter the rest, in keeping with what^N he has said,

> So I swore in my anger,
> "They will not enter my rest,"^O

even though his works have been finished since the foundation of the world. [4] For somewhere he has spoken about the seventh day in this way: And on the seventh day God rested from all his works.^P [5] Again, in that passage he says, They will never enter my rest.^O [6] Therefore, since it remains for some to enter it, and those who formerly received the good news did not enter because of disobedience, [7] he again specifies a certain day — today. He specified this speaking through David after such a long time:

> Today, if you hear his voice,
> do not harden your hearts.^J

[8] For if Joshua had given them rest, God would not have spoken later about another day. [9] Therefore, a Sabbath rest remains for God's people. [10] For the person who has entered his rest has rested from his own works, just as God did from his. [11] Let us then make every effort to enter that rest, so that no one will fall into the same pattern of disobedience.

---

^A 2:11 Or father, or origin; lit all are of one   ^B 2:12 Ps 22:22   ^C 2:13 2Sm 22:3 LXX; Is 8:17 LXX; 12:2 LXX   ^D 2:13 Is 8:18 LXX
^E 2:17 Lit things   ^F 2:17 Or propitiation   ^G 3:6 Other mss add firm to the end   ^H 3:7-11 Ps 95:7-11   ^I 3:14 Or confidence
^J 3:15; 4:7 Ps 95:7-8   ^K 4:1 Lit fear   ^L 4:1 Or that any of you might seem to have missed it   ^M 4:2 Other mss read since it was not united by faith in those who heard   ^N 4:3 Or rest, just as   ^O 4:3,5 Ps 95:11   ^P 4:4 Gn 2:2

[12] For the word of God is living and effective and sharper than any double-edged sword, penetrating as far as the separation of soul and spirit, joints and marrow. It is able to judge the thoughts and intentions of the heart. [13] No creature is hidden from him, but all things are naked and exposed to the eyes of him to whom we must give an account.

OUR GREAT HIGH PRIEST

[14] Therefore, since we have a great high priest who has passed through the heavens — Jesus the Son of God — let us hold fast to our confession. [15] For we do not have a high priest who is unable to sympathize with our weaknesses, but one who has been tempted in every way as we are, yet without sin. [16] Therefore, let us approach the throne of grace with boldness, so that we may receive mercy and find grace to help us in time of need.

CHRIST, A HIGH PRIEST

5 For every high priest taken from among men is appointed in matters pertaining to God for the people, to offer both gifts and sacrifices for sins. [2] He is able to deal gently with those who are ignorant and are going astray, since he is also clothed with weakness. [3] Because of this, he must make an offering for his own sins as well as for the people. [4] No one takes this honor on himself; instead, a person is called by God, just as Aaron was. [5] In the same way, Christ did not exalt himself to become a high priest, but God who said to him,

You are my Son;
today I have become your Father, [A,B]

[6] also says in another place,

You are a priest forever
according to the order of Melchizedek. [C]

[7] During his earthly life, [D] he offered prayers and appeals with loud cries and tears to the one who was able to save him from death, and he was heard because of his reverence. [8] Although he was the Son, he learned obedience from what he suffered. [9] After he was perfected, he became the source of eternal salvation for all who obey him, [10] and he was declared by God a high priest according to the order of Melchizedek.

THE PROBLEM OF IMMATURITY

[11] We have a great deal to say about this, and it is difficult to explain, since you have become too lazy to understand. [12] Although by this time you ought to be teachers, you need someone to teach you the basic principles of God's revelation again. You need milk, not solid food. [13] Now everyone who lives on milk is inexperienced with the message about righteousness, because he is an infant. [14] But solid food is for the mature — for those whose senses have been trained to distinguish between good and evil.

WARNING AGAINST FALLING AWAY

6 Therefore, let us leave the elementary teaching about Christ and go on to maturity, not laying again a foundation of repentance from dead works, faith in God, [2] teaching about ritual washings, [E] laying on of hands, the resurrection of the dead, and eternal judgment. [3] And we will do this if God permits.

[4] For it is impossible to renew to repentance those who were once enlightened, who tasted the heavenly gift, who shared in the Holy Spirit, [5] who tasted God's good word and the powers of the coming age, [6] and who have fallen away. This is because, [F] to their own harm, they are re-crucifying the Son of God and holding him up to contempt. [7] For the ground that drinks the rain that often falls on it and that produces vegetation useful to those for whom it is cultivated receives a blessing from God. [8] But if it produces thorns and thistles, it is worthless and about to be cursed, and at the end will be burned.

[9] Even though we are speaking this way, dearly loved friends, in your case we are confident of things that are better and that pertain to salvation. [10] For God is not unjust; he will not forget your work and the love [G] you demonstrated for his name by serving the saints — and by continuing to serve them. [11] Now we desire each of you to demonstrate the same diligence for the full assurance of your hope until the end, [12] so that you won't become lazy but will be imitators of those who inherit the promises through faith and perseverance.

INHERITING THE PROMISE

[13] For when God made a promise to Abraham, since he had no one greater to swear by, he swore by himself: [14] I will indeed bless you, and I will greatly multiply you. [H] [15] And so, after waiting patiently, Abraham obtained the promise. [16] For people swear by something greater than themselves, and for them a confirming oath ends every dispute. [17] Because God wanted to show his unchangeable purpose even more clearly to the heirs of the promise, he guaranteed it with an oath, [18] so that through two unchangeable things, in which it is impossible for God to lie, we who have fled for refuge

---

might have strong encouragement to seize the hope set before us. [19] We have this hope as an anchor for the soul, firm and secure. It enters the inner sanctuary behind the curtain. [20] Jesus has entered there on our behalf as a forerunner, because he has become a high priest forever according to the order of Melchizedek.

THE GREATNESS OF MELCHIZEDEK

7 For this Melchizedek, king of Salem, priest of God Most High, met Abraham and blessed him as he returned from defeating the kings, [2] and Abraham gave him a tenth of everything. First, his name means king of righteousness, then also, king of Salem, meaning king of peace. [3] Without father, mother, or genealogy, having neither beginning of days nor end of life, but resembling the Son of God, he remains a priest forever.

[4] Now consider how great this man was: even Abraham the patriarch gave a tenth of the plunder to him. [5] The sons of Levi who receive the priestly office have a command according to the law to collect a tenth from the people — that is, from their brothers and sisters — though they have also descended from Abraham. [6] But one without this[A] lineage collected a tenth from Abraham and blessed the one who had the promises. [7] Without a doubt, the inferior is blessed by the superior. [8] In the one case, men who will die receive a tenth, but in the other case, Scripture testifies that he lives. [9] And in a sense Levi himself, who receives a tenth, has paid a tenth through Abraham, [10] for he was still within his ancestor[B] when Melchizedek met him.

A SUPERIOR PRIESTHOOD

[11] Now if perfection came through the Levitical priesthood (for on the basis of it the people received the law), what further need was there for another priest to appear, said to be according to the order of Melchizedek and not according to the order of Aaron? [12] For when there is a change of the priesthood, there must be a change of law as well. [13] For the one these things are spoken about belonged to a different tribe. No one from it has served at the altar. [14] Now it is evident that our Lord came from Judah, and Moses said nothing about that tribe concerning priests.

[15] And this becomes clearer if another priest like Melchizedek appears, [16] who did not become a priest based on a legal regulation about physical[C] descent but based on the power of an indestructible life. [17] For it has been testified:

You are a priest forever
according to the order of Melchizedek.[D]

[18] So the previous command is annulled because it was weak and unprofitable [19] (for the law perfected nothing), but a better hope is introduced, through which we draw near to God.

[20] None of this happened without an oath. For others became priests without an oath, [21] but he became a priest with an oath made by the one who said to him:

The Lord has sworn
and will not change his mind,
"You are a priest forever."[D]

[22] Because of this oath, Jesus has also become the guarantee of a better covenant.

[23] Now many have become Levitical priests, since they are prevented by death from remaining in office. [24] But because he remains forever, he holds his priesthood permanently. [25] Therefore, he is able to save completely those who come to God through him, since he always lives to intercede for them.

[26] For this is the kind of high priest we need: holy, innocent, undefiled, separated from sinners, and exalted above the heavens. [27] He doesn't need to offer sacrifices every day, as high priests do — first for their own sins, then for those of the people. He did this once for all time when he offered himself. [28] For the law appoints as high priests men who are weak, but the promise of the oath, which came after the law, appoints a Son, who has been perfected forever.

A HEAVENLY PRIESTHOOD

8 Now the main point of what is being said is this: We have this kind of high priest, who sat down at the right hand of the throne of the Majesty in the heavens, [2] a minister of the sanctuary and the true tabernacle that was set up by the Lord and not man. [3] For every high priest is appointed to offer gifts and sacrifices; therefore, it was necessary for this priest also to have something to offer. [4] Now if he were on earth, he wouldn't be a priest, since there are those[E] offering the gifts prescribed by the law. [5] These serve as a copy and shadow of the heavenly things, as Moses was warned when he was about to complete the tabernacle. For God said, **Be careful that you make everything according to the pattern that was shown to you on the mountain.**[F] [6] But Jesus has now obtained a superior ministry, and to that degree he is the mediator of a better covenant, which has been established on better promises.

^7:6 Lit *their*   ^7:10 Lit *still in his father's loins*   ^7:16 Or *fleshly*   ^7:17,21 Ps 110:4   ^8:4 Other mss read *priests*   ^8:5 Ex 25:40

A SUPERIOR COVENANT

[7] For if that first covenant had been faultless, there would have been no occasion for a second one. [8] But finding fault with his people,[A] he says:[B]

See, the days are coming,
　says the Lord,
when I will make a new covenant
　with the house of Israel
and with the house of Judah —
[9]　not like the covenant
　that I made with their ancestors
　on the day I took them by the hand
　to lead them out of the land of Egypt.
I showed no concern for them,
　says the Lord,
because they did not continue
　in my covenant.
[10]　For this is the covenant
　that I will make with the house
　　of Israel
　after those days, says the Lord:
I will put my laws into their minds
　and write them on their hearts.
I will be their God,
　and they will be my people.
[11]　And each person will not teach
　his fellow citizen,[C]
　and each his brother or sister, saying,
　"Know the Lord,"
because they will all know me,
　from the least to the greatest of them.
[12]　For I will forgive their wrongdoing,
　and I will never again remember
　　their sins.[D,E]

[13] By saying a new covenant, he has declared that the first is obsolete. And what is obsolete and growing old is about to pass away.

OLD COVENANT MINISTRY

9 Now the first covenant also had regulations for ministry and an earthly sanctuary. [2] For a tabernacle was set up, and in the first room, which is called the holy place, were the lampstand, the table, and the presentation loaves. [3] Behind the second curtain was a tent called the most holy place. [4] It had the gold altar of incense and the ark of the covenant, covered with gold on all sides, in which was a gold jar containing the manna, Aaron's staff that budded, and the tablets of the covenant. [5] The cherubim of glory were above the ark overshadowing the mercy seat. It is not possible to speak about these things in detail right now.

[6] With these things prepared like this, the priests enter the first room repeatedly, performing their ministry. [7] But the high priest alone enters the second room, and he does that only once a year, and never without blood, which he offers for himself and for the sins the people had committed in ignorance. [8] The Holy Spirit was making it clear that the way into the most holy place had not yet been disclosed while the first tabernacle was still standing. [9] This is a symbol for the present time, during which gifts and sacrifices are offered that cannot perfect the worshiper's conscience. [10] They are physical regulations and only deal with food, drink, and various washings imposed until the time of the new order.

NEW COVENANT MINISTRY

[11] But Christ has appeared as a high priest of the good things that have come.[F] In the greater and more perfect tabernacle not made with hands (that is, not of this creation), [12] he entered the most holy place once for all time, not by the blood of goats and calves, but by his own blood, having obtained eternal redemption. [13] For if the blood of goats and bulls and the ashes of a young cow, sprinkling those who are defiled, sanctify for the purification of the flesh, [14] how much more will the blood of Christ, who through the eternal Spirit offered himself without blemish to God, cleanse our[G] consciences from dead works so that we can serve the living God?

[15] Therefore, he is the mediator of a new covenant,[H] so that those who are called might receive the promise of the eternal inheritance, because a death has taken place for redemption from the transgressions committed under the first covenant. [16] Where a will exists, the death of the one who made it must be established. [17] For a will is valid only when people die, since it is never in effect while the one who made it is living. [18] That is why even the first covenant was inaugurated with blood. [19] For when every command had been proclaimed by Moses to all the people according to the law, he took the blood of calves and goats,[I] along with water, scarlet wool, and hyssop, and sprinkled the scroll itself and all the people, [20] saying, **This is the blood of the covenant that God has ordained for you.**[J] [21] In the same way, he sprinkled the tabernacle and all the articles of worship with blood. [22] According to the law almost everything is purified with blood, and without the shedding of blood there is no forgiveness.

[A] 8:8 Lit *with them*　[B] 8:8 Other mss read *finding fault, he says to them*　[C] 8:11 Other mss read *neighbor*　[D] 8:12 Other mss add *and their lawless deeds*　[E] 8:8-12 Jr 31:31-34　[F] 9:11 Other mss read *that are to come*　[G] 9:14 Other mss read *your*　[H] 9:15 The Gk word used here can be translated covenant, will, or testament, also in vv. 16,17,18.　[I] 9:19 Some mss omit *and goats*　[J] 9:20 Ex 24:8

²³ Therefore, it was necessary for the copies of the things in the heavens to be purified with these sacrifices, but the heavenly things themselves to be purified with better sacrifices than these. ²⁴ For Christ did not enter a sanctuary made with hands (only a model^A of the true one) but into heaven itself, so that he might now appear in the presence of God for us. ²⁵ He did not do this to offer himself many times, as the high priest enters the sanctuary yearly with the blood of another. ²⁶ Otherwise, he would have had to suffer many times since the foundation of the world. But now he has appeared one time, at the end of the ages, for the removal of sin by the sacrifice of himself. ²⁷ And just as it is appointed for people to die once — and after this, judgment — ²⁸ so also Christ, having been offered once to bear the sins of many, will appear a second time, not to bear sin, but^B to bring salvation to those who are waiting for him.

THE PERFECT SACRIFICE

10 Since the law has only a shadow of the good things to come, and not the reality itself of those things, it can never perfect the worshipers by the same sacrifices they continually offer year after year. ² Otherwise, wouldn't they have stopped being offered, since the worshipers, purified once and for all, would no longer have any consciousness of sins? ³ But in the sacrifices there is a reminder of sins year after year. ⁴ For it is impossible for the blood of bulls and goats to take away sins.

⁵ Therefore, as he was coming into the world, he said:

You did not desire sacrifice
    and offering,
but you prepared a body for me.
⁶   You did not delight
    in whole burnt offerings
    and sin offerings.
⁷   Then I said, "See —
    it is written about me
    in the scroll —
    I have come to do your will, O God."^C

⁸ After he says above, **You did not desire or delight in sacrifices and offerings, whole burnt offerings and sin offerings** (which are offered according to the law), ⁹ he then says, **See, I have come to do your will.**^D He takes away the first to establish the second. ¹⁰ By this will, we have been sanctified through the offering of the body of Jesus Christ once for all time.

¹¹ Every priest stands day after day ministering and offering the same sacrifices time after time, which can never take away sins. ¹² But this man, after offering one sacrifice for sins forever, sat down at the right hand of God.^E ¹³ He is now waiting until his enemies are made his footstool. ¹⁴ For by one offering he has perfected forever those who are sanctified. ¹⁵ The Holy Spirit also testifies to us about this. For after he says:

¹⁶   **This is the covenant I will make
        with them
    after those days,**
the Lord says,
    **I will put my laws on their hearts
    and write them on their minds,**
¹⁷   and **I will never again remember
    their sins** and their lawless acts.^F
¹⁸ Now where there is forgiveness of these, there is no longer an offering for sin.

EXHORTATIONS TO GODLINESS

¹⁹ Therefore, brothers and sisters, since we have boldness to enter the sanctuary through the blood of Jesus — ²⁰ he has inaugurated^G for us a new and living way through the curtain (that is, through his flesh) — ²¹ and since we have a great high priest over the house of God, ²² let us draw near with a true heart in full assurance of faith, with our hearts sprinkled clean from an evil conscience and our bodies washed in pure water. ²³ Let us hold on to the confession of our hope without wavering, since he who promised is faithful. ²⁴ And let us watch out for one another to provoke love and good works, ²⁵ not neglecting to gather together, as some are in the habit of doing, but encouraging each other, and all the more as you see the day approaching.

WARNING AGAINST DELIBERATE SIN

²⁶ For if we deliberately go on sinning after receiving the knowledge of the truth, there no longer remains a sacrifice for sins, ²⁷ but a terrifying expectation of judgment and the fury of a fire about to consume the adversaries. ²⁸ Anyone who disregarded the law of Moses died without mercy, based on the testimony of two or three witnesses. ²⁹ How much worse punishment do you think one will deserve who has trampled on the Son of God, who has regarded as profane^H the blood of the covenant by which he was sanctified, and who has insulted the Spirit of grace? ³⁰ For we know the one who has said,

---

^A**9:24** Or *antitype*, or *figure* ^B**9:28** Lit *time, apart from sin,* ^C**10:5-7** Ps 40:6-8 ^D**10:9** Other mss add *God* ^E**10:12** Or *offering one sacrifice for sins, sat down forever at the right hand of God* ^F**10:16-17** Jr 31:33-34 ^G**10:20** Or *opened* ^H**10:29** Or *ordinary*

Vengeance belongs to me;
    I will repay,^A,B
and again,
    The Lord will judge his people.^C
³¹ It is a terrifying thing to fall into the hands of the living God.

³² Remember the earlier days when, after you had been enlightened, you endured a hard struggle with sufferings. ³³ Sometimes you were publicly exposed to taunts and afflictions, and at other times you were companions of those who were treated that way. ³⁴ For you sympathized with the prisoners^D and accepted with joy the confiscation of your possessions, because you know that you yourselves have a better and enduring possession.^E ³⁵ So don't throw away your confidence, which has a great reward. ³⁶ For you need endurance, so that after you have done God's will, you may receive what was promised.

³⁷ For yet in a very little while,
    the Coming One will come
        and not delay.
³⁸ But my righteous one^F will live
        by faith;
    and if he draws back,
    I have no pleasure^G in him.^H

³⁹ But we are not those who draw back and are destroyed, but those who have faith and are saved.

LIVING BY FAITH

11 Now faith is the reality^I of what is hoped for, the proof^J of what is not seen. ² For by it our ancestors won God's approval.

³ By faith we understand that the universe was^K created by the word of God, so that what is seen was made from things that are not visible.^L

⁴ By faith Abel offered to God a better sacrifice than Cain did. By faith he was approved as a righteous man, because God approved his gifts, and even though he is dead, he still speaks through his faith.

⁵ By faith Enoch was taken away, and so he did not experience death. **He was not to be found because God took him away.**^M For before he was taken away, he was approved as one who pleased God. ⁶ Now without faith it is impossible to please God, since the one who draws near to him must believe that he exists and that he rewards those who seek him.

⁷ By faith Noah, after he was warned about what was not yet seen and motivated by godly fear, built an ark to deliver his family. By faith he condemned the world and became an heir of the righteousness that comes by faith.

⁸ By faith Abraham, when he was called, obeyed and set out for a place that he was going to receive as an inheritance. He went out, even though he did not know where he was going. ⁹ By faith he stayed as a foreigner in the land of promise, living in tents as did Isaac and Jacob, coheirs of the same promise. ¹⁰ For he was looking forward to the city that has foundations, whose architect and builder is God.

¹¹ By faith even Sarah herself, when she was unable to have children, received power to conceive offspring, even though she was past the age, since she^N considered that the one who had promised was faithful. ¹² Therefore, from one man — in fact, from one as good as dead — came offspring as numerous as the stars of the sky and as innumerable as the grains of sand along the seashore.

¹³ These all died in faith, although they had not received the things that were promised. But they saw them from a distance, greeted them, and confessed that they were foreigners and temporary residents on the earth. ¹⁴ Now those who say such things make it clear that they are seeking a homeland. ¹⁵ If they were thinking about where they came from, they would have had an opportunity to return. ¹⁶ But they now desire a better place — a heavenly one. Therefore, God is not ashamed to be called their God, for he has prepared a city for them.

¹⁷ By faith Abraham, when he was tested, offered up Isaac. He received the promises and yet he was offering his one and only son, ¹⁸ the one to whom it had been said, **Your offspring**^O **will be called through Isaac.**^O ¹⁹ He considered God to be able even to raise someone from the dead; therefore, he received him back, figuratively speaking.^O

²⁰ By faith Isaac blessed Jacob and Esau concerning things to come. ²¹ By faith Jacob, when he was dying, blessed each of the sons of Joseph, and **he worshiped, leaning on the top of his staff.**^R ²² By faith Joseph, as he was nearing the end of his life, mentioned^S the exodus of the Israelites and gave instructions concerning his bones.

---

^A**10:30** Other mss add *says the Lord* ^B**10:30** Dt 32:35 ^C**10:30** Dt 32:36 ^D**10:34** Other mss read *sympathized with my imprisonment* ^E**10:34** Other mss add *in heaven* ^F**10:38** Other mss read *the righteous one* ^G**10:38** Lit *my soul has no pleasure* ^H**10:37-38** Is 26:20 LXX; Hab 2:3-4 ^I**11:1** Or *assurance* ^J**11:1** Or *conviction* ^K**11:3** Or *the worlds were,* or *the ages were* ^L**11:3** Or *so that what is seen was made out of what was not visible* ^M**11:5** Gn 5:21-24 ^N**11:11** Or *By faith Abraham, even though he was past age — and Sarah herself was barren — received the ability to procreate since he* ^O**11:18** Lit *seed* ^P**11:18** Gn 21:12 ^Q**11:19** Or *back, as a foreshadowing,* or *as a type* ^R**11:21** Gn 47:31 ^S**11:22** Or *remembered*

[23] By faith Moses, after he was born, was hidden by his parents for three months, because they saw that the child was beautiful, and they didn't fear the king's edict. [24] By faith Moses, when he had grown up, refused to be called the son of Pharaoh's daughter [25] and chose to suffer with the people of God rather than to enjoy the fleeting pleasure of sin. [26] For he considered reproach for the sake of Christ to be greater wealth than the treasures of Egypt, since he was looking ahead to the reward.

[27] By faith he left Egypt behind, not being afraid of the king's anger, for Moses persevered as one who sees him who is invisible. [28] By faith he instituted the Passover and the sprinkling of the blood, so that the destroyer of the firstborn might not touch the Israelites. [29] By faith they crossed the Red Sea as though they were on dry land. When the Egyptians attempted to do this, they were drowned.

[30] By faith the walls of Jericho fell down after being marched around by the Israelites for seven days. [31] By faith Rahab the prostitute welcomed the spies in peace and didn't perish with those who disobeyed.

[32] And what more can I say? Time is too short for me to tell about Gideon, Barak, Samson, Jephthah, David, Samuel, and the prophets, [33] who by faith conquered kingdoms, administered justice, obtained promises, shut the mouths of lions, [34] quenched the raging of fire, escaped the edge of the sword, gained strength in weakness, became mighty in battle, and put foreign armies to flight. [35] Women received their dead, raised to life again. Other people were tortured, not accepting release, so that they might gain a better resurrection. [36] Others experienced mockings and scourgings, as well as bonds and imprisonment. [37] They were stoned,[A] they were sawed in two, they died by the sword, they wandered about in sheepskins, in goatskins, destitute, afflicted, and mistreated. [38] The world was not worthy of them. They wandered in deserts and on mountains, hiding in caves and holes in the ground.

[39] All these were approved through their faith, but they did not receive what was promised, [40] since God had provided something better for us, so that they would not be made perfect without us.

THE CALL TO ENDURANCE

12 Therefore, since we also have such a large cloud of witnesses surrounding us, let us lay aside every hindrance and the sin that so easily ensnares us. Let us run with endurance the race that lies before us, [2] keeping our eyes on Jesus,[B] the source and perfecter[C] of our faith. For the joy that lay before him,[D] he endured the cross, despising the shame, and sat down at the right hand of the throne of God.

FATHERLY DISCIPLINE

[3] For consider him who endured such hostility from sinners against himself, so that you won't grow weary and give up. [4] In struggling against sin, you have not yet resisted to the point of shedding your blood. [5] And you have forgotten the exhortation that addresses you as sons:

My son, do not take the Lord's
    discipline lightly
or lose heart when you are
    reproved by him,
[6] for the Lord disciplines the one
    he loves
and punishes every son he receives.[E]

[7] Endure suffering as discipline: God is dealing with you as sons. For what son is there that a father does not discipline? [8] But if you are without discipline — which all receive[F] — then you are illegitimate children and not sons. [9] Furthermore, we had human fathers discipline us, and we respected them. Shouldn't we submit even more to the Father of spirits and live? [10] For they disciplined us for a short time based on what seemed good to them, but he does it for our benefit, so that we can share his holiness. [11] No discipline seems enjoyable at the time, but painful. Later on, however, it yields the peaceful fruit of righteousness to those who have been trained by it.

[12] Therefore, strengthen your tired hands and weakened knees, [13] and make straight paths for your feet, so that what is lame may not be dislocated[G] but healed instead.

WARNING AGAINST REJECTING GOD'S GRACE

[14] Pursue peace with everyone, and holiness — without it no one will see the Lord. [15] Make sure that no one falls short of the grace of God and that no root of bitterness springs up, causing trouble and defiling many. [16] And make sure that there isn't any immoral[H] or irreverent person like Esau, who sold his birthright in exchange for a single meal. [17] For you know that later, when he wanted to inherit the blessing, he was rejected, even though he sought it with tears, because he didn't find any opportunity for repentance.

---

[18] For you have not come to what could be touched, to a blazing fire, to darkness, gloom, and storm, [19] to the blast of a trumpet, and the sound of words. Those who heard it begged that not another word be spoken to them, [20] for they could not bear what was commanded: If even an animal touches the mountain, it must be stoned.^ [21] The appearance was so terrifying that Moses said, I am trembling with fear.^ [22] Instead, you have come to Mount Zion, to the city of the living God (the heavenly Jerusalem), to myriads of angels, a festive gathering, [23] to the assembly of the firstborn whose names have been written^ in heaven, to a Judge, who is God of all, to the spirits of righteous people made perfect, [24] and to Jesus, the mediator of a new covenant, and to the sprinkled blood, which says better things than the blood of Abel.

[25] See to it that you do not reject the one who speaks. For if they did not escape when they rejected him who warned them on earth, even less will we if we turn away from him who warns us from heaven. [26] His voice shook the earth at that time, but now he has promised, Yet once more I will shake not only the earth but also the heavens.^ [27] This expression, "Yet once more," indicates the removal of what can be shaken — that is, created things — so that what is not shaken might remain. [28] Therefore, since we are receiving a kingdom that cannot be shaken, let us be thankful. By it, we may serve God acceptably, with reverence and awe, [29] for our God is a consuming fire.

FINAL EXHORTATIONS

13 Let brotherly love continue. [2] Don't neglect to show hospitality, for by doing this some have welcomed angels as guests without knowing it. [3] Remember those in prison, as though you were in prison with them, and the mistreated,^ as though you yourselves were suffering bodily.^ [4] Marriage is to be honored by all and the marriage bed kept undefiled, because God will judge the sexually immoral and adulterers. [5] Keep your life free from the love of money. Be satisfied with what you have, for he himself has said, I will never leave you or abandon you.^ [6] Therefore, we may boldly say,

The Lord is my helper;
I will not be afraid.
What can man do to me?^

[7] Remember your leaders who have spoken God's word to you. As you carefully observe the outcome of their lives, imitate their faith. [8] Jesus Christ is the same yesterday, today, and forever. [9] Don't be led astray by various kinds of strange teachings; for it is good for the heart to be established by grace and not by food regulations, since those who observe them have not benefited. [10] We have an altar from which those who worship at the tabernacle do not have a right to eat. [11] For the bodies of those animals whose blood is brought into the most holy place by the high priest as a sin offering are burned outside the camp. [12] Therefore, Jesus also suffered outside the gate, so that he might sanctify^ the people by his own blood. [13] Let us then go to him outside the camp, bearing his disgrace. [14] For we do not have an enduring city here; instead, we seek the one to come. [15] Therefore, through him let us continually offer up to God a sacrifice of praise, that is, the fruit of lips that confess his name. [16] Don't neglect to do what is good and to share, for God is pleased with such sacrifices. [17] Obey your leaders^ and submit to them, since they keep watch over your souls as those who will give an account, so that they can do this with joy and not with grief, for that would be unprofitable for you. [18] Pray for us, for we are convinced that we have a clear conscience, wanting to conduct ourselves honorably in everything. [19] And I urge you all the more to pray^ that I may be restored to you very soon.

BENEDICTION AND FAREWELL

[20] Now may the God of peace, who brought up from the dead our Lord Jesus — the great Shepherd of the sheep — through the blood of the everlasting covenant, [21] equip^ you with everything good to do his will, working in us what is pleasing in his sight, through Jesus Christ, to whom be glory forever and ever.^ Amen.

[22] Brothers and sisters, I urge you to receive this message of exhortation, for I have written to you briefly. [23] Be aware that our brother Timothy has been released. If he comes soon enough, he will be with me when I see you. [24] Greet all your leaders and all the saints. Those who are from Italy send you greetings. [25] Grace be with you all.

^ **12:20** Ex 19:12 ^ **12:21** Dt 9:19 ^ **12:23** Or *registered* ^ **12:26** Hg 2:6 ^ **13:3** Or *tortured* ^ **13:3** Or *mistreated, since you are also in a body* ^ **13:5** Dt 31:6 ^ **13:6** Ps 118:6 ^ **13:12** Or *set apart*, or *consecrate* ^ **13:17** Or *rulers* ^ **13:19** Lit *to do this* ^ **13:21** Or *perfect* ^ **13:21** Other mss omit *and ever*

JAMES

GREETING

1 James, a servant of God and of the Lord Jesus Christ:
To the twelve tribes dispersed abroad.[A]
Greetings.

TRIALS AND MATURITY

[2] Consider it a great joy, my brothers and sisters, whenever you experience various trials, [3] because you know that the testing of your faith produces endurance. [4] And let endurance have its full effect, so that you may be mature and complete, lacking nothing.

[5] Now if any of you lacks wisdom, he should ask God — who gives to all generously and ungrudgingly — and it will be given to him. [6] But let him ask in faith without doubting.[B] For the doubter is like the surging sea, driven and tossed by the wind. [7] That person should not expect to receive anything from the Lord, [8] being double-minded and unstable in all his ways.[C]

[9] Let the brother of humble circumstances boast in his exaltation, [10] but let the rich boast in his humiliation because he will pass away like a flower of the field. [11] For the sun rises and, together with the scorching wind, dries up the grass; its flower falls off, and its beautiful appearance perishes. In the same way, the rich person will wither away while pursuing his activities.

[12] Blessed is the one who endures trials, because when he has stood the test he will receive the crown of life that God[D] has promised to those who love him.

[13] No one undergoing a trial should say, "I am being tempted by God," since God is not tempted by evil, and he himself doesn't tempt anyone. [14] But each person is tempted when he is drawn away and enticed by his own evil desire. [15] Then after desire has conceived, it gives birth to sin, and when sin is fully grown, it gives birth to death.

[16] Don't be deceived, my dear brothers and sisters. [17] Every good and perfect gift is from above, coming down from the Father of lights, who does not change like shifting shadows. [18] By his own choice, he gave us birth by the word of truth so that we would be a kind of firstfruits of his creatures.

HEARING AND DOING THE WORD

[19] My dear brothers and sisters, understand this: Everyone should be quick to listen, slow to speak, and slow to anger, [20] for human anger does not accomplish God's righteousness. [21] Therefore, ridding yourselves of all moral filth and the evil that is so prevalent,[E] humbly receive the implanted word, which is able to save your souls.

[22] But be doers of the word and not hearers only, deceiving yourselves. [23] Because if anyone is a hearer of the word and not a doer, he is like someone looking at his own face[F] in a mirror. [24] For he looks at himself, goes away, and immediately forgets what kind of person he was. [25] But the one who looks intently into the perfect law of freedom and perseveres in it, and is not a forgetful hearer but a doer who works — this person will be blessed in what he does.

[26] If anyone[G] thinks he is religious without controlling his tongue, his religion is useless and he deceives himself. [27] Pure and undefiled religion before God the Father is this: to look after orphans and widows in their distress and to keep oneself unstained from the world.

THE SIN OF FAVORITISM

2 My brothers and sisters, do not show favoritism as you hold on to the faith in our glorious Lord Jesus Christ. [2] For if someone comes into your meeting wearing a gold ring and dressed in fine clothes, and a poor person dressed in filthy clothes also comes in, [3] if you look with favor on the one wearing the fine clothes and say, "Sit here in a good place," and yet you say to the poor person, "Stand over there," or "Sit here on the floor by my footstool," [4] haven't you made distinctions among yourselves and become judges with evil thoughts?

[5] Listen, my dear brothers and sisters: Didn't God choose the poor in this world to be rich in faith and heirs of the kingdom that he has promised to those who love him? [6] Yet you have dishonored the poor. Don't the rich oppress you and drag you into court? [7] Don't they blaspheme the good name that was invoked over you?

[8] Indeed, if you fulfill the royal law prescribed in the Scripture, **Love your neighbor as yourself,**[H] you are doing well. [9] If, however, you show favoritism, you commit sin and are convicted by the law as transgressors. [10] For whoever keeps the entire law, and yet stumbles at one point, is guilty of breaking it all. [11] For he who said, **Do not commit adultery,**[I] also said,

^1:1 Gk *diaspora* ; Jewish people scattered throughout Gentile lands ^1:6 Or *without divided loyalties* ^1:8 Or *in all his conduct* ^1:12 Other mss read *that the Lord* ^1:21 Or *the abundance of evil* ^1:23 Or *at his natural face* ^1:26 Other mss add *among you* "2:8 Lv 19:18 '2:11 Ex 20:14; Dt 5:18

Do not murder.[A] So if you do not commit adultery, but you murder, you are a lawbreaker.

[12] Speak and act as those who are to be judged by the law of freedom. [13] For judgment is without mercy to the one who has not shown mercy. Mercy triumphs over judgment.

FAITH AND WORKS

[14] What good is it, my brothers and sisters, if someone claims to have faith but does not have works? Can such faith save him?

[15] If a brother or sister is without clothes and lacks daily food [16] and one of you says to them, "Go in peace, stay warm, and be well fed," but you don't give them what the body needs, what good is it? [17] In the same way faith, if it doesn't have works, is dead by itself.

[18] But someone will say, "You have faith, and I have works."[B] Show me your faith without works, and I will show you faith by my works. [19] You believe that God is one. Good! Even the demons believe — and they shudder.

[20] Senseless person! Are you willing to learn that faith without works is useless? [21] Wasn't Abraham our father justified by works in offering Isaac his son on the altar? [22] You see that faith was active together with his works, and by works, faith was made complete, [23] and the Scripture was fulfilled that says, **Abraham believed God, and it was credited to him as righteousness,**[C] and he was called God's friend. [24] You see that a person is justified by works and not by faith alone. [25] In the same way, wasn't Rahab the prostitute also justified by works in receiving the messengers and sending them out by a different route? [26] For just as the body without the spirit is dead, so also faith without works is dead.

CONTROLLING THE TONGUE

3 Not many should become teachers, my brothers,[D] because you know that we will receive a stricter judgment. [2] For we all stumble in many ways. If anyone does not stumble in what he says, he is mature, able also to control the whole body. [3] Now if we put bits into the mouths of horses so that they obey us, we direct their whole bodies. [4] And consider ships: Though very large and driven by fierce winds, they are guided by a very small rudder wherever the will of the pilot directs. [5] So too, though the tongue is a small part of the body, it boasts great things. Consider how a small fire sets ablaze a large forest. [6] And the tongue is a fire. The tongue,

a world of unrighteousness, is placed[E] among our members. It stains the whole body, sets the course of life on fire, and is itself set on fire by hell. [7] Every kind of animal, bird, reptile, and fish is tamed and has been tamed by humankind, [8] but no one can tame the tongue. It is a restless evil, full of deadly poison. [9] With the tongue we bless our Lord and Father, and with it we curse people who are made in God's likeness. [10] Blessing and cursing come out of the same mouth. My brothers and sisters, these things should not be this way. [11] Does a spring pour out sweet and bitter water from the same opening? [12] Can a fig tree produce olives, my brothers and sisters, or a grapevine produce figs? Neither can a saltwater spring yield fresh water.

THE WISDOM FROM ABOVE

[13] Who among you is wise and understanding? By his good conduct he should show that his works are done in the gentleness that comes from wisdom. [14] But if you have bitter envy and selfish ambition in your heart, don't boast and deny the truth. [15] Such wisdom does not come down from above but is earthly, unspiritual, demonic. [16] For where there is envy and selfish ambition, there is disorder and every evil practice. [17] But the wisdom from above is first pure, then peace-loving, gentle, compliant, full of mercy and good fruits, unwavering, without pretense. [18] And the fruit of righteousness is sown in peace by those who cultivate peace.

PROUD OR HUMBLE

4 What is the source of wars and fights among you? Don't they come from your passions that wage war within you?[F] [2] You desire and do not have. You murder and covet and cannot obtain. You fight and wage war.[G] You do not have because you do not ask. [3] You ask and don't receive because you ask with wrong motives, so that you may spend it on your pleasures.

[4] You adulterous people![H] Don't you know that friendship with the world is hostility toward God? So whoever wants to be the friend of the world becomes the enemy of God. [5] Or do you think it's without reason that the Scripture says: The spirit he made to dwell in us envies intensely?[I]

[6] But he gives greater grace. Therefore he says:

> **God resists the proud,**
> **but gives grace to the humble.**[J]

[A] 2:11 Ex 20:13; Dt 5:17   [B] 2:18 The quotation may end here or after v. 18b or v. 19.   [C] 2:23 Gn 15:6   [D] 3:1 Or brothers and sisters   [F] 3:6 Or places itself, or appoints itself   [G] 4:1 Or war in your members   [H] 4:2 Or You desire and do not have, so you murder. You covet and cannot obtain, so you fight and wage war.   [I] 4:4 Lit Adulteresses   [J] 4:5 Or Scripture says: He jealously yearns for the spirit he made to live in us?, or Scripture says: The Spirit he made to dwell in us longs jealously?   [K] 4:6 Pr 3:34

[7] Therefore, submit to God. Resist the devil, and he will flee from you. [8] Draw near to God, and he will draw near to you. Cleanse your hands, sinners, and purify your hearts, you double-minded. [9] Be miserable and mourn and weep. Let your laughter be turned to mourning and your joy to gloom. [10] Humble yourselves before the Lord, and he will exalt you.

[11] Don't criticize one another, brothers and sisters. Anyone who defames or judges a fellow believer[A] defames and judges the law. If you judge the law, you are not a doer of the law but a judge. [12] There is one lawgiver and judge[B] who is able to save and to destroy. But who are you to judge your neighbor?

OUR WILL AND GOD'S WILL

[13] Come now, you who say, "Today or tomorrow we will travel to such and such a city and spend a year there and do business and make a profit." [14] Yet you do not know what tomorrow will bring — what your life will be! For you are like vapor that appears for a little while, then vanishes. [15] Instead, you should say, "If the Lord wills, we will live and do this or that." [16] But as it is, you boast in your arrogance. All such boasting is evil. [17] So it is sin to know the good and yet not do it.

WARNING TO THE RICH

5 Come now, you rich people, weep and wail over the miseries that are coming on you. [2] Your wealth has rotted and your clothes are moth-eaten. [3] Your gold and silver are corroded, and their corrosion will be a witness against you and will eat your flesh like fire. You have stored up treasure in the last days. [4] Look! The pay that you withheld from the workers who mowed your fields cries out, and the outcry of the harvesters has reached the ears of the Lord of Hosts.[C] [5] You have lived luxuriously on the earth and have indulged yourselves. You have fattened your hearts in a day of slaughter. [6] You have condemned, you have murdered the righteous, who does not resist you.

WAITING FOR THE LORD

[7] Therefore, brothers and sisters, be patient until the Lord's coming. See how the farmer waits for the precious fruit of the earth and is patient with it until it receives the early and the late rains. [8] You also must be patient. Strengthen your hearts, because the Lord's coming is near.

[9] Brothers and sisters, do not complain about one another, so that you will not be judged. Look, the judge stands at the door! [10] Brothers and sisters, take the prophets who spoke in the Lord's name as an example of suffering and patience. [11] See, we count as blessed those who have endured.[D] You have heard of Job's endurance and have seen the outcome that the Lord brought about — the Lord is compassionate and merciful.

TRUTHFUL SPEECH

[12] Above all, my brothers and sisters, do not swear, either by heaven or by earth or with any other oath. But let your "yes" mean "yes," and your "no" mean "no," so that you won't fall under judgment.[E]

EFFECTIVE PRAYER

[13] Is anyone among you suffering? He should pray. Is anyone cheerful? He should sing praises. [14] Is anyone among you sick? He should call for the elders of the church, and they are to pray over him, anointing him with oil in the name of the Lord. [15] The prayer of faith will save the sick person, and the Lord will raise him up; if he has committed sins, he will be forgiven. [16] Therefore, confess your sins to one another and pray for one another, so that you may be healed. The prayer of a righteous person is very powerful in its effect. [17] Elijah was a human being as we are, and he prayed earnestly that it would not rain, and for three years and six months it did not rain on the land. [18] Then he prayed again, and the sky gave rain and the land produced its fruit.

[19] My brothers and sisters, if any among you strays from the truth, and someone turns him back, [20] let that person know that whoever turns a sinner from the error of his way will save his soul from death and cover a multitude of sins.

[A] 4:11 Or his brother or sister   [B] 4:12 Other mss omit and judge   [C] 5:4 Gk Sabaoth; or the Lord of Armies   [D] 5:11 Or persevered   [E] 5:12 Other mss read fall into hypocrisy

1 PETER

1 Peter, an apostle of Jesus Christ:
  To those chosen, living as exiles dispersed abroad[A] in Pontus, Galatia, Cappadocia, Asia, and Bithynia, chosen [2] according to the foreknowledge of God the Father, through the sanctifying work of the Spirit, to be obedient and to be sprinkled with the blood of Jesus Christ.
  May grace and peace be multiplied to you.

A LIVING HOPE

[3] Blessed be the God and Father of our Lord Jesus Christ. Because of his great mercy he has given us new birth into a living hope through the resurrection of Jesus Christ from the dead [4] and into an inheritance that is imperishable, undefiled, and unfading, kept in heaven for you. [5] You are being guarded by God's power through faith for a salvation that is ready to be revealed in the last time. [6] You rejoice in this,[B] even though now for a short time, if necessary, you suffer grief in various trials [7] so that the proven character of your faith — more valuable than gold which, though perishable, is refined by fire — may result in praise, glory, and honor at the revelation of Jesus Christ. [8] Though you have not seen him, you love him; though not seeing him now, you believe in him, and you rejoice with inexpressible and glorious joy, [9] because you are receiving the goal of your faith, the salvation of your souls.

[10] Concerning this salvation, the prophets, who prophesied about the grace that would come to you, searched and carefully investigated. [11] They inquired into what time or what circumstances the Spirit of Christ within them was indicating when he testified in advance to the sufferings of Christ and the glories that would follow.[C] [12] It was revealed to them that they were not serving themselves but you. These things have now been announced to you through those who preached the gospel to you by the Holy Spirit sent from heaven — angels long to catch a glimpse of these things.

A CALL TO HOLY LIVING

[13] Therefore, with your minds ready for action, be sober-minded and set your hope completely on the grace to be brought to you at the revelation of Jesus Christ. [14] As obedient children, do not be conformed to the desires of your former ignorance. [15] But as the one who called you is holy, you also are to be holy in all your conduct; [16] for it is written, **Be holy, because I am holy.**[D] [17] If you appeal to the Father who judges impartially according to each one's work, you are to conduct yourselves in reverence during your time living as strangers. [18] For you know that you were redeemed from your empty way of life inherited from your fathers, not with perishable things like silver or gold, [19] but with the precious blood of Christ, like that of an unblemished and spotless lamb. [20] He was foreknown before the foundation of the world but was revealed in these last times for you. [21] Through him you believe in God, who raised him from the dead and gave him glory, so that your faith and hope are in God.

[22] Since you have purified yourselves by your obedience to the truth,[E] so that you show sincere brotherly love for each other, from a pure[F] heart love one another constantly,[G] [23] because you have been born again — not of perishable seed but of imperishable — through the living and enduring word of God. [24] For

> **All flesh is like grass,**
> **and all its glory like a flower**
>   **of the grass.**
> **The grass withers, and the flower falls,**
> [25] **but the word of the Lord**
>   **endures forever.**[H]

And this word is the gospel that was proclaimed to you.

THE LIVING STONE AND A HOLY PEOPLE

2 Therefore, rid yourselves of all malice, all deceit, hypocrisy, envy, and all slander. [2] Like newborn infants, desire the pure milk of the word,[I] so that you may grow up into your salvation,[J] if **you have tasted that the Lord is good.**[K] [4] As you come to him, a living stone — rejected by people but chosen and honored by[L] God — [5] you yourselves, as living stones, a spiritual house, are being built to be a holy priesthood[M] to offer spiritual sacrifices acceptable to God through Jesus Christ. [6] For it stands in Scripture:

> **See, I lay a stone in Zion,**
> **a chosen and honored**[N] **cornerstone,**
> **and the one who believes in him**
> **will never be put to shame.**[O]

[A]**1:1** Gk *diaspora*; Jewish people scattered throughout Gentile lands   [B]**1:6** Or *In this fact rejoice*   [C]**1:11** Or *the glories after that*
[D]**1:16** Lv 11:44-45; 19:2; 20:7   [E]**1:22** Other mss add *through the Spirit*   [F]**1:22** Other mss omit *pure*   [G]**1:22** Or *fervently*
[H]**1:24-25** Is 40:6-8   [I]**2:2** Or *desire pure spiritual milk*   [J]**2:2** Other mss omit *for your salvation*   [K]**2:3** Ps 34:8   [L]**2:4** Or *precious to*
[M]**2:5** Or *you yourselves, as living stones, are being built into a spiritual house for a holy priesthood*   [N]**2:6** Or *precious*
[O]**2:6** Is 28:16 LXX

⁷ So honor will come to you who believe; but for the unbelieving,

> The stone that the builders rejected —
> this one has become the cornerstone,ᴬ

⁸ and

> A stone to stumble over,
> and a rock to trip over.ᴮ

They stumble because they disobey the word; they were destined for this.

⁹ But you are a chosen race,ᶜᴰ a royal priesthood,ᴱ a holy nation,ᶠ a people for his possession,ᴳ so that you may proclaim the praisesᴴᴵ of the one who called you out of darkness into his marvelous light. ¹⁰ Once you were not a people, but now you are God's people; you had not received mercy, but now you have received mercy.

A CALL TO GOOD WORKS

¹¹ Dear friends, I urge you as strangers and exiles to abstain from sinful desires that wage war against the soul. ¹² Conduct yourselves honorably among the Gentiles,ᴶ so that when they slander you as evildoers, they will observe your good works and will glorify God on the day he visits.

¹³ Submit to every human authority because of the Lord, whether to the emperorᴷ as the supreme authority ¹⁴ or to governors as those sent out by him to punish those who do what is evil and to praise those who do what is good. ¹⁵ For it is God's will that you silence the ignorance of foolish people by doing good. ¹⁶ Submit as free people, not using your freedom as a cover-up for evil, but as God's slaves. ¹⁷ Honor everyone. Love the brothers and sisters. Fear God. Honor the emperor.

SUBMISSION OF SLAVES TO MASTERS

¹⁸ Household slaves, submit to your masters with all reverence not only to the good and gentle ones but also to the cruel. ¹⁹ For it brings favor if, because of a consciousness of God, someone endures grief from suffering unjustly. ²⁰ For what credit is there if when you do wrong and are beaten, you endure it? But when you do what is good and suffer, if you endure it, this brings favor with God.

²¹ For you were called to this, because Christ also suffered for you, leaving you an example, that you should follow in his steps. ²² He did not commit sin, and no deceit was found in his mouth;ᴸ ²³ when he was insulted, he did not insult in return; when he suffered, he did not

threaten but entrusted himself to the one who judges justly. ²⁴ He himself bore our sins in his body on the tree; so that, having died to sins, we might live for righteousness. By his woundsᴹ you have been healed. ²⁵ For you were like sheep going astray,ᴺ but you have now returned to the Shepherd and Overseerᴼ of your souls.

WIVES AND HUSBANDS

3 In the same way, wives, submit yourselves to your own husbands so that, even if some disobey the word, they may be won over without a word by the way their wives live ² when they observe your pure, reverent lives. ³ Don't let your beauty consist of outward things like elaborate hairstyles and wearing gold jewelry, ⁴ but rather what is inside the heartᴾ — the imperishable quality of a gentle and quiet spirit, which is of great worth in God's sight. ⁵ For in the past, the holy women who put their hope in God also adorned themselves in this way, submitting to their own husbands, ⁶ just as Sarah obeyed Abraham, calling him lord. You have become her children when you do what is good and do not fear any intimidation.

⁷ Husbands, in the same way, live with your wives in an understanding way, as with a weaker partner, showing them honor as coheirs of the grace of life, so that your prayers will not be hindered.

DO NO EVIL

⁸ Finally, all of you be like-minded and sympathetic, love one another, and be compassionate and humble,ᵠ ⁹ not paying back evil for evil or insult for insult but, on the contrary, giving a blessing, since you were called for this, so that you may inherit a blessing.

¹⁰   For the one who wants to love life
>   and to see good days,
>   let him keep his tongue from evil
>   and his lips from speaking deceit,
¹¹   and let him turn away from evil
>   and do what is good.
>   Let him seek peace and pursue it,
¹²   because the eyes of the Lord are
>   on the righteous
>   and his ears are open to their prayer.
>   But the face of the Lord is against
>   those who do what is evil.ᴿ

UNDESERVED SUFFERING

¹³ Who then will harm you if you are devoted to what is good? ¹⁴ But even if you should

---

ᴬ2:7 Ps 118:22 ᴮ2:8 Is 8:14 ᶜ2:9 Or *generation*, or *nation* ᴰ2:9 Dt 7:6; 10:15; Is 43:20 LXX ᴱ2:9 Ex 19:6; 23:22 LXX; Is 61:6 ᶠ2:9 Ex 19:6; 23:22 LXX ᴳ2:9 Ex 19:5; 23:22 LXX; Dt 4:20; 7:6; Is 43:21 LXX ᴴ2:9 Or *the mighty deeds* ᴵ2:9 Is 42:12; 43:21 ᴶ2:12 Or *among the nations*, or *among the pagans* ᴷ2:13 Or *king* ᴸ2:22 Is 53:9 ᴹ2:24 Is 53:5 ᴺ2:25 Is 53:6 ᴼ2:25 Or *Guardian* ᴾ3:4 Or *rather, the hidden person of the heart* ᵠ3:8 Other mss read *courteous* ᴿ3:10-12 Ps 34:12-16

suffer for righteousness, you are blessed. **Do not fear what they fear^A or be intimidat-ed,**[B] **15** but in your hearts regard[C] Christ[D] the Lord as holy, ready at any time to give a defense to anyone who asks you for a reason for the hope that is in you. **16** Yet do this with gentleness and respect, keeping a clear conscience, so that when you are accused,[E] those who disparage your good conduct in Christ will be put to shame. **17** For it is better to suffer for doing good, if that should be God's will, than for doing evil.

18 For Christ also suffered for sins once for all, the righteous for the unrighteous, that he might bring us to God. He was put to death in the flesh[F] but made alive by the Spirit,[G] **19** in which[H] he also went and made proclamation to the spirits in prison **20** who in the past were disobedient, when God patiently waited in the days of Noah while the ark was being prepared. In it a few — that is, eight people[I] — were saved through water. **21** Baptism, which corresponds to this, now saves you (not as the removal of dirt from the body, but the pledge[J] of a good conscience toward God) through the resurrection of Jesus Christ, **22** who has gone into heaven and is at the right hand of God with angels, authorities, and powers subject to him.

FOLLOWING CHRIST

4 Therefore, since Christ suffered[K] in the flesh, arm yourselves also with the same understanding[L] — because the one who suffers in the flesh is finished with sin[M] — **2** in order to live the remaining time in the flesh no longer for human desires, but for God's will. **3** For there has already been enough time spent in doing what the Gentiles choose to do: carrying on in unrestrained behavior, evil desires, drunkenness, orgies, carousing, and lawless idolatry. **4** They are surprised that you don't join them in the same flood of wild living — and they slander[N] you. **5** They will give an account to the one who stands ready to judge the living and the dead. **6** For this reason the gospel was also preached to those who are now dead,[O] so that, although they might be judged in the flesh according to human standards, they might live in the spirit according to God's standards.

END-TIME ETHICS

7 The end of all things is near; therefore, be alert and sober-minded for prayer. **8** Above all, maintain constant love for one another, since **love covers a multitude of sins.**[P] **9** Be hospitable to one another without complaining. **10** Just as each one has received a gift, use it to serve others, as good stewards of the varied grace of God. **11** If anyone speaks, let it be as one who speaks God's words; if anyone serves, let it be from the strength God provides, so that God may be glorified through Jesus Christ in everything. To him be the glory and the power forever and ever. Amen.

CHRISTIAN SUFFERING

12 Dear friends, don't be surprised when the fiery ordeal comes among you to test you as if something unusual were happening to you. **13** Instead, rejoice as you share in the sufferings of Christ, so that you may also rejoice with great joy when his glory is revealed. **14** If you are ridiculed for the name of Christ, you are blessed, because the Spirit of glory and of God[Q] rests on you. **15** Let none of you suffer as a murderer, a thief, an evildoer, or a meddler.[R] **16** But if anyone suffers as a Christian, let him not be ashamed but let him glorify God in having that name.[S] **17** For the time has come for judgment to begin with God's household, and if it begins with us, what will the outcome be for those who disobey the gospel of God?

18   And **if a righteous person is saved with difficulty, what will become of the ungodly and the sinner?**[T]

19 So then, let those who suffer according to God's will entrust themselves to a faithful Creator while doing what is good.

ABOUT THE ELDERS

5 I exhort the elders among you as a fellow elder and witness to the sufferings of Christ, as well as one who shares in the glory about to be revealed: **2** Shepherd God's flock among you, not overseeing[U] out of compulsion but willingly, as God would have you;[V] not out of greed for money but eagerly; **3** not lording it over those entrusted to you, but being examples to the flock. **4** And when the chief Shepherd appears, you will receive the unfading crown of glory.

---

^A **3:14** Or *Do not fear them*   ^B **3:14** Is 8:12   ^C **3:15** Or *sanctify,* or *set apart*   ^D **3:15** Other mss read *set God*   ^E **3:16** Other mss read *when they speak against you as evildoers*   ^F **3:18** Or *by the flesh,* or *in the fleshly realm*   ^G **3:18** Or *in the spirit,* or *in the Spirit,* or *in the spiritual realm*   ^H **3:19** Or *by whom,* or *in whom,* or *at that time*   ^I **3:20** Or *souls*   ^J **3:21** Or *the appeal*   ^K **4:1** Other mss read *suffered for us*   ^L **4:1** Or *perspective,* or *attitude*   ^M **4:1** Or *the one who suffered in the flesh has finished with sin*   ^N **4:4** Or *blaspheme*   ^O **4:6** Or *those who are dead*   ^P **4:8** Pr 10:12   ^Q **4:14** Or *God's glorious Spirit*   ^R **4:15** Or *as one who defrauds others*   ^S **4:16** Other mss read *in that case*   ^T **4:18** Pr 11:31 LXX   ^U **5:2** Other mss omit *overseeing*   ^V **5:2** Other mss omit *as God would have you*

[5] In the same way, you who are younger, be subject to the elders. All of you clothe yourselves with[A] humility toward one another, because

> God resists the proud
> but gives grace to the humble.[B]

CONCLUSION

[6] Humble yourselves, therefore, under the mighty hand of God, so that he may exalt you at the proper time, [7] casting all your cares on him, because he cares about you. [8] Be sober-minded, be alert. Your adversary the devil is prowling around like a roaring lion, looking for anyone he can devour. [9] Resist him, firm in the faith, knowing that the same kind of sufferings are being experienced by your fellow believers throughout the world.

[10] The God of all grace, who called you to his eternal glory in Christ,[C] will himself restore, establish, strengthen, and support you after you have suffered a little while.[D] [11] To him be dominion[E] forever.[F] Amen.

[12] Through Silvanus,[G] a faithful brother (as I consider him), I have written to you briefly in order to encourage you and to testify that this is the true grace of God. Stand firm in it! [13] She who is in Babylon, chosen together with you, sends you greetings, as does Mark, my son. [14] Greet one another with a kiss of love. Peace to all of you who are in Christ."

[A]**5:5** Or *you tie around yourselves*   [B]**5:5** Pr 3:34 LXX   [C]**5:10** Other mss read *in Christ Jesus*   [D]**5:10** Or *to a small extent*
[E]**5:11** Some mss read *dominion and glory*; other mss read *glory and dominion*   [F]**5:11** Other mss read *forever and ever*
[G]**5:12** Or *Silas*; Ac 15:22-32; 16:19-40; 17:1-16   [H]**5:14** Other mss read *Christ Jesus. Amen.*

2 PETER

1 Simeon[A] Peter, a servant and an apostle of Jesus Christ:

To those who have received a faith equal to ours through the righteousness of our God and Savior Jesus Christ. [2] May grace and peace be multiplied to you through the knowledge of God and of Jesus our Lord.

GROWTH IN THE FAITH

[3] His[B] divine power has given us everything required for life and godliness through the knowledge of him who called us by[C] his own glory and goodness. [4] By these he has given us very great and precious promises, so that through them you may share in the divine nature, escaping the corruption that is in the world because of evil desire. [5] For this very reason, make every effort to supplement your faith with goodness, goodness with knowledge, [6] knowledge with self-control, self-control with endurance, endurance with godliness, [7] godliness with brotherly affection, and brotherly affection with love. [8] For if you possess these qualities in increasing measure, they will keep you from being useless or unfruitful in the knowledge of our Lord Jesus Christ. [9] The person who lacks these things is blind and shortsighted and has forgotten the cleansing from his past sins. [10] Therefore, brothers and sisters, make every effort to confirm your calling and election, because if you do these things you will never stumble. [11] For in this way, entry into the eternal kingdom of our Lord and Savior Jesus Christ will be richly provided for you.

[12] Therefore I will always remind you about these things, even though you know them and are established in the truth you now have. [13] I think it is right, as long as I am in this bodily tent, to wake you up with a reminder, [14] since I know that I will soon lay aside my tent, as our Lord Jesus Christ has indeed made clear to me. [15] And I will also make every effort so that you are able to recall these things at any time after my departure.[D]

THE TRUSTWORTHY PROPHETIC WORD

[16] For we did not follow cleverly contrived myths when we made known to you the power and coming of our Lord Jesus Christ; instead, we were eyewitnesses of his majesty.

[17] For he received honor and glory from God the Father when the voice came to him from the Majestic Glory, saying "This is my beloved Son,[E] with whom I am well-pleased!"[18] We ourselves heard this voice when it came from heaven while we were with him on the holy mountain. [19] We also have the prophetic word strongly confirmed, and you will do well to pay attention to it, as to a lamp shining in a dark place, until the day dawns and the morning star rises in your hearts. [20] Above all, you know this: No prophecy of Scripture comes from the prophet's own interpretation, [21] because no prophecy ever came by the will of man; instead, men spoke from God as they were carried along by the Holy Spirit.

THE JUDGMENT OF FALSE TEACHERS

2 There were indeed false prophets among the people, just as there will be false teachers among you. They will bring in destructive heresies, even denying the Master who bought them, and will bring swift destruction on themselves. [2] Many will follow their depraved ways, and the way of truth will be maligned because of them. [3] They will exploit you in their greed with made-up stories. Their condemnation, pronounced long ago, is not idle, and their destruction does not sleep.

[4] For if God didn't spare the angels who sinned but cast them into hell[F] and delivered them in chains[G] of utter darkness to be kept for judgment; [5] and if he didn't spare the ancient world, but protected Noah, a preacher of righteousness, and seven others,[H] when he brought the flood on the world of the ungodly; [6] and if he reduced the cities of Sodom and Gomorrah to ashes and condemned them to extinction,[I] making them an example of what is coming to the ungodly;[J] [7] and if he rescued righteous Lot, distressed by the depraved behavior of the immoral [8] (for as that righteous man lived among them day by day, his righteous soul was tormented by the lawless deeds he saw and heard)— [9] then the Lord knows how to rescue the godly from trials and to keep the unrighteous under punishment for the day of judgment, [10] especially those who follow the polluting desires of the flesh and despise authority.

Bold, arrogant people! They are not afraid to slander the glorious ones; [11] however, angels,

---

[A] **1:1** Other mss read *Simon*　[B] **1:3** Lit *As his*　[C] **1:3** Or *to*　[D] **1:15** Or *death*　[E] **1:17** Other mss read *my Son, my beloved*　[F] **2:4** Gk *Tartarus*　[G] **2:4** Other mss read *in pits*　[H] **2:5** Lit *Noah, the eighth, a preacher of righteousness*　[I] **2:6** Other mss omit *to extinction*　[J] **2:6** Other mss read *an example of what is going to happen to the ungodly*

who are greater in might and power, do not bring a slanderous charge against them before the Lord.^ [12] But these people, like irrational animals — creatures of instinct born to be caught and destroyed — slander what they do not understand, and in their destruction they too will be destroyed. [13] They will be paid back with harm for the harm they have done. They consider it a pleasure to carouse in broad daylight. They are spots and blemishes, delighting in their deceptions[8] while they feast with you. [14] They have eyes full of adultery that never stop looking for sin. They seduce unstable people and have hearts trained in greed. Children under a curse! [15] They have gone astray by abandoning the straight path and have followed the path of Balaam, the son of Bosor,[c] who loved the wages of wickedness [16] but received a rebuke for his lawlessness: A speechless donkey spoke with a human voice and restrained the prophet's madness.

[17] These people are springs without water, mists driven by a storm. The gloom of darkness has been reserved for them. [18] For by uttering boastful, empty words, they seduce, with fleshly desires and debauchery, people who have barely escaped[D] from those who live in error. [19] They promise them freedom, but they themselves are slaves of corruption, since people are enslaved to whatever defeats them. [20] For if, having escaped the world's impurity through the knowledge of the Lord[E] and Savior Jesus Christ, they are again entangled in these things and defeated, the last state is worse for them than the first. [21] For it would have been better for them not to have known the way of righteousness than, after knowing it, to turn back from the holy command delivered to them. [22] It has happened to them according to the true proverb: **A dog returns to its own vomit,**[F] and, "a washed sow returns to wallowing in the mud."

THE DAY OF THE LORD

3 Dear friends, this is now the second letter I have written to you; in both letters, I want to stir up your sincere understanding by way of reminder, [2] so that you recall the words previously spoken by the holy prophets and the command of our Lord and Savior given through your apostles. [3] Above all, be aware of this: Scoffers will come in the last days scoffing and following their own evil desires, [4] saying, "Where is his 'coming' that he promised? Ever since our ancestors fell asleep, all things continue as they have been since the beginning of creation." [5] They deliberately overlook this: By the word of God the heavens came into being long ago and the earth was brought about from water and through water. [6] Through these the world of that time perished when it was flooded. [7] By the same word, the present heavens and earth are stored up for fire, being kept for the day of judgment and destruction of the ungodly.

[8] Dear friends, don't overlook this one fact: With the Lord one day is like a thousand years, and a thousand years like one day. [9] The Lord does not delay his promise, as some understand delay, but is patient with you, not wanting any to perish but all to come to repentance.

[10] But the day of the Lord will come like a thief;[G] on that day the heavens will pass away with a loud noise, the elements will burn and be dissolved, and the earth and the works on it will be disclosed.[H,I] [11] Since all these things are to be dissolved in this way, it is clear what sort of people you should be in holy conduct and godliness [12] as you wait for the day of God and hasten its coming.[J] Because of that day, the heavens will be dissolved with fire and the elements will melt with heat. [13] But based on his promise, we wait for new heavens and a new earth, where righteousness dwells.

CONCLUSION

[14] Therefore, dear friends, while you wait for these things, make every effort to be found without spot or blemish in his sight, at peace. [15] Also, regard the patience of our Lord as salvation, just as our dear brother Paul has written to you according to the wisdom given to him. [16] He speaks about these things in all his letters. There are some matters that are hard to understand. The untaught and unstable will twist them to their own destruction, as they also do with the rest of the Scriptures.

[17] Therefore, dear friends, since you know this in advance, be on your guard, so that you are not led away by the error of lawless people and fall from your own stable position. [18] But grow in the grace and knowledge of our Lord and Savior Jesus Christ. To him be the glory both now and to the day of eternity.[K]

---

^**2:11** Other mss read *them from the Lord*   [8]**2:13** Other mss read *delighting in the love feasts*   [c]**2:15** Other mss read *Beor*   [D]**2:18** Or *people who are actually escaping*   [E]**2:20** Other mss read *our Lord*   [F]**2:22** Pr 26:11   [G]**3:10** Other mss add *in the night*   [H]**3:10** Other mss read *will be burned up*   [I]**3:10** Or *will not be found*   [J]**3:12** Or *and speed the coming*   [K]**3:18** Other mss add *Amen.*

1 JOHN

1 What was from the beginning, what we have heard, what we have seen with our eyes, what we have observed and have touched with our hands, concerning the word of life — ² that life was revealed, and we have seen it and we testify and declare to you the eternal life that was with the Father and was revealed to us — ³ what we have seen and heard we also declare to you, so that you may also have fellowship with us; and indeed our fellowship is with the Father and with his Son Jesus Christ. ⁴ We are writing these things^ so that our^ joy may be complete.

FELLOWSHIP WITH GOD

⁵ This is the message we have heard from him and declare to you: God is light, and there is absolutely no darkness in him. ⁶ If we say, "We have fellowship with him," and yet we walk in darkness, we are lying and are not practicing the truth. ⁷ If we walk in the light as he himself is in the light, we have fellowship with one another, and the blood of Jesus his Son cleanses us from all sin. ⁸ If we say, "We have no sin," we are deceiving ourselves, and the truth is not in us. ⁹ If we confess our sins, he is faithful and righteous to forgive us our sins and to cleanse us from all unrighteousness. ¹⁰ If we say, "We have not sinned," we make him a liar, and his word is not in us.

2 My little children, I am writing you these things so that you may not sin. But if anyone does sin, we have an advocate with the Father — Jesus Christ the righteous one. ² He himself is the atoning sacrifice^c for our sins, and not only for ours, but also for those of the whole world.

GOD'S COMMANDS

³ This is how we know that we know him: if we keep his commands. ⁴ The one who says, "I have come to know him," and yet doesn't keep his commands, is a liar, and the truth is not in him. ⁵ But whoever keeps his word, truly in him the love of God is made complete. This is how we know we are in him: ⁶ The one who says he remains in him should walk just as he walked.

⁷ Dear friends, I am not writing you a new command but an old command that you have had from the beginning. The old command is the word you have heard. ⁸ Yet I am writing you a new command, which is true in him and in you, because the darkness is passing away and the true light is already shining. ⁹ The one who says he is in the light but hates his brother or sister is in the darkness until now. ¹⁰ The one who loves his brother or sister remains in the light, and there is no cause for stumbling in him.^ᴰ ¹¹ But the one who hates his brother or sister is in the darkness, walks in the darkness, and doesn't know where he's going, because the darkness has blinded his eyes.

REASONS FOR WRITING

¹² I am writing to you, little children,
since your sins have been forgiven
on account of his name.
¹³ I am writing to you, fathers,
because you have come to know
the one who is from the beginning.
I am writing to you, young men,
because you have conquered the evil one.
¹⁴ I have written to you, children,
because you have come to know
the Father.
I have written to you, fathers,
because you have come to know
the one who is from the beginning.
I have written to you, young men,
because you are strong,
God's word remains in you,
and you have conquered the evil one.

A WARNING ABOUT THE WORLD

¹⁵ Do not love the world or the things in the world. If anyone loves the world, the love of the Father is not in him. ¹⁶ For everything in the world — the lust of the flesh, the lust of the eyes, and the pride in one's possessions — is not from the Father, but is from the world. ¹⁷ And the world with its lust is passing away, but the one who does the will of God remains forever.

THE LAST HOUR

¹⁸ Children, it is the last hour. And as you have heard that antichrist is coming, even now many antichrists have come. By this we know that it is the last hour. ¹⁹ They went out from us, but they did not belong to us; for if they had belonged to us, they would have remained with us. However, they went out so that it might be made clear that none of them belongs to us.

²⁰ But you have an anointing from the Holy One, and all of you know the truth.^ᴱ ²¹ I have not written to you because you don't know the

---

truth, but because you do know it, and because no lie comes from the truth. [22] Who is the liar, if not the one who denies that Jesus is the Christ? This one is the antichrist: the one who denies the Father and the Son. [23] No one who denies the Son has the Father; he who confesses the Son has the Father as well.

REMAINING WITH GOD

[24] What you have heard from the beginning is to remain in you. If what you have heard from the beginning remains in you, then you will remain in the Son and in the Father. [25] And this is the promise that he himself made to us: eternal life.

[26] I have written these things to you concerning those who are trying to deceive you. [27] As for you, the anointing you received from him remains in you, and you don't need anyone to teach you. Instead, his anointing teaches you about all things and is true and is not a lie; just as it has taught you,[A] remain in him.

GOD'S CHILDREN

[28] So now, little children, remain in him so that when he appears we may have confidence and not be ashamed before him at his coming. [29] If you know that he is righteous, you know this as well: Everyone who does what is right has **3** been born of him. [1] See what great love[B] the Father has given us that we should be called God's children — and we are! The reason the world does not know us is that it didn't know him. [2] Dear friends, we are God's children now, and what we will be has not yet been revealed. We know that when he appears,[C] we will be like him because we will see him as he is. [3] And everyone who has this hope in him purifies himself just as he is pure.

[4] Everyone who commits sin practices lawlessness; and sin is lawlessness. [5] You know that he was revealed so that he might take away sins,[D] and there is no sin in him. [6] Everyone who remains in him does not sin;[E] everyone who sins[F] has not seen him or known him.

[7] Children, let no one deceive you. The one who does what is right is righteous, just as he is righteous. [8] The one who commits[G] sin is of the devil, for the devil has sinned from the beginning. The Son of God was revealed for this purpose: to destroy the devil's works. [9] Everyone who has been born of God does not sin,[H] because his seed remains in him; he is not able to sin,[I] because he has been born of God. [10] This is how God's children and the devil's children become obvious. Whoever does not do what is

right is not of God, especially the one who does not love his brother or sister.

LOVE IN ACTION

[11] For this is the message you have heard from the beginning: We should love one another, [12] unlike Cain, who was of the evil one and murdered his brother. And why did he murder him? Because his deeds were evil, and his brother's were righteous.

[13] Do not be surprised, brothers and sisters, if the world hates you. [14] We know that we have passed from death to life because we love our brothers and sisters. The one who does not love remains in death. [15] Everyone who hates his brother or sister is a murderer, and you know that no murderer has eternal life residing in him. [16] This is how we have come to know love: He laid down his life for us. We should also lay down our lives for our brothers and sisters. [17] If anyone has this world's goods and sees a fellow believer[J] in need but withholds compassion from him — how does God's love reside in him? [18] Little children, let us not love in word or speech, but in action and in truth.

[19] This is how we will know that we belong to the truth and will reassure our hearts before him [20] whenever our hearts condemn us; for God is greater than our hearts, and he knows all things.

[21] Dear friends, if our hearts don't condemn us, we have confidence before God [22] and receive whatever we ask from him because we keep his commands and do what is pleasing in his sight. [23] Now this is his command: that we believe in the name of his Son Jesus Christ, and love one another as he commanded us. [24] The one who keeps his commands remains in him, and he in him. And the way we know that he remains in us is from the Spirit he has given us.

THE SPIRIT OF TRUTH AND THE SPIRIT OF ERROR

4 Dear friends, do not believe every spirit, but test the spirits to see if they are from God, because many false prophets have gone out into the world.

[2] This is how you know the Spirit of God: Every spirit that confesses that Jesus Christ has come in the flesh is from God, [3] but every spirit that does not confess Jesus[K] is not from God. This is the spirit of the antichrist, which you have heard is coming; even now it is already in the world.

[4] You are from God, little children, and you have conquered them, because the one who is in

---

[A]2:27 Or as he has taught you   [B]3:1 Or what sort of love   [C]3:2 Or when it appears   [D]3:5 Other mss read our sins   [E]3:6 Or not keep on sinning   [F]3:6 Or who keeps on sinning   [G]3:8 Or practices   [H]3:9 Or not practice sin   [I]3:9 Or to keep on sinning   [J]3:17 Lit sees his brother or sister   [K]4:3 Other mss read confess that Jesus has come in the flesh

you is greater than the one who is in the world. [5] They are from the world. Therefore what they say is from the world, and the world listens to them. [6] We are from God. Anyone who knows God listens to us; anyone who is not from God does not listen to us. This is how we know the Spirit of truth and the spirit of deception.

KNOWING GOD THROUGH LOVE

[7] Dear friends, let us love one another, because love is from God, and everyone who loves has been born of God and knows God. [8] The one who does not love does not know God, because God is love. [9] God's love was revealed among us[A] in this way: God sent his one and only Son into the world so that we might live through him. [10] Love consists in this: not that we loved God, but that he loved us and sent his Son to be the atoning sacrifice[B] for our sins. [11] Dear friends, if God loved us in this way, we also must love one another. [12] No one has ever seen God. If we love one another, God remains in[C] us and his love is made complete in us. [13] This is how we know that we remain in him and he in us: He has given us of his Spirit. [14] And we have seen and we testify that the Father has sent his Son as the world's Savior. [15] Whoever confesses that Jesus is the Son of God — God remains in him and he in God. [16] And we have come to know and to believe the love that God has for us.

God is love, and the one who remains in love remains in God, and God remains in him. [17] In this, love is made complete with us so that we may have confidence in the day of judgment, because as he is, so also are we in this world. [18] There is no fear in love; instead, perfect love drives out fear, because fear involves punishment.[D] So the one who fears is not complete in love. [19] We love[E] because he first loved us. [20] If anyone says, "I love God," and yet hates his brother or sister, he is a liar. For the person who does not love his brother or sister whom he has seen cannot love God whom he has not seen.[F] [21] And we have this command from him: The one who loves God must also love his brother and sister.

5 Everyone who believes that Jesus is the Christ has been born of God, and everyone who loves the Father[G] also loves the one born of him. [2] This is how we know that we love God's children: when we love God and obey[H] his commands. [3] For this is what love for God is: to keep his commands. And his commands are not a burden, [4] because everyone who has been born of God conquers the world. This is the victory that has conquered the world: our faith.

THE CERTAINTY OF GOD'S TESTIMONY

[5] Who is the one who conquers the world but the one who believes that Jesus is the Son of God? [6] Jesus Christ — he is the one who came by water and blood, not by water only, but by water and by blood. And the Spirit is the one who testifies, because the Spirit is the truth. [7] For there are three that testify:[I] [8] the Spirit, the water, and the blood — and these three are in agreement. [9] If we accept human testimony, God's testimony is greater, because it is God's testimony that he has given about his Son. [10] The one who believes in the Son of God has this testimony within himself. The one who does not believe God has made him a liar, because he has not believed in the testimony God has given about his Son. [11] And this is the testimony: God has given us eternal life, and this life is in his Son. [12] The one who has the Son has life. The one who does not have the Son of God does not have life. [13] I have written these things to you who believe in the name of the Son of God so that you may know that you have eternal life.

EFFECTIVE PRAYER

[14] This is the confidence we have before him: If we ask anything according to his will, he hears us. [15] And if we know that he hears whatever we ask, we know that we have what we have asked of him.

[16] If anyone sees a fellow believer[J] committing a sin that doesn't lead to death, he should ask, and God will give life to him — to those who commit sin that doesn't lead to death. There is sin[K] that leads to death. I am not saying he should pray about that. [17] All unrighteousness is sin, and there is sin that doesn't lead to death.

CONCLUSION

[18] We know that everyone who has been born of God does not sin, but the one who is born of God keeps him,[L] and the evil one does not touch him. [19] We know that we are of God, and the whole world is under the sway of the evil one. [20] And we know that the Son of God has come and has given us understanding so that we may know the true one. We are in the true one — that is, in his Son Jesus Christ. He is the[M] true God and eternal life.

[21] Little children, guard yourselves from idols.

[A]4:9 Or in us   [B]4:10 Or the propitiation   [C]4:12 Or remains among   [D]4:18 Or fear has its own punishment or torment
[E]4:19 Other mss add him   [F]4:20 Other mss read has seen, how is he able to love . . . seen? (as a question)   [G]5:1 Or loves the one who has given birth   [H]5:2 Other mss read keep   [I]5:7-8 A few late Gk mss and some late Vg mss add testify in heaven: the Father, the Word, and the Holy Spirit, and these three are one. [8]And there are three who bear witness on earth:
[J]5:16 Lit sees his brother or sister   [K]5:16 Or is a sin   [L]5:18 Other mss read himself   [M]5:20 Other mss read the true God

2 JOHN

The elder:
To the elect lady and her children, whom I love in the truth — and not only I, but also all who know the truth — **2** because of the truth that remains in us and will be with us forever. **3** Grace, mercy, and peace will be with us from God the Father and from Jesus Christ, the Son of the Father, in truth and love.

TRUTH AND DECEPTION

4 I was very glad to find some of your children walking in truth, in keeping with a command we have received from the Father. **5** So now I ask you, dear lady — not as if I were writing you a new command, but one we have had from the beginning — that we love one another. **6** This is love: that we walk according to his commands. This is the command as you have heard it from the beginning: that you walk in love.^A

7 Many deceivers have gone out into the world; they do not confess the coming of Jesus Christ in the flesh. This is the deceiver and the antichrist. **8** Watch yourselves so you don't lose what we^B have worked for, but that you may receive a full reward. **9** Anyone who does not remain in Christ's teaching but goes beyond it does not have God. The one who remains in that teaching, this one has both the Father and the Son. **10** If anyone comes to you and does not bring this teaching, do not receive him into your home, and don't greet him; **11** for the one who greets him shares in his evil works.

FAREWELL

12 Though I have many things to write to you, I don't want to use paper and ink. Instead, I hope to come to you and talk face to face so that our joy may be complete.

13 The children of your elect sister send you greetings.

3 JOHN

GREETING

The elder:
To my dear friend Gaius, whom I love in the truth.

2 Dear friend, I pray that you are prospering in every way and are in good health, just as your whole life is going well.^C **3** For I was very glad when fellow believers came and testified to your fidelity to the truth — how you are walking in truth. **4** I have no greater joy than this: to hear that my children are walking in truth.

GAIUS COMMENDED

5 Dear friend, you are acting faithfully in whatever you do for the brothers and sisters, especially when they are strangers. **6** They have testified to your love before the church. You will do well to send them on their journey in a manner worthy of God, **7** since they set out for the sake of the Name, accepting nothing from pagans.^D **8** Therefore, we ought to support such people so that we can be coworkers with the truth.

DIOTREPHES AND DEMETRIUS

9 I wrote something to the church, but Diotrephes, who loves to have first place among them, does not receive our authority. **10** This is why, if I come, I will remind him of the works he is doing, slandering us with malicious words. And he is not satisfied with that! He not only refuses to welcome fellow believers, but he even stops those who want to do so and expels them from the church.

11 Dear friend, do not imitate what is evil, but what is good. The one who does good is of God; the one who does evil has not seen God. **12** Everyone speaks well of Demetrius — even the truth itself. And we also speak well of him, and you know that our testimony is true.

FAREWELL

13 I have many things to write you, but I don't want to write to you with pen and ink. **14** I hope to see you soon, and we will talk face to face.

15 Peace to you. The friends send you greetings. Greet the friends by name.

---

^A**6** Or *in it* ^B**8** Other mss read *you* ^C**2** Or *as your soul prospers* ^D**7** Or *Gentiles*

JUDE

J ude, a servant of Jesus Christ and a brother of James:

To those who are the called, loved^A by God the Father and kept for Jesus Christ.

[2] May mercy, peace, and love be multiplied to you.

JUDE'S PURPOSE IN WRITING

[3] Dear friends, although I was eager to write you about the salvation we share, I found it necessary to write, appealing to you to contend for the faith that was delivered to the saints once for all. [4] For some people, who were designated for this judgment long ago,^B have come in by stealth; they are ungodly, turning the grace of our God into sensuality and denying Jesus Christ, our only Master and Lord.

APOSTATES: PAST AND PRESENT

[5] Now I want to remind you, although you came to know all these things once and for all, that Jesus^C saved a people out of Egypt and later destroyed those who did not believe; [6] and the angels who did not keep their own position but abandoned their proper dwelling, he has kept in eternal chains in deep darkness for the judgment on the great day. [7] Likewise, Sodom and Gomorrah and the surrounding towns committed sexual immorality and perversions,^D and serve as an example by undergoing the punishment of eternal fire.

[8] In the same way these people — relying on their dreams — defile their flesh, reject authority, and slander glorious ones. [9] Yet when Michael the archangel was disputing with the devil in an argument about Moses's body, he did not dare utter a slanderous condemnation against him but said, "The Lord rebuke you!" [10] But these people blaspheme anything they do not understand. And what they do understand by instinct — like irrational animals — by these things they are destroyed. [11] Woe to them! For they have gone the way of Cain, have plunged into Balaam's error for profit, and have perished in Korah's rebellion.

THE APOSTATES' DOOM

[12] These people are dangerous reefs^E at your love feasts as they eat with you without reverence. They are shepherds who only look after themselves. They are waterless clouds carried along by winds; trees in late autumn — fruitless, twice dead and uprooted. [13] They are wild waves of the sea, foaming up their shameful deeds; wandering stars for whom the blackness of darkness is reserved forever.

[14] It was about these that Enoch, in the seventh generation from Adam, prophesied: "Look! The Lord comes with tens of thousands of his holy ones [15] to execute judgment on all and to convict all the ungodly concerning all the ungodly acts that they have done in an ungodly way, and concerning all the harsh things ungodly sinners have said against him." [16] These people are discontented grumblers, living according to their desires; their mouths utter arrogant words, flattering people for their own advantage.

[17] But you, dear friends, remember what was predicted by the apostles of our Lord Jesus Christ. [18] They told you, "In the end time there will be scoffers living according to their own ungodly desires." [19] These people create divisions and are worldly, not having the Spirit.

EXHORTATION AND BENEDICTION

[20] But you, dear friends, as you build yourselves up in your most holy faith, praying in the Holy Spirit, [21] keep yourselves in the love of God, waiting expectantly for the mercy of our Lord Jesus Christ for eternal life. [22] Have mercy on those who waver; [23] save others by snatching them from the fire; have mercy on others but with fear, hating even the garment defiled by the flesh.

[24] Now to him who is able to protect you from stumbling and to make you stand in the presence of his glory, without blemish and with great joy, [25] to the only God our Savior, through Jesus Christ our Lord,^F be glory, majesty, power, and authority before all time,^G now and forever. Amen.

---

^1 Other mss read *sanctified*   ^B 4 Or *whose judgment was written about long ago*   ^C 5 Other mss read *the Lord*, or *God*
^D 7 Or *and went after other flesh*   ^E 12 Other mss read *are like blemishes*   ^F 25 Other mss omit *through Jesus Christ our Lord*   ^G 25 Other mss omit *before all time*

REVELATION

PROLOGUE

1 The revelation of[A] Jesus Christ that God gave him to show his servants what must soon take place. He made it known by sending his angel to his servant John, [2] who testified to the word of God and to the testimony[B] of Jesus Christ, whatever he saw.[C] [3] Blessed is the one who reads aloud the words of this prophecy, and blessed are those who hear the words of this prophecy and keep[D] what is written in it, because the time is near.

[4] John: To the seven churches in Asia. Grace and peace to you from[E] the one who is, who was, and who is to come, and from the seven spirits[F] before his throne, [5] and from Jesus Christ, the faithful witness, the firstborn from the dead and the ruler of the kings of the earth.

To him who loves us and has set us free[G] from our sins by his blood, [6] and made us a kingdom,[H] priests[I] to his God and Father — to him be glory and dominion forever and ever. Amen.

[7] Look, he is coming with the clouds,
   and every eye will see him,
   even those who pierced him.
   And all the tribes[J] of the earth[K]
   will mourn over him.[L,M]
So it is to be. Amen.

[8] "I am the Alpha and the Omega," says the Lord God, "the one who is, who was, and who is to come, the Almighty."

JOHN'S VISION OF THE RISEN LORD

[9] I, John, your brother and partner in the affliction, kingdom, and endurance that are in Jesus, was on the island called Patmos because of the word of God and the testimony of Jesus. [10] I was in the Spirit[N] on the Lord's day, and I heard a loud voice behind me like a trumpet [11] saying, "Write on a scroll[O] what you see and send it to the seven churches: Ephesus, Smyrna, Pergamum, Thyatira, Sardis, Philadelphia, and Laodicea."

[12] Then I turned to see whose voice it was that spoke to me. When I turned I saw seven golden lampstands, [13] and among the lampstands was one like the Son of Man,[P] dressed in a robe and with a golden sash wrapped around his chest. [14] The hair of his head was white as wool — white as snow — and his eyes like a fiery flame. [15] His feet were like fine bronze as it is fired in a furnace, and his voice like the sound of cascading[Q] waters. [16] He had seven stars in his right hand; a sharp double-edged sword came from his mouth, and his face was shining like the sun at full strength.

[17] When I saw him, I fell at his feet like a dead man. He laid his right hand on me and said, "Don't be afraid. I am the First and the Last, [18] and the Living One. I was dead, but look — I am alive forever and ever, and I hold the keys of death and Hades. [19] Therefore write what you have seen, what is, and what will take place after this. [20] The mystery of the seven stars you saw in my right hand and of the seven golden lampstands is this: The seven stars are the angels[R] of the seven churches, and the seven lampstands[S] are the seven churches.

THE LETTERS TO THE SEVEN CHURCHES

THE LETTER TO EPHESUS

2 "Write to the angel[T] of the church in Ephesus: Thus says the one who holds the seven stars in his right hand and who walks among the seven golden lampstands: [2] I know your works, your labor, and your endurance, and that you cannot tolerate evil people. You have tested those who call themselves apostles and are not, and you have found them to be liars. [3] I know that you have persevered and endured hardships for the sake of my name, and have not grown weary. [4] But I have this against you: You have abandoned the love you had at first. [5] Remember then how far you have fallen; repent, and do the works you did at first. Otherwise, I will come to you[U] and remove your lampstand from its place, unless you repent. [6] Yet you do have this: You hate the practices of the Nicolaitans, which I also hate.

[7] "Let anyone who has ears to hear listen to what the Spirit says to the churches. To the one who conquers, I will give the right to eat from the tree of life, which is in[V] the paradise of God.

THE LETTER TO SMYRNA

[8] "Write to the angel of the church in Smyrna: Thus says the First and the Last, the one who

---

^1:1 Or *Revelation of*, or *A revelation of* ^B1:2 Or *witness* ^C1:2 Or *as many as he saw* ^D1:3 Or *follow*, or *obey* ^E1:4 Other mss add *God* ^F1:4 Or *the sevenfold Spirit* ^G1:5 Other mss read *has washed us* ^H1:6 Other mss read *kings and* ^I1:6 Or *made us into* (or *to be*) *a kingdom of priests*; Ex 19:6 ^J1:7 Or *peoples* ^K1:7 Gn 12:3; 28:14; Zch 14:17 ^L1:7 Or *will wail because of him* ^M1:7 Dn 7:13; Zch 12:10 ^N1:10 Or *in spirit*; lit *I became in the Spirit* ^O1:11 Or *book* ^P1:13 Or *like a son of man* ^Q1:15 Lit *many* ^R1:20 Or *messengers* ^S1:20 Other mss add *that you saw* ^T2:1 Or *messenger*, also in vv. 8, 12, 18 ^U2:5 Other mss add *quickly* ^V2:7 Other mss read *in the midst of*

was dead and came to life: ⁹ I know your^ affliction and poverty, but you are rich. I know the slander of those who say they are Jews and are not, but are a synagogue of Satan. ¹⁰ Don't be afraid of what you are about to suffer. Look, the devil is about to throw some of you into prison to test you, and you will experience affliction for ten days. Be faithful to the point of death, and I will give you the crown^B of life.

¹¹ "Let anyone who has ears to hear listen to what the Spirit says to the churches. The one who conquers will never be harmed by the second death.

THE LETTER TO PERGAMUM

¹² "Write to the angel of the church in Pergamum: Thus says the one who has the sharp, double-edged sword: ¹³ I know^c where you live — where Satan's throne is. Yet you are holding on to my name and did not deny your faith in me,^D even in the days of Antipas, my faithful witness who was put to death among you, where Satan lives. ¹⁴ But I have a few things against you. You have some there who hold to the teaching of Balaam, who taught Balak to place a stumbling block^E in front of the Israelites: to eat meat sacrificed to idols and to commit sexual immorality. ¹⁵ In the same way, you also have those who hold to the teaching of the Nicolaitans.^F ¹⁶ So repent! Otherwise, I will come to you quickly and fight against them with the sword of my mouth.

¹⁷ "Let anyone who has ears to hear listen to what the Spirit says to the churches. To the one who conquers, I will give some of the hidden manna.^G I will also give him a white stone, and on the stone a new name is inscribed that no one knows except the one who receives it.

THE LETTER TO THYATIRA

¹⁸ "Write to the angel of the church in Thyatira: Thus says the Son of God, the one whose eyes are like a fiery flame and whose feet are like fine bronze: ¹⁹ I know your works — your love, faithfulness,^H service, and endurance. I know that your last works are greater than the first. ²⁰ But I have this against you: You tolerate the woman Jezebel, who calls herself a prophetess and teaches and deceives my servants to commit sexual immorality and to eat meat sacrificed to idols. ²¹ I gave her time to repent, but she does not want to repent of her sexual immorality. ²² Look, I will throw her into a sickbed and those who commit adultery with her into great affliction. Unless they repent of her^I works, ²³ I will strike her children dead.^J Then all the churches will know that I am the one who examines minds and hearts, and I will give to each of you according to your works. ²⁴ I say to the rest of you in Thyatira, who do not hold this teaching, who haven't known "the so-called secrets^K of Satan" — as they say — I am not putting any other burden on you. ²⁵ Only hold on to what you have until I come. ²⁶ The one who conquers and who keeps my works to the end: I will give him authority over the nations —

²⁷ and he will rule^L them
with an iron scepter;
he will shatter them like pottery^M —

²⁸ just as I have received this from my Father. I will also give him the morning star.

²⁹ "Let anyone who has ears to hear listen to what the Spirit says to the churches.

THE LETTER TO SARDIS

3 "Write to the angel^N of the church in Sardis: Thus says the one who has the seven spirits of God and the seven stars: I know your works; you have a reputation^O for being alive, but you are dead. ² Be alert and strengthen^P what remains, which is about to die,^Q for I have not found your works complete before my God. ³ Remember, then, what you have received and heard; keep it, and repent. If you are not alert, I will come^R like a thief, and you have no idea at what hour I will come upon you. ⁴ But you have a few people^S in Sardis who have not defiled^T their clothes, and they will walk with me in white, because they are worthy.

⁵ "In the same way, the one who conquers will be dressed in white clothes, and I will never erase his name from the book of life but will acknowledge his name before my Father and before his angels.

⁶ "Let anyone who has ears to hear listen to what the Spirit says to the churches.

THE LETTER TO PHILADELPHIA

⁷ "Write to the angel of the church in Philadelphia: Thus says the Holy One, the true one, the one who has the key of David, who opens and no one will close, and who closes and no one opens: ⁸ I know your works. Look, I have placed before you an open door that no one can close because you have but little power; yet you have

---

^A 2:9 Other mss add *works and*   ^B 2:10 Or *wreath*   ^C 2:13 Other mss add *your works and*   ^D 2:13 Or *deny my faith*   ^E 2:14 Or *to place a trap*   ^F 2:15 Other mss add *which I hate*   ^G 2:17 Other mss add *to eat*   ^H 2:19 Or *faith*   ^I 2:22 Other mss read *their*   ^J 2:23 Or *with a plague*   ^K 2:24 Or *the secret things*   ^L 2:27 Or *shepherd*   ^M 2:27 Ps 2:9   ^N 3:1 Or *messenger*, also in vv. 7,14   ^O 3:1 Or *have a name*   ^P 3:2 Other mss read *guard*   ^Q 3:2 Or *strengthen who remain, who are about to die*   ^R 3:3 Other mss add *upon you*   ^S 3:4 Lit *few names*   ^T 3:4 Or *soiled*

kept my word and have not denied my name.
⁹ Note this: I will make those from the synagogue of Satan, who claim to be Jews and are not, but are lying — I will make them come and bow down at your feet, and they will know that I have loved you. ¹⁰ Because you have kept my command to endure, I will also keep you from the hour of testing that is going to come on the whole world to test those who live on the earth. ¹¹ I am coming soon. Hold on to what you have, so that no one takes your crown.

¹² "The one who conquers I will make a pillar in the temple of my God, and he will never go out again. I will write on him the name of my God and the name of the city of my God — the new Jerusalem, which comes down out of heaven from my God — and my new name.

¹³ "Let anyone who has ears to hear listen to what the Spirit says to the churches.

THE LETTER TO LAODICEA

¹⁴ "Write to the angel of the church in Laodicea: Thus says the Amen, the faithful and true witness, the originator^A of God's creation: ¹⁵ I know your works, that you are neither cold nor hot. I wish that you were cold or hot. ¹⁶ So, because you are lukewarm, and neither hot nor cold, I am going to vomit^B you out of my mouth. ¹⁷ For you say, 'I'm rich; I have become wealthy and need nothing,' and you don't realize that you are wretched, pitiful, poor, blind, and naked. ¹⁸ I advise you to buy from me gold refined in the fire so that you may be rich, white clothes so that you may be dressed and your shameful nakedness not be exposed, and ointment to spread on your eyes so that you may see. ¹⁹ As many as I love, I rebuke and discipline. So be zealous and repent. ²⁰ See! I stand at the door and knock. If anyone hears my voice and opens the door, I will come in to him and eat with him, and he with me.

²¹ "To the one who conquers I will give the right to sit with me on my throne, just as I also conquered and sat down with my Father on his throne.

²² "Let anyone who has ears to hear listen to what the Spirit says to the churches."

THE THRONE ROOM OF HEAVEN

4 After this I looked, and there in heaven was an open door. The first voice that I had heard speaking to me like a trumpet said, "Come up here, and I will show you what must take place after this."

² Immediately I was in the Spirit, and there was a throne in heaven and someone was seated on it. ³ The one seated^C there had the appearance of jasper and carnelian stone. A rainbow that had the appearance of an emerald surrounded the throne.

⁴ Around the throne were twenty-four thrones, and on the thrones sat twenty-four elders dressed in white clothes, with golden crowns on their heads.

⁵ Flashes of lightning and rumblings and peals of thunder came from the throne. Seven fiery torches were burning before the throne, which are the seven spirits of God. ⁶ Something like a sea of glass, similar to crystal, was also before the throne.

Four living creatures covered with eyes in front and in back were around the throne on each side. ⁷ The first living creature was like a lion; the second living creature was like an ox; the third living creature had a face like a man; and the fourth living creature was like a flying eagle. ⁸ Each of the four living creatures had six wings; they were covered with eyes around and inside. Day and night they never stop,^D saying,

　　Holy, holy, holy,
　　Lord God, the Almighty,
　　who was, who is, and who is to come.

⁹ Whenever the living creatures give glory, honor, and thanks to the one seated on the throne, the one who lives forever and ever, ¹⁰ the twenty-four elders fall down before the one seated on the throne and worship the one who lives forever and ever. They cast their crowns before the throne and say,

¹¹ 　Our Lord and God,^E
　　you are worthy to receive
　　glory and honor and power,
　　because you have created all things,
　　and by your will
　　they exist and were created.

THE LAMB TAKES THE SCROLL

5 Then I saw in the right hand of the one seated on the throne a scroll with writing on both sides, sealed with seven seals. ² I also saw a mighty angel proclaiming with a loud voice, "Who is worthy to open the scroll and break its seals?" ³ But no one in heaven or on earth or under the earth was able to open the scroll or even to look in it. ⁴ I wept and wept because no one was found worthy to open^F the scroll or even to look in it. ⁵ Then one of the elders said to me, "Do not weep. Look, the Lion from the tribe of Judah, the Root of David, has conquered so that he is able to open the scroll and^G its seven seals."

---

^A 3:14 Or *beginning of God's creation*, or *ruler of God's creation*　　^B 3:16 Or *spit*　　^C 4:3 Other mss omit *The one seated*　　^D 4:8 Or *rest*
^E 4:11 Some mss add *the Holy One*; other mss read *Lord*　　^F 5:4 Other mss add *and read*　　^G 5:5 Other mss add *loose*

[6] Then I saw one like a slaughtered lamb standing in the midst of the throne and the four living creatures and among the elders. He had seven horns and seven eyes, which are the seven spirits of God sent into all the earth. [7] He went and took the scroll out of the right hand of the one seated on the throne.

THE LAMB IS WORTHY

[8] When he took the scroll, the four living creatures and the twenty-four elders fell down before the Lamb. Each one had a harp and golden bowls filled with incense, which are the prayers of the saints. [9] And they sang a new song:

You are worthy to take the scroll
and to open its seals,
because you were slaughtered,
and you purchased[A] people[B]
for God by your blood
from every tribe and language
and people and nation.
[10] You made them a kingdom[C]
and priests to our God,
and they will reign on the earth.

[11] Then I looked and heard the voice of many angels around the throne, and also of the living creatures and of the elders. Their number was countless thousands, plus thousands of thousands. [12] They said with a loud voice,

Worthy is the Lamb who was
slaughtered
to receive power and riches
and wisdom and strength
and honor and glory and blessing!
[13] I heard every creature in heaven, on earth, under the earth, on the sea, and everything in them say,

Blessing and honor and glory
and power
be to the one seated on the throne,
and to the Lamb, forever and ever!
[14] The four living creatures said, "Amen," and the elders fell down and worshiped.

THE FIRST SEAL ON THE SCROLL

[6] Then I saw the Lamb open one of the seven[D] seals, and I heard one of the four living creatures say with a voice like thunder, "Come!" [2] I looked, and there was a white horse. Its rider held a bow; a crown was given to him, and he went out as a conqueror in order to conquer.[E]

THE SECOND SEAL

[3] When he opened the second seal, I heard the second living creature say, "Come!" [4] Then another horse went out, a fiery red one, and its rider was allowed to take peace from the earth, so that people would slaughter one another. And a large sword was given to him.

THE THIRD SEAL

[5] When he opened the third seal, I heard the third living creature say, "Come!" And I looked, and there was a black horse. Its rider held a set of scales in his hand. [6] Then I heard something like a voice among the four living creatures say, "A quart of wheat for a denarius,[F] and three quarts of barley for a denarius, but do not harm the oil and the wine."

THE FOURTH SEAL

[7] When he opened the fourth seal, I heard the voice of the fourth living creature say, "Come!" [8] And I looked, and there was a pale green[G] horse. Its rider was named Death, and Hades was following after him. They were[H] given authority over a fourth of the earth, to kill by the sword, by famine, by plague, and by the wild animals of the earth.

THE FIFTH SEAL

[9] When he opened the fifth seal, I saw under the altar the souls of those who had been slaughtered because of the word of God and the testimony they had given.[I] [10] They cried out with a loud voice: "Lord,[J] the one who is holy and true, how long until you judge those who live on the earth and avenge our blood?" [11] So they were each given a white robe, and they were told to rest a little while longer until the number would be completed of their fellow servants and their brothers and sisters, who were going to be killed just as they had been.

THE SIXTH SEAL

[12] Then I saw him open[K] the sixth seal. A violent earthquake occurred; the sun turned black like sackcloth made of hair; the entire moon[L] became like blood; [13] the stars[M] of heaven fell to the earth as a fig tree drops its unripe figs when shaken by a high wind; [14] the sky was split apart like a scroll being rolled up; and every mountain and island was moved from its place.

[15] Then the kings of the earth, the nobles, the generals, the rich, the powerful, and every slave and free person hid in the caves and among the

rocks of the mountains. [16] And they said to the mountains and to the rocks, "Fall on us and hide us from the face of the one seated on the throne and from the wrath of the Lamb, [17] because the great day of their[A] wrath has come! And who is able to stand?"

THE SEALED OF ISRAEL

7 After this I saw four angels standing at the four corners of the earth, restraining the four winds of the earth so that no wind could blow on the earth or on the sea or on any tree. [2] Then I saw another angel rising up from the east, who had the seal of the living God. He cried out in a loud voice to the four angels who were allowed to harm the earth and the sea: [3] "Don't harm the earth or the sea or the trees until we seal the servants of our God on their foreheads." [4] And I heard the number of the sealed:

144,000 sealed from every tribe
of the Israelites:

[5] 12,000 sealed from the tribe of Judah,
12,000[B] from the tribe of Reuben,
12,000 from the tribe of Gad,

[6] 12,000 from the tribe of Asher,
12,000 from the tribe of Naphtali,
12,000 from the tribe of Manasseh,

[7] 12,000 from the tribe of Simeon,
12,000 from the tribe of Levi,
12,000 from the tribe of Issachar,

[8] 12,000 from the tribe of Zebulun,
12,000 from the tribe of Joseph,
12,000 sealed from the tribe of Benjamin.

A MULTITUDE FROM THE GREAT TRIBULATION

[9] After this I looked, and there was a vast multitude from every nation, tribe, people, and language, which no one could number, standing before the throne and before the Lamb. They were clothed in white robes with palm branches in their hands. [10] And they cried out in a loud voice:

Salvation belongs to our God,
who is seated on the throne,
and to the Lamb!

[11] All the angels stood around the throne, and along with the elders and the four living creatures they fell facedown before the throne and worshiped God, [12] saying,

Amen! Blessing and glory and wisdom
and thanksgiving and honor
and power and strength
be to our God forever and ever. Amen.

[13] Then one of the elders asked me, "Who are these people in white robes, and where did they come from?"

[14] I said to him, "Sir,[C] you know."

Then he told me: These are the ones coming out of the great tribulation. They washed their robes and made them white in the blood of the Lamb.

[15] For this reason they are before the throne of God,
and they serve him day and night
in his temple.
The one seated on the throne
will shelter[D] them:

[16] They will no longer hunger;
they will no longer thirst;
the sun will no longer strike them,
nor will any scorching heat.

[17] For the Lamb who is at the center
of the throne
will shepherd them;
he will guide them to springs of the
waters of life,
and God will wipe away every tear
from their eyes.

THE SEVENTH SEAL

8 When he opened the seventh seal, there was silence in heaven for about half an hour. [2] Then I saw the seven angels who stand in the presence of God; seven trumpets were given to them. [3] Another angel, with a golden incense burner, came and stood at the altar. He was given a large amount of incense to offer with the prayers of all the saints on the golden altar in front of the throne. [4] The smoke of the incense, with the prayers of the saints, went up in the presence of God from the angel's hand. [5] The angel took the incense burner, filled it with fire from the altar, and hurled it to the earth; there were peals of thunder, rumblings, flashes of lightning, and an earthquake.

THE SEVEN TRUMPETS

[6] And the seven angels who had the seven trumpets prepared to blow them.

THE FIRST TRUMPET

[7] The first angel blew his trumpet, and hail and fire, mixed with blood, were hurled to the earth. So a third of the earth was burned up, a third of the trees were burned up, and all the green grass was burned up.

THE SECOND TRUMPET

[8] The second angel blew his trumpet, and something like a great mountain ablaze with fire was hurled into the sea. So a third of the sea became blood, [9] a third of the living creatures in the sea died, and a third of the ships were destroyed.

THE THIRD TRUMPET

[10] The third angel blew his trumpet, and a great star, blazing like a torch, fell from heaven. It fell on a third of the rivers and springs of water. [11] The name of the star was Wormwood, and a third of the waters became wormwood. So, many of the people died from the waters, because they had been made bitter.

THE FOURTH TRUMPET

[12] The fourth angel blew his trumpet, and a third of the sun was struck, a third of the moon, and a third of the stars, so that a third of them were darkened. A third of the day was without light and also a third of the night.

[13] I looked and heard an eagle[A] flying high overhead, crying out in a loud voice, "Woe! Woe! Woe to those who live on the earth, because of the remaining trumpet blasts that the three angels are about to sound! "

THE FIFTH TRUMPET

9 The fifth angel blew his trumpet, and I saw a star that had fallen from heaven to earth. The key for the shaft to the abyss was given to him. [2] He opened the shaft to the abyss, and smoke came up out of the shaft like smoke from a great[B] furnace so that the sun and the air were darkened by the smoke from the shaft. [3] Then locusts came out of the smoke on to the earth, and power[C] was given to them like the power that scorpions have on the earth. [4] They were told not to harm the grass of the earth, or any green plant, or any tree, but only those people who do not have God's seal on their foreheads. [5] They were not permitted to kill them but were to torment them for five months; their torment is like the torment caused by a scorpion when it stings someone. [6] In those days people will seek death and will not find it; they will long to die, but death will flee from them.

[7] The appearance of the locusts was like horses prepared for battle. Something like golden crowns was on their heads; their faces were like human faces; [8] they had hair like women's hair; their teeth were like lions' teeth; [9] they had chests like iron breastplates; the sound of their wings was like the sound of many chariots with horses rushing into battle; [10] and they had tails with stingers like scorpions, so that with their tails they had the power to harm people for five months. [11] They had as their king[D] the angel of the abyss; his name in Hebrew is Abaddon,[E] and in Greek he has the name Apollyon.[F]

[12] The first woe has passed. There are still two more woes to come after this.

THE SIXTH TRUMPET

[13] The sixth angel blew his trumpet. From the four[G] horns of the golden altar that is before God, I heard a voice [14] say to the sixth angel who had the trumpet, "Release the four angels bound at the great river Euphrates." [15] So the four angels who were prepared for the hour, day, month, and year were released to kill a third of the human race. [16] The number of mounted troops was two hundred million;[H] I heard their number. [17] This is how I saw the horses and their riders in the vision: They had breastplates that were fiery red, hyacinth blue, and sulfur yellow. The heads of the horses were like the heads of lions, and from their mouths came fire, smoke, and sulfur. [18] A third of the human race was killed by these three plagues — by the fire, the smoke, and the sulfur that came from their mouths. [19] For the power of the horses is in their mouths and in their tails, because their tails, which resemble snakes, have heads that inflict injury.

[20] The rest of the people, who were not killed by these plagues, did not repent of the works of their hands to stop worshiping demons and idols of gold, silver, bronze, stone, and wood, which cannot see, hear, or walk. [21] And they did not repent of their murders, their sorceries, their sexual immorality, or their thefts.

THE MIGHTY ANGEL AND THE SMALL SCROLL

10 Then I saw another mighty angel coming down from heaven, wrapped in a cloud, with a rainbow over his head.[I] His face was like the sun, his legs[J] were like pillars of fire, [2] and he held a little scroll opened in his hand. He put his right foot on the sea, his left on the land, [3] and he called out with a loud voice like a roaring lion. When he cried out, the seven thunders raised their voices. [4] And when the seven thunders spoke, I was about to write, but I heard a voice from heaven, saying, "Seal up what the seven thunders said, and do not write it down! "

[5] Then the angel that I had seen standing on the sea and on the land raised his right hand to heaven. [6] He swore by the one who lives forever and ever, who created heaven and what is in it, the earth and what is in it, and the sea and what is in it: "There will no longer be a delay, [7] but in the days when the seventh angel will blow his trumpet, then the mystery of God will

---

be completed, as he announced to his servants the prophets.

⁸ Then the voice that I heard from heaven spoke to me again and said, "Go, take the scroll that lies open in the hand of the angel who is standing on the sea and on the land."

⁹ So I went to the angel and asked him to give me the little scroll. He said to me, "Take and eat it; it will be bitter in your stomach, but it will be as sweet as honey in your mouth."

¹⁰ Then I took the little scroll from the angel's hand and ate it. It was as sweet as honey in my mouth, but when I ate it, my stomach became bitter. ¹¹ And they said to me, "You must prophesy again about ᴬ many peoples, nations, languages, and kings."

THE TWO WITNESSES

11 Then I was given a measuring reed like a rod,ᴮ with these words: "Goᶜ and measure the temple of God and the altar, and count those who worship there. ² But exclude the courtyard outside the temple. Don't measure it, because it is given to the nations,ᴰ and they will trample the holy city for forty-two months. ³ I will grantᴱ my two witnesses authority to prophesy for 1,260 days, dressed in sackcloth." ⁴ These are the two olive trees and the two lampstands that stand before the Lordᶠ of the earth. ⁵ If anyone wants to harm them, fire comes from their mouths and consumes their enemies; if anyone wants to harm them, he must be killed in this way. ⁶ They have authority to close up the sky so that it does not rain during the days of their prophecy. They also have power over the waters to turn them into blood and to strike the earth with every plague whenever they want.

THE WITNESSES MARTYRED

⁷ When they finish their testimony, the beast that comes up out of the abyss will make war on them, conquer them, and kill them. ⁸ Their dead bodiesᴳ will lie in the main streetᴴ of the great city, which figurativelyᴵ is called Sodom and Egypt, where also their Lord was crucified. ⁹ And some ofᴶ the peoples, tribes, languages, and nations will view their bodies for three and a half days and not permit their bodies to be put into a tomb. ¹⁰ Those who live on the earth will gloat over them and celebrate and send gifts to one another because these two prophets had tormented those who live on the earth.

THE WITNESSES RESURRECTED

¹¹ But after three and a half days, the breathᴷ of life from God entered them, and they stood on their feet. Great fear fell on those who saw them. ¹² Then they heardᴸ a loud voice from heaven saying to them, "Come up here." They went up to heaven in a cloud, while their enemies watched them. ¹³ At that moment a violent earthquake took place, a tenth of the city fell, and seven thousand people were killed in the earthquake. The survivors were terrified and gave glory to the God of heaven.

¹⁴ The second woe has passed. Take note: The third woe is coming soon!

THE SEVENTH TRUMPET

¹⁵ The seventh angel blew his trumpet, and there were loud voices in heaven saying,

> The kingdom of the world has become the kingdom
> of our Lord and of his Christ,
> and he will reign forever and ever.

¹⁶ The twenty-four elders, who were seated before God on their thrones, fell facedown and worshiped God, ¹⁷ saying,

> We give you thanks, Lord God,
> the Almighty,
> who is and who was,ᴹ
> because you have taken your great power
> and have begun to reign.
>
> ¹⁸ The nations were angry,
> but your wrath has come.
> The time has come
> for the dead to be judged
> and to give the reward
> to your servants the prophets,
> to the saints, and to those who fear
> your name,
> both small and great,
> and the time has come to destroy
> those who destroy the earth.

¹⁹ Then the temple of God in heaven was opened, and the ark of his covenantᴺ appeared in his temple. There were flashes of lightning, rumblings and peals of thunder, an earthquake,ᴼ and severe hail.

THE WOMAN, THE CHILD, AND THE DRAGON

12 A great signᴾ appeared in heaven: a woman clothed with the sun, with the moon under her feet and a crown of twelve stars on her head. ² She was pregnant and cried out

---

ᴬ10:11 Or *prophesy again against*   ᴮ11:1 Other mss add *and the angel stood up*   ᶜ11:1 Lit *'Arise*   ᴰ11:2 Or *Gentiles*   ᴱ11:3 Or *I will give to*   ᶠ11:4 Other mss read *God*   ᴳ11:8 Or *Their corpse*   ᴴ11:8 Or *lie on the broad street*   ᴵ11:8 Or *spiritually*   ᴶ11:9 Lit *And from*   ᴷ11:11 Or *spirit*   ᴸ11:12 Other mss read *Then I heard*   ᴹ11:17 Other mss add *and who is to come*   ᴺ11:19 Other mss read *ark of the covenant of the Lord*   ᴼ11:19 Other mss omit *an earthquake*   ᴾ12:1 Or *great symbolic display*; see Rv 12:3

in labor and agony as she was about to give birth. [3] Then another sign[A] appeared in heaven: There was a great fiery red dragon having seven heads and ten horns, and on its heads were seven crowns.[B] [4] Its tail swept away a third of the stars in heaven and hurled them to the earth. And the dragon stood in front of the woman who was about to give birth, so that when she did give birth it might devour her child. [5] She gave birth to a Son, a male who is going to rule[C] all nations with an iron rod. Her child was caught up to God and to his throne. [6] The woman fled into the wilderness, where she had a place prepared by God, to be nourished there[D] for 1,260 days.

THE DRAGON THROWN OUT OF HEAVEN

[7] Then war broke out in heaven: Michael and his angels fought against the dragon. The dragon and his angels also fought, [8] but he could not prevail, and there was no place for them in heaven any longer. [9] So the great dragon was thrown out — the ancient serpent, who is called the devil and Satan, the one who deceives the whole world. He was thrown to earth, and his angels with him. [10] Then I heard a loud voice in heaven say,

The salvation and the power
and the kingdom of our God
and the authority of his Christ
have now come,
because the accuser of our brothers and
   sisters,
who accuses them
before our God day and night,
has been thrown down.
[11] They conquered him
by the blood of the Lamb
and by the word of their testimony;
for they did not love their lives
to the point of death.
[12] Therefore rejoice, you heavens,
and you who dwell in them!
Woe to the earth and the sea,
because the devil
   has come down to you
with great fury,
because he knows his time is short.

THE WOMAN PERSECUTED

[13] When the dragon saw that he had been thrown down to the earth, he persecuted[E] the woman who had given birth to the male child. [14] The woman was given two wings of a great eagle, so that she could fly from the serpent's presence to her place in the wilderness, where she was nourished for a time, times, and half a time. [15] From his mouth the serpent spewed water like a river flowing after the woman, to sweep her away with a flood. [16] But the earth helped the woman. The earth opened its mouth and swallowed up the river that the dragon had spewed from his mouth. [17] So the dragon was furious with the woman and went off to wage war against the rest of her offspring[F] — those who keep the commands of God and hold firmly to the testimony about Jesus.

THE BEAST FROM THE SEA

[18] The dragon[G] stood on the sand of the sea.[H]

13 And I saw a beast coming up out of the sea. It had ten horns and seven heads. On its horns were ten crowns,[B] and on its heads were blasphemous names.[I] [2] The beast I saw was like a leopard, its feet were like a bear's, and its mouth was like a lion's mouth. The dragon gave the beast his power, his throne, and great authority. [3] One of its heads appeared to be fatally wounded, but its fatal wound was healed.

The whole earth was amazed and followed the beast. [4] They worshiped the dragon because he gave authority to the beast. And they worshiped the beast, saying, "Who is like the beast? Who is able to wage war against it?"

[5] The beast was given a mouth to utter boasts and blasphemies. It was allowed to exercise authority[J,K] for forty-two months. [6] It began to speak[L] blasphemies against God: to blaspheme his name and his dwelling — those who dwell in heaven.[M] [7] And it was permitted to wage war against the saints and to conquer them. It was also given authority over every tribe, people, language, and nation. [8] All those who live on the earth will worship it, everyone whose name was not written from the foundation of the world in the book[M] of life of the Lamb who was slaughtered.[N]

[9] If anyone has ears to hear, let him listen.
[10]   If anyone is to be taken captive,
      into captivity he goes.
      If anyone is to be killed[O] with a sword,
      with a sword he will be killed.
This calls for endurance[P] and faithfulness from the saints.

[A] 12:3 Or another symbolic display [B] 12:3; 13:1 Or diadems [C] 12:5 Or shepherd [D] 12:6 Or God, that they might feed her there [E] 12:13 Or pursued [F] 12:17 Or seed [G] 12:18 Or he; other mss read I [H] 12:18 Some translations put Rv 12:18 either in Rv 12:17 or Rv 13:1. [I] 13:1 Other mss read heads was a blasphemous name [J] 13:5 Other mss read to wage war [K] 13:5 Or to rule [L] 13:6 Or He opened his mouth in [M] 13:8 Or scroll [N] 13:8 Or written in the book of life of the Lamb who was slaughtered from the foundation of the world [O] 13:10 Other mss read anyone kills [P] 13:10 Or Here is the perseverance

THE BEAST FROM THE EARTH

11 Then I saw another beast coming up out of the earth; it had two horns like a lamb,^a but it spoke like a dragon. **12** It exercises all the authority of the first beast on its behalf and compels the earth and those who live on it to worship the first beast, whose fatal wound was healed. **13** It also performs great signs, even causing fire to come down from heaven to earth in front of people. **14** It deceives those who live on the earth because of the signs that it is permitted to perform in the presence of the beast, telling those who live on the earth to make an image^b of the beast who was wounded by the sword and yet lived. **15** It was permitted to give breath^c to the image of the beast, so that the image of the beast could both speak and cause whoever would not worship the image of the beast to be killed. **16** And it makes everyone — small and great, rich and poor, free and slave — to receive a mark on his right hand or on his forehead, **17** so that no one can buy or sell unless he has the mark: the beast's name or the number of its name.

18 This calls for wisdom:^D Let the one who has understanding calculate^E the number of the beast, because it is the number of a person. Its number is 666.^F

THE LAMB AND THE 144,000

14 Then I looked, and there was the Lamb, standing on Mount Zion, and with him were 144,000 who had his name and his Father's name written on their foreheads. **2** I heard a sound^G from heaven like the sound of cascading waters and like the rumbling of loud thunder. The sound I heard was like harpists playing on their harps. **3** They sang^a a new song before the throne and before the four living creatures and the elders, but no one could learn the song except the 144,000 who had been redeemed from the earth. **4** These are the ones who have not defiled themselves with women, since they remained virgins. These are the ones who follow the Lamb wherever he goes. They were redeemed^I from humanity as the firstfruits for God and the Lamb. **5** No lie was found in their mouths; they are blameless.

THE PROCLAMATION OF THREE ANGELS

6 Then I saw another angel flying high overhead, with the eternal gospel to announce to the inhabitants of the earth — to every nation, tribe, language, and people. **7** He spoke with a loud voice: "Fear God and give him glory, because the hour of his judgment has come. Worship the one who made heaven and earth, the sea and the springs of water."

8 And another, a second angel, followed, saying, "It has fallen, Babylon the Great has fallen.^J She made all the nations drink the wine of her sexual immorality,^K which brings wrath."

9 And another, a third angel, followed them and spoke with a loud voice: "If anyone worships the beast and its image and receives a mark on his forehead or on his hand, **10** he will also drink the wine of God's wrath, which is poured full strength into the cup of his anger. He will be tormented with fire and sulfur in the sight of the holy angels and in the sight of the Lamb, **11** and the smoke of their torment will go up forever and ever. There is no rest^L day or night for those who worship the beast and its image, or anyone who receives the mark of its name. **12** This calls for endurance from the saints, who keep God's commands and their faith in Jesus."^M

13 Then I heard a voice from heaven saying, "Write: Blessed are the dead who die in the Lord from now on."

"Yes," says the Spirit, "so they will rest from their labors, since their works follow them."

REAPING THE EARTH'S HARVEST

14 Then I looked, and there was a white cloud, and one like the Son of Man^N was seated on the cloud, with a golden crown on his head and a sharp sickle in his hand. **15** Another angel came out of the temple, crying out in a loud voice to the one who was seated on the cloud, "Use your sickle and reap, for the time to reap has come, since the harvest of the earth is ripe." **16** So the one seated on the cloud swung his sickle over the earth, and the earth was harvested.

17 Then another angel who also had a sharp sickle came out of the temple in heaven. **18** Yet another angel, who had authority over fire, came from the altar, and he called with a loud voice to the one who had the sharp sickle, "Use your sharp sickle and gather the clusters of grapes from the vineyard of the earth, because its grapes have ripened." **19** So the angel swung his sickle at the earth and gathered the grapes from the vineyard of the earth, and he threw them into the great winepress of God's wrath. **20** Then the press was trampled outside the city, and blood flowed out of the press up to the horses' bridles for about 180 miles.^O

---

^a **13:11** Or *ram*   ^b **13:14** Or a *statue,* or a *likeness*   ^c **13:15** Or a *spirit,* or *life*   ^D **13:18** Or *Here is wisdom*   ^E **13:18** Or *count,* or *figure out*   ^F **13:18** Other Gk mss read *616*   ^G **14:2** Or *voice*   ^a **14:3** Other mss add *as it were*   ^I **14:4** Other mss add *by Jesus*   ^J **14:8** Other mss omit the second *has fallen*   ^K **14:8** Or *wine of her passionate immorality*   ^L **14:11** Or *They have no rest*   ^M **14:12** Or *and the faith of Jesus,* or *and faithfulness to Jesus*   ^N **14:14** Or *like a son of man*   ^O **14:20** Lit *1,600 stadia*

PREPARATION FOR THE BOWL JUDGMENTS

15 Then I saw another great and awe-inspiring sign[A] in heaven: seven angels with the seven last plagues; for with them God's wrath will be completed. [2] I also saw something like a sea of glass mixed with fire, and those who had won the victory over the beast, its image,[B] and the number of its name, were standing on the sea of glass with harps from God. [3] They sang the song of God's servant Moses and the song of the Lamb:

Great and awe-inspiring are your works,
    Lord God, the Almighty;
just and true are your ways,
    King of the nations.[C]
[4] Lord, who will not fear
    and glorify your name?
For you alone are holy.
    All the nations will come
    and worship before you
because your righteous acts
    have been revealed.

[5] After this I looked, and the heavenly temple — the tabernacle of testimony — was opened. [6] Out of the temple came the seven angels with the seven plagues, dressed in pure, bright linen, with golden sashes wrapped around their chests. [7] One of the four living creatures gave the seven angels seven golden bowls filled with the wrath of God who lives forever and ever. [8] Then the temple was filled with smoke from the glory of God and from his power, and no one could enter the temple until the seven plagues of the seven angels were completed.

THE FIRST BOWL

16 Then I heard a loud voice from the temple saying to the seven angels, "Go and pour out the seven[D] bowls of God's wrath on the earth." [2] The first went and poured out his bowl on the earth, and severely painful sores broke out on the people who had the mark of the beast and who worshiped its image.

THE SECOND BOWL

[3] The second[E] poured out his bowl into the sea. It turned to blood like that of a dead person, and all life in the sea died.

THE THIRD BOWL

[4] The third[E] poured out his bowl into the rivers and the springs of water, and they became blood. [5] I heard the angel of the waters say,

You are just,
    the Holy One, who is and who was,
because you have passed judgment
    on these things.
[6] Because they poured out
    the blood of the saints and the prophets,
you have given them blood to drink;
    they deserve it!
[7] I heard the altar say,
    Yes, Lord God, the Almighty,
true and just are your judgments.

THE FOURTH BOWL

[8] The fourth[E] poured out his bowl on the sun. It was allowed to scorch people with fire, [9] and people were scorched by the intense heat. So they blasphemed the name of God, who has the power[F] over these plagues, and they did not repent and give him glory.

THE FIFTH BOWL

[10] The fifth[E] poured out his bowl on the throne of the beast, and its kingdom was plunged into darkness. People[G] gnawed their tongues because of their pain [11] and blasphemed the God of heaven because of their pains and their sores, but they did not repent of their works.

THE SIXTH BOWL

[12] The sixth[E] poured out his bowl on the great river Euphrates, and its water was dried up to prepare the way for the kings from the east. [13] Then I saw three unclean spirits like frogs coming from the dragon's mouth, from the beast's mouth, and from the mouth of the false prophet. [14] For they are demonic spirits performing signs, who travel to the kings of the whole world to assemble them for the battle on the great day of God, the Almighty. [15] "Look, I am coming like a thief. Blessed is the one who is alert and remains clothed[H] so that he may not go around naked and people see his shame." [16] So they assembled the kings at the place called in Hebrew, Armageddon.[I]

THE SEVENTH BOWL

[17] Then the seventh[E] poured out his bowl into the air,[J] and a loud voice came out of the temple[K] from the throne, saying, "It is done!" [18] There were flashes of lightning, rumblings, and peals of thunder. And a severe earthquake occurred like no other since people have been on the earth, so great was the quake. [19] The great city split into three parts, and the cities of the

[A] **15:1** Or and awesome symbolic display [B] **15:2** Other mss add his mark [C] **15:3** Other mss read ages [D] **16:1** Other mss omit seven [E] **16:3,4,8,10,12,17** Other mss add angel [F] **16:9** Or authority [G] **16:10** Lit They [H] **16:15** Or and guards his clothes [I] **16:16** Some mss read Armagedon; other mss read Harmegedon; other mss read Mageddon; other mss read Magedon [J] **16:17** Or bowl on the air [K] **16:17** Other mss add of heaven

nations[A] fell. Babylon the Great was remembered in God's presence; he gave her the cup filled with the wine of his fierce anger. [20] Every island fled, and the mountains disappeared. [21] Enormous hailstones, each weighing about a hundred pounds,[B] fell from the sky on people, and they blasphemed God for the plague of hail because that plague was extremely severe.

THE WOMAN AND THE SCARLET BEAST

17 Then one of the seven angels who had the seven bowls came and spoke with me: "Come, I will show you the judgment of the notorious prostitute[C] who is seated on many[D] waters. [2] The kings of the earth committed sexual immorality with her, and those who live on the earth became drunk on the wine of her sexual immorality." [3] Then he carried me away in the Spirit[E] to a wilderness.

I saw a woman sitting on a scarlet beast that was covered[F] with blasphemous names and had seven heads and ten horns. [4] The woman was dressed in purple and scarlet, adorned with gold, jewels, and pearls. She had a golden cup in her hand filled with everything detestable and with the impurities of her[G] prostitution. [5] On her forehead was written a name, a mystery: BABYLON THE GREAT, THE MOTHER OF PROSTITUTES AND OF THE DETESTABLE THINGS OF THE EARTH. [6] Then I saw that the woman was drunk with the blood of the saints and with the blood of the witnesses to Jesus. When I saw her, I was greatly astonished.

THE MEANING OF THE WOMAN AND OF THE BEAST

[7] Then the angel said to me, "Why are you astonished? I will explain to you the mystery of the woman and of the beast, with the seven heads and the ten horns, that carries her. [8] The beast that you saw was, and is not, and is about to come up from the abyss and go to destruction. Those who live on the earth whose names have not been written in the book of life from the foundation of the world will be astonished when they see the beast that was, and is not, and is to come. [9] This calls for a mind that has wisdom:[H] "The seven heads are seven mountains on which the woman is seated. They are also seven kings: [10] Five have fallen, one is, the other has not yet come, and when he comes, he must remain for only a little while. [11] The beast that was and is not, is itself an eighth king, but it belongs to the seven and is going

to destruction. [12] The ten horns you saw are ten kings who have not yet received a kingdom, but they will receive authority as kings with the beast for one hour. [13] These have one purpose, and they give their power and authority to the beast. [14] These will make war against the Lamb, but the Lamb will conquer them because he is Lord of lords and King of kings. Those with him are called, chosen, and faithful."

[15] He also said to me, "The waters you saw, where the prostitute was seated, are peoples, multitudes, nations, and languages. [16] The ten horns you saw, and the beast, will hate the prostitute. They will make her desolate and naked, devour her flesh, and burn her up with fire. [17] For God has put it into their hearts to carry out his plan by having one purpose and to give their kingdom[I] to the beast until the words of God are fulfilled. [18] And the woman you saw is the great city that has royal power over the kings of the earth."

THE FALL OF BABYLON THE GREAT

18 After this I saw another angel with great authority coming down from heaven, and the earth was illuminated by his splendor. [2] He called out in a mighty voice:

It has fallen,[J]
Babylon the Great has fallen!
She has become a home for demons,
a haunt for every unclean spirit,
a haunt for every unclean bird,
and a haunt[K] for every unclean
and despicable beast.[L]
[3] For all the nations have drunk[M]
the wine of her sexual immorality,
which brings wrath.
The kings of the earth
have committed sexual immorality
with her,
and the merchants of the earth
have grown wealthy from her sensuality
and excess.
[4] Then I heard another voice from heaven:
Come out of her, my people,
so that you will not share in her sins
or receive any of her plagues.
[5] For her sins are piled up[N] to heaven,
and God has remembered her crimes.
[6] Pay her back the way she also paid,
and double it according to her works.
In the cup in which she mixed,
mix a double portion for her.

[A]**16:19** Or *the Gentile cities*   [B]**16:21** Lit *about a talent*; talents varied in weight upwards from 75 pounds   [C]**17:1** Traditionally translated *the great whore*   [D]**17:1** Or *by many*   [E]**17:3** Or *in spirit*   [F]**17:3** Or *was filled*   [G]**17:4** Other mss read *earth's* [H]**17:9** Or *Here is the mind of wisdom*   [I]**17:17** Or *sovereignty*   [J]**18:2** Other mss omit *It has fallen*   [K]**18:2** Or *prison* [L]**18:2** Other mss omit the words *and a haunt for every unclean beast.* The words *and despicable* then refer to the *bird* of the previous line.   [M]**18:3** Some mss read *collapsed*; other mss read *fallen*   [N]**18:5** Or *sins have reached up*

⁷ As much as she glorified herself
  and indulged her sensual and excessive
    ways,
give her that much torment and grief.
For she says in her heart,
"I sit as a queen;
I am not a widow,
and I will never see grief."
⁸ For this reason her plagues will come
    in just one day —
death and grief and famine.
She will be burned up with fire,
because the Lord God who judges her
    is mighty.

THE WORLD MOURNS BABYLON'S FALL

⁹ The kings of the earth who have committed
sexual immorality and shared her sensual and
excessive ways will weep and mourn over her
when they see the smoke from her burning.
¹⁰ They will stand far off in fear of her torment,
saying,

Woe, woe, the great city,
Babylon, the mighty city!
For in a single hour
your judgment has come.

¹¹ The merchants of the earth will weep and
mourn over her, because no one buys their cargo any longer — ¹² cargo of gold, silver, jewels,
and pearls; fine linen, purple, silk, and scarlet;
all kinds of fragrant wood products; objects
of ivory; objects of expensive wood, brass,ᴬ
iron, and marble; ¹³ cinnamon, spice,ᴮ incense,
myrrh,ᶜ and frankincense; wine, olive oil, fine
flour, and grain; cattle and sheep; horses and
carriages; and slaves — human lives.
¹⁴ The fruit you craved has left you.
    All your splendid and glamorous things
        are gone;
    they will never find them again.

¹⁵ The merchants of these things, who became
rich from her, will stand far off in fear of her
torment, weeping and mourning, ¹⁶ saying,
Woe, woe, the great city,
dressed in fine linen, purple, and scarlet,
adorned with gold, jewels, and pearls;
¹⁷ for in a single hour
such fabulous wealth was destroyed!

And every shipmaster, seafarer, the sailors,
and all who do business by sea, stood far off
¹⁸ as they watched the smoke from her burning
and kept crying out: "Who was like the great
city?" ¹⁹ They threw dust on their heads and
kept crying out, weeping, and mourning,

Woe, woe, the great city,
where all those who have ships
    on the sea
became rich from her wealth;
for in a single hour she was destroyed.
²⁰ Rejoice over her, heaven,
and you saints, apostles, and prophets,
because God has pronounced on her the
    judgment she passed on you!

THE FINALITY OF BABYLON'S FALL

²¹ Then a mighty angel picked up a stone like a
large millstone and threw it into the sea, saying,
In this way, Babylon the great city
will be thrown down violently
and never be found again.
²² The sound of harpists,
    musicians,
flutists, and trumpeters
will never be heard in you again;
no craftsman of any trade
will ever be found in you again;
the sound of a mill
will never be heard in you again;
²³ the light of a lamp
will never shine in you again;
and the voice of a groom and bride
will never be heard in you again.
All this will happen
because your merchants
were the nobility of the earth,
because all the nations were deceived
by your sorcery.
²⁴ In her was found the blood of prophets
    and saints,
and of all those slaughtered
    on the earth.

CELEBRATION IN HEAVEN

19 After this I heard something like the
loud voice of a vast multitude in heav-
en, saying,
Hallelujah!
Salvation, glory, and power belong
    to our God,
² because his judgments are trueᴰ
    and righteous,
because he has judged
    the notorious prostitute
who corrupted the earth
    with her sexual immorality;
and he has avenged the blood
    of his servants
that was on her hands.
³ A second time they said,
Hallelujah!
Her smoke ascends forever and ever!

ᴬ**18:12** Or *bronze,* or *copper*   ᴮ**18:13** Other mss omit *spice*   ᶜ**18:13** Or *perfume*   ᴰ**19:2** Valid; Jn 8:16; 19:35

⁴ Then the twenty-four elders and the four living creatures fell down and worshiped God, who is seated on the throne, saying,

Amen! Hallelujah!

⁵ A voice came from the throne, saying,

Praise our God,
all his servants, and the ones
   who fear him,
both small and great!

⁶ Then I heard something like the voice of a vast multitude, like the sound of cascading waters, and like the rumbling of loud thunder, saying,

Hallelujah, because our Lord God,
   the Almighty,
reigns!

⁷ Let us be glad, rejoice, and give him glory, because the marriage of the Lamb
   has come,
and his bride has prepared herself.

⁸ She was given fine linen to wear, bright and pure.

For the fine linen represents the righteous acts of the saints.

⁹ Then heᴬ said to me, "Write: Blessed are those invited to the marriage feast of the Lamb!" He also said to me, "These words of God are true." ¹⁰ Then I fell at his feet to worship him, but he said to me, "Don't do that! I am a fellow servant with you and your brothers and sisters who hold firmly to the testimony of Jesus. Worship God, because the testimony of Jesus is the spiritᴮ of prophecy."

THE RIDER ON A WHITE HORSE

¹¹ Then I saw heaven opened, and there was a white horse. Its rider is called Faithful and True, and he judges and makes war with justice. ¹² His eyes were like a fiery flame, and many crownsᶜ were on his head. He had a name written that no one knows except himself. ¹³ He wore a robe dipped in blood, and his name is called the Word of God. ¹⁴ The armies that were in heaven followed him on white horses, wearing pure white linen. ¹⁵ A sharpᴰ sword came from his mouth, so that he might strike the nations with it. He will ruleᴱ them with an iron rod. He will also trample the winepress of the fierce anger of God, the Almighty. ¹⁶ And he has a name written on his robe and on his thigh: KING OF KINGS AND LORD OF LORDS.

THE BEAST AND ITS ARMIES DEFEATED

¹⁷ Then I saw an angel standing in the sun, and he called out in a loud voice, saying to all the birds flying high overhead, "Come, gather together for the great supper of God, ¹⁸ so that you may eat the flesh of kings, the flesh of military commanders, the flesh of the mighty, the flesh of horses and of their riders, and the flesh of everyone, both free and slave, small and great."

¹⁹ Then I saw the beast, the kings of the earth, and their armies gathered together to wage war against the rider on the horse and against his army. ²⁰ But the beast was taken prisoner, and along with it the false prophet, who had performed the signs in its presence. He deceived those who accepted the mark of the beast and those who worshiped its image with these signs. Both of them were thrown alive into the lake of fire that burns with sulfur. ²¹ The rest were killed with the sword that came from the mouth of the rider on the horse, and all the birds ate their fill of their flesh.

SATAN BOUND

20 Then I saw an angel coming down from heaven holding the key to the abyss and a great chain in his hand. ² He seized the dragon, that ancient serpent who is the devil and Satan,ᶠ and bound him for a thousand years. ³ He threw him into the abyss, closed it, and put a seal on it so that he would no longer deceive the nations until the thousand years were completed. After that, he must be released for a short time.

THE SAINTS REIGN WITH CHRIST

⁴ Then I saw thrones, and people seated on them who were given authority to judge. I also saw the souls of those who had been beheaded because of their testimony about Jesus and because of the word of God, who had not worshiped the beast or his image, and who had not accepted the mark on their foreheads or their hands. They came to life and reigned with Christ for a thousand years. ⁵ The rest of the dead did not come to life until the thousand years were completed.

This is the first resurrection. ⁶ Blessed and holy is the one who shares in the first resurrection! The second death has no powerᴳ over them, but they will be priests of God and of Christ, and they will reign with him for a thousand years.

SATANIC REBELLION CRUSHED

⁷ When the thousand years are completed, Satan will be released from his prison ⁸ and will go out to deceive the nations at the four corners of the earth, Gog and Magog, to gather them for battle. Their number is like the sand of the sea. ⁹ They came up across the breadth of the earth and surrounded the encampment

---

ᴬ**19:9** Probably an angel; Rv 17:1; 22:8-9   ᴮ**19:10** Or *the Spirit*   ᶜ**19:12** Or *diadems*   ᴰ**19:15** Other mss add *double-edged*
ᴱ**19:15** Or *shepherd*   ᶠ**20:2** Other mss add *who deceives the whole world*   ᴳ**20:6** Or *authority*

of the saints, the beloved city. Then fire came down from heaven[A] and consumed them. [10] The devil who deceived them was thrown into the lake of fire and sulfur where the beast and the false prophet are, and they will be tormented day and night forever and ever.

THE GREAT WHITE THRONE JUDGMENT

[11] Then I saw a great white throne and one seated on it. Earth and heaven fled from his presence, and no place was found for them. [12] I also saw the dead, the great and the small, standing before the throne, and books were opened. Another book was opened, which is the book of life, and the dead were judged according to their works by what was written in the books. [13] Then the sea gave up the dead that were in it, and death and Hades gave up the dead that were in them; each one was judged according to their works. [14] Death and Hades were thrown into the lake of fire. This is the second death, the lake of fire.[B] [15] And anyone whose name was not found written in the book of life was thrown into the lake of fire.

THE NEW CREATION

21 Then I saw a new heaven and a new earth; for the first heaven and the first earth had passed away, and the sea was no more. [2] I also saw the holy city, the new Jerusalem, coming down out of heaven from God, prepared like a bride adorned for her husband.

[3] Then I heard a loud voice from the throne:[C] Look, God's dwelling[D] is with humanity, and he will live with them. They will be his peoples,[E] and God himself will be with them and will be their God.[F] [4] He will wipe away every tear from their eyes. Death will be no more; grief, crying, and pain will be no more, because the previous things[G] have passed away.

[5] Then the one seated on the throne said, "Look, I am making everything new." He also said, "Write, because these words[H] are faithful and true." [6] Then he said to me, "It is done! I am the Alpha and the Omega, the beginning and the end. I will freely give to the thirsty from the spring of the water of life. [7] The one who conquers will inherit these things, and I will be his God, and he will be my son. [8] But the cowards, faithless,[I] detestable, murderers, sexually immoral, sorcerers, idolaters, and all liars—their share will be in the lake that burns with fire and sulfur, which is the second death."

THE NEW JERUSALEM

[9] Then one of the seven angels, who had held the seven bowls filled with the seven last plagues, came and spoke with me: "Come, I will show you the bride, the wife of the Lamb." [10] He then carried me away in the Spirit[J] to a great, high mountain and showed me the holy city, Jerusalem, coming down out of heaven from God, [11] arrayed with God's glory. Her radiance was like a precious jewel, like a jasper stone, clear as crystal. [12] The city had a massive high wall, with twelve gates. Twelve angels were at the gates; the names of the twelve tribes of Israel's sons were inscribed on the gates. [13] There were three gates on the east, three gates on the north, three gates on the south, and three gates on the west. [14] The city wall had twelve foundations, and the twelve names of the twelve apostles of the Lamb were on the foundations.

[15] The one who spoke with me had a golden measuring rod to measure the city, its gates, and its wall. [16] The city is laid out in a square; its length and width are the same. He measured the city with the rod at 12,000 *stadia*.[K] Its length, width, and height are equal. [17] Then he measured its wall, 144 cubits according to human measurement, which the angel used. [18] The building material of its wall was jasper, and the city was pure gold clear as glass. [19] The foundations of the city wall were adorned with every kind of jewel: the first foundation is jasper, the second sapphire, the third chalcedony, the fourth emerald, [20] the fifth sardonyx, the sixth carnelian, the seventh chrysolite, the eighth beryl, the ninth topaz, the tenth chrysoprase, the eleventh jacinth, the twelfth amethyst. [21] The twelve gates are twelve pearls; each individual gate was made of a single pearl. The main street[L] of the city was pure gold, transparent as glass.

[22] I did not see a temple in it, because the Lord God the Almighty and the Lamb are its temple. [23] The city does not need the sun or the moon to shine on it, because the glory of God illuminates it, and its lamp is the Lamb. [24] The nations[M] will walk by its light, and the kings of the earth will bring their glory into it.[N] [25] Its gates will never close by day because it will never be night there. [26] They will bring the glory and honor of the nations into it.[O] [27] Nothing unclean will ever enter it, nor anyone who does what is detestable or false, but only those written in the Lamb's book of life.

[A] 20:9 Other mss add *from God* [B] 20:14 Other mss omit *the lake of fire* [C] 21:3 Other mss read *from heaven* [D] 21:3 Or *tent,* or *tabernacle* [E] 21:3 Other mss read *people* [F] 21:3 Other mss omit *and will be their God* [G] 21:4 Or *the first things* [H] 21:5 Other mss add *of God* [I] 21:8 Other mss add *the sinful,* [J] 21:10 Or *in spirit* [K] 21:16 A *stadion* (sg) = about 600 feet; 12,000 *stadia* = 1,400 miles. [L] 21:21 Or *The public square* [M] 21:24 Other mss add *of those who are saved* [N] 21:24 Other mss read *will bring to him the nations' glory and honor* [O] 21:26 Other mss add *in order that they might go in*

THE SOURCE OF LIFE

22 Then he showed me the river[A] of the water of life, clear as crystal, flowing from the throne of God and of the Lamb [2] down the middle of the city's main street. The tree of life was on each side of the river, bearing twelve kinds of fruit, producing its fruit every month. The leaves of the tree are for healing the nations, [3] and there will no longer be any curse. The throne of God and of the Lamb will be in the city, and his servants will worship him. [4] They will see his face, and his name will be on their foreheads. [5] Night will be no more; people will not need the light of a lamp or the light of the sun, because the Lord God will give them light, and they will reign forever and ever.

THE TIME IS NEAR

[6] Then he said to me, "These words are faithful[B] and true. The Lord, the God of the spirits of the prophets,[C] has sent his angel to show his servants what must soon take place."

[7] "Look, I am coming soon! Blessed is the one who keeps the words of the prophecy of this book."

[8] I, John, am the one who heard and saw these things. When I heard and saw them, I fell down to worship at the feet of the angel who had shown them to me. [9] But he said to me, "Don't do that! I am a fellow servant with you, your brothers the prophets, and those who keep the words of this book. Worship God!"

[10] Then he said to me, "Don't seal up the words of the prophecy of this book, because the time is near. [11] Let the filthy still be filthy; let the righteous go on in righteousness; let the holy still be holy."

[12] "Look, I am coming soon, and my reward is with me to repay each person according to his work. [13] I am the Alpha and the Omega, the first and the last, the beginning and the end.

[14] "Blessed are those who wash their robes,[D] so that they may have the right to the tree of life and may enter the city by the gates. [15] Outside are the dogs, the sorcerers, the sexually immoral, the murderers, the idolaters, and everyone who loves and practices falsehood.

[16] "I, Jesus, have sent my angel to attest these things to you for the churches. I am the root and descendant of David, the bright morning star."

[17] Both the Spirit and the bride say, "Come!" Let anyone who hears, say, "Come!" Let the one who is thirsty come. Let the one who desires take the water of life freely.

[18] I testify to everyone who hears the words of the prophecy of this book: If anyone adds to them, God will add to him the plagues that are written in this book. [19] And if anyone takes away from the words of the book of this prophecy, God will take away his share of the tree of life and the holy city, which are written about in this book.

[20] He who testifies about these things says, "Yes, I am coming soon."

Amen! Come, Lord Jesus!

[21] The grace of the Lord Jesus[E] be with everyone.[F] Amen.[G]

[A] **22:1** Other mss read *pure river*   [B] **22:6** Or *trustworthy*   [C] **22:6** Other mss read *God of the holy prophets*   [D] **22:14** Other mss read *who keep his commands*   [E] **22:21** Other mss add *Christ*   [F] **22:21** Other mss read *with all the saints*   [G] **22:21** Other mss omit *Amen.*

ARE YOU READY TO RECEIVE GOD'S OFFER OF ETERNAL LIFE AND HOPE?

If so, please pray the following prayer. Remember, it is not the words that you use, but the attitude of your heart. If you pray this prayer sincerely, Jesus will come into your life, and in him you will have eternal life and hope.

"Dear God, I know that Jesus is your Son and that he died on the cross and was raised from the dead. Because I have sinned and need forgiveness, I ask Jesus to come into my heart. I am willing to change the direction of my life by acknowledging Jesus as my Lord and Savior and by turning away from my sins. Thank you for giving me forgiveness, eternal life, and hope. In Jesus's name, Amen."

YOU ARE ASSURED OF ETERNAL LIFE AND HOPE BECAUSE:

You can trust God's promise.

"For everyone who calls on the name of the Lord will be saved" (Romans 10:13).

Did you sincerely ask Jesus into your heart as Lord and Savior? Where is he right now? What does God's Word promise?

You are a member of God's family.

"The Spirit himself testifies together with our spirit that we are God's children" (Romans 8:16).

Your life is eternally secure in God.

"For I am persuaded that neither death nor life, nor angels nor rulers, nor things present nor things to come, nor powers, nor height nor depth, nor any other created thing will be able to separate us from the love of God that is in Christ Jesus our Lord" (Romans 8:38-39).

WHAT HAPPENS AFTER YOU RECEIVE
HOPE FROM GOD?

You will begin to live for God (Romans 12:1-2,9-18).

You will publicly profess your faith by being baptized (Matthew 28:19-20; Luke 3:21; Romans 6:4).

You will share with others what Jesus has done for you (Romans 10:14).

You will get to know God better through prayer, Bible study, and fellowship with other Christians as a member of a local church (Romans 15:4-6).

MY RECORD OF SALVATION

On _____ , I _____ trusted
        (date)   (name)

Jesus as my Savior and gave myself to him to be Lord of my life.

Witnessed by: _____